# THE
# VENTURE
# ALCHEMISTS

Sandy—

I hope that this book sheds new light.

Also, hope you enjoy!

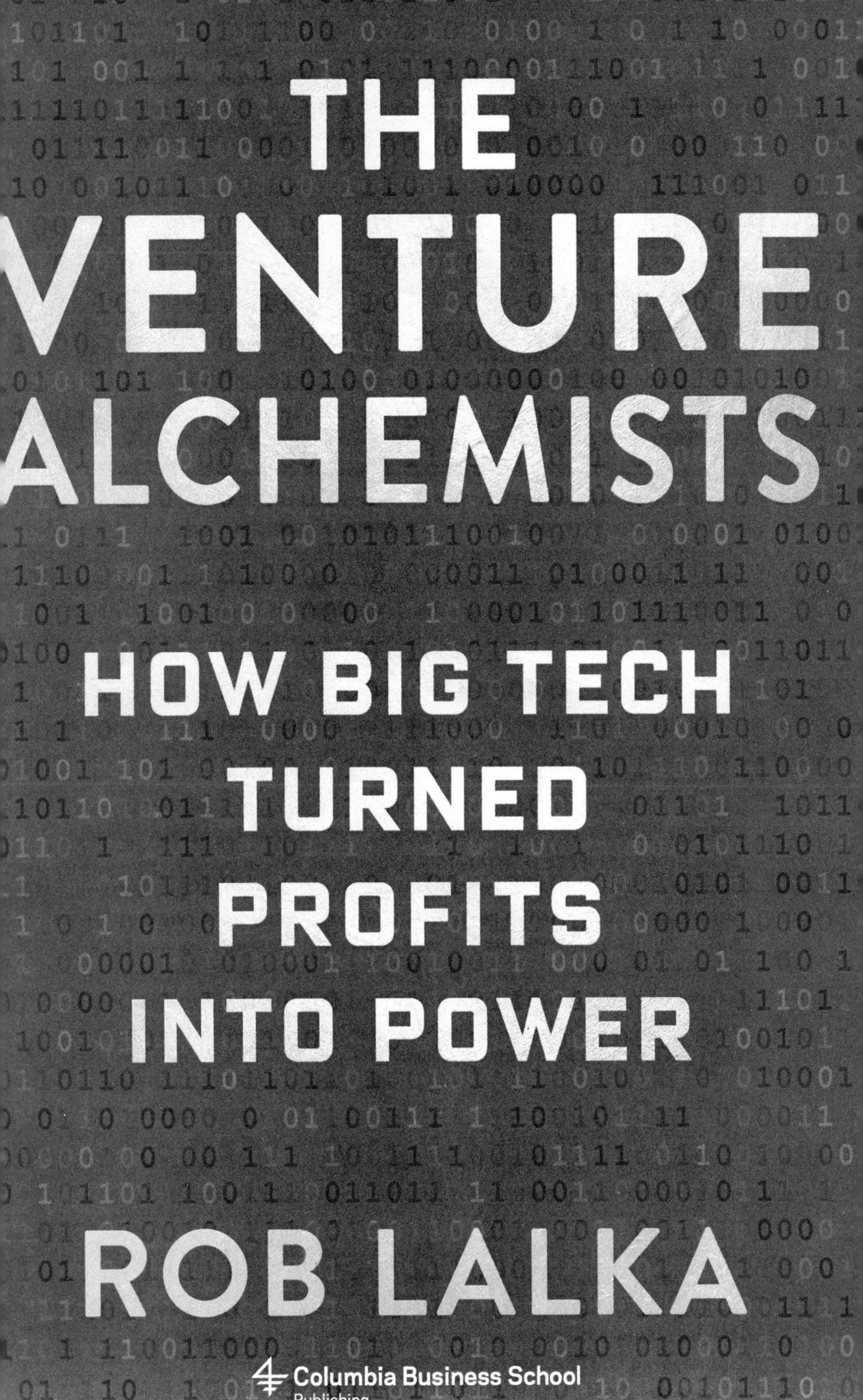

THE
VENTURE
ALCHEMISTS
HOW BIG TECH
TURNED
PROFITS
INTO POWER
ROB LALKA
Columbia Business School
Publishing

Columbia University Press
*Publishers Since 1893*
New York   Chichester, West Sussex
cup.columbia.edu



Library of Congress Cataloging-in-Publication Data
Names: Lalka, Rob, author.
Title: The venture alchemists : how big tech turned profits into power /
    Rob Lalka.
Description: New York : Columbia Business School Publishing, an imprint of
    Columbia University Press, [2024] | Includes bibliographical references
    and index.
Identifiers: LCCN 2023042635 (print) | LCCN 2023042636 (ebook) |
    ISBN 9780231210263 (hardback) | ISBN 9780231558334 (ebook)
Subjects: LCSH: High technology industries—Biography. | Capitalists and
    financiers—Biography. | Venture capital.
Classification: LCC HC79.H53 L355 2024  (print) | LCC HC79.H53  (ebook) |
    DDC 338.4/760922—dc23/eng/20231220
LC record available at https://lccn.loc.gov/2023042635
LC ebook record available at https://lccn.loc.gov/2023042636

Printed in the United States of America

Cover design: Noah Arlow
Cover image: Shutterstock

*For my sons and for my students.*

*Moving fast and breaking things*
*created chaos and confusion,*
*heat, not light.*

*To fix things,*
*seek the truth.*
*Be the light of the world.*

*It was the best of times, it was the worst of times. It was the age of wisdom, it was the age of foolishness, it was the epoch of belief, it was the epoch of incredulity, it was the season of light, it was the season of darkness, it was the spring of hope, it was the winter of despair.*

—Charles Dickens, *A Tale of Two Cities*
1859, or 165 years ago

# CONTENTS

**ACT III. POWER**

# ACKNOWLEDGMENTS

Call me "ordinary." That's just fine by me. No one in my family is wealthy or famous. My grandfather, born on December 20, 1905, came from South Carolina. My grandmother was born in rural Alabama on September 1, 1916. They died in 2003 and 2014 and rest in peace in the Roanoke Valley's Blue Ridge Memorial Gardens. Our family remembers them, lovingly, but their lives are forgotten by public memory.

Yet we are history's luckiest ones. Simply because my grandparents were born in America in the twentieth century, we've enjoyed a standard of living far greater than most. Throughout their lives, my grandparents remained humble, taking nothing for granted. As tyranny spread, their calling became clear. They believed in fairness. They fought for freedom. The world turned against them, so they changed the world. My grandparents were "ordinary" people. They accomplished heroic deeds. They truly were the Greatest Generation.

The way my grandmother was welcomed into this world seems so utterly strange to us now. A country doctor drove his horse-drawn carriage many miles to deliver her at home. She worked the cotton fields and grew her own food. She got power thanks to the Tennessee Valley Authority and could vividly remember when her family got that first Model-T, their first GE Monitor Top refrigerator, their first black-and-white TV. She studied in a one-room Alabama schoolhouse for white children only, then taught in Virginia's first integrated classrooms. She helped build bombers that attacked fascists and married the soldier who had become her pen pal. With each note they wrote or read, they fell more in love. Their words mattered, amid such senselessness. They would've told you, as a matter of fact, that those cherished letters meant the world even when its end seemed ever nearer.

I learned civics outside the classroom, growing up with a family of public school teachers who were also Red Cross volunteers, polling station workers, Lions Club members, and Sunday school instructors. I discovered that democracy is about doing. It takes work, but it works. It's hard-earned, and it's well worth it. Everyone around me was constantly contributing to our community—not because anyone asked them to, but because it was the reason why we are here.

This book begins with my family, and it's fitting, because I need to acknowledge the lessons they taught me from the start. My grandmother told me stories of the prettiest Easter dresses she'd handmade, with bleached-out sackcloth that was better than any store-bought Sunday best; of better August rest outside on a screened-in sleeping porch, in a time without air conditioning; of the thousands more stars you could see before ambient light muted the heavens. She marveled that we didn't need to roll up the car windows by hand or pay that nice man at Ewald-Clark to develop rolls of film anymore. So many innovations—from her American life to ours today—are worlds apart.

In her final years, she was in awe of it all. She was stunned by the sudden speed of the early Internet. She cherished all the late-in-life minutes that modern medicine gifted her. In many ways, technology seemed magical. But she had worries, too. She warned about quick conveniences replacing what's most important. She was a perpetual storyteller. She knew the power of the tales we tell about our lives and the virtues and values they furnish for us. It's only right to begin this book by sharing in her awe about modern innovations, while also sharing with you her main concern: we should seek out things that mean the most. They'll matter more.

My favorite photo from childhood shows me, age two, with a colander on my head. I'm sitting next to my grandfather, reading the *Wall Street Journal*, with a colander on his head, too. He told stories of men jumping from Chicago's skyscrapers during the Great Depression. As markets came crashing down, their worlds had suddenly fallen apart. But they'd made choices, too. They'd borrowed money they couldn't pay back and spent money they didn't have. It was all too much. They couldn't start over again, so they ended up choosing to end it all.

Those people must have known the dignity of a day's work at some point, enjoyed an honest wage's rewards. They dreamed of a better life, made possible by America and earned by their efforts. But something good in this world had become corrupted, as people made far too many compromises, the greediest took and took, and the neediest lost out and lost hope. Across America, dreams died, so all our losses grew. Yet my grandfather remained a passionate capitalist, a prudent investor, and an incredible inventor. He worked as a railroad engineer and tracked the markets. He charted trends on graph paper with a draftsman's hand. He often smelled of sawdust from long hours of woodworking and whittling. I watched him in wonder.

Today I run the entrepreneurship and innovation center at Tulane's business school and teach classes about creating companies to solve the world's toughest problems. I'm here only because of my family and Glenda Gilmore, Anne-Marie Slaughter, Tom Taylor, Jim Thompson, and other teachers and mentors who helped to raise me. They taught me to defy limitations, while instilling ethics that grounded me. My work, in its best moments, exists on the borderline of those two intersecting ideas, where unrelenting curiosity meets principled decisions. That's the approach I now teach. It made this all possible.

I often thought about my mom's influence as I worked on this project. Years ago we spent long afternoons with pastels and paint in her basement studio or tending to the kiln at the high school where she taught. For her, all life is art. Each breath, a brief refreshing of an everlasting promise, where we encounter each moment as a new creation. I was raised on an all-American idea: to fulfill a dream, it takes imagination and ambition, humility and hard work. Others will doubt or hurt you. Seek understanding. Choose wonder. Take a deep breath. Do your very best.

I look back in amazement. She did it all as a single mom, on one public schoolteacher's salary. But she was on a mission of her own, and she lit a fire in me (and countless other students) that money can't buy. We kept our heads held high as we moved onward. But we didn't look down on anyone. *Love thy neighbor. All men are created equal. Resilience and resolve pay off, but always pay it forward.* Those simple principles were our way of life.

We didn't have much money, but I never knew it. Money ain't rich. With each new day, we valued things that mattered, like love, laughter, and time together. Those blessings felt immeasurable. I was taught to count them anyway, pray for those who hurt, forgive unfairness, fight injustice, and give to those with less than us. Mom, your teachings appear throughout.

This book also wouldn't exist without Lynn. You helped me endure each time I felt like quitting: when the research seemed too daunting, when pandemic lockdowns felt too frustrating, or when I hurt my back by hunching over my laptop. It all added to my self-doubts, which grew into a destructive disbelief about this effort not being worth it. You knew how much it mattered. Your support made such a difference. My greatest endeavors—with this book, as in our lives—are in the hard challenges we help each other through and the good things we nurture together.

I've come to believe that a person is fortunate if they can count their true lifelong friends on more than one hand. Many meaningful relationships exist, but real friends are set apart from great acquaintances. I feel blessed to know that kind of unfailing love. I want to thank the people who have always been by my side: Drew Bender, Gordon Bronson, Howard Buffett, Aaron Dalton, Brent Jones, Mark Newberg, Tim O'Shea, and Eric Sapp. All of you contributed feedback, inspiration, and insights to this book from the first moment onward, as you've done throughout all parts of my life. I am especially thankful for Howard's many contributions. Before I knew what questions to ask, you did; once I figured out the right way to tell the story, you listened and encouraged, then listened and challenged, then listened some more; and when I nearly gave up, you kept at it: asking, listening, challenging, encouraging. Howard, I am forever grateful.

The Columbia University Press team was tremendous from start to finish, especially Brian Smith and Myles Thompson. Anita O'Brien's careful attention sharpened the manuscript during copyediting. I'm thankful for the folks at Stanford's Special Collections and University Archives, particularly Tim Noakes. And I'm indebted to Ben Kalin, whose fact checking and recommendations made this book clearer, cleaner, and far more compelling. Ben is a master at his craft, and I feel very fortunate to have worked with him. I owe Jill Filipovic for introducing me to Ben, which was an unanticipated gift when I needed it most, and I'm eternally thankful for Ty McCormick, who helped from the earliest outlines. Jill and Ty are two of the most insightful thinkers I've ever met, and they were incredibly generous throughout this project.

Thank you to Paulo Goes, Albert Lepage, Ira Solomon, and so many smart colleagues at the A. B. Freeman School of Business. I am grateful for advice from others at Tulane, including Brian Edwards, Matt and Nicole Escarra, and Walter and Cathy Isaacson. And I deeply value the community that supported this book, including Chessie Brittain, Josh Brittain, Sandy Cohen, Bela Cormier, Lee Cormier, Daryn Dodson, Jonah Evans, Breck Heidelberg, Adam Karlin, Jacob Landry, Kate McCrery, Daniel McGee, Andy Rabens, Merin Rajadurai, Scott Shalett, Drew Sokol, and Amelia Willits-Smith. Your love of ideas and your dedication to the greater good made this book better—both richer and more enriching. I can never repay your generosity. But to honor each of you, and to pay it forward, I will be giving 27 percent of net profits to charity. (For the reason behind that number, read on.)

I dedicate this book, especially the endnotes, to my students. The year before I started this project, I asked a roomful of Tulanians: "How do you define 'research'?" One reply bothered me so much, I still remember it verbatim: "Research is finding information to back up what you want to argue." That only seems right in a world that rewards you for making declarations forcefully, regardless of their legitimacy. I've seen those debates turn into diatribes, which shed more heat than light, especially online. Today we experience a constant barrage of uncompromising opinions and overheated arguments. It can cause us all to feel burned out. Decency dissipates; disputes worsen. We engage each other less; we enrage each other more.

Fortunately, I've taught far more Tulane students who have dug in, searched deeper, and opened up new worlds with the breakthroughs that resulted. They are amazingly bright students, and when their eyes light up, it's spectacular and inspiring, and it will forever motivate me. A few words of encouragement to each of you: explore every competing idea, question every assumption, wring every drop out of your education, and have so much fun here—and while you do, be kind to strangers and tip generously. New Orleans is paradoxical. It's whimsical, it's loyal, it's impossible. You're lucky to know this place. This book of contradictions couldn't have been written anywhere else. (Plus, WWOZ played in the background during much of it.)

My students dream big dreams, and that gives me hope. I have loved being part of your journeys, as entrepreneurs and as leaders. My research assistant, Matt Yam, collaborated closely with me up until his graduation, right before I submitted the manuscript for fact checking. You've just begun imagining a new path into the future. Illuminate what's possible for us all.

To Tice and Taylor, my wonderful and wonder-filled sons, this book is for you. As I wrote this, you were just learning to read. You were on my mind as I typed every word. In one sense, this book felt like the most forthright discussion, which went straight on until dawn, between me and the world that welcomed you. In another way, it's a quiet prayer that you will find purpose, that you might repair the world. My greatest hope in publishing these words is that you and yours will eventually leave this place better off than how my generation leaves it to you.

Father's Day 2023, New Orleans, Louisiana

# THE
# VENTURE
# ALCHEMISTS

| | | |
|---|---|---|
| Mark Zuckerberg | Larry Page | Sergey Brin |
| Keith Rabois | Peter Thiel | David Sacks |
| Travis Kalanick | Bill Shockley | J. D. Hamel |

# ACT I

---

# SILICON

Zuckerberg. Page and Brin. Kalanick.

These are not the names of "ordinary" men.

They seem like living gods.

Their odysseys have exceeded anything we experience as mere mortals. And the extraordinary technology they've created has remade the world we live in.

The people who bet on these companies are called venture capitalists. In 1984 the *New York Times* traced the invention of the phrase to the mid-1900s, a uniting of "adventure" and "capital."[1] Yet only in recent decades did venture capital reach such scale—first billions, and now hundreds of billions of dollars invested globally each year.[2]

People usually stop there. We focus on the adventure, the daring heroism of it all. We admire the entrepreneurs who overcame all obstacles to fulfill their destinies. And, of course, we worship the wealth they made for themselves and their investors. They've become modern day legends, the kings of the Silicon Age.

The Stone Age lasted for more than two million years. The Bronze Age and the Iron Age took over a thousand years each. The many metals of the Machine Age, as well as the chemistry and physics that put them to work, created incredible innovations in far swifter succession.[3] The first long-distance phone call, flicker of a light bulb, long-distance car trip, and airplane to go airborne all altered the course of history—and all of that took place in less than twenty-seven years.[4]

The Silicon Age has accelerated the pace of change even faster. But the impacts of venture capital go beyond the adventure. They mean more than money. These Great Men of History turned novel ideas into incredible wealth, silicon into gold.

And as we'll discover, they then turned that money into influence, profits into power. There's a word for this.

*Alchemy, noun*: a medieval chemical science and speculative philosophy aiming to achieve the transmutation of the base metals into gold, the discovery of a universal cure for disease, and the discovery of a means of indefinitely prolonging life.[5]

---

**Figure I.1**  Mark Zuckerberg.
Source: Photo by Elaine Chan and Priscilla Chan, CC BY 2.5, https://commons.wikimedia.org/wiki/File:MarkZuckerberg-crop.jpg.

**Figure I.2**  Larry Page.
Source: Photo by Andreas Weigend, CC BY-SA 2.0, https://commons.wikimedia.org/wiki/File:Larry_Page_laughs.jpg.

**Figure I.3**  Sergey Brin.
Source: Photo by Allen Lew, CC BY-SA 2.0, https://commons.wikimedia.org/w/index.php?curid=6978715.

**Figure I.4**  Keith Rabois.
Source: Photo by Yaniv Golan, CC BY 2.0, https://www.flickr.com/photos/24901154@N00/291739522.

**Figure I.5**  Peter Thiel.
Source: *TechCrunch*, CC BY 2.0, https://www.flickr.com/photos/techcrunch50-2008/2841658864/.

**Figure I.6**  David Sacks.
Source: *TechCrunch*, CC BY 2.0, https://www.flickr.com/photos/techcrunch50-2008/2869154108/.

**Figure I.7**  Travis Kalanick.
Source: *TechCrunch*, CC BY 2.0, https://commons.wikimedia.org/w/index.php?curid=106127154.

**Figure I.8**  Bill Shockley.
Source: Nobel Foundation courtesy of Wikimedia Commons, https://commons.wikimedia.org/wiki/File:Shockley.jpg.

**Figure I.9**  J. D. Hamel.
Source: Middletown High School Optimist Yearbook, 2003.

# CHAPTER 1

# SOPHOMORIC EXPLOITS

Mark Zuckerberg, Facemash and Thefacebook

The boy's name was Mark. Dusk was falling as he walked back to his dorm. He felt angry, as the sun set on a very bad day. He knew that a sleepless night was going to be ahead of him anyway, so he sat down at his computer and opened a beer. He gave into a temptation to get into a little mischief. He began to break into Harvard's computer systems, so he could steal the student ID pictures stored on its various sites. Then, he had a choice to make. Should he compare girls to each other or to pigs in barnyard slop? He drank, he coded, and he decided.[1]

Mark Zuckerberg blogged about the prank, to brag in real-time, as he attempted to crack the digital safe of each house at Harvard. He chronicled his exploits in an entry titled, "Harvard Face Mash | The Process," written as both a technical treatise of his exploits and a running commentary about just how easy it was to infiltrate the university's systems. His writing dripped with teenage scorn and smarter-than-everybody condescension. He bragged about his cyberattack, detailing his precise methods, and he posted it all online for his peers to read.

Harvard undergraduates cared about the opinions of the 2,067 other kids in their class. They were already the best of nearly twenty thousand who'd applied that year, but these were Harvard kids, so they held themselves to the highest possible standards, including when it came to the subjective sentiment of their social standing.[2] They obsessed over their "status." Zuckerberg blogged to show off his skills, to assert his dominance. He was superior to his fellow man, far better than the machines they'd made to protect all those pictures.

He started at 8:13 p.m. on October 28, 2003, and by 9:48 p.m. he wrote: "I'm a little intoxicated, not gonna lie. So what if it's not even 10 p.m. and it's a Tuesday night? What?" Zuckerberg finished the mischief about six hours later. It was hacking, and he knew it was. He called it that—"let the hacking begin"—in fact, he deemed it "child's play" compared to his prior efforts.[3] He hijacked Harvard's system and stole hundreds of student ID photos; many of them were unflattering, like the ones taken at the DMV with that awkward deer-in-headlights look. Zuckerberg then uploaded them to a website that asked people to choose which photo was more attractive. Unlike the one-to-ten rankings on a popular site that preceded it, hotornot.com, this time it was a true head-to-head contest. Zuckerberg opted to compare girls to other girls, boys to other boys. He did all this without consent. He made that choice.

Facemash debuted the week of Halloween. At the top of the page, the header read, "Were we let in for our looks? No. Will we be judged on them? Yes." Then, above two pictures of teenagers selected by a computer program written by Mark Zuckerberg himself—two images of Harvard students whom we all hope had been accepted because of incredible academic achievements, inspiring talents, and merit alone—the prompt demanded: "Who's Hotter? Click to choose." People responded. They clicked. They chose. And it all started with the choices Mark Zuckerberg made, history writ with code.[4]

## Mark asks: Are Harvard girls or farm animals more attractive?

One of the most powerful businessmen of all time got his start with a cyberattack, which was popularized in Aaron Sorkin's movie *The Social Network* in 2010 but has since been well documented in deeply researched books, most notably in Steven Levy's *Facebook: The Inside Story* (2020) and Sheera Frenkel and Cecilia Kang's *An Ugly Truth: Inside Facebook's Battle for Domination* (2021). Zuckerberg wrote an algorithm to evaluate college kids, like they were objects to be compared and chosen. He put people on display, for others to gawk at and mock, without their permission. Here's what he thought when he drank and blogged: "I almost want to put some of these faces next to pictures of farm animals and have people vote on which is more attractive."[5]

If it seems sophomoric, that's probably a fair assessment. After all, he was a sophomore in college.

It would be his last year at Harvard. He'd drop out and leave the rest of his education to what his investors and other mentors in the business world would teach him. Soon enough, Silicon Valley's venture capitalists would instruct that revenues and growth, and the power they created, truly mattered. They were the priorities, even more than profits or changing lives, because world domination was the way of the Silicon Age. But early on, before investors had any influence, he coded the math that powered Facemash. In those 1s and 0s, yeses or noes, hot or not, Zuckerberg determined a path. We'd be judged, for our looks, as better or worse. We'd judge others, for how things looked, online—not how they are, for real—from there on out. Other prerogatives are obvious now, too. In his not-so-innocent Halloween prank, we can see his utter disregard for the privacy of complete strangers, his disrespect for the dignity of each real person because it was *just online*, and even his obvious obliviousness toward the ways that judging others caused pain and self-doubt—it was all there early on.

But most of all, we can see what Facemash revealed about humanity: judging each other could become so captivating, so engrossing. Judgment was entertainment. In the coming decades, for Thefacebook, then Facebook, and finally the company called Meta, the business model would depend on enjoying judging others. By 2022, 74 percent of people with access to the Internet would be on one of Meta's platforms. Globally, around 35 percent of humanity used Facebook at least monthly. Of those, over two-thirds used Facebook every single day.[6]

Zuckerberg turned computers across Harvard's campus into scoreboards of self-worth. He set the stage to put us on display; he let the bidding begin without asking for permission. On a Tuesday night in Kirkland House, Room H33, Zuckerberg drank beers at age nineteen *just like so many college kids do*, he stole and posted other people's photos *just for a college prank*, and he publicly bragged about it. *Forgive the kid, he was so young then.* It silently left the students whose pictures Zuckerberg posted without their permission wondering, *How attractive am I?*, as they checked the site to see how they ranked. So many people clicked, the traffic overwhelmed Harvard's servers. The IT staff had to cut off the Internet to all of Kirkland.[7]

Long before Facebook became Meta Platforms, Inc., with its Menlo Park headquarters address at One Hacker Way, there was Facemash. We usually remember its origins as a "mashup" of pictures from Harvard's various residential house facebooks. But there's a better definition.

*Mash, transitive verb*: to reduce to a soft pulpy state by beating or pressure.[8]

Ivy League college life was already pressurized. Getting an elite education was just the start of it, because by itself, getting in was never good enough. Facebook would expand through the .edu sites first, because Zuckerberg had an easy early market at Harvard before expanding through the Ivy League. At America's most selective schools, "status" mattered.

The main arbiter of popularity at the time was the *Harvard Crimson*, the student newspaper. It was how the Harvard community decided who was hot or not, before the Internet existed. Founded in 1873, it was intended to be authoritative from the start, with that unique blend of wry wit (aged seventeen to twenty-one years) that campus newspapers are known for.[9] "At length the College Bible is placed before us, containing the instructions by which the undergraduate is to be guided clear of the shoals and quicksands which surround his course," an anonymous author explained irreverently in one of its earliest articles. "Its commandments, though not written on tablets of stone, are, however, more numerous, and intended, if possible, to be more binding than those of Biblical history. Its beatitudes address themselves to our better nature, and can all be summed up in one,—Blessed are the obedient, for they shall obtain marks."[10]

But getting good grades wasn't good enough. Over a century later, marks mattered, but other factors also determined who excelled among the most elite. At Harvard, "having it all" also meant doing it all: being smart, athletic, and beautiful, being a musical virtuoso or artistic genius, becoming the leader of every kind of club, and the list went on, as the competition to be the best-of-the-best only increased in the rare air of the elite institution. Still, as Zuckerberg learned, superficiality was as quick as a click. Regardless of résumés, "our looks" were what we'd be judged by. This system was engineered to exploit fears we've all experienced: worrying we're not enough, not good enough. Facemash encouraged objectification and comparison, demanding: worthy or unworthy. It asked us to approve or reject each other, one picture after another put on parade. Each choice taught the comparison engine underneath what we wanted, what we'd click. This is an origin story about control and influence, superficiality and judgment.

## What Facebook knew about its impact

In September 2021 a former Facebook employee named Frances Haugen leaked hundreds of screenshots of internal documents developed in 2018 and 2019 to the *Wall Street Journal*. The evidence was striking. One chart explained that teenagers' ambitions like "the perfect image, feeling attractive, and having enough money are the most likely to have started on Instagram," with 39 percent of U.S. teens and 51 percent of UK teens reporting that believing they "have to create the perfect image" started on Instagram. Over 40 percent of teens in both the United States and Britain answered that feelings of "Not attractive" and "Don't have enough money" began on Instagram. "Content on IG makes teens feel very bad," another chart was titled. How bad was "very bad?" It was staggering: 76 percent of teens in the United States and 53 percent of teens in the UK responded, "they wanted to hurt themselves," and 70 percent in the United States and 46 percent in the UK reported, "they wanted to kill themselves," after seeing content about self-injury and suicide.[11]

Other slides described the ways that "social comparison creates a negative feedback loop" and that "social comparison makes teens feel very bad," with 64 percent of U.S. teens and 67 percent of UK teens saying Instagram made them feel that "your life isn't as good" and 68 percent of U.S. teens and 79 percent of UK teens feeling "that you will be judged." As one teenager in the UK told Facebook, "But it's clear you need boobs, a booty, to be thin, to be pretty. It's endless and you end up feeling worthless and shitty about yourself. I'm never going to have that body without surgery."[12]

Facebook's analysts observed that "as young people compare themselves to others, their feelings of self-doubt grow," and "in some cases, they can get addicted to things that make them feel bad." One girl in the UK wrote, "Flat stomach, bigger boobs, bigger bum. My friends started working out & not eating. A load of people tried weight loss teas or weight trainers. Even teeth whitening. It all causes pressure." Another British girl worried about "the pressure to be present." She didn't mean being with friends in real life; instead, she was on Instagram all the time, where she felt compelled "to share things about your life constantly or feeling pressured to have a public account," which allowed strangers to see her posts. An American male worried that any mistake he made would ruin his reputation: "I just feel on the edge a lot of the time. It's like you can be called out for anything you do. One wrong move. One wrong step." Our children experienced a Catch-22 where they were damned if they did, damned if they didn't. The evidence was damning for Facebook.[13]

Employees at Facebook also knew that their algorithms—the math that determined what posts and stories people saw—were showing more of this harmful content to the teens who were most at risk. "Teens who are unsatisfied with their lives are more likely to see content related to mental health on Instagram," one slide reported. But that didn't mean content to encourage better mental health. People who admitted they were unsatisfied with life were twice as likely to see content on Instagram about "being down, sad, or depressed," "they're not attractive," "they're not good enough," "they don't have enough friends," and "their friends are not really their friends." Young people who felt unsatisfied with their lives were more than twice as likely to see content about self-injury and suicide, too.[16]

Girls were impacted in unique ways, and Facebook employees knew it. Only about half of teens on Instagram reported having positive feelings of well-being, 70 percent said they'd felt "Not good enough" or "Not attractive," and 21 percent of teens in the UK and 14 percent in the United States admitted that they "wanted to hurt themselves" or "wanted to kill themselves"—but it was worse for girls than boys. "It's a vicious cycle," one American girl explained. "You see content that encourages you to criticize yourself. But I rush to judge people as well. Standards are totally based on looks."[15]

When did we go wrong?

## Mark thinks: People might be offended.
## Maybe we can control that.

Control creates influence. Power produces prestige. That's nothing new. Earlier world-changing innovations also upended social norms through social pressure. Right around the time that Johannes Gutenberg printed the Bible that made his name famous, he also used a jerry-rigged winepress to print indulgences for the Catholic Church. Those documents meant wealth and power for the church's priests. The Bibles that people read expanded the Vatican's influence; the indulgences that people bought meant money for the church. But every innovation has unintended consequences. Who could have guessed why that institution—and all its influence and authority—would suddenly become destabilized by Martin Luther some sixty years later? The reason: his ideas spread as quickly as they could be printed. It was too fast to stop.[16]

Zuckerberg changed his world as he cracked the code of this treasure trove of student ID photos. He created more public dialogue and more freedom of expression—about the physical appearance of college kids whose pictures he'd hacked to get. But no one could anticipate what came next, and how quickly what he'd originally coded would grow into such a popular public forum, at Harvard and beyond. His site wasn't just effective. It was addictive. People kept coming back, to judge others based on their looks. Instead of studying or partying on the autumn evening when Facemash launched, 450 students basked in the glow of their computer monitors. They clicked on twenty-two thousand photos in one night.[17]

Harvard students first went online in 1992. Zuckerberg hacked *our* system in less than half of the time from Gutenberg to Luther.[18] And it was intentional, but originally it was more of a social experiment than a startup. "We weren't looking to start a company," Zuckerberg reflected at Y Combinator's Startup School in 2012. "I thought that over time someone would definitely go build this version of this for the world but it wasn't gonna be us," he recalled discussing over pizza with a friend. "It was gonna be, you know, Microsoft or you know someone who builds software for hundreds of millions of people. Who were we? We were college students. We're not qualified in any way to build this."[19]

He didn't think it was going to be him. But he knew *someone* was going to connect the world through a social network powered by the ever-expanding Internet. And it all started as a joke, but it was far from innocent and not by accident. He hacked Harvard, and the results of the cyberattack showed that people would quickly become addicted to judging each other online. Today, four of the top seven social media apps are owned by Meta Platforms, Inc.: Facebook has nearly 3 billion users; WhatsApp has 2 billion; Instagram has 2 billion; and Facebook Messenger has 931 million.[20]

This Halloween tale portended a new future where we'd watch each other and worry, where impulses and judgment would muddle together into intense peer pressure and we'd share performative versions of our lives. Yet we can't say we weren't warned. Alarms went off, even back in 2003, but no one was listening for them. Two decades ago, many of the young women Zuckerberg pitted against each other for entertainment felt that they'd been wronged. The e-mail list-servs of two student groups, Fuerza Latina and the Association of Harvard Black Women, caught fire with Facemash backlash.[21] "I heard from a friend and I was kind of outraged. I thought people should be aware," Fuerza Latina president Leyla R. Bravo said, carefully, to the *Crimson*.[22] Zuckerberg searched for the right answer to the criticisms he'd received, saying, "I think people might be slightly offended but whatever, maybe there's a way to control that."[23]

*Kind of. Slightly. I think. Maybe.* These are the words of people grasping to understand something that was so new, didn't quite know how to feel. In 2003 they didn't realize that the Internet would become so powerful, that our digital lives would overtake our actual lives, or that what happened online wasn't truly separate from what affected someone's real-life feelings, or even their overall self-worth. The Internet was still, *kind of,* a place of anonymity and mischief. It was still where you could, *slightly,* get away with behind-a-screen behavior that shouldn't be taken so seriously by anyone, because *I think* that world would be over as soon as you powered down. *Maybe.*

This origin story was premised on proving something: who was hotter, better. It was based on a false belief that interactions online wouldn't lead to horrible unintended consequences for people in the real world. Maybe something misfired due to antisocial enmity, where the power from the mysterious math done by machines mattered more than the actual impacts on human beings. At least, that was how Zuckerberg said he saw the world at the time. "I thought the site was interesting mathematically, theoretically," he told the *Crimson* as he tried to explain himself. In another interview, he rationalized, "I'm a programmer and I'm interested in the algorithms and math behind it." He'd hoped to calm the campus controversy over Facemash, but it created problems that quickly grew far beyond what any single person could control.[24]

For Zuckerberg, it was all just for fun originally, just another game with points on a virtual scoreboard adding up on a computer screen. That was just like Civilization III, the computer game you won when your empire dominated any others that got in your way. Civ had sold more than half a million copies the year before and won PC Game of the Year. It was Zuckerberg's favorite right around this time. How do we know? It was the game he was playing when he got his Harvard admissions decision. His dad taped a home video that showed the very moment when Zuckerberg opened the e-mail. He typed a message on AOL Instant Messenger, asked his dad, "So you want me to open this?" and then did. He began to read, then started to scroll. His dad excitedly asked, "What does it say?" Zuckerberg announced, unenthusiastically, "Yay. I got accepted," in a too-cool-for-even-that-school monotone.[25]

## Mark brags: After all, they "trust me." Dumb fucks.

At the time, Mark Zuckerberg also loved *Ender's Game,* a novel whose main character, Andrew "Ender" Wiggin, was a child prodigy who mastered computer war simulations. Zuckerberg's college pal Joe Green told Steven Levy a story about the book's importance. When Sheryl Sandberg became Facebook's chief operating officer (COO), Green remembered, "I gave her a copy of *Ender's Game* and said, 'Read this to understand Mark.'"[26] Ender was being trained by the military to bomb virtual targets. He realized, much later, that what happened on his computer affected the real world. People actually died.[27]

Back in 2003, few people could explain why so many unpermitted pictures of kids being posted online, and such a barrage of judgment, should matter so much in reality. It had only happened on the Internet, where normal rules supposedly didn't apply. Yet Orson Scott Card knew the risks in 1985. "The power to cause pain is the only power that matters, the power to kill and destroy," he wrote in *Ender's Game,* "because if you can't kill then you are always subject to those who can, and nothing and no one will ever save you."[28] But here's the thing: when Ender's computer program led to mass destruction, it was *intended* as a cautionary tale.

Facebook was not simply a college prank that got wildly out of hand after it grew into one of the most powerful businesses in world history. Social media's risks were seen early on, and Zuckerberg got into trouble for it. "I understood that some parts were still a little sketchy," Zuckerberg wrote with a searching tone, in an email to Fuerza Latina and the Harvard Association of Black Women that the *Crimson* published. *Some parts. A little.* "I hope you understand, this is not how I meant for things to go, and I apologize for any harm done as a result of my neglect to consider how quickly the site would spread and its consequences thereafter," he wrote. "I definitely see how my intentions could be seen in the wrong light."[29] As Zuckerberg apologized for Facemash, he hedged. He confessed, then he self-justified.

The *Crimson* printed Zuckerberg's apology. That made it official, since the student newspaper influenced opinions on campus. The *Crimson* was so powerful, in fact, that Zuckerberg searched for the private login information that student reporters had submitted for their accounts on Thefacebook, and he used those same passwords to access their school email accounts, so he could read what they were going to write about him before the paper went to press.[30] He didn't need to conduct a new cyberattack that time; he already had their data.

That was part of a pattern. Early on, Zuckerberg seemed to view his access to private information as a convenient path to power, not as a weighty responsibility, as his AOL Instant Messenger chats would later reveal, when *Business Insider* released them in 2010:

*Zuck:* Yeah so if you ever need info about anyone at Harvard
*Zuck:* Just ask.
*Zuck:* I have over 4,000 emails, pictures, addresses, SNS [screennames]
*[Redacted Friend's Name]:* What? How'd you manage that one?
*Zuck:* People just submitted it.
*Zuck:* I don't know why.
*Zuck:* They "trust me"
*Zuck:* Dumb fucks.[31]

Zuckerberg's cavalier approach to data and user trust meant that breaches would occur, which would become problematic after the company was a global force over a decade later: data from 50 million users leaked in September 2018, then 600 million in March 2019, 540 million more in April, 419 million in September, and 309 million in December.[32] All those times they failed to protect people's data were just the sins of omission. Yet there were far worse issues, beyond even what Frances Haugen shared, that directly resulted from what Facebook and other social media companies did to us, on purpose, to keep us clicking.

On May 23, 2023, the U.S. surgeon general, Vivek Murthy, issued an official public statement imploring the American people to pay attention to an urgent public health issue. "Children are exposed to harmful content on social media, ranging from violent and sexual content, to bullying and harassment," Murthy explained. "And for too many children, social media use is compromising their sleep and valuable in-person time with family and friends. We are in the middle of a national youth mental health crisis, and I am concerned that social media is an important driver of that crisis—one that we must urgently address."[33]

In the official advisory, which was the kind of report "reserved for significant public health challenges that require the nation's immediate awareness and action," the surgeon general noted that 95 percent of children ages thirteen to seventeen were on social media, with a third of them "almost constantly." Despite the rules at Facebook and Instagram that officially restricted kids younger than thirteen from joining the platforms, the surgeon general's advisory found that 40 percent of children ages eight to twelve used social media. "Frequent social media use may be associated with distinct changes in the developing brain in the amygdala (important for emotional learning and behavior) and the prefrontal cortex (important for impulse control, emotional regulation, and moderating social behavior), and could increase sensitivity to social rewards and punishments." The surgeon general especially warned about the dangers "in early adolescence, when identities and sense of self-worth are forming, brain development is especially susceptible to social pressures, peer opinions, and peer comparison."[34]

The risks weren't just about data lost to the dark web. The concern was not a few cyberbullies who left crude or cruel comments. Social media posed health risks, impeding the cognitive growth, personality development, and self-esteem of children. By the time the college kids who had first joined Facebook around 2005 and 2006 had grown up and had kids of their own, the dangers of social media had become intergenerational—and they'd gotten way worse. These technologies had already begun to take time away from active engagement and learning during playdates, as adults took pictures, edited and cropped them, and scrolled on their phones to interact online. If some at Zuckerberg's company had their way, that "social" experience wouldn't just be meant for adults but for their toddlers and elementary schoolers, too.

Other documents Frances Haugen leaked to the *Wall Street Journal* showed that Facebook had created a team to study preteens as "a valuable but untapped audience." It was a startling revelation. Facebook had begun to develop plans to engage our youngest children with their products. "With the ubiquity of tablets and phones, kids are getting on the internet as young as six years old. We can't ignore this and we have a responsibility to figure it out," explained a confidential Facebook strategy document from 2018. "Imagine a Facebook experience designed for youth." By "youth," the company meant kids ages nine and younger. The research team had even strategized new ways for its products to engage children in preschool and elementary school during playdates.[35]

When did we go wrong? Early on.

## Mark decides: People will think what I tell them to think

The publishing titan William Randolph Hearst also attended Harvard. He got kicked out for playing too many pranks. Eventually, other schools honored him with an honorary degree, but Harvard never did.[36] Just like Zuckerberg's barnyard musings about Facemash, many of Hearst's pranks also involved animals. He kept a pet alligator named Champagne Charlie in his dorm room. After being put on probation, he bought a donkey, then left it in a classroom for a professor he disliked. He'd tied a note around the actual jackass's neck that read, "Now there are two of you."[37] The final straw came when he chiseled images of his professors' faces into pisspots.[38]

It seemed all in good fun then. But soon enough, he'd gone from managing Harvard's humor publication, the *Harvard Lampoon,* to growing his family media business into an incredible empire, conquering other publications to become one of the true marvels of the Gilded Age.[39] He owned more magazines and newspapers than anyone else in the world; he controlled information flow and orchestrated what could be said and who could be trusted, holding easy sway over opinions, all the world 'round. Doesn't that sound familiar?

Hearst was the inspiration for Orson Welles's classic film, just as Aaron Sorkin's *The Social Network* was deemed by *Esquire* as the "Citizen Kane for the Internet age" and "the movie of our new millennium."[40] The lessons from the lines spoken by Charles Foster Kane echo throughout the ages. When Kane's mistress fretted about their affair becoming public, she admonished, "Charlie, you got other things to think about. Your little boy, you don't want him to read about you in the papers." His response: "There's only one person who's going to decide what I'm going to do and that's me." And when his wife worried aloud about what "people will think," he interjected, "What I tell them to think."[41]

Back in 2003, Mark Zuckerberg defended Facemash to the *Harvard Crimson*, saying, "I didn't mean for it to be released so quickly because I wanted to control peoples' being offended by it." He'd also admitted, "It was basically a mistake."[42] This endeavor wasn't about creating the world's largest social network—and all the responsibility that entailed. Not for Zuckerberg, that would be beyond his control. He was just a math whiz college kid. Who would become the Citizen Kane of the Silicon Age? That would be Bill Gates at Microsoft, or someone like that. But Zuckerberg's earliest choices had profound implications. They would change the world.

Perhaps, with hindsight, we can now more fully understand the lessons Zuckerberg took away from his college experience, which seemed to be less about harms done and rules broken, and more about what will keep people addicted and coming back for more—or at least not feeling so offended that they'd shut him down. As Zuckerberg instructed his employees, which became a Silicon Age mantra: "Move fast and break things." Early on, when he saw the points go up on Thefacebook's scoreboard, showing the number of users and how often they checked the site, he'd figured out how to capture attention. He fed the impulses and insecurities of those judging others, along with those who kept checking to see how they were judged. He learned that a prank could cause 450 people to click on twenty-two thousand photos in a night, and he started working on a new version, one where he wouldn't have to hack servers to get pictures, because people would post the photos themselves.

But before that happened, how did the regulators, the authorities, and his community respond? That's important, too. Because even though the leaders who were responsible at the time were the Harvard IT Department and the President's Office, and the first people affected were his fellow undergraduates, the ways Zuckerberg got away with this are just as important as what he learned (and refused to learn) from it.

## Mark realizes: "People are more voyeuristic than I would have thought"

Zuckerberg met his future wife, Priscilla Chan, at the "Goodbye, Mark" party his fraternity threw for him before his potential expulsion due to the Facemash hack. He told her, "I'm going to get kicked out in three days, so we need to go on a date quickly."[43] They went to a chocolate shop called L.A. Burdick's, and Zuckerberg's cell phone rang halfway through the date. He told the caller that he had to decline the invite. He lied: no, he couldn't attend the party, no matter how much fun it was going to be, since he was on a date with a great girl he'd recently met. It was all a ploy to impress Chan. There was no party that night. The entire scheme had been carefully planned with the friend who had introduced Chan to Zuckerberg in the first place.[44] As another Silicon Valley mantra goes: "Fake it till you make it."

The university had restored the Internet to Kirkland, including room H33, but Zuckerberg worried that the Administrative Board of Harvard College, the "ad board," would expel him. He maintained it was all due to something pretty harmless. He looked forward to a future with more independence, and no overbearing administrators, telling a friend via AOL Instant Messenger that "there are no school newspapers and ad boards after you graduate. Only the new york times and the federal courts haha."[45] Harvard didn't kick him out. It placed him on "disciplinary probation" for "improper social behavior." (That was despite the extensive school rules and state laws he likely had broken, which the *Crimson* detailed at length in its reporting of the case.)[46]

The real lessons Zuckerberg took away from the Facemash incident didn't involve ethics and risks, or his mistakes and their consequences; rather, he was stunned by how much people liked looking at pictures of friends. When he was later asked about what Facemash taught him, Zuckerberg replied, under oath, "People are more voyeuristic than I would have thought."[47] He'd also learned how to get out of trouble, to repent and repeat.

To make amends, Zuckerberg extended an olive branch to Harvard's Association of Black Women in the fall of 2003. He offered to code a new website for the group, another great *Mark Zuckerberg Production*, free of charge. They accepted his offer.[48] We didn't know it, but in Cambridge that fall, something was taken from all of us. We definitely shouldn't blame a few college kids for the avalanche of domino effects that soon ensued, but it taught Zuckerberg valuable lessons about how to apologize and move on, how to maintain control. He'd worried people might be slightly offended, but with a small penance, he was proven right in that easy answer that "maybe there's a way to control that."[49]

What if Zuckerberg would have understood the harm he'd caused after invading others' privacy and urging people to judge others without anyone's permission? What if those who felt violated would have been listened to when they spoke out? Did the leaders at Harvard teach Zuckerberg the wrong lessons?

Should everything have been absolved after a school club website, then a weak apology in the student newspaper?

Zuckerberg opted not to ask permission, barely for forgiveness. He faked it. He made it. He moved fast, broke things, and learned on his own terms. Within a few months, Zuckerberg quit school anyway. And in 2017 Harvard gave him an honorary degree for hacking them and then creating the technology that encouraged all of us to judge each other by making it so very entertaining. Harvard didn't just give him the bachelor's degree that he never earned. For dropping out and eventually becoming a centibillionaire, it awarded him a doctorate.[50]

He'd coded the pronouncement, at the top of the page: *Will We Be Judged? Yes.*

He had set the stage. We'd all play our parts. *Click to Choose.*

And we did.

We all made choices. Our decisions about devoting our time—and ourselves—to Facebook and Instagram and Meta's other applications could have led to different outcomes earlier on. But now, we are hooked. The average American social media user spends thirty-three minutes a day on Facebook, twenty-eight minutes a day on Instagram, and over fifteen minutes a day on WhatsApp—totaling over an hour a day across all Meta-owned platforms.[51] The Like button fed a visceral need for appreciation, as we counted the people who approved of how we looked, what we did, what we wrote. So did the comments on our posts, initially from friends on our wall and then in groups both public and private, where we agreed or argued with strangers about news stories, articles, and opinions. Notifications alerted us about all of them; every action we took lured us back in, nudged us to participate more.

And if we tried to quit, Facebook reminded us what we'd lose. Your 713 friends will no longer be able to keep in touch with you, early versions of the site warned. We wouldn't want to make that mistake. There would be real-world consequences. But if that wasn't convincing enough, we'd see pictures of five friends, visual cues of our loss, which we'd have to scroll past to cancel our accounts. The text below each one read: *Angela will miss you. Tammie will miss you. Nina will miss you.*[52] Our choices would hurt other people. That's what Facebook told us. We wouldn't want to do that to them. We couldn't lose those connections. We'd never get them back. Because the data was the company's, not ours, just as we'd agreed from the start.

## Mark asserts: "I'm CEO, bitch"

This all began with Facemash, which Mark Zuckerberg hacked out of defiance, even out of spite. The first words he hid in the code, which would appear in case the site ever went down, were, "My mommy told me to take down this page, so it's down temporarily." He set the font size, put the date at the top in bold, and put the starting time in italics. Then he wrote the next line, words he coded and hid so no one would see them unless they looked at the source, which lawyers eventually did. According to a lawsuit, Zuckerberg coded: "Jessica Alona is a bitch. I need to think of something to make to take my mind off her."[53] When Zuckerberg left Harvard, he maintained that same swagger; it was apparent even on his business cards. In the spot where you'd normally see "Chief Executive Officer," it read, "I'm CEO, Bitch."[54] He sure was confident.

By the end of 2004, there were over a million users of Thefacebook. By 2005, there were 5.5 million.[55] That summer, Rupert Murdoch's NewsCorp, which owned both the *Wall Street Journal* and Fox News, purchased MySpace, which had around 16 million users at the time, paying $580 million in the deal.[56] The CEO of MySpace had tried to buy Facebook a few months before, in early 2005, but Zuckerberg showed up late to the meeting and seemed uninterested. After the NewsCorp acquisition and flush with cash, they tried again. Zuckerberg rebuffed the offer once more, later telling Murdoch that in the future more people wouldn't read the *Wall Street Journal* each morning or watch Fox News each night—they'd get their news through links shared by their friends online, on his platform.[57] He sure was right.

Murdoch missed it, but Donald Graham, whose family owned the *Washington Post*, saw Facebook's potential after a colleague's daughter had raved about its popularity at Harvard. "I was absolutely blown away. The first thing I said was, 'Mark, I think this is the best business idea that anybody's brought to this table,'" he told Alex Kantrowitz for the Big Technology podcast. "A lot of people in their late teens and early twenties are quite shy and awkward, including some very interesting ones," Graham observed. "Mark Zuckerberg in January 2005 in this conversation was the shiest, most awkward young person I've ever seen."[58]

But Graham was impressed, because Zuckerberg was clearly brilliant, and he put serious thought into every response about the company's strategies. "Well, there goes the *Crimson*," Graham joked. "Well, it's true," Zuckerberg laughed, but he explained that the plan wasn't to make money right away. It was to expand massively before anyone else built something better. Soon, the two had a handshake deal for Graham to invest in Facebook, but then the venture firm Accel Partners offered more money. "I will release you from your moral dilemma," Graham told Zuckerberg, "Go get every cent you can out of those guys."[59] Graham would join Facebook's board in 2008, receiving one million shares of stock that he committed to donate to charity after the company went public. His daughter Molly joined Facebook as an employee in 2009.[60]

In 2006 Viacom attempted to buy Facebook. Zuckerberg said no. Then Google made a bid. Again, the answer was no. When Yahoo asked, rumors began circulating that it might go as high as $3 billion. "I was like, *Well, okay,*"

Zuckerberg recalled. He genuinely considered it, but the actual offer came in lower. "When it got down to it, they were talking about a billion dollars." While not as jaw-dropping, that offer was still unprecedented for such an early-stage company. Zuckerberg later heard that Doug Hirsch, a former Yahoo executive, had given his old colleagues private details about Facebook's growth numbers. He was Facebook's head of product at the time—but only for a short while longer. Zuckerberg fired him, and when a new employee saw Hirsch packing up his things, he turned to the CEO, asking how he might avoid the same fate. "Don't try to sell my company out from under me," Zuckerberg replied. He was cutthroat. That's for sure, too.[61]

Not long after that, Zuckerberg walked into a board meeting. He looked at his watch and declared, "Eight-thirty seems as good a time as any to turn down a billion dollars."[62] It was a defining moment for the company. That choice also changed the future of the Internet, and with it, the course of world history. Max Kelly, Facebook's chief security officer, remembered: "We literally tore the Yahoo offer up and stomped on it as a company! We were like, 'Fuck those guys, we are going to own them!' That was some malice-ass bullshit."[63]

On May 18, 2012, Facebook went public. It was valued at $104 billion and had 900 million users.[64] Mark Zuckerberg became rich and famous. He had discovered that silicon offered control. It created greater power, in pursuit of further world domination. It could then be transformed back into gold, which created greater scale, and far more riches and influence.

# CHAPTER 2

# DARK ARTS

Larry Page and Sergey Brin, Backrub and Google

At 12:47 p.m. on May 10, 1869, Leland Stanford, Sr., drove the Golden Spike into the ground of Promontory Summit, Utah. He'd finished the transcontinental railroad and begun the first mass media moment in American history, as the messages spread at light speed via telegraph, electrified the nation, and sparked festivities nationwide with these four letters: D-O-N-E. The spike itself bore engravings, including this message: "May God continue the unity of our Country as this Railroad unites the two great Oceans of the world."[1] Or rather, the story was supposed to go like that.

Only four years after the Civil War had torn America apart, private industry could become a salve, which made Stanford and his business partners our saviors. Due to the exceptional drive of these Great Men of History, they'd achieved the unimaginable. Then because of technology, we all knew about it in an instant, so we could celebrate together. That's what they'd hoped would happen. The inspiring words of Stanford's speech might even be remembered as magnificent as the promise he fulfilled, not just to reunite America but, truly, to stitch the nation together even better, once and for all. At least, that was the plan.

In this retelling of history, Leland Stanford's railroad legacy should have been the one that every American of his era would have been gauged by: without him, Carnegie might have flamed out, for you needed Stanford's railways to sell such steel; we'd never know Rockefeller, who couldn't transport all that oil without Stanford; and Vanderbilt would've been foolhardy to shift from steamboats to trains, unless pioneers like Stanford had not already proven it was profitable.[2] Again, that was how it was all supposed to have gone. That was the myth they'd hoped to make.

They tried to hammer it out, once and for all, using a precious metal. The spike didn't stay in the ground for long. It was far too expensive for that, exquisitely made of 17.6 carat gold that weighed over 14 ounces. They sent it back to California, where it would eventually be displayed at the grand, innovative university that would bear the Stanford name.

What actually happened was a bit more complicated, as it always is. After an overly long introduction that was remembered as "arduously verbose," Stanford prepared to drive in the Golden Spike. He took the heavy hammer into his hand, held it aloft, and let gravity take over—and he missed, striking the tie instead. Next, the Union Pacific's Thomas Durant, who was too hungover to give the speech he'd planned, not only missed the spike but the tie, too, hammering a useless thud against the earth. The wealthy men, exasperated and no doubt embarrassed, asked one of their workers to drive home the spike. He did so without breaking a sweat, and his name was soon forgotten. Yet there's much more to be learned from the true story than there is from the mythology: a forgotten worker swung the heavy hammer with ease, while the ultrarich profited. At a self-congratulatory affair, hungover from their excesses, they defined progress and made history. And they'd be remembered for it instead of the laborers who did the work.

But where is the truth in the great American triumph of our transcontinental railroad? The unknown laborers didn't decide what would be remembered. The hands that did the work are now long gone. Their names are erased, as if they'd never even existed. Instead, they're replaced by oversimplifications, a single paragraph in a museum next to the Golden Spike, or a picture, a caption, and a paragraph in a high school textbook about Great Men of History. That was decided for us by whom—by the powerful dead? The permanently prestigious? The wealthy from another long-gone era? Where is the truth in that history?

As we dig deeper, we discover that Stanford wanted to hire only white-skinned laborers, but he faced a dilemma when they refused the dangerous, backbreaking work.[3] In January 1864 Central Pacific started with a crew of twenty-one workers—all of Chinese descent. Over the next five years, fifteen to twenty thousand Chinese immigrants built the railroad. They worked six days a week, digging away earth and exploding through mountains, and they were originally paid $26 a month, about $470 in 2023. They made up 90 percent of the workforce. The other 10 percent, who were white, were hired at much higher rates for the same work, making $40 monthly, or $723 in 2023.[4]

Can we still believe in the supposed moral of the story, about "the unity of our Country," when we learn that the hand-me-down fairytale about Great Men of History who got it "D-O-N-E" was overstated and embellished all along? What reality are we left with, if those who wrote the history (and promoted it, to glorify themselves) weren't the ones who accomplished the most heroic deeds, and those who did were exploited, then mostly forgotten? How often do we do this, pleasantly remembering American greatness—when it was, in fact, a miscellany of missing information, if not outright misinformation? Is the U.S. history we know now merely a romanticization written by the victorious, by and about corporate titans and civic heroes? Was their destiny manifested not because these Great Men of History were exceptional, not because they were more virtuous, but because they were more powerful, and the rest of us were taught the history that they wanted us to learn?

That would match the origin of the word "prestige," after all.

*Prestige, noun*: widespread respect and admiration felt for someone or something on the basis of a perception of their achievements or quality. Origin: mid-seventeenth century (in the sense "illusion, conjuring trick"): from French, literally "illusion, glamour," from late Latin praestigium "illusion," from Latin praestigiae (plural) "conjuring tricks.[5]

In any case, their power persists. In some ways, their enduring prestige still controls how we remember them. Or maybe we secretly prefer their noble myths, their tales of triumph? Does that feel better than admitting to any injustices, from a bastard reality we misremembered? Even if we wanted to, is there enough information out there to learn what actually happened? What is possible, even knowable, if we wanted to try to discover the capital-A, capital-T Absolute Truth? Could we ever catalogue all the world's knowledge? Or should we just accept that most history will exist as a collection of happy misremembrances, cheerfully cherished, in our collective selective memory?

## Stanford and Olmsted: The conqueror and the gardener

Leland Stanford, Sr., was a determined man. He had strict, even stern views about who decided what was right and true. The university that many people think was named after him was, in fact, named after his son. It was a way to honor the boy who succumbed to typhoid in 1884, two months before his sixteenth birthday.[6] The next year, Stanford founded the university "to promote the public welfare by exercising an influence in behalf of humanity and civilization."[7] He wanted this university to influence others, and to have a reputation for advancing the common good, for that would be virtuous. That would be a beautiful thing. It would represent, for him, something meaningful. It would be an undying tribute in his son's memory, something true that would leave a lasting legacy.

Stanford spared no expense for the new school, seeking out the great landscape architect Frederick Law Olmsted, the genius behind those magnificent rambles of New York's Central Park and the glorious grounds of the United States Capitol.[8] Olmsted and his sons planned for the university to have the same aesthetic that was later used to build many of the most beloved campuses across America, all with a similar pastoral feel: the Ohio State University, the University of Notre Dame, Louisiana State University, the University of Florida, and numerous others.[9] Stanford's vision for a great university, "in behalf of humanity and civilization," was for a gorgeous campus designed by the very best, the virtuoso who orchestrated America's great outdoor spaces, the father of modern landscape architecture.[10]

But unlike those other projects, Leland Stanford objected to Olmsted's campus plans and attempted to micromanage its development; he wanted fewer sunny walkways to amble along and more courtyards shaded by stately towers. Olmsted asked for $10,000 up front—seemingly daring Stanford not to hire him—but Stanford didn't flinch at the cost, and he didn't waver in his demands to the famous architect. When Olmsted presented the final blueprints, Stanford overhauled the entire undulating design and insisted on a colossal Memorial Arch to cover the north entrance to the university. The quarrel was about more than bricks and mortar, however. Stanford's and Olmsted's ideas of a university clashed. In the tension of their argument, we could see a great debate about who determined the future, and who had the right to decide what was beautiful and true.

Stanford's business success had taught him that civilization could be built up; he knew that, because he had done it. It was Western civilization hammered out in iron through westward expansion, a conquest won by charging hard in one direction without being distracted by damages done. Alternatively, Olmsted believed the civilized mind was cultivated and grown by turning inward in contemplation or seeking inspiration all around the fertile grounds. Education, for Olmsted, meant exploring life's mysteries, wandering the promenades alone, or learning and questioning in near-and-dear conversation. Olmsted's ideal was to nurture and prune new theories as they grew, being better than one's own ego by gathering ideas together, subtly, with craft and care.[11]

Stanford was the hunter, the conqueror. Olmsted was the gardener, the gatherer.

Like many other businessmen of his era, Stanford prospered due to order and organization. By setting the rules, corporate control sought to make sense of chaos. Money aligned everything. In 1869 there was greater dysfunction than we could imagine today. On the date the Golden Spike connected the Atlantic to the Pacific, there were around one hundred different time zones across the

United States.[12] As Jack Beatty explained in *Age of Betrayal: The Triumph of Money in America, 1865–1900*, several places created the most confusion. Wisconsin had thirty-eight separate local zones. There were twenty-seven in Indiana and twenty-three in Illinois. In the nineteenth century, few Americans had traveled beyond their hometowns, so this unruly patchwork didn't matter. But the business of nationwide railroads required greater certainty and, with it, a more universal definition for everyone to agree on. To make sense of it all, businessmen sought dominion over the clock, just as they had with weights and measures. The U.S. government resisted at first. Only the sun above at midday could dictate noontime, policymakers maintained. God should determine the world's natural order, not business interests.[13]

At a convention held in downtown Chicago in April 1883, William F. Allen, editor of the *Official Railway Guide*, proposed establishing four equal time zones across the country. Using two brightly shaded maps, he first showed a chaotic clash of colors as "the barbarism of the past," while the clean, clear, consolidated stripes of the second map promised America "the enlightenment we hope for in the future." The railroad companies all agreed to the new rules, which took effect at 12:01 a.m. on November 18, 1883. Thirty years later, Congress came around. It made the boundaries set by the railroads the official law of the land, nationwide.[14] The earlier mind-boggling contradiction of clocks seems unfathomable today. Likewise, Stanford's effort to make sense of the world, through the founding of Stanford University, meant bringing order to a world that seems so strange, disconnected, and disordered to us today.

This was an era when the truth was supposedly decided by the Great Men of History, the businessmen who'd won out. Hesitant legislators protested that they shouldn't use technology and math to reorder what was, naturally, God's alone to decide. They lost the argument. The prior patchwork became the four distinct continental American time zones. The skeptics who dared to question the corporate order were relegated to a distant past.

They were from a different time altogether.

## Larry meets Sergey: Backrub scratches an unquestionable itch

The time zones across America today make so much sense to us that they go unquestioned. Our phones and laptops automatically switch over once we cross an imaginary line. It's a decided issue. Yet while some Americans might believe we set the rules and have everything figured out, when spring arrives we change everything for daylight savings time, but most of the world does not.[15] The certainty of the clock is a recent creation, which people decided. Time zones and the twenty-four-hour day represent choices that became social norms. But daylight savings time shows they aren't universal. These ideas are manmade, not Absolute Truth.

When it comes to topics with even less consensus, the campus resulting from the Stanford/Olmsted compromise has hosted an array of thinkers and doers who have believed in both the conqueror's and the gardener's approach, along with many who try to navigate the world in the gradations between either extreme. Few of those discussions were more important than the lively debates between a couple of students that started in the fall of 1995. That year, a Stanford computer science master's degree student in his second year welcomed a prospective new graduate student to campus. They had much in common. They shared a passion for computers and a vision for the world that the early Internet could create, which was informed by their upbringing as professors' kids who went west to study at Stanford. They admired the eventual compromise of the rectangular courtyards and undulating walkways, which led to debates. Their time together at Stanford inspired them—to argue. "I thought he was pretty obnoxious. He had really strong opinions about things, and I guess I did, too," Larry Page remembered in an interview with *Wired*. "We *both* found each other obnoxious," Sergey Brin countered.[16]

They'd grown up in the long shadows of the towers and spires of college campuses, and in other shadows, too, as super smart kids of college professors. They contemplated ideas in those early days, about science and reason, corporate greed and evildoing, what's believed in and built, the dark arts, and those who bring the truth to light. These Stanford Students would argue about all that—and much more—and one of their discussions would lead to the decision to develop a computer program that would map the connections that held the early Internet together. As documented in Adam Fisher's oral history collection *Valley of Genius: The Uncensored History of Silicon Valley (as Told by the Hackers, Founders, and Freaks Who Made It Boom)*, they brainstormed other ideas before that. They sketched out concepts for self-driving automobiles or a rock that would orbit the earth and be tied to a tether anchored to us, so we could attach an elevator and climb into space just like the fairytale of Jack and his beanstalk.[17]

But the one great idea that would alter the Internet, and affect all humanity, came from a dream Larry Page had, which he woke up from but kept thinking about: "What if we could download the whole Web," he wondered, "and just keep the links and . . .," what would happen then?[18] What if he could just retrace the steps from there, to backtrack all the paths taken on the early Internet? What if we could index all that is known?

Then we could search it!

All those links would teach us what was most important, they realized. As more information went online, they could then track new paths, too. Page and Brin started to download the entire Internet onto Stanford's computers. As Brin told Fisher, "we had stolen these computers from all over the department, sort of," by building a network of machines to map everything, or at least to try to do that. Because it measured how many sites referenced back to a given website, the project was originally called Backrub.[19] At first they'd figured out how to download one hundred pages at a time, but then a fellow graduate student, Scott Hassan, helped out by coding a new program to download thirty-two thousand all at once. They had begun a world-changing project. "It was mostly just Sergey and I from 2 a.m. to 6 a.m. in the morning," Hassan later told Fisher. "We just worked on it in the middle of the night, mainly because, if I worked on it during the day, I would get yelled at by my boss, because building a search engine was not considered research."[20]

Search might not have been "research," but it was what fascinated many top computer scientists back then. Just five years before Brin met Page, the World Wide Web was born. Tim Berners-Lee worked at CERN, Conseil Européen pour la Recherche Nucléaire, the European Council for Nuclear Research, which was established after World War II as a scientific research institute for multinational collaboration on particle physics. Berners-Lee worked as a software engineer and systems architect. His bosses tasked him with finding a way to manage all the data and reports developed by researchers who were seeking to unravel the universe's greatest mysteries through knowledge about atomic energy and beyond. On August 6, 1991, he debuted the very first website at http:// info.cern.ch/hypertext/WWW/TheProject.html.[21] Under "WorldWideWeb—Summary," he wrote: "The WWW project merges the techniques of information retrieval and hypertext to make an easy but powerful global information system." He traced its origins in academia: "The project is based on the philosophy that much academic information should be freely available to anyone."[22] Right then and there, the bedrock of the Internet was established: with a global purpose from the start, for knowledge, not for profit. We owe so much to that ethos of both freedom and fairness; the Internet was intended to be free, for all, forever. In fact, when colleagues encouraged Berners-Lee to patent the idea of the World Wide Web, he refused. "Berners-Lee didn't try to cash in on his invention and rejected CERN's call to patent his Web technology," historian Elizabeth Nix explained. "He wanted the Web to be open and free so it could expand and evolve as rapidly as possible."[23]

Even with all the sleek corporatization to come, that early decision was pivotal. The Internet would cost nothing to use. Internet access providers would eventually charge customers for their services, but we would never have to pay a penny to access each website. As a result, the World Wide Web began as an economic system that incentivized openness and equal access, for abundant content creation and freedom of expression. Even Berners-Lee's sprawling vision for a "powerful global information system" would be a drastic underestimation. Yet he clearly grasped the values that underpinned his efforts. "And mostly, the

Internet thrives on lack of regulation. But some basic values have to be preserved," he wrote in a blog in 2006. He reasoned, "Democracy depends on freedom of speech. Freedom of connection, with any application, to any party, is the fundamental social basis of the Internet, and, now, the society based on it."[24]

Those were the founding principles for this new online experience, built for enhancing democracy everywhere through more freedom to connect. But Berners-Lee didn't call it the Internet at first. He instead used "WorldWideWeb," abbreviated as "W3," to describe "a wide-area hypermedia information retrieval initiative aiming to give universal access to a large universe of documents." Berners-Lee began with instructions about how links could take you from one site to the next: "a reader clicks with a mouse (or types in a number if he or she has no mouse)." That remains such a wonderful, innocent phrase, like a glimpse of Eden before the Fall. Then Berners-Lee wrote this: "To search and index, a reader gives keywords (or other search criteria)." It made the Internet's universality and interconnectedness, and the ability to search all that knowledge, indispensable from day one. It's obvious now why Page and Brin would want to expand on that idea, with the code they wrote building off of Berners-Lee's ideas. Then Berners-Lee wrote a third sentence, never fathoming how true it would become: "These are the only operations necessary to access the entire world of data."[25]

It was an auspicious and ambitious beginning if there ever was one, and when Brin and Page published their Stanford thesis as a joint effort, they wrote it as a technical treatise of their new endeavor to index and search all the world's online data. The Internet was already growing exponentially: Berners-Lee's site debuted on August 6, 1991, and by the end of 1992 there were only ten websites. By 1994 there were three thousand, including the first version of Yahoo, which Jerry Yang and David Filo built after meeting at Stanford in 1989. They came up with the concept for "Jerry and David's Guide to the World Wide Web," decided to call it Yahoo, and registered yahoo.com on January 18, 1995.[26] Calling themselves "Chief Yahoos" rather than cofounders or CEOs, they priced the stock at $13 a share for an initial public offering (IPO) on April 12, 1996, and it soared to $43 before ending the day at $33. Yahoo's first-day gains were the third highest in stock market history, and just fifteen months after they'd bought the website, their tech startup that indexed the early Internet was worth $848 million.[27] To ensure quality, Yahoo had hired experts to list the best results. In fact, the name was an acronym, which stood for "Yet Another Hierarchical Officious Oracle."[28]

Page and Brin's Internet indexer was different, though, because they relied on networks, not hierarchies and experts. They began their project in a more democratic and open fashion, and they didn't intend to start a company with it. When these Stanford Students started downloading the earliest twenty-four million websites, the Chief Yahoos already had an impressive head start. But both companies would have an incredible first-mover advantage as the Internet grew, with those twenty-four million pages representing only 1.3 percent of the nearly two billion websites today.[29]

Page and Brin published their plans openly because they wanted others to review their work. Their peers were big-brained computer science graduate students who loved technology. These scholars cared about the citations of their publications, which was how they sought objectivity. The idea of retracing the connections between websites might have come in a dream, but it was inspired by Page's upbringing. Carl Victor Page, Sr., was one of the first faculty members of the Department of Computer Science and Engineering at Michigan State. He started there in 1967. For decades he researched what we now know as artificial intelligence.[30]

During those same years, Michael Brin taught mathematics at the University of Maryland, where he explored ways to graph different systems by using data, formulas, and network mapping. Looking back, both the Page and Brin families had been working for decades on the theories that became reality once the World Wide Web of connected computers made the Internet possible. Based on the environments they were raised in, and who raised them, it is now clear why the Stanford Students knew how to make the most of the early Internet—how they integrated mathematical concepts with the formulas that formed their first algorithms; where they learned the network theory to connect computers as nodes and edges; why it made so much sense to index all they could early, since millions of sites could exponentially scale to become billions; and how citation counts decided influence in ways that could be adapted to determine what was most important online. They were raised by professors who taught these concepts every day.[31]

Building Backrub especially depended on this last factor, the power of citation counts. Knowing who was smartest, and who was best, was something you could try to measure. Because that was important, professors did. The number of times you were cited, and by whom, wouldn't actually determine the Absolute Truth about who was most influential. But it sure came close, so citations proved worthiness, a collectively accepted social norm. Publications helped decide progress at every career stage, since that was how professors compared their achievements to other big brains everywhere else. Those numbers helped determine whether they would have gotten tenure, that cherished lifetime contract. As a result, academia's approach to faculty personnel matters would inspire the strategies behind the ideas that made Backrub, which became the graduate thesis for these two Stanford Students. It led to the company that started as a nonsense word, a riff on the largest number imaginable, which became a verb that meant summoning all the world's information in an instant: Google.[32]

## Larry and Sergey go on a vision quest . . . for truth?

The Stanford Students' thesis, "The Anatomy of a Large-scale Hypertextual Web Search Engine," explained their earliest results. They'd crawled the web to gather all its data, determining exactly what page linked to another, and then they ranked the results just like paper citations in academia. Their thesis detailed the technical ins and outs of their approach to map the World Wide Web, and it revealed their love of knowledge and research, of classification and organization, of consensus and facts. The words that Page and Brin used were all scientific—even the first noun, anatomy, implied a biological evaluation of these connected computers—but this wasn't just a technical treatise by computer science graduate students.

Their thesis was also a principled document written by two philosophers who walked the Olmsted/Stanford grounds during fierce debates. They had decided to take a moral stand, together, against what they already regretted was happening to the World Wide Web. "Aside from tremendous growth, the Web has also become increasingly commercial over time," they complained, with .com domains covering 60 percent of the Internet in 1997 compared to only 1.5 percent four years prior. They also criticized the similar expansion of commercial search engines like Yahoo because no one knew what influenced the results. "This causes search engine technology to remain largely a black art and to be advertising oriented," they warned. "With Google, we have a strong goal to push more development and understanding into the academic realm."[33] In other words, Page and Brin believed they were too committed to knowledge to be prejudiced by wealth, to be warped by corporate influences.

Even during the first five years of the World Wide Web, fact and fiction had already begun to blur. The Stanford Students despised that trend. As a response, their project wasn't neutral at all. To be unbiased, it was an *anticorporate* effort. With the first words of the founding documents that would become Google, Page and Brin deemed ads to be evil. Ads distorted the truth. They were the twisted result of dark arts practiced by corrupt corporations.

In 2006 Berners-Lee warned, "Let's see whether the United States is capable as acting according to its important values, or whether it is, as so many people are saying, run by the misguided short-term interests of large corporations."[34] That was exactly what Page and Brin were worried about in 1997, and their moral vocabulary of right and wrong focused on unseen biases, ominous risks, and undue influences. It wasn't just that they lacked a business plan—they loudly, even brashly, rejected any profit-making in this undertaking—because they'd agreed that corporate America's answers to people's questions would bias the results toward the interests of individual businesses, not commonly agreed on facts.[35]

* * *

In appendix A of their thesis, Page and Brin gave a striking example that showed exactly why they were so concerned. In their prototype, one of the links that returned the most matches for "cellular phone" was an academic study that addressed the risks of distracted driving. Any commercialization of their search engine would ruin the project, they reasoned, because "we expect that advertising funded search engines will be inherently biased towards the advertisers and away from the needs of the consumers." This type of bias was, to use the phrase chosen by Page and Brin, "particularly insidious."[36]

On November 10, 1997, Brin explained his rationale further in an email to a list-serv, which was first published in the book *How Data Happened: A History from the Age of Reason to the Age of Algorithms* (2023) by Columbia University's Chris Wiggins and Matthew Jones:

> As scientists in the field of data mining, it is important for us to periodically take a step back from the technology and consider the ethics of using it. . . . auto insurance companies analyse accident data and set insurance rates of individuals according to age, gender, vehicle type. . . . If they were allowed to by law, they would also use race, religion, handicap, and any other attributes they find are related to accident rate. Health insurance companies also use similar data. . . . All of these can be seen as results of data mining and they have a significant affect [*sic*] on people's lives.[37]

These two Stanford Students took an ethical stand, in honor of intellectual honesty, in pursuit of agreed on and commonly accepted facts. They also, clearly and directly, warned about the risks of corporations using data to target people based on their demographics or other attributes. And then, to make their point even clearer, they explicitly warned in their thesis about an even more egregious commercial takeover they'd noticed on search engines like Yahoo that were ad-funded. Companies advertised at the top of the website, with a banner ad, which replaced the results someone was expecting to find there. "This type of bias is much more insidious than advertising," Page and Brin explained, "because it is not clear who 'deserves' to be there, and who is willing to pay money to be listed."[38]

Taking profits in exchange for search results would cost Page and Brin far too much, in terms of true-to-the-facts academic integrity, so they rejected letting any financial factors impact their decision-making or alter the code that would power this search engine. The World Wide Web had been built by scholars for the common pursuit of knowledge, not for the .com takeover that Page and Brin complained about in their thesis. They hoped Google could return the Internet to its origins, which were freer, more open, and more transparent.

Jerry and David hired experts to create their guide to the World Wide Web, whom they paid with money from the companies that advertised on the site to promote their products as the best results.[39] If Yahoo was becoming where the corporate conquerors took over the new frontier of the World Wide Web, then the results from Google would yield what naturally emerged, instead of what businesses wanted everyone to see. Rather than hunting and killing for a profit, Google would garden and wait to see what grew. Page and Brin would use computers to map connections based on what people cited, thus nurturing the Internet in its original ethos: for a university's purpose, for a more universal purpose. While the Yahoo model relied on the "black art" of "insidious" business, which listed what was true because Great Men of History had decided it, for the purpose of profits, the Stanford Students agreed with Olmsted, and they gathered input from everyone in their quest for truth. That felt more natural, more organic.

Mark Zuckerberg's business began as people made choices between two pictures, which created a ranking system that seemed objective (while objectifying). But Facemash was totally subjective, as thoughtless as our most impulsive reactions. Page and Brin started with a commitment to advancing knowledge, to actual answers, by designing a ranking system they intended to be unbiased, public, and auditable. From its very start, Google was meant to be a solution machine that provided accurate information. They sought global agreement about facts, in an open and democratic fashion by asking everyone what belonged. At least originally, they refused to be compromised by unfair influences or have their results ruined by subjectivity.[40]

To the Stanford Students, the truth wasn't some academe fantasy; it was a noble pursuit based on a higher calling. Consider the words the mottoes of these universities used: *Veritas*, truth (Harvard); *Lux et Veritas*, light and truth (Yale); *Lux Libertas*, light, liberty (University of North Carolina at Chapel Hill); *Veritate Duce Progredi*, to advance with truth as our guide (Arkansas); *Et Facta est Lux*, and there was light (Morehouse).[41] Michigan State's mission, in the Page family lineage, was "advancing knowledge and transforming lives."[42] The one that best described the early Internet that the Stanford Students dreamed of, before Brin and Page crashed Stanford's servers and then left to start their new venture, was *Esse Quam Videri*, to be rather than seem (Appalachian State, among many other schools).[43] For Brin and Page, Absolute Truth wasn't just an abstract idea. Pursuing knowledge and seeking the truth were the reasons Google first existed. And in case you're about to look it up on your phone before you turn the page, which might risk you getting distracted by some advertisement, Stanford's is "the wind of freedom blows"—not in Latin, but in German: *Die Luft der Freiheit weht*. That slogan, preferred by its founding president, David Starr Jordan, won out over "truth and service."[44]

Page and Brin wanted to crawl the entire Internet to answer any possible question. Like Tim Berners-Lee, that was the original purpose of search, with far more meaning than money. So they actively rejected profits. Their anticorporate approach played out in numerous ways early on. In fact, Scott Hassan told Adam Fisher that Google even gave their largest competitors free exposure on their site. Alongside the search results that came from the earliest version of Google, they listed other outcomes for the same search term from Excite, Lycos, AltaVista, Infoseek, and Inktomi (but, notably, not Yahoo).[45] Neither Page nor Brin wanted to start a business of their own, so Page set up meetings with the leaders at other search engines to show off what they'd done. No one wanted to license it. For a year they talked to more suitors. In 1998 Yahoo had the chance to license Google's technology for $1 million, but David Filo told them to strike out on their own and introduced them to investors instead.[46]

Early on, Page and Brin met rejection after rejection. That was because they were trying to sell search to companies as the users, not selling what its users searched to companies.

$$* * *$$

They began to meet with investors, and Andy Bechtolsheim, one of the founders of SUN Microsystems, wrote a check for $100,000 to invest in this new technology and the business he hoped it could create. There was only one problem. The check was made out to "Google, Inc.," which didn't exist. Page and Brin started this project to resist the corporate takeover of the World Wide Web, but now they had a decision to make. They tried to license what they'd built for $1 million. They'd failed, so now they needed to incorporate a business so they could deposit Bechtolsheim's check. "It was pretty unreal," Page remembered, and Brin agreed: "It was like, *That was pretty easy!*"[47] These Stanford Students would eventually have a net worth of over $100 billion each.[48] So, check in hand, what did they decide to do first?

Instead of going to the bank, they loaded up for Burning Man. On August 30, 1998, they created the first Google Doodle. It was a Burning Man stick figure, arms raised behind the yellow O.[49] As employee number twenty, Marissa Mayer, later recalled, it was an out-of-office message while they were out in the desert, relaxing, partying, and eating MREs.[50]

## Larry and Sergey go on a venture quest . . . for wealth

Soon Google received a full $1 million seed round, adding Jeff Bezos (Amazon's founder), Ram Shriram (Amazon's vice president of business development at the time, who was also an early executive at the Internet browser Netscape), and

David Cheriton (a Stanford professor who led the computer science department's Distributed Systems Group).[51] They still didn't have a real business model, but the search engine was working wonderfully. As Brin stated on June 7, 1999, in a press release announcing they'd raised $25 million more, "A perfect search engine will process and understand all the information in the world. That is where Google is headed."[52] From the absolutes—"perfect," "all," and "in the world"—to the definitiveness of the direction they envisioned for the company, Brin was wholeheartedly optimistic about what was possible. Google just didn't have a way to make money with it yet.

Sequoia Capital and Kleiner Perkins led Google's $25 million round, but other big names joined, too: Shaquille O'Neal, Tiger Woods, Henry Kissinger, and Arnold Schwarzenegger.[53] As the press release also noted, "Google's innovative user interface includes dynamic summaries, a cached web, and the time-saving 'I'm feeling lucky' button."[54] That last part was a quirky, quick click to some, an overt innuendo to others. Both explanations held up. Early on, Brin wanted to give out Google-branded condoms to high schoolers as an early marketing scheme, and the company had fishbowls full of "I'm feeling lucky" condoms, in the company's trademarked primary colors, free for employees.[55]

The "I'm feeling lucky" button lasted until 2010, but it didn't go away because an employee complained about the sexualization of search, or due to backlash from the political right or left, from a conservative legislator concerned about biblical principles or a liberal media pundit concerned about toxic masculinity. The button disappeared because clicking it would take you instantly to the first result. That meant it bypassed all the places where Google wanted to advertise to you. The button went away when greater profit-making became paramount.[56] Google eventually added it back to searches on web browsers, but that was only after they'd created the instant search that automatically populated the words that Google's artificial intelligence had guessed you wanted next, which would take you to a page where you'd see ads. More often than not, people started searching using their phones, where there was no search button whatsoever. You just typed in what you wanted, hit return, and algorithms provided your answer—and often several advertisements to compete for your attention as well.[57]

Having written derisively in their thesis about the insidiousness of search engines like Yahoo, Google was soon powering Yahoo, too. They grew and grew, proving that their software-focused business model did not need so many people to scale. This was transformative. In the June 26, 2000, press release announcing the agreement with Google, Yahoo executives still made their business case for the hierarchical, in-person, and made-by-hand world, rather than the networked, digital, and machine-powered one to come: "Unlike search engines, which use automated 'spiders' to electronically crawl the Web to capture and store sites in the search engine's index," it stated, "Yahoo!'s staff of experts appropriately categorizes Web sites into an intuitive hierarchical organizational structure."[58] Yahoo remained true to its name, celebrating how it was a real business with hierarchy and experts; at the time, that was working just fine, because Yahoo was worth more than Ford, Chrysler, and GM combined.[59] But the Silicon Age was just getting started, and the future favored Google: with the automation and algorithms doing the work, with value from the data they mined for free, and with such exponential growth possible at astonishing speeds in this newly networked world.

Google built a democratized system where inputs would be distributed and intelligence would be artificial. Yahoo emphasized that their advantages existed in the expertise of the Great Men of History who knew better. While Google used algorithms to refer everyone to other sites throughout the World Wide Web, Yahoo built its directory with expert opinions, hoping to keep everyone clicking on Yahoo-owned sites as the be-all and end-all. But Google would win not just because of their algorithms but because of all of us. They didn't just create a great online search engine. They beat Yahoo, which depended on paid labor, with a better search engine that benefited from all our unpaid human effort. As the Internet grew, the machines learned what was most important based on what we looked at, clicked on, and cared about.

Page and Brin knew this, even back then. In the June 26, 2000, press release, the cofounders of the underdog search company Google, only a few months old, explained why they were so excited for different reasons. "We're extremely proud that Yahoo! has selected Google to complement its existing directory and navigational guide," said Brin. "This is a significant milestone for Google and a strong validation of our business strategy," which was one that was interconnected, automated, and exponential, because it didn't need to pay people to power it like Yahoo did.[60] It also clearly worked. People loved the service: "Google led all search engines with 97 percent of its users indicating that they would recommend Google to a friend."[61] That number wasn't just statistically significant. It was financially important.

Brin and Page had used words of morality earlier—describing the dark arts of deception, of disguising the truth, of insidious business—but now these incredible Stanford Students had become the Google Boys. That's what the media had started calling them.[62] By developing the ranking software that would index the Internet, using other websites to do the work for them, and then relying on code and clicks instead of paid people to yield the answers, the Google founders had discovered something transformational. In 2002 Yahoo again tried to buy Google, this time for $3 billion. Page and Brin wanted $5 billion.[63] Yahoo walked away, making a terrible mistake. Two years later, Google had its IPO with a market value of more than $23 billion.[64]

Ultimately, the donation by Leland Stanford, Sr., paled in comparison to the deal struck with the Google cofounders: "The university owns the technology," the director of Stanford's Office of Technology Licensing told the *New York Times* as the company prepared its IPO. "We license it to Google, which back then was just these two kids. They pay Stanford royalties annually. We also took a bit of stock in the deal." Her use of "these two kids" seemed patronizing, but that was likely meant for a reason. It sent a clear signal to Brin and Page not to do anything stupid like try to back out, now that they'd made it. The same went for her disclosure of the terms of the initial deal: somewhere between a third and one half of royalties went to Page and Brin, with the rest being shared by Stanford's computer science department and engineering school.[65]

Stanford owned over 1.8 million shares of Google stock when the company had its IPO in August 2004.[66] The university's trustees ordered the sale of 10 percent immediately, selling 184,207 shares on that first day. While that netted them over $15.6 million, if Stanford had kept all of their shares invested until 2021, it would have been one of the best bets in world history. That's because Google became one of capitalism's greatest success stories ever. If Stanford had left all 1,842,070 shares invested for those seventeen years, they would have been worth over $10 billion before the end of 2021.[67]

That was more money than anyone at Stanford could have imagined would have resulted from this project, perhaps Page and Brin most of all. Stories like theirs have caused many university administrators across America to think twice about needing to take the moral high ground of prioritizing truth over money, too, no matter what their mottos encourage. After the Stanford Students became the Google Boys, and they became centibillionaires, many leaders in academia also began to rethink their priorities. Universities have increasingly focused on tech transfer, or patenting and licensing their innovations, to benefit society and to create new revenue streams for the inventors and their institutions. In 1991 U.S. universities spent less than $12 billion on research and there were around five thousand invention disclosures. Three decades later they spend beyond $80 billion on research and make over twenty-five thousand disclosures each year, more than a fivefold increase in both respects.[68]

Universities have also changed the allocations of their investment portfolios during the Silicon Age. In recent years, many schools have taken on riskier bets with their endowments. That has often paid off massively. "University Endowments Mint Billions in Golden Era of Venture Capital," the *Wall Street Journal* headline read on September 29, 2021. The subheading said even more: "Some schools, including Washington University in St. Louis and Duke University, gained more than 50%."[69] That same year, the University of North Carolina's venture capital portfolio returned 142 percent, which contributed to overall gains exceeding 42 percent. Harvard's $53 billion endowment trailed others—logging a return of 34 percent that year—because their portfolio had a smaller allocation to venture capital. That was "the opportunity cost of taking lower risk," their endowment manager explained.[70] By putting more money into riskier venture funds, Brown has recently outperformed its peers by two or three times—and even five or six times for brief periods after venture-backed companies sold.[71] In 2016 Yale had less than one-sixth of its endowment in high-growth venture funds; five years later that allocation grew to more than one-quarter.[72]

Combining the endowments of four Ivy League schools—Columbia, Brown, Dartmouth, and Cornell, which were founded in 1754, 1764, 1769, and 1865, respectively—would be less than what Stanford's has become, even though it was founded in 1885. In other words, those four schools had nearly eight hundred years more of combined history, almost eight centuries of a head start on Stanford to grow their endowments. But now, Stanford was winning.[73] That's all due to the speed of the Silicon Age. A mere 152 years after the Golden Spike, and 136 years after the university's founding in the Golden State, the vast wealth and influence created by a single company like Google would have been unthinkable for the Great Men of the Gilded Age. Today, the success of startups coming out of Stanford has become one of the greatest legacies left by Leland Stanford, Sr.—and Jr.

Stanford's endowment is behind only Harvard and Yale.[74] In the black and white of a balance sheet, that's an irrefutable fact. You can Google it.

It's the best way we know to seek the Absolute Truth.  Or is it?

# CHAPTER 3

# YOU'RE GOING TO GET WHAT'S COMING TO YOU

Keith Rabois, Peter Thiel, and David Sacks, PayPal

Throughout the morning of January 8, 1992, a group of faculty, staff, and students from Stanford visited Mosswood Chapel, a Spanish-style building in Oakland with hardwood floors and exposed wood ceiling beams. Daylight flowed through the nine rectangular skylights above. The guests were all there to pay their respects to a colleague, teacher, and friend. He had died five days before, at the age of forty-three, after a difficult fight with a disease that stole his strength and ended his life. Nevertheless, the difference he made in others' lives remained.[1]

When Stanford announced the funeral arrangements for Arthur Hall, the university noted that "Hall had lived with AIDS for a long time, and he'd spoken openly about his illness and his sense of gratitude while living on 'borrowed time.'" He spent that time helping others, teaching freshmen English and creating new courses to help Stanford employees improve their on-the-job writing. His obituary also quoted from the admissions essay for his doctorate at Stanford, a program he ran out of time before completing: "No matter how much I may crab in certain moods about the low pay, the lack of job security, the weekend hours, the never-ending stacks of papers, the annoyance of coming across the phrase 'in this fast-moving world of today' for the 189th time in the concluding sentence of a student essay," he'd written, "there's something about teaching that attracts me and brings me back with renewed enthusiasm every September, no matter how burned-out I may have felt in June." He concluded, "At the risk of sounding dewy-eyed, I have never found anything else to do that I love or that rewarded me half as much."[2]

A month prior to his death, Arthur Hall had made a choice. In the precious moments before his hospital admission on December 6, he went back to campus one last time to pay his respects to his colleagues and students.[3] His last wish was to visit Stanford one more time, just so he could see them all. He wanted to say goodbye and to express his thanks. He found dignity in death by sharing those final few hours with loved ones who lived on, reflecting his love in their own lives, long after he was gone. A Stanford colleague honored his strength and grace to show gratitude to others in his final days. She memorialized his courage with these words: "He was such a teacher, such a teacher, even about how to live and how to die."[4]

* * *

Late at night on January 19, 1992, Keith Rabois had a decision to make, too. He had been shouting, and he'd paused to catch his breath. "Faggot! Hope you die of AIDS!" That was the first thing he'd screamed. What should he yell next? "Can't wait until you die, faggot." That's what he chose. He then continued, "You're going to get what's coming to you. You're going to get what's coming to you. Damn faggot!"[5]

The person Rabois screamed at, Dennis Matthies, was a respected Stanford faculty member. He had received the university's top teaching honor just a few years earlier, for "distinctive and exceptional contributions to undergraduate education or the quality of student life at Stanford." He taught English literature and lived on campus as a resident fellow. And, for what it mattered, he was heterosexual.[6]

That quarter, Matthies had been assigned two new courses, on "Learning Strategies" and "Reading Rate Improvement." He'd been asked to take on those responsibilities over winter break. The regular instructor had just died sixteen days before Rabois's late-night rant.[7]

His name was Arthur Hall.

## Keith creates controversy on campus and Stanford PR denounces him

Keith Rabois was a first-year law student at Stanford. He'd also been an undergrad there. That winter night, to get within shouting distance of Matthies's home, he joined sophomores Bret Scher and Mike Ehrman as they walked through Otero House in Wilbur Hall (which was then freshmen housing and is now Stanford's Public Service and Civic Engagement Theme dorm). Scher and Ehrman were later questioned about the incident, but they denied saying anything.[8] Rabois admitted to the student newspaper, the *Stanford Daily*, that he'd yelled the slurs.

In an official Stanford press release, issued on February 12, 1992, Rabois defended himself on the grounds of free speech. "Admittedly, the comments made were not very articulate, not very intellectual nor profound," he explained. Yet Rabois held his ground, because he believed the First Amendment allowed screaming slurs and wishing disease and death on someone. Having studied Stanford's handbook, the *Fundamental Standard*, he also felt he was within his rights: "The intention was for the speech to be outrageous enough to provoke a thought of 'Wow, if he can say that, I guess I can say a little more than I thought.'"[9]

It may seem strange that a university would issue a formal statement to the media about this incident, but Stanford likely wanted to get in front of a worsening crisis, by proactively managing public perception on its own terms. The dean of students confirmed that "this vicious tirade is protected speech" but then emphasized, "We must loudly reject their mean-spirited actions against a resident fellow and a valued member of the Stanford community."[10] Compared to the tactful language that the Stanford PR shop had quoted, Rabois was far more forthcoming with the rest of the words that the *Stanford Daily* had printed on February 5, 1992, from its interview with him. "I'm a first-year law student. I know exactly what you can say and what you can't," he'd insisted. When asked about what he *did* say, Rabois responded that the reports were "reasonably close" to what he'd yelled out. He recalled that his comments were, in his words, "mostly about faggots being bad in general."[11]

Numerous Stanford students sent letters to the *Stanford Daily*, in a chorus of astonishment mixed with condemnation, with many arguing that just because you're within your rights to say something, it doesn't make it right. Others observed that Rabois was unnecessarily incendiary, and his choices were as confusing as they were inappropriate: as a law student, he had decided to go to the freshman dorms, to scream slurs at a faculty member, and then to brag about being justified in doing so.[12] "Rabois' misguided belief that his actions have made a significant contribution to the debate about free speech and his attitude for self-congratulation for illuminating previously unclear aspects of the Fundamental Standard are laughable," Stanford junior Susannah Jech wrote to the *Stanford Daily*. "I can only hope that through future years of study at the Stanford Law School, Rabois will develop a sense of decency and will learn to act respectfully and rationally, not only towards individuals whose views he does not share, but also with regard to the laws and Constitution to which he owes so much."[13]

In the official press release, Stanford's dean of students had assessed: "This speech may have been 'free,' but it was also juvenile and brutal."[14] That sentiment was echoed by Robin Kennedy, the associate university counsel and the wife of Stanford president Donald Kennedy. She wrote a letter to the *Daily*: "I hope the Bar Association of whatever state in which Rabois elects to practice is informed of his behavior in this incident and aware that such behavior represents a violation of this community's values." She added: "As an attorney and Stanford alumna, I am deeply disturbed that a person of Rabois' character—and with his obvious disrespect for human dignity—may someday become qualified as a member of my profession, displaying two Stanford degrees on his office wall."[15]

This controversy raised so many important questions. Did Rabois personally loathe Matthies? Had he stirred up trouble to test if he could get away with the taboo speech? Or was it something else—perhaps Matthies wasn't even the target of the attack? Was it supposed to be Hall? After all, no one was home when it happened. Was Rabois using such extreme language because he believed it was the right thing to do? Did he think that it was somehow honorable to say what he did, because he was promoting free speech by testing the furthermost limits of the First Amendment? Was this a noble act? Even patriotic?

Continuing this line of inquiry, what about the other side? Was it right to denounce Rabois? Did they have a moral obligation to speak out? Was silence complicity? Did defending human dignity require them to return the fire? Why did Stanford, without any due process beyond the blistering exchanges in the *Stanford Daily*, issue a press release that definitively condemned a student? Was it meaningfully pursuing justice by calling Rabois's words juvenile and brutal? Were administrators mad at him? Or were they merely seeking to forestall further reputational damage from an ugly incident? What was really going on here?

Matthies was slow to anger. According to the *Stanford Daily*, he thought that "everyone seems to have an answer and an opinion, but no one is asking questions." Looking back on it, that same assessment applied both to Rabois's words *and* the words chosen by Stanford, given the unequal power dynamics once the authorities had so quickly issued their press release. Matthies worried that people had become disagreeable without even truly disagreeing. They were yelling past each other, refusing to listen to the other side. "All the discussion is debate, not dialogue," he fretted.[16] He was concerned that both sides would lose out. As the battle escalated, their anger had created new problems in the heightened passions about the controversy. Pursuing what was right had devolved into proving that you were right, and any righteousness was lost to self-righteousness, as arguing shut down honest discussions.

Matthies remained nuanced in his response. He rejected black-and-white reappraisals, which might "end the process of observation and questioning," in part because "That's not fundamentally different from what it is that you're making your judgments about." The *Stanford Daily* summed up Matthies's viewpoint this way: "He said he believed that external acts such as condemning a comment or constructing a speech code are easily implemented but do not remove bias from our society."[17] Matthies wasn't ignoring the offense. Yet neither did he call for Rabois's complete condemnation and quick cancellation. He sought answers in the gradations.

As the debate intensified at Stanford, Keith Rabois refused to apologize. In the ensuing weeks, he continued to justify his insults. He wrote an opinion piece in the *Stanford Daily* on February 7, 1992, to maintain that he was right to say what he did, because "quite simply, this school has subverted its educational mission to the establishment of a radical, destructive, and (surprisingly) anti-liberal agenda." He explained, "Labelling was the tactic. Every time a genuine intellectual challenge was made to the multicultural mythology, the person making the argument was declared to be insensitive, racist, sexist, homophobic, etc." Justifying his slurs, Rabois wrote: "The entire point was to expose these freshmen ears to very offensive speech."[18]

As more students vilified Rabois as ignorant, even abhorrent, Matthies asked them not to. Students posted flyers with Rabois's face, captioned with "Just because its [*sic*] legal doesn't make it right."[19] Then they went further by attacking Rabois personally, crossing out his face and writing "Homophobia is Ugly" beneath the picture.[20] They were almost reveling in their righteousness. Matthies disapproved. "For the last fifteen years I have spent about half my time with my students, trying to cajole them into living with questions instead of answers and trying to coax them into answering questions with categories that go beyond 'yes' or 'no,' the two blind mice," Matthies wrote in the *Stanford Daily*. The controversy inflamed passions from all sides, creating an overheated climate on campus. Matthies encouraged the students who'd attacked Rabois to pause, reflect, question, and discern: "Perhaps we should start with the word 'bigot'—is this a dangerous oversimplification? Or 'homophobia'—is this a word that obscures more than it reveals?"[21]

As for Rabois, the issue was more black-and-white for him. In the *Stanford Daily* that same day, he declared that the other students were the ones who had committed the worst offenses. He justified his reasons behind screaming, "You're going to get what's coming to you" and other threats with a simple rationale: when gay people had sex, it could cause AIDS and lead to death. It was a personal choice, which had preventable consequences. "Actually, I truly don't care nor think too much about the issue," he claimed. "I don't necessarily hate homosexuals, but do believe in Jack Kemp's suggestion that they may not be the best teachers of young children in public schools and recognize that the spread of AIDS has a direct causal link back to their activity." To drive home his point, Rabois took a political stance, insisting, "I hate Democrats, not homosexuals; they're the ones who have hurt the country."[22]

## Peter and David decide to challenge fundamental taboos

Throughout the late 1980s and early 1990s, political debates had been intensifying on America's college campuses, with significant outside funding going toward the effort. Two of Keith Rabois's friends at Stanford, Peter Thiel and David Sacks, were fellows at the Independent Institute, a right-wing think tank in the Bay Area that funded conservative student leaders and their campus organizations.[23] In 1987 this group of friends had started the *Stanford Review*, which competed with the *Stanford Daily* by "offering alternative views on a wide range of issues."[24] According to Sacks, they were joined by other "new campus radicals" who, unlike the liberal activists of the 1960s, saw themselves as a new generation that was ready to resist left-leaning culture and instruction, challenge overreaches by overbearing administrators, and restore Stanford's curriculum to the canon of Western civilization, those proudly inherited traditions they felt had created the modern world.[25] But the battle over free speech, curriculum decisions, and campus culture didn't only happen at Stanford. It was nationwide, and it kept escalating.[26]

Another conservative organization, the Intercollegiate Studies Institute, had been founded in 1953 by Frank Chodorov and William F. Buckley. It supported student-run papers like the *Stanford Review* across the country, including the *Dartmouth Review*, which debuted in 1980 and featured a column by Dinesh D'Souza, and the *Cornell Review*, which debuted in 1984 with Ann Coulter as its founding editor.[27] In fact, just a few months before all this controversy at Stanford, D'Souza had published *Illiberal Education: The Politics of Race and Sex on Campus*. In chapter 1, "The Victim's Revolution on Campus," he had argued that "most university presidents and deans cooperate with the project to transform liberal education in the name of minority victims" and objected to how "diversity, tolerance, multiculturalism, pluralism—these phrases are perennially on the lips of university administrators. They are the principles and slogans of the victim's revolution." In chapter 8 he took umbrage that "instead of liberal education, what American students are getting is its diametrical opposite, an education in close-mindedness and intolerance, which is to say, illiberal education," and warned, "If the university model is replicated in society at large, far from bringing ethnic harmony, it will reproduce and magnify the lurid bigotry, intolerance, and balkanization of campus life in the broader culture."[28]

Thiel and Sacks decided to write a book about politics on campus, too. In *The Diversity Myth: Multiculturalism and Political Intolerance on Campus*, which came out in 1995, they described the West Coast version of the dismal picture of college life from D'Souza's *Illiberal Education*. Both books were in the tradition of William F. Buckley Jr.'s *God and Man at Yale: The Superstitions of "Academic Freedom"* from 1951. At age twenty-five, Buckley had blamed Yale for abandoning its religious values.[29] In 2011 *God and Man at Yale* was named one of *Time Magazine*'s one hundred best and most influential nonfiction books since 1923, or the beginning of *Time*.[30] Thiel, Sacks, and D'Souza sought that same kind of notoriety at an early age, too, through more secularized morality tales about their corrupted alma maters.

*The Diversity Myth*'s book jacket showed pictures of Thiel and Sacks as recent Stanford graduates, dressed in suit jackets and crisp, white collared shirts. Their chosen mien was, in a word, conservative. The blurb above the photos touted Sacks's stellar résumé (attending the University of Chicago Law School, conducting research for Judge Robert H. Bork, and being one of Capitol Hill's "rising stars" according to the *National Journal*) and Thiel's impressive achievements (working as a derivatives trader at Credit Suisse Financial Products, being rated as a National Master by the U.S. Chess Foundation, and writing speeches for Ronald Reagan's secretary of education, William J. Bennett).[31] They were hard-working and supersmart students, and their biographies for *The Diversity Myth* listed serious accomplishments at elite institutions and mainstream conservative organizations. Yet the book wasn't about lower taxes, free markets, or reducing government regulations. It was instead positioned at the front lines of the culture wars, focusing on issues like homosexuality, race relations, and women's rights.

The Independent Institute published *The Diversity Myth*, and other conservative funders and organizations also supported the effort. The Young America's Foundation promoted *The Diversity Myth*, and the John M. Olin Foundation gave a $40,000 grant to market the book. Fifteen years before, the Olin Foundation had also supported the libertarian treatise that economist Milton Friedman coauthored with his wife, Rose, *Free to Choose: A Personal Statement*, and four years earlier, it had backed D'Souza's *Illiberal Education*.[32] The new book by Thiel and Sacks was filled with libertarian, antiauthority messages that echoed Friedman in a few ways and D'Souza in many more. They wrote that the problem with Rabois's actions was that "his demonstration directly challenged one of the most fundamental taboos: To suggest a correlation between homosexual acts and AIDS implies that one of multiculturalists' favorite lifestyles is more prone to contracting the disease and that not all lifestyles are equally desirable."[33]

Rabois's taboo speech gave Thiel and Sacks a perfect case-in-point. The authors argued that the outburst was just one incident among several "periodically interrupting the day-to-day calm of the multicultural regime" that they contended the Stanford administration maintained over its students. Multiculturalism, unreasonable accommodations, and acceptance to a point of excess—those were the real problems, according to Thiel and Sacks—not bigotry, indignities, or death threats.[34] In an interview on April 3, 1996, at the conservative Heritage Foundation, Thiel spoke about why he thought the incident mattered. "Keith was—perhaps this was the wrong thing to do—but he attempted to create a test case of the speech code." He continued: "It was, strictly speaking, still protected under the speech code at Stanford. But, at the same time, the point is that there are very few people who say things like Keith, who feel free to say those things, or who would say those things if they were not trying to create a test case." At that same event, Thiel contended, "The problems of racism, sexism, other forms of oppression have been vastly exaggerated, and as a result, people get unjustly accused. A culture of complaint leads to a culture of blame, and that is ultimately the real problem with it."[35]

In the book, Thiel and Sacks complained about how homosexuals at Stanford were engaging in anonymous, promiscuous sex acts. They wrote, "The university is also willing to tolerate excesses by members of the homosexual community that would never be tolerated in any other group. In men's bathrooms throughout campus, but particularly in libraries and the history department, holes have been drilled between the walls of toilet stalls to facilitate 'anonymous bathroom sex.'" Thiel and Sacks left no room for misinterpretation about what they meant. They admonished administrators with these words: "Apparently unwilling to anger members of the homosexual community, the university has failed to reseal 'glory holes' in a number of the campus's public bathrooms, despite the discomforting effect on people seeking to use toilets for more prosaic purposes."[36]

Thiel and Sacks claimed that Stanford purposefully left holes in the men's bathrooms to encourage anonymous gay sex. Heterosexuals were the victims, they argued, not homosexuals whom they felt Stanford administration supported at the expense of other groups. In these situations, "nobody dared to challenge the claim that homosexuals truly were oppressed. Their fragile identities had been thoroughly reaffirmed," they mocked. That same scornful tone carried on throughout *The Diversity Myth* toward liberals at Stanford. The authors wrote: "The denizens of the multicultural community could be reassured that they were 'good citizens' because they were helping victimized homosexuals to confront and overcome their 'oppressor.'"[37]

Later in life, Thiel and Sacks would become renowned for launching new ventures and identifying innovative ideas before anyone else saw them, but everything about their political endeavors at Stanford—including the contrarian *Review* they started, the book they wrote, the funding sources for both, and the arguments they made all throughout—relied on a proven model. They'd learned from people who were a few years older and had tried this before, and they used many of the same arguments and even phrases that others, like Dinesh D'Souza, had already made. Thiel, Sacks, Rabois, and their *Stanford Review* friends found common cause by using taboo language and battling the ensuing campus backlash in the late 1980s and early 1990s. They'd keep working together in the years to come, creating and supporting scores of disruptive ventures that defied the status quo during the Silicon Age.

Thiel cofounded an unorthodox financial technology company, which they named Confinity, a mashup of infinite and confidence, because theirs was.[38] It became PayPal, which made Thiel rich when it was sold to eBay, and then he became far wealthier after reinvesting those earnings as the first investor in Facebook.[39] Sacks became PayPal's COO and later founded Yammer, which sold to Microsoft for $1.2 billion.[40] Thiel and Sacks brought on Rabois as PayPal's executive vice president for business development, public affairs, and policy, where he led public relations and community engagement efforts for the company. Rabois later served as an executive-in-residence at Thiel's Clarium Capital and a partner at Founders Fund, which was also started by Thiel (along with other PayPal alums and Facebook's first CEO, Sean Parker).[41] Over the coming decades, Founders Fund invested in Airbnb, Lyft, Palantir, and Wish (all of which Rabois also invested in personally) as well as dozens of other top tech businesses, including Affirm, Anduril, Credit Karma, DeepMind, Oculus, Postmates, and SpaceX.[42]

That last one was founded by Elon Musk, whose payment company X.com merged with Confinity early in 2000.[43] As Jimmy Soni recounted in *The Founders: The Story of PayPal and the Entrepreneurs Who Shaped Silicon Valley*, Musk had almost accidentally killed Thiel on the way to a meeting to discuss their deal that would create PayPal and earn them both millions. Musk sped down Sand Hill Road in his Magnesium Silver McLaren F1. Thiel asked, "So, what can this thing do?" and Musk replied, "Watch this." He took too tight of a turn, and the supercar went airborne. Thiel wasn't wearing his seatbelt. The vehicle was wrecked, but miraculously, neither was hurt. Thiel hitchhiked to the meeting.[44]

Back then, a brand-new McLaren F1 would have cost around $1 million.[45] Musk had purchased the car with earnings from his first startup, but astonishingly, "all he could do was laugh about the fact that he had failed to insure it," according to Sebastian Mallaby in *The Power Law: Venture Capital and the Making of the New Future*. Mallaby wrote: "Such extremes and eccentricities were actually good signs, Thiel contended; VCs should celebrate misfits, not coach them into conformity."[46] Whether the McLaren incident showed dangerous impulsiveness, which risked lives, or a rebel spirit that was praiseworthy, things worked out for Musk in this instance. He paid out of pocket to repair the vehicle, drove it for several more years, and then sold it for a profit. In an interview with CNN that showed Musk driving the car for the first time, Musk claimed that "X.com could absolutely be a multibillion-dollar bonanza" and explained why starting company after company appealed to him: "It's sort of like a series of poker games. And now I've gone onto a more high stakes poker game and just carried those chips with me."[47]

A story that Thiel biographer Max Chafkin recounted in *The Contrarian: Peter Thiel and Silicon Valley's Pursuit of Power* typified the intense corporate culture at PayPal under Musk and Thiel. Employees at PayPal had a tracker on their computer screens that gave a running count of its users in real-time. Whenever a new account was created, the tally would go up and a bell would chime. Above the counter, the words read: "World Domination Index."[48]

The combined company of Confinity and X.com would indeed expand exponentially, but the new union did not mean happily ever after. When the company went public in 2002, Thiel and Confinity cofounder Max Levchin both donned crowns, a visual reminder that they were the kings. Levchin wore a white t-shirt with the PayPal emblem, but Thiel's had Confinity's old logo, seemingly implying that it was Confinity's day of victory, not the combined company's.[49] Ultimately, the sale to eBay netted $1.5 billion.[50] Thiel then conspired to oust Musk from the CEO role—while he was on his honeymoon to the 2000 Summer Olympics in Australia, so that he couldn't stop them—which caused Musk to write, "This whole thing is making me so sad that words fail me."[51]

Over time, the men made amends. Thiel, Sacks, Rabois, and Musk continued collaborating and investing together over the decades to come. In fact, when Musk bought Twitter in 2022, the *Wall Street Journal* reported that these same friends were "The Shadow Crew Who Encouraged Elon Musk's Twitter Takeover."[52] Even if that conspiratorial tone overstated matters, it's clear that Musk valued David Sacks's input, bringing him on as a key advisor during Twitter's transformation to X.com (which was notable because Musk was taking a second run at making X.com a "multibillion-dollar bonanza"). With the platform under new management, Musk and Sacks hosted interviews with Ron DeSantis and Robert F. Kennedy, Jr.—two presidential candidates that Sacks had supported and would host fundraisers for in mid-2023.[53]

Why did Musk make this $44 billion purchase? This went beyond a rare second chance at a once-in-a-lifetime business opportunity: Musk had become convinced that freedom of speech was at risk. "This is a battle for the future of civilization," he tweeted on November 28, 2022. "If free speech is lost even in America, tyranny is all that lies ahead."[54] Censoring taboo ideas meant tyranny. The stakes couldn't be higher.


## The PayPal Mafia's gambles pay off

PayPal's alumni, known as the PayPal Mafia, have launched companies that have raised over $37.5 billion from more than a thousand different investors.[55] By comparison, ventures founded by Facebook alumni have raised $11.5 billion, and Twitter alumni have raised $4.9 billion. Put another way, PayPal didn't just produce more entrepreneurs than the other leading Bay Area firms. Its former employees have been so successful, they've raised more than twice the *combined* venture capital that went to the alumni from two of Silicon Valley's giants.[56]

Jeremy Stoppelman and Russel Simmons, two early engineers with Pay-Pal, went on to found Yelp in 2004.[57] They received investment from another PayPal founder, Max Levchin, who had been the company's chief technology officer (CTO) and was later a board member for Yahoo and the CEO of Affirm.[58] Keith Rabois served as a board member at Yelp from the very start until its IPO eight years later, when it went public with a $1.47 billion valuation.[59]

Luke Nosek was vice president of marketing and strategy for PayPal and Ken Howery was PayPal's chief financial officer (CFO), and the two of them helped Thiel start Founders Fund in 2005.[60] Rabois would become a general partner at Founders Fund in 2019.[61] Andrew McCormack was Thiel's assistant and later joined Thiel Capital before launching Valar Ventures.[62] Joe Lonsdale interned at PayPal while still in college, then he cofounded Palantir with Thiel, which Rabois, Sacks, and Stoppelman invested in.[63]

Reid Hoffman was friends with Thiel, Sacks, and Rabois at Stanford, but after college he went overseas to pursue a master's degree in philosophy. "The thing that I realized, within three to six months of being at Oxford, was that it was a scholarly pursuit, not a public intellectual pursuit. So I was like, 'Oh, no, no. I actually want to have a much broader canvas,'" he later told *CNBC*. "It was thinking back to my time at Stanford, where I was like, 'Oh wait, software is this new medium by which we interact with each other, by which we kind of parse the universe. I could go work on that!'"[64] He rejoined his friends in the Bay Area and became a board member for PayPal. He soon stepped down to take a more active role and serve as COO.[65] He found a nearly limitless canvas for his creative endeavors by investing in Facebook with Thiel, as well as Flickr, Zynga, and many others. He built his own social media site, LinkedIn, which sold to Microsoft for $26.2 billion.[66] Rabois was a key early member of Hoffman's senior team, serving as LinkedIn's vice president of business development and corporate development.[67]

After Howery left, Roelof Botha became PayPal's CFO, a position he maintained until the company went public. He then joined the venture capital fund Sequoia Capital.[68] During his wildly successful career there, Botha led many of the firm's best investments. Instagram debuted in October 2010, and eighteen months later, Sequoia invested in their B Round. The deal, which gave Instagram a valuation of $500 million, was announced on a Friday. By Monday, they'd doubled their money once Facebook acquired the company for $1 billion.[69] Botha led the investment in Square, where Rabois became the COO in 2010 and which went public in 2015 with a value of $2.9 billion (it would be worth over $100 billion by 2020).[70] And he put money into Xoom, where Rabois served on the board from its inception in 2003 until PayPal bought it for $1.1 billion in 2015.[71] But Botha's most astonishing early-stage investment was one of his very first for Sequoia; it was a bet on his fellow PayPal Mafia members.

After learning about YouTube from a friend in June 2005, Botha reached out to Jawed Karim (architect of PayPal's real-time antifraud system), Chad Hurley (designer of the first PayPal logo), and Steve Chen (who wrote much of the code that powered PayPal early on).[72] The first YouTube video, uploaded on April 23, 2005, showed Karim commenting on the attributes of San Diego Zoo elephants: "The cool thing about these guys is that they have these really, really, really long trunks."[73] YouTube then nearly failed when it debuted as a video dating site in its first iteration, but it scaled at blinding speed once it changed course by focusing on videos of all kinds and allowing corporations (and everyday users) to upload content.[74]

In Botha's memorandum recommending that Sequoia Capital should invest, he wrote, "Launched June 11th. Has already overtaken all previously existing competitors and is now the dominant player in this space." Beneath that description, Botha included a line graph showing YouTube's daily reach. Starting at zero in mid-June, the line spiked to thirty million daily viewers within a few days and then dipped below ten million viewers by early July. By August there were over fifty million daily viewers. The tally kept climbing, up and to the right. A month later YouTube reached two hundred million people. In three months they'd gone from zero to nearly two hundred million people watching videos each day. It was the dream scenario for what was possible with the exponential growth of the Silicon Age.[75] Before Sequoia looked at it, Rabois had already invested in YouTube. He put money in well before it had even launched.[76]

Botha joined YouTube's board late in 2005 as part of Sequoia's investment and stayed on until it sold to Google just a year later. That seemed astonishingly fast, even by Silicon Valley standards. The rewards were just as awe-inspiring. YouTube sold for $1.65 billion only eighteen months after launching.[77] Google had seemingly paid top dollar for the startup, but over fifteen years later, YouTube makes $7 billion every quarter. Every minute, people upload 500 hours' worth of videos while others stream 694 hours of video.[78] Today nearly every American uses YouTube monthly (an astonishing 98 percent of us) and usually at least once a week (92 percent).[79] Buying YouTube for $1.65 billion turned into an absolute bargain for Google.

Many individual investors and venture funds have found success during the Silicon Age, but truly none compares to the PayPal Mafia and the immense wealth they have generated together.[80] In college, Rabois had written, "When all the resources of the multicultural agenda are directed against you, you quickly find out who your real friends are. In that way, this has been one of the most valuable experiences of my life."[81] Even though he transferred from Stanford after the controversy on campus, his time there was indeed a valuable experience, at least in financial terms.[82] That went for others in the PayPal Mafia, too.

Rabois, Thiel, and Sacks, as well as Botha, Hoffman, Howery, and Lonsdale, all went to Stanford.[83]

Rabois became one of the most successful early-stage venture capitalists of all time through these investments, with ten of his early-stage bets turning into "unicorns," or companies valued at more than $1 billion.[84] Yet Thiel was, by far, the most active investor in the PayPal Mafia, through the funds he ran and his personal investments. He backed dozens of successful companies, going far beyond Facebook, PayPal, and Palantir. Personally, he invested in companies like Alchemy, Clearview AI, and Quora, along with over fifty others. Nineteen of his companies have exited (the term for successfully selling your venture, either by going public or by being bought by a larger corporation).[85] Thiel's Founders Fund placed bets on tech across industries: Credit Karma, Hinge, Mint, Postmates, SoFi, TaskRabbit, Twilio, Xero, Zocdoc, and over 750 others. More than one hundred Founders Fund companies have exited.[86]

Looking back, some of the most successful Silicon Valley stories trace their earliest funding, mentorship, and connections to Thiel, Sacks, Rabois, and their tight-knit network. In fact, Andrew Granato's in-depth study for *Stanford Politics* in 2017 connected nearly three hundred relationships, involving both investments and employment, among *Stanford Review* alumni. Of the newspaper's fifty-eight former editors-in-chief, twenty-five have worked or interned for at least one company started by Thiel or Lonsdale.[87] Throughout their lives, this same peer group invested in companies together, and in recent years several of them have done so politically, too. But it went beyond betting on candidates they liked: they identified emerging talent, encouraged them, and connected them to powerful people. They met many of these *newer* "new campus radicals" before their careers even began—young people like Blake Masters at Stanford and J. D. Hamel at Yale—and helped the next generation of antiauthority students become venture capitalists, too, on their way to being antiestablishment politicians. Masters, Hamel, and others were hired, set up for success, and funded with millions.

Later this book will reveal the many ways they've gained and wielded power. But, importantly, it all began decades earlier. When this social group formed at Stanford, they first came together around shared ideas about politics, and especially cultural values and social standards, not business. Their friendships began with late-night rants and dorm room debates, when Thiel, Sacks, and Rabois were outspoken rabble-rousers on campus. The careers of the wildly successful PayPal Mafia did not begin with Founders Fund's bets throughout the 2000s, 2010s, and 2020s. Their astonishing journeys should not even be traced to the entrepreneurial adventures at PayPal in the late 1990s. Instead we should go back further, to the messages in *The Diversity Myth* in the mid-1990s and everything Thiel, Sacks, and Rabois started at the *Stanford Review* in the late 1980s and early 1990s. Before their financial success, and over a decade before Peter Thiel met college-aged Mark Zuckerberg, many in the PayPal Mafia found their common cause by challenging taboo issues and defying the "political correctness" that they worried would result in in closed-mindedness and intolerance.

* * *

In *The Diversity Myth*, Thiel and Sacks came up with all kinds of analogies for the troubled situation they saw at Stanford. In one chapter, they equated Rabois to the Rebel Alliance heroes from Star Wars. The heading for this section of the book was "The Empire Strikes Back," because of how forcefully the Stanford administration and like-minded students had denounced Rabois. After reading Robin Kennedy's letter, some students were demanding for Rabois to be denied access to the state bar preemptively, before finishing law school, and had begun a letter-writing campaign to his potential employers.[88] Rabois's fraternity put out a statement that "his comments violate all modicum of humanity and decency." Rabois wouldn't apologize, so his fraternity brothers did instead: "We extend to the entire University our deepest apologies and regrets for Rabois' comments." They distanced themselves from him, stating, "We cannot emphasize enough, however, that his actions were undertaken independently of our organization and should in no way be construed as indicative of our membership."[89]

Thiel and Sacks used this denunciation to show how the "Evil Empire" had quickly turned against their friend. What they mentioned in their citations (and couldn't have anticipated at the time) was that the author of the statement, "Fraternity Founded on Principles of Tolerance," would go on to become another one of most successful venture capitalists of the Silicon Age. As managing partner of Andreessen Horowitz, Scott Kupor was there from day one along with Marc Andreessen and Ben Horowitz. He played a leading role in its top-tier performance. Colloquially, Andreessen Horowitz is referred to as "a16z," and it's fitting because of their team's early bets literally on everything from A to Z, from Asana to Zynga, with Facebook, Groupon, Pinterest, Skype, Slack, and many more in between.[90]

As of 2023, Andreesen Horowitz had raised $32.4 billion across twenty-seven funds, making 1,398 investments with 202 of those being major exits. Thiel's Founders Fund had raised $13.1 billion for their twelve funds, leading to 839 investments and 138 exits. Founders Fund and a16z invested together in dozens of startups, including many big winners: Airbnb, Lyft, and Stripe. They both backed Anduril, Flexport, Oculus, and OpenAI, all ventures addressed further later in this book.[91]

## Dennis encourages a more patient, gentle, honest, and accurate approach

Thiel and Sacks had claimed that the homosexual community on campus over-reacted, along with others who came to their defense, including university administrators, professors, and student leaders like Scott Kupor. They argued that "these actions injured nobody physically, and any psychological wounds were largely self-created." Thiel and Sacks claimed that "in every case, the multiculturalists behaved far more inappropriately" than Rabois, because the backlash against Rabois fostered such a negative environment that he felt he had no choice but to leave Stanford.[92] The sacrifice he'd been forced to make, to be clear, was transferring to Harvard Law School.[93]

At the time, few would have believed Rabois had yelled such slurs out of a desire to create reasonable discourse. He had a history of antagonizing others. "The Stanford College Republicans, purported champions of free and vigorous debate, have lately produced nothing of the sort," Alex Grant wrote in the *Stanford Daily* in 1990, while both he and Rabois were undergraduates, two years before Rabois had screamed anything late one winter night. "Instead, they have only displayed a spirit of intolerance in speaking out about issues concerning the gay community," Grant explained, specifically rebuking Rabois for saying, during a recent college debate, that he refused to accept that "a homosexual lifestyle is as valid as a heterosexual one."[94]

That same year, Rabois agreed with students who told the *Stanford Daily* that Martin Luther King, Jr., was overrated. "There are certainly other American leaders in the past who have accomplished as much as or more than King who don't have their own holiday," he'd chided, adding, "Reagan is the greatest champion of civil rights in the 20th century."[95]

In another odd analogy from *The Diversity Myth*, Thiel and Sacks compared Rabois to a woman who was publicly executed during the Salem Witch Trials in the 1690s. They twisted history, in a brazen attempt at revisionism to make that one work: "The accused women likely were not angelic people. Quite the contrary, many of the accused were probably rather unpleasant people who had behaved imperfectly in the past and were partially to blame for the negative attention they received." In this case, they managed to blame the victims, while also turning Rabois into the abused one, all in a single, mangled analogy.[96] The chapter where Sacks and Thiel claimed Rabois was the victim of a witch hunt was titled, "Welcome to Salem."

Through it all, Dennis Matthies refused to condemn Rabois. As the *Stanford Daily* reported, "His main concern is that an incident like the one in Otero makes people hide behind their versions of 'correct' positions instead of revealing what they think personally."[97] Matthies upended the idea of "Political

Intolerance on Campus," as Thiel and Sacks had termed it, rejecting the us-versus-them disagreements from both the left and the right. He cautioned that the quick, harsh, and personal rejections of Rabois were "simplistic" and "self-righteous." He asked Stanford students to take a more compassionate and thoughtful approach, one that was "patient, gentle, honest and accurate," which sought, to use his word, "truth-telling."[98]

"I would like people to ask more questions about who Keith Rabois is," Matthies said. He encouraged students to avoid easy denunciations and asked them to pursue greater tolerance, more critical thinking, and deeper awareness. "This is not simple bigotry," he noted, adding that the situation was "more complicated than that." In doing so, he found the way to achieve two things at once: he rejected the slurs for their mean-spiritedness and refused efforts to "wrap in a neat package" any quick verdicts about Rabois personally. Instead, he advised, "you'd find the threads of Keith Rabois in yourself."[99]

It was a prudent approach. We're all fallible. Humans are complex. We make choices based on our hopes and dreams, but we also react due to fear and pain. Matthies neither condemned Rabois nor condoned harmful actions. These two opposed ideas added up to work in tandem, in inquiry: not to find quick fixes or easy answers, but to sit in the unease, to seek the deeper causes underneath it all, and to discern the meaningful lessons that might teach.

To achieve that kind of balance—to gain a sense of greater understanding, and with it, wisdom—it took a first-rate emotional intelligence that could process two contradictory feelings at once. In this case, that meant rejecting the cruelty in Rabois's words, yet having empathy about the turmoil that might cause him to act out like that. Instead of issuing a denunciation via press release, maybe there was a better way. As Matthies urged, the Stanford community might ask more questions about this complicated, confusing, and maybe even irresolvable mystery behind Keith Rabois's antigay screed toward a heterosexual faculty member, who wasn't even home at the time. There were many possible causes, conflicts, and motivations behind this incident. For instance, as we'd learn in due time, Rabois was gay but not yet public about it. And the same went for Peter Thiel.[100]

## For Keith, Jacob, and Pete, the power cycles turn

Leading up to the 2020 election, Keith Rabois and his husband, Jacob Helberg, gave a total of $749,100 in political donations.[101] Before their marriage, Rabois almost exclusively gave to Republicans; Helberg had never donated. Over the next four years, Helberg contributed more than $2.2 million, mostly to Democrats, and Rabois gave over $4 million (compared to less than $479,000 from the prior twenty-four years). In 2020 they both gave to one candidate.[102]

That politician was a rising star in the Democratic Party who had captivated audiences with his Harvard intellect, his military experience, and his small-town bona fides. He'd left corporate consulting with McKinsey & Company and returned home to run for local office. He protested the Iraq War in college; he later deployed to Afghanistan. Then he made history. He was the first openly gay person to run for president, declaring his candidacy in April 2019, and he seemed well on his way once he won the Iowa Democratic Caucus the following February.[103]

His name was Pete Buttigieg.

Rabois and Helberg hosted a fundraiser for Buttigieg in San Francisco on July 24, 2019. Their support was widely reported by the *Financial Times*, *Politico*, *Vox*, and *Yahoo*, and one journalist linked to Helberg's Twitter feed with pictures showing the candidate and his husband with Rabois and Helberg.[104] Yet the media completely failed to mention that Buttigieg had welcomed support at a fundraiser (then accepted additional contributions on December 10, 2019) from a man who once yelled, "Faggot! Hope you die of AIDS!" and "Can't wait until you die, faggot." No one brought up that Rabois had said homosexuals shouldn't be schoolteachers, or his assertion "about faggots being bad in general."[105] Journalists did not report that Rabois had rejected that "a homosexual lifestyle is as valid as a heterosexual one" or insisted, "I hate Democrats, not homosexuals; they're the ones who have hurt the country."[106] After so many at Stanford sought to ruin Rabois's career before it began, which was unmistakably documented by Peter Thiel and David Sacks in *The Diversity Myth* a quarter-century before, the American public, its politicians, and the media all seemed to forgive—or at least forget.

In 2019, ostensibly an era where all past deeds would be severely scrutinized, no one spoke up. The Otero incident had occurred more than ten thousand days before the Buttigieg fundraiser, and Rabois's comments had resurfaced even more recently than that, when he'd resigned as Square's COO and the company said he showed "poor judgment" after a younger male employee accused him of sexual harassment.[107] On that same day, January 25, 2013, Rabois wrote a Tumblr blog to explain himself. "With increasing frequency, we hung out, drank wine, and I helped prepare him for interviews with tech startups," he wrote. "As our friendship deepened, we spent more time together, and our relationship became physical." He admitted, "I realize that continuing any physical relationship after he began working at Square was poor judgment on my part." Rabois stated that the relationship was welcome, but Square did not know it was going on until a lawsuit was threatened. He explained that no one received nor was denied benefits based on the relationship and emphasized that he "did not do the horrendous things I am told I may be accused of," which remained unmentioned. He then apologized to his colleagues, writing, "While I have certainly made mistakes, this threat feels like a shakedown, and I will defend myself to the full extent of the law."[108] Three years later, that Tumblr post was taken offline.[109]

By 2013, arguments over "political correctness" had begun to heat up, especially on far right and far left TV talk shows; several years later, those disputes had transformed into even more intense feuds about "cancel culture" and "woke-ism." The controversies they caused kept coming to an angry boil nationwide, intensified by a new burn every instant on social media. But the two-party battlefield didn't decide who ultimately won or lost in America. That was where the media focused, as they detailed the barbs traded between extreme factions of the left and right, or, more essentially, as they documented the daily distrust between Democrats and Republicans. But the "woke" and "antiwoke" controversies didn't tell the full story, nor was "cancel culture" meted out with consistency. Corruption in government and corporate America, and the power that technologists and politicians consolidated and wielded, couldn't be easily explained in a simple soundbite or an oversimplified label. This wasn't about truth-telling, or even truth-seeking, anyway. Both sides were up to no good. The ground beneath us had shifted during that decade, as prior skirmishes over "political correctness" became a blistering, all-out war of "woke" or "antiwoke"—each past transgression either being an unforgettable, unconcealable cruelty that still mattered, or merely bluster or a blunder from long ago that no longer did. Both were dangerous oversimplifications.

Through the smoke, one insight became clear. Power was determined not only by what the mainstream journalists and social media mobs had found, but also what they'd missed or ignored. Some could say what they felt, even scream it, only to expand their power, profits, and prestige. Party didn't seem to matter. Apparently, neither did well-documented facts, statements, and events. We must now ask ourselves: Has all this finger-pointing and name-calling improved society in any meaningful way? If not, then ultimately, what good did that do?

All the while, for a select few, silicon turned into gold. It began to turn into power, and then the cycles moved even faster. In 2022 Keith Rabois was ranked eighth on *Forbes*'s Midas List of the wealthiest venture capitalists in the world, ahead of Thiel at tenth, Botha at thirty-sixth, Hoffman at fortieth, and Horowitz at eighty-seventh. For all their many successes, the other investors and entrepreneurs mentioned here—Andreessen, Chen, Howery, Karim, Kupor, Levchin, Lonsdale, Nosek, Sacks, Simmons, and Stoppelman—didn't make the top one hundred.[110]

# CHAPTER 4

# A SELF-FULFILLING PROPHECY

Travis Kalanick, UberCab

A college dropout partied in Paris late into the midwinter night. "Amongst the amazing food, the copious amounts of wine and inevitable nightlife crawls there were all kinds of discussions about what's next," he wrote in a blog about the LeWeb conference, an annual gathering for high-tech ventures, entrepreneurs, and investors. "Jamming on ideas, rapping on what's next is what entrepreneurs do."[1] Were these the words of a bottom-line-driven businessman who hustled hard, got results, and achieved greatness? Or was it all just bluster? He'd quit UCLA to work at a startup called Scour, a platform to share music and video files online for free. It went bankrupt due to a barrage of multimillion-dollar lawsuits from movie studios and record labels.[2] He then decided that he could turn those plaintiffs into clients, by altering the software to serve businesses rather than illegally giving away their content. It was called Red Swoosh, which he sold for $18.7 million.[3] But he wasn't satisfied. He needed a new idea.

Bounding about Paris during the conference, he wondered what new venture he could get involved with that might truly change the world. "Garrett's big idea was cracking the horrible taxi problem in San Francisco—getting stranded on the streets of San Francisco is familiar territory for any San Franciscan," he explained, which he found promising for this reason: "Garrett's m.o. fits the Uber brand. He likes to roll in style, comfort and convenience. His over-the-top idea in Paris that winter started as a limo timeshare service."[4] And, eureka, Uber was born. Or, at least, that's how Travis Kalanick's story went about one snowy night in Paris.

Garrett Camp had previously founded StumbleUpon, which eBay bought for $75 million. He'd stayed on as CEO and then bought the company back from eBay in 2009.[5] Nearly a year before seeing Kalanick at LeWeb, after a late night of partying on New Year's Eve and with no taxis available in San Francisco, Camp paid $800 for a private driver to take him home.[6] The seed of an idea had been planted by that point, possibly even earlier, but months would pass before Camp discussed the concept with Kalanick. Even so, Kalanick claimed he was present at the creation, writing on the corporate blog that Camp's "original pitch had me and him splitting the costs of a driver, a Mercedes S Class, and a parking spot in a garage, so that I could use an iPhone app to get around San Francisco on-demand. Hilarious! Obviously things have changed quite a bit." That line was followed by an emoji (a winking face), which would be the second consecutive paragraph that he'd conclude that way, for emphasis, before posting it to Uber's website.[7]

Kalanick credited the Parisian debauchery with their lightning-in-a-bottle moment in 2008, but they weren't the first to think of this business idea. They weren't even the first to try it and find some success. Zimride debuted over two years earlier as a better way for Cornell students to get to the airport instead of posting ride requests on a flyer-covered corkboard on campus. It would rebrand as Lyft in 2013.[8] The founder of another ridesharing venture, Sidecar, came up with the first on-demand ride-hailing app.[9] Six years and nine months before Kalanick and Camp were at LeWeb, Sidecar's founder Sunil Paul had patented a computerized "System and Method for Determining an Efficient Transportation Route." In the application, he'd described "a peer-to-peer system for linking drivers to passengers," as well as "a more precise method of hailing a taxi." He'd imagined that "the user may request a vehicle to perform a delivery in lieu of arranging for the delivery by a delivery service." All those ideas were included in U.S. Patent 6,356,838, awarded to Paul on March 12, 2002.[10] Uber's network linking drivers to passengers, using a wireless device to hail a ride, even UberEats—the concepts were nothing new.

Paul had gotten there first with so many ideas, and he brought them into the world earlier, too: Sidecar was the first business to let anyone drive and ride rather than relying on professional drivers. Back when Uber still built its business around high-end services and licensed black car drivers, Sidecar raised $10 million from Google Ventures and Lightspeed.[11] Those firms made a bet that Sidecar might win out, not Uber, but Sunil Paul wasn't guaranteed success just because he saw the future first or because he believed in what was possible earlier. Just as Uber wasn't the direct result of Parisian bacchanalia, or even due to buyer's remorse over an $800 limo ride, neither was Sidecar fulfilling a destiny. Nothing was predetermined. The race was on.

Mark Zuckerberg warned Kalanick that Facebook employees loved Sidecar—a friendly suggestion that was almost certainly life-changing.[12] Kalanick tried out Sidecar after hearing that. According to Mike Isaac's *Super Pumped:*

*The Battle for Uber,* he quickly realized that Uber's elitism was far too limiting. It needed to shift toward a peer-to-peer approach, so UberX was born, where anyone could drive everyone anywhere.[13] At the same time, Kalanick also saw a clear advantage. He quickly realized that Sidecar's interface was far too complicated. Every driver could set their own price, and riders could choose their own driver, which made the entire experience a complete mess. "The legacy of Sidecar is that we out-innovated Uber but still failed to win the market," Paul later confessed. "We failed—for the most part—because Uber is willing to win at any cost and they have practically limitless capital to do it."[14]

"Win at any cost" and "practically limitless capital" are two very important ideas. There is more, much more, to discuss regarding the implications of both. But Uber's main innovation, ridesharing with a few clicks on an app, has been misremembered as an entrepreneurial epiphany, inspired by Kalanick's personal frustrations in snowy Paris. One of the cofounders of LeWeb bought into the myth himself during an interview at the conference in 2013. He claimed Kalanick thought, with a singular revelation there a few years earlier, "How about a service I would use on my phone?" and Kalanick confirmed to him and everyone in attendance, "We actually came up with the idea at LeWeb in 2008. . . . The story is what everybody here knows." Then, just to make sure the lie held up, he emphasized each part of the next sentence: "It is hard. To get a cab. In Paris." He then summarized, "I couldn't get a cab. So, Paris was the inspiration for Uber."[15]

According to Kalanick, Uber started with their frustrations in Paris, not because of what Camp realized on New Year's Eve, which Kalanick had learned about almost a year later. No one interrupted to mention the fact that Sunil Paul had patented the concept over half a decade before. "Never let the truth get in the way of a good story," the old saying goes, which is often attributed to Mark Twain. But that might just be apocryphal, too, because there's no evidence he ever said it.[16] "Paris was the inspiration for Uber" became legitimized as official history on the corporate blog and in a public interview at the conference where it all began (or, more factually, where it did not). But it went over just fine. Uber's founder believed in the folklore, where he was the daring hero. The interviewer encouraged him, and the crowd sat back and listened to the mythmaking. The story worked, so reality skewed. Soon, the deceptions, the daringness, and the audience would all expand, too, and the wider world would shift along with them.

## Travis celebrates "the awesomest job post and response I've ever seen"

Kalanick and Camp were joined by Ryan Graves, who had been leading up the Information Technology group for GE's Information Management Leadership

Program at the time.[17] Kalanick didn't need an executive search firm to find Graves. All it took was a tweet from @KonaTbone: "Looking 4 entrepreneurial product mgr/biz-dev killer 4 a location-based service . . . pre-launch, BIG equity, big peeps involved—ANY TIPS?"[18] In Kalanick's words, "What resulted was the Awesomest job post and response I've ever seen," which was this response from @ryangraves: "heres a tip. email me :) graves.ryan[at]gmail.com." That reply, with little punctuation and no capitalization, but with a smiley emoji, was the first step Graves took on the path to being a billionaire within the next decade.[19] It's a fascinating thing, Travis Kalanick's Twitter feed. More on that soon, too.

At a key decision point for the new venture, Kalanick and Camp had both felt too burned out from their prior startups to run a new company, so they made Graves the first CEO. Yet Kalanick quickly had a change of heart. He decided he wanted the job, so a few months later, he had it.[20] The earliest pitch deck for "UberCab" touted a high-end black car service that relied on chauffers' willingness to make extra money after-hours, much like how an off-duty security guard might moonlight as a nightclub bouncer. From day one, the company's ethos was elite and, unabashedly, elitist. The number one differentiator they pitched for the business? "Members Only—Respectable clientele." To attract customers, luxury automobiles (Mercedes Sedans, the pitch deck specified) and "Great drivers" were among the other top ways Kalanick's new startup would create value.[21]

The largest market they could imagine, Kalanick told investors back then, involved "professionals in American cities," who would pay a premium for a deluxe service: the "NetJets of car services" to enjoy the "experience of a professional chauffer."[22] They'd abandon the comparison to NetJets (the Berkshire Hathaway–owned business that allowed wealthy customers to rent a private jet without having to own one) in order to expand even faster, once the company began allowing anyone to drive everyone. Their world domination wasn't because these rides were profitable; in fact, the company lost more and more money as it grew, funded by astonishing amounts of high-growth venture capital.

The investors in the company's earliest round in August 2010 were among the Bay Area's best. Uber went through the Techstars accelerator program (whose notable alumni and investments included Class Pass, DataRobot, and Remitly).[23] They raised an angel round from Chris Sacca (who had invested in Instagram, Stripe, and Twitter), DCVC (Elastic, Square, Zoom), Gary Vaynerchuk (Birchbox, Medium, Path), and several others.[24] The fear of missing out in Silicon Valley increased when Cyan Banister (Buffer, Thumbtack, Wardrobe), First Round Capital (Blue Apron, TaskRabbit, Ring), Kapor Capital (Bitly, Life360, Thrive Market), and more invested just a few months later, in October 2010.[25] Uber kept bringing in huge sums of venture capital.

How did Kalanick raise so much money, so quickly, from so many top investors? They saw the potential in his idea, they saw his drive, but most of all, they didn't want to miss striking it rich. Kalanick used that to his advantage. In a blog post on March 19, 2009, titled, "Startup Seed Raising Skilzzz," he advised: "If you're doing a startup, you're trying to change the world, you've kicked your cushy job to the curb, you've had Ramen noodles for breakfast lunch and dinner as far as you can remember, and maybe you've moved back in with the 'rents. You've definitely got the passion . . . why else would you be doing this?"

Calling "Passion/Charisma" "the X-factor," he explained, "Don't be afraid to show it. Every pitch could be your last one (i.e., the dude across the table writes you a check!), know that . . . give it your all . . . listen to some music that pumps you up before you get into the meeting, think about all of the great shit you're doing and could do. Focus on the positive, have confidence, be amped, bring passion to your game, and share the love with the person across from you."[26] Travis Kalanick wrote all that right before UberCab sought its first funding. It described his signature approach to entrepreneurship, which soon became a corporate core value. It was one of the "Uber Competencies" along with "Fierceness" and to "Always Be Hustlin.'" It meant going to any extreme to get what you wanted. Growth at any cost, regardless of the rules broken or the norms you ignored. The term Kalanick used was "Super Pumpedness."[27]

## Travis's investors see money in the madness

What did these venture investors see in Kalanick that others lacked? What convinced them that he would emerge from a crowded field of ridesharing start-ups? His win-at-all-costs attitude had something to do with it. That's because venture math required it. The typical venture funds keep 20 percent of the money they earn for their investors, and they take 2 percent of everything, as a management fee, *each year*. Here's an example: investors in a $100 million, ten-year fund would pay up to $2 million every year for a decade, just to let other investors bet on new ventures on their behalf.[28] Being a venture capitalist is a great job if you can get it, because the fees are so high (an average financial advisor charges half that).[29] But while the day-to-day money is good, the potential payouts for success exceed few other careers on the planet.

The "2 and 20" model that's become the standard in venture investing, with 2 percent fees plus 20 percent upside, means that if you can turn this $100 million fund into $1 billion, then $200 million of it stays with the venture firm. So you've just made quite a haul: up to $20 million over ten years to make investments, and then $200 million from the investments, all for investing other people's money.[30] Venture capitalists rarely risk their own money: only 1 percent of venture funds include a single penny from the venture investors' own bank accounts.[31] This, of course, is even though they're guaranteed salaries to take highly risky gambles with other people's money, for a decade at a time, no matter how they perform.

It's not always this straightforward, many fund structures have different nuances, and sometimes venture capitalists will only get 1 percent or 1.5 percent in fees after the first four or five years. More recently, investors have taken less than 2 percent for the entire life of the fund, in order to negotiate up to 30 percent of the returns. But the entire system incentivizes the same goals: incredible risk-taking on audacious, even outlandish entrepreneurs. That can be a good thing because it encourages outsized ambition and out-of-the-box thinking. But it could also have seriously negative impacts, as we'll soon see. For better and for worse, hypergrowth and exponential expansion are the top priorities; if you hit it big with other people's money, then you can raise more of it all over again.[32]

This last point is an important one. The better your fund does, the more of a chance you'll have to raise another fund—an even *bigger* fund. So, even though you have up to a decade to invest, you're incentivized to turn investor money into incredible wealth as soon as possible, so you can go back out and raise that second, even larger fund. If your portfolio appears to have a big winner or two, even if the potential outcomes are just "on paper," it's more likely investors will put more into your next fund, so you try to raise your newest and larger fund only three or four years after your first.[33] For simple math, let's say you raise a second fund of $250 million. That means that for a decade, you'd get $2 million a year to run that first fund, and then for the next decade, you'd have $5 million each year to run the next fund. Guaranteed.

If the fees go down for a few of those years, even cut nearly in half, this still works out great for venture capitalists. A full 2 percent across the two funds in this scenario would have been $70 million in fees. Even a lower amount of $40 million or $50 million, all to invest other people's money, is an incredible haul over two decades. Of course, that is even though your only results thus far involved the story you told about the first fund and then, quite possibly, a story you're telling about the second fund. The companies you'd invested in earlier might still be unrealized bets; perhaps they haven't become profitable or have exited yet. But massive revenues and hypergrowth create a track record, so you can make a case about estimated worth "on paper," or their predicted value once they exit. Hindsight is 20/20. For venture capitalists who win over the investors, foresight is 2/20, which is worth millions. It makes for a great gig if you can get it.

This approach incentivizes extreme urgency, and Kalanick knew that. He appealed to venture capitalists' needs for revenue- and growth-maximalization:

Every communication you have with prospective investors must include a sense of momentum and urgency in the deal process. "Things are moving quickly." "My day is packed with meetings." "Many parties are interested." "This deal could come together quickly." You back this up with hard work and serious hustle. Keep your update conversations short. Make the Urgency a reality by working your ass off. It will become a self-fufilling [*sic*] prophecy and your deal will get done.[34]

How does a startup get financed? Convince them you're a visionary, you're even a bit crazy. Demand urgency. Tell them time is running out. Fear of missing out is still rooted in fear, after all. But more than anything, tell them you will make them an insane amount of money. How? Because you will do whatever it takes to win.

## Travis finds success in growth, not profits

After the Angel Round, UberCab transformed into Uber, and Universal Music gave Kalanick the website Uber.com in exchange for shares. At the time, that unique address was worth $107,148, which Universal sold off during the A Round for $863,000. It was a handsome profit at the time. Those same shares, if Universal would have held onto them, would have been worth $532 million less than a decade later.[35]

By February 2011, less than six months after Uber's first round was raised and two months after Kalanick had stepped into the CEO role, it was on to more venture funding: Benchmark (which had bet on Dropbox, eBay, Glassdoor, Grubhub, Snapchat, Stitch Fix, Twitter, Upwork, and Zillow), Sequoia Capital (Airbnb, Apple, Cisco, Doordash, Google, Instagram, Snapchat, Square, Zoom), and Scott Banister (Cyan's husband and an early PayPal board member who had invested in Zappos, among others), along with more money from Chris Sacca.[36] Then, in December 2011, Menlo Ventures (PillPack, Poshmark, Roku, Siri), CrunchFund (now Tuesday Capital: Airbnb, Redfin, Tumblr), Jeff Bezos, Goldman Sachs, and others joined in.[37] Camp had put $220,000 into the company to get started. In those three rounds, Uber had raised, respectively, $1.3 million, $11 million, and then $37 million—in under fourteen months.[38] This was because the company wasn't seeking profitability. It spent investors' money on growth and then used that growth to prove why it deserved more investors' money.[39]

GV (previously known as Google Ventures) would lead the next round less than two years later, injecting $258 million, and then Fidelity, BlackRock, and other investors would pour in $1.4 billion less than a year after that.[40] Uber became one of the fastest growing companies in world history, and it was also one of the quickest to raise over a billion dollars in venture capital. After its first test run in 2010, fueled by venture capital, the startup quickly dominated the taxi market in the first cities it took on. That was the best-case scenario that it had told investors at first. It took Uber six years to complete the first billion rides. Everything accelerated from there. Six months later, it announced that it completed its two billionth ride. In fact, 147 rides across five continents tied for that record, because they all finished at 4:16 a.m. GMT on June 18, 2016.[41] By the end of 2019 Uber was completing 1.91 billion rides in a single quarter—yes, nearly 2 billion in just three months.[42] By 2022 the company was worth over $112 billion, yet it remained unprofitable.[43]

All that mattered was growth and revenues, not profits. So the people it hired were the most ambitious, who would work long hours, stopping at nothing to expand Uber into new markets. Traditionally, companies cared about character, experience, decision-making, and expertise; by most accounts, Uber's top priorities were intense loyalty, competitiveness, and the willingness to work toward the company's growth goals—at almost any cost. That was, after all, what "Fierceness," "Super Pumpedness," and "Always Be Hustlin'" were all about.

Several of the most sophisticated investors of the Silicon Age conducted due diligence on the company, and in Kalanick, they saw his aggressiveness, even arrogance. They'd read the tweets from @KonaTbone. In fact, Rob Hayes, a partner at First Round Capital, found out about Uber from Garrett Camp's Twitter feed. On June 15, 2010, he sent a two-word email to Camp: "I'll bite." By the July 4 weekend, Hayes and Camp were finalizing the deal for Uber's angel round.[44] Uber would turn the $510,000 that Hayes invested into $2.5 billion.[45] Uber's investors had surely seen when Kalanick had posted, "in my vegas pad quest, I found ultimate pad . . . formally named the PIMP HOUSE, equipped with a stripper pole AND stage," followed by a link to vegaspartyhouse.com. The Vegas Party House was owned by a company named "Nine Deep Enterprises, LLC," seemingly referring to the mental, emotional, no, the spirit-ual state that one is in after consuming nine alcoholic drinks.[46] Uber's investors evaluated the risks of this purposefully pugilistic, endlessly energetic, and utterly Alpha-male entrepreneur.

They liked what they saw. Some of them even joined in on the debauchery they'd funded, such as when he was "Throwing down a 2004 Colgin magnum," chugging a bottle of wine worth several hundred dollars, with investor Gary Vaynerchuk.[47] Kalanick went to extremes, and his hard-partying, hard-charging ways were more than a raging lifestyle. It was his way of life, a daily devotion, which he updated with moment-by-moment missives in real time. He narrated his nights out on Twitter, from "Tbones skollin those mutha fuckas on the dance floor yo," to the final 4:13 a.m. denouement of "KTB is oooowwwwwwwww-wuuuuuuuuuttttttte," to the encore six hours later of "Headache . . . now twittering."[48] But some investors didn't need social media to know about Kalanick's nightlife; Chris Sacca partied with Kalanick at the strip club, according to Kalanick's tweets.[49] They were all along for this wild ride, as it ran wild. On his personal blog, Kalanick wrote, "When you've got the kind of crew we've got, the party is wherever we are." That comment was about the time that Kalanick, Camp, and Sacca flew to Washington to attend Barack Obama's inauguration in January 2009. Kalanick joked, "Like it or not, the big balls (I'm talking about events not anatomy) require the black tie."[50]

One after another, Travis Kalanick's blogs, tweets, and other public pronouncements left no one to wonder why Emily Chang would choose *Brotopia* as the title of her 2018 book, a blistering reappraisal of Silicon Valley, where she decried how "from its earliest days, the [tech] industry has self-selected for men: first, antisocial nerds, then, decades later, self-confident and risk-taking bros."[51] From Mark Zuckerberg hacking Harvard while getting buzzed on cheap beer to Travis Kalanick tweeting from the nightclub while downing fine wine worth hundreds of dollars, Silicon Valley culture embraced it all without slowing down to ask questions, just so long as there was so much money to be made.

The virtues of this pseudo-religion: selfishness, urgency, and excess. Its main mantra was Work Hard Play Hard. Its only savior was the Self. Its trinity, Me, Me, Me. Kalanick was more than just egoistic. His proclamations neared messianic, and that's according to his own self-assessment. Kalanick called it "the church of creative capitalism," in tweets where he bragged about people who "just showed up for church @konatbone about to give a sermon."[52] Kalanick had an evangelical fervor about entrepreneurship. For a pilgrimage to its holiest site, investors just needed to visit @JamPadHQ, the Twitter feed Kalanick created for his apartment.

Who were their prophets, the philosophers whom Kalanick and his crew revered the most? The profit maximalists, the capitalist absolutists, the people who turned rugged individualism into something far more extreme. They were willing to sacrifice almost anything as they praised the ultrarich. The ideologies that had inspired the Church of Creative Capitalism flowed from sacrosanct texts written by Milton Friedman and Ayn Rand.[53]

## Milton and Ayn: The Prophets of Profits

As the first priest of the Church of Creative Capitalism, Milton Friedman argued that making as much money as quickly possible was a business's *sole* duty —that moneymaking mattered far more than the costs of its actions to anyone else— and that mandate meant maximizing the returns to shareholders as the only stakeholders that mattered. With this rationale, employees, contractors, partners, and suppliers always came second to shareholder profits, if those other people were considered at all. The same went for any intended or unintended negative impacts on the customers to whom a business provided products or services, the communities where they operated, or the overall environment that enabled them (both the business environment and our natural one). In

Friedman's view, it was always profits first. Usually that meant profits second through last, too. It didn't matter what happened to workers, families, communities, and society.[54]

Of course, someone has to pay those other costs eventually. But based on Friedman's teachings, corporate responsibility meant *socialism*. Or, as the @JamPadHQ account tweeted on February 7, 2010, several months before Uber raised its first round, "socialism bleeds into the heart of the wounded capitalist."[55] Rather than be wounded, weakened, and worried about others, Kalanick believed that business required an all-encompassing focus on what was good for oneself. This idea largely came from Friedman's essay in the *New York Times Magazine* in 1970, "The Social Responsibility of Business Is to Increase Its Profits," where he argued that the main duties of businesses were toward their shareholders, while minimizing any obligations to society, employees, and customers.[56] Today that view might seem mainstream, but it represented a drastic shift away from prior beliefs. Promoting unbridled business practices that prioritized only shareholders would have been controversial, even heretical at the time, but Friedman was, to use his word, an "extremist" who preferred black-and-white absolutes. Historian Angus Burgin explained: "Friedman maintained a relentless faith in the ability of unpopular ideas to gain recognition and, over the course of decades, to effect political change."[57] During the coming decades, Friedman's faith was rewarded. But before he was culturally celebrated, even exalted as a Prophet of Profits, most mid-twentieth-century businesspeople would have considered his ideas not only "extremist" but also bizarre.

When Harvard Business School was founded in 1908, its mission was to educate leaders who "make a decent profit—decently."[58] That purpose was put into practice in the decades to come. After the euphoria of the 1920s and the trauma of the Great Depression, many leading thinkers had argued that concerned consumers, organized labor, legislators, and government regulators all played necessary and important roles in curbing the excesses of corporations as they grew, created jobs, and, in turn, expanded economic opportunities. Harvard corporate law professor E. Merrick Dodd (along with many other scholars and corporate executives of his day) would have heard the "Greed is Good" belief, and likely responded, with nuance: *yes, profits are really good, but they can also cause problems, even unintentionally, and someone has to pick up the tab eventually if costs are ignored.*

This approach viewed business as a vibrant part of American society, where entrepreneurs and executives were vital civic leaders who contended with real-world complexities as they made valuable decisions that shaped the nation. For long-term well-being—of not only their individual businesses, but also the economy and society overall—they'd take into account the impacts on the stakeholders beyond just shareholders, such as their employees, customers, and communities where they did business. They rejected false choices of business versus society, where focusing on profits meant disregarding people. They deemed decency a virtue. More than that, it was a necessary way of doing business.

Dodd wrote in 1932 that the notion that "stockholders who have no contact with business other than to derive dividends from it" was "hardly thinkable." Instead, he believed businesses "should become imbued with a professional spirit of public service" that went beyond a black-and-white bottom-line calculation.[59] This approach allowed for a longer-term time horizon. Considering business as vital part of a healthy society would take more factors into account than venture capital's instant gratification and urgent hypergrowth. In some ways, the Silicon Age's short-termism was more straightforward and far simpler.

But fifty years after Friedman, new technologies meant massive scale was possible, like never before. As a result, his ideology served venture capitalists' goals—it came down to math, where venture investors needed huge wins to make the entire portfolio—and so they narrowed capitalism's aims to focus on extreme returns in the extremely short term. If the entrepreneurs could raise more and more venture money, and their massively valuable (yet still unprofitable) enterprises grew enough, they'd make out like bandits. They just needed to sell or go public before they'd spent everything, which would ensure huge returns for their investors and themselves. Everyone would win. Well, seemingly, everyone who mattered.

Silicon Valley's "Move Fast and Break Things" ethos encouraged entrepreneurs to do almost anything to win, privatizing most gains, while socializing many risks and losses. This approach encouraged excesses by high-risk startup founders, as they sought rapid expansion no matter the long-term consequences. To turn silicon into gold, the excess reagents didn't matter. And these growth-at-all-costs investors absolutely loved winner-take-all entrepreneurs like Travis Kalanick. They offered him practically limitless capital so he would win at any cost.

Kalanick viewed business like an extreme sport: "He wasn't satisfied with winning," a former Uber executive later told Mike Isaac for *Super Pumped*. "He needed to rub your nose in it. Like a master training a dog to submit. It was intense."[60] Most Silicon Valley companies have embraced rule-breaking as inevitable, but Kalanick went further than most. And this wasn't just a business decision, it was a personal commitment. Kalanick's Twitter avatar wasn't a picture of himself. When he referred to "T-Bone," it was a riff on his first name and the profile picture he'd chosen, a T-bone steak. At another point, a different image popped up next to each of his tweets. It was the cover of Ayn Rand's *The Fountainhead*.[61] Long before Friedman, she was the priestess of the Church of Creative Capitalism, the earliest Prophetess of Profits.

"Every man creates his meaning and form and goal," Rand wrote in that book, in the words of the main character, the architect Howard Roark. "Why is it so important—what others have done? Why does it become sacred by the mere fact of not being your own?"[62] Roark was Rand's greatest man, the model for all to follow. Because of his self-centered approach to life, Rand wrote in her letters that "Roark is the genuine human being, because he exemplifies a man who has reached perfection."[63] Not "a genuine human being" because of his humanity, because "he has empathy for others." Not even, "he strives for perfection." It was an extreme statement, "Roark is *the* genuine human being," because he cared only about himself. He was perfect because he couldn't care less about other people. To be selfish, uncompromising, superior—those were Rand's ultimate virtues.

When financiers questioned the viability of one of his designs, Roark quit, rejecting both wealth and prestige—and the power that would come with them—in the ultimate Randian act of integrity. He'd created something pure, and when they critiqued it, his fidelity to that ideal made him perfect. He refused to revise the design, which they deemed "sheer insanity!" and called him "fanatical." Roark just smiled and said, "That was the most selfish thing you've ever seen a man do," and walked out.[64] For Rand, this rejection of society's norms made Roark virtuous. Roark was Rand's ideal man because he reshaped the world in the way he wanted, in his own image. At the climax of *The Fountainhead*, he destroyed Cortlandt Homes, the model housing project he'd built, because his design specifications were not followed (importantly, this was even though Rand made the point that it would have created positive social impact by providing affordable and safe housing for low-income renters).[65]

In America, capitalism often inspires individualism and democracy encourages free enterprise, but Rand went even further than Friedman's most radical statements. She believed in a kind of capitalism where prior vices like selfishness became virtues. Entrepreneurs took this so far in the Silicon Age that their aims became more important than free enterprise itself. It neared antiauthority anarcho-capitalism, where rules didn't matter and markets needn't be free for everyone, because the individual came first. Likewise, markets did not have to be fair for anyone.

As Dallas Mavericks owner Mark Cuban, a mentor to Kalanick, once told the *New York Times*: "Travis's biggest strength is that he will run through a wall to accomplish his goals. Travis's biggest weakness is that he will run through a wall to accomplish his goals."[66] Like Roark, Kalanick seemed ready to break any rule. It was codified in that core Uber value of "super pumpedness." Officially: "'Super pumpedness' is all about moving the team forward, working long hours—pretty much a do-whatever-it-takes attitude to move the company in the right direction."[67] Do-*whatever*-it-takes.

Capitalism often entails intense competition, but we've reached new extremes more recently. Near the end of the twentieth century, Freidman seemed to have prevailed, and Rand had too, as Americans trusted that disrupting the status quo in pursuit of business goals was *always* a good thing even when there were serious costs. As new ventures grew and grew, venture capitalists deemed dominance a duty, so entrepreneurs' self-serving pronouncements were made virtuous. They were evidence of improved odds of winning, rather than risks about a company culture that could harm people. Yet we're starting to have doubts as the twenty-first century unfolds. Did winning at all costs have to be the gospel truth? The way Kalanick ran Uber, and the corporate culture he created, gave clear reasons for concern.

## Ayn discovers Friedrich, and Uber is born from Superman

When literary scholars sifted through Rand's personal files, they found numerous instances where she derided empathy, rejected social responsibility, and lauded characters who served their own interests. It went far beyond destroying low-income housing, even extending to some of the worst crimes imaginable. In Rand's notes about one character from the summer of 1927, she wrote that murder wasn't evil. She celebrated, as a positive good, that he'd slaughtered a beloved pastor: "He does not understand, *because he has no organ for understanding*, the necessity, meaning or importance of other people."[68] In clinical terms, that is called an antisocial personality disorder. Colloquially, we might call someone a "sociopath" if they demonstrate a pervasive disregard for societal norms, rules, and the rights of others, while often acting aggressively or impulsively. We'd use the word "psychopath" to describe a similar disregard for others when accompanied by more calculated, manipulative behavior, or an ability to mimic emotional connections for their own advantage.[69]

Rand called this character "An extreme 'extremist.' A clear, strong, brilliant, mind. An egoist, in the best sense of the word." All his selfishness was praiseworthy, including his murderous ways, because "other people have no right, no hold, no interest or influence on him. And this is not affected or chosen—it's *inborn*, absolute, it can't be changed, he has 'no organ' to be otherwise. In this respect, he has the true, innate psychology of a Superman. He can never realize and feel 'other people.'"[70] It wasn't even his choice. He was born with it.

We might recognize the term "Superman" from the comic books, but what are its origins? It was first translated into English as "overman," and later as "beyond-man," but the name that stuck was George Bernard Shaw's, popularized by his play *Man and Superman*. The comic book hero, introduced in 1938, turned the name into a cultural icon.[71] But Ayn Rand had used the word eleven years before that, quoting Nietzsche's *Beyond Good and Evil* to describe the ideal character who had murdered a pastor: "The noble soul has reverence for himself." It was the same line she included at the start of *The Fountainhead*.[72] The German word Nietzsche had used, in *Beyond Good and Evil* from 1886, was

*Übermensch*.[73] Before anyone was "superpumped," before Uber put us all on an app that would take us anywhere, Kalanick was a Randian. That was almost certainly where Uber got its name. But more important, "the true, innate psychology of a Superman" shaped the ideals that Kalanick read about and pursued with Uber.

As Kalanick conquered city by city, he seemed to approach the government like Rand had, as the enemy in all circumstances. He used his business to organize against it. He gained power from his wealth, using both to gain access, not only to exclusive parties in Washington, but also to an entirely new world of power over people that was now possible technologically. In the years to come, he'd put all that power to use. With a few lines of code, he could push out online petitions, encourage floods of emails, spark rallies, and wage an assault on the phone lines of local officials. Did it matter if these outspoken advocates represented the way most people really felt? If they were loud enough, on message enough, and powered by the speed and reach of the Internet, Uber would win. As we'll see, they did. Kalanick and his colleagues did whatever it took, to win at all costs.[74]

∗ ∗ ∗

One time Kalanick was asked for book recommendations. He answered: *Atlas Shrugged* and *The Fountainhead*.[75] They were both books he'd read again and again as a teenager. As CEO of Uber, he would taunt underperforming colleagues with this criticism: "You're a Peter and not a Howard."[76] That meant that instead of seeking greatness, like the heroic Howard Roark, someone was being weak-willed like his foil in *The Fountainhead*, Peter Keating. As a teenager, Rand's own intellectual development was heavily influenced by Friedrich Nietzsche, who died in 1900 in Weimar, Germany, five years before she was born.[77] At age fifteen, Rand boldly declared that individualism was the only thing that mattered in the world; her cousin told her that Nietzsche had already come to that same conclusion. "Naturally, I was very curious to read him," Rand recalled over forty years later. "I certainly was enthusiastic about the individualist part of it. I had not expected that there existed anybody who would go that far in praising the individual."[78]

Nietzsche went quite far in his praise, hailing the Übermensch as supreme, while arguing against any philosophies or spiritual practices that taught otherwise:

> We should not deck out and embellish Christianity: it has waged a war to the death against this higher type of man, it has put all the deepest instincts of this type under its ban, it has developed its concept of evil, of the Evil One himself, out of these instincts—the strong man as the typical reprobate, the "outcast among men." Christianity has taken the part of all the weak, the low, the

botched; it has made an ideal out of antagonism to all the self-preservative instincts of sound life; it has corrupted even the faculties of those natures that are intellectually most vigorous, by representing the highest intellectual values as sinful, as misleading, as full of temptation."[79]

Those words appeared in Nietzsche's second-to-last book, *The Antichrist*, from 1895. American writer H. L. Mencken deemed it a magnum opus, "a statement of some of his most salient ideas in their final form."[80] Nietzsche didn't hold back. "I condemn Christianity; I bring against the Christian church the most terrible of all the accusations that an accuser has ever had in his mouth," he wrote. "I call Christianity the one great curse, the one great intrinsic depravity, the one great instinct of revenge, for which no means are venomous enough, or secret, subterranean and *small* enough,—I call it the one immortal blemish upon the human race."[81]

Rand rejected Christianity with similar denunciations. She believed it made life "flat, gray, empty, lacking all beauty, all fire, all enthusiasm, all meaning, all creative urge," and she claimed that the Bible, due to its lessons about charity, empathy, and love, "is the best kindergarten of communism possible."[82] Man's purpose should not be found in service to others, she thought, but in service to himself. By rejecting the self-sacrificing values taught by society, which many of us had simply absorbed in Sunday school or civics classes, Rand offered an alternative: personal values were up to the individual. If a man pursued his own ideas against all odds—demonstrating his superiority—then society would model itself after the best and strongest. Others would follow his lead and mimic his success. For Rand, this created a moral duty to seek greatness, not ordinariness, to be a producer, not a moocher.

Ayn Rand called her approach "objectivism," since objective reality could be understood through individual values and rational knowledge—most visibly, in the logical outcomes of an unfettered market. Freedom of choice was the meaning of life, according to Rand, the earliest Prophetess of Profits. But Rand's cousin taunted that an earlier book by Nietzsche had "beat you to all your ideas."[83] To any free thinker, that was the ultimate putdown. The book was *Thus Spoke Zarathustra,* which challenged traditional morality as dogmatism and religion as superstition. In their place, Nietzsche embraced the "will to power" and established a new morality of man through "self-overcoming."[84]

"God is dead! God remains dead! And we have killed him!" Nietzsche proclaimed, with words so renowned they'd become pop culture.[85] In an all-time power move, Nietzsche used the stroke of a pen to kill God. The result? People could create a world based on their own aims and ambitions. "How can we console ourselves, the murderers of all murderers! The holiest and the mightiest thing the world has ever possessed has bled to death under our knives: who will wipe this blood from us?," Nietzsche asked. "With what water could we clean ourselves? What festivals of atonement, what holy games will we have to invent for ourselves? Is the magnitude of this deed not too great for us? Do we not ourselves have to become gods merely to appear worthy of it?"[86] Men could become godlike, as word spread about their superiority. This cult of personality motivated celebrity heroes to try to become living deities, or more. Some even believed that with enough power, they could replace God.

If all this sounds scarily familiar—Germans in Weimar promoting ideas of their superiority over others, at all costs, as people became so cutthroat that they'd murder and massacre to become godlike supermen—it's because those ideas left a deadly legacy. It started harmlessly enough, just some ideas on a page. Yet, clearly, words do matter.

Nietzsche's sister, Elisabeth, curated and published his manuscripts to match her own extremist, anti-Semitic, and nationalist views (even though Nietzsche himself had strongly rejected anti-Semitism, once writing that he "would have all anti-Semites shot"). Adolf Hitler's rise in following decades was premised on these same concepts, on "race betterment," based on the belief that the Aryan race, not Jews, were true descendants of God's chosen people.[87] The same word, "Übermensch," would be used to justify good genes (eugenics) and good deaths (euthanasia), all in the pursuit of the Nazis' Aryan ideal, one of history's worst extreme outcomes. They slowly eroded each red line between right and wrong, graying and blurring them, then crossing them. They created confusion, then resignation, with each new right-thing-to-do made uncertain and every new wrong already done. As moral frameworks frayed, vices became virtuous and ethical options became unenviable, and then unviable. And the extreme ideology of Aryan "race betterment" became an abominable easy answer, which millions believed in.

That's what happened. But it's important not to overreach and make comparisons where they're unmerited. In 1963 Ayn Rand did just that, in a speech where she read lines from speeches by Hitler and John F. Kennedy to make the case that the listener couldn't tell the difference between them. She argued against Kennedy's New Frontier policy agenda, claiming that any government intervention eventually becomes a slippery slope toward totalitarianism: "The basic moral political principles running through all of these statements is clear: the subordination and sacrifice of the individual to the collective. That principle, derived from the ethics of altruism, is the ideological root of all statist systems, in any variation, from welfare statism to a totalitarian dictatorship." There is no middle ground in this thinking, it's an all-out war for all-out individualism, and that's why Rand originally wanted to call the collection of essays *The Virtue of Selfishness* by the same title as her speech: "The Fascist New Frontier."[88]

Rand had written some of the most popular titles ever published by Random House, and she got along wonderfully with Bennett Cerf, its cofounder and publisher. "She was a veritable golden goose for the house," Jennifer Burns explained in her Rand biography *Goddess of the Market*. Rand's books had sold hundreds of thousands of copies, and Cerf and Rand were personal friends, too. Cerf's wife had even taken the dust jacket photo of the author. He worried that Rand had gone too far this time, so he asked her to tone it down, maybe even refrain from comparing JFK to Hitler. As Burns chronicled, Rand became apoplectic and accused the publisher of breach of contract. She split from Random House and published the book with a division of Penguin. The lost revenues hurt Cerf's company, but he'd acted on principle, and he remained good natured about it all. "How wonderful it must be to be so sure you are right!" he later mused about Rand's worldview to a colleague.[89]

Those beliefs would change the world. As venture capital fueled hypergrowth, Rand's followers went to such extremes, world domination upended traditional capitalism. Her objectivism became a form of nihilism. Once the leaders of the Silicon Age put this theory into practice, selfishness became supercharged. Their "will to power" was disruptive, and then destructive. Over time, on all our devices, it became more like annihilism.

* * *

Bennett Cerf was a distant cousin of Vint Cerf, the Father of the Internet, who designed its earliest architecture while working at the Defense Department.[90] The free and open Internet, and the democratic and meritocratic values it was founded on, was first built in government labs and university campus offices. Many of the people who contributed to its creation, like Cerf, did so on the U.S. taxpayer's dime. From time to time, history harmonizes. But it can also blare jarringly.[91]

According to the Church of Creative Capitalism, existing laws weren't worth preserving; rules could be broken for your own objectives. Government was too big, a waste of resources; bureaucrats thought too small, a limit on progress. Diversity was worthless. Why listen to others who differ from you? Compromise was weakness. Why alter your egocentric ideals?

The rule-breaking of the Silicon Age moved us away from considering societal good and toward the orderless interests of extremist individualism. In that light, Rand's wildly popular writings from the 1930s and 1940s weren't just precursors to Friedman's profits-only declarations in the 1970s and the "Greed is Good" culture of the 1980s. Today, her words seem like the earliest warnings about the excesses of Big Tech and the do-whatever-it-takes culture it encouraged, years before a Stanford professor discovered the transistor—or, at least, he claimed he did—and then spent most of his career promoting "race betterment," eugenics, and his plans to create a master race by forcibly sterilizing people.

# CHAPTER 5

# WHITE LIES

Bill Shockley, Foundation for Research and
Education on Eugenics and Dysgenics

In 1951 there were transistor companies headquartered in Boston, Camden, New York, and Syracuse. Five years more, and twenty-two cities were home to innovators who dreamed of silicon-enriched futures. Kokomo, Indiana, was one of them.[1] What if history had pivoted? What would America have become, if the Silicon Heartland had sprung up in that rural town between Indianapolis, South Bend, and West Lafayette? Back then, there were no transistor companies in Northern California. If not for a renowned physicist who was too paranoid to keep a team intact, it might have stayed that way. Instead, California's apple orchards transformed into Silicon Valley, which created the greatest wealth in the world. Regrettably, the Midwest weathered the worst economic decline of any region in America, as its steel mills eroded into the Rust Belt.[2]

In 1955 William Shockley moved from the East Coast to be nearer to his ailing mother. She lived in Palo Alto, California.[3] That was where he started Shockley Semiconductor Laboratory, located at 391 San Antonio Road, in nearby Mountain View.[4] In 1946 he'd received the Medal for Merit, America's highest civilian decoration at the time, for contributions during World War II.[5] That same year, alongside an essay from Albert Einstein warning that "all the people living in cities are threatened, everywhere and constantly, with sudden destruction," Shockley had a very different message. He called the atomic bomb "profitable," based on his cost-benefit analysis that the price of the bomb was outweighed by the even more extraordinary carnage it wreaked and the deaths it caused. Shockley ran the numbers. He tallied a net benefit.[6]

A decade later, on November 1, 1956, Bill Shockley woke up to news that changed his life forever: he'd won the Nobel Prize as part of the team that invented the transistor. When he got to the office, he immediately called off work for the day and took everyone to a champagne breakfast at Dinah's Shack.[7] Californians went to Dinah's for a heaping dose of southern hospitality. Charles and Hazel McMonagle had named their restaurant after a Black woman who helped to raise Hazel during her childhood—not in the postbellum South but in Kansas. Even so, the recipes they embraced, and the traditions that they traced back to, were all Deep South.[8]

They served fried chicken, biscuits from scratch, and waffle fries. The restaurant's brand was based on the mammy image, a popularized depiction of a Black woman who worked in white homes to help raise the children. When two white Californians made a mammy's face their logo, it was for marketing purposes. They hoped it would convey a sense of hospitality and warmth, reminiscent of home-cooked family meals where guests were waited on and cared for. But with Jim Crow in full force elsewhere in America, and with California having only recently outlawed public accommodation segregation, not everyone felt welcomed.[9]

A few years after Shockley's celebration, civil rights advocates arrived at Dinah's front door to demand that the McMonagles change the logo and remove other objects they'd placed outside the restaurant: Black lawn jockeys, another Jim Crow Era relic.[10] Historian Kenneth Goings had once described these figurines as "an attempt to show African Americans as comical and miniature human beings and, more importantly, still happy to be working for their masters."[11] The restaurant owners reacted to this backlash by declaring, "If they really feel it's necessary, we'll paint them white or make them Indians." And then, incredibly, they did. Altering the face of the mammy logo on the sign, the owners turned up the brightness and down the contrast on the image. Then they whitewashed the statues.[12]

Rather than learning by listening, the McMonagles reacted. That may have silenced the protestors, but their quick fix didn't get to the root causes. They didn't pause and reflect, instead showing exasperation, even indignation. Race relations in America have often meant fear, resentment, misinterpretations, and indignities—and that's not exclusive to the South. It can be seen in the choices made by West Coast restaurateurs, as they cooked southern food for Californians, inspired by a nanny from Kansas, who became a mammy for their marketing. Racism has never been just a "southern thing," and neither has it solely been a lost cause idea in the minds of uninformed Americans, people who were uneducated, rural, and lower class. "Racism is a worldwide problem," the musician Patterson Hood once declared, even though "it's always a little more convenient to play it with a Southern accent."[13] And, as Bill Shockley's story reveals, racist ideologies were protected and promoted by the powerful—throughout

Silicon Valley, across America, and at elite institutions, especially Stanford University.

## Eight entrepreneurs reject Bill's toxicity, then set the world on fire

The fact that Bill Shockley offered to pay for everyone's breakfast at Dinah's might give the impression that he was a generous man, but that was far from the truth. He regularly berated and belittled his team. He was paranoid, once hiring private detectives to investigate his staff and demanding they take polygraphs because he was convinced someone was sabotaging his work.[14] No one had. But he still harbored doubts. "I don't think 'tyrant' begins to encapsulate Shockley," one employee put it.[15] "When he hired you, you were the greatest person in the world," another colleague told the *Los Angeles Times*. "Then slowly you worked your way down the line. First you were brilliant. Then, 'You're doing a good job.' Then, 'You're capable, but I'm unsure about you. . . . Now I'm really unsure. . . . Now I think you're inadequate. I don't think you can do the job for me.' He kept a black book on everybody."[16] He was known to ridicule his employees by often demeaning their intellect, asking, "Are you sure you have a PhD?"[17]

Shockley felt he was superior to his peers, too. He shared the Nobel Prize with two collaborators, John Bardeen and Walter Houser Brattain, who seethed at the horrible way he'd treated them. They complained that Shockley did almost none of the work but took all the credit.[18] When they posed for a publicity photo, Shockley sat in in the center, placing both hands on the test equipment. Brattain claimed that was "the first and last time William Shockley ever laid hands on it."[19] One September day in 1957, eight scientists had finally hit their limit. Shockley's relentless abuse had become too suffocating. They resigned from Shockley's lab en masse. Suddenly out of work, they decided to create the region's very first transistor company, Fairchild Semiconductor. Shockley dubbed them the "Traitorous Eight."[20]

Fairchild grew from eight to four thousand employees over the next decade. Nowadays, an astonishing 70 percent of public Bay Area technology companies have some connection to Fairchild and those eight entrepreneurs, according to Rhett Morris and Mariana Penido at the global nonprofit Endeavor.[21] The breakthroughs they discovered soon led to all kinds of new innovations. The Traitorous Eight left behind Shockley's toxicity and changed the world.

These eight men had numerous venture-backed successes early on, with thirty-one spinoffs in their first dozen years.[22] But it went beyond that. By creating the Silicon Age machines that would enmesh the entire world in an online network, they also created a powerful social network. Just as the PayPal Mafia would accomplish over half a century later, they built the next generation of ventures together in Northern California—sending investment opportunities to each other, sharing ideas about the next breakthrough, and recommending talented young people for jobs at each other's ventures. Morris and Penido found that ninety-two public companies today, which employ more than 800,000 people, trace back to Fairchild. They're worth over $2 trillion, more than the GDP of Canada, India, or Spain.

These men started Silicon Valley, but their achievements went beyond even that. They also helped to invent the modern American entrepreneur. No one has better shown just how important high-tech ventures, and the venture capital that funds them, have been for the U.S. economy than the man who cofounded AOL and is now the chair and CEO of Revolution, Steve Case. Half of all Fortune 500 companies turn over every twenty-five years, Case has noted. What replaces them? New ventures that grow into massive successes. Nearly all these startups are powered by technology, and most are backed by venture capital.[23] While big corporations have grown and shrunk over time, and local small businesses have too, Case has convincingly shown that venture-backed startups have created all net new jobs in America. Research by Tim Kane for the Kauffman Foundation has gone even further, writing that larger and older American corporations are, in fact, "net job destroyers, losing 1 million jobs net combined per year," while "startups create an average of 3 million new jobs annually."[24]

So while growth-maximization has often had negative impacts on society overall, the jobs and wealth created by new ventures are undeniably valuable. They're creating millions of *net* new jobs a year. But as Case has often emphasized, only a few places in America have benefited from that growth. "Venture capital just started about 50 years ago. It's a relatively new idea, and actually started in New York and in Boston and San Francisco, and it got built up around those places," he explained, with 75 percent of venture investing still happening in those three states: California, Massachusetts, and New York.[25] That has already transformed the U.S. economy and reshaped our world, but as Case predicted in his book *The Rise of the Rest: How Entrepreneurs in Surprising Places Are Building the New American Dream*: "Over the next decade, a *majority* of the iconic startup companies—the ones that create tens of thousands of jobs and end up being worth billions of dollars—will *not* be in Silicon Valley, but all across the country."[26] Perhaps the startup story of Kokomo, Indiana, is just in its earliest iterations.

That creates an inspiring opportunity for job creation throughout America, but success is not guaranteed. "Thirty to 40 years ago, 90 percent of global venture capital went to the United States, and now it's under 50 percent, so we have seen a globalization of entrepreneurship," Case explained. If communities are unable to support startup founders in all parts of the country, or venture investors invest only on the coasts and don't back startups nationwide, Case warns that others could outpace us in entrepreneurial activity: "Many other countries have figured out that, in some ways, the 'secret sauce' that made America is innovation and entrepreneurship. Other countries are trying to win the industries of the future and make policies that create the right environment for the entrepreneurs in their countries to succeed."[27] That is a warning worth heeding. But no matter what happens next, the growth of venture-backed technology startups will undoubtedly determine the future of economies and societies around the world—and it all traces back to one invention, the transistor.

$*\ *\ *$

"I would put it on the [same] level as fire, in terms of its importance to what modern life is like today," said physicist and science historian Michael Riordan. "It has enabled this global civilization."[28] The transistor ushered in a new era of transformational change. Two Fairchild cofounders, Robert Noyce and Gordon Moore, also cofounded Intel.[29] Eugene Kleiner started one of the most storied venture capital firms, Kleiner Perkins Caufield & Byers, which backed Amazon, Compaq, Netscape, Sun Microsystems, Symantec, and many others.[30] Shockley's defectors figured out how to make these novel deals work, with their high-risk nature and super-high returns. In many ways, these better rebels who rejected Shockley and created Fairchild and its children deserve the credit for making the Silicon Age possible.

They built technology using digital networks. They developed real-world personal networks that enhanced their successes, too, as they mentored and invested in the next generation. Venture capital backs only a tiny fraction of the companies that pitch them, but those investments account for over half of all public U.S. companies founded since 1979.[31] Today every dollar invested in new ventures yields three times the number of patents of traditional corporate research and development.[32] None of that would have happened without the eight men who founded Fairchild.

The transistor was truly one of humankind's greatest inventions. The Nobel winners discovered fire. Then Fairchild fanned the flames. The world has never been the same.

After his lab ignited it all, Shockley abandoned the field of physics altogether. This was at the exact time that transistors and the businesses built from them created wealth, opportunities, and innovations that were, without hyperbole, unprecedented in human history. From the mid-1960s until the day he died in 1989, Shockley committed the remainder of his life's work not to transistors and the Silicon Age they ushered in. Instead, he focused on what he thought made people superior to others. He advanced ideas about eugenics and dysgenics, theories that elites were born better due to their genetic lineage, particularly because of race.[33]

## After eight great entrepreneurs abandon him, Bill makes new friends

With the Nazis' Aryan ideal, eugenics had been pursued to horrific effect just a decade before Shockley won the Nobel. Dysgenics was its opposite, where human suffering was supposedly attributable to poor and lazy people having too many children.[34] "We're living in a society in which the achievements of the human mind have made it possible for people to survive with the help of machines and technology and welfare," Shockley told *US News & World Report* on November 22, 1965. "Therefore, adverse things may take place genetically, and the unfit may increase faster in our population than ever was true in the past." He then gave an example of a sixteen-year-old girl whose parents received welfare; Shockley claimed she had three illegitimate children of her own and they all were supported by the U.S. taxpayer. He worried, "How is our democracy going to work if a large fraction of the electorate must be supported by the community and also lacks the brains and moral sense needed for good citizenship?"[35]

Shockley sent copies of this interview to colleagues, claiming that he had received significant support for his arguments. One of the people who endorsed him was the chairman of the Executive Committee of Planned Parenthood, Cass Canfield, who wrote that "it seems to me that in the public interest the interview should be printed."[36] Canfield's support brought with it a great deal of legitimacy; he has been praised as "one of the most influential publishers of the 20th century," considering his roles as chairman of the board of directors of *Harper's* and as a cofounder of *Foreign Affairs*.[37] Across the top of Shockley's letter that cited Canfield's support, the letterhead read, in bright red font, "Stanford Electronics Laboratories."[38] He was using Stanford's resources to promote his theories about race. That was just the start of it.

Earlier that year, an official Stanford press release celebrated Shockley's Nobel symposium on "Genetics and the Future of Man," where he'd made a similar argument. "Many thoughtful people are now concerned about possible genetic deterioration due to selective multiplication of less gifted members of society through extremely large families or high rates of illegitimacy," he declared. "Where survival of the fittest would have selected only the best of these in past centuries, our abundant American society assures all the privilege of reproducing their kind." Shockley found hope in one policy solution: "wiser eugenic laws," such as "the laws for sterilization of mental defectives in many states."[39] That included the state of California, he noted, where officials forcibly sterilized thousands of patients in state-run mental institutions, in accordance with eugenics laws that had been on the books since 1909.[40] By the time those rules were repealed, in 1979, more than twenty thousand people had been sterilized against their wishes.[41]

The faculty at Stanford who *had* studied genetics protested when they read about Shockley's plans, after the Stanford School of Medicine republished the *US News* interview in January 1966. Seven faculty from the Department of Genetics responded in an open letter the next month, writing, "This kind of pseudo-scientific justifications for class and race prejudice is so hackneyed that we would not ordinarily have cared to react to it," but they worried that his "standing as a Nobel laureate and as a colleague at Stanford, and now the appearance of his article with a label of Stanford medicine, creates a situation where our silence could leave the false impression that we share or even acquiesce in his outlook, which we certainly do not."[42]

They admonished, "We deplore his innuendoes about the hereditary basis of purported intellectual and social deficits of Negroes, and the tone of his entire discussion about 'bad heredity,'" because they felt those assertions had no scientific merit. Instead, they believed real impetus for his effort "falls between mischief and malice." They also condemned his plan to sterilize people with lower IQ scores, because he'd ignored the possibility of "useful careers for the whole wonderful variety of human beings."[43] On April 12, 1966, Shockley responded to his colleagues—chastened, at least for the moment—and wrote that "this subject needs study and public discussion, not as much by worried amateurs like me who are not geneticists, but by the best scientists in genetics and other relevant scientists."[44]

That sentiment didn't last. Just two years later, Shockley stopped working on transistors completely. The self-described "amateur" would put his tenure to use, by saying what others could not—at least, that was his rationale.[45] He dedicated his entire research agenda to eugenics and dysgenics, as we will discover from the documents in Stanford's Special Collections & University Archives, most of which are being published here for the first time.

Early on, Shockley's department rejected his proposals to stray so far from his field of expertise. On June 14, 1968, the associate dean of the School of Engineering wrote a memo to the dean, raising numerous concerns that "the subject is outside of Bill's area of demonstrated research competence and it would be fruitless (even dangerous) for an amateur to dabble in an undertaking of such sensitivity." He warned that "there is a real danger in carrying out such research because it is not inconceivable that the consequences would only serve to exacerbate an extremely delicate situation." Ultimately, the associate dean concluded that "it seems clear that this program falls outside of the research scope of the School of Engineering; it is properly a matter for the Provost."[46] The dean of the School of Engineering wrote to Shockley: "As you know, the subject has some controversial aspects and represents a venture into a new field of activity beyond that contemplated at the time of your initial appointment to the faculty," closing his letter with these words: "I would suggest you address it directly to Provost Lyman."[47]

Shockley had already gone straight to the top anyway. Two days earlier, he sent a formal memo to the provost that outlined his plan for "Research on Methodology to Reduce the Environment-Heredity-Uncertainty, Including Ethnic and Racial Aspects." In other words, he would study what's now called the "nature versus nurture" debate, but with a specific focus on whether certain ethnicities or races were superior to others.[48] Shockley was determined to get the permission he needed. Throughout the spring of 1968, he had already begun to lobby the President's Office about the importance of his research—and not just with words, but with dollars, because it's money that talks, after all.

The first major donation came from Bill Lear, who was best known for his success with Learjets, but who also invented eight-track cassettes and developed the first car radio, an innovation that eventually grew to become the company Motorola.[49] Lear wrote the first check of $10,000 (over $86,000 today) to support "Dr. Shockley's interests in exploring new ways to establish objective facts about the hereditary aspects of our national human quality problems." He specified that supporting Shockley's work on inherited greatness or inferiority would "represent the only interest I would have in contributing to Stanford activities at the present time."[50] Stanford president J. E. Wallace Sterling responded, "Thank you for your letter and for the generous offer to contribute $10,000 for the support of research proposed by Professor William Shockley." He asked Lear to "bear with the rather bureaucratic procedures that have had to evolve for dealing with sponsored research supported by these customary sources," and demurred that "I trust that the delay occasioned by compliance with these procedures will not discommode either you or Professor Shockley."[51] Clearly, fundraising made a difference in the decision-making by Stanford administrators; in fact, they specifically instructed Shockley to account for the overhead that he would owe the university with all the new funding that he would be bringing in.[52]

Before Stanford approved Shockley's plans, several key donors also sent checks to the university to fund Shockley's investigations into racial superiority. These initial donations weren't small dollar gifts from uneducated racists; on the contrary, Stanford accepted thousands of dollars from wealthy and influential Americans to support Shockley's yet-unauthorized project. "I am greatly impressed with Professor Shockley's view that genetic factors have not been adequately weighed in consideration of the Black problem," one Manhattan-based benefactor wrote to a Stanford trustee. He hoped that "a genetic study of intelligence among races" might "speed the solution of our race problem by helping us to help the Negroes on a rational basis."[53] Those words were written by Paul J. Kern, the president of the Municipal Civil Service Commission under New York Mayor Fiorello H. LaGuardia and a corporate board director for Western Pacific Railroad. He sent Stanford $1,000.[54]

"Money doesn't talk," Bob Dylan corrected the old saying. "It swears."[55] And Stanford's capitulation to the almighty dollar came in its final form with a mundane memorandum titled, "Research Account for Professor William Shockley," from the Controller's Office to the associate dean of the School of Engineering on August 30, 1968. "Will you please transfer $1,000 from the Engineering General Gifts account 172G010-1-DAA-612 to this new account," came the request. "The title of this research is 'Research to reduce Racial Aspects of the Environment-Heredity Uncertainty.'"[56] On September 11, 1968, the donation from Kern was added to Shockley's new account, with the university's official ledger recording a transfer from the School of Engineering's General Gift Account, 1-DAA-612-68517, to the newly established account assigned to Shockley's research, 2-XX0-601-68117.[57] On September 17 Shockley wrote to Kern, informing him that "Yours was the wedge which opened this project at Stanford," enclosing Xerox copies of the transaction. Shockley then celebrated, "In a sense these are historic items since they are the quite possibly the first fund expenditures in the present half century on such a project in a major university."[58]

As additional donations began rolling in, Shockley had learned that money was the best way to meet Stanford's requirements for its "rather bureaucratic procedures," as President Sterling had put it, while overcoming objections from the School of Engineering and the faculty with actual expertise in genetics.[59] Money solved problems. And in the routine paperwork sent between Stanford's School of Engineering and the Office of the Controller, one thing became clear: the utterly appalling, yet completely official, banality of evil. All the other faculty were overruled. Shockley had the permission he'd desired and could pursue his own agenda.

## The physics professor promotes his opinions about genetics

Bob Dylan was right, and Patterson Hood was, too: money can be obscene, and hate is worldwide, festering both on the streets and in the suites. Racism is often talked about as a backward idea from the backwoods, but history shows otherwise. During the seventeenth, eighteenth, and nineteenth centuries, immense riches were created from American soil through the toil of men, women, and children held as subhuman property. "Major companies and universities profited off of the institution of slavery," according to the Alabama-based Equal Justice Initiative, "including Aetna, Inc., and New York Life Insurance Company, JP Morgan Chase, Harvard, Columbia, Princeton, and Yale."[60] And the reality is that throughout the twentieth century, long after slavery ceased, numerous foundations, universities, and scholars advanced not just elitism but "race betterment." They thought that white people were inherently superior.[61]

For decades, Stanford had already served as an epicenter for ideas like Shockley's. Its founding president, David Starr Jordan, believed that "the blood of a nation determines its history" and "the history of a nation determines its blood."[62] He promoted that concept decades before the Nazis, whose phrase for it was "*Blut und Boden*" or "Blood and Soil," which "was an early Nazi slogan used in Germany to evoke the idea of a pure 'Aryan' race and the territory it wanted to conquer," according to the United States Holocaust Memorial Museum.[63] Jordan also served on the initial board of trustees for the Human Betterment Foundation, a pro-eugenics organization that promoted legislation in the United States for compulsory sterilization based on IQ scores.[64] This went far beyond the Ivy League finishing-school version of education for white students only. At Stanford, racism relied on the scientific method, technology, and testing.[65]

As a young boy, Shockley's mother took him to one of the first testing centers for talented children, and he received merely average scores on the Stanford-Binet Intelligence Scale. At age nine, he demanded to retake the test. He refused to believe that he was not "gifted," to use the word coined by Stanford psychology professor Lewis M. Terman.[66] The test that Shockley took as a young boy was one of the earliest IQ tests, which French psychologist Alfred Binet developed along with Terman, whose "ardent promotion of the gifted few was grounded in a cold-blooded, elitist ideology," as *Stanford Magazine* later explained. Like Shockley in the 1960s, 1970s, and 1980s, Terman thought the future of humanity depended on limiting who had children. *Stanford Magazine* noted: "Especially in the early years of his career, he was a proponent of eugenics, a social movement aiming to improve the human 'breed' by perpetuating certain allegedly inherited traits and eliminating others. While championing the intelligent, he pushed for the forced sterilization of thousands of 'feebleminded' Americans."[67]

This plan for "progress" had savage outcomes. "In the United States, the movement peddled a topsy-turvy form of Darwinism," *Stanford Magazine* concluded, "claiming that the 'fittest' (defined as well-to-do Whites of Northern European ancestry) were reproducing too slowly and in danger of being overwhelmed by the inferior lower strata of society." This influenced U.S. social programs, immigration policies, and foreign affairs. To reduce poverty, the government could forcibly sterilize the "underclass" of people who were supposedly less ethical or intelligent. To keep America pure, they'd restrict immigration, including from Southern and Eastern Europe, while welcoming Northern and Western Europeans.[68] It was a toxic philosophy, promoted by professors, scientists, politicians, and business leaders, with cruel consequences.

"The man in the street has had experience and knows what to expect from blacks in business," Shockley said in one interview. "If one were to randomly pick ten blacks and ten whites and try to employ them in the same kinds of things, the whites would consistently perform better than the blacks."[69] Shockley promoted what he called the "Voluntary Sterilization Bonus Plan." In essence, he thought the U.S. government should pay people to be sterilized if they had low IQs or hereditary diseases. He recommended "a bonus of a thousand dollars for every point you score below 100 on an IQ Test."[70] Based on Shockley's "research," he estimated that 85 percent of Black Americans would qualify.[71]

Shockley claimed that any criticisms against him represented suppression of free speech and evidence of the intolerance of academia. "Our intellectuals won't think objectively about the poor illegitimate slum babies—both black and white—that come from parents without much foresight," Shockley told the *Detroit News* in 1974. "There is a very high probability that these children will get a bad shake from the unfairly loaded genetic dice of their parents. Statistically, they have little likelihood of being able to lead satisfactory, rewarding lives in our society."[72] Shockley justified his views with convoluted math and complicated statistics, all to advance his "loaded genetic dice" argument about humanity: white people, except perhaps Appalachians and others from chronically poorer areas, were inherently superior to Black people in America.

Shockley took this idea to extremes, such as when he asked the managing editor of *Ebony* magazine to send him blood samples so that he could prove that the most successful Black Americans had white ancestors. "We are not interested in participating in your proposed project that would determine the fraction of White ancestry in one-half of 'The 100 Most Influential Black Americans,' and we seriously doubt that any of 'The 100 . . .' would offer you samples of their blood for your project," came the reply. That happened in the summer of 1980.[73]

Shockley continued to conduct this kind of "research," and other projects like it, well into the 1980s—all out of his Stanford office, Room 202 in the McCullough Physics Building.[74]

## Stanford supports Bill's "research" on eugenics and dysgenics

After the Department of Engineering created Shockley's research account, the floodgates opened. Some checks were made out to Shockley himself, some were for Stanford University, others listed the Stanford Electronics Laboratories, and still others were made out to FREED, the Foundation for Research and Education on Eugenics and Dysgenics, a nonprofit that Shockley started to accept tax-deductible donations.[75] He raised funding for FREED using his official Stanford Electronics Laboratories letterhead, and Stanford directly received and processed checks that were deposited into 2-XX0-601-68117, Shockley's account.[76] Between 1968 and 1977, individual contributions and large foundation grants—totaling what today would be millions of dollars—went toward

Shockley's "research." Rather than funding studies on the transistor, or anything else that had to do with electrical engineering, this money supported Shockley's work on eugenics and dysgenics. It came from a few of the wealthiest, most successful, and most prominent leaders in America. Stanford accepted many of these checks, processed them, disbursed them, and never renounced or returned them.[77]

Shockley and his wife, who worked as his administrative assistant, also pursued small-dollar fundraising campaigns for FREED through annual "membership dues." They sent out publications, for ten cents for a page or two and fifty cents apiece for longer articles, which addressed topics like "models, mathematics, and the moral obligation to diagnose the origin of negro IQ deficits," and "population control or eugenics."[78] Throughout the 1970s Stanford regularly hired students to work with Shockley as part of their work/study program, at the university's standard rate of $500 per month.[79] Shockley told candidates to write an essay about why they wanted to become his protégés and asked them to propose ideas for creative projects they could undertake. One hoped to "make a film comparing the apparent retardation of black and white children in homes for the retarded," while another wanted to "check 1890 census in which this question was asked: 'Number of idiots in household and head size.'"[80] One student worker, Sandra Froman, gave Shockley advice about ways to get more attention from journalists. Decades later she would serve on the corporate board of Sturm, Ruger & Company, one of the world's largest gun manufacturers, and on the board of the National Rifle Association.[81]

On January 23, 1978, FREED mailed out a letter titled, "An Appeal for FREED by Student Office Personnel." The students explained, "We've learned a lot in this past year, not only about the man and his work but also about his 'context': the academic community, the mass media, the general public." They had decided that "the most fundamental injury is the damage done to Dr. Shockley's freedom of speech," based on their beliefs that they were "confident that Dr. Shockley is a scientist of integrity," and that "the racial component of his theories has been sensationalized." They ended the letter by declaring that "FREED, the foundation that supports Dr. Shockley's research, is in desperate need of funds," and then solicited, "Can you ensure that this vital research continue by making a tax-deductible contribution to FREED?"[82]

Hundreds of donations arrived. They came in various forms, from a few quarters taped to a letter, to tens of thousands of dollars wired in from afar. They came from all over America, several foreign countries, and people of all walks of life.[83] One churchgoer wrote, "I am sharing my church contribution with you and what you are doing," while the pastor of Christ Presbyterian Church in Lakewood, California, sent six dollars and wished Shockley, "Good luck in your work."[84] Contributions arrived from the former Confederate states, accompanied with overtly racist letters written by southerners—and they also came from the North, East, and West with the exact same arguments of abhorrent bigotry.[85] Donations from came from Austria, Canada, Mexico, and Sweden.[86] Many letters, which touted the intellectual advantages and racial superiority of white people, were riddled with misspellings and poor grammar.[87]

A professor at the University of California, Berkeley, wrote, "I agree with your opinion of the superiority of the white race. Furthermore, I think the historical record proves this superiority more completely and convincingly than any experimental tests." He also contended, "If it be concluded that the negro is inferior to the white, the question is what can we do about it. Sterilize all criminals and all recipients of relief. The public would not consider such a law, although less than 100 years ago it was considered patriotic to murder Indians and steal their land." Those words were written by John H. Northrop. He had won the Nobel Prize in 1946. He was trained as a chemist, not a historian.[88]

At Shockley's request, Northrop signed onto a public statement that Shockley drafted in April 1969 titled, "An Analysis Leading to a Recommendation Concerning Inquiry Into Eugenic Legislation." They quoted from an article by Arthur Jensen in *Harvard Educational Review*, where he asked, "Is there a danger that current welfare policies, unaided by eugenic foresight, could lead to the genetic enslavement of a substantial portion of our population?" and admonished, "The possible consequences of our failure seriously to study these questions may well be viewed by future generations as our society's greatest injustice to Negro Americans."

Put another way, Jensen thought that "genetic enslavement," which was what he called *allowing* Black Americans to have children—who would supposedly be inevitably inferior to white Americans—would be worse than actual enslavement—where white Americans shackled, bought, sold, raped, whipped, and otherwise terrorized them and their children. Shockley and Northrop, Nobel Laureates at the two most prestigious academic institutions in California, supported eugenics and dysgenics because they deemed it the humanitarian thing to do. They claimed that children were being "born enslaved in a slum environment and probably genetically enslaved by inherited mental traits causing lack of foresight and responsibility," based on their conclusion that "irrefutable evidence continues to accumulate for the inheritance of genetically controlled, socially maladaptive traits."[89]

But it was even worse than that, the letter claimed. "We fear that 'fatuous beliefs' in the power of welfare money, unaided by eugenic foresight, may contribute to the decline of human quality for both the black and white segments of our society," they warned. To replace the social safety nets of the New Deal, the New Frontier, and the Great Society, they told legislators to consider a nationwide campaign of "sterilization for IQ below 75 and release of completely incorrigible prisoners only after their agreement to sterilization," which they thought would prevent "human quality problems, including their racial aspects" that they otherwise believed "might '. . . hasten the end . . .' of civilization." In addition to Shockley and Northrop, Walter C. Alvarez (emeritus head of the Division of Medicine of the Mayo Clinic), John Bertrand deCusance Morant Saunders (first chancellor of the University of California San Francisco), Sheldon Glueck (emeritus professor at Harvard Law School), and Dwight Ingle (chair of the Department of Physiology at the University of Chicago) all endorsed these mass sterilization policies.[90] They were among the most accomplished and respected scholars of their generation, the elites from America's most respected institutions, in the Northeast, Midwest, and West, not the Deep South.

## Bill receives donations, large and small, from far and wide

To raise additional money for FREED, Shockley traveled across America to lecture about his "race betterment" theories. He gave dozens of speeches at universities each year, including paid appearances at New York University (for $350), the University of Texas at Dallas ($550), the University of Virginia ($693.50), the University of Wisconsin ($700), Virginia Tech ($1,050), and Denison University ($1,251.84). In today's dollars, those amounts would be about six to seven times higher, ranging from $2,000 to over $8,000 per appearance.[91] After receiving funding from Bill Lear, the corporation that resulted from his research sent checks of $402.37 and $500.[92] The money came from Motorola's Semiconductor Products Division for talks given to its Science Advisory Board, but it specified that funding should "be used for Dr. Shockley's research," which had focused on eugenics and dysgenics for nearly a decade.[93]

Numerous well-respected entrepreneurs, attorneys, and business leaders across the country donated to Shockley. Wallace W. Knox, whose name would eventually adorn the clubhouse of the Boys & Girls Club of Oakland, gave him $1,000 for "the uphill battle you are fighting."[94] Robert Klark Graham, an optometrist who had invented shatterproof eyeglasses and founded the company that became Armorlite, sent thousands of dollars, writing, "The attached may help to mitigate certain consequences encountered by an honorable man in meeting commitments which he would only have made in the first place had he not been in earnest about informing his countrymen of certain of their basic problems."[95] The F. M. Kirby Foundation sent $500 on December 26, 1974, $750 on December 26, 1975, and $1,200 on December 23, 1976, to FREED as "an expression of interest in your work by the Board of Directors."[96] The New Jersey–based foundation had been created after Fred Morgan Kirby merged his five-and-dime business with the stores owned by Frank Woolworth in 1912, which brought ninety-four stores together to start the F. W. Woolworth Company.[97]

But the largest donations to Stanford came from the Pioneer Fund, totaling $188,700 from 1968 to 1977, worth more than a million dollars today. The Pioneer Fund might sound like a modern venture capital group on Sand Hill Road, but it wasn't. In fact, it was a foundation established in New York City in 1937, and the "pioneers" referenced in its name were the colonists from Western Europe. Its purpose was twofold:

1.  To advance research and programs supporting scholars "descended predominantly from *White persons who settled in the original thirteen states* prior to the adoption of the Constitution of the United States and/or from related stocks," and

2.  To support "research into the problems of heredity and eugenics in the human race generally . . . and study into the *problems of race betterment* with special reference to the people of the United States." (Emphases in original)[98]

The Pioneer Fund has received tax-free treatment from the U.S. government since its founding and remains an active grant-making foundation.[99] In 2013 the organization's website celebrated the "cutting-edge research" it had funded through "grants to 64 different institutions, located in eight different countries, including to some of the most prominent universities in the world," but today the organization has very limited presence online.[100] (The web address, www .pioneerfund.org, was taken over in 2014 by a direct-to-consumer generic drug company called Pioneer Pharmacy; another group recently purchased the URL, and the site now lists the pros and cons of trading cryptocurrencies.)[101]

In his proposal to the Pioneer Fund in 1969, Shockley asked for nearly twice as much money for himself as went to Stanford, including requesting that the Pioneer Fund commit $11,000 a year toward his personal pension and $10,500 a year toward an allowance for out-of-pocket expenses (which would now be approximately $95,100 and $90,780, respectively). He explained that he was willing to abandon his focus on transistors only for this reason: "a significant probability of advancing by months or years the date at which appropriate and humane social programs may reduce the number of illegitimate, slum, non-white births."[102] Shockley pointed to the Pioneer Fund's donations to Stanford as a key reason the university should permit him to continue his work on eugenics and dysgenics. "The Pioneer Fund, the chief contributor to the Project last year," Shockley wrote on September 9, 1969, to the dean of the Engineering Department, "has placed funds at my disposal for transmission to Stanford that would carry the project at the going rate through the 1969–70 Academic year."[103]

The earliest contributions from the Pioneer Fund were made out to Shockley personally and to Stanford University; later their checks were made out to FREED. The receipts, letters, and audio recordings in Stanford's archives showed that Shockley treated the nonprofit he'd established, his personal bank account, and his account at Stanford almost interchangeably. During a phone call with Harry F. Weyher, president of the Pioneer Fund, on July 11, 1974, Shockley requested that funding go both to FREED and to Stanford. He offered to submit two proposals for the same "research" project and asked, "Should I send you two then, one for Stanford and one for FREED?" The donor agreed that would be a good idea, saying, "Yeah, that's alright, let's do it that way."[104]

If there was any question about whether Shockley should be using Stanford's resources to research genetics and formulate race theories while working out of an entirely different department altogether, the letters Shockley sent to Stanford administrators clarified just how directly he sought support from Stanford—and how clearly he received it. "Some weeks ago you wrote about continuing your research," the dean of the School of Engineering responded to Shockley on November 4, 1969. "As I told you the other day, I am not aware of any reason for you to discontinue this study."[105] That was the reply, in its entirety. The funding kept coming. When the Pioneer Fund reached out to Stanford via its banker at a division of JP Morgan, they received quick confirmation from the legal department that the grant would support Shockley's work on eugenics and dysgenics, in fulfillment of its mission for "race betterment."[106]

## Bill proposes paying bounty hunters to forcibly sterilize his fellow citizens

It was more than a century after the Thirteenth Amendment abolished slavery throughout the United States. It happened decades after Hitler's Aryan ideal had been purportedly been vanquished in Europe by Allied Forces. Many years had elapsed since the Civil Rights Act had ended America's de jure Jim Crow. Yet this was the de facto reality in California: one of America's greatest research institutions gave safe harbor to a physicist so that he could work outside of his field, spread unsubstantiated ideas about race, and advocate for public policies of mass sterilization based on skin color and IQ test scores. He did this for the better part of three decades at Stanford, even while some of the world's most talented electrical engineers and computer scientists (who actually chose to focus on their fields of study) built Silicon Valley all around them. The university prospered as a result.

By the 1980s Shockley had devised a new scheme: for the government to set aside money for a payout pool, to "put into action the native American genius for entrepreneurship." What for? "Well, if somebody were to ask me if this meant 'bounty hunters,' I'd say, 'I would never put it that way,'" he said slyly to an auditorium full of students. Shockley then publicly called for the federal government to pay Americans to hunt down other Americans and turn them in, so that they could be forcibly sterilized.[107] These people hadn't committed a crime. But

Shockley's scheme was no longer voluntary. He'd worked on "race betterment" for three decades at Stanford, starting with a plan to pay volunteers to be sterilized. He now theorized that a government-run, *involuntary* initiative was more workable, with eligibility being determined by some bounty hunter's best guess that the victim had a below-average IQ. For Shockley, their skin color would be a good indicator of that, based on his earlier estimates that 85 percent of Black people in America would qualify for mandatory sterilization.[108]

Shockley confirmed this during a lecture in 1986, at an event meant for public dissemination. The discussion was hosted in a lecture hall on Stanford's campus. A videographer and professional photographer were there to document it.[109] Did Shockley ever deserve a platform like this at Stanford? Some would argue certainly not, and many students protested his speeches when he came to their campuses.[110] But one of the great virtues of a university is that it is a place for discussion and disagreement. Even words that go against norms can add to the overall vibrant exchange of ideas. Free speech in academia is a necessity because ideas are best when they're debated, perhaps especially when they are unusual, they challenge existing authorities, or they might make people uncomfortable.

But we should ask what went wrong in this instance, since Shockley kept his position in the Department of Electrical Engineering while his sole focus was eugenics and dysgenics—even though Stanford's genetics faculty had objected. The First Amendment protects free speech, but what happens when tenure protects someone to spread unfounded fictions in the wrong department entirely? Should someone have acted when Shockley and other leading scholars of his era warned that "genetic enslavement" would be the worst injustice to befall Black Americans? What about when Shockley publicly advocated to pay bounty hunters to carry out mass forced sterilization to create a superrace? Should Stanford administrators have accepted funding on his behalf, reassured him that his project was acceptable, and protected him for decade after decade? Should the IEEE—"the world's largest technical professional organization dedicated to advancing technology for the benefit of humanity"—have awarded him their Medal of Honor in 1980? What about its 100th Anniversary Medal in 1984?[111] Did it benefit humanity to focus on the positive parts while disregarding Shockley's many other statements and schemes? What was negligible? What was negligence? Who holds the scales of justice? And who chose to be willfully blind to injustice?

Many of Shockley's assertions were baseless, but he made his claims as a tenured Stanford faculty member and Nobel Laureate. That position of authority helped to legitimize his views, and Stanford supported him, accepting the equivalent of millions from donors to this effort, and endorsing Shockley until his final breath—and as he frequently told people, he'd hoped that his very last thought, on his deathbed, would be about race betterment.[112] When Shockley died, in 1989, Stanford celebrated him. "It's a great loss for Stanford," said Joseph W. Goodman, chair of the electrical engineering department. Professor William E. Spicer, Shockley's colleague for thirty-three years, lauded him. "I would say he would have to be compared to people who opened up huge new areas, such as Pasteur or the Salk vaccine," he told the Associated Press. Spicer commented that "in his later years, Shockley tried several times to befriend blacks he came into contact with," adding, "I think he very much would have liked to have found a black person who would be a personal friend."[113]

If Spicer was right about that, then what Bill Shockley needed all along was a special friend, a Black one. That was the answer he gave, not in 1891 when Stanford's founding president had argued that there were better bloodlines of the "governing classes inherently superior to the sons of other men," but ninety-eight years later, after Shockley had used Stanford's resources to promote "race betterment" for decades. Stanford took in donations and protected Shockley, all while the university's senior leadership apparently chose to value money from wealthy donors over the objections of their own genetics faculty.

That happened after Shockley had vilified the most important entrepreneurs of his time, who had rejected his cruelty, trusted their talents, created Silicon Valley, and changed the world. Stanford profited massively from the wealth and power that resulted. But Shockley's story teaches other lessons, too, because Stanford's support of him was only a precursor. They would invite other technologists to teach about topics far outside of their field of expertise, because there was far more power to be gained and money to be made.

Mark Zuckerberg

Larry Page

Sergey Brin

Keith Rabois

Peter Thiel

David Sacks

Travis Kalanick

Bill Shockley

J. D. Vance

# ACT II

## GOLD

hey weren't always honest, and it certainly doesn't seem fair, but what in life is?" you could be wondering by this point.

"Maybe these entrepreneurs were just born with it." That's one possible verdict. "They were made of something special that the rest of us didn't have. We just couldn't cut it in the cutthroat world of business. That's why we lost out."

They are the crazy ones who took the risks, so they reaped the rewards. They are the misfits and rebels who dreamed bigger. Were they better than us? Potentially.

Even if they lied, it worked. They made the future what they wanted it to be.

That's just how things go. It's how they've always gone.

And, if we are honest about it, we don't mind so much. We get so much for free.

Why focus so much on the damages done? We love the likes.

Why be so negative?

Who cares if a few emperors have no clothes?

Why does it matter if there are some skeletons in their closets?

The system is rigged. So what? What difference could I make if I wanted to?

Even if it did matter, if we wanted to make a difference, where would we even begin?

**Figure II.1**  Mark Zuckerberg.
Source: Photo by Guillaume Paumier, https://commons.wikimedia.org/wiki/File:Mark_Zuckerberg_at_the
_37th_G8_Summit_in_Deauville_018_square.jpg.

**Figure II.2**  Larry Page.
Source: Photo by Herkko Hietanen, CC BY 2.0, https://www.flickr.com/photos/51035575028@N01/242199269.

**Figure II.3**  Sergey Brin.
Source: Photo by Joi Ito, https://commons.wikimedia.org/w/index.php?curid=79158941.

**Figure II.4**  Keith Rabois.
Source: *TechCrunch*, CC BY 2.0, https://www.flickr.com/photos/52522100@N07/15203178585.

**Figure II.5**  Peter Thiel.
Source: Fortune Live Media, CC-BY-ND-2.0, https://flic.kr/p/cywLm9.

**Figure II.6**  David Sacks.
Source: Photo by Robert Scoble, CC BY 2.0, https://commons.wikimedia.org/w/index.php?curid=13353736.

**Figure II.7**  Travis Kalanick.
Source: Official Leweb Photos, CC BY 2.0, https://www.flickr.com/photos/86704644@N00/11315226723.

**Figure II.8**  Bill Shockley.
Source: Wikimedia Commons, https://commons.wikimedia.org/wiki/File:Shockley.jpg.

**Figure II.9**  J. D. Vance.
Source: New America, CC BY 2.0, https://commons.wikimedia.org/wiki/File:Small_Talks_DC-_Securing_the
_American_Dream_for_Young_Children_(37629711710).jpg.

# CHAPTER 6

## TRUST US

Mark Zuckerberg, Thefacebook and Facebook, Inc.

In high school, Mark Zuckerberg and his friends wore t-shirts that read: "[[my brain is better than yours]]." They made them to market Synapse-ai, a plug-in for the digital music player WinAmp. It would keep track of songs you heard, suggest similar songs, and add them to your play-list—a digital DJ that predated both Pandora and Spotify by many months. The slogan was a joke about Synapse-ai's artificial intelligence capabilities, but it doubled as an obnoxious boast about Zuckerberg's superior intellect.

As Steven Levy chronicled in *Facebook: The Inside Story,* the same sentiment would resurface years later at Facebook headquarters. Microsoft CEO Steve Ballmer told the young CEO that every employee should easily recognize the company's corporate values, so Zuckerberg scrawled two words—"high IQ"—on a piece of paper and pinned it to the office refrigerator. In all these early *Mark Zuckerberg Productions,* antisocial enmity manifested as brash superiority.[1] (As often happens, underneath that lay a bleaker reality that revealed social immaturity and, very likely, some deeply rooted insecurities as well.) Ezra Callahan, Thefacebook's first product manager, told Adam Fisher, "We had company parties all the time, and for a period in 2005, all Mark's toasts at the company parties would end with 'Domination!'" He added, with concern: "'How much was the direction of the internet influenced by the perspective of nineteen-, twenty-, twenty-one-year-old well-off white boys?' That's a real question that sociologists will be studying forever."[2]

Synapse-ai caught the attention of the leading corporations in online music—including MusicMatch and Windows Media Player—but Zuckerberg even turned down Microsoft's offer to purchase the technology.[3] The *Harvard Crimson* attributed that decision to the Internet's open and equitable ethos, explaining that "Zuckerberg's software populism goes beyond simply turning down big-money corporate offers." He told the paper that "it's important to us that people are able to use the software for free," because he believed, "software belongs to everyone. No matter what kind of deal we get into, we're going to try to keep it free." The *Crimson* published those words on October 23, 2003, five days before Facemash debuted.[4]

* * *

Zuckerberg also collaborated on a project called Buddy Zoo with Adam D'Angelo, who would become Facebook's chief technology officer (CTO) and, later, the CEO of Quora. They had hacked AOL Instant Messenger so that people could upload their Buddy List to see who they had in common with their friends. Buddy Zoo helped Zuckerberg develop tools that he soon applied to Thefacebook, which could "measure how popular you are," "detect cliques you're a part of," and "view your Prestige, computed the way Google computes Page-Rank to rank webpages."[5] All these other projects—Synapse-ai, Buddy Zoo, and Facemash—provided a basis for the algorithms that ran the earliest versions of Thefacebook, which traced connections and determined social worth. Behind every page, the systems churned, and its artificial intelligence learned about each new user by calculating, in essence, *Who's Hotter? Click to choose*, while mapping an ever-growing friend list to *Measure how popular you are.*

Within a year, Thefacebook would have a profile page that represented every user. Zuckerberg emblazoned three words across the top of each profile page: "This Is You."[6] But, then again, wasn't that obvious? Who else would it be? Your name, your picture, your email were all there. But that phrasing was on purpose. With Thefacebook, Zuckerberg was cultivating our online experiences with a new values system: Your digital life was now just as important as your real life. Maybe more. "This Is *You.*" This is where you get to define your identity, even redefine a better version of yourself.

Importantly, Facebook required everyone's real names and not just an anonymous avatar, which they enforced at the beginning by requiring a unique .edu email account to get started. That worked. Thefacebook was far more successful than Synapse-ai or Buddy Zoo had been. Soon it became more successful than other social networks on the college campuses where it was available, too. What worked so well? Unlike most other social networks at the time, where you could create an account in anonymity online without verifying who you actually were, Thefacebook was built through existing real-life social networks on college campuses.

Zuckerberg and his friends didn't build the *first* online social network. They just built the first one that really mattered by starting in communities where people cared about what happened on the site. Then everyone who joined made those online experiences as important, if not more important, than their real-life interactions. People could now measure their popularity by tracking the number of friends they had on Thefacebook. It was brilliant. All that social pressure encouraged each new user to invite their friends, so everyone spent more time online. The people who'd done the actual work, students who made their pages and sent out so many invitations, grew Thefacebook at an astonishing rate.

Larry Page and Sergey Brin had created a better search engine that, unlike Yahoo, didn't need paid human labor to build and scale it. The Google Boys knew it, too. In their press release announcing their partnership with Yahoo, they'd even said that the network effects would make all the difference. Initially, Mark Zuckerberg didn't realize what he'd achieved with Thefacebook as college kids built his business one friend request after another. In fact, he almost gave up on the fast-growing social network altogether so he could focus on another idea.

He called it Wirehog.

***

Similar to Scour and Red Swoosh, Wirehog was designed to share data between computers, but it was built for larger files such as business documents. Thefacebook was growing rapidly, but Zuckerberg seemed to worry it was just like everything else he'd made. Maybe it *was* just child's play, which depended on some juvenile need for affirmation felt by high schoolers or college kids. Perhaps he thought that Wirehog could be more useful, more of a "real" business that adults would use. In a way, Zuckerberg was ahead of his time with this idea; Wirehog predated widespread cloud computing by almost a decade.[7] His new friend Sean Parker had another name for it. He called it Dropbox.[8] Unbeknownst to Parker at the time, a company that went by that name would eventually pursue this exact strategy. Dropbox launched at TechCrunch Disrupt in 2008, and its IPO a decade later put its price at $21 a share, valuing the company at $8.2 billion. By 2021 Zuckerberg's company earned nearly that much quarterly.[9]

"Mark was like, 'Well college kids seem to like this Facebook thing. But what they really would like is having access to each other's media content,'" Aaron Sittig told Steven Levy.[10] Sittig had worked for Parker at their first startup, the popular music sharing platform Napster. As Facebook's first designer, he came up with tagging photos and the Like Button.[11] With Thefacebook, these college kids had built an incredibly addictive way for other college kids to connect with friends. Sittig recalled, "Facebook would launch at a school, and within one day they would have 70 percent of undergrads signed up. At the time, nothing had ever grown as fast as Facebook."[12] By December 2004 Thefacebook had over a million users, and according to Levy, around 80 percent of them were visiting the site *every single day*.[13]

Kids checked the site, repeatedly, incessantly. But Thefacebook still lacked a business model. Could they sell addictiveness? They sure hoped so, based on the company's earliest marketing materials. They quoted a UPenn student who, on March 25, 2004, described his feelings about the site with these words: "I have a new addiction. It is powerful. It is disturbing. It is thefacebook.com." On the next slide, they told advertisers: "We will help you identify the most effective placements to reach the goals of your campaign," including by targeting students by using the information already gathered on them: college/university, gender, sexual orientation, personal interests, clubs and jobs, and, to use their phrase, "Political Bent."[14]

## Mark discovers a business model built on attention and addiction

The software businesses of the Silicon Age are truly different from any that came before. Unlike traditional companies that we're all familiar with—where a restaurant makes money from customers, but then profit margins are quickly diminished because the restaurateur needs to cover equipment, rent, and other fixed costs as well as to pay for ingredients, employees to make and serve the meal, and other costs that go up with each new diner—a software business like Facebook doesn't have many of those expenses. In fact, it has very few variable costs; the price to run the site does not change significantly as the number of users increases. After designing and coding the software, you need to keep it updated and make revisions over time. But just so long as you're able to provide the same great experience online to the millionth user as you are to the first few, it costs the company relatively little to provide the service to so many of them. As a result, profitability doesn't matter at first. Neither does revenue, at least for a while. What matters, above all, is growth.

Unlike traditional businesses, high-growth software companies are encouraged to expand massively early on. Venture capitalists will bet on every software company with the potential for massive growth, because they're not working in a world where it costs more to serve more meals. Likewise, when someone invites a friend to try a new restaurant, the best possible outcome for the owner is that they'll gain one new fan who might (or might not) visit again one day, often weeks or months later. Online, it all happens much faster and more frequently. Adding ten students at a college will incentivize each to send invites to ten more, so that everyone can keep clicking to *Measure how popular you are.*

Let's run the math on that. Assuming you're at a school with ten thousand students, do you know how many rounds of invitations it would take if you were the last person to join a service like Thefacebook? The answer might surprise you. If each person added ten others, then everyone would be on the platform in just three rounds. The first ten would add ten each, leading to one hundred. Once everyone adds ten more each, that'd be one thousand. By the third round of invites, all ten thousand students would be signed up. This is why exponential growth works so well for tech companies. Given that the cost to serve ten thousand people is nearly the same as serving the first ten, you have the potential to scale from obscurity to ubiquity practically overnight.

Taking the approach that users matter while profits don't encourages tech companies to pour every dollar into growth, so that everyone's attention and data can eventually be sold to advertisers. That explains why software companies will use money that they make to attract more users, who check the site addictively, rather than taking home the profits, especially in the early years. That's also why companies like Facebook can give so much to us "for free," while eventually making the money from advertisers who want to be in front of so many eyeballs. It's a way of doing business that is built for two things: to capture our attention as often as possible, and to achieve rapid (even total) world domination before someone else distracts your audience.

The *Harvard Crimson* ran a story on October 20, 2004, which touted that Thefacebook had hit half a million users, but Zuckerberg used the milestone moment to discuss file sharing, saying, "I think Wirehog will probably spread in the same way that Thefacebook did." He even hoped that advertisements on Thefacebook would cover the costs to develop Wirehog. When an intrepid journalist from the *Crimson* then talked to the spokesperson for the Recording Industry Association of America, who warned that copyright law violations would ruin Wirehog's business model, Zuckerberg replied, "I honestly don't think it should be a problem," in his usual devil-may-care tone, crediting "tricks" he'd come up with (quotes in the original article). The headline read, "Facebook Creator to Debut Wirehog."[15]

When Zuckerberg met with Peter Thiel and Reid Hoffman to pitch Thefacebook, both investors were blown away by its growth. At Harvard, two-thirds to three-quarters of the students joined Thefacebook in the first two weeks, and that trend continued as the platform expanded to new schools in 2005 and 2006, according to an interview Zuckerberg gave for Y Combinator's Startup School in 2012. "We'd open it up at a school and within a couple of weeks, the vast majority of students would be on the service," he explained.[16] But in 2004 Parker pitched the business's potential, and according to Levy, "Zuckerberg maintained a mysterious silence." He spoke up at least once, though. He interjected that if

Thefacebook wasn't interesting, he had an idea about ways to help people share files. Hoffman stopped him. "No, no, no," he said. "Facebook's the good idea. Abandon Wirehog."[17] The investors saw the jaw-dropping trend lines, with such growth and addictiveness, even when Zuckerberg did not.

Zuckerberg continued to pursue Wirehog even after Thefacebook's first investors urged him not to. He and Parker flew to Los Angeles to meet with Warner Music Group's top executives, hoping they'd invest—not in the value of Thefacebook but instead in the promise of Wirehog. They refused. In fact, they told Zuckerberg and Parker: "Shut this fucking thing down." Parker recounted, with pride and probably a great deal of relief, "We put a bullet in that thing."[18]

Well, they did, and they didn't. Zuckerberg then visited Sequoia Capital (investors in Apple, Cisco, Google, and many others) to discuss Wirehog. He showed up late to the 8 a.m. meeting, still wearing his pajamas. According to Sebastian Mallaby in *The Power Law*, it wasn't that Zuckerberg had actually overslept. "Zuckerberg appeared fresh from a shower, his hair had not dried yet," which could only mean one thing. "Zuckerberg had risen, washed and then *decided* to dress up in pajamas and show up insolently late," Mallaby explained. "A deliberate snub was worse than an unintended one."[19]

It seems so arrogant it's outlandish, but keep in mind that this was around the same time Zuckerberg carried around "I'm CEO, Bitch." business cards.[20] Rather than a traditional pitch to the Sequoia partner—Roelof Botha of the PayPal Mafia—and his colleagues, Zuckerberg delivered "The Top Ten Reasons You Should Not Invest in Wirehog," in the style of David Letterman. The first few reasons seemed plausible enough. By the end, the venture capitalists couldn't ignore it: they were being mocked to their faces. Number three: "We showed up at your offices late in our pajamas." Number two: "Because Sean Parker is involved." As everyone knew, Sequoia had invested in Napster, and it didn't end well. In true Letterman style, the top reason wasn't funny at all: "We're only here because Roelof told us to come."[21] But Zuckerberg didn't just embarrass Botha that day. He mocked the entire process. "I assume we really offended them," he later admitted to David Kirkpatrick for *The Facebook Effect: The Inside Story of the Company That Is Connecting the World*, "and now I feel really bad about that."[22] Just another ridiculous act, overlooked, even laughed at, all due to how fast Thefacebook grew.[23]

In 2005 a reporter named Bambi Francisco asked Zuckerberg how he raised his Series A Round, which was a good question given that he didn't exude the pitch-perfect skills of other wildly charismatic entrepreneurs. He seemed flummoxed. "Oh, we didn't do any pitch, but, um, yeah, I mean," he replied. "I wouldn't say that I prepared anything formal for that. I dunno, I mean. I think that the attractive component of this was probably that the base was so localized and that we could target stuff and provide functionality for users at such a granular level . . . and I think the time spent on the site was just around the highest on the Internet."[24]

That last line said it all. One day, formal business terminology would define all this activity: ad targeting for core audiences, custom audiences, and lookalike audiences, as well as omni-channel analyses of average session length, median session length, and median time per user.[25] It would eventually make the company tens of billions of dollars every quarter.[26] But the addictiveness mattered most. "I think the time spent on the site was just about the highest on the internet." That was why Thefacebook was such a special investment.[27]

## E. Jean's website: Be evil

Mark Zuckerberg bought the URL for Thefacebook.com on January 11, 2004.[28] Word about the website spread so far and so fast that E. Jean Carroll—a writer for *Saturday Night Live* and author of the popular "Ask E. Jean" column at *Elle*, the longest-running advice column in any American magazine—registered a website of her own that July. Catch27.com debuted in November.[29] It was intended as a parody, but Carroll put serious resources behind it. She paid Chantelle Farmer, a coder with the Cyrus Company, to create the website. She hired a full-time public relations staffer, a recent Stanford graduate named Lindsey Johnson, to field inquiries from college kids and reporters.[30] Once you signed up, which you could do only if you were between the ages of eighteen and twenty-seven, you began collecting digital trading cards of faux "friends." A pack of three cost ninety-nine cents.[31]

Was this real? Fake? Did it matter? Had the Internet changed all that, and could you reinvent yourself on Catch27? Unfazed, Johnson played each interview straight, to further the ruse. "It's like Facebook, except with a wicked twist. Instead of just networking your friends, you trade your friends for hotter, smarter ones," she told Pitt's student newspaper. "It's kind of an elite, edgy group of hot minds and hot bodies. If they're not, we kick them off the site."[32] The more you used the site, the more Catch27 rewarded you. As the *Yale Daily News* reported, you would sign up and create a digital persona on Catch27, just like on Thefacebook. Then your value fluctuated based on "your looks, smarts, number of hot people in your pack," as well as the "number of page-views you're getting and the number of people buying and trading you."[33]

Why Catch27? The site's instructions page began with "don't read these instructions," explaining that "instructions suck." For those who kept reading anyway, they were told that Catch27 was the same as real life. "You play this game every single day of your life. You meet a bunch of new friends, you get tired of them, you trade them for hotter, smarter friends."[34] You could buy bitches and brains, freaks and geeks, stars and sluts. The more people who bought a card, the higher its price went. The goal was to collect the twenty-seven cards that appreciated the most; they'd mail prizes to the people with the most valuable sets. The Catch27 team awarded bonus points for creativity, such as everyone in your pack having exposed midriffs and bellybutton rings. Similar to the algorithms behind Thefacebook, the Catch27 team refused to divulge how their points system worked, so people wondered if they were just giving out rewards at random.

But why not catch-22? As Johnson explained to the *Pitt News*, "basically your life as you know it is over at 27."[35] The website took the joke further, noting that Kurt Cobain, Jimi Hendrix, Janis Joplin, and Jean-Michel Basquiat all died at twenty-seven, and that Usher hadn't died yet but he was twenty-seven (his new album had sold over a million copies in its first week, one of the fastest of all time).[36] Just like Thefacebook, Catch27 spread like wildfire, doubling month-over-month.[37] Curious journalists pressed Johnson about how Catch27's calculations worked behind-the-scenes. She replied, "The voting is subjective, objective and everything in between."[38]

Carroll had funded the site personally at first, but in less than a year, the business was already making money based on just how many people were paying 99 cents for packs. When Carroll was asked about revenues, she refused to give exact figures and instead replied, "Let's put it this way: I'm lying on the floor losing consciousness."[39] Because of these digital assets, they didn't need to sell advertisements, unlike Facebook. They owned the intellectual property, unlike Scour or Napster. Catch27 had a viable business model from day one, because of those ninety-nine-cent digital collectible cards. That was nearly a decade before the first nonfungible token (NFT) was created in 2014, which would lead to a multibillion-dollar marketplace for digital assets before the market crashed in 2022.[40]

Yet Carroll, Johnson, and Farmer told us something we never heard from Scour, Napster, Thefacebook, and so many others: "Anyway, Catch27 is evil. The less you know about it, the better. Trust us."[41]

## E. Jean's parody feels too real

Catch27 was Thefacebook's "evil twin," as Carroll and Johnson called it, but the joke site continued to gain serious attention on college campuses. In the same era when students were first signing up for Thefacebook and filling out profiles describing their majors, favorite music, and relationship statuses, many of them also created profiles on Catch27, answering edgier questions about "living human beings you really loathe," "number of hearts broken," and "most hideously humiliating social moment." According to William & Mary's student magazine, "You can also create a blog for yourself on the site in order to record all the exciting events that happen to you each day, for the viewing pleasure of everyone else."[42] Long before Thefacebook rolled out status updates, Catch27 had the feature first.

Thefacebook's prompts were relatively benign. This caused the creators of Catch27 to claim that Thefacebook censored content and limited free expression. When asked about Thefacebook by the Colorado State student paper, Carroll exclaimed, "Jesus! I thought. It was boring." Johnson told the reporter, "It's like an address book and it's too policed." On Catch27, people could answer far more *interesting* prompts than what Thefacebook offered, like "How I lost it," which meant their virginity, and "Sin I'd like to try."[43] Those disclosures might go too far for some people, but decades later, amid unresolved debates about what must be allowed and what should be censored on social media, we'd mostly forgotten about Catch27. Back in 2004 they encouraged free speech, no matter how wild, on a site that was fully open to anything people wanted to share.

Johnson and Carroll joked that Catch27 had more authenticity than its competitors. "Just like popularity in real life, it's how popular you are, how fast your car is, how fashionable you are and how hot you are," Johnson told the Colorado State student paper. "It's the reality of the social world. Just like the categories on the site, it's all very real and we're mocking it."[44] Carroll agreed. "Catch27 is real," she told William and Mary's student paper. "You play this game every day of your life, trading your friends for hotter ones."[45]

Some college students didn't find the joke humorous. "It's a destructive process, and it only perpetuates culture's standards of beauty, which are problematic," Pitt's Campus Women's Organization vice president Melissa Patti told the student newspaper. "It kind of decreases the work that women have created in the past to be looked at as equals in society's eyes." The *Pitt News* reported that "Patti also explained that rejection based on appearance and on society's standards of beauty encourages problems like eating disorders," because, in her words, "It goes back to everything in culture that tells women that their only value is them as sex objects." Again, Patti said this about Catch27, not Facemash or Thefacebook.[46] Still, her warnings applied to the entirety of social media throughout its earliest days—as well as over the decades to come.

Other students found different reasons to criticize Catch27, worrying about the power of capitalism to change society in dangerous ways. The business of encouraging people to judge one another for entertainment bothered them. A Northeastern student wrote a piece in the *Boston Globe* claiming that E. Jean Carroll "is either really desperate for friends or is laughing all the way to the bank," while also expressing unease about the longer-term impacts of all of these new sites: "It's not that we don't know this compulsive behavior is unhealthy; it's just another one of those guilty pleasures you know is bad for you but that you don't care enough about to stop doing."[47] Similarly, a Colorado State student worried, "I'm afraid people will get carried away and it will become a huge moneymaking endeavor. It's a way to suck people into perpetuating the materialism ideals of our society."[48] That was about Catch27, not Thefacebook, much less products like Instagram, WhatsApp, and Oculus, which would come many years later.

In perhaps its ultimate irony, Catch27 sought absolution for its evils from the very start. As the Colorado State student newspaper reported, "Catch27 is not all fun and games, however. With the money used to purchase people, 27 percent of donations will go to a charity that has yet to be determined."[49] Here again, the company was ahead of its time, foreshadowing the "purpose and profit" social enterprises launched throughout the early twenty-first century, such as B Corporations like TOMS that had a legal duty to pursue their mission and not just profits.[50] In 2019 TOMS expanded its charitable efforts, promising to give away $1 for every $3 made.[51] It almost exactly mirrored Catch27's giveback commitment from over fourteen years before.

A *Yale Daily News* columnist, Sarah Mishkin, wrote this about Catch27: "Obnoxious and useless, the site still has promise, it could still be one giant work of elaborate social commentary."[52] She voiced concerns about Thefacebook's approach to dating, where students would "poke" each other, such an awkward way to get attention, and where they announced that they were "Single," "In a relationship," "In an open relationship," or "Whatever I can get."[53] Mishkin wrote, "But instead of mocking those who check off 'Whatever I can get' on Thefacebook and mean it, Catch27 members don't seem to have gotten the joke."[54] The real site's inside jokes were funny, in that teenage way where parents wouldn't know the real meaning, almost like locker room banter. The edgy parody site felt too raunchy and real, too truthful about things you weren't supposed to discuss. In this era of the early Internet, everything felt kind of confusing.

In February 2005 a Tufts student called Thefacebook "kind of creepy and stalkerish," noting that "people use it to look at pictures of and find out information about people that they don't even know, just as entertainment." Catch27 was described as having the same effect, although it was "even more repellent than Facebook."[55] By March a Towson University columnist explained, "On The Facebook you hoard friends like precious commodities, on Catch27 you throw them out to acquire new ones." He wondered, "Whatever happened to meeting people at a bar or through work, or meeting friends through friends? I didn't know tending to social relationships translated to sitting in front of a computer screen."[56] Those words seemed prescient, but the change was already well underway: 2005 was the year when people started meeting online about as frequently as they did in bars or through work. By 2017, 39 percent of couples met online, nearly double the number who met through friends.[57]

A strange thing happened though, and real-life romance started sparking on Catch27, too. The site soon added a feature called an "Itch List" for people to write profiles about their perfect matches. "This is where you describe exactly what you want in a sig.other," it encouraged. "If you're itching for a red-headed manicurist with an IQ of 167, ask for it." Those itches, which we just had to scratch, were based on an impossible ideal from an online image. But as more real users signed up, they began to message each other. It wasn't called an instant message or a direct message, though. Each digital note sent was called, in a perfect prophecy, "a wiretap."[58]

Catch27 had begun to take off, just like Thefacebook had. Both seemed quirky and fun. Even the addictiveness felt innocent enough, just like a game, as they grew exponentially by becoming a hot topic with college kids. Mark Twain is often quoted as saying, "A lie can travel halfway around the world while the truth is still putting on its shoes." That's been proven in numerous studies, which have shown that lies spread faster than facts, especially online, through social networks like Facebook.[59] But the joke is on us.

Twain never actually wrote or said that.[60]

* * *

In April 2005 Catch27 entered the mainstream public consciousness, with coverage in the *Wall Street Journal*. It was taken seriously as part of "The Gated Online Community," a "new wave of exclusive sites" defining the beginnings of social media. The *Journal* reported that these new digital communities were forming quickly and that on Catch27, "which claims thousands of users and touts itself as the 'most hip,' member profiles appear as baseball cards."[61] At first, Thefacebook only allowed students from Stanford and the Ivy League to join, so it met the "A-List" elitism of the initial audiences the *Journal* identified as social media's early adopters. But at the time, Thefacebook seemed too insignificant to include.

The next month, Thefacebook finally appeared in the *Journal*, but it was just a passing mention.[62] The paper's first in-depth coverage of the company appeared nearly two months later, when it described Thefacebook's rapid growth in an article about Rupert Murdoch's purchase of MySpace for $580 million.[63] That December, the *Journal*'s reporters wrote more extensively about the company, but the coverage took a negative turn. The headline ran: "Too Much Information? Colleges Fear Student Postings on Popular 'Facebook' Site Could Pose Security Risks." The article inventoried recent backlash against Zuckerberg's company: the University of New Mexico had banned the site after breaches of the school's computer systems; the University of Virginia sent an email warning students to "use caution" due to privacy risks since the site publicly listed cell phone numbers and physical addresses; and the University of Missouri formed a task force to address safety issues related to this popular new platform. Parents, too, had concerns. "I have not been pleased with their venture into these sites, as I feel they contain too much personal information," one parent wrote in the *Journal*. "My thoughts immediately turn to fear about identity theft, stalking, etc. My kids think I'm paranoid and overprotective—although isn't that my job?"[64]

In hindsight, those were healthy premonitions. Yet the most prescient words came from a Penn State administrator quoted in the *Journal* article. The university had used pictures from Thefacebook to identify and censure fifty students after a big win. They'd stormed the football field, which was against school policy. The assistant director of police operations reassured the reporter that further surveillance wouldn't occur: "We don't have the time and the resources to sit on the Web looking at Facebook all day."[65] Soon enough, the company's business model required others to pay it to advertise to us, so it would find more ways to encourage us all to spend our time and resources looking at Facebook all day.

Moreover, the facial recognition that Penn State campus police had likely done one-by-one, by squinting at a screen to match student IDs to Facebook photos, would be automated by another tech business Peter Thiel would invest in. Without widespread public knowledge of what was happening, federal, state, and local law enforcement, including security personnel at colleges nationwide, would that use that software. We'll learn more about that later. But at Penn State that day, social media had already become a powerful new surveillance tool. Students were punished who, at the time, likely never thought that a few pictures uploaded to Thefacebook would be used against them. The world had changed. But who could fathom the implications of the loss of our privacy? When should we have realized it? When did Facebook's leadership? "Move Fast and Break Things," Facebook's motto proclaimed.[66] But it all moved too fast for anyone to recognize what was being broken.

## The price of abandoning oneself

E. Jean Carroll knew the perils of popularity, which included less anonymity and forfeited privacy; she was one of the popular ones. She was a college cheerleader, became Miss Indiana University, and even won Miss Cheerleader USA, long before writing one of the most renowned relationship advice columns in the world.[67] She designed Catch27 to satirize the ways people bought digital representations with real money, all while treating real-life friends like trading cards. But Catch27 had found a market in 2005. It had national media attention and regular revenues, with those 99-cent packs of three—well before Thefacebook had either steady revenues or coverage by mainstream journalists. Yet profits and press clippings mattered less now; the Silicon Age was about exponential growth, clicks, and attention. Even if it was addicting, it was utterly entertaining, so maybe the tradeoffs were worth it. With Thefacebook, the Internet became a place to create your identity. "This *Is* You."[68]

The company's first CEO, Sean Parker, understood just how fast technology could supercharge hypergrowth: twenty-two months after Napster launched in 1999, upward of eighty million people used it.[69] Napster was a music-sharing platform similar to Scour that became far more popular, but it took just a few days for the service to be shut down forever.[70] Copyright law enforcement, to the tune of $20 billion, destroyed the company before Parker could make enough money to fight back.[71] Parker had a flameout with Napster as legendary as Icarus's own.

Whether he realized it or not, he had discovered a profound breakthrough: if you build the technology to allow people to connect their computers, break the rules, and grow exponentially, you might be able to figure out how to profit from all that attention. Still, you must figure out how to profit from all that attention. That mattered more than Parker ever realized at Napster. To change the way the world works, it takes more than just power. It required personal networks to scale through, interesting content to captivate us, and nudges to urge us to keep coming back—and it would take money, so much money—to ultimately change how everyone experienced our lives on the Internet. It took silicon, power, *and* gold.

That's why Parker would never fly too close to the sun again. What an insight it was: you could make the universe revolve around you. For Thefacebook, and for all of us, this revelation was revolutionary. Everything suddenly shifted away from others to refocus on ourselves: the identities we invented, the way we felt, and how much praise we saw others get compared to our numbers. All that kept us coming back for more, as we sought approval and stayed online for longer. Our self-worth was tallied in friend counts and likes and comments; our lives existed in a stream of status updates. Once they began to run ads, each one more specific to each of us, they turned the artifice of the Internet into real-world spending power. E-commerce became commerce.

Suddenly, the universe revolved around you. The change was Copernican.

In April 2023 Deloitte asked thousands of people if they agreed with this statement: "I believe online experiences are meaningful replacements for in-person experience." Only 19 percent of Gen X Americans agreed, compared to 50 percent of Millennials and Gen Z. Then it asked what people thought about "I spend more time interacting with others on social media than in the physical world." Likewise, 20 percent of older Americans said yes, compared to 48 percent of Millennials and Gen Z. Consider the implications of this: "I socialize more in video games than I do in the physical world." For that one, 9 percent of older Americans agreed, compared to 40 percent of Millennials and Gen Z.[72]

We weren't just different people on social media. Ultimately, social media made people different. It altered our sense of being. Instead of how we felt around other people, we'd begun to care more about how we looked online. We valued a representation of reality online more than the living, breathing reality in our lives. "*This* Is You." Our sense of self had shifted.

Even now, decades later, we don't fully understand the consequences, but when Jonathan Haidt from NYU and Jean Twenge of San Diego State sifted through hundreds of studies, here's what they found from the most reliable ones: of the eighteen experiments testing a causal effect of social media use on mental health outcomes, thirteen found a significant effect on a measure related to mental health (usually anxiety or depression), and of the six quasi-experiments, all six found that "mental health got worse as soon as Facebook came to campus—or high speed internet came to town."[73] Three clever scholars at MIT, Bocconi University, and Tel Aviv University even compared colleges that had Thefacebook to those that did not from 2004 to 2006. They found that 20 percent of students on campuses with Thefacebook had severe anxiety and depression, compared to 7 percent everywhere else.[74] Increasingly, the Internet became our existence. And that was dangerous.

Someone had warned us about this before it happened. "But no representation of reality is ever the same as reality, and one must never lose sight of the larger framework within which the representation exists," he'd written in July 2004. "The price of abandoning oneself to such an artificial representation is always too high, because the decisions that are avoided are always too important." At a symposium at Stanford the summer after the Facemash prank, it had already been predicted: "By making people forget that they have souls, the Antichrist will succeed in swindling people out of them."[75] Peter Thiel wrote that, right around the time he'd invested in Sean Parker, Mark Zuckerberg, and their new venture.[76]


## Sean makes a confession

As the company's first CEO, and the person who secured the investment from Thiel, Sean Parker helped build the business that took the ideas of Synapse-ai, Buddy Zoo, Facemash, and Thefacebook and created the Facebook, Inc.[77] He saw the early addictiveness of this college website and, just as he'd done with Napster, helped it grow exponentially. By the time the Apple App Store debuted in 2008, Facebook was available beyond campus, open for everyone, and it had begun to spread around the world.[78] These young technologists weren't chemists in the traditional sense, creating tablets for us all to swallow to change the chemistry in our brains. Instead, we absorbed Facebook visually, from a website on a desktop in a college computer lab. Eventually, everyone could take it all in, everywhere they went, through apps on our tablets and our smartphone screens, too. Yet we still struggle to grasp Facebook's ubiquity today; in fact, the vast majority of Americans don't know that Facebook, now Meta, owns Instagram.[79]

Haidt and Twenge have cautioned against "the risk of repeating previous moral panics over comics, TV, video games, etc.," because "those stories play well in a media environment that thrives on eliciting fear in parents. Later research often shows that there was no detectable harm."[80] This time, however, there were serious reasons for concern. Ever so subtly, social media altered how we thought and felt, based on findings from the newest and best studies.[81] As they concluded, after cataloguing more than two hundred single-spaced pages of results and analysis from research conducted since 2014: "Many studies, using a variety of methods, have found associations between heavy social media use and bad mental health outcomes, particularly for girls."[82]

Nicholas Carr had worried about this in a best-selling book from 2010, arguing the ease of the Internet "turns us into lab rats constantly pressing levers to get tiny pellets of social or intellectual nourishment," which prevents us from reading, reasoning, and ruminating deeply.[83] The way we process words and images became hasty, hurried, distracted, and sporadic, with every bit of it in quick hits. We're sprinting to the information we want, then lingering not an instant longer, before hurrying to something else entirely that we've become distracted by. All that meant the marathons of the mind became harder. As we built fast-twitch muscles to jump from one task to the next, one click to the next, one dopamine hit to another, we risked losing the metaphorical muscle tone it takes to think critically, read deeply, and decide reasonably. We went from being reasonable to being reactive. "Once I was a scuba diver in the sea of words," Carr regretted. "Now I zip along the surface like a guy on a Jet Ski."[84] Thus his book's title: *The Shallows.*

Others felt the same way. "Steve Jobs wasn't exaggerating when he described the iPhone as a kind of magical object," *New York Times* technology and business columnist Kevin Roose explained in 2019, "and it's truly wild that in the span of a few years, we've managed to turn these amazing talismanic tools into stress-inducing albatrosses. It's as if scientists had invented a pill that gave us the ability to fly, only to find out that it also gave us dementia."[85] Sean Parker helped formulate one of those very first pills as the founding president of Facebook at age twenty-four, when he was five years older than Mark Zuckerberg yet far more experienced in business and tech. And in 2017 he gave an interview that felt more like a confessional.

Parker told Mike Allen at *Axios* that he'd tried to overhaul how we thought, and he'd done so on purpose. From the outset, "The thought process that went into building these applications, Facebook being the first of them . . . was all about: 'How do we consume as much of your time and conscious attention as possible?,'" he explained. "And that means that we need to sort of give you a little dopamine hit every once in a while, because someone liked or commented on a photo or a post or whatever," Parker admitted. "And that's going to get you to contribute more content, and that's going to get you . . . more likes and comments."[86]

Dopamine hits might have seemed, to these hackers, like a cheat code that unlocked the human psyche. But it's not, of course. We're making choices, too, as that student at Northeastern had realized: "It's not that we don't know this compulsive behavior is unhealthy; it's just another one of those guilty pleasures you know is bad for you but that you don't care enough about to stop doing."[87] Facebook was engineered to create an itch we simply *had* to scratch, but which always caused a greater rash each time we did. According to Parker, the entire system was built to feed our brains feel-good juices through positive social stimuli, based on representations of reality, as we clicked for pleasure even when we knew it wasn't healthy.

But we were the ones making those choices. We claimed we were somehow unable to control our compulsions, because of how it all made us feel, even when it felt wrong. It worked on the smartest young minds in the world; in fact, it especially worked on them, at Harvard, at Stanford, at Yale, and then at every .edu. "It's a social-validation feedback loop," Parker explained, "exactly the kind of thing that a hacker like myself would come up with, because you're exploiting a vulnerability in human psychology."[88] If they'd actually hacked our brains, it amazed them just how much we loved it. We seemed to value representations more than real life. We weren't just hacked. We were hooked. Parker went on for several minutes in response to a single question, a full-on admission that our obsession with social media—and our addiction to our devices more generally—had been planned. He fretted most about "the unintended consequences of a network when it grows to a billion or 2 billion people and it literally changes your relationship with society, with each other. . . . It probably interferes with productivity in weird ways."

Then, the final confession: "God only knows what it's doing to our children's brains."[89]

## Mark was wrong: "People don't trust us"

"Why the Past 10 Years of American Life Have Been Uniquely Stupid." That's how Jonathan Haidt put it in the title of an essay for the *Atlantic* in May 2022.[90] "Something fundamentally changed in the nature of this social universe in the early 2010s, and everything got *weird* and kind of *stupid* after that," he explained during an interview with Christiane Amanpour on PBS. "What happened, beginning in 2012, was that rates of depression, anxiety, self-harm, and suicide all began going up. I mean, it wasn't a gradual thing, it was like they were sort of stable until 2012 and then it's like a hockey stick." That's how exponential growth looks on a chart. Haidt continued, "They're now, most of them are 100 percent higher. We kind of double it, of the rates of suicide, self-harm, depression and anxiety."[91]

From the start, it was a catch-22 for us all. Actually, it was worse than that. E. Jean Carroll was right when she'd upped it five levels. The parody site she had created as social commentary exaggerated the paradox, because even when you were winning, you lost. The website listed twenty-seven reasons why the site was named that—and why the joke was funny, but actually not. The final reason? "The number of days it took Catch27 players to turn the game completely evil . . . 26. Ah, well."[92]

Carroll's prior Internet projects, GreatBoyfriends.com and GreatGirlfriends .com, had been featured on *Oprah* and sold to The Knot a couple of years prior. The sites allowed people to review people they'd enjoyed dating even if it didn't work out. Carroll claimed on her Catch27 biography that Oprah had called that the "best idea I've ever heard" about twenty-seven times.[93] As the press release touted, Carroll's websites were "unique referral-based e-dating services that offer singles access to 'pre-approved' potential suitors."[94] As we now know, most of the Internet companies that took that kind of an approach—by caring about safeguards or prioritizing decency—usually faded into the graveyard of good intentions, while the social media sites that succeeded during the first two decades of the new millennium were built for hypergrowth. That meant offering us content to keep us hooked, even when that made us feel inferior or insecure, angry or anxious, and even when that caused serious real-world pain and suffering.

    ✳ ✳ ✳

Facebook knew that it could even control how we felt; in fact, it tested this out just to prove how well it worked. For a week in January 2012, Facebook ran a study on its users unbeknownst to them—689,003 of them. The company claimed that by signing up for Facebook, these people had signed up for the study, too. At least technically and legally, they were right. By agreeing to the Terms of Service, each user had permitted the company to do this, but they were all unwitting participants in the mood manipulation.[95] Facebook's data scientists worked with a professor at Cornell University and tweaked an algorithm, which altered the number of positive or negative posts in people's feeds. They wanted to see if they could prompt people to post more positive or negative content.[96]

It worked just like we'd expect: depressing content made people feel bad so they posted more pessimistic status updates, while uplifting content made people feel more upbeat and they began using words with happier connotations. The most interesting finding, though, was how valuable extreme emotions were for Facebook. When researchers made the experience of Facebook more neutral, by removing more of the status updates that evoked emotion, they found that a person became "less expressive." That meant they created less content and thus became less valuable to Facebook. As a result, there was a stronger business case for Facebook's algorithms to amplify the most extreme and emotion-producing content.[97]

In the end, all the information Facebook gathered, as with so much of the data it has collected on us, was not shared with the participants. In fact, none of them to this day even know that their moods might have been affected one way or the other.[98] The journal where the findings were published issued a rare "Editorial Expression of Concern," stating that, in retrospect, Facebook's Terms of Service agreement was not enough to ensure the participants had given their permission: "It is nevertheless a matter of concern that the collection of the data by Facebook may have involved practices that were not fully consistent with the principles of obtaining informed consent and allowing participants to opt out."[99]

Facebook's founders learned that people love to hate, like to judge, and react out of fear. It's no surprise that when distortions from both sides of the political spectrum fill our Facebook newsfeeds and Facebook groups, social media becomes an echo chamber for increasingly extreme groupthink.[100] That has also happened on cable TV and in so many other areas of our lives on the Internet, but Facebook's internal documents revealed that it knew what it was doing to polarize us, to spread lies, and to keep us coming back.[101] As views that were more extreme got more views, Facebook's algorithms encouraged more extremism.

"Our algorithms exploit the human brain's attraction to divisiveness," explained a slide from a presentation in 2018 that Frances Haugen leaked to the *Wall Street Journal.* "If left unchecked," it warned, users would see "more and more divisive content in an effort to gain user attention & increase time on the platform." One internal Facebook report revealed that "64% of all extremist group joins are due to our recommendation tools."[102] In other words, it wasn't an extreme meme, a viral video, a cruel status update, or even an angry advertisement that caused people on the far left and far right to join radical groups. Instead, Facebook's algorithms were telling people "You might like to join this group," and people did. In fact, some Facebook employees even told their bosses that "people don't trust us," insisting that the company needed to do more to rebuild trust, lessen polarization, and reduce extreme content. It might be "antigrowth." But they believed the company needed to "take a moral stance." By the summer of 2018, a group of these employees took their concerns to management, advocating for "Sparing Sharing," which would decrease the virality of dangerous content and lessen people's exposure to extreme articles, videos, and memes.[103]

Feeling pressure from his team, Zuckerberg agreed to tweak the algorithm, but he told them that he wasn't happy about it. According to the *Journal,* "Mr. Zuckerberg also signaled he was losing interest in the effort to recalibrate the platform in the name of social good, they said, asking that they not bring him something like that again."[104] It was Zuckerberg's choice to make, because even after Facebook went public, he maintained control over 56 percent of voting rights. That remains the case today, through what is known as a dual-class structure. Zuckerberg controls the vote even though he retains 18 percent of the company's shares.[105]

Over the years, investors and shareholder advocates have pushed back on Zuckerberg's unusual voting power, as well as the lack of controls being placed on the violent and extremist content that kept spreading on the site. In 2018 Christopher Ailman, the chief investment officer of the California State Teachers' Retirement System, deleted his personal Facebook account in protest, declaring, "We think that there's a problem with having one person in charge of the company" and "Their lack of oversight and poor management is offensive." Likewise, CalSTRS portfolio manager Aeisha Mastagni asked, "Why does Mr. Zuckerberg need the entrenchment factor of a dual-class structure? Is it because he does not want governance to evolve with the rest of his company? If so, this American dream is now akin to a dictatorship."[106]

Zuckerberg made decisions based on what he thought was best. When the platform encouraged judgment as entertainment, gave us reality-fixing photo filters, and nudged us with notifications, it all fueled growth early on; then later, emotional content was encouraged, then extremist views and foreign propaganda were promoted by its algorithms, because limiting them was "antigrowth." That was all justified, according to one of the most stunning admissions by a Facebook executive. Andrew Bosworth had worked with Zuckerberg since 2006 and is now Meta's CTO. His internal memo dated June 18, 2016, leaked to *BuzzFeed*:

So we connect more people. That can be bad if they make it negative. Maybe it costs a life by exposing someone to bullies. Maybe somebody dies in a terrorist attack coordinated on our tools. And still we connect people. The ugly truth is that we believe in connecting people so deeply that anything that allows us to connect more people more often is *de facto* good. It is perhaps the only area where the metrics do tell the true story as far as we are concerned.[107]

To rephrase Kevin Roose's formulation, in this context, it's as if technologists invented a way to connect everyone in the world, only to find out that it also gave communities cancer.[108]

Or, if not cancer, at least an arsenal of weapons, and lots more reasons to rage and to act on that anger. That's what Jonathan Haidt observed in his *Atlantic* essay, where he quoted one of the engineers who had worked on creating Twitter's retweet button—"We might have just handed a four-year-old a loaded weapon." Haidt explained, "As a social psychologist who studies emotion, morality, and politics, I saw this happening, too. The newly tweaked platforms were almost perfectly designed to bring out our most moralistic and least reflective selves. The volume of outrage was shocking."[109]

## Mark makes a confession

Haidt's essay in 2022 wasn't the first time someone compared social media to a loaded firearm. Back in 2005, Mark Zuckerberg was a recent Harvard dropout with a startup that was new to Silicon Valley. He awkwardly struggled through an interview in front of an auditorium of Stanford MBAs. One student addressed the ethical implications of Facebook directly. He only gave his first name, Mike, so scholars will be hard pressed to find this prescient person when twenty-first-century technology is eventually studied by historians (or sociologists). But we could see the social media's fatal flaws, identified during the dawning days of the Silicon Age through Mike's thoughtful line of questioning.

"I'm curious about what you're actually, what you're actually having the people do. Because, they're browsing around, and, and it seems as if it's, it's essentially a stalking tool, if I'm not mistaken," Mike asked. Uncomfortable laughter filled the auditorium. Zuckerberg smiled, quickly, almost mechanically. Then he didn't. His face tightened. His lips pursed. "And so what are the sort of ethical implications when it comes to developing a tool where, you know, you're leaving it up to the user to use." Mike then added, "You're not saying . . . You know, it's like the gun manufacturers make the gun. They don't tell you to, to point it at people." Zuckerberg smiled again, more nervous laughter echoed in the auditorium, then he was again straight-faced, no smile. "But, um, ultimately, when you have a tool like this, and it's venture funded, and it's backed, there are certain ethical implications and possibly, you know, uh, legal implications in the future."[110]

Zuckerberg paused before answering. We can only guess what he was thinking. "There was a strong sense back then—certainly you heard it from Mark and the people around him—that wiring the world was good in and of itself," Facebook cofounder and Zuckerberg's roommate Chris Hughes later told Sheera Frenkel and Cecilia Kang. "There was a widespread belief in the inevitable forward march of history. I don't know that that came from books, or from anywhere in particular—I think it was just understood." Others noticed that, too. "I never saw Mark reading a book, or expressing any interest in books," another friend remembered. "And he definitely didn't have a broader interest in philosophy, political thought, or economics. If you asked, he would say he was too busy taking over the world to read."[111]

"I remember a ton of conversations in which the introduction of our tools was compared to the advent of the hammer, or the light bulb," Hughes told the

*New Yorker*'s Andrew Marantz in 2019. "We could have compared it to a weapon, too, I suppose, but nobody did."[112] Come to think of it, someone did compare it to a weapon.[113] We just didn't pay close enough attention to the Stanford MBA who had only introduced himself as Mike. It was not immoral but amoral, and just like any tool, it was intended for a purpose. This one was more destructive, like a gun. And what we would do with that tool was predicted, too. "The price of abandoning oneself to such an artificial representation is always too high," Peter Thiel told us.[114] But even though we didn't listen to him—or to Mike at Stanford, the creators of Catch27, and all those college kids who wrote in their student newspapers about why they felt uncomfortable—we *were* warned.

Back in 2005, Zuckerberg broke the silence by answering Mike's ethical dilemma with a few different ideas peppered into each sentence. "So, I mean, we do a lot of stuff with the data that's collected," he began, making the understatement of the young century, "and a lot of that is aimed towards proactively defending the user base, and, I mean, making sure that we have analyzed a pattern, which is like the typical user heartbeat, right? Or like what their use looks like." Zuckerberg worried most about fake accounts, spam, and other concerns that would diminish the quality of the user experience on Facebook. He worried about nuisances that would be antigrowth. He didn't weigh the broader moral consequences.

Zuckerberg circled around an answer. The gears turned in his mind—as he rambled for ten, twenty, thirty, then forty seconds—then he contemplated the real issues that would embroil the entire world over a decade later. He swallowed deeply and said, "But I mean, in terms of, of like the ethical implications of creating this, I mean, what I kind of saw this as is enabling a freer flow of information. You know, I mean, people are interested in this stuff, we're not asking anyone to put anything out there that they wouldn't be comfortable putting out there, we're not forcing them to publicize any information about themselves."

He couldn't fully fathom the personal, much less societal, impacts of social media.

In the years ahead, Facebook would monetize what people bought and with whom they interacted. Zuckerberg's company would personalize advertisements to each of us by gathering data about where we were, what we watched and read, how often and for how long, what we shared and wrote, how often and how much. So, "we do a lot of stuff with the data that's collected." That was the real answer. But it still didn't address the massive consequences of social media.

Zuckerberg believed that the value of free-flowing information would ultimately justify any other issues. The rest of his answer revealed that he was skeptical about the magnitude of any harmful results: "And, I mean, I think that, just like putting people in control of what they put out there, we are kind of putting it in their hands, but we're not necessarily putting it in the hands of the person who will misuse it. We're putting it in the hands of the person who could potentially be the victim if it ever came to that. But, I mean, we're not really finding that much." Those last words were said with concern. His brow furrowed. He shook his head no.

Later Zuckerberg was asked about his greatest challenges and what he lost sleep over. He paused, looked down at the ground, didn't respond. The question was repeated by the interviewer, "The question, of course, is what keeps you awake at night. What's the biggest challenge? Endless number of challenges, of course, but what would the top three or four be?" Zuckerberg responded that he wanted to maintain the site's quality and continue to improve its growth. He cited the statistic that 70 percent of the people came back to the site every day. "That's a very vague answer, so I kind of apologize," he concluded. But nowhere in his response did he say a word about the significant ethical concerns raised earlier.[115]

The evening's final question was the most pointed. "Uh, if I may ask this," the audience member began. He then asked Zuckerberg what caused the greatest tension between him and investors. Like Parker's confession years later, Zuckerberg answered honestly. It began with his hands on his knees, and a long deep pause. Like waiting for an Excel file to compute a null equation. Then a few words, a false start, and an even longer pause. But the ultimate answer was clear and unfiltered. It was authentic. He leaned forward, elbows on his knees, his feet tapping rhythmically in his signature three-striped Adidas sandals. "I think that they kind of look at this investment and say, we have this twenty-one-year-old kid running it. We should at least try to complement him with someone who has more experience running a business. You know."[116] He laughed, and it was heartfelt. The tone of his voice became more dynamic, more engaging.

"And honestly, that's something I'm a little afraid of, even though it's probably really good." He said he was being honest. He was. "I'm not sure when that point is. And I mean, I think that they probably think that point is now, where you want to get that person in as soon as possible, and, I mean, to me it's unclear. . . . I don't know, it's not like really tense at all, because we haven't found that person."[117] Zuckerberg laughed, with a big smile on his face. In front of a roomful of strangers, he'd replied truthfully. It was a genuine human interaction, in-person, showing imperfections in a social setting with other living, breathing people.

For a moment, it felt really good.

# CHAPTER 7

# ANYTHING IT LIKES

Larry Page and Sergey Brin, Google, Inc.

Early on, Google was supposed to answer any question by returning unbiased results. But that changed when it began allowing ads on October 23, 2000.[1] After the Stanford Students turned their school project into a business, they did not accept corporate dollars for ads for over two years. They still worried about the dangers of "dark arts." So they made a new pledge in 2000: "Don't Be Evil."[2] It was a phrase that never made much sense.

Why didn't Sergey Brin and Larry Page make their motto, "Be Good," simple as that? If truth was inherently good, couldn't they make that their slogan? Or if "Be Good" was too much to ask, why not say, "Do the Greatest Good for the Greatest Number," or something like that? That would have worked well. After all, Google came from "googol," a child's neologism for the biggest number anyone could imagine.[3] Utilitarianism would not only sound more positive, but that approach would also align with the values statement they'd debut during their IPO in 2004, about "significantly improving the lives of as many people as possible."[4] Instead, they chose this strange slogan. Why settle for "Don't Be Evil"?

Presumably, they'd decided Google couldn't *possibly* be good if they displayed ads, but that was a necessary evil now. In 1995 they'd written that "advertising funded search engines will be inherently biased towards the advertisers and away from the needs of the consumers," which they called "insidious."[5] Page and Brin had begun as anticorporate graduate students, who believed that the novel technologies of an open Internet would help facts triumph over business interests. Now they were tech entrepreneurs who needed ads to succeed. If they couldn't do good, they'd at least be anti-evil. If the unbiased truth wasn't possible, because it wasn't profitable, they'd try to limit the damage done from corporate control over search results.

Before Google went public in 2004, they promised potential shareholders that "Google is not a conventional company." Brin and Page swore that "our goal is to develop services that improve the lives of as many people as possible—to do things that matter." But wasn't the actual reason for this pre-IPO letter to recruit investors? Were they saying that improving lives should take precedence over profits? The Google Boys answered those questions by focusing on long-term value creation, arguing that "a management team distracted by a series of short term targets is as pointless as a dieter stepping on a scale every half hour." The cofounders emphasized that "the ads we provide are relevant and useful rather than intrusive and annoying."[6]

But wait a second. Wouldn't that make them an "advertising-funded search engine," which could be biased toward corporate interests? Wouldn't that be, to use their word, "insidious," and wouldn't that be, well, evil? Not so, according to Page and Brin, who reassured the world in 2004 that "we will live up to our 'don't be evil' principle by keeping user trust and not accepting payment for search results."[7] As Google grew, the company never charged us for each search. Instead, people kept seeing and clicking on ads. That's how Google got paid.

We were never its customers. The advertisers were, and our search habits and all our data were what was so valuable. So Google sold our attention. Advertisers loved it.

In 2004 Google was the search engine of choice for 47 percent of Americans, while 26 percent preferred Yahoo, according to Pew. By 2012 Google had the answers for 83 percent of Americans and only 6 percent used Yahoo. Google managed to maintain that dominance over many years to come, while its revenues soared. It held over 87 percent of market share for the better part of a decade.[8] In 2005 Google's yearly ad revenues added up to just over $6 billion; by 2012 they were over $43 billion, and in 2022 they'd exceed $224 billion.[9] Yes, one company, which so many of us use without ever directly paying for its products, makes almost a quarter of a trillion dollars each year.

Our attention and data are valuable.


## Advertisements: A necessary evil?

Once ads appeared, they were clearly marked at first, with a bright blue background behind them. In 2007 Google changed the background from blue to yellow. Over the next few years, it changed to green, light blue, violet, and then back to yellow. In 2013 Google got rid of the background color entirely. From that point forward, every ad looked exactly the same as other search results except for a little icon next to the link that said "Ad." At first, the word "Ad" was surrounded by a bright yellow box followed by green text with the link. Then, in 2016, it changed to a green box that matched the green text. In 2019 "Ad" was in black and so was the link, which looked like every other search result on the page. Over time it meant a steady erosion of Google's honest delineation of ads from answers.[10]

"Harmony." That's the word Sundeep Jain, Google's director of search ads quality, used to describe these changes, positing at a marketing conference in 2016 that the new layout was clearer and would "make it easier for users to digest information on the search results page." By information, he meant both ads and answers. He also professed that it wasn't about what Google wanted; people were asking for the change because they were making more impulsive decisions as they flicked through sites on their phones, compared to when they browsed on their computers. The changes were necessary "as users move more of their activity on mobile, where they have much, much lower attention span," he said. He claimed that those behaviors justified Google's changes: they were "gradually trying to reduce the number of deviations of colors and other patterns on the page, and bring a little bit more harmony and rhythm to the page."[11] That "harmony" of information would blur any distinction between unbiased results and biased ads.

Page and Brin had asked users to trust them—a truth-telling machine must be built on trust, after all—and then they told investors to trust them, too. But there was a conflict. What people wanted (the unbiased answers from the knowledge of everyone who clicked on the content on the Internet) clashed with what investors wanted (the revenues from companies paying not merely for people to see their adds but, more profitably, for them to click on those ads instead of the unbiased answers). What mattered more? The Google Boys had started making decisions that went against their original anticorporate ethos. They learned it created incredible value for businesses that commingled their commercials with unbiased information.

Page and Brin had warned in their pre-IPO letter that "the standard structure of public ownership may jeopardize the independence and focused objectivity that have been most important in Google's past success and that we consider most fundamental for its future," so they'd decided to pursue a dual-class share structure, which concentrated voting power with Google's executive team, not shareholders.[12] Over the next two decades, users saw the lines blur between ads and facts, as Google's artificial intelligence learned what made people click. So much had changed since the days of Backrub. Gradually, the more we wanted to know something, the more corporations got results. By the time Google became the multinational conglomerate Alphabet in 2015, it was often hard to tell the difference between ads and unbiased answers, and the more corporations trained Google's algorithms that their results were what we wanted, the more their content appeared near the top anyway.

Over time, Google's algorithms also learned how to entice people to click on the results paid for by advertisers. That same approach was then applied to other popular products, such as Google Maps, where it became nearly impossible to delineate what was an ad. Did the restaurant that just popped up when you searched for the best local Mexican food appear because it was the nearest to you, the highest rated by people who ate there, or because the restaurateur ran ads promoting the margarita happy hour specials with an online coupon, so people kept clicking, and Google's algorithms learned that's what everyone wanted? We can never be sure. What's happening behind the scenes with the complex algorithms, and the factors that influence them, is unknown by anyone but Alphabet.

We do know this: our data is mined, presented to advertisers, and optimized for their benefit. Of course, the restaurants promoting cheap margaritas on Google don't always serve the tastiest Mexican food, too. But whenever we click on an ad, Alphabet gets paid more, so it's in their financial interest to blur the lines between what the rest of the Internet might have otherwise recommended as the best answer and what companies would want us to click on. Alphabet's business model requires our attention and data. We get all these services for "free" because our time and behaviors online are so valuable.

How valuable? Alphabet's family of companies have gone beyond revenues from search ads; they also earn money from running the cloud computing technology that stores data for corporations and people. Decades of data on billions of people became astonishingly valuable as Alphabet's artificial intelligence learned more about each of us individually, then all of us collectively. It fueled their expansion into more aspects of human life. Alphabet's products now include Google Maps, Gmail, Google Drive, and Google Photos, as well as an array of other companies it had bought along the way: YouTube, Waze, Nest, Waymo, and Verily Life Sciences.[13] Google's revenues were just $400 million in 2002. A decade later, they topped $50.1 billion. By 2022 Alphabet's overall revenues exceeded $279.8 billion.[14] Today the ads appearing on Google's search engine are just one part of how it makes money. But it still makes Alphabet far more than all its other business lines combined, and its growth has accelerated as ads and answers mix and we all keep clicking.[15]

Here's something else astonishing about its dominance: the majority of websites don't get accessed by anyone, and that's decided for us by Google as well. According to one estimate, 90 percent of the content on the Internet gets no traffic from Google because it is buried beneath other search results.[16] The corporatization of the World Wide Web that Brin and Page had fretted about as graduate students was, as it turned out, the outcome of their life's work as businessmen. This leads to an all-important question that also has gone unnoticed, yet might never be answered. Which is worse, visionaries whose only founding ideals were to get rich at any cost, or entrepreneurs who knew what was wrong and swore by "Don't Be Evil" but then targeted us all with ads anyway? Which is more of a deception: creating fake scoreboards to tally up our status, or blurring facts with ads to make it harder to tell what was sponsored and what was not?

## The surveillance economy feeds on cookies

There are little bits of code that make it possible for Alphabet's commercialization of our attention and data. They're called "cookies." But while that word makes them seem innocent, they're ensuring that each of us are surveilled by corporations even after we've clicked away from the site we were on. The private sector's surveillance of our lives runs on cookies. As the evolution of Google's approach to search results reveals, our attention and data are the "free" Internet's currency, and the massive companies that trade in that currency are finding all new ways to mine and monetize it. Alphabet is now worth over $1.2 trillion, mostly funded by ads and fueled by our attention and data.[17] Alphabet craved cookies. We've fed it a steady diet.

In recent years, Alphabet executives have talked about getting rid of cookies altogether. One of the leaders in this effort, David Temkin, took on a very interesting role as the director of product management for ads privacy and trust. On March 3, 2021, Temkin wrote an essay on the Alphabet corporate blog titled, "Charting a Course Towards a More Privacy-First Web." In it, he admitted that there had been "an erosion of trust: In fact, 72% of people feel that almost all of what they do online is being tracked by advertisers, technology firms or other companies, and 81% say that the potential risks they face because of data collection outweigh the benefits, according to a study by Pew Research Center." Temkin explained that Alphabet wanted to get rid of cookies by seeking "to build innovations that protect anonymity while still delivering results for advertisers and publishers." Then he directly promised that "today, we're making explicit that once third-party cookies are phased out, we will not build alternate identifiers to track individuals as they browse across the web, nor will we use them in our products." It was a massive change for the company, which could be transformative for the future of the Internet. "If digital advertising doesn't evolve to address the growing concerns people have about their privacy and how their personal identity is being used," Temkin warned, "we risk the future of the free and open web."[18]

Some skeptics, such as Sara Morrison at *Vox*, didn't think that it will make much of a difference in terms of our privacy or Google's abilities to surveil us. The same day as Temkin's blog went live, she responded with a contrasting perspective. "Meanwhile, Google will still track and target users on mobile devices, and it will still target ads to users based on their behavior on its own platforms, which make up the majority of its revenue and won't be affected by the change," she wrote. "In other words, while the announcement will have huge implications for the digital ad industry, it probably won't for Google itself."[19] This public pronouncement might have sounded good, at least in terms of mitigating the backlash against the corporate surveillance of our lives, but the implementation would be what mattered most.

Given Google's market share in Internet search and the revenues that came from targeted advertising, it was fair to wonder whether this new strategy was even a way for the company to maintain its dominance. With over two decades' worth of data on us all already, and with its ad targeting becoming more mature and sophisticated throughout that entire time, there was a distinct possibility that Alphabet already had the data it needed from us to achieve its goals. If it could successfully build data models without cookies, and people loved it for suddenly protecting privacy, then that might give it an unbeatable offering.

At least thus far, however, Alphabet has been unable to achieve this dream. Developing an alternative to cookies—such as by using the data it already has on all of us to target advertisements at people similar to you, but not you individually—has proved harder than it had thought. In the summer of 2021 it delayed going cookie-less until late 2023. In 2022 it pushed the rollout to late 2024.[20] How did we end up here, where our time and attention are monetized, where it harvests our data, and where companies can constantly surveil us? How is all this legal? The answer to that question might be the most amazing ruse of the twenty-first century.

## The surveillance economy relies on terms of service that nobody reads

Tech companies have convinced us that our data is theirs, not ours, so we give it away for free. But the reality is: we all signed up for this, through Terms of Service we never read. We're constantly asked, "Do you agree to abide by our terms of service?" Hardly anyone stops to read what that means. We just accept, an act of trust, but also a little white lie. With every unread Terms of Service, we fib to the Internet every day. They ask us, directly, whether we have read the agreement. Even though we haven't, we click accept anyway.

The lawyers for tech companies have made it impossible for us to even try to understand what we're signing up for. Let's imagine the opposite scenario: that the average Internet user stopped to read all the privacy policies he or she was asked to agree to in a given year. It would take seventy-six workdays, according to two scholars at Carnegie Mellon. The median word count of the top seventy-five websites' agreements totaled 2,514 words—that's close to what you've read in this chapter thus far. That takes about ten minutes each, and such a mind-numbing ten minutes at that, which really starts to add up when we come across about 1,462 privacy policies annually.[21]

Other studies are even more astonishing. Take NameDrop, Inc., which wasn't even a real business. Jonathan Obar of York University in Toronto and Anne Oeldorf-Hirsch of the University of Connecticut invented the social media company for a study. Only 11 of the 543 people caught the trick hidden in the made-up company's fake Terms of Service. That meant that about 98 percent, the other 532 people, agreed to share information with the National Security Administration to use at its discretion. Buried in the legalese, they would have read that their data could be used to affect future "employment, financial service (bank loans, insurance, etc.), university entrance, international travel, the criminal justice system, etc."[22]

Oh, and one more thing. Those 532 people also agreed to give up their first-born children to the researchers' fake company. Only 11 participants who read what it actually meant that "by clicking Join, you agree to abide by our terms of service" were able to avoid that fate. The others clicked to proceed, agreeing to the following: "all users of this site agree to immediately assign their first-born child to NameDrop, Inc. If the user does not yet have children, this agreement will be enforceable until the year 2050. All individuals assigned to NameDrop automatically become the property of NameDrop, Inc. No exceptions."[23]

No exceptions, indeed. Most of us like to think of ourselves as honest. We try to be decent people in our daily lives. But we're busy, and we're not going to waste our time reading complex legal documents on the Internet. When the European General Data Protection Regulation (GDPR) law took effect in May 2018 as "the toughest privacy and security law in the world," its earliest impact meant more websites asked you to agree to something you'd never read.[24] "This website uses cookies to ensure you get the best experience on our website," the pop-ups explained, innocently enough. We quickly click "accept," also innocently enough. But we never know what we've agreed to, and companies know that, so they take more from us without us noticing. "There's a real concern that consumer protection law is basically being swallowed by click-by-agree clauses," the University of Pennsylvania Law School's David Hoffman told the *Guardian*.[25] Cookies sounded harmless, even delicious. But they're not.

* * *

Speaking of mouthwatering mistakes, if you come up with the idea for the next great milkshake, don't think Sonic will pay you for it. Their lawyers made sure you signed off on this statement, among others: "SONIC may use and own your submission for any purpose whatsoever now and in the future without any obligation to obtain your permission or to compensate you."[26] Many of our favorite companies hide surprises like those in their terms of agreement. They are not as bad as surrendering our firstborn children, but they are still astonishing. "Modern cars are a privacy nightmare and it seems that the Fords, Audis, and Toyotas of the world have shifted their focus from selling cars to selling data," reported a team of Mozilla Foundation researchers who found that our personal and car sensor data gets sold for a profit, shared with the government, and resold on data marketplaces. It's nearly impossible to opt out.[27]

God knows the number of hairs on your head, but the world's most visited Christian website for searching the Bible and devotionals, Bible Gateway, knows every other website you visit, thanks to what you agreed to in its privacy policy.[28] Signing up for the free educational services offered by organizations like Khan Academy means waiving your right to a class-action lawsuit against them.[29] *National Geographic* owns the rights to anything you say or do on its site, including pictures you post or other content you upload. Like many similar websites, it gets to keep "a worldwide, perpetual license" even if you shut down your account.[30] When you post something to the BBC, "you give up your moral rights to it," according to its Terms of Use. Think that phrase sounds ominous? Well, it certainly is. As the BBC explains, "That means we can: Use your creation without identifying you as the creator" or "edit or change your creation and you won't be able to say we've treated it in a 'derogatory' way."[31] So if you say something brilliant, the BBC can take it—and take credit for it. If you write something it misinterprets, misrepresents, or even edits, you have no recourse, at least based on what you agreed to.

While we browse the Internet, we make these agreements with companies from around the world. The business most responsible for the expansive corporatization of the Internet was the one that made more money from online advertisements than any other company: Alphabet. In recent years, it has made over forty-five times more than what Twitter (now X) made from digital advertising and almost twice what Meta has.[32] "Your search query, your keystrokes, your voice imprint and face in a Google Chat video chat, your sent emails in Gmail—those are all pieces of content that you have submitted to their Services," James Ward, a lawyer who specializes in privacy law and data security, told the *New York Times* in July 2019. "This was how we all 'consented' without having a clue that we had done so."[33]

Alphabet has used your GPS coordinates, your unique IP address, and sensor data from technologies like the accelerometer in your phone, as well as "information about things near your device, such as Wi-Fi access points, cell towers, and Bluetooth-enabled devices."[34] That's a direct quote from its privacy policy. As the Internet of Things connects up more of our devices and data floods out of our everyday actions into the cloud, Alphabet gladly harvests from these "things," as in *all the things*, anywhere near our device. When Alphabet acquired Fitbit for $2.1 billion in 2019, it got the data from every Fitbit ever worn. That included step counts, heart-rate readings, sleep time, menstrual cycles, and other health information from people who never knew Alphabet would eventually have all that data. "What is Google going to do with your Fitbit data?" one article inquired. The rest of the headline answered the question: "Anything it likes."[35] Unsurprisingly, one of the first new devices that Fitbit launched after being acquired by Alphabet also had GPS capabilities to track you everywhere you go.[36]

Meta tracks what other websites you visit, including what you look at and how long you do, even after you've left Facebook.[37] How valuable is our data and content? Here is one perspective: even GDPR's most significant fine, a whopping $1.3 billion penalty in May 2023, amounted to only 1 percent of the total revenues Meta was on pace to make that year.[38] To be clear, it's not like just one of these companies has duped us into signing off on these agreements. The same kind of legal language is all over the Internet. So we shouldn't blame one bad actor. While cookies are stored on your computer, the data they contain can be accessed by a website's server while you browse the Internet. You create this data, but the monetizable value it creates becomes theirs, and you do not share in the economic benefits. In fact, you instead experience a range of unnoticed losses: the loss of knowing who has access to your data, and of your privacy as companies track you online and in real life. You lose power over who has your data, as it gets sold and resold. One party sells it to a third party, who then sells it to a fourth party, to a fifth one, and our data makes more money for more companies through unknown networks from there. Our data is spread exponentially rather than linearly, and everyone profits from it along the way. Well, everyone except for you.

So maybe it isn't an overstatement to say that your freedom to decide is lost in this equation. Your power over your data certainly is. There's a reason so many tech companies have made so much money with this business model. They don't have to pay you anything for the data they're mining and all the value they're gaining from your attention and experiences.

Do you know how many times you've visited your grandparents, your in-laws, or your nieces and nephews? Because of geolocation on your phone, these companies almost certainly do. And they know where you stayed each time, how long you stayed there, and how often you checked your phone while with them. Do you know what times of the year or what life situations cause you to spend more money? Online retailers probably do. And so does everyone else they decide should have that information. Do you know how often you've spent browsing websites about not being able to find a boyfriend or girlfriend, or not being able to have children, or struggling with anxiety? It's a fair bet that social media companies do. They know how often, for how long, at what times of day, and what you wrote when you did.

Now that you think that over, does it bother you? Well, there's not much you can do. You've signed away any agency. That's because when it comes to all the Terms of Service that we've agreed to the entire time we've used the Internet, we'll never know what we once signed up for. We are functionally illiterate when it comes to our data. Should we blame the tech entrepreneurs and their Silicon Valley lawyers? No. We all agreed to this. But it is about time we begin asking more questions, about the power they've gained and what we've given up.

## Data: So valuable, it's the new oil

"Why Data Is the New Oil," ran the headline in *Fortune* in 2016.[39] "The world's most valuable resource is no longer oil, but data," the *Economist* claimed the following year.[40] The companies that profit from all this "oil of the digital era" engage in a new form of business, which scholars, politicians, and business leaders have attempted to describe with various formulations and phrases. We are still searching for the right verbiage, but one phrase that has become increasingly popular is "surveillance capitalism," a term that Harvard Business School professor emerita Shoshana Zuboff came up with and used in a paper she published in 2015. "Surveillance capitalism challenges democratic norms," she contended, "and departs in key ways from the centuries-long evolution of market capitalism." These technologies seemed inevitable and automatic, but Zuboff knew that they never were. While the machines were mindless, never knowing why they swept up our data, serious thought went into the plans made by corporate executives, starting with the Google Boys. In other words, surveillance capitalism was mostly about people's choices, not technology's pre-destined progress. The result: "a new economic order that claims human experience as a free source of raw material."[41]

That economic order depended on agreements we'd made that we never read, data that was mined from us in ways we never fully realized, and algorithms that would never be revealed to us but that worked in ways we could never comprehend (and even tech executives would never fully fathom, because they'd become so complex). As Zuboff testified to Congress in February 2022: "Over these last two decades, I've observed the consequences as fledgling internet companies morphed into surveillance empires founded on the premise that *privacy must fall* and powered by global operations of behavioral monitoring, analysis, targeting, modification, and prediction that I have called 'surveillance capitalism.'"[42] The Google Boys had originally worried that the information from advertisers would be worse for people than the answers offered by the rest of the Internet. "Aside from tremendous growth, the Web has also become increasingly commercial over time," they'd fretted in their thesis.[43] As Google expanded, with ever greater profits, prestige, and power, they'd abandoned their first principles of creating an easy way for anyone to search the Internet to find unbiased answers. Tim Berners-Lee hoped to create "an easy but powerful global information system."[44] As the Stanford Students became the Google Boys, they changed their minds about the compromises they'd make with that power.

By blurring the lines between what's an advertisement and what's not, one result is undeniable: it sure has been profitable. When Google went public, its Class A shares traded at $2.71. By the time it got rid of the colored background for ads in 2013, nine years later, the stock had reached $20. Two years after that, the company renamed itself Alphabet. By the time it chose "harmony" over clarity in 2019, with no background and only that little "Ad" icon, its stock topped $60. In the next three years, the share price tripled, to over $140. From $2.71 to over $140 a share.[45] Silicon had become gold.

"In an information civilization, societies are defined by questions of knowledge—how it is distributed, the authority that governs its distribution, and the power that protects that authority," Zuboff told Congress. *Who knows? Who decides who knows? Who decides who decides who knows?* Surveillance capitalists now hold the answers to each question, though we never elected them to govern." Silicon became gold and then profits created more power. "Digital territories that most people have assumed to be public," she explained, "are now owned, operated, and mediated by private commercial interests for maximum profit while almost entirely unconstrained by public law."[46] Power cycled into more profits, which turned into even more power.

The transmutation was complete, and so was the transformation. The Stanford Students decided to make money from their project, making them the Google Boys. They turned our interests into business interests. Then they became the Alphabet Men, as they gained value from so many aspects of our lives: whenever we wanted answers, whatever we watched, and everywhere we went. The company once called Google, which determined knowledge itself, had become Alphabet, which was the very substance of which our entire understanding of the world was made.

## Focusing on the issues that matter

On April 30, 2011, President Barack Obama stood behind the microphone at the annual White House Correspondents' Association dinner and smiled. It was an annual Gatsby-esque celebration, colloquially referred to as "nerd prom," based on that popular DC saying that "Washington is Hollywood for ugly people."[47] But the self-effacing jokes belied the wealth, power, and prestige of the people in that one room, where dozens of the most influential politicians and journalists gathered all in one place.

These leaders thought that they understood the truth; they felt that they knew the answers. Some had probably even convinced themselves that they got to decide what was true or right for other people, with their policies and press releases, their investigations and interviews. The Fourth Estate convened that evening to celebrate their top-notch truth-telling, their news-making fact-finding, and their many witty analyses. Washington politicians and its media establishment took turns giving speeches, roasting each other with so-smart sarcasm blended with self-satisfied narcissism. When he took the stage, Obama seemed at ease. A few weeks before, he'd announced his plans to seek reelection for a second term.[48] And just a few days earlier, the White House had posted his long-form birth certificate online.[49]

A conspiracy theory had been circulating on the Internet that Obama was ineligible to be president because he was born in Kenya, not Hawaii. It was all based on an outright lie, but many Americans believed it.[50] In fact, the state director of health for Hawaii claimed that the influx of inquiries they'd received were "disruptive to staff operations and have drained State resources."[51] Obama addressed the topic directly. "Now, I know that he's taken some flak lately, but no one is happier, no one is prouder to put this birth certificate matter to rest than The Donald," Obama said midway through his speech. "And that's because he can finally get back to focusing on the issues that matter—like, did we fake the moon landing? What really happened in Roswell? And where are Biggie and Tupac?" he asked. Donald Trump laughed along.[52]

Yet despite all the power and insider knowledge in that room, few in attendance truly understood the two great ironies of what they experienced that evening. The first one was obvious in retrospect. Obama and the DC elites dining together that night failed to grasp the incredible potential for artificial representations to replace reality. That would occur more and more online, with social media's mean memes and incendiary comments, its alternative facts, viral videos, and conspiracy tweets, and soon, its Truths, ReTruths, and outright mistruths.

Obama mocked Trump, feigning seriousness: "But all kidding aside, obviously, we all know about your credentials and breadth of experience." The crowd laughed, and the president twisted the knife further. "For example—no, seriously, just recently, in an episode of 'Celebrity Apprentice'—at the steakhouse, the men's cooking team did not impress the judges from Omaha Steaks. And there was a lot of blame to go around. But you, Mr. Trump, recognized that the real problem was a lack of leadership. And so ultimately, you didn't blame Lil Jon or Meatloaf. You fired Gary Busey. And these are the kind of decisions that would keep me up at night."[53]

But the power of celebrity was real, too. Trump would prove that and more. The media and the establishment politicians believed they had the control. But the Internet had already changed things by eroding the business models of the traditional press and upending institutions that had once been the arbiters of facts. The Democrats, the party in power that evening, seemed self-satisfied with their shared ideas about the world, the security of their stature, and the accuracy of their polling. Their unquestioned vote tallies gave them a sense of control. That turned out to be illusory, or perhaps a self-delusion. Either way, it didn't last.

The second great irony that evening was less apparent. Obama had just approved the secret raid to take out Osama bin Laden, which happened the next day. He truly *did* know something that others there did not, because of the power of the presidency. For the moment, the decision remained a necessary secret. That evening, Obama calmly joked about "the kind of decisions that would keep me up at night," which only he knew applied to more than firing Gary Busey, given that he'd just ordered the raid to kill the mastermind behind 9/11. He dismissed Trump with this presidential proclamation: "Well handled, sir. Well handled."[54]

Despite being a president who was known for his carefully considered choices, with the bin Laden operation among the most historic, Obama miscalculated with Trump, as did most of the political establishment. They failed to grasp the ways the institutions they derived such power from were losing out to new dynamics created in California, both in Silicon Valley and in Hollywood. Power could be fueled by popularity, enhanced by controversy, and quickened by technology. Crisp editorial control and elegant speechwriting mattered so much less than the constant content that was massively entertaining and utterly instantaneous. Donald Trump had become universally recognizable and had built a very real-world following during fourteen seasons of *The Apprentice*. The show portrayed him as someone powerful in ways that others weren't, because he seemed like the ultimate boss of all these other celebrities. America had seen them before, too, and they had previously answered to no one. But then they cowered before Trump. It was designed to make him look decisive, as the ultimate executive.[55] That status proved fungible for other purposes.

The American public knew that these actors, athletes, and other popular people didn't report to Trump in real life. It was for entertainment, just part of a grand show. But the fact that he wasn't their boss did not matter; the film was edited, and compelling, and on demand. The charade was beamed into our living rooms and streamed to our phones. This counterfeit reality became a fresh canvas, a new frontier, allowing new experiments in reality. By working outside entrenched power structures, reality TV meant a freer world, a blank screen where Trump's image was projected, his power on full display. And as for the Washington elites, with all their inside jokes and self-referential power? They were on C-SPAN.

That evening, Donald Trump was not yet a Republican. He had been a Democrat from 2001 to 2009 and had had no party affiliation since December 2011.

In April 2012, a year after the White House Correspondents' dinner, he registered as a Republican.[56]

"I do understand it's all basically a game. We're all here to play the game and we're all hopefully going to play it well. But some people obviously can't play it well." Those were the words of Donald Trump in 1980. "I think that the world is made up of people with either killer instincts or without killer instincts," explained Trump in an interview for *Rona Barrett Looks at Todays $uperRich*. At age thirty-four, he shared this wisdom about how the world works: "And the people that seemed to emerge are the people that are competitive and driven and with a certain instinct to win."[57] Thirty years after saying that, Trump put his killer instinct to work, by tweeting that Barack Obama's presidency was illegitimate. From October 2011 until November 2015, he tweeted about this conspiracy sixty-seven times.[58] For his political debut, Trump used technology to get everyone spun up with a web of lies. Because here's a fact: all of that came *after* Barack Obama had released officially authenticated evidence on the White House website to disprove the claim.[59]

Trump stirred up new controversies, then he redoubled his accusations despite the facts. He tweeted in all caps and entertained on Facebook Live and built a massive following. Trump advisor Roger Stone admitted the plan in an interview about *Celebrity Apprentice* in 2000: "Think how he looked in that show: high-backed chair, perfectly lit, great makeup, great hair, decisive, making decisions, running the show. He looks presidential. Do you think that voters, nonsophisticates, make a difference between entertainment and politics?"[60] It was a game Trump kept playing for higher stakes, "sort of like a series of poker games," like Elon Musk had done. But Trump turned the tables, shifting from business to politics, "onto a more high stakes poker game," as he "just carried those chips" from one game to the next.[61]

Or, rather, maybe the right analogy was theater. Politics became entertainment, as the *Art of the Possible* meant *Anything Goes*. "Here's the fundamental question," Stone asked. "Is the pop culture in this country more influential now than its institutions?"[62] It wasn't in 2000 or even that evening in April 2011. It would be soon, though. Fact or fiction, reality or advertisement, actual event or total spectacle, real-life evidence or artificial representation.

It kept getting harder to tell the difference.

# CHAPTER 8

# WORDS DO MATTER

Keith Rabois, Peter Thiel, and David Sacks,
PayPal and Founders Fund

On the final night of the Republican National Convention (RNC) in 2016, minutes before Donald Trump accepted the nomination, Peter Thiel took the dais. He made three declarations about his identity: "I am proud to be gay. I am proud to be a Republican. But most of all, I am proud to be an American." He told the crowd, "When I was a kid, the great debate was about how to defeat the Soviet Union. And we won. Now we are told that the great debate is about who gets to use which bathroom. This is a distraction from our real problems. Who cares?"[1]

Thiel had come out as gay and gotten married; he was now a proud member of the homosexual community he'd once disparaged for their "excesses." He boasted about American victories over Russia, even while Vladimir Putin was consolidating power and had illegally seized Crimea from democratic Ukraine just two years prior.[2] And by chiding his opponents for being overly concerned with bathrooms, Thiel warned that political intolerance had expanded beyond campus life and was now directed at every American. "I don't pretend to agree with every plank in our party's platform," he admitted, "but fake culture wars only distract us from our economic decline, and nobody in this race is being honest about it except Donald Trump."[3]

Months after Thiel's RNC speech, he gave a major donation supporting the Trump campaign.[4] According to America's very best data scientists and political pollsters at the time, Hillary Clinton was heavily favored to win—near the end, their consensus reached 85 percent.[5] Thiel defied the oddsmakers and bet on a longshot upset just three weeks before the election, spending $1.25 million on this unorthodox campaign being waged by the contrarian candidate. After learning about the donation, even those people who usually refrained from political debates protested. Numerous investors, business executives, and other leaders in Silicon Valley called for a boycott of Facebook, of PayPal, of anything Thiel had supported.[6] The media skewered him. *Fortune* levied this criticism: "If savvy investment is all about timing, Peter Thiel may have lost his touch."[7] Even Jeff Bezos spoke out. He had generally avoided making any kind of political commentary after buying the *Washington Post* from Donald Graham's family in 2013, but during a public interview with Walter Isaacson on October 20, 2016, he reassured, "Peter Thiel is a contrarian, and you have to remember that contrarians are usually wrong."[8]

Thiel donated more to Trump than the combined contributions by all employees at top tech firms, by many orders of magnitude. CNN found just fifty-two tech company employee donations to Trump that year, worth $21,000. It had searched the records of two hundred tech corporations, even including "Uber driver" as the profession listed for one, although we know that Uber doesn't consider drivers employees.[9] *NBC News* reported that everyone at Apple, Google, Microsoft, Facebook, and Amazon, combined, had given Trump $50,000.[10] A third analysis by *Wired* showed that the Trump campaign received $250 from all Google employees; they gave over ten times that much to candidates from both the Libertarian Party and the Green Party, who had even less of a chance to win.[11] By every measure, Thiel's $1.25 million was dozens of times greater than the combined individual contributions to Trump from the employees of Silicon Valley's top companies.

Thiel's support angered many Facebook employees, some of whom had also protested when Trump promised to ban all Muslims from immigrating to the United States. They believed that such statements qualified as hate speech, a violation of company policy, so his Facebook account should be suspended.[12] Fortunately for them, Zuckerberg agreed. He felt disgusted and wanted the post removed. According to the *Washington Post*, he asked his top advisors whether Trump had violated (you guessed it) the Terms of Service, the legalese that few ever read.[13] In other words, Zuckerberg didn't want to change Facebook's rules, but he wondered if Facebook could justify taking action against a presidential candidate, since at one point Trump had agreed to the Terms of Service just like everybody else.

Monika Bickert, Facebook's vice president for policy, offered Zuckerberg several options in a memo that leaked to the *Post*. She proposed ideas across a spectrum of possibilities, ranging from deleting posts on a case-by-case basis to changing the company policy entirely and allowing all comments that would've previously been off-limits, such as "No blacks allowed" and "Get the gays out of San Francisco." Beneath those choices, Bickert listed "PR Risks," which included, "Would Facebook have provided a platform for Hitler?"[14] Ultimately, Facebook didn't censor Trump's Muslim ban statements. The company eventually changed its policies, leaving up posts for "newsworthiness," which meant that public figures like Trump could say what they wanted, even when that violated Facebook's rules.[15]

That lasted for most of the Trump presidency, but not all of it. Years later, Zuckerberg banned Trump from Facebook entirely, while he was still in office.[16] Shortly thereafter, Trump sued Zuckerberg for "illegal and shameful censorship of the American people" and for limiting his ability "to act as head of the Republican Party, campaign for Republican candidates, fundraise, and lay the groundwork for his own potential campaign run for the 2024 Republican Party nomination for President of the United States."[17] But in 2016 Zuckerberg had agreed with his employees that Trump's statements were hate speech. He'd still commanded that they stay up, because Facebook was a forum for free speech—some of it, at least temporarily, and for some people, some of the time.

## Mark defends Peter and promises "our community will be stronger"

In October 2016 Peter Thiel spoke to the National Press Club. "No matter what happens in this election, what Trump represents isn't crazy and it's not going away," he said, foreshadowing the ensuing turmoil of the Grand Old Party. "He points toward a new Republican party beyond the dogmas of Reaganism." Thiel admitted that such a transition was not going to be easy for conservatives, or for America, but he considered it necessary. "Everybody knows we've been living through a crazy election year. Real events seem like they're rehearsals for Saturday Night Live. Only an outbreak of insanity would seem to account for the unprecedented fact that this year a political outsider managed to win a major party nomination."[18] He spoke on Halloween, of all days. Mark Zuckerberg had debuted Facemash thirteen years before.

Despite his outspoken disgust about Trump's beliefs, Zuckerberg defended Thiel with an internal, all-company message. It was made public on Y Combinator's blog, *Hacker News*, and Facebook officials soon confirmed its authenticity with other media outlets.[19] "Our community will be stronger for all our differences—not only in areas like race and gender, but also in areas like political ideology and religion," he promised, attempting to quell the discontent over the donation while likely also not wanting to aggravate Thiel. But with another line in the statement, it became clear Zuckerberg had not read *The Diversity Myth: Multiculturalism and Political Intolerance on Campus*. Zuckerberg contended, "There are many reasons a person might support Trump that do not involve racism, sexism, xenophobia or accepting sexual assault."[20]

That was true. There were many other reasons someone might support Trump for president. But let's revisit what Thiel and David Sacks had written on each topic, one at a time.

## Peter and David: Rapes are seductions that are later regretted

In 1995 Thiel and Sacks wrote that "when verbal pressure means coercion and coercion means rape, then the number of rapes will become as large as the number of seductions that are later regretted." The coauthors cast doubt on all women who spoke out about assault, as if *they* were the problem, not rapists. They continued, "Indeed, the purpose of the rape crisis movement seems as much about vilifying men as about raising 'awareness.'" Recall that in another chapter, they wrote the following about the Salem Witch Trials that "many of the accused were probably rather unpleasant people who had behaved imperfectly in the past and were partially to blame for the negative attention they received."[21] Just as witches in the 1600s had likely deserved being tortured, mutilated, and murdered, so too were the victims to blame here.

They went even further: "Since women are trained to submit to men, no possibility of consent exists for one of the parties, and rape becomes intrinsic to all heterosexual relations." By this rationale, sex wasn't about love, intimacy, or consent. It was about power, and the dynamics of domination and submission made permission irrelevant. Rather than empathizing with people who had been raped, Thiel and Sacks mused about ways to render their words powerless by making consent meaningless. They also challenged the influential words of the college administrators who sought to protect and support victims. Stanford was at fault because "instead of blaming a failed ideology, they blame these problems on a mythical 'culture of rape.' This rape culture supposedly socializes men to be aggressors and women to submit helplessly."[22]

This section of *The Diversity Myth* has attracted the most attention since 1995. Tech reporter Julia Carrie Wong wrote a scathing article in the *Guardian* about Thiel and Sacks in 2016 that cited this passage, arguing the book "suggests that he may sympathize more with Trump—who has recently been accused of sexual assault and misconduct by several women—than with his victims."[23] There were numerous examples to support Wong's critique, including *Stanford Review* articles where Sacks had criticized women who "see phallocentrism in everything longer than it is wide" and cautioned that "if you're male and heterosexual at Stanford, you have sex and then you get screwed."[24] But the full story, which went beyond a few flippant comments, answers the earlier mystery behind why Keith Rabois screamed slurs at Dennis Matthies.

* * *

On January 21, 1992, the *Stanford Review* published a special issue: "RAPE AT STANFORD." A month before, a Stanford upperclassman and former basketball star named Stuart Thomas had pled guilty to charges of statutory rape and providing alcohol to a minor after he'd gotten an underage girl drunk and then assaulted her.[25] Regarding the "verbal pressure" that Thiel and Sacks said shouldn't have been considered rape? The first-year student told him that she was a virgin and had a boyfriend, but he'd insisted they have sex anyway. As for the so-called coercion that Thiel and Sacks said shouldn't have been considered rape? She'd told him that she'd only had alcohol once before, then Thomas gave her eight servings of Peppermint Schnapps, according the police report.[26] It was a disgustingly bitter yet far too common story.

She never said yes. He got her drunk, undressed her, and raped her. That old and ugly idea, again: *He wanted it, and she was there, so she must have too.* But she never gave consent. He was six-foot-seven and she later told police that she felt "a certain coercion from Stuart's presence." The Casa Zapata Resident Advisor informed police that Thomas had planned it all out, heading into the night with the goal of getting a first-year student drunk. Thomas had allegedly told the RA that it would be better "if these girls get wasted and get fucked during their first week here at Stanford, so they learn not to do it the rest of the time they are here."[27]

Thomas was engaged when it happened; they'd made arrangements to get married in the springtime. When he met with Stanford's residence dean, Angela Rickford, he begged her to let him see the victim again. She asked him if he'd committed the crime, which he denied at first. But according to the *Stanford Daily*'s coverage of the police report, "When Mrs. Rickford insisted that Thomas tell her the truth, he then put his head in his hands, broke down and admitted the offenses to her." Dean Rickford refused to let him see the freshman girl, so he instead left a letter he wanted delivered to her, with a photograph of his fiancée inside. He wrote on the envelope, "Please read this and let me have the picture of my fiancée back."[28]

The victim was seventeen. Thomas was six years older than her.[29]

✳ ✳ ✳

The "RAPE AT STANFORD" issue included an article by David Sacks where he described the encounter in graphic detail, claiming that "if she still had the physical coordination to perform oral sex, she presumably could have uttered the word, 'no.'"[30] To be clear, the victim never, ever, said "yes," according to her testimony to police and other contemporaneous accounts.[31] Thomas was twenty-three years old when he raped an inebriated underage girl who had been at college for less than a month. He was the first student charged with sexual assault in the university's history. Stanford published a press release to address the issue, which quoted the school's president: "This incident requires me to make plain what ought to be understood by everyone in this community: sex by force or coercion, including coercion through the use of alcohol, is absolutely unacceptable here." He then warned, "Those who are found in violation of university policy in this regard will face maximum institutional sanctions, in addition to any prosecution the district attorney may undertake through the courts."[32]

Stuart Thomas was only a few credit hours away from graduating, which led David Sacks to write that "to refuse you your last four units would be extreme, not to mention cruel and unusual, punishment. So, Stu, take the degree—and run." But Sacks and his friends went beyond just defending Thomas's Eighth Amendment rights; they then proceeded to mock the victim. "She obviously was not so drunk that she passed out," Sacks wrote about "the minor, who turned eighteen a mere month after the incident," as if that made any of this somehow acceptable. Those words appeared in a section titled "Consent, Responsibility, and Oral Dexterity." He mused that statutory rape should not be considered a crime in the first place, writing that it was "a moral directive left on the books by pre-sexual revolution crustaceans," and declaring that "Most students at Stanford know that 'statutory rape' is a silly crime."[33]

Thirty years later the U.S. Sentencing Commission guidelines provided the following data: "99.5% of sexual abuse offenders were sentenced to prison; their average sentence was 211 months," or over 17.5 years, and what Sacks called a "silly crime"—the one Thomas pled guilty to, statutory rape—usually meant an average sentence of 41 months, nearly 3.5 years.[34] The laws and corresponding punishments for rape have gotten far clearer and often tougher since the 1990s. We now have words to describe getting someone too drunk to consent and then raping them. That is a Diminished Capacity Rape. Americans' cultural tolerance for such crimes has changed too. In the two decades after this particular crime was committed, sexual violence fell by half. Our laws, and our choices, prove that words do matter.[35]

But back in 1991, Stuart Thomas went free on an $80,000 bail and then reached a deal with the district attorney to receive no jail time, two years of probation, one hundred hours of community service, and a $1,000 fine. As for the "maximum institutional sanctions" from the university? The Stanford Judicial Council allowed him to graduate. They delayed his degree by two years. That was it. There were no further consequences for his actions.[36]

* * *

Keith Rabois wrote a humor piece about "The Lighter Side" of the "RAPE AT STANFORD" issue. He was joined by a sophomore student, Mike Ehrman, as they joked about the various reasons why "You Absolutely Know You Go to

Stanford When. . . ." They answered that prompt with several antigay statements, including that "males should be more weary [*sic*] of walking alone at night than females," and "the LGBCC [Lesbian Gay Bisexual Community Center] requested $110 of student money to show a pornographic how-to-be-gay video," and that "they actually might get it."[37]

The context of these statements matters. Rabois and Ehrman's older brother, Kenny, had been at Stanford together. During the spring semester of their freshman year, in May 1988, Kenny Ehrman was evicted from Otero. According to the *Stanford Daily*, "he got drunk and vandalized the house lounge," then yelled that Resident Fellow Dennis Matthies was a "fucking wimp." He then turned to Resident Advisor Jeff Sloan, who was gay, and called him "a 'faggot,' culminating months of verbal abuse of the RA."[38] The broader context matters, too, considering the ever-present threats of both the AIDS epidemic and antigay violence. Arthur Hall's death a few weeks earlier was a somber reminder of the former; as for the latter, the LGBCC had received this bomb threat a few months before: "I have planted a bomb in your building. I have planted a bomb in your building. It is set to go off at 10 a.m. tomorrow morning. That would be Monday, October 1st. I am going to kill all you faggots. Fuck you."[39]

The specific timing matters as well. Rabois, Ehrman, and Sacks had worked on the *Stanford Review*'s "RAPE AT STANFORD" publication until just days, maybe hours, before the late-night rant at Otero by Rabois, where he'd screamed, "You are going to die of AIDS" and "You're going to get what's coming to you. Damn faggot!"[40] It's possible that Rabois and Ehrman had been out partying that night to celebrate the publication being sent to the printers, but it's almost certain that the words and place Rabois chose for the outburst were motivated by the similar language Ehrman's brother had used at Otero during their freshman year.

Words do matter, both spoken and printed. Keith Rabois's slurs were not just an impulsive outburst; they were years in the making. Rabois tested the limits of taboo speech in person, just as he and Mike Ehrman had done in print, and just as Kenny Ehrman had done in Otero four years before. Rabois yelled these words to show Mike Ehrman what you could get away with if you relied on destructive words rather than destructive acts like Kenny had.[41] And so, with all that as the full background, we can now understand the most disturbing answer to "You Absolutely Know You Go to Stanford When. . . ."

Keith Rabois and Mike Ehrman suggested that Stuart Thomas's actions were somehow beneficial when he took his victim's virginity by raping her. They wrote, "You Absolutely Know You Go to Stanford When . . ." and answered, "the solution to asexually frustrated freshmen evidently lives in Zapata," the dorm where the assault took place.[42]

* * *

Julia Carrie Wong's article in 2016 renewed the controversy over sexism and accepting sexual assault in *The Diversity Myth*, and three days after it appeared in the *Guardian*, David Sacks apologized. He told Kara Swisher, then at *Recode*, that "it does not represent who I am or what I believe today. I'm embarrassed by some of my former views and regret writing them." In her article about the apology, Swisher cited only a few words from the part of *The Diversity Myth* that Wong had written about, which Swisher deemed "a truly disturbing section." She referred to Stuart Thomas as "the alleged perpetrator," even though he'd pled guilty. Beyond that, she mostly skimmed over the contents of the book, summing up that the authors had "also criticized Stanford for a number of cultural changes aimed at improving campus life for minorities, gay and lesbians and women." Swisher wrote that "the pair tried to be geek-clever, noting: 'Real diversity requires a diversity of ideas, not simply a bunch of like-minded activists who resemble the bar scene from Star Wars.'" Then she parenthetically teased, "(My opinion: That was an *epic* bar scene.)" All the other statements in *The Diversity Myth* described in this chapter went unnoticed by Swisher, and the same went for other journalists who didn't revisit what these men had written decades before.[43]

In response to Wong's article, Peter Thiel told *Forbes*: "More than two decades ago, I co-wrote a book with several insensitive, crudely argued statements. As I've said before, I wish I'd never written those things. I'm sorry for it. Rape in all forms is a crime. I regret writing passages that have been taken to suggest otherwise."[44] Thiel apologized directly with the first four sentences of that statement, but then in that last line, he claimed that others had misinterpreted his words. There was no room for misinterpretation. Thomas had pled guilty and his case was closed years before Sacks and Thiel wrote *The Diversity Myth,* but they defended a rapist anyway. "Of course, it is ludicrous to believe that anyone who had been forcefully violated would not know it and bear physical marks," they wrote in 1995. "But since a multicultural rape charge may indicate nothing more than belated regret, a woman might 'realize' that she had been 'raped' the next day or even many days later."[45] In that context, it was as if women just like this seventeen-year-old never could have been raped; she was drinking, so she had put herself in that situation.

It wasn't just crudely argued. It was cruelly argued.

By 2016 progress had been made for women's rights, and those kinds of views were far more unacceptable. This argument from any man had always been as despicable as it was harmful, but by 2016 it was widely condemned socially, so Thiel regretted "writing passages that have been taken to suggest otherwise." Even so, he only apologized for the words Wong had focused on, which stirred up controversy immediately prior to Election Day in 2016. But there was so much more in that book, which many people missed entirely, and some must have purposefully permitted. In fact, the excerpts in the following pages are the first time that most of these lines from *The Diversity Myth* have reappeared in print since the Independent Institute first published the hardcover book in 1995 and the paperback in 1998.

That matters, since Thiel eventually reached an entirely different conclusion about the book from what he told Wong. At a gala honoring him in April 2023, he reflected, "When I look back on *The Diversity Myth*, almost three decades later, I still think that almost every point we made was right. There's very little that's wrong, which is both gratifying and depressing."[46] Likewise, in an interview from August 2023 with Founders Fund's chief marketing officer to "unpack what the book got right and wrong," Thiel attested: "The specific arguments in *The Diversity Myth*, I stand by. The vast majority of them, I think they were right. The people we argued against, I think they were wrong." He claimed, "It now feels prophetic. I suppose I'm kind of proud that I wrote it, that I can say I was right about everything."[47]

## Condoleezza: Peter and David's words were "demagoguery, pure and simple"

This brings us to the next concern cited by Zuckerberg in his all-company memo about Donald Trump: racism. Speaking about *The Diversity Myth* in April 1996, Thiel claimed, "There is no problem with racist speech on campus. There is no problem with racism. There is no problem with sexism. Or, to the extent that there is a problem, it is not very big." He added, "The reason we have racial tensions in our society, the reason we have other kinds of tensions, is not because there is a problem with racism or other forms of oppression, but because people are looking for these things too much." When it came to addressing racism, he felt, "In many ways, the cure is worse than the disease at this point."[48]

In the years leading up to that declaration, Bill Shockley remained an emeritus faculty member who had been protected by Stanford's administrators and faculty for decades. He had proposed that the U.S. government pay bounty hunters to forcibly sterilize citizens with low IQs, and he estimated that 85 percent of Black Americans would qualify. In fact, he said that in a public lecture in 1986, Thiel's freshman year.[49] While Thiel worried that "people are looking for these things too much," the fact was that Stanford had endorsed and promoted Shockley's "race betterment" theorizing for decades. The university still did so while Thiel was a student. In fact, the organizers didn't just allow Shockley to lecture on campus about bounty hunters; a videographer and photographer were there, to ensure it was recorded and saved for posterity.[50]

When talking about the book, Thiel worried that "the great multicultural experiment" at Stanford had "dumbed down" its curriculum by adding more content from African American writers, scholars, and leaders throughout

American history.[51] In addition, Thiel and Sacks wrote that Stanford had diminished its educational value by creating experiential learning opportunities in partnership with community nonprofits in the Bay Area. For homework in freshman English, a professor had asked students to write grant proposals that could benefit local groups of their choosing, including "homeless advocacy projects, AIDS support groups, and environmental action leagues."[52] This eroded the value of a college education, according to *The Diversity Myth* authors, who thought that knowledge came from the writings by dead Great Men of History on the bookshelves, not the wisdom of more recent (and more overlooked) scholars or the "ordinary" men and women living in the local community. Years later Thiel would create the Thiel Fellowship, where he paid talented young people to drop out and start new ventures instead of pursuing a college degree.[53] But in the mid-1990s, he believed college was vitally important and had lost its way, so he demanded that Stanford adhere to the traditional coursework of the Western canon.[54]

Thiel and Sacks felt offended by the new additions to Stanford's curriculum, which prompted the authors to ask why, "all too often, 'multiculturalism' really means antipathy for the West." They argued that these nontraditional courses were not just a distraction; they were harmful, even anti-American: "As recycled anti-Western banalities substitute for a genuine study of Western and non-Western cultures, multiculturalism effectively is wasting some of the best years of America's brightest students. In this regard, the new curriculum exacts a steep price from liberals and conservatives, believers and heretics alike." They warned Stanford faculty and administrators: "The new canon delivers everything but the one educationally justifiable thing it promised—the serious study of other cultures."[55]

"That commentary was demagoguery, pure and simple," replied Stanford president Gerhard Casper and Stanford provost Condoleezza Rice. "They concoct a cartoon, not a description of our freshman curriculum."[56] A decade later Rice would be named the nineteenth U.S. national security advisor to the U.S. president, then the sixty-sixth American secretary of state, becoming the second woman and first African American woman to hold that post.[57] In 2017 *Politico*'s Susan B. Glasser interviewed Rice at length to get her perspective on the presidency of Donald Trump. "American democracy will survive Donald Trump," the article began. "At least Condoleezza Rice hopes so."[58] In the course of that lengthy interview, one phrase stood out.

"Words do matter," Rice declared. "I hope that we will say even more that the world is a dark place when the United States of America is not involved. It's a dark place when we don't stand up for those who just want to have the same basic values that we have." Rice had just published *Democracy: Stories from the Long Road to Freedom*. She wrote the book prior to Election Day 2016, and it became an instant bestseller. The book was "a repudiation of Trump's America First worldview," according to Carlos Lozada for the *Washington Post*.[59] Based on her interview, Glasser wrote that the book conveyed Rice's "alarm about the political wave of rising populism, nativism, protectionism and isolationism that helped boost Trump's election," which she deemed "the Four Horsemen of the Apocalypse."[60]

In 1995 Sacks and Thiel, both recent Stanford graduates, did not stand up for "the same basic values" as most Americans, not only in terms of protecting rape victims but also when it came to being "One Nation, Under God" where diversity was not a myth but a strength, and we were out of many, one. They did, however, call out Rice, as "Sovietologist and Stanford Provost Condoleezza Rice" when they quoted her in the chapter titled "Welcome to Salem" and accused Stanford administrators of treating Rabois unfairly.[61] *Words do matter.* By calling Rice a Sovietologist, were they implying that her field of research raised questions about her character? Was she, in fact, a communist? Did they mean to portray her as untrustworthy? Even anti-American?[62]

## Peter and David's views on South African apartheid

In 1977 more than a thousand Stanford students had protested apartheid when the university's leadership refused to divest from South Africa. The sit-in led to 294 arrests. The next day, 900 students showed up, chanting, "Apartheid means profit, Stanford won't stop it."[63] South African corporations had given Stanford securities worth $18.9 million at the time, and the university had a range of investments in South African companies, mining operations, and other assets. Students ran the numbers, estimating that it would cost Stanford $125 million in endowment assets to fully divest, spread among fifty-nine corporations (adjusted for inflation, all those amounts would be worth nearly five times that today).[64]

A group of enterprising seniors came up with an idea: if Stanford wouldn't divest, they'd launch a campaign to proactively invest in ways that aligned with their values.[65] In May 1986 several students created an "alternative endowment" to encourage graduates to donate to a Free South Africa Fund in lieu of a traditional alumni donation. If Stanford divested, the university would get the money. If the school didn't divest within a decade, then the funding would go toward Black South African students to pursue their education wherever they wished.[66] Soon after Nelson Mandela became president of a multiracial, democratically elected government in South Africa, all the funding raised through the alternative endowment was deposited into Stanford's Amy Biehl Fund. It had been established just months prior, in memory of a Stanford graduate and

Fulbright scholar who was murdered while doing research and volunteer work with predominantly Black communities in South Africa.[67] Stanford never fully divested from apartheid.[68]

In context, Thiel and Sacks were writing about experiences on campus that they'd had during the apartheid era, where Black South Africans endured a system of legalized racial segregation and economic discrimination, not the post-apartheid world we've lived in ever since. As *The Diversity Myth* went to print, it remained a time of uncertain outcomes, as the Mandela-led government took control, and South Africans began their search for healing through the Truth and Reconciliation Commission.[69] The moments they discussed in the book occurred in the midst of the controversies on campus about the ways the Stanford endowment profited from South Africa's system of racist oppression and financial exploitation.

Specifically, the coauthors critiqued a Stanford campus ministry for opposing apartheid: "Memorial Church's new mission focuses on social and political work, pursued with evangelical zeal—for example, writing sexual harassment policies on campus, organizing divestment efforts from South Africa, and providing sanctuary for potential conscientious objectors during the Persian Gulf War." To Thiel and Sacks, this meant that "the new multicultural religion becomes transformed into a religion of antireligiosity." They claimed: "The efforts of the official campus ministry closely resemble the social engineering pushed through the curriculum and Residential Education."[70] By arguing a campus ministry should keep quiet, Thiel and Sacks took a side in three debates at once. To them, Christians shouldn't seek equality and object to apartheid; they shouldn't work toward a safer campus culture and help victims of rape, assault, and other sex crimes; and they shouldn't protest war and promote peace.

Apparently, such activities were not Christlike.

* * *

In 2016 one of Thiel's freshmen dorm mates at Stanford, Julie Lythcott-Haims, claimed that he had told her that "apartheid was a sound economic system working efficiently, and moral issues were irrelevant." She continued, "He made no effort to even acknowledge the pain the concept of apartheid could possibly raise for me, a Black woman."[71] A spokesperson for Thiel responded to the accusation by saying that "Peter has no recollection of a stranger demanding his views on apartheid. He has never supported it, but he can easily see how a conversation might be misremembered 30 years later."[72] The language here, about "a stranger," and about the length of time since anything was said, was meant to obfuscate, marginalize, and minimize. *Words do matter.* And there were more recent publications and public statements worth reconsidering, which might clarify the matter further.

In an essay in 2009 titled "The Education of a Libertarian," Thiel wrote, "The 1920s were the last decade in American history during which one could be genuinely optimistic about politics. Since 1920, the vast increase in welfare beneficiaries and the extension of the franchise to women—two constituencies that are notoriously tough for libertarians—have rendered the notion of 'capitalist democracy' into an oxymoron." While he served on Facebook's board of directors, before the company went public, Thiel publicly argued that elections that included *women* and *welfare beneficiaries* (his words) harmed America. He went on to assert: "I no longer believe that freedom and democracy are compatible."[73] This antidemocracy sentiment was not just a one-off idea he expressed in 2009. At a conference in Miami a dozen years later, he stated that "I am probably mildly antidemocracy in all these ways" and supported the notion that "there's always some distrust of simply having voting plebiscites in this country, a somewhat healthy distrust of the mob."[74] When the choice was between universal suffrage that included people who might not share his political views, and being antidemocracy altogether, Thiel seemed to prioritize his dreams of electing more libertarian politicians over the fundamental constitutional rights of all Americans.

In three of the areas Zuckerberg cited in his message to Facebook colleagues about Donald Trump—sexual assault, racism, and sexism—Peter Thiel had made antagonistic, radical statements during the 1990s and well into the 2000s. Thiel and Sacks had minimized the pains of historically oppressed groups throughout *The Diversity Myth*—underplaying the concerns of homosexuals, rape victims, and Black South Africans during the horrors of apartheid.[75] In his 2009 essay, Thiel instead pined for a return to the bygone glory days in America where wealthy white men ruled, serving their own interests, from over a century ago.

What did he mean when he questioned the legitimacy of the God-given, constitutionally guaranteed rights of women and "welfare beneficiaries" in America? This much was clear: Thiel preferred a time before 1920, when they lacked significant influence in policymaking. He wanted to return to a less democratic era. He preferred when women, Black people, and poor white people were disenfranchised in America due to sexist, racist, and elitist laws and poll taxes.[76]

## Peter joins Stanford's faculty to teach about startups

These statements did not stop Thiel from gaining influence, as an investor and board director at scores of companies. He understood how to secure and wield power, but he also studied power in ways that many entrepreneurs and investors never do. One of the great influences on his worldview was a Stanford philosophy professor named René Girard, whom Thiel credited with inspiring him to stop copying the careers of his peers. Instead, he would quit his high-paying law-firm job and move to San Francisco. In 2016 Thiel said: "Looking back at my ambition to become a lawyer, it looks less like a plan for the future and more like an alibi for the present. It was a way to explain to anyone who would ask—to my parents, to my peers, and most of all to myself—that there was no need to worry. I was perfectly on track. But it turned out in retrospect that my biggest problem was taking the track without thinking really hard about where it was going."[77]

Girard taught at Stanford from 1981 to 1995, and he remained a mentor and friend to Thiel throughout his life. When Girard died in 2015, three people spoke at his memorial service: one of his sons, a colleague at Stanford, and Thiel.[78] Thiel credited Girard for helping him understand the concept of mimesis: that all human beings are, by our nature, imitators. Consciously defying that impulse, and rejecting what others thought, would become integral to Thiel's trademark contrarianism; he claimed it helped him succeed as an entrepreneur and investor. He left the law firm and saw the potential for Facebook to change the world—because it exploited our desires as social creatures. "Facebook first spread by word of mouth, and it's about word of mouth, so it's doubly mimetic," Thiel explained. "Social media proved to be more important than it looked, because it's about our natures."[79] With Facebook, Zuckerberg and Thiel tapped into the underlying weaknesses of our psychology and, in this light, of the fundamental flaws inherent in being human.

There is a deep history behind this school of thought about human nature. During Shakespeare's era, the word "ape" already meant both "primate" and "to imitate," as Thiel noted in an essay he wrote for a philosophy conference at Stanford hosted with Girard in 2004.[80] He argued that even before Darwin, this dual meaning of "ape" revealed a "more comprehensive account of human nature." Thiel explained, "According to Girard, all cultural institutions, beginning with the acquisition of language by children from their parents, require this sort of mimetic activity, and so it is not overly reductionist to describe human brains as gigantic imitation machines."[81]

Girard believed, and Thiel agreed, that this intrinsic urge to imitate led to rivalries, which caused violence. Thiel retold the Genesis story of Cain and Abel: both sons made sacrifices to God, but Abel gave God the very best he had, and God favored Abel. It was a surprise choice given that Cain was the firstborn. Instead of showing remorse and remedying his mistake, Cain became angry at Abel. Thiel summarized Girard's conclusion: "The war of all against all culminates not in a social contract but in a war of all against one, as the same mimetic forces gradually drive the combatants to gang up on one particular person." Cain murdered Abel, which Thiel noted was humankind's first social act after expulsion from Eden. "The war continues to escalate and there is no rational stopping point, at least not until this person becomes the scapegoat whose death helps to unite the community and bring about a limited peace for the survivors. That murder is the secret origin of all religious and political institutions."[82]

In this context, we can see that Facebook was not just an addictive college pastime that became the unplanned startup for a socially awkward college dropout. With Peter Thiel's influence and investment, it developed based on ancient ideas. Facebook proved a theory about humankind's tendencies toward mimicry and anger, and against social cohesion. Resentment and violence were central to it all along, not remorse or redemption. This tale from Genesis still worked astonishingly well in the Silicon Age. Thiel's theories about rivalries came true.

Why is humankind more like Cain than Abel? Thiel gave two reasons, based on Girard, during an interview in November 2014 with *Business Insider*: "(1) competitors tend to become obsessed with their rivals at the expense of their substantive goals, and because of that (2) the intensity of competition doesn't tell you anything about underlying value. People will compete fiercely for things that don't matter, and once they're fighting they'll fight harder and harder."[83] You just need to replace the words "rivals" with "Facebook friends" and "things that don't matter" with "likes" to have an almost complete synopsis of why Facebook worked so well.

* * *

In 2014 Thiel collaborated with Blake Masters, one of his Stanford students, to write the book *Zero to One: Notes on Startups, or How to Build the Future*. It became a #1 *New York Times* bestseller.[84] In the preceding years, Thiel had paid $200,000 to more than sixty students to drop out of college, even as Stanford students simultaneously paid tuition to take classes with him.[85] Masters attended Stanford for college and had returned for law school, too, following a brief stint at Duke. After turning his class notes into a bestseller, Masters continued his career with Thiel, first by working at Founders Fund, and eventually becoming COO of Thiel Capital and president of the Thiel Foundation.[86]

During his undergraduate years, Masters often espoused libertarian and antigovernment sentiments—even celebrated anarcho-capitalistic, antidemocracy extremists—as documents obtained by *Mother Jones* later revealed. Before Election Day in 2005, he groused about why voters "must worship that miserably peculiar American diety [*sic*] called Democracy" in an email to his fellow students where he encouraged them to read an essay by German economist (and self-described "libertarian/anarcho-capitalist philosopher") Hans-Hermann Hoppe.[87] "First, the idea of democracy and majority rule must be delegitimized," Hoppe wrote in *Democracy: The God That Failed*. He declared that "the historic transition from monarchy to democracy represents not progress but civilizational decline," because democracies rejected the "natural order" where the elites ruled when society "voluntarily acknowledged 'natural' elite—a *nobilitas naturalis.*"[88]

With childish simplicity, Hoppe assessed, "men commit more crimes than women, the young more than the old, blacks more than whites, and city dwellers more than villagers. Accordingly, changes in the composition of the sexes, age groups, races, and the degree of urbanization can be expected to have a systematic effect on crime." For Hoppe, monarchies were better than democracies, due to genetics: "because of selective mating and marriage and the laws of civil and genetic inheritance, positions of natural authority are more likely than not passed on within a few noble families." He praised monarchs who were supposedly born better due to their "long-established records of superior achievement, farsightedness, and exemplary personal conduct." He hoped that a similar political system could one day be rediscovered anew after democracy died out, resulting in "an 'anarchic' private law society" where "territorially smaller governments" would be ruled by an elite but decentralized order of leaders with "economic independence, outstanding professional achievement, morally impeccable personal life, and superior judgment and taste."[89]

According to Thiel and Masters, Hoppe's theories about superior groups of people and their elite rulers could never work in the modern world, however, because maddened mobs would unjustly kill even the best leaders. In *Zero to One*, they mused: "Perhaps every modern king is just a scapegoat who has managed to delay his own execution."[90] That was something Thiel had taught Masters in Computer Science 183, during the eighteenth class of the 2012 spring semester. In that class, "Founder as Victim, Founder as God," Thiel taught that scapegoats were often worshipped first before being sacrificed, and "kings became scapegoats who had not yet been killed. Every king was a living god. Every god was a murdered king." According to Masters's notes, Thiel cited everyone from Steve Jobs to John F. Kennedy to "the Forever 27 club, whose members include Janice Joplin, Jimi Hendrix, Jim Morrison, Kurt Cobain, Amy Winehouse, etc." Masters jotted down: "This is the set of famous musicians who all died at age 27."[91] It was an unintentional echo of E. Jean Carroll's Catch27 (and, just maybe, the universe's way of hinting that Thiel's ideas about mimesis were correct, since history's common refrains often reemerge in surprising ways).

The term "scapegoat" is commonly used, but its origin might be surprising. It all went back to Leviticus, where on the Day of Atonement, two goats were chosen for sacrifice. One was slain, but the other had the sins of the community symbolically transferred to it by the high priest, and then it would be sent into the wilderness. The root word literally meant the "escape goat," the goat that went away.[92] Nowadays, we say a person or group is being "scapegoated" when they've been unfairly persecuted, usually for something they never did or for a situation that is more complex than the blame suggests, which becomes even more compelling in the context of Girard's theories and Thiel's "secret origin of all religious and political institutions" when a leader "becomes the scapegoat whose death helps to unite the community and bring about a limited peace for the survivors."[93]

This brings us to the final concern cited by Zuckerberg in his all-company memo about Donald Trump: xenophobia.

## Peter returns to Stanford's faculty to teach about nationalism

Did Peter Thiel ever think he'd become a scapegoat himself? The full arc of his career told a different story than being falsely accused and having everything he'd touched boycotted. Even when that was threatened after he gave $1.25 million to Trump, his bet paid off. While fretting about political correctness, cancel culture, and witch hunts—about having to take the fall for something you *didn't* do, as the scapegoat—Thiel gained power as he started and invested in the companies that became some of the biggest in Big Tech, as he coached and donated to political candidates to Make America Great Again, and as he taught and mentored Stanford students whom he'd hire for Thiel Capital and his many startups. With success after success, Thiel seemed almost immune to any ugly accusation (or fact) despite his worries about unfair witch hunts—and he counseled Donald Trump, who did the same. No matter what he'd written or said since the early 1990s, Thiel gained influence, in business, politics, and society. It was as if words against him were meaningless, with no power over him.

By understanding mimesis, rivalries, unjustified scapegoating, and unjust murders, Thiel almost seemed invincible against even legitimate concerns and well-documented facts, even becoming some kind of antiscapegoat. The same went for Donald Trump. Earlier, Stanford had given Bill Shockley a platform to espouse views far outside his field of study. Then, at the height of Trump's America First presidency, Peter Thiel taught a couple of new courses at Stanford, not about venture capital at the Graduate School of Business or technology in the Computer Science Department, but about nationalism in Stanford's German Department.[94]

In 2019, two years into Donald Trump's term in office, Thiel taught about why "the current historical moment appears to be marked by opposition to globalization, which has emerged in many countries in the various forms of populism, restrictive trade policies, attacks on 'neo-liberalism,' protest parties, and localism."[95] This was also after Thiel had received New Zealand citizenship, after spending 12 days there rather than the required 1,350 days. He didn't meet the criteria for citizenship, but he received an "exceptional circumstances" waiver based on his investments. That made him a citizen of New Zealand,

Germany, and the United States.[96] In the coming years, Thiel would also apply for citizenship from the island nation of Malta.[97] As he gained citizenship in places he'd barely visited, it gave new meaning to his course title: "German 270: Sovereignty and the Limits of Globalization and Technology."

At Stanford, students could learn firsthand from the man who promised that a "political outsider" would take America "beyond the dogmas of Reaganism."[98] Just across campus from Condoleezza Rice's Stanford office, they could hear Thiel's perspective on what she had warned about in the "rising wave of populism, nativism, protectionism and isolationism that helped boost Trump's election," which she had called "the Four Horsemen of the Apocalypse."[99] In the midst of the Make America Great Again presidency that he helped make a reality, Thiel was in front of the classroom, sharing thoughts with German majors about Friedrich Nietzsche, whose Superman ideal was distorted to such evil ends, and Carl Schmitt, who was an actual member of the Third Reich and became known as "the philosophical godfather of Nazism."[100] During week nine, the topic was "Why Chinese Mothers Are Superior," an essay by Yale Law professor Amy Chua.[101] Deciding to include Schmitt's writings was especially notable, considering that Schmitt had argued in favor of burning not only "un-German" books but also texts by authors who had been influenced by "Jewish ideas" in an effort to "cleanse public life of non-Aryan, foreign elements." Among his many odious anti-Semitic writings, Schmitt asserted, "The Jew's relationship to our intellectual work is parasitical, tactical, and commercial."[102]

Thiel co-taught this course with a professor who had taught at Stanford since 1979, Russell Berman, who during this same time simultaneously advised the Trump administration by serving as a member of the State Department's policy planning staff.[103] Berman invited Thiel back for another course in 2020, "German 277: Technology and Culture Between Stagnation or Progress," which was an "examination of relations between technology and culture through a series of conversations with Peter Thiel, concerning the conditions and limits of progress." That course also included readings from Schmitt.[104] In the book that Berman and Thiel selected, *The Crisis of Parliamentary Democracy*, Schmitt claimed that diversity corrupted nations, arguing, "Democracy requires, therefore, first homogeneity and second—if the need arises—elimination or eradication of heterogeneity."[105] He wrote those words in 1923, where he also called for authoritarian leader who would take charge and enforce that homogeneity, because "the people can be brought to recognize and express their own will correctly through the right education."[106] Inflation had already spiraled out of control, with 4 million German marks equaling only 1 U.S. dollar that year.[107] A decade later, Schmitt's vision came true once Adolf Hitler became German chancellor and the Reichstag became a "one-party parliament" following a series of electoral victories that destroyed German democracy and resulted in fascism.[108]

Considering that Peter Thiel had written in 2009 that "the 1920s were the last decade in American history during which one could be genuinely optimistic about politics," and that his field of expertise was venture capital, it's a fair question to ask why he was the best person to lead discussions about Schmitt's writings in a Stanford German class in both 2019 and 2020.[109] Peter Thiel is one of the greatest entrepreneurs and venture capitalists of all time, and we can now see how his personal scholarship informed decisions throughout his wildly successful career, including the early bet on mimetic Facebook. But in the same way that Stanford supported Bill Shockley not because of his expertise in genetics, but because he'd won a Nobel Prize in an entirely different field, when Stanford undergraduates hoped to take classes with Thiel and Berman they did not care about learning philosophy. "I admire Mr. Thiel for helping found the modern financial payments system with PayPal and for supporting and inspiring hundreds of entrepreneurs through the Founders Fund and the Thiel Scholarship," one student wrote in their application for the German seminar, unironically praising Thiel for paying people to quit school. "I admire Mr. Thiel's integrity to stand by his ideas," the student explained, "and believe that this course will add unparalleled breadth to my Stanford education."[110]

In high school history and civics classrooms across America, students had heard about ideals that were different from what those Stanford students read in Schmitt, Nietzsche, and even Chua. Instead, they'd studied stories of people who make America great, truly the greatest, with their goodness. These better rebels had remarkable integrity, as they stood up for principles like freedom and fairness, yet they were flawed and sometimes failed, because even heroes make mistakes and we're all human. They were imperfect in their pursuits of liberty and justice, but homogeneity was never the goal. Their imperfections revealed our common humanity, and the moments when they'd failed created new moments for grace and understanding. That was how we all became more perfect—in our reunions and redemptions, not our retributions—for we became a more perfect people through individual good faith efforts, which would heal divisions and bring more freedom and fairness to more people.

This basic high school history might have been too rosy, a Norman Rockwell depiction of America. But that could work out just fine once teachers went beyond the 1940s with his Four Freedoms series and debated the ones about justice from the 1960s, too, which revealed the troubles of integration as the *New Kids in the Neighborhood* were met with skeptical expressions on young white faces, in Rockwell's famous painting, or when violence around Ruby Bridges reified *The Problem We All Live With* when all she wanted to do was go to school.[111]

Those classroom conversations across America showed how neighbors solved problems despite differences, in communities of all kinds, not through some final solution resulting from the superior judgment of like-minded elites. America was great, because its people could be so good, and when they weren't, we believed in second chances. Because while each of us is imperfect, we're in this together. And nothing could diminish our inherent equality under God.

This wider and weirder—yet more nuanced and noble—story of America taught lessons about how everybody mattered while walking the *Long Road to Freedom* together, in a vibrant, multicultural nation where victims could be liberators, democracy would be messy, but diversity was no myth. At least for now, our students still pledged allegiance as "one nation, under God, indivisible, with liberty and justice for all." Both liberty *and* justice. Not for one, but for *all*.

Recently, democracy has seemed too angry, too cruel, with too many disputes over differences. We tire of the bitter rivalries of this two-party system, where both sides have become twin Cains constantly trying to murder each other. Our politicians live as enemies, while the media thrives on the armies at war. Nevertheless, our ugly debates and overheated election seasons are far more attractive than Carl Schmitt's antidemocratic homogeneity of the 1920s, 1930s, and 1940s. It was an era Thiel longed to return to, when America First had originally meant keeping us out of World War II. Knowing that history, in fullness, can help us.

A couple of Yale Law students had come up with the name, "The Emergency Committee to Defend America First," but that was a mouthful. They needed something more memorable for their nationwide campaign. They shortened it to the America First Committee, and more than 800,000 people would join their isolationist movement by the early 1940s.[112] Many were pacifists, but others joined due to sinister, racist nativism. In fact, its spokesman believed inaction against the Nazis was the wise course of action due to "race betterment."

"Our bond with Europe is a bond of race and not of political ideology," declared Charles Lindbergh, the famous aviator and spokesman for America First, in October 1939. "We had to fight a European army to establish democracy in this country. It is the European race we must preserve; political progress will follow." To Lindbergh, fighting the Germans would be like fighting ourselves: "If the white race is ever seriously threatened, it may then be time for us to take our part in its protection, to fight side by side with the English, French, and Germans, but not with one against the other for our mutual destruction." He urged his listeners to join the battle only if it became a race war against "Asiatic intruders"—he warned about the Russians, Persians, Turks, or Jews—who defiled America's "most priceless possession: our inheritance of European blood." Lindbergh asserted, "Racial strength is vital, politics is a luxury."[113]

America entered the war after the Japanese attacked Pearl Harbor, which was just over two years after Lindbergh's speech. His white nationalism, and the xenophobia of the first America First, seems shocking today. So perhaps those details belong in our high school curriculum, too? It's all part of America's rich and complex story, right along with the date that still lives in infamy, our personal family lore about those who fought in the Second Great War, and our collective public memory about the Greatest Generation's fight for liberty and justice for all.[114]

## Thielology: A collection of random contrarian impulses?

Between the time when Peter Thiel called Provost Condoleezza Rice a Sovietologist and accused Stanford of teaching a "dumbed down" curriculum full of "recycled anti-Western banalities" and when he stood at the front of a Stanford German classroom during the twenty-first century's America First presidency while paying students to drop out of college, he had made many iconoclastic statements, some of them shocking and hurtful. This was more than contrarianism. This was contradictory, confounding, and downright confusing, a churning and mighty force made of somewhat controlled creative chaos. But that was Peter Thiel.

Did Thiel operate based on a coherent ideology, or, as Thiel biographer Max Chafkin has wondered, was his core philosophy too hard to pin down? Was it just "a collection of random contrarian impulses," with "aspects of Thiel's politics that aren't libertarian at all; they're closer to authoritarianism," as Chafkin believed?[115] Was that it? As Chafkin concluded in *The Contrarian: Peter Thiel and Silicon Valley's Pursuit of Power*: "Thiel's ideology is not especially coherent, but to the extent there was an ideology, it was that a less democratic America, purged of its multicultural delusions and pieties, would somehow lead to economic and technological progress. A critic might call this fascistic; Thiel called it going 'back to the future.'"[116] Was Thiel a fascist? Was this incipient totalitarianism? Or was his antigovernment and profreedom philosophy more libertarian, even reflecting ideas about business and society that many Americans share?[117] Was this more mainstream? Was "back to the future" just another way to describe Donald Trump's promise to Make America Great Again?

While Thiel's philosophies might seem enigmatic, he has made statements over the years that shed light on his beliefs. Thiel was raised in an Evangelical Christian family, and he stated, "I believe Christianity is true" in a 2011 interview with the *New Yorker*'s George Packer where he was quick to add that he didn't want to convert others to his beliefs.[118] A decade later he warned against being "hyper-Christian or an intensification of certain Christian ideas." That line came during an interview at the Culture, Religion, and Technology conference with Bambi Francisco Roizen in 2021.[119] With his words that evening, we could gain deeper insights into his beliefs and their impacts.

Thiel told Roizen: "If you lose faith in Christ and in the resurrection of Christ, in one sense, in theory, everything goes. I mean, you can become a Nietzschean

Superman, you can become a relativistic person who just plays video games in the basement. In theory, everything goes. Ayn Rand, all these different things."[120] With Rand's freedom-above-all-else philosophies, that approach made logical sense. If there was no God, people could live and let live. To each his own. The individual could be all that mattered.

Yet, Thiel continued, people *weren't* opting to do whatever they wanted. "In practice, the overwhelming tendency seems to be towards something like politically correct wokeness, hyper-Christianity, communism, different things like this, and I would suggest that there's nothing that new about it." He then claimed that communism had its origins in this so-called hyper Christianity, where "what animated these things was always some idea like we're going to be more Christian than the Christians."[121] That idea mirrored Rand's sentiment that Jesus's teachings were "the best kindergarten of communism possible."[122] Empathy could become a slippery slope, Thiel argued, because in his view, the Marxists eventually became mass murderers by thinking: "The Christians aren't doing enough for the poor and we're going to do *even more*, and we're going to have heaven on earth, and we're going be prepared to kill millions of people to show how serious we are and we're doing *more*."[123]

As a result, Thiel also had concerns about Christians who tended to the suffering or showed a preferential option for the poor. "There is something about the Judeo-Christian tradition in history where it always takes the side of the victim," he said. "You know, it's Cain and Abel versus Romulus and Remus: same story, different perspective." Here, Thiel was referring to the founding myth of Rome, where the gods favored Romulus (who proceeded to consolidate his power and kill his brother, unlike Abel who won divine approval then was unfairly murdered). "There is something that is essentially Christian about this concern for victims and then there is something about that that could get weaponized and radicalized." The result would be, as he'd put it earlier, "politically correct wokeness, hyper-Christianity, communism, different things like this."[124]

✳ ✳ ✳

How can we decipher Thiel? How do we understand his ideology, his theology? He has already told us the solution. Thiel thought that "the secret origin of all religious and political institutions" was discovered in one phenomenon: the scapegoat.[125] Yet according to Christian teachings, Jesus broke humanity's unending cycle to need unwarranted scapegoats and merciless slaughter. It meant putting down your weapons, whether they had been used in sin or atonement, to murder your own brother like Cain had or to sacrifice animals like God once required.

"To believe in the crucified one is to want no other victims," S. Mark Heim, a religious studies professor at Yale Divinity School, has explained in an essay titled "The End of Scapegoating." "To depend on the blood of Jesus is to refuse to depend on the sacrificial blood of anyone else. It is to swear off scapegoats."[126] God subverted people's expectations about who should be favored; the first became last and the last would be first, an enduring lesson that went back to Abel's better offering and his victory in victimhood with God favoring him.[127] God surprised us once more after Jesus's death, because Christians were no longer required to sacrifice animals to seek redemption. They were asked to become living sacrifices, forfeiting their self-interests to serve God and others.[128]

The historical events that culminated in Jesus's execution might have ended with his death. But that didn't happen. "Instead, an odd new counter-community arises," Heim noted, "dedicated both to the innocent victim whom God has vindicated by resurrection and to a new life through him that requires no further such sacrifice."[129] More than man's vengeful politics, rather than us-versus-them, this counter-community came together and invited others in. For Heim, this taught Christians another lesson that was timeless, about how people should live in community and not for themselves alone.

That *was* odd. It was countercultural and against human nature. Because instead of the normal power dynamics of domination over others—instead of obeying egocentric impulses, of greediness, quarrelsomeness, and selfishness—this was, indeed, a victim's revolution. Stanford Memorial Church encouraged students to choose self-sacrifice, to decide to forgive, and to work to repair. Nothing about it was *weaponized*: the Christian life meant doing justice, loving mercy, and walking humbly; and if along the road you came upon a wounded stranger, you'd help them up, then pay others to help them heal; and if someone slapped you, you'd turn the other cheek, you'd give them the shirt off your back, you'd go the extra mile; and then you'd need to find it in your heart to forgive, not just once, not even seven times would be generous enough, but Jesus encouraged forgiveness seventy times seven times, limitless love.

So Thiel was wrong about caring for victims becoming weaponized, but he was right about the radical difference it could make. Nothing was more *radical* than Christianity, in sacrifice, in forgiveness, and in love.[130]

＊＊＊

In 1995 Thiel and Sacks had criticized Stanford Memorial Church when students spoke out against apartheid and ministered to women who had been assaulted.[131] Those Christians had aided the ailing, such as a seventeen-year-old girl who had been raped by a man six years older than her. They'd tried to prevent sexual assault through new codes of conduct, and they were there with mercy, helping victims in their darkest hours. They also cared for "a stranger," to use the words from Thiel's spokesman when a woman accused him of asserting that "apartheid was a sound economic system working efficiently, and moral issues were irrelevant."[132] Based on their actions, these Christians at Stanford showed that every person mattered, all were equal, and that they had moral duties toward someone they'd never met suffering under apartheid a world away. Jesus told his followers that this was life's purpose all along, to love God and neighbor, not to pursue prestige or power or wealth. That was the real Golden Rule, not that "he who has the gold makes the rules."[133] Stanford's campus ministry showed mercy and love to the oppressed. Thiel and Sacks condemned them for it.

In fact, blaming a student ministry for protecting innocent people who had been treated inhumanely, including people under apartheid's terrors or fellow Stanford students who had been raped, was Thiel's own scapegoating of those who were, to quote First Peter, tending to the flock.[134] It was a sad irony. These Christians were living like Jesus, who chose to spend his time with the outcasts, the diseased, the wayward, and the loneliest. He was anti-elite, because he left no one out. He was antiauthoritarian, a better rebel who taught radical love and loved all. He ministered everywhere he went. That was why the Christians at Stanford were provictim and antiapartheid, not because they were promised power or fame or money for it, but because it was a small self-sacrifice compared to Jesus's tragic trials, the most unjust in history. He took everyone's place, as "the goat that goes away," taking away all sins as the ultimate scapegoat. Every other priest had to sacrifice something else to get right with God. No one needed to do that now, because Jesus lived a perfect life of sacrifice and then sacrificed himself. That's what these Christians believed.

*Words do matter*, since the scriptures taught that Jesus was there long before Romulus and Remus or Cain and Abel. He was the Word from the start.[135] Soldiers dressed him in a fake royal robe and a crown formed from thorns; they hurled slurs at him, spat on him, and spurned him; they gambled for his garments—every action, a new abuse against the King of the Jews. Then the sinless was slain for all sinners.[136] Believing in redemption by grace is why Stanford Memorial Church counseled rape victims and protested apartheid. Their acts weren't insincere or some form of performative moral posturing to further the "social engineering" of a "new multicultural religion." *Words do matter*, because the people's words, not just the government's decrees, decided Jesus's fate. The priests and other elites of the ruling class urged them on. Pontius Pilate had turned to the people and asked if they wanted Jesus to go free, knowing the elites had turned him in out of their own self-interest, but the priests riled up the angry crowd to demand Jesus's death.[137] The crowds had sung hosannas on Jesus's way into Jerusalem; the mobs screamed "Crucify Him!" on his way to

Golgotha. They lynched a blameless man for sedition and freed Barabbas, the insurrectionist.[138]

In 2009 here was Thiel's assessment: "Politics gets people angry, destroys relationships, and polarizes peoples' vision: the world is us versus them; good people versus the other." The bitter irony would only grow in intensity over the next decade of embitterment, once Thiel become a kingmaker for an extraordinary politician who had often decried being the victim of a witch hunt, a frequent scapegoat. Years before, in 2009, Thiel had argued: "Politics is about interfering with other people's lives without their consent."[139]

*Words do matter. Without their consent.* It was a bold statement from the man who, over a decade prior, had defended a rapist and then criticized a church group when they showed mercy to sexual assault victims. This was the man who'd founded Palantir in 2003, a year before he invested in Facebook. Later he'd also invest in Anduril and Clearview AI. We all became increasingly surveilled, with wiretapped lives and intensifying unease about what they knew about our private information. We'll discover more about that in the third section of this book, and we'll learn how Thiel profited both coming and going. But as we find out more, we should pause before making judgments.

As Mark Heim concluded, "One of the crucial things that makes the Church a new community is its constitution in solidarity not *against* some sacrificial victim, but by identification with the crucified one. The moment we point a finger at some 'they' as Jesus' killers, we have enacted the sin that the very particularity of the cross meant to overcome."[140] In other words, "That's not fundamentally different from what it is that you're making your judgments about," as Dennis Matthies had once said.[141] We must explore these concerns deeply, thoughtfully, carefully—and humbly. We must resist the self-satisfied urge to blame others and revel in righteousness.

Because this is not simple bigotry. It is more complicated than that.

# CHAPTER 9

# RAPE WITH AN ENGRAVED INVITATION

Travis Kalanick, Uber

As Uber grew, its employees crossed many lines. They defied city and state laws, social norms, and prior expectations about privacy. In 2012 an Uber data scientist wrote a post for the company website titled "Rides of Glory," where he boasted about surveilling people who had been part of one-night stands, because the data indicated they'd taken a late-night Uber then ordered another ride from near that destination early the next morning. "The world has changed, and gone are the days of the Walk of Shame," he wrote. "We live in Uber's world now."[1]

The surveillance capitalism of the Silicon Age has prevailed in moments like those because we signed up for it. We didn't know we had, because we'd agreed to hundreds of thousands of pages of legal agreements that we never looked at. But they can surveil us because we've allowed them to—in fact, because we've actively agreed to it. Uber analyzed the data to track "anyone who took a ride between 10 p.m. and 4 a.m. on a Friday or Saturday night, and then took a second ride from within 1/10 of a mile of the previous night's drop-off point 4–6 hours later (enough for a quick night's sleep)." Instead of the walk of shame, the people who partook in a "Ride of Glory" were nicknamed RoGers.[2]

In a not-all-that-scientific and utterly invasive analysis, the author reached a conclusion that said more about the company's culture than what he'd learned in his "study." He blogged about how Uber's data showed that more people did this on Cinco de Mayo than on April 20. That was just so he could force a bad joke about tequila versus marijuana. There were more one-night stands in early May, so maybe liquor had been a factor. But a few days earlier, on 4/20, he wondered whether there was "something happening that day such that people are otherwise too preoccupied?"[3]

When a stranger uses state-of-the-art monitoring devices to track people without their knowledge, tags their account as someone who had a one-night stand (to use his term, "Brief overnight weekend stays"), and then maintains that information on them to see how often and when they repeat that pattern of behavior—most of us would consider that alarming, and possibly deserving of a search warrant. It might seem like a far-fetched perversion of tech's powers, almost a poorly designed plot to a bad sci-fi horror movie, about a nerd-turned-psycho-stalker. But it wasn't fiction. And these weren't the private journals of some pervert. This entire account was made public on purpose. In fact, it was expressly written to be publicized, on Uber's official company website at http://blog.uber.com/ridesofglory.[4]

And it wasn't confined to that one analysis. They called their map of all active Ubers "God View," a name that showed how they felt about the powers at their fingertips. And, as we now know, they used it regularly. A few months prior, in September 2011, Uber launched in Chicago.[5] It was their first location between the coasts, shortly after expanding to Seattle and New York City and before they took on Boston and DC. To show off their power, there was allegedly a giant screen at the party that monitored thirty celebrities, venture capitalists, and politicians in God View.[6] Without their knowledge, the map would have shown their whereabouts in real-time throughout the night to the partygoers in Chicago (whether Uber employees or not).[7]

This attitude prevailed at Uber in the coming years, until one executive used God View in 2014 to track Johana Bhuiyan, a journalist from *BuzzFeed*. He used the tool to see which car she was arriving in. "There you are," he greeted her, then gestured to the iPhone in his hand and boasted, "I was tracking you."[8] During their conversation, he shared with her the complete list of every recent ride she'd taken, to demonstrate the power of the technology.[9] All that was without her permission.[10]

Just a few weeks earlier, another *BuzzFeed* reporter, Charlie Warzel, had published screenshots from Uber's website. Uber's Lyon office debuted a new promotion: a chance to take a twenty-minute Uber ride with a French supermodel. The words *Avions de chasse* translated as "fighter jets," but the #UberAvions campaign meant "the colloquial term to designate an incredibly hot chick," according to the company. In American slang, the term was "bombshell." Uber's website listed the steps to sign up for the app and make a request to be driven around by one of eight gorgeous women, who were pictured on the site in bikinis and lingerie, promising to make the rider "the luckiest co-pilot of Lyon." The Uber website promised: "Lucky you! the world's most beautiful 'Avions' are waiting for you on this app. Seat back, relax and let them take you on cloud 9!" and asked, "Who said women don't know how to drive?"[11]

Sarah Lacy, a former senior editor at *TechCrunch* and the founder and editor of *PandoDaily*, read Warzel's story and decided that she had reached her limit. In a scathing article, she blamed Uber's "asshole culture" as the reason she'd deleted the app from her phone. "I've never had much of an issue with Kalanick's hard charging competitive nature or libertarian beliefs," she wrote. "But this sexism and misogyny is something different and scary."[12] Kalanick had already felt unfairly targeted by the media. But Lacy's criticisms struck a nerve, according to Mike Isaac in *Super Pumped*. He asked Uber's senior vice president of business, Emil Michael, "How would they like it if we did it to them?"[13]

A few weeks after Lacy's article appeared online, Kalanick and Michael attended a dinner together, where Kalanick continued to grouse that the negative publicity was unmerited. Michael went even further, proposing that Uber spend a million dollars to hire researchers and journalists to dig up dirt on people like Sarah Lacy. They already knew that they could "prove a particular and very specific claim about her personal life," according to Ben Smith, *Buzzfeed*'s editor-in-chief. In fact, Michael even argued that Lacy should be held "personally responsible" for any woman who followed her lead, deleted the Uber app, and then was sexually assaulted in a taxicab. We know all this because another *BuzzFeed* journalist had also been invited to the dinner, and no one had told him that the comments were to be off the record, so what Kalanick and Michael told the group became public information.[14]

This was not during the startup's earliest days; in fact, Uber's revenues would reach $495.3 million in 2014.[15] But as Mike Isaac revealed, it had required subterfuge: Uber's software engineers had camouflaged its app on iPhones to monitor all kinds of data from individual iPhones without anyone knowing. That way, once the app had been deleted, or even when the device itself had been wiped clean, Uber could gather data unnoticed. This was part of a pattern. On another occasion, Apple's CEO Tim Cook asked about the governance concerns resulting from a Google executive being on Uber's board, since Google was competing with Apple (and Uber for that matter). "I know what the hell I'm doing," Kalanick retorted, according to Isaac. "The board is irrelevant. I hand pick all these guys. They do what I tell them, and the way I've structured things, I do what I want."[16]

Still, there was mounting evidence that Uber's God View posed legal concerns. Under oath, Uber's former forensic investigator, Ward Spangenberg, stated that "Uber's lack of security regarding its consumer data was resulting in Uber employees being able to track high profile politicians, celebrities, and even personal acquaintances of Uber employees, including ex-boyfriends/girlfriends, and ex-spouses," all in violation of government regulations and the data privacy and consumer protection laws on the books.[17] Spangenberg had sounded the alarm when he realized that every Uber employee, not just the small security team he was a part of, could access this data. He then decided to sue Uber after he claimed that the company had terminated him after he'd raised these concerns about privacy violations.[18] The New York attorney general decided to take action, too, and pursued the case throughout 2015. On January 6, 2016, Uber settled out of court for $20,000.[19] The fine equated to 0.0003 percent of its revenues that year.[20]

Unfortunately, Spangenberg's warnings that Uber wasn't adequately protecting people's data came true. In fact, it would all become blackmail fodder for decades, since fifty-seven million driver and rider accounts leaked in a cyberattack later in 2016. Kalanick ordered for that scandal to be kept secret, and Uber paid a $100,000 ransom. Once it had paid up, Uber tracked down the hackers, got them to sign nondisclosure agreements, and hid the issue from the public. No one knew their data had leaked until November 21, 2017, when the company conducted an internal review that had been mandated by its board.[21] "None of this should have happened, and I will not make excuses for it . . . we will learn from our mistakes," came the response.[22] Uber followed the Silicon Valley PR playbook: say you're sorry, gather data and grow at all costs, go too far with it and make mistakes, repent, and repeat. Get data and grow, make mistakes, get called out, repent, and repeat. Silicon into gold and power.

Years later a federal jury convicted Uber's chief security officer for his role in the coverup.[23] He was the first corporate executive in history to be found guilty of crimes related to a data breach by outsiders. During sentencing, U.S. District Judge William Orrick stated that he believed that Travis Kalanick also shared in the blame. From the bench, he wondered aloud why the CEO had not also been charged.[24]

* * *

In March 2010 Travis Kalanick had published "The Whole Truth and Nothing but the Truth, So Help Your Reputation" on his personal blog. In it, he argued, "we are fooling ourselves into thinking that indiscretions will be completely forgotten—the best case is that the most common indiscretions get pushed off the indiscretion list," in other words, social mores and morals will fade away while everyone gives up all their expectations of privacy. They might even embrace hedonism as he had. He explained: "Now some of us may hate that all of this information gets out there, that all of these reviews are so easily created, that we are so exposed to the public . . . that cheating on a wife, or a business colleague no longer can happen in the dark, but hyper-transparency is the world we are increasingly living in and we all better get used to it."[25] The sin wasn't the problem. Nor was it that the sin was now known, and that the sinner was seen. Kalanick believed that adultery, or any other form of cheating in life or in business, would be "pushed off the indiscretion list" and no longer be considered wrong.

"We live in Uber's world now," they thought, where Uber's powers seem to ensure that whatever it declared was right would be right. God View justified all, money vindicated the excesses, and expansion absolved the costs. Or so they thought. "Its [*sic*] just that those of us that are adults right now are carrying an old belief that what happens in the past stays there," Kalanick concluded in the blog post. "That's a luxury that is about to die and we all better get used to it." Ryan Graves responded with a comment, beginning by quoting the overused aphorism, "the truth shall set you free." Then he wrote a prophecy of his own about reputations: "it's time we start embracing this change. i really can't see how someone can say rep is dead . . . rep is just as important as it ever was, it's just more accessible now." Graves was one of the first recruits to the Church of Creative Capitalism, or maybe it should have been called the JamPad Cult of Excess. He had just prophesied the downfall of its founder, the man who had created such superpowers with Uber's God View. The extremes of Kalanick's vision—of a world of complete surveillance, where all was seen and everything became known—would increasingly become reality. He got that right.

But what was wrong was still wrong. And his indiscretions would ruin him.

## Ayn's perfect man, the rapist protagonist

Early in *The Fountainhead*, Howard Roark built the Stoddard Temple, but the project was put on hold right before its debut due to his unorthodox design. Hopton Stoddard sued him for breach of contract and malpractice and he won, but Ayn Rand made it clear that Roark was the moral victor. He'd received support during the court proceedings from the femme fatale Dominique Francon. Some literary critics have argued that she was even a co-protagonist in book. While Roark was the Übermensch, Francon was the one who recognized his virtues. Yet she did this only once she came around, by the end of the book, to Rand's individualist ideals: that what mattered, above all else, was the self-serving, dominant man.[26]

At first, Francon married Roark's foil, Peter Keating, a man who conformed to the status quo and seemed successful to the outside world for doing so. In an audacious move for that era, Francon asked Keating to marry her. He accepted, they did the I do's, and then she went off and cheated on him with Roark. Only after they had sex did she tell Roark two things: first, that she loved him, and second, by the way, she was also married to the man who was his exact opposite. She eventually left Keating, married someone else, left him, and then married Roark.

*Words do matter*, even when someone contends that vows do not, and rules don't apply to them. Given that, how should we describe Uber, a business that maximized growth with its do-whatever-it-takes approach to world domination that seemed to influence every decision? What word best defines a venture where growth and dominance are the main goals, and where clear consent is nonexistent, due to inscrutable agreements we eagerly agree to but never read? What word works, if we invited them into our lives like that? When we hate the way it feels to lose our privacy but cannot do anything about it? Uber's God View "hyper-transparency" meant its executives could boast about surveilling celebrities, stripping them of their privacy, while Uber's engineers tracked former partners, ex-spouses, and anyone with the app on their iPhone even after it was deleted. Consider how invasive Uber became, by surveilling strangers who had one-night stands then bragging about it on the corporate blog. What word worked best?

Instead of one word, perhaps we should start with a phrase. How should we think about such intense individualism-above-all-others, the astonishing acceptance of might-makes-right at all costs? One of Kalanick's favorite quotes was Alec Baldwin's famous line in *Glengarry Glen Ross* from the "Coffee is for closers" scene, where he told business leaders to remember their A-B-Cs, "A-Always, B-Be, C-Closing. Always be closing!" (Less well remembered was the fact that the ABCs came during the same scene when Baldwin's character screamed, "You can't close the leads you're given, you can't close shit, you are shit!" called his employees "you fucking faggots," and yelled, "You think this is abuse? You think this is abuse, you cocksuckers?").[27] Kalanick repeated the ABC mantra himself, as he raised round by round and conquered city after city. He even made a version of this phrase a corporate value at Uber: "Always Be Hustlin.'"[28] But the word that best describes such dominance-at-any-cost is neither closing nor hustling. It is not scoring or conquering, or even domination or conquest. It's not quite, but it's nearly . . . rape.

Or, to use Ayn Rand's phrase, it's "rape with an engraved invitation."[29]


✳ ✳ ✳


When *The Fountainhead* first came out in 1943, the American public was confronted with two extremely controversial moments in the book: the detonation of a public housing complex and what became popularly known, quite simply, as "the rape scene." Both sections fulfilled an ideological commitment Roark had made to himself, and which made him Rand's ideal man. Destroying public housing symbolized Rand's message, about the virtue of selfishness, as did "the rape scene," which was an extreme moment for American literature.

In the early 1940s such explicit erotica was risqué, the most scandalous part of *The Fountainhead*, and one reason for the novel's vast influence and wildfire popularity. Rand talked about it with similar words on different occasions, as "rape with an engraved invitation" and "rape by engraved invitation."[30] Following the breakthrough success of *The Fountainhead*, this same kind of sadomasochistic spectacle reappeared in other Rand works: *Atlas Shrugged*'s heroine, Dagny Taggart, had sex with three different men in similar scenes. Rand's characters often treated sex as a tool, which got them what they wanted, no matter what others desired. As Rand biographer Jennifer Burns put it, for Rand, sex was not about consent, intimacy, and love but power through control. Sex was an act of dominance. As Burns noted, in Rand's world, "Lovers don't hold hands, they hold wrists."[31]

In Rand's debut novel, Roark forced himself on Francon after a wordless back-and-forth of dominance and submission.[32] In the original drafts of the book, Rand included dialogue between Francon and Roark (her: "What do you want?" him: "You know what I want") and then repeated it in another scene before their first sexual encounter (him: "What do you want?" her: "You know what I want"). But during the editing process, Rand made the choice to cut out those words. She left any mutuality unspoken, entirely deleting verbal consent from the narrative.[33] Instead, Rand replaced it with thoughts of violating, followed by acts of violence.

Rand made clear Francon's fear: "her eyes wide, colorless, shapeless in terror." Rand described Roark's pleasure at her horror: "He was laughing. There was the movement of laughter on his face, but no sound." Rand detailed Francon's resistance: "She tried to tear herself away from him. The effort broke against his arms that had not felt it," and "she thrust her elbows at his throat, twisting her body to escape." Rand told how he asserted himself, violently: "Her fists beat against his shoulders, against his face. He moved one hand, took her two wrists and pinned them behind her, under his arm, wrenching her shoulder blades."[34]

This was rape, no doubt about it.

＊＊＊

What about the "engraved invitation" part? There were no words, because Rand edited them out, so the consent was supposedly implicit. Before the encounter, Francon's mind had wandered to Roark, who had taken a job as a lowly stonecutter but had kept his integrity intact: "She thought of the quarry worker. She thought of being broken—not by a man she admired, but by a man she loathed. She let her head fall down on her arm; the thought left her weak with pleasure." On the very next page, Rand mentioned that some of Roark's coworkers had jail records, which led Francon to think, "She wondered whether they whipped convicts nowadays. She hoped they did." Violence had precipitated and predicted the rape scene in numerous ways: Francon scratched a marble fireplace and called on Roark to fix it, all in a ruse to get him into her bedroom. Then he broke it into pieces. He described how marble formed: "Pressure is a powerful factor. It leads to consequences which, once started, cannot be controlled."[35]

Days passed, and Francon went out on horseback to search for Roark, but he was gone. Furious, she whipped her horse into a frenzy. When she encountered Roark, she whipped him across the face. All that wordlessly foreshadowed the rape scene. Rand described the assault with gruesome imagery: "she fought like an animal," "the hatred, the helpless terror in her blood," and "the sudden pain shot up, through her body, to her throat, and she screamed." Afterward, she considered taking a bath, but then she noticed the bruises on her body, so she chose not to, lying on the floor until dawn.[36]

Rand later reflected on Francon's choices: "Like most women, and to a greater degree than most, she is a masochist and she wishes for the happiness of suffering at Roark's hands." Rand also explained that her "man who has reached perfection" was now a rapist but remained flawless. He was justified due to a sadistic form of machoism that Rand praised: "It is primarily a feeling of wanting her and getting her, without great concern for the question of whether she wants it. Were it necessary, he could rape her and feel perfectly justified. Needless to say it is she who worships him, and loves him much more than he loves her. He is the god. He can never become a priest. She has to be the priestess."[37]

*He is the god*, Ayn Rand said. And Roark was irresistible, even though Francon resisted, because as Rand explained in a letter, "A man who would force himself on a woman against her wishes would be committing a dreadful crime."[38] Rand could claim that Francon's wishes had been left unspoken, since she'd had the words in there but then took them out. But what was left as a result? This wasn't "rape in all forms is a crime," as Peter Thiel had said. This was not: "I regret writing passages that have been taken to suggest otherwise."[39] No, this wasn't Thiel circa 2016, when he expressed regret. This was remorseless and selfish. As a result, for Rand, it was virtuous. That was how powerful men justified thinking that "the number of rapes will become as large as the number of seductions that are later regretted," and "rape becomes intrinsic to all heterosexual relations," which "socializes men to be aggressors and women to submit helplessly."[40] That's what Thiel and David Sacks wrote in the 1990s, after Stuart Thomas, age twenty-three, raped a first-year student, age seventeen. She didn't consent, but she didn't say no, and she had supposedly said yes to all those boozy drinks.[41] *Hadn't she been asking for it?*

The words from Thiel and Sacks in the early 1990s had echoed Rand's heroine, where she wrote that women wanted it all along, even when Francon did not consent, even when she fought back.[42] Yet were Thiel and Sacks, as well as Rabois and all the other contributors to the *Stanford Review*'s "RAPE AT STANFORD" issue, being contrarian, or were their ideas more mainstream in modern America than we wanted to admit? Wasn't Rand's approach the same justification given by too many men? Were they just addressing a culture-wide corruption regarding consent, the insidious poison of permissionlessness, the unspoken acceptance of "she wanted it," "she liked it," or "she was asking for it," although she said nothing? Even if she never said yes? That was how these actions were justified, according to scholars who studied the topic. The conclusion from 183 interviews with rapists: "Rape supportive attitudes, expectations for having sex, misperceptions of sexual intent, victims' alcohol consumption, attempts to be alone with her, and the number of consensual sexual activities prior to the unwanted sex were significant predictors of perpetrators' post-assault use of justifications."[43]

When silence supposedly affirmed, did words matter anymore? And what about the words that came after? That was all just locker room banter. For Rand, rape became a masculine right, even a manly achievement, so she justified an evil act. It wasn't *wrong*. It wasn't even something she deemed *vaguely acceptable*. Instead of an unequivocal evil, rape became good—*a positive good*, a 1, not a 0. Too few people rejected that thinking. For example, when Donald Trump was a first-time political candidate in April 2016, he declared that he was an Ayn Rand fan who identified the most with Howard Roark and he believed the Bible's best lesson was about vengefulness, to "take life for life, eye for eye, tooth for tooth."[44]

One time Rand was asked, "In the event that you re-wrote your novels, would you liberate your heroines, and change the way they subject themselves to passive behavior in romance?" She responded, scornfully, "Dagny is very passive: In *Atlas Shrugged*, she's nearly raped three times, by the three men in her life. Dominique, the heroine of *The Fountainhead*, is raped. If this is passivity, make the most of it."[45] So, there we have it. This was rape after all.

Make the "most" of being raped, Rand encouraged decades ago. But is modern American culture any different? What's popular today? What are people reading now? The best-selling book of the twenty-first century so far sold 15.2 million copies from 2011 to 2020. Along with its two sequels, total sales were 35 million print copies and e-books.[46] This provocative trilogy showed that sex still sells, just like Rand's scandalous bestsellers, not as part of a healthy and respectful relationship but rather as power over another person: beginning when an innocent young virgin named Steele found no strength to resist the controlling demands of a troubled, twisted, and maybe even sociopathic billionaire.

There was no right or wrong, just *Fifty Shades of Grey*, with nothing in black-and-white. As every choice became a relativistic gray, there were no lines the powerful wouldn't cross as they made choices to take what they believed to be theirs—and everything was and every woman could be, too. "If this is passivity, make the most of it," Rand instructed. As no one stopped them, black became gray to them, and power didn't corrupt but instead seemingly purified, making all those grays turn white, with violent and vengeful acts becoming not just good but great again and again.

## Travis: "We seek to make Uber a just workplace for everyone"

In February 2017 a former Uber employee named Susan Fowler wrote a blog that spread quickly on social media. She explained that during her first day working with a new manager, he sent her a message to share something completely irrelevant to her professional onboarding. "He was in an open relationship, he said, and his girlfriend was having an easy time finding new partners but he wasn't," she wrote. "He was trying to stay out of trouble at work, he said, but he couldn't help getting in trouble, because he was looking for women to have sex with." She explained that she took screenshots of the chat and sent them to HR. According to Fowler, "Upper management told me that he 'was a high performer' (i.e. had stellar performance reviews from his superiors) and they wouldn't feel comfortable punishing him for what was probably just an innocent mistake on his part."[47] Over time, Fowler said she had learned that other women had complained about him, too, and that he had kept bringing up his polyamory in the workplace. In fact, after Fowler left that team, she was told that her former manager propositioned yet another colleague. This wasn't an isolated incident.[48]

After Fowler went public with her story, Travis Kalanick emailed a statement to media outlets: "What she describes is abhorrent and against everything Uber stands for and believes in. We seek to make Uber a just workplace for everyone, and there can be absolutely no place for this kind of behavior at Uber— and anyone who behaves this way or thinks this is O.K. will be fired."[49] He did not refute what she'd said, nor did he recognize that her courage to speak out gave him a second chance, to pause, reflect, discern, and question—then to evaluate and overhaul the company's broken culture and processes. He didn't do that, carefully. Instead, this was a PR problem. It needed a quick fix, so he reacted immediately, deeming the incident an isolated case, nothing more. Repent and repeat, but not repair.

Yet so many facts contradicted Kalanick's statement. Uber executives had enabled, even promoted, the culture that Fowler critiqued. Very early on, when Uber's revenues in only five cities exceeded the rest of their global operations combined, *GQ*'s Mickey Rapkin had asked Kalanick about his popularity.[50] "When I tease him about his skyrocketing desirability," Rapkin explained, "he deflects with a wisecrack about women on demand: 'Yeah, we call that Boober.'"[51] That same attitude seemed to infiltrate much of the company culture. Uber executives frequently expensed parties at strip clubs on the corporate account, as Mike Isaac chronicled in *Super Pumped*. Officially, the billing codes were "client entertainment" or "business development." Informally, it was called "Tits on Travis."[52]

Before an all-team, all-expenses paid trip to Miami in 2013, Kalanick sent an email to the entire company that listed a series of party rules, which was published by *Vox* in 2017 after it was shared with Kara Swisher and Johana Bhuiyan. It was the kind of email you'd expect from an obnoxious fraternity brother the week before their biggest party of the year. The admonitions included: "Do not throw large kegs off of tall buildings. Please talk to Ryan McKillen and Amos Barreto for specific insights on this topic." He also insisted, "We do not have a budget to bail anyone out of jail. Don't be that guy. #CLM," meaning "career limiting move." And speaking of careers, the most revealing declaration of all: "Do not have sex with another employee UNLESS a) you have asked that person for that privilege and they have responded with an emphatic "YES! I will have sex with you AND b) the two (or more) of you do not work in the same chain of command. Yes, that means that Travis will be celibate on this trip. #CEOLife #FML," with #CEOLife being the worst humble brag imaginable, and #FML, or "fuck my life," showing how Kalanick truly felt about not being able to have sex with his employees.[53]

When Kalanick offered advice to his employees about how to have sex, or even an orgy, at a company event—when he encouraged verbal consent yet also regretted that he couldn't join them—it wasn't during the dorm room startup phase, when the company culture was still taking shape, amid all the late-nights-and-pizza-boxes. Uber really never had that phase, because its founders were all successful before this and had raised investment from top angel investors and venture firms blindingly fast. This was in October 2013, after more than fifty different venture firms and other investors had already backed them, including larger institutional players like Goldman Sachs, Google Ventures, and several of the world's most renowned venture capitalists, including David Sacks and Gary Vaynerchuk.[54] A few months later, Uber raised even more money. It was a massive round, of $1.2 billion, but one detail seemed almost laughable in the aftermath of Kalanick's sex advice email. One of the company's newest backers was Fidelity.[55]

Kalanick was in his late thirties when he sent that message before the retreat in Miami. He'd dropped out of UCLA over fifteen years before.[56] He had plenty of time to mature. He just didn't. Sometimes maturity doesn't correlate with age. That's because it's not about destiny. It's about decisions.

One email might mean these words were out of context. A single message doesn't define an entire company's culture; he could have been joking, or he could've been drinking. But these instructions were just one example among many; it was part of a "culture of sexual harassment and retaliation against individuals who complained about such harassment" according to the U.S. Equal Employment Opportunity Commission in 2019.[57] Beyond its hubristic and immature tone, Kalanick's prideful flexing of his power over others showed his approach: from the admonition of "You better read this or I'll kick your ass" in the opening of the email to its closing line: "If someone asks to meet the CEO and Founder of Uber, kindly introduce him to Max Crowley." Crowley was nowhere near the c-suite. His companywide role involved "management and distribution of all marketing materials (and Uber swag) and pop-up launches such as the Democratic National Convention (Charlotte) and SXSW (Austin, TX)," events from the year before. In other words, Crowley was the person in charge of throwing the party, so as far as Kalanick was concerned, Crowley was the CEO for the weekend.[58]

The Miami trip was a vacation for everyone to celebrate a victory—and quite a victory it was, because Uber had reached a billion-dollar run rate, meaning the company would make a billion dollars in revenues at its current performance levels.[59] Anyone who didn't want to party didn't have to be there. They had won, after all. "The first right on earth is the right of the ego. Man's first duty is to himself. His moral law is never to place his prime goal within the persons of others," Ayn Rand wrote in *The Fountainhead*. "His moral obligation is to do what he wishes, provided his wish does not depend primarily upon other men."[60] When "other men" got in the way—namely, government officials, permit issuers, regulators, city council members, union leaders, citizens groups, and others— Uber executives saw only one clear and absolute moral choice: to build Uber there anyway.[61] Once they had enough users, whenever the city pushed back, Kalanick's team could rally them to join his effort to defy the laws. "Men have been taught that the ego is the synonym of evil, and selflessness the ideal of virtue. But the creator is the egoist in the absolute sense," Rand explained in *The Fountainhead*, adding "the creator is the man who disagrees," "who goes against the current," and "who stands alone."[62]

* * *

As Uber expanded from city to city, its employees resorted to dirty tricks. They started ordering rides from other services, then canceling and ordering again, and they repeated that hundreds of times. They got caught, and the company issued a statement promising that they'd "tone down their sales tactics."[63] But after Lyft drivers complained that Uber recruiters were ordering rides, all in an effort to tell them about how great Uber was and to encourage them to switch, Lyft analyzed the data from those cell phone numbers, which it shared with Erica Fink of CNN. From August 2013 until August 2014, Lyft claimed it could identify 177 Uber employees who had initiated and then canceled 5,560 rides, which not only cost their drivers what they could've earned on legitimate passengers but also meant they wasted both time and gas on people who never intended to use the service. In response, Uber didn't deny the underhanded tactics. Instead, the company defended itself: "We recruit hundreds of thousands of entrepreneurs to build their own small businesses on the Uber platform, where the economic opportunity for drivers is unmatched in the industry."[64] *Entrepreneurs. Small businesses.*

*Words do matter.* The fact was, U.S. entrepreneurial activity had neared a forty-year low at the time, and the recovery after the Great Recession was not evenly distributed nationwide.[65] Throughout much of the 2010s, nearly 60 percent of new businesses were formed in only 25 percent of the most prosperous ZIP codes. Everywhere else, there were more companies shutting down than being started.[66] One tragic irony of that same decade was that so many Americans did so much work for the tech companies. We became convinced that Uber was helping "hundreds of thousands of entrepreneurs."[67] We thought their hustling meant they were hard-working *small businesses* because the company had used that word. But they weren't. They were 1099 contractors. Uber paid them that way, so it didn't have to provide health insurance, retirement, paid time off, or other benefits and protections. As a result, Uber drivers, as contractors, had no right to sue the company if they were victims of sexual harassment or workplace discrimination.[68]

Women filed lawsuits with harrowing stories of assault and abuse. "Uber's whole business model is predicated on giving people a safe ride home," an attorney representing over 500 women explained, "but rider safety was never their concern—growth was, at the expense of their passengers' safety."[69] These cases came from across America, but Uber came under the deepest scrutiny in their home state. "Uber receives a complaint, investigates the complaint, makes a finding and handles said finding internally and privately," a California assistant district attorney told the *New York Times.* "Uber has essentially carved out its own justice system."[70] In 2019 the California Public Utilities Commission demanded that Uber release more data about sexual assaults resulting from Uber rides. The company failed to comply, and the state fined it $59 million, but during lengthy legal battles, lawyers argued the fine down to $150,000. After a public outcry, Uber agreed to donate an additional $9 million to a victims' relief fund.[71]

That was less than 0.04 percent of its revenues that year.[72]

## Uber: Just a workplace for everyone . . . who does cocaine?

Overseas, Uber took even more combative approaches than it did in the United States, especially when it encountered resistance. "Sometimes we have problems because, well, we're just fucking illegal," one Uber director wrote. In the efforts to "avoid enforcement" in foreign countries, another executive said: "We have officially become pirates." Those emails and thousands of others all came to light in July 2022 when a team from the *Guardian* reported on the worst offenses from more than 124,000 leaked Uber documents.[73]

Yet at the time, the public stance taken by the company was one of celebration, even sheer exultation. Uber expanded into Nairobi, Kenya, as one of its first markets in Africa, which it announced on its blog with glamorous photos of an "awesome launch party which jived with sweet beats" where it hosted "everyone from hardcore bankers to socialites, from tech startup jocks to fashionistas," with a clear emphasis on the *hardcore* and far less importance on the *everyone* in that phrase. The revelry that defined Uber's culture in America raged on when the company expanded abroad—which it promoted on the company's blog, in the official photos and the self-promotional marketing that described this see-and-be-seen spectacle.[74]

But while the Party Hard culture had hurt people in America, matters got way worse overseas, as Mike Isaac detailed in *Super Pumped*. When a female employee with Uber Malaysia left work late one night, she noticed a group of men following her. Frantic and worried that she was about to be raped, she texted her colleagues to ask for help. "Don't worry, Uber has great health care," her manager wrote back. "We will pay for your medical bills." At Uber Thailand, colleagues stayed up late drinking and doing cocaine long after the workday had ended. One female employee chose to abstain from taking any drugs, but then her manager demanded that she join in. He grabbed her and shook her, leaving bruises, and then he yanked a fistful of hair and pushed her face down on the table. Right there, in the office in front of her colleagues, her manager forced her to snort cocaine.[75]

"He needed to rub your nose in it," an Uber employee had once said about Travis Kalanick. "Like a master training a dog to submit."[76]

## Travis: "If it's easy I'm not pushing hard enough"

As Uber's employees overseas partied so hard, with such horrible harms resulting, the people who did the work for them had a different experience altogether. In Nairobi, long after the "awesome launch party," drivers made $5 after working ten-hour days, with the company charging $2.90 per ride—one of the lowest fares worldwide, according to the *New York Times*. Even then, the company decided to allow older, more rundown vehicles onto its network, for a $1.45 minimum fare.[77] Drivers' protests became so violent that Uber's twenty full-time employees (rather, the twenty it chose to pay as full-time employees) worked from home rather than risking going to the office.[78] The Ministry of Transport got involved, and Uber gave in to the pressure, raising its fares just slightly.[79] Even so, it still continued with the plan to undercut its own drivers with the lower-quality vehicles and the lower minimum fare.[80]

Then it got even worse. As Uber expanded in Nairobi, bringing on new drivers, the company encouraged them to take out loans that were sometimes promoted, arranged, or even financed by Uber. The rates the company offered were algorithmically optimized to be exactly what drivers could afford. But problems emerged when Uber later changed its rates or undermined the same drivers who had nice new vehicles by flooding the market with lower rates. One Uber driver asked an honest question after ending up financially underwater: "When you have a family to feed, kids to pay school fees for, rents to pay, a loan to pay and your work is too much and exploitative, what happens?"[81]

Many drivers complained that *this* wasn't what they'd signed up for. The harder they worked, the more value they created for the company, the lower the fares and their pay went. Alissa Orlando, who used to oversee Uber's East African operations, admitted as much to *NBC News*: "The primary metric used to assess the growth and success of a city was the number of trips, as opposed to revenues or profits. So there was every incentive to drive prices as low as possible."[82]

"Be your own boss," Uber drivers were promised. When our every need is met, on-demand, we called it the "sharing" economy, yet the math showed that the wealth went to the companies and investors—not us. "Ordinary" people did the hard work for companies like Uber. In exchange, they made a pittance compared to what corporate executives did from so many trips and food deliveries. While Uber profited from Big Data and the massive scale that made it so much money, who did real work here? "Ordinary" people did. They are the company's labor—almost. That's an official legal classification, so Uber drivers don't count as the official workforce, and they don't get any of the benefits that come with labor rights. Yet the drivers put in so much effort. In a sense, the same went for all the Silicon Age entrepreneurs who benefited so much from our time, work, and attention, as they extracted so much value from the data we create. Nothing is ever "free," except what we've given up.

"Data is the new oil," we were told. But that's not quite right. While so much wealth is being extracted by outsiders a world away, we are left behind to deal with the lasting impacts.

"Oil" is the wrong word here. Do you remember the phrase Sergey Brin used in the email he sent on November 10, 1997? He and his friends were "scientists in the field of data mining."[83] In a world of surveillance capitalism, data is the new *coal*.

And we're being strip-mined. While outsiders profit, we're exploited like Appalachia was. The more you think about that, the stronger the analogy becomes. We're also left behind worse off, unhealthier, and anxious about what it might mean for our children. *Data is the new coal*. That's a better comparison, because if we're not feeling pressured—the raw resource of our time and talent placed under stress—then the Big Tech executives feel like they must push even harder. Otherwise they might be losing money that could fuel more growth, which they could turn into more wealth and power.

That's how they see it, or at least one of them did.

We know that because Travis Kalanick admitted it in the back of an Uber on February 5, 2017. The Super Bowl had just ended, after one of the biggest meltdowns in sports history. The Atlanta Falcons led 28–3 with 2:12 left in the third quarter. The world watched in disbelief as the Falcons' hopes for their first Super Bowl Championship slipped away. But, moments later, Uber's CEO rivaled quarterback Matt Ryan for the worst unforced errors that night. The Falcons lost in overtime after the worst collapse in Super Bowl history.[84] Then Kalanick seemed to say, *"Hold my beer."*

By the looks of him, he'd already had many that evening. "It takes twenty years to build a reputation," Warren Buffett famously advised, "and five minutes to ruin it."[85] As it turned out, Uber took less than ten years to create an unbearably toxic culture during the Silicon Age. Fittingly, it took Kalanick only a couple of fully honest minutes to implode. That quickly, Kalanick lost his company. It happened in the back of an Uber.[86]

Seated between two girls, Kalanick swayed back and forth to the music. Even then, one of his companions told him to "loosen up." He certainly did. As an Uber driver named Fawzi Kamel drove across the San Francisco–Oakland Bay Bridge, Kalanick rubbed against the shoulder of one girl and then the other. One of them mentioned that she'd heard Uber is having a tough year. The CEO retorted, "Nah, nah. I make sure every year is a hard year," he smiled. Both girls giggled gleefully at that. "That's kind of how I roll." Then, for effect, out of drunkenness, or both, he repeated, "I make sure every year is a hard year. If it's easy I'm not pushing hard enough."[87]

That put a big smile on Kalanick's face. The entire time, he cradled his iPhone between his knees, thumbing the screen in his hands even though he never looked down at it, mindlessly caressing a device that had helped him become a multibillionaire, while ensuring we all lived in Uber's world now, where drivers like Kamel had a hard year every year. But Travis Kalanick had read a warning long ago that these conditions could not last. "Pressure is a powerful factor," Ayn Rand wrote. "It leads to consequences which, once started, cannot be controlled."[88]

On a video captured from the dashboard of an Uber, surveilled by a camera placed there by a man who worked for him but was not employed by him, Travis Kalanick smiled wide.[89] His own prophecy from seven years before was about to come true, too. "Now some of us may hate that all of this information gets out there," he'd written, "but hyper-transparency is the world we are increasingly living in and we all better get used to it."[90]

## A kinglet, dethroned

After they'd arrived at their destination, and the girls had gotten out of the Uber, the dashcam video recorded Fawzi Kamel challenging the company's CEO. When Kamel made that choice, he stood up for every person who has ever driven someone else, which gave Uber Technologies, Inc., upward of 25 percent of the fare, only to have the terms change on them without them knowing, and to have all the value of the data they'd created taken away without ever knowing how much they'd lost and the corporation gained.[91] "I saw the email, it's all about the rating," Kamel began, complaining about a recent email blast. "You're raising the standards and you're dropping the prices."[92]

"We have to. We have competitors. Otherwise we go out of business," Kalanick responded, sounding agitated. The facts told a different story. His company had created $19.24 billion in gross bookings in 2016, leading to $3.85 billion in revenues.[93] That year, Uber's closest competitor, Lyft, had gross bookings of $1.9 billion and revenues around $340 million.[94] On December 31, 2015, Sidecar had shut down completely.[95] So let's be precise: during the twelve-month period that concluded prior to when Kalanick got into the Uber that would end his tenure as CEO, his next closest competitor had less than a tenth of the gross bookings and less than a tenth of the revenues than the company he'd founded, and the entrepreneur who first patented the idea for ridesharing went totally out of business.

At over $34 billion, Uber's gross bookings in 2017 would end up over $15 billion higher than the prior year, with revenues more than doubling to nearly $8 billion.[96] Less than a decade earlier, Kalanick wouldn't have complained about that kind of "competition," because he couldn't have imagined that level of market dominance and the wealth it would make him. He led a company that would decimate the taxi industry across more than six hundred cities globally by 2017, and he'd begun working toward the greatest cost-cutter of all: putting all drivers out of work, so that a network of self-driving, all-electric vehicles could move anything or anyone to anywhere—for the right price.[97] It had been a technological impossibility ever since the Stanford Students had dreamed about this same idea two decades earlier before they built Backrub. But by early 2017, Uber's self-driving car fleet was already on the road in Pittsburgh.[98] By the end of that year they'd struck a deal with Volvo to purchase as many as twenty-four thousand automated vehicles.[99] Yet in that critical moment in the back of an Uber, Travis Kalanick failed as a leader because he asserted dominance instead of choosing to listen. He instead decided to defend the price hikes to the man who told him they hurt him.

When Kalanick had said, "I make sure that every year is a hard year," even as Uber vanquished the competition and pursued automation, we could finally begin to understand: Uber hoped to make as much money as possible from the riders, while paying the drivers only what they had to, in order to keep enough of them driving to meet the demand. They didn't want drivers to make too much money. Then they'd stop driving. They wanted the American economy to do well, so that people kept ordering Ubers, but they needed the American economy to not do too well, so that no one would be willing to drive an Uber.

That was just reality, the cost of doing business, based on the growth-at-all-costs business model.

But as the company explored the next frontier of innovation—to create machines that could think like people and replace human labor—every Uber driver's complaints became a necessary but temporary nuisance before it created a world of automation. Uber had acted as if it would all last forever: the growth and power, the binging and rule-breaking, the sex and subterfuge, and the data it gained so much value from, while drivers never did. It was almost like the basic physics of free and fair markets had somehow vanished. It was as if all that growth meant gravity was gone. It would be, with Uber's artificial intelligence and the automated vehicles it powered. They could reach escape velocity.

∗ ∗ ∗

But as the rest of Travis Kalanick's conversation with Fawzi Kamel revealed, his unfounded fear of close competitors and his drive for total domination had other costs. Kalanick couldn't hear the hurt in Kamel's voice. Even as he worked toward a world where artificial intelligence might put Kamel out of work entirely, Kalanick couldn't recognize the pain that a recent price hike had caused. In fact, he seemed surprised Kamel would dare to question him, with a tone that conveyed: *"Don't you know who you are talking to?"* It was not quite what Rand wrote, but close: "for don't they wish for the happiness of suffering at his hands."[100]

Kamel looked down at the phone that Kalanick cradled in his left palm and continued to mindlessly rub with his right thumb. Kamel grumbled, "Competitors, man. You have the business model in your hands. You put the prices you want. But you choose...." Kalanick interjected, "No, you misunderstand me. We started high-end. We didn't go low-end because we wanted to. We went low-end because we had to."[101] In other words, Uber served the general public (and hadn't stuck to the original business model as a premium limo service) only because it *had* to squeeze every last dollar from each customer and driver to stay in business. In reality, Uber could have remained an elite service that was far more expensive and exclusive, but it had chosen to go "low-end" with "ordinary" people driving around other "ordinary" people because it meant it could grow bigger and faster.

But recent price adjustments had squeezed the drivers, which Kamel told Kalanick directly: "I lost $97,000 because of you. I'm bankrupt because of you. Yes, yes, yes, you keep changing every day," he insisted, addressing the fact that Uber's pricing was never set and so drivers struggled to know how to budget to not fall behind, much less get ahead. The lyrics on the radio went: *Wasted (wasted)/And the more I drink the more I think about you.*[102]

"But people are not trusting you anymore," Kamel told Kalanick. With those words, the fuse on Kalanick's temper was lit. Trust was a trigger word. The confrontation escalated. "You changed the whole business," Kamel complained, arguing that Uber kept adjusting fares while the driver's take-home pay kept dropping. Kalanick interjected: "Bullshit. Bullshit!" Kalanick couldn't know the irony at the time, given the fateful lyrics he'd shimmied to:

> *I don't wanna know, know, know, know*
> *Who's taking you home, home, home, home*[103]

It wasn't poetic. But it was profound.

* * *

"Perhaps every modern king is just a scapegoat who has managed to delay his own execution," Peter Thiel and Blake Masters once wrote.[104] Upon reflection, that notion was misguided, by presupposing that these modern kings always know what's best for the rest of us. It also implied that their virtue grows as power does, not that power corrupts. It assumed that their power brought wisdom, and that to end it was the unthinking act of a mindless mob. It asserted that the freedom to do anything, for the elite few, mattered more than the liberties of the great many they held power over. Maybe that was why they didn't put faith in equal rights, or why Thiel instead believed, "I no longer believe that freedom and democracy are compatible."[105]

For another take, consider what W. E. B. DuBois wrote in *Black Reconstruction in America* long ago. He worried about the abuse of authority, reasoning that the most powerful people all, eventually, "became arrogant, strutting, quarrelsome kinglets; they issued commands; they made laws; they shouted their orders; they expected deference and self-abasement; they were choleric and easily insulted. . . . As the world had long-learned, nothing is so calculated to ruin human nature as absolute power over human beings."[106]

Was Uber's power absolute? When we saw how far it would go to feed the bottom line, along with the rules it broke, the surveillance it carried out, and the authorities it bested, we could discern the ways that it had gained immense power over people. But no, its power was not yet absolute. In some moments, it came close. But this wasn't Rand's perfectly selfish Übermensch, even though Uber seemed unrelenting in its pursuit of domination, even though artificial intelligence could bring it closer.

The Silicon Age was all about growth, because command created control, and passivity meant more power. Uber could then wield that influence, expand further, and be almost everywhere by the time its greatest cost driver (the drivers themselves) went away entirely. "The primary metric used to assess the growth and success of a city was the number of trips, as opposed to revenues or profits. So there was every incentive to drive prices as low as possible." In this way of the world, everyone who dared to challenge entrepreneurs like Kalanick needed to get out of the way of progress, because "Man's first duty is to himself, and the creator is the man who stands alone." By this logic, if workers' lives were worse off because they weren't CEOs, they needed to work harder. Business ordered society. Innovation was the purpose, no matter the price of progress. At the Church of Creative Capitalism, might made right. Power didn't corrupt; it purified and made virtuous.

It was rapidly becoming Uber's world now. The moral math had become scrambled. As automation loomed, some elites began to believe they had a duty to motivate poor people to work harder. This so-called mob of voting plebiscites, the underclass, would need to do more to keep up, after all. These kinds of attitudes about how to deal with the weaker ones have become more popular than you might think, and in the next chapter, we'll discover that they reflect the same condescension from elites of decades ago: "*When everything is mechanized, there's no place for them. They're piling up by the hundreds of thousands,*" even while "*thrift was inimical to their being.*" Instead of getting up by their bootstraps, elites fretted that these poor people would become "*cowardly, self-indulgent, and pathetic,*" while "*self-reliance and initiative deteriorated into self-pity.*" They needed to "*wake the hell up.*" If yelling at them worked, if it might jolt them from their listlessness, and maybe that was the decent thing to do.

So Travis Kalanick yelled, "Bullshit!" as a reality check to the Uber driver who failed to recognize that he was in the presence of a Great Man of History. Kamel, an "ordinary" man who kept worrying aloud about going bankrupt, failed to see the great tide of history that Kalanick had unleashed—at least that's how the world seemed from the CEO's vantage point. He'd won, no matter what it took, at any cost. But then, he lost it.

Kalanick was just about to leave Kamel's car, but he paused for one final declaration. "You know what?" the CEO asked the driver who, along with so many other people, had made him wealthier beyond imagination. "Some people don't like to take responsibility for their own shit," he sneered. "They blame everything in their life on somebody else. Good luck!"[107]

But that wasn't the final word, after all. Once Kamel sent the video to *Bloomberg News*, the public outrage over how Kalanick treated the driver resulted in his undoing. In his email to the reporter, Kamel explained the simple reason why he was willing to share the video: he felt not just disrespected but morally wronged. "Cause he   cheated the drivers who promoted his  idea at the beginning and made him   who he   is   today," he emailed, from his iPhone, extra spaces and all. Kamel was angry at Kalanick, but he was disappointed in him, too. He put it bluntly: "Didn't seem as an answer of a CEO."[108] With those words, something changed: the indiscretions that Travis Kalanick thought weren't wrong, and the culture he'd created where anything goes, all came crashing back against him.

The morning after the video appeared online, Kalanick issued a public statement, titled "A Profound Apology," where he confessed, "To say that I am ashamed is an extreme understatement. My job as your leader is to lead . . . and that starts with behaving in a way that makes us all proud. That is not what I did, and it cannot be explained away." He then went even further: "It's clear this video is a reflection of me—and the criticism we've received is a stark reminder that I must fundamentally change as a leader and grow up."[109] Kalanick admitted that Kamel was right. He'd learned a lesson and—to rephrase how he'd explained away the mistakes in the Susan Fowler press release just a few weeks before—this *was* how he'd behaved and what he'd thought was OK. But it was *not* OK.

The apology seemed genuine. Yet the timing mattered. Fowler posted her blog on February 19, 2017, fourteen days after Kamel took his video. Even though he'd already cursed out Kamel two weeks before, Kalanick didn't apologize until the dashcam video *and* Fowler's blog were both going viral on the Internet.[110] After stepping down as CEO, Kalanick sold his Uber shares for more than $2.5 billion. The company remained unprofitable. By the second quarter of 2019, Uber's stock had declined significantly, and the company had posted record losses of $5.2 billion.[111] Within a year, company would rebound under a new CEO's leadership. Kalanick had left at least $1 billion on the table by selling his shares.[112]

# CHAPTER 10

# GREED IS GOOD

J. D. Vance, Mithril Capital and Narya Capital

Hundreds of letters arrived at Bill Shockley's Stanford post office box to share toxic ideas and terrible messages about Black people being inferior to white people. But a few had to do with place, not race. A man from Knoxville, Tennessee, explained, "My interest stems from our highly personal & terribly agonizing experience with two adopted children from Appalachia. We have found that we are not along [*sic*] in this—a high percentage of children adopted by other than their immediate family become major problems—they become criminals, prostitutes, etc."[1]

Other letters echoed that message. "The federal government has poured out lavish sums for food, repairing homes, welfare and pension grants of numerous kinds," a Kentuckian named Harry Caudill explained. "To a large extent the 'War on Poverty' centered here in east Kentucky. And yet, IQ scores have been declining steadily and the Appalachian poverty that was so widely written about in the '60s has persisted." Caudill had given up: "The poverty that is associated with our region is accompanied by passivity and dependence and I see no present hope for allaying it. I have come full circle in my thinking and have reluctantly concluded that the poverty that called into being the Appalachian Regional Commission is largely genetic in origin and is largely irreducible."[2]

Caudill wasn't some wide-eyed kook, whose empty head clouded with moonshine fumes, only to then conclude that genetics doomed his fellow citizens from birth. He was a respected lawyer, legislator, professor, and author.[3] Beliefs in "race betterment" aren't just hidden away in the hollers of America, only to bubble up from the muck, but instead they flow from a mighty source. They can come from "science," from the educated, from the elites. Caudill wrote:

> In conclusion I will say that I know absolutely nothing about the issue of white vs. black intelligence. We have few blacks in this area and practically all my observations have dealt with whites. There is no doubt in my mind at the present time that our welfare programs and general humanitarian principles and practices have contrived to effectively repeal the first law of nature so that young and old alike survive to procreate. The dull, dependent and welfare-supported are outbreeding the intelligent and the ambitious. This has, in my opinion, planted a deadly genetic time bomb in our society.[4]

In response to the letter, Shockley called Caudill on July 29, 1974. He began by praising the Kentuckian for his leadership and vision, hoping to flatter him. "If we could find a suitable place to go in, and poll some people, and find out whether they could be induced for money, or in other ways, to be sterilized—that is this Voluntary Sterilization Bonus Plan—and if we could actually get some test cases where this was done," Shockley encouraged, "this I am absolutely certain would probably make a large splash in national news and get people to thinking."[5]

Caudill told Shockley that he'd be happy to help with the sterilization program. He explained, "If we think we have problems in this country now, after another generation has passed, we are going to have an absolutely unmanageable situation, in my opinion. Because, well, we're just going to have multitudes of people who cannot possibly compete in a highly technological world." Technology had reshaped the workforce, and millions of farming, coal mining, and other blue-collar jobs had been replaced by tractors and combines, by wheel loaders and blast hole drills. People who had previously earned an honest wage were being left behind. "When everything is mechanized, there's no place for them. They're piling up by the hundreds of thousands," Caudill warned. Shockley responded, "Well, civilizations have gone down the drain in the past," and then fretted about "a genetic pool of people who might be regarded as human refuse."[6] How hopeless. How helpless. How cynical.

How undignified, too, by ignoring the dignity of others. As a result: how inexcusable. That must be stated clearly, since many prior assessments have failed to do so. For instance, a PBS documentary in 1999 gently explained away Shockley's views as "allowing himself to be painted a racist." PBS protected his reputation by stating that "he had slipped into eugenics," and that during the *US News & World Report* interview in 1965, "he fell into the trap of discussing race." Even worse, in 2016 the Computer History Museum's semiconductor curator excused Shockley's "well-meaning but socially unacceptable theories of race, intelligence, and eugenics." Today, that's still how the Computer History Museum portrays Shockley's career, as part of an article on "The Birth of Silicon Valley."[7] If we try to soften the past by blurring the facts, we risk neither learning from our mistakes nor improving in the future. During the Silicon Age, fixing that starts with ensuring the most respected Silicon Valley institutions do not defend the toxicity of Shockley's ideas about eugenics, white nationalism, and "race betterment."

* * *

After his discussions with Caudill, Shockley traveled to Whitesburg, Kentucky, to meet him in person. Caudill wanted to collaborate not just by studying poverty—"This region is a laboratory for the study of genetic decline," Caudill had informed Shockley—but also to do something about it through Shockley's project. The two strategized about how much money it would take to give poor Kentuckians sufficient incentives to volunteer to be sterilized. The poll that they hoped to conduct, to determine the right payout amount for voluntary sterilizations, was also meant to identify participants in their eugenicist campaign. They met in Caudill's living room, but both had a flair for the dramatic and thought they were onto something important. They invited others to join them, calling it "The Whitesburg Conference."[8]

One of the attendees, Memphis attorney J. W. Kirkpatrick, had supported FREED for many years. He'd sent Shockley checks both from his personal account and from his law firm.[9] Several years later, court testimony linked him to supporting the Ku Klux Klan and financing a failed attempt to overthrow the government of the Caribbean island nation of Domenica in 1981 by white supremacists who hoped to replace the local leadership with their own white-people-only government.[10] Soon after that, he killed himself.[11] That was something else these men had in common. Shockley had attempted suicide years earlier but had survived.[12] After a Parkinson's diagnosis in 1990, Caudill killed himself: a bullet in his brain under a hemlock tree, overlooking the Blue Ridge Mountains.[13]

In their later years of life, these men struggled with disillusionment and mental anguish. A friend of Caudill's lamented that despite all the good he'd inspired through his writings, lectures, and teaching, "he acknowledged nothing—no progress, no reforms," which led Caudill eventually to reach a harrowing conclusion, that the only answer was mass sterilization.[14] Fortunately, unlike the surgeries that took place in more than thirty U.S. states due to the twentieth century's widespread eugenics laws, the Whitesburg Conference failed to achieve its stated goals. No Kentuckians were sterilized, forcibly or otherwise, after their plans for "race betterment."[15] But the impact of their ideas, and their cynicism and hopelessness, could still be felt well into the twenty-first century. The same went for other lessons we can take from these stories, as elite institutions supported influential figures who tried to speak on behalf of the poorest people in America.

## From "rich in potential" to "evidence of genetic decline"

When Bill Shockley first called Harry Caudill in 1974, he praised the book that the Kentuckian had written, *Night Comes to the Cumberlands: A Biography of a Depressed Area*, which had recently become a popular sensation (and which Shockley's wife had made sure he'd read).[16] Caudill's bestseller brought the Appalachian region into intense focus when it was published in 1963, as so many Americans "discovered" Appalachia through the tales about the suffering and resilience of the people whose lives were chronicled in this *Biography of a Depressed Area*. The words chosen for that subtitle speak volumes. "No Kentucky book ever brought the state more attention or more firmly established its image in the eyes of outsiders," wrote John Cheves and Bill Estep of the *Lexington Herald-Leader* just before Christmas 2012, in their third article as part of a yearlong series documenting the impact of Caudill's message and the immense legacy of "Fifty Years of *Night*."[17]

As Cheves and Estep rightly noted, Caudill considered the message of *Night* as part of a moral quest, with real lives hanging in the balance. "If a man has a foremost duty, it is to pass this land and culture on to his child in better condition than he found it because the unborn can't defend themselves," he told a reporter when *Night* was published. "The waste in Eastern Kentucky is immoral. In a sense, we're destroying the home of people yet unborn."[18] In the 1960s Caudill saw the world with moral clarity and with determination, faith, and optimism. A decade later he had a more defeatist attitude in the conversation with Shockley, as he claimed these problems were genetically inherited and, amid so much hopelessness, the only solution was to stop poor people from having children to prevent further intergenerational poverty.

President John F. Kennedy read the book and insisted his aides do so, too.[19] Motivated by the possibilities of improving the lives of so many, and inspired by Caudill's moral convictions, President Kennedy declared, "The Appalachian region is an area rich in potential. Its people are hard-working, intelligent, resourceful, and capable of responding successfully to education and training." He told the Conference of Appalachian Governors, "They are loyal to their homes, to their families, to their States, and to their country," and he announced a joint federal-state committee to develop "a comprehensive program for the economic development of the Appalachian region."[20] JFK saw potential, not problems. He saw dignity and, in it, richness.

On November 22, 1963, JFK was assassinated. Less than sixteen months later, on March 9, 1965, President Lyndon B. Johnson signed into law the

Appalachian Regional Development Act, echoing Kennedy's language: "Congress finds and declares that the Appalachian region of the United States, while abundant in natural resources and rich in potential, lags behind the rest of the Nation in its economic growth and that its people have not shared properly in the Nation's prosperity."[21] Kennedy's former vice president made good on his commitment, and Kennedy's brother, Robert F. Kennedy, picked right up on the crusade. He told reporters that it was "indecent" that America, with a gross national product of $800 billion, had "large pockets of unemployment."[22]

Caudill invited RFK to Kentucky; after visiting Appalachia for the first time, he professed, "I love these people. This is a terrible thing. It's terrible to have all this in a country as affluent as ours." Caudill wrote to RFK that, following his trip, "instinctively millions of people like those whom you saw here look to you ... for leadership and guidance."[23] Another terrible thing happened next, though. Just sixteen weeks after he'd visited Eastern Kentucky—and hours after he'd won the California primary in his own bid for the presidency—RFK was assassinated on June 5, 1968.[24]

Over the coming years, the implementation of the Appalachian Regional Commission (ARC) also caused Caudill to become deeply disenchanted. He had hoped for a focused jobs program, which would retrain the workforce of Appalachia for a more modern economy. That way, the people from the heart of coal country—its central counties in Eastern Kentucky, East Tennessee, Southwestern Virginia, and all of West Virginia—could have a fighting chance. Instead, the ARC funded traditional public works projects, which were spread out from New York to Mississippi. In the decades to come, billions of dollars in federal aid flowed through these new government programs; by 1985 the ARC had spent $656 million in Kentucky, with two-thirds of it going to roads and bridges that, in Caudill's view, only accelerated the job loss, land loss, toxic pollution, and social costs wrought by the robber barons who strip-mined the majestic mountains with their machines. "I think the ARC ought to be put to work or abolished," Caudill lamented.[25]

Shockley took a different lesson from Caudill's bestseller than the Kennedys did. "He's concerned in this book with what essentially would be dysgenics in this area of Appalachia," Shockley told a donor on July 11, 1974.[26] On their first phone call, later that month, Caudill agreed with Shockley: "Our good, bright people get up and leave, and then those who don't have the ambition, or the courage, or the strength, or whatever, stay behind. And that process has been repeated so many times that my wife and I frequently discuss what we think is very apparent evidence of genetic decline, or whatever one might call it." It was a bitter, even embittered, assessment, especially compared to the hopes for workforce reskilling he'd dreamt of years before, which had inspired so many, including the president of the United States.

## We qualified because of poverty, not because we're Appalachian

On October 8, 2008, President George W. Bush signed S.496 into law, and "Appalachia" officially expanded by nearly five thousand square miles, a vast expanse that spread resources even farther away from the targeted efforts Caudill had hoped would improve the mountainous region he cherished so much. The territory covered by the ARC grew by thirteen counties, stretching much farther into Ohio, Kentucky, Tennessee, and Virginia.[27] Ohio senator George Voinovich, a Republican, had written the bill. Congressman Tim Ryan, an Ohio Democrat, had been pushing for the designation for years, working in a bipartisan fashion with another Ohio member of Congress, Republican Steven LaTourette. Ryan explained to the local paper, quite candidly, that this was far more about money than culture or geography, much less identity: "It is a designation that makes us eligible for certain federal grants out of the Appalachian Regional Commission's Area Development Program and Highway Program." The director of Youngstown State's Center for Urban and Regional Studies agreed: "We qualified because of our high level of poverty, not because we're at the Appalachian region by any means."[28]

While new funding sounded great, local leaders noted that there were downsides to branding the Youngstown area as part of Appalachia. "The concern has been that we would be perceived as a stereotypical Appalachian county out of the movies," explained Reid Dulberger, the executive vice president of the Youngstown-Warren Regional Chamber. "Quite frankly, I'm not too concerned about that," he said, noting that people "know that Northeast Ohio is not what you think of when you typically think of Appalachia."[29] It certainly wasn't. The same went for most of the state, which culturally felt like the Heartland and topographically was more like the rest of the Midwest than the mountains of Appalachia.

In 2008 a college student named J. D. Hamel attended Ohio State University. He was originally from north of Cincinnati.[30] To travel from Appalachia to where Hamel was raised, you'd drive for hours after seeing the foothills of Pennsylvania or West Virginia fade in your rearview mirror. You'd pass through a few of those parts that were added as "Appalachia" so they could get more government money, then you'd keep going through other parts of Ohio that didn't get added. Eventually, you'd reach a suburb called Middletown.[31]

Not Georgia's Middleton that's halfway from Athens to Greenwood, South Carolina, or the one in Alabama, east of Birmingham and north of Talladega. Those two qualify as Appalachia according to the ARC's map.[32] The Middletown we're talking about was likely first called that because it's halfway to Dayton from Cincinnati.[33] This midwestern Middletown isn't where Appalachians— neither the mountains nor their people—can be found.

When you're brought up some forty miles north of Cincinnati, you've stretched things *real far* to call yourself a hillbilly. But that's what Hamel did. He married a Yale Law classmate in 2014, and when she changed her name, he changed his, too.[34] Then he published a book that would make that name famous. Everyone who'd known him previously had called him James Donald Bowman (his birth name) or James David Hamel (the name he'd gone by for most of his life).[35] But those names were nearly forgotten two years later, when the books hit the shelves. More than thirty years into life, he changed his name. It was just in time for his memoir.[36] He called it *Hillbilly Elegy*. The subtitle mirrored Caudill's. Instead of *A Biography of a Depressed Area*, this time it was *A Memoir of a Family and Culture in Crisis*.

"My name is J. D. Vance," the book began. Two pages later, he wrote, "To understand me, you must understand that I am a Scots-Irish hillbilly at heart."[37] It didn't matter where he was actually from. What mattered was how he *identified*. "I may be white, but I do not identify with the WASPs of the Northeast," he wrote. "Instead, I identify with the millions of working-class white Americans of Scots-Irish descent who have no college degree."[38] This was, of course, in direct contradiction to the fact that Vance did have a college degree, and he'd also just earned a law degree from Yale. He was no longer working class, having written much of the manuscript while employed by Peter Thiel's venture firm, which was located several blocks from the San Francisco Palace of Fine Arts.[39] He'd started a blog in 2010 during his first year at Yale (claiming it was "like a diary, only far more masculine"), and he'd named it *The Hillbilly Elite* (in his words: "That explains the blog's name: I am an Appalachian white boy in style and disposition, but I've just begun training at the world's premier center for elites.").[40] A few years later he'd decided that the world of the exclusive, educated, and privileged WASPs wasn't for him, or at least that's what he claimed in his memoir. He wanted to be seen as a hillbilly instead.

## With elegy, night gets darker

"We spend our way to the poorhouse," Vance wrote. "We buy giant TVs and iPads. Our children wear nice clothes thanks to high-interest credit cards and payday loans. We purchase homes we don't need, refinance them for more spending money, and declare bankruptcy, often leaving them full of garbage in our wake. Thrift is inimical to our being."[41] Vance had decided that the Appalachian people's deficiencies were inherent, even inherited, by writing *to our being*. The outlook of *Elegy* resembled the pessimism of the 1974 Caudill-to-Shockley letter. It was a world away from the Kennedys' efforts in the 1960s, where leaders recognized the intrinsic dignity, and the promise and potential, of poor Appalachians who had suffered for too long.

Vance followed the Caudill formula in more ways than just the book's title. "Bit by bit, his self-reliance and initiative deteriorated into self-pity," the story went about a lazy freeloader. "He reasoned that it was unfair for one child to eat because his father was crippled while another starved because his father was able-bodied. If disability and ill health were the magic keys that would open the Welfare portal he could, perhaps, find them."[42] That was from Caudill, not Vance. But it was the same message. Both men blamed poor people's moral failings for their suffering, and Vance took a dismal tone as he reintroduced Appalachia to America, fifty years later and all over again. Vance claimed that Appalachia's residents had embraced "a culture that increasingly encourages social decay instead of counteracting it" and that "many folks talk about working more than they actually work."[43] He insisted, "We hillbillies must wake the hell up."[44]

* * *

In addition to Caudill's writings, Vance's approach also echoed the same message and tone of another bestseller, which was written by his mentor at Yale, Amy Chua. Vance told Karen Heller of the *Washington Post* that Chua was the "authorial godmother" of *Hillbilly Elegy*. She returned the praise. "He's such a true person," she gushed. "You can tell an honest voice." Heller's article was reprinted in local newspapers across the country with this title: "Author Has Become a Reluctant Spokesman for Poor White Americans."[45] But was it *reluctance* if it had all been strategized ahead of time? Could reluctance be planned, as Chua coached Vance on how to create controversy like she had for her best-selling book, even introducing him to her agent, Tina Bennett, who would also represent Vance?[46]

During Vance's first year of law school, Chua published her memoir, *Battle Hymn of the Tiger Mother*. She started a cultural firestorm using a strikingly similar message to Vance's. In lieu of exhorting people dealing with a *Culture in Crisis*, she contrasted American norms against another hard-line approach. "Chinese mothers can say to their daughters, 'Hey fatty—lose some weight.' By contrast, Western parents have to tiptoe around the issue," she wrote in her book. "Chinese parents can say, 'You're lazy. All your classmates are getting ahead of you.' By contrast, Western parents have to struggle with their own conflicted feelings about achievement, and try to persuade themselves that they're not disappointed about how their kids turned out." When kids were struggling with an assignment, here was Chua's advice: "The solution to substandard performance is always to excoriate, punish, and shame the child."[47]

The same aggressive tone that Vance took in *Elegy* could be found in his professor's approach to parenting, such as when her daughter, Lulu, struggled to play the piano: "I threatened her with no lunch, no dinner, no Christmas or Hanukkah presents, no birthday parties for two, three, four years. When she still kept playing it wrong, I told her she was purposely working herself into a frenzy because she was secretly afraid she couldn't do it. I told her to stop being lazy, cowardly, self-indulgent and pathetic."[48] This seemed to cross over to verbal abuse as a parenting strategy, but it revealed something more profound about Chua's approach to the world. She taught her daughters the world was zero-sum and hypercompetitive. This view was nothing new. In the seventeenth century, philosophers talked of living in "continual fear, and danger of violent death," because life was "solitary, poor, nasty, brutish, and short."[49] But in the modern era of such abundance, the Hobbesian jungle of might-makes-right felt shocking to many readers—especially when children would get *both* Christmas and Hanukkah presents until their Tiger Mother abruptly took them away. The shock value captured people's attention. Chua's book spent three months on the *New York Times* bestseller list.[50]

## The "honest" voice of J. D. Vance

The *Lexington Herald-Leader* published its series about Harry Caudill's *Night* in 2012, right around the same time that Vance, as a third-year student at Yale Law School, had decided to write his book. Amy Chua later told the *Atlantic* that she knew it would be a better idea than applying to clerk for a Supreme Court Justice; plus, she said, he should prioritize his girlfriend above his career ambitions, since he was clearly smitten by her.[51] So, after graduation, Vance worked for Peter Thiel at Mithril Capital and wrote his memoir. His girlfriend, Usha, clerked for Chief Justice John Roberts.[52]

"She seemed some sort of genetic anomaly, a combination of every positive quality a human being should have: bright, hardworking, tall, and beautiful," Vance wrote in *Hillbilly Elegy*. "I joked with a buddy that if she had possessed a terrible personality, she would have made an excellent heroine in an Ayn Rand novel but she had a great sense of humor and an extraordinarily direct way of speaking."[53] What kind of a compliment was Vance aiming at here, by calling his wife the better version of a Rand heroine? Why celebrate your spouse not primarily for the wisdom, kindness, and character she learns and lives by, but because a "genetic anomaly" gave her "every positive quality a human being should have"? Were some people truly destined for greatness? Perhaps they were just born better?

As the book reviews came pouring in, they praised Vance for his account about how poor people were too lazy, with thrift inimical to their being, while he'd exceeded expectations, gotten out against all odds, and married a Yalie who seemed to be genetically superior. Few questioned why Vance could be trusted to speak for all Appalachia by writing *A Memoir of a Family and Culture in Crisis*.[54] The opening pages of the book were filled with effusive endorsements. The *Economist* claimed, "You will not read a more important book about America this year." Bill Gates praised "Vance's bravery in telling it." David Brooks called it "essential reading for this moment in history."[55] Apparently, Vance's approach had appealed to some powerful people.

As the media, universities, and other "elites" elevated him, he was celebrated for looking down on others. People bought it up, quite literally. A million copies sold in the first year, then Oprah endorsed it.[56] As historian Douglas Brinkley put it, "The reason 'Hillbilly Elegy' became such a high-octane book was academics, professors, cultural arbitrators—liberals—embraced it as explaining a forgotten part of America." The text became required summer reading for colleges across America, all on the way to selling over three million copies.[57] He'd taken the most dismal messages from *Night*, then made them even darker, and that darkness spread.

Sarah Jones reviewed Vance's book for the *New Republic*, explaining, "In the rise of Donald Trump, it has become a kind of Rosetta Stone for blue America to interpret that most mysterious of species: the economically precarious white voter," before criticizing the book: "*Elegy* is little more than a list of myths about welfare queens repackaged as a primer on the white working class."[58] But many Democrats didn't read it that way. The book reduced complexity and provided certainty, even offering long-lost "lived experiences" and "authenticity" in its narrative, which leftists loved. *Elegy* seemingly served a purpose, by helping liberals understand these Trump-loving strangers who had voted against their candidate. Colleges paid Vance upward of $20,000 each, along with Vance's contractually mandated best-in-class hotel accommodations and first-class airfare, so he'd meet their students and share his ideas about Appalachia.[59] *Elegy* spent seventy-four weeks on the *New York Times* bestseller list.[60]

* * *

Was J. D. Vance "such a true person" with "an honest voice," to use Amy Chua's words, which were reprinted across America? Let's remember Dennis Matthies's wisdom, rephrased here as, "I would like people to ask more questions about who J. D. Vance is." That's because this is not a simple coming-of-age tale, where a young man went off to the Ivy League, faced an identity crisis, forgot where he came from, and became a "Hillbilly Elite" when other highly educated people celebrated his success story. It was far more complicated than that. *Hillbilly Elegy* became a sensation, which created wealth and prestige. And just as Peter Thiel gained citizenship in far-flung places like

New Zealand that he'd only visited, J. D. Vance was made into a native son of Appalachia by powerful people.

In her postelection memoir about her loss to Donald Trump, Hillary Clinton cited Vance's argument as the perfect explanation for *What Happened*, the title of her book. "A culture of grievance, victimhood, and scapegoating has taken root as traditional values of self-reliance and hard work have withered," she wrote, looking to *Elegy* to explain her loss.[61] In her book, Clinton cribbed from Vance's notes: "There's a tendency toward seeing every problem as someone else's fault, whether it's Obama, liberal elites in the big cities, undocumented immigrants taking jobs, minority groups soaking up assistance—or me." It was basically the same line Vance had used in *Elegy*, where he told America, "I don't know what the answer is, precisely, but I know it starts when we stop blaming Obama or Bush or faceless companies and ask ourselves what we can do to make things better."[62] Few paused to fact check where he was from. He only *identified as* an Appalachian in his book; Ohio was his native state. Yet Clinton gave Vance legitimacy, turning *identifying* into born-and-bred *identity*. She began her praise with this line: "As Appalachian natives such as author J. D. Vance have pointed out."[63]

Clinton agreed with Vance's theories about lazy victimhood and excuse-making scapegoating, while she disregarded the fact that Appalachia was nowhere near Vance's hometown. But why *did* she lose? It *could* have been that she ran a disunified and bumbling campaign, or that she put too much trust in polls that were way off. It *might* have involved the fact that Trump's message and his promises to voters connected with how they felt in ways that hers didn't. It *should* have at least been mentioned that Facebook had embedded its employees with the Trump campaign to help them buy more ads more effectively, while Clinton refused their support.[64] In fact, she did mention most of those mistakes, but she didn't stop there. Clinton concluded that part of *What Happened* in 2016 was due to "a tendency toward seeing every problem as someone else's fault," leading to "a culture of grievance, victimhood, and scapegoating." In other words, a *Culture in Crisis*.

Vance criticized Trump throughout the book tour for *Elegy*, starting with an article for *USA Today* before the book came out, where he lamented that "a reality TV star might become president" and declared, "I quickly realized that Trump's actual policy proposals, such as they are, range from immoral to absurd." That won friends and influenced people in liberal circles. "What unites Trump's voters is a sense of alienation from America's wealthy and powerful," he argued.[65] Suddenly, Democrats had answers for Trump's popularity: Maybe the poor and powerless people were just envious of their successes, jealous of their money and influence?

In many big city, blue state book clubs, readers sought out *Hillbilly Elegy* as a palliative to a bewildering electoral loss and painful ideological rejection. The analysis almost felt like sociology, or even anthropology, as journalists used words like "underclass" to describe their fellow Americans. For example, the AP's Jake Coyle deemed Vance's book "an election-year explainer to liberal America about the white underclass that fueled Donald Trump's rise."[66] But before the election in 2016, Vance had sided with the "elites." He seemed out of touch with millions of "ordinary" Americans who made Trump even more popular and so very powerful.

Back then, Vance sent this note on Facebook Messenger to a Yale Law classmate: "We are, whether we like it or not, the party of the lower-income, lower-education white people," Vance wrote, beginning by attributing Trump's influence to voters' poverty and ignorance. He then explained, "I'm not surprised by Trump's rise, and I think the entire party has itself to blame." He proceeded to call Trump "a demagogue" who posed risks to democracy, concluding with these words: "I go back and forth between thinking Trump is a cynical asshole like Nixon who wouldn't be that bad (and might even prove useful) or that he's America's Hitler."[67]

During his 2016 book tour, Vance warned that Trump was "leading the white working class to a very dark place."[68] In the pages of *Hillbilly Elegy* itself, Vance rejected the lies that Trump had circulated about Obama's birth certificate. "But if a third of our community questions the president's origin—despite all evidence to the contrary—it's a good bet that the other conspiracies have broader currency than we'd like," he wrote. "This isn't some libertarian mistrust of government policy, which is healthy in any democracy. This is deep skepticism of the very institutions of our society. And it's becoming more and more mainstream."[69] On television and on Twitter, and throughout his book tour, Vance targeted Trump: "reprehensible," "I never liked the guy," and, with exasperation, "My God what an idiot."[70] On NPR in August 2016, Vance conceded, "I might have to hold my nose and vote for Hillary Clinton."[71] He later said that he didn't vote for either of them; he went with a third-party candidate.[72] On the *Charlie Rose Show* that October, Vance said, "The elites were right about Donald Trump, right? I'm a Never Trump guy."[73] But at the time, the "elites" and Vance had *all* underestimated Trump.

On July 4, 2016, Vance attacked Trump in a scathing essay for the *Atlantic Monthly*. He warned of a new pain reliever for America, the "opioid of the masses," which "enters minds, not through lungs or veins, but through eyes and ears, and its name is Donald Trump." Vance was alluding to the famous phrase by Karl Marx, who had called religion "Opium des Volkes," the opium of the people. Then Vance attacked Trump. He didn't hold back: "There is no self-reflection in the midst of a false euphoria. Trump is cultural heroin. He makes some feel better for a bit. But he cannot fix what ails them, and one day they'll realize it."[74]

## The untold suffering in the opioid overdose epidemic

In 2016 many Americans were enduring an *actual* opioid overdose epidemic, which received far too little notice at the time. Purdue Pharma eventually pled guilty to three federal felonies and agreed to an $8.3 billion settlement with the Justice Department.[75] When the books by Vance and Clinton went to print, the words that corporate leaders had written hadn't been made public yet. But court records soon revealed odious evidence (the drug distributor emailed, "It's like people are addicted to these things or something. Oh, wait, people are." The drug manufacturer replied, "Just like Doritos keep eating. We'll make more.").[76] Somehow, prescribing life-altering addictions had become just some kind of joke, for profit. But in reality, the true costs meant hundreds of thousands of lives lost.

We all needed to dig deeper, reject easy answers, and study the facts. From 1999 to 2015, before Vance and Clinton published their books, nearly 350,000 Americans had died of opioid overdoses. For all but the first three of those years, over *half* of overdose deaths across America were due to opioids.[77] Many people trusted the doctors who prescribed too many pain pills that numbed them to life's joys. Evidently, accountability started only once that pill reached those people's pockets or called to them from their cabinets—not with any of the decisions that came before that. That was even though around one out of four people who got opioids misused them (maybe *that* should have been a warning that so much use was misuse).[78] That was even though three out of four people who ended up on heroin started with prescription pills that came from doctors who swore to "maintain this Oath faithfully and without corruption."[79] *Words do matter.* At least, they should. So should someone's word—that they'll do what they swear to—because it can be a matter of life or death.

For many opioid users, it wasn't that they didn't love their families enough, it was that they were addled with addiction. It's not that they didn't try to stop taking the pills, not that they lacked moral fortitude, and certainly not that they're genetically inferior—it's that chemicals were concocted that made them ill if they didn't get more. Each first prescription became a possible life sentence. Scientists knew it, and too many businesses promoted it, seemingly without caring about the costs. So many people made choices to create this human-caused epidemic.

Opioid prescriptions quadrupled between 1999 and 2010.[80] But here's the worst part of all. Even after Big Pharma admitted wrongdoing and prescriptions declined—by 60 percent between 2011 and 2020—overdose deaths continued to surge.[81] In fact, they doubled between 2015 and 2021, as people turned to illegally manufactured fentanyl, which is fifty to one hundred times more potent than morphine, and carfentanil, which is one hundred times stronger than that.[82] More than a million Americans died from 1999 to 2021 due to drug overdoses.[83] By 2021 over 100,000 Americans were dying every single year due to these exponentially more powerful drugs.[84]

As we consider the facts, we should recognize that *everyone* made choices. Some people might have merely wanted to chase a fleeting feeling of euphoria no matter the consequences, but many were addicted to incredibly powerful drugs because they trusted that doctors knew what they were doing. There were choices made by the pharmaceutical executives who pushed it, the drug manufactures who made it, the drug distributors who sold it, the doctors who prescribed it, the regulators who didn't regulate it, the legislators who didn't legislate against it, and all the other people in power who didn't stop it. Instead of dealing with the many tangled threads that made up that complicated web, far too many hurting people were blamed for the situations they ended up in. Ultimately, "ordinary" men and women faced a daily dilemma as their bodies became chemically in need of drugs that addicted them, as withdrawal sickened them, and as despair enveloped them.[85]

Then the powerful people at the microphones had the gall to blame so many suffering people for not working hard enough, for social decay, for victimhood, for a culture in crisis, for complaining that it was always someone else's fault. Many in Appalachia couldn't *wake the hell up*. The truth was, they were too dopesick.[86] But the challenges they faced were nuanced and hard to solve, with no quick fix. It may have felt good to moralize and scold them. And you might even say that they made for a convenient scapegoat.

* * *

In context, the challenges of the Silicon Age are complex: venture-backed technologies enhanced the U.S. economy for too few, which was exacerbated by multiple global economic collapses, an unprecedented nationwide opioid epidemic, and a once-in-a-generation pandemic. All along, economic opportunities have been affected by deeply unfair educational disparities, including the reality that where you live almost always decides the quality of your education. When it comes to upward mobility and the promised-to-all American Dream, the twenty-first century has been decidedly un-American thus far.[87]

Americans know it, too. The current generation is the first in U.S. history to believe that the next generation will have it worse off than they do, and that's not just in Appalachia. According to Pew, a full 61 percent of Americans believe that, putting their own American Dreams in doubt.[88] We have reasons to feel unsure, insecure, even inept. Americans' deepening pain over the past two decades didn't simply come from not hustling hard enough. In reality, advancements in science and technology meant that machines replaced many jobs, and people fell behind on far too many bills. In more American homes, both parents had to work because of the rising costs of mortgages, childcare, and basics like groceries and household goods.[89] Most good jobs weren't nearby anymore, nor was anyone trained for them.[90] Harry Caudill had been right about that decades before. Education could create new opportunities. But rather than doing what worked, the politicians mostly talked about working, while our government underinvested in the future. The machines gained intelligence and skills. Literally and figuratively, the roads to elsewhere were built, and strip mining was big business.[91] Greed was good, at least for a few. So while outsiders prospered, in their elite circles, people struggled. People suffered.

And they were the only ones left behind for anyone to blame.


## J. D. makes a name for himself

The morning after Donald Trump defeated Hillary Clinton, the *New York Times* published an article titled "6 Books to Help Understand Trump's Win," compiled by the paper's critics and reviewers "for those trying to understand the political, economic, regional and social shifts that drove one of the most stunning political upsets in the nation's history on Tuesday." Vance's book was called "a compassionate, discerning sociological analysis of the white underclass that has helped drive the politics of rebellion, particularly the ascent of Donald J. Trump."[92] There was that word again, *underclass*, dripping with superiority. Vance used it, too, in a piece for *National Review* on August 29, 2016. In that article, "Why Race Relations Got Worse," he claimed that the "black underclass" and the "white underclass" represented two "tribes" in America. Vance concluded, "Trump's policies, such as they are, offer little substance to those suffering from addiction, joblessness, and downward mobility."[93]

In retrospect, it does seem not very compassionate to label anyone as part of an "underclass." So let's be more discerning. As "ordinary" men and women in Appalachia have faced increasingly difficult prospects, should we blame them for doubting the American Dream? What should we say about the exceptions: the prodigies who exceeded every expectation and went off to a great university; the idealists who imagined a completely different life for themselves and then made it happen; and the innovators who relentlessly pursued their own ideas until their dreams came true? Do the pain or sacrifices made along the way matter? Or are those badges of courage? Should we celebrate them for convincing the academics, professors, and cultural arbitrators, the investors and business leaders—the "elites in the big cities"—to believe in their potential, which led to riches and fame beyond even their wildest dreams? Should we glorify the most exceptional of all, the Great Men of the Silicon Age? Disagree with them? Vilify them?

How should we measure their accomplishments? How do we count the costs to the rest of us? In that respect, should we adore or deplore J. D. Vance, after he identified as "Hillbilly Elite" and self-styled as "an Appalachian white boy in style and disposition," which impressed all the right people, even if his path to success meant running strangers' good names through mud he'd rarely set foot on? Does it matter if their lives improved as result of *Hillbilly Elegy*?

His surely did. But what if being embraced by liberals wasn't Vance's real goal after all? Perhaps he got what he'd wanted all along, as he gained wealth and acclaim, while moving ever closer to power. As he'd discovered, the money he made was fungible and could be used toward other goals. The same went for notoriety. That's what J. D. Vance's story would prove.

Peter Thiel has shaped Vance's career in significant ways. After they met at a guest lecture at Yale, Thiel invested both time and resources into Vance's ascent.[94] That included allowing Vance to write *Elegy* despite the demands of his job at Mithril Capital in San Francisco and then investing in Vance's own venture firm, Narya Capital, along with putting millions more toward Vance's political ambitions.[95] Mithril was named after a precious metal worth ten times its weight in gold from J.R.R. Tolkien's stories, and the name Narya also came from *The Lord of the Rings*. It was the Red Ring, the Ring of Fire, which came with the encouragement, "with it you may rekindle hearts in a world that grows chill."[96]

That choice seemed fitting, since Vance was a red state Republican who made a name for himself starting with an embittered memoir. All it would take was a move home (not to Kentucky, but to a $1.4 million mansion on the Ohio River), a lucrative movie deal, a few remarkable investments by Narya, and one more astounding reinvention of his identity.[97] He needed to purge his past by erasing everything he'd just said as a "Never Trump guy."[98] He'd have to turn the riches he made from *Elegy* into millions more.


## The biggest biotech IPO in history: Too good to be true

After attending Yale Law School with Usha and J. D. Vance (then, Usha Chilukuri and J. D. Hamel), one of their former classmates started a new company, Axovant, where he tried to use gene therapies to cure Alzheimer's disease.[99] Vivek Ramaswamy raised money from a Harvard College classmate, C. R. Sincock II, whose venture firm was called Transhuman Capital, a word that traced back to Dante's concept, "to transcend human nature."[100] More recently, Silicon Valley investors have used the word to describe gene-editing innovations to cure illnesses, to create superhuman abilities, or to live forever.[101] When Peter Thiel invested in these innovations, he hoped to defy evolution itself—in his words, "to try to escape it or transcend it in our society."[102]

*Transhuman*: we all know what *human* means. That's the essence of who we are: who we are each, uniquely, and also who we are, all together. *Trans* means "across, beyond, through, on the other side of, to go beyond."[103] In other words, better than "race betterment," even more super than any Superman among us. It was the same idea as Übermensch, but even more, because it included antiaging and even immortality.

In addition to Vivek, his brother, Shankar, and their mother also worked for Axovant.[104] After just fifteen months in business, their new venture had the most lucrative biotech public offering in U.S. history.[105] But, quite simply, the drug didn't work. They were caught making miscalculations and then they failed their Phase III trials.[106] Experts had warned that their cure was too good to be true. Most notably, biotech journalist John Carroll sounded the alarm as this company "with no track record, no experience and one questionable product, leaped onto the market worth much more than $1 billion," when Ramaswamy's venture debuted on the stock market. Carroll was clear: the entire "bonanza should scare the hell out of you." He added, "The fact that someone can make something of this size out of virtually nothing should be of concern to everyone in the industry" and that when "perfectly legal schemes like this rain money, the pitfalls start to look like the Grand Canyon."[107] He wrote that on June 11, 2015.

Investors didn't listen that day. They pumped up the stock price, all the way to $239.20 on its first day as a public company.[108] "Vivek Ramaswamy may not know anything about biotech and even less about treating Alzheimer's," Carroll wrote, "but he just provided a master class on the current state of public investing and executing IPOs in the field."[109] Carroll was right. Once reality set in, the stock plunged to 23 cents, a loss of over 99.9 percent.[110] Even so, the Ramaswamy family made out just fine. Vivek's company had made them all millionaires for just fifteen months of work—on something that never worked.[111] Vivek Ramaswamy then launched numerous new biotech ventures through Roivant, a holding company. His millions grew into hundreds of millions more, as Roivant's market value grew to $6.6 billion.[112] In 2016 *Forbes* named him one of the twenty-five richest entrepreneurs under age forty, with a net worth of $600 million.[113] Roivant remained unprofitable, according to *Forbes*, with a net loss of $975 million and only $33 million in revenue over the nine months ending in December 31, 2022.[114] On April 5, 2023, over 99 percent of shareholders of Axovant (rebranded as Sio Gene Therapies, Inc.) chose to liquidate and dissolve the company, by a vote of 46,030,603 to 393,418.[115]

As technologists have become so wealthy attempting to rewrite our genetic code, we should pause, reflect, question, and discern. We must understand the power they have gained, and the greater power they seek. That is especially true for Vivek Ramaswamy, who then published three best-selling books in 2021, 2022, and 2023. He worried America was becoming a *Nation of Victims* (which reiterated the antivictimhood messages from *Hillbilly Elegy*, along with earlier books like Charles Sykes's *A Nation Of Victims: The Decay of the American Character* from 1993), and he warned in *Woke, Inc.* and *Capitalist Punishment* about corruption among Wall Street investors and big corporations. He did not mention Axovant in his books.[116] During those same years, he launched an "anti-woke" investment firm backed by Narya Capital, Founders Fund, and Peter Thiel, then he announced he was running for president on an "anti-woke" platform.[117] Likewise, we should also understand the choices Vance made. He'd soon rewrite his story again, making personal and professional changes, as he pursued greater political power.

## As greed gets glorified, power corrupts

After moving back to Ohio, Vance underwent another transformation. He launched a venture fund of his own, but even more important for his career, he also completely reversed his opinion about Donald Trump, which would aid in his political ascent.[118] By this point, Vance had spent roughly four years in venture capital, working at Mithril in 2016 and then with Steve Case at Revolution from 2017 to the end of 2019. He still managed to raise a whopping $93 million for his first-time fund (more than 2.5 times the median size of U.S. venture funds at the time, according to PitchBook). His investors included some of the Silicon Age's marquee names—Thiel, former Alphabet board chairman Eric Schmidt, and Andreesen Horowitz's Marc Andreessen.[119]

Assuming the traditional 2 and 20 model, that meant Vance, his fellow managing director, Colin Greenspon, and their team would get paid up to $1.86 million a year to invest other people's money.[120] On its website, Narya promoted itself as "a thesis-driven, early-stage venture capital firm based in Ohio." A key part of that thesis came from Steve Case's playbook; both Vance and Greenspon had left Revolution's Rise of the Rest Seed Fund to start their own fund, seeking to invest in ventures between the coasts.[121]

Despite its stated goals, the first company Narya backed was based on the West Coast, Kriya Therapeutics. Its founder was Shankar Ramaswamy, Vivek's brother.[122] Even though the Ramaswamys were born and raised in Cincinnati, Shankar did not come back home to Ohio to start his new gene-editing company after the riches of Axovant's "billion-dollar bonanza."[123] Instead, he based his new venture in Redwood City, California.[124]

In 2009 Shankar had written an op-ed for the *Harvard Crimson* titled, simply, "Greed Is Good."[125] At the time, the worst financial crisis since the Great Depression devastated America after subprime mortgage lenders repackaged bad debts as investment-worthy, offered loans to borrowers who had shown zero ability to repay them, and then never clearly told customers what they'd signed up for—sure, they might have technically and legally done so, but hardly anyone knew what those reams of complicated documents actually said.[126] The answer to such growth-at-all-costs greed? More greed, according to Ramaswamy. "Wall Street CEOs and financial kings have never had any professional interest other than making as much money as possible," he wrote. "And, until now, we thought that was just fine."[127]

Businesspeople *never* had "any professional interest" other than shareholder returns? And "we thought that was just fine," *did* we? No. Both statements were demonstrably false. Recall that E. Merrick Dodd, who taught corporate law at Harvard, had approached the Great Depression completely differently. In the midst of a horrible economic situation, he'd argued for multistakeholder approaches. He thought that business served a much greater purpose in society, rather than solely focusing on making every possible dollar for distant shareholders. Dodd wasn't some clueless socialist, whose ill-informed ideas would undermine prosperous businesses. Instead, when a business was more ethical by design, making decisions based on values, it would become a better place to work. A good reputation would attract loyal employees and more customers. The company should perform better over the long term.[128]

Perhaps Shankar Ramaswamy's Harvard economics classes hadn't mentioned Dodd, because Milton Friedman's approach to fiduciary duty had the greatest influence on his *Crimson* article in 2009. "The primary goal of a financial firm has always been to maximize monetary profits; unlike 'nonprofits,' a financial company exists solely to make as much money as possible for its executives, employees, and shareholders," he wrote. Apparently, Ramaswamy only saw a world of either/or, for-profit or nonprofit, good for business or good for society, 1 or 0, with no nuance in between. He argued, "Don't blame the only thing that can save Wall Street." In his opinion, to fix the Great Recession, we needed more greed.[129]

But what about Ramaswamy's absolutist claims about business "always" being about maximizing returns for shareholders? Friedman had published "The Social Responsibility of Business Is to Increase Its Profits" in the *New York Times* in 1970, and at the time it seemed extreme, which Friedman himself acknowledged.[130] A quarter century later, the cultural changes he'd hoped for had become common practice. The prominent national association of CEOs, the Business Roundtable, declared in 1997 that the main purpose of a business was "shareholder primacy—that corporations exist principally to serve shareholders."[131] Shankar Ramaswamy was eight years old when that definition was finalized, and Friedman had died before Ramaswamy had graduated from high school. So, it made sense that, in Ramaswamy's world, the sole purpose of a business had *always* been reduced to profiting at all costs. That was the case for most of his sentient life, when he wrote that argument at age twenty. But it was a great big lie—or at least a truly false belief—for him to assert that Friedman's approach to business was the Absolute Truth throughout all American life, much less world history.[132]

What's more, the Business Roundtable wouldn't even maintain that position forever. On August 19, 2019, 181 of America's top CEOs redefined the purpose of business: not just to create wealth for a few shareholders but instead to benefit other stakeholders—with the purpose of business being about customers, employees, suppliers, communities, *and* shareholders—through "a modern standard for corporate responsibility," which it called "stakeholder capitalism."[133] For Ramaswamy, all those people didn't factor into the bottom-line math. What counted was maximizing profit, no matter the cost. "One might rightly characterize this profiteering spirit as 'greed,' but, prior to the recent economic meltdown, such greed was never an issue for the public," he argued.[134] Again, he was wrong. Long before the Great Recession, many Americans worried about the greediness of the ultrarich. Nonetheless, Ramaswamy went even further. He defended a man whose actions were indefensible.

Bernie Madoff pled guilty to an investment scheme that defrauded people around the world of billions. In eight different distributions, the Madoff Victim Fund would make direct cash payments to over forty thousand victims, exceeding $4 billion in total.[135] Madoff received 150 years in prison for the injustices he'd committed against the "ordinary" people in 136 countries he'd deceived.[136] The payments were part of an effort to provide "justice for victims of history's largest Ponzi scheme."[137] Put another way, freedom alone was kept in check. It needed to be in better balance. We also needed fairness in American enterprise.

The grateful responses came pouring in. "Your commitment to righting this horrific injustice makes me have faith again in our judicial system and humanity," one stated. From overseas, another wrote, "I just wanted to thank you, your organization, your laws, your public servants and in general your country, for all the time, dedication and determination in trying to recover value for investors involved in the Madoff scam worldwide, regardless their nationality, creed and origin. Pursuing justice, domestically and abroad is one of the things that make[s] your country great. You all should be very proud of it."[138] At least in this instance, fairness and freedom in tandem was what made America great, and good, in the world.

But in 2009 Ramaswamy sided with Madoff instead. He chose the most extreme example, to defend the most excessive version of capitalism, all to prove his point that "Greed Is Good." "Bernard Madoff's investors did not care if their money fueled a Ponzi scheme as long as they received their regular returns," Ramaswamy wrote.[139] No, they actually *did* care quite a bit about being cheated out of billions of dollars, as the letters to the Madoff Victim Fund clearly showed. In the end, the U.S. district judge deemed Madoff's scheme "extraordinarily evil"—so greed didn't justify the damages done or make Madoff's actions okay, as Ramaswamy had argued.[140] Ultimately, free enterprise must have its limits; otherwise, scores of "ordinary" Americans will suffer and democracy will erode and we will all, rightfully, lose trust in how free markets function. We needed fairness—alongside, interspersed with, and always involved in—the great endeavor of American free enterprise.

They'd blurred too many lines, accepted too many grays that were just shades of wrong. It'd been the same since the extraordinarily evil ideas to addict people to opioids "like Doritos" so they kept coming back; to use the notoriety gained from winning a Nobel Prize to advance sinister schemes to track, hunt down, and sterilize people without their consent; to brag about surveilling "ordinary" men and women who'd had one-night stands, journalists, and celebrities, all without their permission or knowledge—these and so many other similar moments throughout recent American history, they all sounded discordant notes. History didn't rhyme, much less harmonize. Taken together, the cacophony clanged jarringly.

To the technologists of the twenty-first century, greed wasn't merely good, it was more than that. Their math wasn't addition, where one plus one only equaled two. It wasn't even multiplication. The formula for venture capital, made possible by the increasingly intelligent machines of modern times, was exponential. The power it created? That was exceptional. In the Silicon Age, greed seemed better than good. Greed meant greatness. It made men feel godlike.

Or so they believed. They focused on freedom, not fairness, once their riches and roles also gave them fearful power over women they supervised, overwhelming power over people who worked for them but who didn't count as employees, surveillance powers over so many unsuspecting people. It enabled them to alter the traits we inherit. And it would create political power over all of us. While fairness required thinking about at least one other person, freedom was all about you. Technology simplified everything. "This Is You." Life is all about you and no one else, they asserted. But we felt deceived. Deep down, we knew it was unfair. Nothing in life is free. Not when the costs go uncounted.

As tech scaled greed with few limitations, these men seemed to gain superhuman strength, so they lusted for even more of that kind of power. What did that result in?

*Predictably, that power corrupted.*

* * *

What were the true costs, not to them but for all us? The vulnerable suffered the worst, and the ultrarich and famous found ways to profit from what they'd decided was progress. Few of us would have called it all good. Even fewer of us made money as a result. Whether we were directly harmed or not, we all suffered in other ways, as people lost trust in our social contract. We were working more than ever before, two jobs, even three jobs, both parents working, hustling harder for less take-home pay than our parents once had.

Our social fabric started to come apart at the seams, began to become more threadbare. If others suffered more, we didn't end up better off. We lost too. Economic disparities widened.[141] The average American died sooner, while the richest sought to become immortal.[142]

And "ordinary" men and women were right.[143] *The American Dream had begun to die.*


## Hollywood in Kentucky

When J. D. Vance sold the movie rights to his story, he gained more fortune and fame, beyond the millions of copies of his book that college kids and lost liberals bought to discover his version of Appalachia. Netflix doubled the bid of the next closest competitor. The movie deal for *Elegy* totaled $45 million. And Ron Howard produced it.[144] Yes, Vance got Opie Taylor himself, an Academy Award winner, to help tell his story about small-town hillbilly life.[145]

It was life imitating art all along. An outward projection of a made-up image, for everyone to see. Identifying, rather than identity. Just a staged production, of play-acting and pretend, of mythmaking and make-believe.

We should have seen right through it.

For two years before *Elegy* hit bookstore shelves, and six years before the Netflix movie arrived in our living rooms, plenty of people heard all about this when Country Radio stations had played Black Stone Cherry's "Hollywood in Kentucky."[146] The band had greater claim to Appalachia than Vance, coming from Metcalfe County, one of three counties added to Kentucky's expanded ARC map in 2008.[147] They'd sung, "You'd mix champagne with mountain dew/You'd keep the name that was given to you."[148] That song appeared on the album Magic Mountain, which came out on May 6, 2014.[149] Forty days and forty nights later, J. D. married Usha and changed the name that was given to him.[150] As it turned out, Vance wouldn't want Hollywood in Kentucky anyway. J. D. Vance brought Ron Howard to the middle of Ohio to film his life story.[151]

*Hillbilly Elegy* the movie was not filmed in the Blue Ridge and Allegheny Mountains of Virginia and West Virginia, the Black Mountains of North Carolina, or the Great Smoky Mountains of Tennessee. Some footage came from around Atlanta and the nearby foothills, mainly due to Georgia's 30 percent film tax credit.[152] But most of it was filmed in the Midwest.[153] Howard and Vance visited sites in Appalachia, too, but Vance encouraged them to set up shop north of Cincinnati.[154] As a result, *Hillbilly Elegy* was largely filmed where Vance is from—a midwestern town with no mountain range or hillbillies anywhere around. They certainly weren't the mighty Appalachians.[155]

It'd just be a whisper from the past, but you can almost hear the words from long ago. "The concern has been that we would be perceived as a stereotypical Appalachian county out of the movies. Quite frankly, I'm not too concerned about that . . . Northeast Ohio is not what you think of when you typically think of Appalachia."[156] Those worries were unfounded. Soon the facts just faded away anyway, like some make-believe identity invented from overextending Appalachia, which was made official federal policy in 2008 to get more money to help poor people. Twelve years later, *Hillbilly Elegy* hit Netflix. Critics hated it, but the film was popular with viewers.[157]

J. D. Vance's hometown, Middletown, became Appalachia to America.

The singer/songwriter Sturgill Simpson put it best: "I'll give this to J.D.—like so many coastal elites that have come to eastern KY to point out all its problems, much like them he offered no solutions, but just found a way to get fucking paid for it. Twice."[158] Everyone should listen to Sturgill Simpson, especially at a moment like that one. He was actually born in Breathitt County, Kentucky, where Vance's grandparents lived.[159] Yet even given Simpson's exasperation, Ron Howard still asked if *Elegy* could use his music as part of the score for the film. Simpson's incredulous, once-hell-freezes response about their caricature of Appalachia: "You should have seen the credits, the characters are like 'holler girl one and two.'"[160]

Mark Zuckerberg

Larry Page

Sergey Brin

Keith Rabois

Peter Thiel

David Sacks

Travis Kalanick

Bill Shockley

J. D. Vance

# ACT III

# POWER

Now we know: technology has created incredible short-lived financial returns shockingly quickly, especially for a few. They gained extraordinary power, too.

Our arguments got uglier. Reality got mixed up with conspiracies. Our lives felt more insecure. It all intensified, then everything spiraled into uncertainty. All the while, men who sought to be godlike monitored and profited off what we did, saw, and wrote. Surveillance. Capitalism. They surveilled us. They capitalized off us.

As we'll learn, this creates serious risks for the constitutional rights and shared values of many Americans. It already has. Chaos and confusion after an election led to violence, after all. Their insurrection failed. But has the threat passed?

That's a good question. Here's another: Has technology blurred lines we shouldn't cross? The next innovations of the Silicon Age might be irreversible. They're now coding artificial intelligence smarter than any of us. They're editing humankind, too, by changing our DNA. What happens next, once coders go from our screens to our genes and machines code for themselves?

We might feel betrayed, deceived, desperate, or even worthless. We could despair. We must expand ourselves beyond those initial emotions. We should shift as far as we possibly can away from reacting and begin to inch toward understanding.

It could get better. To find a way forward, we must first sit with the uncertainties, the complexities, and the challenges that don't offer us instant gratification.

We must pause and reflect. Stop clicking and think.

Peruse deeply and explore the consequences thoroughly.

Understand them thoughtfully. Question and discern.

There are no easy answers.

Protecting free and fair markets, and ensuring free and fair elections, will ultimately depend on choices we make in the coming years about increasingly out-of-control technology—which we all helped to create.

---

**Figure III.1**  Mark Zuckerberg.
Source: Photo by Anthony Quintano, CC BY 2.0, https://commons.wikimedia.org/wiki/File:Mark_Zuckerberg_F8_2018_Keynote_(41793468502).jpg.

**Figure III.2**  Larry Page.
Source: Photo by Marcin Mycielski, CC-BY-SA 4.0, https://commons.wikimedia.org/wiki/File:Larry_Page_in_the_European_Parliament,_17.06.2009_(cropped1).jpg.

**Figure III.3**  Sergey Brin.
Source: U.S. Secretary of Defense, https://flic.kr/p/WoFvz2.

**Figure III.4**  Keith Rabois.
Source: Fortune Live Media, CC-BY-ND 2.0, https://www.flickr.com/photos/63750402@N07/5955831107.

**Figure III.5**  Peter Thiel.
Source: Photo by Gage Skidmore, CC BY-SA 2.0, https://commons.wikimedia.org/wiki/File:Peter_Thiel_(51876609719).jpg.

**Figure III.6**  David Sacks.
Source: *TechCrunch*, CC BY 2.0, https://www.flickr.com/photos/52522100@N07/29552154672.

**Figure III.7**  Travis Kalanick.
Source: *TechCrunch*, CC BY 2.0, https://www.flickr.com/photos/52522100@N07/15159429776.

**Figure III.8**  Bill Shockley.
Source: Wikimedia Commons, https://commons.wikimedia.org/wiki/File:Shockley.jpg.

**Figure III.9**  J. D. Vance.
Source: Photo by Gage Skidmore, CC BY-SA 2.0, https://commons.wikimedia.org/wiki/File:JD_Vance_(51128031756).jpg.

# CHAPTER 11

# WHAT IMPORTANT TRUTH?

Mark Zuckerberg and Peter Thiel, Meta Platforms, Inc.

Peter Thiel had been wrong before. While many envy the incredible bet he made on Facebook in 2004, most don't realize how clouded Thiel's crystal ball became starting in 2008, right as Facebook first achieved world domination online. After the Great Recession, Thiel thought the early recovery would falter. He maintained that dim view of the world for many years. He doubted global growth, and he bet against America. In particular, he wagered the U.S. dollar would decline; he kept shorting the markets (specifically, U.S. public markets); and he predicted far more volatility than occurred.[1] Under the headline, "Pessimism Exacts a Price on the Skeptics," a *Wall Street Journal* piece featured Thiel.[2] The date was September 28, 2009, and the Dow Jones had just reached 9,789. Facebook had 305 million monthly users.[3]

"The recovery is not real," he asserted then, when he was asked about the Dow's 51 percent increase since the nadir of the Great Recession, at 6,469.95.[4] "Deep structural problems haven't been solved and it's unclear how we will create jobs and get the economy growing again—that's long been my thesis and it still is."[5] Concerns about deep structural problems persisted throughout the next decade, and stock market gains certainly didn't create Silicon Valley's level of prosperity for "ordinary" Americans. But Thiel made objectively terrible wagers in 2008, 2009, and beyond. He remained an early skeptic of the longest bull market in world history, which lasted for almost eleven years, starting in March 2009 and ending in February 2020.[6] By January 2022 the Dow reached 36,934.84, up more than 470 percent since its 2008 low point.[7] That year Facebook had over 2.9 billion monthly users, up over 860 percent.[8]

Warren Buffett had predicted the recovery's success, arguing for a balanced approach that eschewed overreacting. On October 17, 2008, he wrote in the *New York Times* that "fear is now widespread, gripping even seasoned investors," which described Thiel at the time, but those "fears regarding the long-term prosperity of the nation's many sound companies make no sense." Amid the panic, Buffett outspokenly bet on the U.S. economy. His op-ed was titled, bluntly, "Buy American. I Am." And even though 2008 was Berkshire Hathaway's worst year ever, he kept investing. "These businesses will indeed suffer earnings hiccups, as they always have. But most major companies will be setting new profit records 5, 10 and 20 years from now," Buffett maintained.[9] He was right.[10]

And Thiel was wrong. In a postmortem assessing Thiel's hedge fund, Clarium Capital, Bloomberg's Lizette Chapman explained it was "infamous for a spectacular collapse that vaporized more than $6 billion in value between 2008 and 2012."[11] In 2008 Thiel also began to dedicate time and money to the Seasteading Institute, a nonprofit that pushed for an extreme version of libertarianism. Thiel gave $1.25 million to support this far-out-there idea: seasteading meant constructing manmade islands on the ungoverned seas and then building villages there. This went beyond reducing taxes: it was anarcho-capitalism, with no government, just markets.[12] This initiative to escape America was a passion project led by Milton Friedman's grandson, Patri.[13]

Patri Friedman sought a different way forward. "Starting a new country is actually a much less hard problem than, say, a libertarian winning a U.S. election," he told Katherine Mangu-Ward at *Reason* magazine in 2008. Rather than elect a radical individualist candidate, he'd break away from America. "What was intriguing to us," one of Thiel's partners at Clarium Capital explained, "was that here was somebody proposing to shift the canvas to a relatively neutral space by recreating a frontier." Thiel told Mangu-Ward, "We're at a fascinating juncture: the nature of government is about to change at a very fundamental level."[14] In 2008 that was more than a prediction. It was a promise. But it wouldn't work out the way that Friedman imagined.

Friedman worked at Google, but in his free time, he'd planned out Ephemerisle, a portmanteau of ephemeral and island, as an early experiment in seasteading.[15] The *San Francisco Chronicle* deemed it "Burning Man on Boats."[16] Alexandra Wolfe, the daughter of journalist and novelist Tom Wolfe, wrote about how Thiel and Friedman had first brainstormed a coast-to-coast bus tour to encourage college students to drop out and start companies, akin to the Merry Pranksters in Tom Wolfe's *The Electric Kool-Aid Acid Test*. Alexandra Wolfe deemed it "a countrywide call to reject the lax, coddling environment plaguing America's higher education system." After that idea fizzled, Thiel and Friedman collaborated on Ephemerisle, which aimed to create a libertarian free-for-all on the high seas and beyond the reach of any government. In describing

Friedman's relationships with the Thiel Fellows who lived nearby, and as an example of "his rather uncaring disrespect for authority," Wolfe mentioned that Friedman had been in a polyamorous relationship with his wife for a decade, and they'd been married for six of those years. She noted that the entire time, their Facebook profile pages advertised that they were "in an open relationship."[17]

Seasteading was first dreamed up in the 1970s by the multimillionaire businessman Robert Klark Graham, who had financed Bill Shockley's Foundation for the Research and Education on Eugenics and Dysgenics.[18] He'd also funded one of the very first sperm banks, called the Repository for Germinal Choice. He'd hoped to create superior children from celebrity and high-IQ donors, which began with Shockley's sperm. To address dysgenics (to use Shockley's term, or "retrograde humans," as Graham claimed) and advance eugenics, Shockley and Graham wanted to create a superior genetic line.[19] The lab was nicknamed the Nobel Prize Sperm Bank, which became a joke nationwide because of Shockley's involvement, causing two other Nobel winners to back out.[20] Protestors picketed outside of Graham's home, according to David Plotz, who wrote *The Genius Factory: The Curious History of the Nobel Prize Sperm Bank*. To defend himself, Graham "hired guards to protect his precious vats of frozen sperm."[21]

The Repository for Germinal Choice also drastically affected the science and business of addressing infertility, with far more choices available to clients than prior experiences where doctors would choose the donor. As Kat Eschner wrote in *Smithsonian Magazine*, "Today, sperm banks are more like Graham's approach than the previous one, and they offer significant donor details to prospective parents. The lure of choice is one of the marketing strategies of sperm banks, which are, after all, businesses. But the question of whether sperm banks are engaging in eugenics on some level has never really gone away."[22]

In 2011 Patri Friedman interviewed a candidate for a new job at the Seasteading Institute. He made quite an impression on her, according to her *New York Times* story. Rosalie Radomsky had worn a pearl necklace and matching earrings to the interview; he had on yoga pants decorated with flames, moons, and stars. His t-shirt read, "I Am Jon Galt," the protagonist in *Atlas Shrugged*. She got the job, and a few months in, Friedman asked his new employee on a date—to Burning Man. His marriage was falling apart, and he thought they had similar views on the world. "She was really enthusiastic about the political movement, which I started," Friedman told Radomsky, deeming seasteading a movement, not just an experiment. They shared an interest in transhumanism, too. What if, instead of Ephemerisle, they could build a new civilization, defy death through genetic modifications, and live forever on an ungoverned island? "We were committing to marriage to multiple human lifetimes if we have that opportunity," Friedman explained. Radomsky's story appeared in the Vows section under this headline: "A Commitment for More than One Lifetime."[23]

A year after Peter Thiel helped fund Friedman's Seasteading Institute, Friedman also wrote an essay in the same special issue of *Cato Unbound* where Thiel wrote that "I no longer believe that freedom and democracy are compatible."[24] In a section titled "Democracy Is Not the Answer," Friedman observed that only 16 percent of people had libertarian beliefs like he did. After concluding that others would never come around to his views, he'd decided to bail on democracy altogether. "Libertarians are a minority, and we underperform in elections, so winning electoral victories is a hopeless endeavor," he assessed. Instead, to get his desired outcome, Friedman thought the best possible path forward for humanity was seasteading, "to open the oceans as a new frontier, where we can build new city-states to experiment with new institutions," and to "make systemic changes, outside entrenched power structures, that could realistically lead to a freer world."[25]

Instead of advancing these ideals in a robust democratic dialogue, or attempting to rework existing institutions, he was quitting and starting elsewhere. For Friedman, the answer wasn't going to be found in democracy—it wasn't even in America. Friedman believed that, for the future frontier of radical libertarianism, seasteading represented the best answer to their difficulties with democracy. They needed to abandon America entirely. This was an extreme view of how the world should work, but Thiel was intrigued by the possibilities. If freedom and democracy were no longer compatible, and Thiel had a feeling that the nature of government was about to change at a fundamental level, what would come next?

Or *who* would?

## A wild wager and a power grab

Looking back on the Great Recession a decade later, Warren Buffett told the *Wall Street Journal* that "people talk about a fog of war, but there's a fog of panic, too. And during that panic, you're getting inaccurate information. You're hearing rumors." In the case of the crash in 2008, investors' overconfident sense of inevitable gains was replaced by an overwhelming fear of endless losses, and the crisis caused markets to decline far beyond the actual value of the assets. "Fear spread in the month of September 2008 at a rate that was like a tsunami," Buffett said. Asked who was responsible, he replied, "Bubbles are always hard to ascertain the originators of it—there really aren't any originators—everybody got caught in it. Some were foolish, some were crooked, and some were both. But you had a mass illusion that it could go on forever."[26] Even after the fog cleared for most, Thiel stuck to his contrarian impulses. When they went long, he stayed short. They bet on America. He bet against it. And, as Bloomberg's Lizette Chapman had put it, billions vaporized, as the money managed by Thiel went up in smoke.[27]

Thiel made mistakes with his stake in Facebook during these years, too. As the first investor in Zuckerberg's college connection website, Thiel's Founders Fund put in $500,000 for 7 percent of the company.[28] When the company went public seven years later, it became the largest venture-backed IPO ever, valued at $104 billion.[29] Founders Fund sold 16.8 million shares in a prearranged stock-trading plan—at an average price of less than $20 each—then sold 20 million more later that year, as soon as legally allowed.[30] By September 2021 Facebook's stock traded above $380, making it worth over a trillion dollars.[31] Thiel owned 2.5 percent of Facebook when it went public; less than a decade later, he had 0.000004 percent.[32]

But in 2016 another Thiel bet paid off wildly, when he backed a world-renowned entrepreneur who shared his doom-and-gloom views. Where there is smoke, there must be fire, the saying goes. And where there is fog, there might be war, or panic. As risky as this Thiel bet seemed at the time, his decision now makes sense in context. It aligned with his worldview.

Thiel and Blake Masters began their bestseller *Zero to One* with a job interview question Thiel loved asking: "What important truth do very few people agree with you on?" The answers always proved enlightening, because "brilliant thinking is rare, but courage is in even shorter supply than genius."[33] For decades, this entrepreneur who received funding from Thiel in 2016 had truly been one-of-a-kind. Like Patri Friedman in his polyamory while married, he had demonstrated a particularly outrageous kind of courage that rebelled against social norms. One example of that had just come to light eight days before Thiel announced his investment.

"I just start kissing them. It's like a magnet. Just kiss. I don't even wait," the American public heard Donald Trump say, in a recording by *Access Hollywood* from a decade prior.[34] He was married when he'd tried to do this, as well as when he recounted it.[35] That didn't seem to matter.

"And when you're a star, they let you do it. You can do anything. Grab 'em by the pussy," Trump boasted. "You can do anything." He bragged about his unwanted advances toward television anchor Nancy O'Dell when they'd gone shopping for furniture together. "I did try and fuck her," Trump recalled. "She was married," he explained. He emphasized that part not to underscore the sanctity of marriage but rather to bolster the brazenness of his actions. We know that, because he reemphasized, "I moved on her like a bitch, but I couldn't get there, and she was married."[36] Apparently, he would cross any line. He seemed proud of that. It showed power, authority, control, and dominance.

E. Jean Carroll later alleged he'd attacked her in a similar manner, in a Bergdorf Goodman store, located at 754 Fifth Avenue.[37] Campaigning in Iowa,

Trump had said, "I could stand in the middle of Fifth Avenue and shoot some-body, and I wouldn't lose any voters, okay? It's, like, incredible."[38] He claimed he could do anything he wanted. Years later, on May 9, 2023, a jury in a civil trial would unanimously agree that Trump had sexually abused Carroll, awarding her $5 million.[39] The night after the verdict, Trump mocked Carroll further during a CNN town hall, bragging, "My poll numbers just came out. They went up, okay?" and disparaging her as "a whack job." The audience laughed.[40] "I am upset on the behalf of young men in America," Carroll countered. "They cannot listen to this balderdash and this old-timey view of women, which is a caveman view."[41]

Trump had been demeaning Carroll and denying her claims for years by that point, ever since an interview with the *Hill* in 2019, when he declared, "I don't know anything about her. I know nothing about this woman," adding, "Number one, she's not my type. Number two, it never happened."[42] Carroll had been Miss Indiana University and Miss Cheerleader USA; Nancy O'Dell had been Miss South Carolina.[43] Yet with Trump's boasts about O'Dell that leaked in 2016, there was no he said/she said that needed to be adjudicated by a jury. The audio was evidence. There was only he said.

Many Republicans felt horrified, and morally convicted, by Trump's words.

The sound quality was clear. What he'd meant by what he'd said was clear. And many key Republican leaders felt the implications were clear, too. As the scandal engulfed Trump's campaign, polls showed that approximately two out of five voters, and one in five Republicans, believed that Trump's boasts about attempting to rape a married woman (and how easily he could get away with it all) disqualified him.[44] House Speaker Paul Ryan counted himself in that number. He had practical reasons in addition to moral ones. Ryan believed the statements doomed Trump's chances of winning. "This is fatal," he told Reince Priebus, the Republican National Committee chairman. "How can you get him out of the race?," he asked.[45]

Trump sought to make it an attack on his opponent: "This was locker room banter, a private conversation that took place many years ago. Bill Clinton has said far worse to me on the golf course—not even close. I apologize if anyone was offended."[46] Again, anytime a public apology is followed by making it more about the accuser—"how my intentions could be seen in the wrong light," as Zuckerberg said about Facemash; "have been taken to suggest otherwise," when Thiel spoke about how he'd doubted rape victims in *The Diversity Myth*; or "if anyone was offended," as Trump said about his statements about rape—alarms should go off about it being an attempt to repent-and-repeat with little genuine meaning behind it.[47] That's a moment when the cycles that had created such power, wealth, and prestige had suddenly hit a screeching halt. When the powerful strain like this—to minimize, to normalize, to marginalize—they're trying to resume their power cycles and get everyone else to move on. Hillary Clinton worked in reverse, putting the audio into ads that blanketed the airwaves, using her two-to-one cash advantage.[48] As the election approached, nearly 90 percent of newspapers endorsed her, which was around 30 percent higher than the prior election cycle, according to the bipartisan political consulting firm Mehlman Castagnetti Rosen & Thomas.[49]

During the final month of the campaign, Trump's running mate stayed at home to pray for an entire weekend, refusing to return calls. Mike Pence grappled with his own emotions and then expressed them to Trump in a handwritten note. He conveyed how hurtful Trump's words had been to him and his wife. *Politico* later revealed that top Republican leaders wanted Pence at the top of the ticket, and Condoleezza Rice was a frontrunner to become his vice president.[50] Trump apologized to the Pence family in private, then took full responsibility in public.[51] This time, he was direct about taking complete personal responsibility: "Anyone who knows me knows these words don't reflect who I am. I said it. I was wrong. And I apologize."[52]

Less than a week after that, Peter Thiel made his bet. The timing mattered: Thiel's funding arrived when Trump needed it most. If anyone thought he was acting solely on principle, it was important to note that Thiel had also given to one of the most liberal Democratic candidates, Ro Khanna, earlier in the summer.[53] Thiel's contribution to Trump in 2016 was his largest donation, but it was certainly not his first. From 2000 to 2015 he gave over $7 million to political candidates, and while most went to Republicans, he also gave to Democrats. Thiel had twice before supported Khanna's candidacy, in 2011 and 2013, for the congressional seat representing Silicon Valley.[54] Khanna had lost both times, but he won in 2016.[55] He would go on to vote against Trump 97 percent of the time.[56]

The amount of Thiel's donation mattered, too. He gave $1.25 million to support Trump, just like he'd given $1.25 million to Patri Friedman several years earlier.[57] It was a wild wager with unlikely odds, in an attempt to upend the status quo because, as happened with Friedman, "here was somebody proposing to shift the canvas to a relatively neutral space by recreating a frontier."[58] Only eleven donors gave more to Trump's election efforts in 2016 than Thiel's Clarium Capital.[59]

Thiel's $1.25 million donation was legal due to the *Citizens United* court case, which allowed it and the record $1 billion that ultrawealthy individuals and corporations donated, without limits, to powerful political action committees (Super PACs) in 2016. This was all possible because the Supreme Court decided that money should be regarded as free speech, corporations were treated as people, and wealthy businesses and their owners could fund efforts they hoped would sway election outcomes—leading to public policies that reflected their values (and, of course, their interests).[60] In America, dollars became just like words. Rich people and businesses could cycle their prestige into wealth, wealth into more influence, and all of it into power over policymakers and the policies they make.

Donald Trump was not forced out of the race, after bragging that he tried to cheat on his wife with a married woman (again, to use his exact words, "I did try and fuck her. She was married."). Instead, Trump transformed philandering into evidence that he was willing to defy the status quo, crossing lines others wouldn't, to get what he wanted. He even used this incident, shocking as it was, to blame his enemies, real and perceived. "The media and establishment want me out of the race so badly," Trump tweeted. "I will never drop out of the race, will never let my supporters down! #MAGA."[61] It was a turning point.

Even disregarding marital fidelity and other moral constraints suddenly seemed a show of strength, not weakness. By ignoring established rules, you'd find new frontiers, remaking reality into a blank canvas. By saying the most extreme slurs, by taking the most contrarian position, you'd attract attention and upend the status quo. Each line crossed meant other boundaries blurred. Voters began to distrust polls as lies, while witnessing so many instances of unbelievable outrage, amid other examples of outrageous courage.

That didn't make it morally right. But at least in some cases, people were drawn in by the taboo speech. They tuned in for the drama. They rewarded the fury.


## Hoan meets Peter

Before Peter Thiel spoke at the Republican National Convention in 2016 and put $1.25 million behind Trump to defeat Hillary Clinton, a man named Hoan Ton-That created an iPhone app so that people could take selfies and then put a cartoon image of Trump's hair on their head, like a king's crown. It was called, simply, TRUMP HAIR. And it was free, or so people thought.[62]

Just like the other apps he'd built, TRUMP HAIR was designed to gather photos. Months before that, in February 2015, Ton-That had released "Topshot ~ Rate your photos," an app designed to show people their attractiveness on a scale of one to five.[63] It was hotornot.com or Facemash all over again, and not much was new about the approach a decade later. Except this time, Ton-That wanted the photos for far more privacy-destroying aims than the judgment of the early Internet that Mark Zuckerberg had encouraged.

In 2009, six years after Zuckerberg's sophomore year exploits, Ton-That had tried to hack Harvard, too. He created a phishing worm using Google's instant messenger service that invited unsuspecting users to click on a link to ViddyHo

.com, a website that would scoop up their data and steal their passwords. That cyberattack ended up being discovered by student journalists for the *Harvard Crimson*, which caused Bay Area police to look into the matter, so Ton-That shut it down.[64] Yet within weeks he was at it again, using the same scheme to lure people to a new malicious website.[65]

Those hacking schemes faltered, but Ton-That kept at it for many years. TRUMP HAIR and Topshot weren't accomplishing what he wanted. In April 2015 Ton-That debuted another photo app, Flipshot. That failed. In July he launched a fourth, Shimmer. It was a disaster, too.[66] Each new app was free and easy to use, but they didn't take off. He'd failed every single time. Why would he want so many photos? What was he doing?

By March 2016 his phishing worms and photo upload apps had all yielded disappointing results. People were more cautious about data and more hesitant to sign up than Ton-That had surmised, so he kept trying new ways to get photos that he could connect to personally identifiable information. "Now, sharing today's photos may sound a little scary," explained the description for his fifth app, Lifestream. But, not to worry: "Here's a better way to think of it. Have you ever use [*sic*] Find My Friends, where it lets you see where your friends are at any given moment? It's a little like that, except for your photos. You trade off a little bit of privacy for a whole lot of awesome."[67]

He claimed was all just for fun, completely innocent. Just like Facemash had been, after Zuckerberg had hacked Harvard, too. But given the people behind Ton-That's efforts, and the power he sought, we had reasons to pay closer attention this time. Ton-That began to surround himself with some of the most outspoken supporters of American white nationalism, who promoted various antidemocracy and proautocracy conspiracy theories.[68] Then he met Peter Thiel.

Chuck Johnson introduced Ton-That to Thiel during the Republican National Convention in 2016, according to emails Johnson shared with Kashmir Hill of the *New York Times*. Johnson was a right-wing activist known for incendiary behaviors, online and in real life. He had once written, during a Reddit "Ask Me Anything" session, "I do not and never have believed the six million figure," referring to the Holocaust. He instead had insisted, "I think the Red Cross numbers of 250,000 dead in the camps from typhus are more realistic." Johnson claimed that the Allied bombing of Germany was the real war crime. He came out in favor of "Auschwitz and the gas chambers not being real."[69] After being denounced for these statements, Johnson said that no one really knew what he believed: "On Twitter, like, I have a certain kind of personality, a pugnaciousness, like an alter ego. You know, like when Spider-Man puts on the costume, for instance, he's no longer a mild-mannered photographer. He has an attitude. I do that because I want my content to really go viral." He proclaimed that he was only testing social media platforms' commitment to free speech.[70] Johnson unknowingly echoed Keith Rabois from three decades earlier: "The entire point was to expose these freshmen ears to very offensive speech."[71]

A belief that Johnson held strongly—at least strongly enough to meet with two members of Congress to discuss it in January 2019—involved eugenics and dysgenics. He'd once claimed that "the empirical evidence is overwhelming" that Muslims were "genetically different in their propensity for violence or rape," disregarding the fact that people of many racial and ethnic backgrounds practice Islam. Johnson also asserted that Black Americans "possessed a 'violence' gene," and that "They mean to exterminate us."[72] He'd posted these comments on Facebook, and they attracted attention, because they got him the clicks he craved.[73] Racist ideas were nothing new, but when they spread like wildfire on Facebook—that part *was* new.[74]

In one of the emails Johnson shared with Hill, Ton-That asked if he could stay with him in Cleveland. "Yes, of course," Johnson replied. "Want to meet Thiel?" Ton-That responded, "Of course!"[75] They drank together and discussed the possible merits of physiognomy, or whether a person's character could be determined based on their facial features, as they debated what had gone wrong with Ton-That's prior failed apps. Rather than waiting for everyone to upload their photos and data to his apps, Ton-That decided to change his approach with a new app called Smartcheckr, which would soon rebrand as Clearview AI. The idea was simple. What if we could download the photos that were already publicly available on the Internet? If someone found out and then changed their social media privacy settings, it would be too late. Clearview AI's database already had their photos.[76]

Ton-That's business strategy had begun to take shape. "That was where a lot of ideas that became Smartcheckr, and then Clearview, began," Johnson explained to Hill.[77] Resonances of the Stanford-Binet test from 1908—where intelligence was determined by choosing which face was superior—echoed hauntingly from decades past.[78] So, too, did the words Mark Zuckerberg coded for Facemash in 2003: "Were we let in for our looks? No. Will we be judged by them? Yes."[79] But Clearview AI's database of faces would have astounded any researcher of Lewis Terman's era, and the speed at which they'd built it even caught Zuckerberg and his team by surprise. After meeting Ton-That at the RNC in the summer of 2016, Peter Thiel invested $200,000 in his startup the next February.[80] Ton-That began mining the Internet for photos to connect faces to other personally identifiable information.[81] "A lot of people are doing it," Ton-That told Hill. "Facebook knows."[82] Facebook's leadership did not know, or they pretended not to know, because they responded with multiple letters to ask Clearview AI what exactly they were doing and how they'd done it.[83] At the time, Thiel served on Facebook's board. He had just become the chairman of its governance committee.[84]

## Catastrophically bad judgment

The person who chaired Facebook's Compensation, Nominating, and Governance Committee prior to Peter Thiel was Netflix founder and CEO Reed Hastings. On August 14, 2016, he wrote an email to Thiel about Trump. "I see our board being about great judgment, particularly in unlikely disaster where we have to pick new leaders," Hastings wrote. "I'm so mystified by your endorsement of Trump for our President, that for me it moves from 'different judgment' to 'bad judgment.' Some diversity in views is healthy, but catastrophically bad judgment (in my view) is not what anyone wants in a fellow board member." Hastings closed the email by telling Thiel, "No response necessary. I just didn't want to say this stuff behind your back."[85] Hastings sent that email a few weeks after Thiel's RNC speech and two months before Thiel's $1.25 million donation. Thiel then forwarded the email to Chuck Johnson, who leaked it to the *New York Times*, as Elizabeth Dwoskin later reported in the *Washington Post*.[86] Even if Hastings genuinely intended to be forthcoming, as he said, it only added fuel to the fire. It meant more fog of war, or panic, for everyone.

Hastings's words resembled others that had felt right to write, nearly the same as "His comments violate all modicum of humanity and decency," as others had admonished in years gone by. But did that just feel good, or did it actually do any good? Those voices would be drowned out by the flood of current events, and just like so many denunciations from long ago, they'd be mostly forgotten, buried deep in the past.[87] The *Wall Street Journal* later reported that Zuckerberg had called both Thiel and Hastings to confront them about who had leaked the email to the press. Worried about the incident being too much of a distraction for the company, Hastings offered to resign. Thiel told Zuckerberg the opposite: He wouldn't step down voluntarily.[88] They both stayed on Facebook's board until April 12, 2019, when Hastings left. Thiel not only stayed on the board of directors; he took Hastings's place as chair of the governance committee.[89] Right or wrong, Thiel held firm about his bet on Trump, remained on the board, and eventually gained more power.

A week after America first heard Trump say, "I did try and fuck her. She was married," his campaign scheduled an event preceding the final presidential debate. Trump created a media frenzy, as only he knew how to do, like he'd done with global beauty contests and celebrity apprentices. He sat with four women who accused Bill Clinton of rape and other assaults. As cameras clicked, a reporter asked, "Mr. Trump, does your star power allow you to touch women without their consent?" Trump coldly replied, "Thank you very much for coming. These four very courageous women have asked to be here. And it was our honor to help them," and then they each read from a written statement.[90]

Trump broadcast in real-time on Facebook Live. He received hundreds of thousands of reactions and comments. The most popular were "Don't look so sad. You have done so much for this country!!" and "Donald you're our only hope left. The blue-blooded Americans that have poured blood sweat and tears into achieving the American dream need you to win."[91] Perhaps that person meant to write "red-blooded," suggesting that "ordinary" Americans were counting on Trump's campaign. Typically, the term "blue-blooded" relates to wealthy families, often with undertones of elitism, aristocracy, or royal lineage. Then again, considering the power and wealth at play, maybe Facebook had become an unlikely source—unintentionally and ironically—of a starkly honest assessment of U.S. politics.

Could a different, or even bad, judgment turn into a "great judgment" after all?

## A questioned election: "I'll keep you in suspense"

During the final presidential debate in 2016, Trump attacked the mainstream media and Hillary Clinton—portraying both as a corrupted establishment rigged against him—and he responded to the claims from women who accused him of assaulting them. He sharpened his killer instinct. "First of all, the stories have been largely debunked. Those people, I don't know those people. I have a feeling how they came. I believe it was her campaign that did it," Trump said into the camera, blaming Clinton. He added, "It was all fiction. It was lies and it was fiction."[92]

Why apologize to the Pence family, if the accusations were all lies? Why admit to taking part in "locker room banter, a private conversation that took place many years ago," if he didn't say it? Why confess, "I said it. I was wrong. And I apologize," if it *didn't* happen?[93] Once he was president of the United States, Trump would take this even further. He'd claim that tape was doctored, that "we don't think that was my voice." In an era of voice actors and deepfakes—where increasingly advanced artificial intelligence can create videos and images depicting people saying or doing things they never said or did—there might have even been a reason to believe him.[94] But to admit to it, deny it, then claim that it was all made up?[95]

Other politicians had lied or hidden the truth from the American public before. But while reality might get distorted from a typo in a telegraph, during a game of telephone, or even filtered by what producers at CBS, NBC, or ABC wanted to broadcast, we now lived in an era where everything fought for our attention. Honest facts competed with dishonorable deceptions, and accurate accounts mixed with misleading information. It created irrepressible entertainment value—at a faster pace and in so many places, on all our screens and the feeds on our phones, as no one had seen before. These new mediums helped Trump triumph.

What emerged was a dark vision of the world, full of fear and fire, with fog thickened by conspiracies and contradictions. Many didn't know what to believe, for the conflict was confusing, but it all became so mesmerizing. Others found it funny, relishing in how Trump made a mockery of the establishment and traditional norms. But it worked. It was frenetic, fantastical, and, above all, influential. As the smoke worsened, with the Internet ablaze in rumors and fear, identifying arsonists meant far less than chasing after each new wildfire.

When the dust settled, Trump had done something unprecedented. True, he would go on to win the presidency. But during that final debate, on October 16, 2016, he did something else that no major candidate had done before: he refused to commit to accept the election results prior to votes being cast.[96] No major candidate had tried this before, no matter how close the race.[97] And, to be clear, some from recent history had been astonishingly close: Al Gore lost to George W. Bush by 537 votes in 2000. In an analog era of paper ballots that weren't fully punched through, Gore sought a recount. He took his case to the Florida State Supreme Court, and he won on December 8, 2000. Florida's recount began. Every state needed to certify results by December 12, so time was precious. The U.S. Supreme Court stopped the recount on December 9 so it could make its own ruling, then it sent the case back to the lower court—but it was too late to recount the votes. Congress's deadline for states to choose electors held true, so Bush had won Florida based on the original vote tally. Gore conceded the next day.[98]

Now, in 2016, weeks *before* Americans went to the polls, Trump was already unwilling to accept the outcome unless he won. At the vice presidential debate, Mike Pence had promised he'd do otherwise, as did Trump's daughter earlier in the day. They swore that the election results would be honored if the Trump-Pence ticket lost.[99] Trump responded that "first of all, the media is so dishonest and so corrupt, and the pile on is so amazing," and then he added, "they've poisoned the minds of the voters, but unfortunately for them, I think the voters are seeing through it." Trump claimed the election was already "rigged" against him and then, adding to the Hollywood-style drama, declared, "I'll tell you at the time. I'll keep you in suspense."[100] Long before Trump questioned the results of the 2020 election, he had already doubted the 2016 election, before the voters made their decisions.

Tim Alberta, the chief political correspondent at *Politico Magazine*, later deemed the final Trump-Clinton debate "without question, the ugliest and most vitriolic presidential debate in the mass-communication era. And it was exactly what Trump needed."[101] A few weeks later, 62,985,106 Americans went to their polling places to vote for Donald John Trump. That night, every major pre-election poll seemed part of one great conspiracy, as so many little misleading data points added up to one big miscalculation, which felt more like a deception by a mainstream media establishment intent on preserving the status quo. Every poll seemed rigged, and Trump was proven correct, in the fight over who knew the true beliefs of American voters.

Thiel was right about his contrarian bet, and in the surprise upset, Trump seemed vindicated, too. The press and political elite had mocked him. So he'd questioned everything, bravely, brazenly. As he did, we learned something about America. We already knew anger could be profitable for Big Tech. Despite costs to society, companies like Facebook had often maximized extreme content. Our experiences online fueled feelings of outrage and aggrievement, as tempers flared in an already heated political climate. The earlier norm had been to act with decency, but many now didn't. We'd also been told that bragging about sexual assault would hurt people, which made it wrong. In 2016 we learned that it wasn't unpopular enough to disqualify Donald Trump. He became the forty-fifth president of the United States, with the victory decided by 77,747 votes in three key states, which was less than 0.06 percent of total votes cast nationwide.[102]

Trump credited the debate, and his ability to redirect anger back against those who'd attacked him, for winning him the election. It made him look stronger. It proved that he would stop at nothing. "Do you think that voters, nonsophisticates"—that's what Roger Stone had called "ordinary" Americans in 1980—"make a difference between entertainment and politics?"[103] Both were about popularity, and Trump was going to win at that, so everyone he battled he bludgeoned. It was as if to ask, "Are you not entertained?," and America sure was.

Perhaps a more memorable, and lasting, reply to the enraptured audience would've been, "Is that not why you are here?" since politics was blood sport, elections were battlefields, and killer instincts prevailed.[104] Politics was upended by a man made famous by his wealth: a casino entrepreneur, a risk-taker, a reality TV star. Trump produced another kind of show entirely, taking the stage and surprising us all with an unpredictable and different script. He'd completely shifted the canvas, a much broader canvas, re-creating the frontier. Democracy was entertainment. It had become a showman's game to win, and the nature of government was about to change at a very fundamental level.[105]

"What important truth do very few people agree with you on?" Thiel always asked, seeking courage in reply, which was in short supply even compared to genius. Trump packaged together so many misdirections, memes, and alternative facts—tied together with enough politically incorrect it-was-just-a-jokes, tall tales, and locker room talk—to give America a more entertaining version of reality. He convinced people who'd doubted him initially to follow along, to doubt themselves instead and question the facts, to challenge all those powerful people with their boundaries, their rules, and all their other claims to what was real. Disregard earlier ideas of right and wrong and begin to believe in him over them. That was courageous, for sure. But also, in its own way, it was genius.

That's because it worked.

## Peter's gamble pays off

During an interview for the *New York Times,* Maureen Dowd asked Peter Thiel why he donated to Donald Trump. "Maybe I do always have this background program running where I'm trying to think of, 'O.K., what's the opposite of what you're saying?' and then I'll try that," he told her. "It works surprisingly often."[106] He said it was "Pyrrhonian skepticism," the fourth-century BC philosophy that the meaning of life was happiness and flourishing (*eudaimonia*), and the way to achieve it was through equanimity, or making decisions without the haze of emotions, only being influenced by tranquil logic (*ataraxia*).[107] It meant fewer fires because of less fog.

Dowd reminded Thiel that the Obama years were nearly scandal-free. Thiel replied, "But there's a point where no corruption can be a bad thing. It can mean that things are too boring." Dowd then asked about potential corruption in the Trump administration. "I don't want to dismiss ethical concerns here, but I worry that 'conflict of interest' gets overly weaponized in our politics," Thiel replied. "I think in many cases, when there's a conflict of interest, it's an indication that someone understands something way better than if there's no conflict of interest. If there's no conflict of interest, it's often because you're just not interested."[108]

Thiel was, in fact, quite interested. His donation arrived as many influential people in the Republican Party wrote Trump off, in favor of an eleventh-hour Pence-Rice ticket.[109] As Thiel had written two years earlier, in *Zero to One,* "If you can identify a delusional popular belief, you can find what lies hidden behind it: the contrarian truth."[110] This time, with Donald Trump, he absolutely had. When it seemed that it couldn't get much worse for the Trump campaign, Thiel's timing couldn't have been better. "The election had an apocalyptic feel to it," Thiel told Dowd. "There was a way in which Trump was funny, so you could be apocalyptic and funny at the same time. It's a strange combination, but it's somehow very powerful psychologically."[111] It was all a crude joke, a controversial prank, an Internet meme about origins in Africa, just meaningless and raunchy chatter, locker room banter, some taboo stories that weren't politically correct, but that was the point, after all—until the Trump presidency became serious, which meant serious opportunities for Thiel and his friends, his mentees and employees.

At one of the first official meetings hosted by the incoming Trump administration, staffers sat Thiel right next to Donald Trump, closer to the president-elect than even Tim Cook, despite the fact that Apple would soon be the first publicly traded corporation to reach a $1 trillion market cap (on August 2, 2018) and would later become the first to reach the $2 trillion and $3 trillion marks, too (breaking those barriers on August 19, 2020, and January 3, 2022, respectively).[112] Thiel joined the executive committee for the Trump White House transition.[113] As a favor to Thiel, Chuck Johnson supported the effort, too, later claiming that he'd vetted at least a dozen people who would get in jobs in the Trump administration. "The election was won by a bunch of people making memes," Johnson bragged at the time. "We memed the President into existence."[114] To Johnson, that often meant trying to get a rise out of others. For Thiel, it meant more people imitating others, sharing a meme on a meme machine. Naturally, the better name for Facebook, which was rebranded on October 28, 2021, would be Meta. It was exactly eighteen years to the day when Zuckerberg had hacked Harvard and debuted Facemash. Facebook had come of age.[115]

## Dangerously naïve

Peter Thiel recommended several of his top confidants for top roles in national security and federal policy. After college, all of them had extensive experience—working for Thiel. None had a robust record in diplomacy, international aid, the Pentagon, the Peace Corps, or any other aspect of foreign affairs. They all took on senior roles that far exceeded what was customary, given their ages, backgrounds, and experiences.[116]

Thiel's former chief of staff became the United States chief technology officer (CTO) for the Trump administration. In fact, he was America's fourth CTO of all time and was unanimously confirmed by the U.S. Senate.[117] Here were his professional credentials: Michael Kratsios worked as an analyst for one year at Barclays investment bank, taught a principles in economics course at Tsinghua University in Beijing, and then spent seven years and one month working for Thiel.[118] Before that, he'd graduated from Princeton and interned for Republican senator Lindsey Graham, from his home state of South Carolina.[119] The only other experiences he listed on his conflict-of-interest form included being the comptroller of a student organization, the International Model United Nations Association, from April 2013 to March 2016, as well as the trustee of a Princeton undergraduate organization.[120]

That career experience—most significantly, just over seven loyal years working for Peter Thiel—was what it took to earn Kratsios the top role for deciding America's technology policy.[121] In fact, he wasn't given the job at first. He was originally tapped to be the CTO's second-in-command, but then the Trump administration didn't fill the top post, so he was promoted.[122] Scott Waldman at

*Scientific American* criticized Kratsios as wholly unqualified for the position, writing, "A job that's been held by some of the nation's top scientists is now occupied by a 31-year-old politics major from Princeton University."[123]

The prior CTO, Megan Smith, had joined Google in 2003, while Kratsios was in high school. She was elected to the board of her alma mater, MIT, in 2006; she'd graduated from there with her master's degree in 1988 and her undergraduate diploma in 1986, several months before Kratsios was born.[124] The CTO of the United States who preceded her, Todd Park, had cofounded two tech companies prior to entering government, athenahealth in 1997 and Castlight Health in 2008. The first venture, an early pioneer in cloud-based software for the healthcare industry, had launched before Kratsios was a teenager.[125] In 2011 the second one became the *Wall Street Journal*'s top venture-backed company in America.[126] Before Smith and Park, Aneesh Chopra had been in the role. His qualifications included starting and consulting with an array of tech companies and serving as the Commonwealth of Virginia's secretary of technology.[127]

But the U.S. CTO job wasn't enough for Kratsios. He took on a second concurrent position, as acting undersecretary of defense for research and engineering at the Pentagon.[128] The prior person in that position, Michael D. Griffin, had been an Eminent Scholar at the University of Alabama Huntsville and then headed up the Space Department at the Johns Hopkins University Applied Physics Laboratory. He'd served as the administrator of NASA, president and COO of In-Q-Tel, and chairman and CEO of the Schafer Corporation, a top national security and technology company—but he'd only done one of those jobs at a time.[129] He'd received more accolades than could be listed in a brief bio, including the Department of Defense's highest honor for a private citizen.[130] He'd had an asteroid named after him in recognition of his contributions to the Pluto New Horizons mission.[131] But even he couldn't do two jobs at once. That took Thiel's protégé, Kratsios. He served as America's chief technology officer and concurrently took on one of the top jobs at the Pentagon.

Kratsios was just one of several beneficiaries of Thiel's influence. Another key appointment went to Kevin Harrington. On Thiel's recommendation, he served on Trump's "landing team" at the Commerce Department, where he helped decide the jobs other political appointees received.[132] Harrington became deputy assistant to the president, a midlevel role at the White House. "Harrington has a conspicuous lack of foreign policy experience in a role that typically values extensive tenure in the field," wrote Kate Brannen and Luke Hartig, the editors of *Just Security* at NYU School of Law's Reiss Center on Law and Security.[133] After college at Stanford, the entirety of Harrington's work experience was under Peter Thiel, at Thiel Macro LLC and Clarium Capital Management. They had a very close working relationship; in fact, Harrington had once claimed, "Peter is my foil, and I'm his foil."[134]

Harrington's inexperience in national security soon became apparent, once he was asked to lead the effort to rewrite the all-important National Security Strategy for the White House.[135] Early in the Trump administration, Harrington wanted to remove all troops from eastern Europe and lift all sanctions on Russian oil, according to the *Daily Beast*'s Spencer Ackerman.[136] At the time, these proposals would have been Vladimir Putin's best possible outcome, but it would have demoralized democracies throughout the former Soviet Union. That included the Republic of Georgia, whose South Ossetia and Abkhazia provinces had been invaded by Russia in August 2008, as well as Ukraine, which Putin had attacked in 2014 to annex the territory known as Crimea and would invade again in 2022, with truly devastating humanitarian consequences as twelve million people fled their homes.[137] Listening to Harrington, removing U.S. troops from eastern Europe, and lifting all sanctions—it all wouldn't just have been short-sighted, it would have been totally blind. According to many foreign policy experts, that would have led to only one outcome: pandering to Putin while putting America's democratic allies in harm's way.[138]

At the time, one national security official told Ackerman that the advice was "dangerously naïve," explaining that "we were giving something and it wasn't clear what we were gaining in return."[139] That person spoke on condition of anonymity. But from the political left, right, and center, numerous national security experts were more outspoken about the implications. They weren't shy about publicly opposing the idea, adding their name, title, and rank to the record, calling out Harrington for weakening America and strengthening Putin.[140]

In the summer of 2017, the U.S. Congress voted 419–3 in the House and 98–2 in the Senate to pass the Countering America's Adversaries Through Sanctions Act, which solidified support for Ukraine and ensured that Congress maintained oversight to prevent the executive branch from lifting sanctions on Russia.[141] Trump called the bill "seriously flawed" but signed it into law since it had been passed by near-unanimous, veto-proof majorities.[142] Congress prevented Harrington and others from lifting sanctions on Russia. "We passed this legislation along with a clear message for the White House: if you don't hold Russia accountable, we will," said Elliot Engel, the ranking member on the House Committee on Foreign Affairs. He added, "I hope Congress doesn't need to invoke the review provisions written into this law, but if the President continues to cozy up to Russia, lawmakers won't hesitate to act."[143]

Two years later, during a phone call with Ukrainian president Volodymyr Zelensky, President Trump threatened to halt military support to Ukraine, which would directly benefit Russia.[144] The former Soviet country of Ukraine was a democratic republic, where the president and legislature were elected by popular vote and there was an independent judiciary, all of which were modeled much like the American political system. The freedom and fairness of its elections and economy were better than several countries in Russia's backyard (Freedom House ranked Ukraine above other Russian neighbors, such as Azerbaijan, Belarus, Georgia, and Kazakhstan, but lower than other bordering nations like Estonia, Finland, Lithuania, and Norway).[145] Lieutenant Colonel Alexander Vindman had previously worked as a foreign affairs officer in both Ukraine and Russia; now he served alongside Harrington at the National Security Council and was frustrated by the unforced errors being made.[146] He recalled, "We'd long been confused by the president's policy of accommodation and appeasement toward Russia. But now there were new concerns rapidly emerging. This time the issue was the president's inexplicable hostility toward a U.S. partner crucial to our Russia strategy: Ukraine."[147] This put at risk one of the most promising (but fragile) democracies near Russia.[148]

"I will say that we do a lot for Ukraine," Trump told Zelensky on July 25, 2019. "We spend a lot of effort and a lot of time. Much more than the European countries are doing and they should be helping you more than they are. Germany does almost nothing for you."[149] This was completely off-script, having nothing to do with the original reasons the National Security Council had set up the call, according to Vindman. President Zelensky responded, "I would also like to thank you for your great support in the area of defense. We are ready to continue to cooperate for the next steps specifically we are almost ready to buy more Javelins from the United States for defense purposes."[150]

Then President Trump made the requests that would lead to his first impeachment. The White House had put a hold on $391 million in military aid to Ukraine, which had already been approved by the U.S. Congress. In 2017 and 2018 the Trump administration had already given the previous Ukrainian president, Petro Poroshenko, a total of $869 million in aid. Additionally, the administration had already approved the sale of Javelin missiles to Ukraine in December 2017 and then more in June 2019.[151] But that day, Trump asked Zelensky for something first before he would deliver the aid package. "I would like you to do us a favor though," Trump began, before repeatedly asking Zelensky to launch investigations into his opponent, Joe Biden, and Biden's family.[152]

Vindman deemed this "a wholly improper effort to subvert U.S. foreign policy in order to game an election."[153] On August 16, 2019, he wrote a memorandum to his bosses explaining that the consensus view of the National Security Council, the State Department, and the Defense Department was that the military assistance to Ukraine should be released. Trump rejected their recommendation. But weeks later Congress was notified of a whistle-blower complaint, which led to an investigation into the matter. The White House reversed its course, and Ukraine received the aid.[154] The next month the trial began for Donald Trump, and he was impeached for abuse of power and obstruction of Congress.[155] The editor of *Christianity Today*, Mark Galli, summarized the results: "The facts in this instance are unambiguous: The president of the United

States attempted to use his political power to coerce a foreign leader to harass and discredit one of the president's political opponents."[156]

Less than a month after the impeachment proceedings had begun, Kevin Harrington was promoted—from his midtier White House role to join its senior ranks—where he'd gain more influence on policymaking and greater exposure to the president. Throughout the rest of the Trump administration, he'd serve on the National Security Council as strategic counselor to the national security adviser. With the promotion, Harrington got a raise.[157]

# CHAPTER 12

# THERE WILL BE BLOOD

Larry Page and Sergey Brin, Alphabet Inc.

There are two novels that can change a bookish fourteen-year old's life: *The Lord of the Rings* and *Atlas Shrugged*," screenwriter John Rogers once mused. "One is a childish fantasy that often engenders a lifelong obsession with its unbelievable heroes, leading to an emotionally stunted, socially crippled adulthood, unable to deal with the real world. The other, of course, involves orcs."[1] Rogers wrote the story for *Transformers*, the Michael Bay and Steven Spielberg version from 2007. It is a fantasy that depicts mankind struggling between good robots and bad ones, which starts with a car that has a life of its own and grows into an inescapable dilemma of "their war, our world."[2] The same might be said about the risks of artificial intelligence. If that seems hyperbolic, just tell that to the family of Elaine Herzberg.

At 9:58 p.m. on Sunday, March 18, 2018, Herzberg, age forty-nine, crossed a road in Tempe, Arizona, walking with her bike beside her. It wasn't very safe. It was dark. Yet what happened next was far more complicated than any accident that came before it. That's because, for the first time in human history, a self-driving car killed a human being.[3] The vehicle maintained its speed of 45 miles per hour until 2.5 seconds before impact, and it began initiating a plan to slow down only 0.2 seconds before hitting Herzberg nearly at full speed.[4]

Uber had developed this Volvo XC90's high-tech monitoring system, which had picked up an object in its path six seconds before impact, first considering the woman an unknown object, then a vehicle, perhaps slow-moving traffic, then, a mere 1.2 seconds before impact, a bicycle. It was too late to brake. According to a federal investigation, the computer's records showed it never recognized Herzberg as a human being.[5] The news media all paused the video a split second before impact, so technically their YouTube channels didn't show it either.[6] Yet people couldn't help themselves from clicking the link and watching disturbing content—right after a brief advertisement, of course, targeted toward them.

"Violent or gory content intended to shock or disgust viewers, or content encouraging others to commit violent acts, are not allowed on YouTube," the company's policies stated, but the video of Herzberg's death could remain up, just so long as it didn't show the collision.[7] Likewise, Facebook's policies prohibited "videos that show the violent death of a person or people by accident or murder."[8] But when twenty-eight-year-old Antonio Perkins was streaming on Facebook Live and someone shot him in the head and neck, the company didn't take the video down. People couldn't see the gore, even though what had happened was grotesquely clear.[9] This was a seemingly impossible dilemma of content moderation: Where do you draw the line? What should stay? What shouldn't? As Steven Levy noted in *Facebook: The Inside Story*, the day before Perkins died, a French man killed two police officers and then loaded up Facebook to rant on video for thirteen minutes. Again, it was free speech and didn't show the murders, so they'd left it up. There weren't even warnings about the content. The line they'd decided on wasn't ever crossed, which meant it was considered free expression. So, the company didn't do anything.[10]

Google had purchased YouTube in 2006 and then acquired the ad service DoubleClick the next year. That one-two punch would change Google's business model forever and fast track the Internet toward corporate interests.[11] By giving contributors the opportunity to make a small slice of revenues, made possible through their Partner Programs starting in December 2007, it encouraged anyone to do almost anything to become famous on the Internet.[12] Even though creators only shared in a tiny portion of the value of the content they created, it worked. YouTube increasingly became an obsession. By 2022, 77 percent of U.S. Internet users between fifteen and twenty-five years old would use the site.[13]

In isolated cases, people who sought stardom attempted utterly stupid stunts, like the one by a Minnesota teenager named Monalisa Perez. She shot and killed her boyfriend with their three-year-old watching (along with a couple dozen YouTube viewers) because they'd thought that an encyclopedia would stop a bullet.[14] Or there was the twenty-year-old Tennessean who approached a family trampoline park, wielding knives as a "prank." He was shot and killed by a man who wanted to protect the children inside.[15] YouTube attempted to restrict life-threatening challenges, but they kept happening. Each edgy online stunt became a new incentive for the next person to seek fame through a more dangerous prank. More people saw YouTube's millions of views on the counter prominently placed next to their videos than read the fine print buried in the Terms of Service.[16]

Early on, social media companies had celebrated how fast they could grow, without needing humans to change the outcomes. That was how the Google Boys designed their search engine, so it could overtake Yahoo and its army of experts, after all. It was how Facebook inspired people to upload their own photos, after the Facemash hack when Mark Zuckerberg did all that work by himself. And it was how Clearview AI would soon harvest all of our pictures, which we'd made freely available online, so its artificial intelligence could find each of us in its database of faces. But where did that leave us over a decade later?

We'd used the Internet to buy and sell things or approve and dislike what people posted. The Internet had learned about us as consumers and recognition seekers because that was what we had taught it. For artificial intelligence to function responsibly in a complex, real world, we would now need to teach ethics, and empathy, and deeper understanding. We faced a grave dilemma as we relied more and more on Big Tech's machines and trusted in their math. At least until this point, humans could revise the code they wrote. But artificial intelligence has become increasingly sophisticated, as machines gained more autonomy and learned complex skills like how to drive. Soon the computers could be writing the code themselves. They might make decisions based only on what they'd already learned, even if it meant mistakes like what led to Elaine Herzberg's death or other unforeseeable tragedies.

Superintelligent machines that self-code, autonomously and without us asking, don't exist yet. But when an automated Uber killed Elaine Herzberg in 2018, we should have pressed pause. *Let's stop and think about it.* The self-driving vehicle wasn't inherently evil, and neither was Google or Facebook by that logic. They were just tools. Just as a gun doesn't kill people; Monalisa Perez did. YouTube didn't kill people or start dangerous trends. In that same way, cars don't kill people. Drivers do. *Well, hold on a second.* Except with Uber's self-driving cars. We'll have to recalculate this moral equation. Herzberg died on impact, not when some Bay Area coder made a miscalculation months before.

Her death wasn't a bug on a screen that needed fixing. Or was it?

## Big things can happen when government gets out of the way

In Herzberg's case, an alarm was supposed to signal for the person behind the wheel to act.[17] Something clearly went awry. That's because the programmers had also taught the Volvo XC90 to avoid pedestrians, or at least they thought they did. As it turned out, they designed the algorithm to recognize people whenever they were in an area marked off in the white-and-black pattern of a crosswalk. According to what the artificial intelligence had learned, jaywalking pedestrians weren't within the realm of possibility. That's how it had been trained.[18] So, technically, they had told the car to brake automatically when it neared people. They just hadn't considered a scenario like this one.

Our machines will only be as smart as we teach them to be. They'll be "ethical" only to the extent that we can delineate the wide array of decision matrices they'll need to calculate. But let's pump the brakes. Is that even possible? Whose morals do we use as inputs? All technologies are tools, and tools aren't intrinsically good or evil. This gets complicated quickly—because of us, not the machines.

The people who design these systems could have honorable or evil motivations. Sometimes they might luckily make the right predictions; on the other hand, they could fail due to terrifying yet completely unintended errors. Or they might code in beliefs and biases they aren't even aware they had. Do good intentions matter if innocent people die by accident anyway? Does selfishness matter if they happen to survive?

Artificial intelligence, as a tool, could have positive or negative outcomes. But by itself, it is not inherently good or bad. A tool is amoral. How it gets made, and why it gets used—that's what is good or bad. Still, we can't expect there to be universal agreement about the exact moment when the right level of "good" becomes palatable enough to justify a stomachable amount of "bad." Life's tough tradeoffs are seldom straightforward. Regardless, from here on out, many more of history's outcomes will be writ with code.

If the Volvo XC90 wasn't ethically responsible, who was? Strategic decisions were made at Uber. The self-driving team subscribed to Uber's aggressive, do-whatever-it-takes culture, which came straight from Travis Kalanick. "Autonomous transportation is very possibly winner-take-all and, thus, existential for Uber," Kalanick told his employees, according to Alex Davies's book *Driven: The Race to Create the Autonomous Car.* Uber executives worried that they were going to lose the race. "We started from a huge gap with Google, and I think we've all been sobered by how hard it is to close that gap, even with exceptional effort," Jeff Holden, Uber's chief product officer, wrote in an email to Kalanick. The head of Uber's Advanced Technologies Group, John Bares, wrote, "My strain, personal strain, increasing pressure to catch up seven years and deploy 100,000 cars in 2020."[19] Mistakes were made in Uber's drive to grow fast. The company didn't take time to weigh all the necessary precautions. But should we have expected it to? Or is speed required to progress?

"It starts with understanding that the world is going to go self-driving and autonomous," Kalanick told Biz Carson of *Business Insider* in August 2016. "So if that's happening, what would happen if we weren't a part of that future? If we weren't part of the autonomy thing?" he asked rhetorically. "Then the future passes us by basically, in a very expeditious and efficient way," he warned. At the time, not only was he concerned about Google's advances in artificial intelligence and automated vehicles; Apple and other competitors worried him, too.

Carson asked him if Uber could ever catch up. Kalanick replied that it was existential: "Well, it's not about whether I think it is—it's that it has to be. So, if we are not tied for first, then the person who is in first, or the entity that's in first, then rolls out a ride-sharing network that is far cheaper or far higher-quality than Uber's, then Uber is no longer a thing."[20]

In the months before Herzberg's death, Uber's self-driving cars in Arizona logged 84,000 miles a week. "We were trying to ramp up really quickly, which at the time was what Uber was good at—or able to do," Uber's Jonathan Barentine, who at the time was responsible for training the nondriver operators, told Lauren Smiley of *Wired*. His choice of words was meaningful: revising "good at" to "able to do" midthought showed a moral reckoning, which had come with time to pause and reflect after leaving Uber. He likely had little chance to do that while under the pressures of his job, considering the "Always Be Hustlin' " culture, where performance metrics incentivized more self-driving miles even when it meant taking greater risks. According to Barentine, "These were pretty purposely outrageous goals."[21]

That much was clear in the slogan Uber executives told employees: "crush miles." One of the shortcuts they'd considered was to have just one person in the vehicle. Rather than asking two Uber employees to monitor for safety, they'd just trust a single operator. In the fall of 2017, weeks before Kalanick resigned, Uber decided to do just that.[22]

So, was the former CEO to blame, even though he wasn't around anymore? What about Uber managers who demanded that their employees strive for ridiculous goals and then changed policies that increased risks? Or what about Rafaela Vasquez? She was in the driver's seat, after all. According to police reports and a federal investigation, Vasquez was supposed to take over controls of the car at a moment's notice to prevent this from happening. She was expected to be as attentive as any of us would have been behind the wheel—when driving the car normally.[23]

Except that was not her expectation, because the car was autonomous. She told the police that when they arrived. "The car was in auto-drive," she spontaneously self-exonerated. "And all of a sudden, the car didn't see it. I didn't see it. And all of a sudden it was just there." She kept using "it" to describe a person, the same determination the self-driving Uber had made, that Herzberg was just an object in the road. Then, haltingly, Vasquez used words that were more personal, more responsible: "But, shot out in front, and then I think, *I know*, I hit them."[24]

*　*　*

Back at headquarters in Northern California, Uber knew there were problems. In fact, just five days prior, the head of the company's autonomous testing division, Robbie Miller, sent an email warning that "the cars are routinely in accidents resulting in damage."[25] Amir Efrati of the *Information* published his email, which then received coverage in numerous media outlets.[26] He cited multiple cases where operators were poorly trained; they hadn't been fired, even if they'd made repeated mistakes. "A car was damaged nearly every other day in February," he noted. "Repeated infractions for poor driving rarely results in termination. Several of the drivers appear to not have been properly vetted or trained."[27] As for Vasquez, she'd received recent citations for speeding, failing to stop at a red light, driving with a suspended license, lacking a current registration, and not having insurance.[28] She had previously served almost four years in prison for attempted armed robbery when she and an accomplice tried to rob a Blockbuster Video coworker.[29]

Once journalists learned those facts—and police called the crash "entirely avoidable" and assessed that if Vasquez had been focused on the road, she could have stopped 42 feet in front of Herzberg—the public narrative changed. Instead of blaming Herzberg's death on Uber's failure to address known problems, many journalists began to accuse Vasquez. As *Wired*'s Lauren Smiley wrote, "The media focus shifted from Uber to Vasquez, sometimes in cartoonishly villainous terms."[30] Many of those same stories that condemned Vasquez failed to mention what Smiley reported: Herzberg struggled with mental health issues and addiction, had been homeless for many years, and had also previously spent time behind bars. Few of the journalists who criticized Vasquez also included these details about the jaywalking victim: toxicology tests revealed Herzberg had methamphetamine and marijuana in her system when she died.[31]

* * *

The solutions Robbie Miller offered likely would have saved Elaine Herzberg's life. For example, he called for every vehicle to have two Uber employees in the car at all times, until the company could fix the technical problems that kept happening.[32] Reverting to Uber's earlier policies would have required the operator to call out obstacles and traffic signs, and the person in the passenger seat would then confirm that the vehicle's artificial intelligence had correctly registered each of them by using a laptop connected to Uber's systems. In any case, this would have at least created a basic safeguard against the operator not paying attention while behind the wheel.[33]

Vasquez had been told to watch out, be ready, stay alert. That was what she was being paid to do, and that's what Uber had told the Arizona officials that she would be doing, when elected politicians and career public servants had all ensured that their state would become home to this new technology.[34] That's what the public was promised. These public officials were supposed to govern wisely, and to protect and serve only the public interest, with "true faith and allegiance." That was in the oath that they'd taken.[35] Arizona policymakers, in their public statements and their regulatory frameworks, embraced Uber's risk-taking and shortcuts. It's fair to ask whether they were somewhat responsible, too.

Uber had first launched the self-driving cars in San Francisco, following its standard playbook to act first, then figure things out. The state of California had already updated the laws to require companies to apply for autonomous vehicle testing permits, but Uber ignored the application process. That gambit backfired when the state revoked registrations for Uber's test vehicles, which had been caught on camera running red lights citywide. That didn't stop Uber. It put the cars on a flatbed truck, destined for Arizona. "Arizona welcomes Uber self-driving cars with open arms and wide open roads," announced Governor Doug Ducey. "While California puts the brakes on innovation and change with more bureaucracy and more regulation, Arizona is paving the way for new technology and new businesses."[36]

This fit with Ducey's governing philosophy. As he later proclaimed, "Big things can happen when government gets out of the way of innovation, creativity, and entrepreneurship."[37] That's what Travis Kalanick believed, too, and he not only wanted government out of the way—he wanted to destroy all competitors, breaking rules when necessary. That was clear in the text messages he sent to Anthony Levandowski, whose self-driving trucking company, Otto, had recently been acquired by Uber after Otto completed the longest continuous journey by a driverless and autonomous semitruck, 131.99 miles long.[38]

Levandowski had previously worked on autonomous vehicles for Google (which, again, became Alphabet in 2015). After he left, the company branded that project as Waymo, and it accused Levandowski of stealing files. Alphabet sued Uber for theft of trade secrets. Uber's meeting notes and text messages between Kalanick and Levandowski became public during court proceedings. They included Kalanick's instructions to Levandowski in March 2016 to "burn a village," and declarations he reportedly made at a strategy meeting about self-driving cars a month later: "The golden time is over. It is war time," and "Cheat codes. Find them. Use them."[39] Levandowski texted Kalanick, "We do need to think through the strategy to take all the shortcuts we can find," and "I just see this as a race and we need to win, second place is first loser."[40] Lawyers also discovered that Levandowski had sent Kalanick a link to a YouTube video of the 1987 movie *Wall Street*, saying, "Here's a speech you need to give;-)."[41]

It was the often-quoted Gordon Gekko speech, and it makes sense in retrospect. "Greed is good" taught people like Travis Kalanick and Anthony Levandowski, who were teenagers in the late eighties and early nineties, that business success was the end-all-be-all, then they went to new extremes. Hollywood took rugged individualism, polished it up, and made it shine: "Greed is right. Greed works. Greed clarifies, cuts through, and captures the essence of the evolutionary spirit," Michael Douglas installed in the national operating system of America in 1987, right before Kalanick and his peers were teenagers.[42] Milton Friedman's moneymaking-at-all-costs philosophy had come of age as they did, becoming an unquestioned maxim in most of corporate America. Paired with Ayn Rand's virtue of selfishness, it became a moral imperative: greed was a positive good. The Church of Creative Capitalism had created the belief system that justified Big Tech's excesses and rule-breaking early in the twenty-first century, and then the Silicon Age's entrepreneurs put those ideologies on hyperdrive.

But we didn't notice, possibly because we were too busy staring down at our phones, like Rafaela Vasquez was. For the 11.8 miles before the Uber hit Elaine Herzberg, she kept getting distracted.[43] That's too charitable of a word. Vasquez looked down over two hundred times at her device, according to police reports. In a twenty-two-minute span, she spent six minutes and forty-seven seconds focused on her phone, which rested on her right knee. Detectives estimated that 85 percent of motorists could have seen Herzberg 143 feet down the road.[44]

Vasquez didn't see Herzberg. She was looking down. The car didn't recognize a human in the road. Neither did Vasquez. Right before 10 p.m., when the vehicle struck Herzberg, Vasquez had been streaming something on Hulu.[45] "My mother Elaine Herzberg is loved and missed by everyone that knew her. R.I.P. mom until I see you again I love and miss you," wrote Herzberg's daughter in response to a blog post about her mom's death. She added, "There is not a day that goes by that I don't think about her or about what her and I would be doing right now of [sic] she was still alive."[46]

Elaine Herzberg was run over by an autonomous Uber that failed to stop, while Vasquez streamed an episode of *The Voice* on her phone.[47]

Whether we blamed the technology or human beings for this death was more complicated. If we said technology, then was it somehow the phone's fault, or should we blame the self-driving car? If we said people, then who was responsible? Was it the distracted operator of the "driverless" car, whom the media excoriated for her criminal past? Was it the jaywalker who was an ex-convict, too, on drugs at the time and homeless, meandering across the road at night? As we think about their histories, should we also consider why their past choices mattered so much in our decision? Who are we to judge?

What about Uber's software programmer who wrote the code, which preset it so that the vehicle could not recognize her as a living being in the final moments of her life? Was Travis Kalanick and his growth-at-all-costs culture to blame, or the Uber managers who established the incentives to "crush miles"? Was it the definition of success in Silicon Valley, and of American capitalism more generally, that urged, "Greed is good"? Or was it Robbie Miller, who led Uber's autonomous testing and had warned about the malfunctioning machines but didn't get them shut them down? Was it the regulators back in California who put laws in place limiting self-driving cars, which led Uber to go elsewhere rather than comply, or was it the Arizona politicians, who knew about those risks and had welcomed Uber anyway? Who should be held accountable? Should we blame the laws or those who wrote them? Were the drivers at fault or were the cars? Was it the fast-paced businesses or those who steered them? Should we blame the machines or those who made them?

What caused Elaine Herzberg's death? Who, or what, was at fault?


## He just changes the rules as he goes

At Uber, it kept getting more expensive to win the race to a driverless future. Acquiring Otto had cost $680 million.[48] But years earlier, and six weeks before he left to start the company, Levandowski "downloaded over 14,000 highly confidential and proprietary design files for Waymo's various hardware systems, including designs of Waymo's LiDAR and circuit board," according to Waymo. It claimed Levandowski "downloaded 9.7 GB of Waymo's highly confidential files and trade secrets, including blueprints, design files and testing documentation."[49] Soon after Waymo's accusations, Uber fired Levandowski.[50] A few months after that, Uber announced that it would shut down the self-driving trucks unit and focus on freight and logistics more generally.[51]

It was a quintessential example of the close-knit world of Silicon Valley's elites: Google Ventures had invested in Uber's Series C round. Putting $258 million into Uber was the largest investment Google Ventures had ever made, and it was a huge bet at the time, considering that it had only committed to deploy $300 million in total.[52] When Uber went public, Google Ventures had 5.2 percent of the company, which was worth billions, in addition to its separate 5.3 percent stake in Lyft, which was worth around $780 million.[53] Ultimately, Uber would settle the case for $245 million and apologize with these words: "To our friends at Alphabet: we are partners, you are an important investor in Uber, and we share a deep belief in the power of technology to change people's lives for the better. Of course, we are also competitors. And while we won't agree on everything going forward, we agree that Uber's acquisition of Otto could and should have been handled differently."[54]

They were friends, they were enemies; they were investors, they were competitors. Lines had blurred and roles had reversed. Even after this feud, Waymo and Uber would make amends. On May 23, 2023, they jointly announced a multiyear deal to "bring together Waymo's world-leading autonomous driving technology with the massive scale of Uber's ridesharing and delivery networks." The first self-driving Ubers would soon be available, with a tap on a screen, in Phoenix, Arizona, thanks to the partnership with Alphabet's Waymo.[55]

Rivalries faded, rules were rewritten, and ethics were recalculated. And that odd but memorable line, perhaps the most idealistic three words of the Silicon

Age—it had vanished, too. Weeks after Elaine Herzberg took her last breath, Google deleted this entire paragraph from its Code of Conduct: "'Don't be evil.' Googlers generally apply those words to how we serve our users. But 'Don't be evil' is much more than that. Yes, it's about providing our users unbiased access to information, focusing on their needs and giving them the best products and services that we can. But it's also about doing the right thing more generally—following the law, acting honorably, and treating co-workers with courtesy and respect."[56] "Don't be evil" had been a part of the company's Code of Conduct since Page and Brin wrote it in 2000. In fact, that phrase had been prominently featured as the very first words in its preface. Warnings against various manifestations of "evil" had appeared in four different ways throughout the document, too. By early May 2018, that had all been wiped away. What remained, as an afterthought, were these words at the very end: "And remember . . . don't be evil, and if you see something that you think isn't right—speak up!"[57]

In 2019 Larry Page and Sergey Brin left the company entirely, observing that "since we wrote our first founders' letter, the company has evolved and matured." They still believed, "Nonetheless, Google's core service—providing unbiased, accurate, and free access to information—remains at the heart of the company."[58] Were they lying to themselves, or lying to all of us, or both? One thing was for sure: the little project initially developed every night from 2 a.m. to 6 a.m. called Backrub now governed so much of our digital experience—whether unbiased or evil or not. It decided our understanding of the world; it determined what we saw, learned, and believed to be true. It was hard to see the difference clearly anymore between reality or fiction, ads or answers, facts or opinions, or evil or good—and who knew if it mattered either way? In the end, they were all just words, words, words. And these words had seemed to lose all meaning, or at least power.

That was the outcome with Alphabet in our world. "Don't Be Evil" became more part of company history than present practice. All that was left of the Stanford Students' early actions against the dark arts of insidious businesses was now reduced to an inert seventeen-word "see something, say something" afterthought, which seemed to fade away, losing significance, a pale last remembrance, a boyish ideal's final dying whimper.

*** ***

Anthony Levandowski's troubles had just begun. As Alex Davies documented in *Driven*, Levandowski sent an email to Larry Page days before he quit Google, around the time of his illegal actions: "I want to be in the driver seat, not the passenger seat, and right now feels like I'm in the trunk."[59] That statement was soaked in irony, given that he was one of the world's experts in self-driving cars. It also revealed his, well, my-way-or-the-highway attitude.

"He plays above board," a Google colleague later recalled. "He just changes the rules as he goes." Another remembered that Levandowski often wore a t-shirt that said, "I Drink Your Milkshake."[60] It was a reference to the final lines of the film *There Will Be Blood* (2007), which celebrated how the meek will lose the earth and only the strong survive: "Here, if you have a milkshake and I have a milkshake, and I have a straw . . . my straw reaches acroooooooss the room and starts to drink your milkshake," the greedy oil baron played by Daniel Day Lewis seethed in the final scene. Then, for emphasis: "I. Drink. Your. Milkshake! I drink it up!"[61]

After Google and Uber settled out of court, federal prosecutors charged Levandowski with thirty-three counts of theft.[62] The U.S. district judge deemed it the "biggest trade secret crime I have ever seen," declaring that "billions [of dollars] in the future were at play, and when those kind of financial incentives are there good people will do terrible things, and that's what happened here."[63] In fact, Alphabet wanted Levandowski to return the $120 million he'd earned at Google before he resigned and started Otto (or, more accurately, which he'd earned while developing the technology he'd then steal to start Otto).[64] On August 4, 2020, Levandowski confessed to his crime. He pled guilty to one of the thirty-three counts and was sentenced to eighteen months in prison. The Department of Justice dropped all remaining charges.[65]

But Levandowski never went to prison. His lawyers argued that since he had pneumonia, incarceration would be a "death sentence" due to COVID-19.[66] The judge agreed, stating that he didn't need to report to prison until the worst of the pandemic had passed. Then, on January 20, 2021, minutes before Joe Biden took the oath of office, Donald Trump pardoned Anthony Levandowski. As a result, he never spent a single moment behind bars.[67]

## Anthony's supporters, the debt collectors

The Trump administration defended the president's choice with these words: "This pardon is strongly supported by James Ramsey, Peter Thiel, Miles Ehrlich, Amy Craig, Michael Ovitz, Palmer Luckey, Ryan Petersen, Ken Goldberg, Mike Jensen, Nate Schimmel, Trae Stephens, Blake Masters, and James Proud, among others."[68] The sequence mattered: Ramsey was one of Levandowski's lawyers, then came Thiel. Ehrlich and Craig were two of Levandowski's other lawyers.[69] Most of Levandowski's other supporters had strong ties to Thiel.

Ovitz had cofounded Creative Artists Agency, which represented many of Hollywood's biggest names, from Martin Scorsese and Sean Connery to Steven Spielberg and David Letterman. Over the years, he had brokered the sale of numerous major Hollywood studios. He ran marketing and advertising for the Coca-Cola Company, including by creating the lovable, memorable polar bear campaign. He'd run Disney from October 1995 to January 1997.[70] And, on top of all that, he was an early investor in Thiel's company Palantir, where he'd also served as a senior advisor for over a decade.[71]

James Proud joined the first class of Thiel Fellows; at age nineteen, he'd skipped college, and Thiel paid him $100,000 annually for two years. He decided to build an alarm clock and sleep tracker called Sense.[72] Thiel invested $2 million in the company, which Proud named Hello.[73] This was a rarity because most Thiel Fellows didn't also receive an investment from Thiel, but he made an exception because, as he told Brian Solomon of *Forbes*, "James stood out from the start as extremely tenacious and determined." Solomon's article was titled, "Peter Thiel's Chosen One." Proud appeared on the magazine's cover for the *Forbes* "30 Under 30" list, standing next to Olympic legend Michael Phelps. Motivated to be even brasher than the other Thiel Fellows, the young entrepreneur more than lived up to his name, showing incredible arrogance in the interview with Solomon. During their lunch conversation, Proud mocked Silicon Valley for its "airy-fairy bullshit about changing the world," and he declared, "No one can make me do what I don't want to do." When Solomon asked him about competitors like Google, Apple, and Amazon, his outrage was outrageous: "Looking up from his lamb ribs and roast pork, he lifts both hands in a double-middle-finger salute." The magazine hit newsstands on January 23, 2017.[74]

On June 12, 2017, Proud shuttered his startup, firing all fifty employees.[75] "The past few months have been incredibly tough, especially on the team of Hello," Proud wrote with contrition. "For that I'm incredibly sorry."[76] On CBInsight's rankings of over 250 "of the biggest, costliest startup failures of all time," Proud's failure was in the top half.[77] He'd raised $52.9 million for a $149 alarm clock that wouldn't even charge reliably. As Solomon had reported, the power cable didn't fit the device. He explained, "When I brought a Sense home, I nearly abandoned the set-up process after an hour of trying and failing to plug in the charging cable."[78] Proud struggled to sell off the leftover assets. The competitors he'd mocked, like Google, Apple, and Amazon, didn't want his scraps.[79]

Ryan Peterson founded Flexport, a logistics company whose $20 million Series A round was led by Thiel's Founders Fund in August 2015.[80] Flexport was described as a logistics startup that would bring "an Uber-like experience" to shipping and freight, resulting in "a really rich dataset to look into and understand traffic patterns."[81] In June 2016 Peterson was asked during an interview at TechCrunch Shanghai if he would have taken Founders Fund's investment if he knew Thiel would support Donald Trump. "Probably not, actually," he replied. "Well, it depends on how desperate we were. I don't think that supporting Donald Trump is an acceptable position, honestly. For our business, it would be disastrous."[82]

He was mistaken on both of those points. On September 26, 2016, Flexport raised $65 million in its Series B round. Its lead investor was Founders Fund.[83]

On September 21, 2017, Flexport raised its $110 million Series C round. Founders Fund invested yet again.[84] What about the "disastrous" consequences? In August 2020 Peterson told Danny Fortson on the *Danny in the Valley* podcast, "Trump got elected, and you had trade wars, tariffs, all through '17, '18, '19, and '20 is COVID. So I think our company was kind of battle tested. Like, we're used to chaos." The changing rules meant an unpredictable environment not only for Flexport but also other logistics firms: "Every time Trump would launch a new tariff, within five minutes, we're figuring out, okay, here are the customers that are going to be affected; within an hour, their account managers have the names of every customer to call and here's the dollar amount, let's start strategizing and reaching out."[85]

By staying flexible, true to its name, Peterson's company solved the problems posed by each new trade restriction. Flexport also paid far higher taxes due to the Trump administration's policies: "The average tariff that is paid really went up substantially, it's now in the double digits and it used to be less than 2 percent in tariffs being paid. We paid a billion dollars to the U.S. Government last year on behalf of our customers, in taxes."[86] But by remaining agile, it continued to grow, despite the Trump administration's unpredictable orders. Flexport's responsiveness gave it an advantage over less nimble corporations that dominated the shipping industry. By 2022 it was worth over $8 billion.[87]

Others on the White House's list were also close to Peter Thiel. As mentioned, Blake Masters worked for him, at Thiel Capital and as president of the Thiel Foundation. Trae Stephens had worked for him at Founders Fund, then Stephens and Luckey had cofounded Anduril with two of the earliest hires at Palantir (one of whom also worked for Thiel at Mithril Capital).[88] Previously, Luckey had built the virtual reality headset Oculus—by duct-taping together a prototype for Kickstarter and securing an investment from Founders Fund— and then he sold the company, nineteen months after its debut, for $2 billion to Facebook.[89]

Many more billions would follow, because Mark Zuckerberg reoriented the future of Facebook towards the metaverse. He even changed the company's name to reflect its importance. Over a three-year period, $36 billion went towards developing the technology needed to create immersive virtual worlds.[90] That exceeded what the United States had spent, adjusted for inflation, on the Manhattan Project to develop the atomic bomb, as Farhad Manjoo noted in the *New York Times*.[91] Even after so much investment, virtual reality remained highly unprofitable. Reality Labs, the company's virtual reality division, had annual operating losses of $13.7 billion by 2022.[92]

Zuckerberg had bet that the money brought in from the company's "Family of Apps," including Facebook, Facebook Messenger, Instagram, and WhatsApp, could pay for all this research and development. But Wall Street disagreed. Just about a year after becoming Meta, its stock price had dropped 75 percent, leading to $800 billion in market value lost. That cost Zuckerberg, personally, $76.8 billion, over half of his fortune according to *Forbes*.[93] "There Has to Be a Better Way to Lose $800 Billion," Ben Cohen's *Wall Street Journal* headline read on November 3, 2022. The subheading read: "Intelligent failures in business are based on small bets. Meta bet the company."[94] Six days after that article, Facebook announced it had laid off eleven thousand people. "I got this wrong, and I take responsibility for that," Zuckerberg confessed in a message to employees, explaining that he'd hoped online commerce would continue to accelerate after COVID-19 subsided. He'd miscalculated. Too many shoppers returned to stores in real life.[95]

Zuckerberg still stuck to his decision to bet the company on the metaverse, though. He told the remaining employees, "We do historically important work," and he explained that they would concentrate on "a smaller number of high priority growth areas," which involved both Reality Labs and the company's Family of Apps. "Our core business is among the most profitable ever built with huge potential ahead," he explained. But instead of solely focusing there, Meta would still push forward in "developing the technology to define the future of social connection." He concluded, "I believe we are deeply underestimated as a company today."[96] Just four months later, in March 2023, Zuckerberg announced an additional ten thousand Meta employees would lose their jobs.[97]

Palmer Luckey was not on the Reality Labs team; Meta had let him go much earlier, back when it was still Facebook. Luckey claimed it was "for no reason at all," hinting, "I gave $10,000 to a pro-Trump group, and I think that's something to do with it."[98] Even so, Luckey took credit for Facebook's shift to the metaverse. "When we were acquired, people told me Oculus would be taken over and turned into Facebook," he told Steven Levy for *Wired*. "I think it's been the other way around: Facebook got taken over by Oculus, and it turned into Oculus."[99]

At Anduril, Luckey shifted from building virtual worlds for everybody and instead focused on creating high-tech surveillance tools for police and military forces. In July 2020, less than three years after its founding, Anduril signed a five-year contract with U.S. Customs and Border Protection to develop a "virtual border wall" of surveillance towers powered by artificial intelligence designed to detect illegal immigrants, through a deal worth several hundred million dollars.[100] It also soon debuted a new "ghost" drone that could noiselessly fly above the border.[101] In January 2022 the U.S. Department of Defense announced that Anduril beat out eleven other bidders to win a ten-year, $1 billion contract for surveillance using drones, "in various locations within and outside the continental U.S."[102] Founders Fund was Anduril's first investor, too.[103]

The executives at Anduril benefited from the insights and perspective Thiel had gained over many years with Palantir, another surveillance company we will learn about in the next chapter. The names of both companies came from J.R.R. Tolkien's series *The Lord of the Rings*. The palantír was a "seeing stone" that allowed people to communicate across long distances or see into the past when they looked into it.[104] Andúril was the name given to an extremely powerful sword wielded by one of Tolkien's greatest heroes, Aragon, who had carried around the broken pieces of an ancient weapon and then had them reforged before several of the greatest battles in Tolkien's books. The name meant "Flame of the West," appropriate for a company based in Costa Mesa, California.[105] But first we will learn more about a Thiel-backed surveillance company that debuted around the same time as Anduril, with a simpler name that said what it did directly: using artificial intelligence to search a massive database of our photos, Clearview AI.

## A facial recognition tool that could eliminate public anonymity

According to revelations in Kashmir Hill's book *Your Face Belongs to Us: A Secretive Startup's Quest to End Privacy as We Know It*, Hoan Ton-That, Chuck Johnson, and the other entrepreneurs who were building the first prototypes of Clearview AI (then known as Smartcheckr) claimed they'd partnered with Anduril when both companies were in the startup phase. In 2017, before Anduril had launched, Smartcheckr pitched the Hungarian government on "a unique joint venture with Oculus Virtual Reality founder Palmer Luckey," promoting that Anduril's drone software would be "technologically integrated with the Smartcheckr search platform." They told the Hungarians that the combined offering would provide "instant background reviews of individuals attempting to cross the border." Based on the evidence Hill reviewed, she critiqued these as brazen overpromises. "These surreal claims were far beyond what Smartcheckr was actually capable of at that time, judging from internal emails," she wrote, adding, "but that is what startups do: fake it till they make it."[106]

And with that, the line between "secretive" and "deceptive" blurred even further.

In the months after Hill's *New York Times* exposé "The Secretive Company That Might End Privacy as We Know It" in early 2020, *BuzzFeed* published numerous stories about the startup, including one in which a spokesperson for Anduril disavowed any relationship with Clearview AI.[107] Then Luke O'Brien published further revelations on April 7, 2020, in a *HuffPost* article titled "Far-Right Extremists Helped Create the World's Most Powerful Facial Recognition Technology." O'Brien had been handed a trove of corporate files, private Facebook posts, Slack Channel screenshots, and other documents, which led him to conclude that Chuck Johnson was not the only person close to Peter Thiel who helped with Clearview AI and its precursor Smartcheckr; Jeff Giesea, who had been editor of the *Stanford Review* before working at Thiel Capital Management, had also helped Hoan Ton-That. O'Brien also concluded that the earliest brainstorming discussions had involved several of America's most well-known conspiracy theorists and even a few white nationalists.[108]

According to O'Brien, Mike Cernovich, who promoted the near-deadly PizzaGate rumors, had helped with the startup. Weeks before the Republican National Convention in 2016, he'd tweeted a photo of Johnson and Ton-That flashing the "OK" sign (which could've simply meant "OK," but according to the Anti-Defamation League was also being promoted online as a way to signal "White Power," typically to provoke overreactions from liberal critics).[109] O'Brien reported that Douglass Mackey had been hired as a consultant for Smartcheckr. In March 2023 Mackey was convicted by a jury of his peers for interfering with the 2016 election by conspiring to "disseminate fraudulent messages that encouraged supporters of presidential candidate Hillary Clinton to 'vote' via text message or social media which, in reality, was legally invalid," according to the Department of Justice. "Today's verdict proves that the defendant's fraudulent actions crossed a line into criminality," U.S. Attorney Breon Peace declared, "and flatly rejects his cynical attempt to use the constitutional right of free speech as a shield for his scheme to subvert the ballot box and suppress the vote." Mackey faced up to ten years in prison for "attempting to deprive individuals from exercising their sacred right to vote."[110]

O'Brien's documents also connected Ton-That to Tyler Bass, a member of a white nationalist group in Northern Virginia. O'Brien reported that Bass had been hired at Smartcheckr just weeks after bringing his eight-year-old son to the "Unite the Right" rally in Charlottesville, Virginia, where hundreds of far-right extremists would—less than a year after Thiel invested in Smartcheckr—march with tiki torches and chant, "Russia is our friend," "You will not replace us," and the Nazi slogan, "Blood and soil."[111] Another extremist who was not on the Smartcheckr payroll, but who had frequently collaborated with Chuck Johnson, was Andrew "weev" Auernheimer, the webmaster of the white nationalist website the Daily Stormer.[112] The website had been named after the Nazi propaganda paper *Der Stürmer.* It was home to pro-eugenics, anti-Semitic, antigay, misogynistic, and other pestilential content until it was taken offline due to posts that viciously mocked the woman who was murdered on August 12, 2017, after the Unite the Right march.[113] Her killer deliberately drove into a crowd of peaceful counterdemonstrators, ending her life and injuring many others. He was found guilty of twenty-nine federal hate crimes and was sentenced to life in prison plus 419 years.[114]

Nonetheless, Auernheimer and the Daily Stormer both profited, receiving donations in Bitcoin worth millions of dollars from their supporters afterward.[115] In another surprising turn of events, Chuck Johnson began to spread lies on his website that an unrelated person—who was attending a family wedding at his home in Michigan at the time—had been behind the wheel.[116] The misidentified man and his father were forced to flee their residence after incessant death threats. Following many months of undeserved hardship, they sued Johnson for defamation and prevailed. Johnson paid them a settlement and shut down his website.[117]

* * *

Throughout the early months of 2020, Facebook, YouTube, Twitter, LinkedIn, Vimeo, and Venmo had all demanded that Clearview AI stop harvesting images from their sites—with several sending formal cease-and-desist letters.[118] "Scraping people's information violates our policies," a spokesperson for Facebook said, "which is why we've demanded that Clearview stop accessing or using information from Facebook or Instagram."[119] In this instance, we apparently hadn't signed up for *this* in the Terms of Service. Members of Congress wrote them, too. "I write regarding disturbing reports that your company, Clearview, is selling a facial recognition tool that could eliminate public anonymity in the United States," Senator Ed Markey wrote in a letter to Ton-That in January 2020. "Widespread use of your technology could facilitate dangerous behavior and could effectively destroy individuals' ability to go about their daily lives anonymously."[120]

But by the time Congress and these other tech companies knew what had happened, it was too late. Clearview AI had already downloaded so much publicly available data. By that point, the company's internal presentations touted that it had already harvested 2.8 billion photos.[121] By cataloging pictures from Instagram, Facebook, and across all parts of the Internet via Google, Clearview AI had connected the identities of real people to images of faces they had "sourced from public-only web sources, including news media, mugshot websites, public social media, and other open sources."[122] On its website, Clearview AI explained that the service was "search, not surveillance," since it had just gathered the pictures that were already online.[123] After Thiel invested, it had gathered billions of them. It only worked because Clearview AI's systems could pair our pictures to our real identities, which traced all the way back to when Facebook had told us "This Is You" and we'd believed it, so we signed up using unique .edu email addresses to create individual profile pages.

More than six hundred U.S. law enforcement agencies had started using the facial recognition software, with few Americans ever knowing.[124] A Government Accountability Office report in 2021 confirmed that the Departments of Homeland Security, Justice, Health and Human Services, and the Interior all used Clearview AI. The Department of Defense had starting using an operational pilot of its systems in June 2020, and the Departments of Agriculture and

Commerce planned to begin pilots in 2023.[125] By October 2021 Clearview AI's website promoted that it had more than ten billion photos in its system, and it proudly quoted Kashmir Hill's *New York Times* article, with a banner on its website showing the newspaper's logo and boasting that its database "goes far beyond anything ever constructed by the United States Government or Silicon Valley giants."[126] All these photos were harvested by Clearview AI and used by our government without anyone's consent for this purpose. Clearview AI claimed its data collection system had ingested 1.5 billion images a month, according to a deck obtained by the *Washington Post* that revealed that Clearview AI had pitched investors on plans to harvest one hundred billion photos for its database, which would allow it to accurately recognize every person on the planet.[127] Its new slogan: "BUILDING A SECURE WORLD ONE FACE AT A TIME."[128]

Even though Clearview AI promised that it cared about "providing the most cutting-edge technology to law enforcement to investigate crimes, enhance public safety and provide justice to victims," that wasn't the whole truth.[129] Journalists soon revealed that the U.S. government wasn't the only client it had pursued. Private businesses across America and their employees—hundreds of people who had never undergone police training or been vetted for a security clearance—all gained access to Clearview AI's database of billions and billions of photos that connected to the identities of tens of millions of people, completely without their knowledge.

Clearview AI's technology created extraordinary power. From early 2018 until February 2020, 1,803 different local entities accessed Clearview AI's systems. Officials in Mountain Brook, Alabama, population twenty thousand, ran nearly 590 searches, according to a *BuzzFeed* exposé.[130] That was one of twenty articles *BuzzFeed* published over several years to keep track of developments at the company.[131] In one, it publicly disclosed an email from Clearview AI to an officer in Green Bay, Wisconsin, which asked, "Have you tried taking a selfie with Clearview yet? It's the best way to quickly see the power of Clearview in real time." The message encouraged, "Try your friends or family. Or a celebrity like Joe Montana or George Clooney. Your Clearview account has unlimited searches. So feel free to run wild with your searches."[132]

*BuzzFeed* found that more than two hundred prospective corporate clients had done just that. Kohl's and Walmart personnel looked up shoppers. Wells Fargo and Bank of America employees searched for information about their clients. Madison Square Garden security learned more about their guests, as had the NBA. Employees at AT&T, Verizon, and T-Mobile queried Clearview AI. The Las Vegas Sands and Pechanga Resort Casino compared its surveillance videos against Clearview AI's records. Equinox had looked into what it could learn about the lives of its members when they weren't at the gym. The campus police at Columbia University, Southern Methodist University, the University of Alabama, Florida International University, and the University of Minnesota had explored what this powerful platform could do for them as they searched Clearview AI's database for information on students, faculty, staff, and guests of their schools. Those were just five educational institutions among more than fifty, across twenty-four states, that had used the tool without asking or informing anyone.[133] The free trial became more like a free-for-all, as people gained surveillance powers and ran wild with their searches.[134]

Overseas, the police force and employees of the United Arab Emirates sovereign wealth fund had used Clearview AI, according to *BuzzFeed*.[135] Privacy violations in America had caused concerns, but there were additional human rights implications in places like the UAE. The U.S. State Department had cautioned: "Significant human rights issues included allegations of torture in detention; arbitrary arrest and detention, including incommunicado detention, by government agents; political prisoners; government interference with privacy rights."[136] Then again, was it worse if an oppressive government began to do any of that with Clearview AI's capabilities, or if this aggressive American venture gained these powers, then sold surveillance back to our government, paid for with taxpayer dollars and without our knowledge at the time? What was the difference? By early 2023 Clearview AI updated its website. Where it had once advertised that it had ten billion faces in the system, it had tripled to thirty billion.[137]

It is now time for a music lesson. This one comes from a few years earlier, before Clearview AI had downloaded billions of photos of our faces, at a time when we posted freely to Facebook and Instagram, before they were Meta.[138]

Late one night in January 2017, Sturgill Simpson had a message for America. It was a particular moment in time: this was a few months after Peter Thiel's investment in the Trump campaign had been announced, and ten days after the inauguration of the forty-fifth president of the United States; months had passed since Thiel and Hoan Ton-That had first met to discuss the business idea for Smartcheckr, but it was before they'd launched the facial recognition company that would become Clearview AI. Palmer Luckey still worked at Facebook, and Anduril did not yet exist; across America, *Hillbilly Elegy* had been a bestseller for several months, while J. D. Vance remained a "Never Trump guy." Sturgill's band performed a song from his new album, *A Sailor's Guide to Earth*, for *Saturday Night Live*.

One of the most popular comments on the YouTube video put it best: "I have a feeling Sturgill told the band that we probably ain't ever gonna be invited back to SNL so let's just go out and burn the whole damn place down."[139] That person sure had it right. It was barnburner as the band railed on their instruments, in the bright red key of E, to light up *Saturday Night*.

The lead guitarist struck the strings of his Gretsch Billy-Bo Thunderbird like flint for fire. The drummer pummeled his kit with such ferocity, he didn't just keep time, he'd bent it; they played at such velocity, they wouldn't just change your mind, they'd dent it. The trumpeter took your breath away, too, with a roaring "dah-dah *dahhhh* dah, dah-dah *dahhhh* dah," interpolation from "Tequila." While serving up the outro, the organist surfed on his instrument, which Sturgill soon kicked in a riot of rock and roll revolt.

This is a different kind of revolution from the one you're probably imagining—not one with mobs raging or renegades rampaging—but it feels somehow sacred, like something set apart. Because if you believe in evil at all, you'd better have faith that there are better rebels out there, too. When they're banging on those instruments, like gavels, for justice, that's when we'll know the time has come. We'll rejoice once they rouse us. As each note sounds to burn it all down, they'll build us all up, one good word at a time. Sturgill's twenty lines of lyrics, *like ninety-five theses*, electrified and amplified, revamped into melodies, history here in harmony, *finally*. That night, *and what a night it was*, because . . .

*That night, they nailed it.*

They say you can never step in a river twice, because the river's changed and so are you. With that song, those instruments ended up too torn up. The way they were played, it was never the same. *And also with you.*

Their rebel song was called "Call to Arms." In the first two verses, Sturgill sang about the lives wasted from worsening wars, then his protest hit home with the third stanza. As drones buzzed overhead, unnoticed, we'd kept our heads bowed. We worshipped false idols in our devices. We ignored the unmerciful machinations by modern masters of war.

But something changed that Saturday night, like a sudden flash of blinding light that revealed the anguish that awaited us. Sturgill slammed his hand on his woodgrain Telecaster with a Rebel Alliance logo on it, until it all reached a crescendo. He held his guitar high, like some hardworking hammer, and then pounded it down to the ground, *like an answer*. He stared out at America, a prizefighter in his prime, ready for another round, confrontationally, uncompromisingly, in a glorious frenzy and a fit of beauty, with a glint in his glare, as if to ask, *is that all y'all got?*

He'd just sung:

> Well, nobody's looking up to care about a drone
> All too busy looking down at our phone
> Ego's begging for food like a dog from a feed
> Refreshing obsessively until our eyes start to bleed
> They serve up distractions and we eat 'em with fries
> Until the bombs fall out of American skies.[140]

# CHAPTER 13

# A NEW CRUSADE

Peter Thiel, Palantir

Americans' diminishing privacy due to surveillance capitalism, the erosion of our civil liberties by digital means, and the constant scrutiny of our daily lives by private companies can be traced back to when the twenty-first century began. That was not at a tick past midnight on December 31, 1999, because the Y2K catastrophe never happened. A truly barbaric and far more horrible one soon did, though. "The 21st century started with a bang on September 11, 2001," Peter Thiel wrote in an essay for a symposium hosted with René Girard at Stanford. He was correct about that. "And what was needed to be done, given that technology had advanced to a point where a tiny number of people could inflict unprecedented levels of damage and death?"[1] He was right to ask that, too. A few radicals hadn't suddenly become rocket scientists. They'd turned planes into bombs that felled skyscrapers, blasted the U.S. Pentagon, and terrorized us all.

But for all that he got right, Thiel had the wrong answer about "what was needed to be done." He contended, "Overnight, the fundamentalist civil rights mania of the American Civil Liberties Union (ACLU), which spoke in the language of inviolable individual rights, was rendered an unviable anachronism."[2] Calling fundamental civil rights "fundamentalist" is an extreme statement all by itself. But 9/11 and its aftermath altered the usual left-versus-right political divides in America. Republicans and Democrats rallied around a new multitrillion-dollar, multifront war effort, while civil rights advocates and anti-government libertarians found common cause in their dissent.[3] Thiel speculated on whether *more* war was needed; he claimed privacy was obsolete. In his essay, which he wrote on July 12, 2004, and was published in *Politics & Apocalypse: Studies in Violence, Mimesis, and Culture* in 2007, he turned to Carl Schmitt's philosophies to make sense of the post-9/11 world. He wondered if the West might unite after 9/11 in a "civilizational war," with America leading a modern-day crusade against Islam:

> When bin Laden declares war on the "the infidels, the Zionists, and the crusaders," Schmitt would not counsel reasoned half-measures. He would urge a new crusade as a way to rediscover the meaning and purpose of our lives, perhaps borrowing the exhortation from Pope Urban II at the Council of Clermont, who urged his eager listeners on to the First Crusade back in 1096: "Let the army of the Lord, when it rushes upon his enemies, shout but that one cry, *'Dieu le veult! Dieu le veult!'*" Whatever its shortcomings, Schmitt's account of politics captures the essential strangeness of the unfolding confrontation between the West and Islam.[4]

Thiel explained that "The Islamic side retains a strong religious and political conception of reality," and that "Bin Laden would quote with approval" these appeals for an all-out religious war. Yet he added that many in America and its allies still doubted "why there should be a civilizational war at all." More than a year after American troops had invaded Iraq, Thiel considered an even more aggressive approach than the United States had already taken in the Global War on Terror. He entertained a religious war where "we understand Islam as the providential enemy of the West; and that we can then respond to Islam with the same ferocity with which it is now attacking the West." Reflecting on Schmitt's writings from pre-Hitler Germany, he wondered if a firmer approach was needed to combat Muslim extremists, because "when one runs away from an enemy that continues to fight, one is ultimately going to lose—no matter how great the numerical or technological superiority may appear at the outset."[5]

Thiel presented an oversimplification and a false dichotomy here. He equated the religion of 1.25 billion people, or about one-fifth of the world's population, with the most radical group of violent terrorists who'd gone into hiding in caves and compounds, in faraway places like Afghanistan and Pakistan. He ignored the reality that Muslims lived all around the world; thus referring to the "Muslim world" was a senseless descriptor.[6] Early in the twenty-first century, the country with the largest population of Muslims, which represented 88 percent of its 219 million people, was not even in the Middle East. It was Indonesia, a nation of over 17,500 islands in Southeast Asia led by a secular government with an elected legislature.[7] The third largest population of Muslims globally, with nearly 161 million, wasn't an Arab nation. It was the world's largest democracy, India. In fact, most Muslims lived outside of the Middle East and North Africa.[8] Muslims came from many ethnicities, conversed in numerous languages and dialects, held a wide array of conservative and liberal theological views, and lived all around the world—including nearly forty-seven million Muslims in Europe and the Americas, living throughout the Western World, contributing to contemporary Western civilization.[9]

Taking the Global War on Terror to such extremes, and considering "Islam as the providential enemy of the West," would have been radical, nonsensical, and antithetical to U.S. policy; as President George W. Bush had said in November 2001, "The Islam that we know is a faith devoted to the worship of one God, as revealed through The Holy Qur'an. It teaches the value and importance of charity, mercy, and peace."[10] Yet, after the United States had invaded Iraq and toppled Saddam Hussein, many Muslims feared that the conflict would spread as Thiel conjectured. "Anti-Americanism has deepened, but it has also widened," Andrew Kohut, the director of the Pew Research Center at the time, told the *New York Times* in June 2003. "You now find it in the far reaches of Africa—in Nigeria, among Muslims—and in Indonesia. People see America as a real threat. They think we're going to invade them."[11]

At that time, many Muslims put greater trust in the leader of the Taliban than in the U.S. president. Pew's global survey found that "solid majorities in the Palestinian Authority, Indonesia and Jordan—and nearly half of those in Morocco and Pakistan—say they have at least some confidence in Osama bin Laden to 'do the right thing regarding world affairs.'"[12] So while many people in Muslim communities, from Nigeria to Indonesia, thought the U.S. military was coming after them post-9/11, Thiel mused that it might not be a bad thing for "a new crusade as a way to rediscover the meaning and purpose of our lives."[13] (And, not to bury the lede: he'd just launched Palantir, with the CIA's support, which would be prepared to help with just that.)

## Euro-Americans, do you want to become minorities?

As Americans worried about being attacked again, feelings of patriotism surged, too. Americans' trust in government reached heights that hadn't happened in the three decades prior—or in the two decades since.[14] Seizing the moment, the federal government gained new powers. While serving as a White House fellow in the Bush administration, a Kansan named Kris Kobach helped to start the Department of Justice's National Security Entry-Exit Registration System.[15] This government program created new limitations for *legal* immigrants from Muslim-majority countries (mostly across the Middle East and North Africa, but also encompassing Indonesia) that required them to undergo additional screening and ongoing surveillance.[16] "There are many reasons a person might support Trump that do not involve racism, sexism, xenophobia, or accepting sexual assault," Mark Zuckerberg had reassured his employees in the internal all-company message in 2016.[17] But of all the concerns raised about Trump, the one that Zuckerberg said caused him the greatest personal concern was Trump's proposed "Muslim ban," and he'd asked his team if it violated Facebook's Terms of Service.[18]

During his campaign, Trump had promised "a total and complete shutdown of Muslims entering the United States until our country's representatives can figure out what is going on."[19] Yet that idea wasn't just Trump's, nor did it originate in 2016. Kobach had laid the groundwork for the so-called Muslim registry in the immediate aftermath of 9/11.[20] Fourteen years later, he joined the Trump administration's transition team to focus on immigration issues, which raised concerns from civil rights advocates.[21] CNN called him "a lightning rod for critics who have accused him of extreme racism and having ties to white nationalists" and explained that "Kobach is almost single-handedly responsible for some of the nation's strictest immigration laws in at least a half-dozen states—he not only writes the laws, but advocates for them and battles on their behalf in court."[22] That same year, while Kobach served as Kansas's secretary of state, the ACLU sued. Kobach warned about election fraud, then blocked more than thirty-five thousand eligible voters from participating in elections. The ACLU won, which cost taxpayers in Kansas $1.9 million in legal fees.[23]

As for Kobach? He ran for U.S. Senate in 2020, receiving $850,000 from Peter Thiel in a single contribution, the largest one he'd made since his $1.25 million donation to Trump. Kobach also benefited from a fundraiser at Thiel's Park Avenue penthouse.[24] Thiel kept the funding flowing to the Super PAC supporting Kobach's campaign. He gave and gave, and in the end, all but $30,000 of the $2.13 million they'd raised came from Thiel.[25] Some commentators believed this was a follow-up to Thiel's bet on Trump. In reality, it was a prelude to his support for candidates who were far closer to him—in their ideology and their work history.

Most of the Super PAC's expenditures were standard practice, with its first quarterly report of 2020 listing a series of payments: $70,050 in ad production by the Magnolia Media Group of Mobile, Alabama; $26,250 for consulting services by the Logan Circle Group in Washington, DC; and $40,000 in digital advertising and other media placement services from Red Dog Media in Henderson, Nevada. Then there was a $1,500 charge from Daniel Schwartz of Evanston, Illinois, for "research."[26] That one stood out. Glaringly.

Evanston police had caught a man with that name, at the same address, when he spray painted alarming messages as graffiti on the walls of overpasses. He was charged with six misdemeanor counts of criminal defacement of property. He didn't deny it. He defended his actions to the *Chicago Tribune*: "I was not motivated by hatred of any group. I was motivated by my concerns over immigration policies that I think are hurting the short- and long-term interests of all Americans, regardless of race." He told the *Tribune* that he chose to target areas near metro stations in Chicago's wealthy suburbs, where lawyers and bankers lived, because he wanted them to think twice about the "stranglehold of political correctness" on America.[27] He'd scrawled: "Whites, do u want to become a minority? If so, support mass immigration," "Demography is Destiny," "Euro-Americans, do you want to become minorities? If so support mass immigration," and "circa 2042 Face difficult truths or be dispossessed."[28] Kobach lost his U.S. Senate race, but in the next major election cycle, anti-immigration sentiment intensified.[29]

These fears would only deepen in the years to come. "The Democrats want to change the demographics of this country," a different Thiel-backed politician argued during his Senate campaign in 2022. "They think that if they can bring in millions and millions and millions of illegal aliens, someday they'll be able to grant them amnesty to grant them citizenship and make them reliable Democrat voters. I think it's an electoral plan."[30] Another Thiel-supported candidate agreed. "You're talking about a shift in the democratic makeup of this country that would mean we never win, meaning Republicans would never win a national election in this country ever again," he argued.[31] During that same campaign, he declared that Democrats could not win elections "unless they bring in a large number of new voters to replace the voters that are already here."[32]

The first candidate was Blake Masters. The second was J. D. Vance. The $32.5 million that Thiel gave to the Super PACs for Masters and Vance in 2022 were the largest donations supporting any candidates for Congress that year.[33] David Sacks gave Vance $1 million and donated $500,000 to a Super PAC supporting Masters.[34] Before that, his political contributions ran the gamut. He'd donated to both Republicans and Democrats, including by backing Hillary Clinton over Donald Trump in 2016; he'd supported Gavin Newsom for governor in 2018, then backed the effort to have him recalled in 2021. Yet the donations to Masters and Vance were by far the largest contributions he'd ever made.[35] The huge sums Thiel and Sacks gave to these two campaigns showed just how much money was now influencing American democracy in the Silicon Age, and this book will soon contend with the implications of these anti-immigration platforms. But for the time being, we should recognize that these fear-of-being-replaced concerns didn't appear out of thin air. There was a long and difficult history behind all this scaremongering and finger-pointing, tracing back to Stanford decades ago, with important lessons about power, wealth, and privilege.[36]

* * *

In the article Thiel wrote in 2004 for the Stanford conference honoring René Girard, he explained that the outcomes of Carl Schmitt's clash would have been too much to bear. He worried that a Western world versus "Muslim world" conflict would be a war that America lost, even by winning. "This would be a Pyrrhic victory, for it would come at the price of doing away with everything that fundamentally distinguishes the modern West from Islam." Thiel concluded: "If one agrees with Schmitt's starting assumptions, then the West must lose the war or lose its identity."[37]

What aspects of that identity *were* at risk because of America's wars in Afghanistan, Iraq, and related military engagements throughout the Middle East and North Africa during the first decades of the twenty-first century? In retrospect, the "inviolable individual rights" that groups like the ACLU had stood for should have never been declared an "anachronism" like a few powerful people kept insisting—no matter what Thiel thought, Hoan Ton-That did, or Travis Kalanick believed about making privacy an expendable luxury, which "is about to die and we all better get used to it."[38] Unfortunately, too many Americans failed to recognize the consequences of our overreach, which included not only the erosion of liberties due to acts by our own business leaders and legislators but also (and with even more severe moral consequences) the cruel treatment of prisoners and other staggering human costs, which have been tallied by a team of thirty-five researchers, legal experts, human rights practitioners, and physicians at Brown University. They began their work on the Cost of War project in 2011 and started publishing its most important findings a decade later.[39]

For citizens across the nation, September 11 became a midmorning U.S. civics class, interrupted by two towers in flames. America watched as people jumped, in a free fall we couldn't unsee. So we fought back. We upended 38 million lives, ended 937,000 others, and put $8.6 trillion on our collective credit card (according to the Costs of War estimates, that consisted of $2.1 trillion in debt and $6.5 trillion in interest).[40] Those were the costs of our decisions, which eroded many of the very values we were supposed to fight for all along.

We acted, and reacted, out of formless fear. As just one example, the September 20, 2001, speech when George W. Bush had declared, "Either you are with us, or you are with the terrorists," was billed as the "Freedom at war with fear" speech.[41] How do you fight a war against an emotional response? How could you declare war against terror? Painfully, the twenty-first century started in such trauma that fear became a driving force in U.S. policymaking—and, as we will learn, that meant big business opportunities.

Most of us didn't end up going to war, but we still forfeited ourselves to the constant surveillance of our whereabouts at every moment. We waived many rights that we should've been learning about in that civics class in the first place. We didn't realize the powers the government gained at the time, nor the business interests at work. Fear escalated on all sides, worsening the ever-angrier world we lived in, leading to more fire, fog, and war.

The USA PATRIOT Act passed with astounding bipartisanship, and with even more astonishing speed.[42] It took two days to convince over 87 percent of Congress to allow government officials to detain immigrants indefinitely without trial and to wiretap Americans without warrants, passing 357–66 in the House on October 24, 2001, then 98–1 in the Senate the next day. President George W. Bush signed it into law the day after that.[43] Later, some in Congress admitted that—just like the Internet Terms of Service that we don't read—evidently the same went for one of the most impactful pieces of legislation that Congress passed early in the Silicon Age.[44] As fast as that, our rights eroded. Our privacy seemed an unviable anachronism.

## Before private companies surveilled us, the U.S. government set the stage

The USA PATRIOT Act gave broad new surveillance and detention powers to law enforcement agencies following 9/11. It ushered in sweeping changes, which altered not only how America conducted intelligence on foreigners but also how our government treated Americans.[45] Peter Thiel had just turned thirty-five, and he'd just become a millionaire from the PayPal sale.[46] Mark Zuckerberg was eighteen, just out of high school, and developing his WinAmp plug-in, Synapse-ai.[47] And Jennifer Newstead was in her early thirties, a rising star in the Bush administration. Senior Department of Justice officials had assigned her to lead the efforts to get the law passed.[48]

Two decades later, Patrick Eddington, a senior fellow at the libertarian Cato Institute, denounced the entire process of passing the USA PATRIOT Act as hasty and irresponsible. In a *Detroit News* article, "The PATRIOT Act Has Threatened Freedom for 20 Years," he noted that "the 130-page bill with more than 150 provisions was rushed through both chambers without any meaningful oversight or extensive hearings despite enabling the most sweeping federal surveillance powers ever." In Eddington's view, this created a "government-sponsored dragnet" that led to "the most sweeping forms of surveillance in the history of the republic," with the government acquiring new authorities, ranging from gaining access to your online purchase history to receiving notifications from your bank if you deposited more than $10,000—all without telling you they'd done so.[49]

Several of the decisions made following the USA PATRIOT Act, including the bulk collection of Americans' phone records, have since been deemed unlawful.[50] According to the ACLU, the law "made it easier for the government to spy on ordinary Americans by expanding the authority to monitor phone and email communications, collect bank and credit reporting records, and track the activity of innocent Americans on the Internet. While most Americans think it was created to catch terrorists, the Patriot Act actually turns regular citizens into suspects."[51] And Newstead was given the credit for it. In 2002 the Justice Department honored her for "her enhanced leadership duties and her excellent service on a range of issues—including helping craft the new U.S.A. Patriot Act to protect the United States against terror."[52] In fact, John Yoo praised Newstead in 2006 as the Bush administration's "day-to-day manager of the Patriot Act in Congress."[53] He was the Bush administration lawyer whose memoranda were used to justify "enhanced interrogation techniques"—legalese for the dehumanizing actions against detainees that many deemed to be torture.[54] While senior U.S. government leaders rushed to give themselves new surveillance and interrogatory powers, even when it meant by brutal force, they didn't pause to ask "Should we?," instead focusing on "Could we?" Like so many investors and entrepreneurs during the Silicon Age, they found a way to do it. So they did it.

They also failed to stop and ask this question: "Why weren't plans in place before 9/11, to prevent it?" Years later the CIA inspector general conducted an in-depth report asking just that. It did not conclude that the United States needed to be wiretapped coast-to-coast in new ways, ensuring the federal government and the private companies they contracted with could monitor what American citizens were doing 24/7. Their answer, instead, was that U.S. intelligence leaders failed to plan ahead; we didn't question our assumptions enough; and our analysts lacked the imagination about what extremist groups might do. In fact, the former head of the CIA, George Tenet, had instructed the agency to develop new strategies to address the threat of Al-Qaeda, but it did not follow up on his order in time. The inspector general determined that Tenet, "by virtue of his position, bears ultimate responsibility for the fact that no such strategic plan was ever created, despite his specific direction that this should be done."[55]

One major initiative that Tenet did see through to completion before 9/11, however, was the creation of In-Q-Tel, the CIA's own venture capital group. He tapped Gilman Louie to run it. Louie had a fascinating career trajectory. Prior leading In-Q-Tel, he sold his company to the toys and games company Hasbro, where he was then put in charge of licensing the world's most popular computer game, Tetris, from the Soviet Union.[56] He designed and developed numerous video games, including *Star Trek: The Next Generation—"A Final Unity"* and the *F-16 Fighting Falcon* flight simulator series in the late 1980s, and he was an advisor for *Top Gun: Fire at Will!*, *MechCommander*, and *MechWarrior3* in the late 1990s.[57]

Louie offered Silicon Valley an incredible opportunity. He'd present the problems that the government faced; he'd help entrepreneurs figure out the solution; he'd invest with In-Q-Tel's money that would provide further validation, which would encourage other venture funds to invest, too; and then he'd help them get their first contracts at the Pentagon.[58] With the USA PATRIOT Act in place, the U.S. government could do so much more with the massive troves of data it had access to, but it needed the technology to make sense of it all. Enter Palantir.

***

In his essay making the case for "a new crusade" in 2004, Thiel didn't mention his role with the new antiterrorism startup he'd cofounded the year before. Along with Joe Lonsdale and Stephen Cohen, both recent Stanford computer science graduates, Thiel developed Palantir's business model based on the realization that the antifraud detection algorithms developed at PayPal could have broader applications for all kinds of data—especially post-9/11—to stop terrorists and help banks and law enforcement identify illegal activities.[59] Over the next decade the company developed two main products: Palantir Gotham (which found patterns in data to help intelligence, police, and homeland security officials identify and track down criminals and terrorists) and Palantir Metropolis (which analyzed datasets to find fraud so Wall Street banks and hedge funds could make more money).[60] National security and financial success both mattered to Thiel. "I believe, as a libertarian, that if the security problem is not solved, we will end up with a society with terrorism and no civil liberties at all," he told Oliver Chiang at *Forbes* in 2011, adding, "It should be worth on the order of tens of billions in a few years' time."[61]

According to a talk Gilman Louie gave at Stanford in 2017, Thiel's new venture came out of brainstorming sessions with In-Q-Tel about using PayPal's algorithms to combat terrorism. Louie had already seen how casinos could find collusion between dealers and patrons via patterns in data.[62] He'd tested those tools on the information that the CIA had gathered from intelligence sources in the Middle East, especially Saudi Arabia, where the majority of the hijackers had originated.[63] Louie concluded that many 9/11 hijackers would have been caught by running the casino's algorithms against data they already had about prior terrorist activity, especially intelligence gathered after the World Trade Center attack from 1993.[64] So although other venture capitalists had passed on investing in Palantir, they were right to surmise that the CIA's venture group might be interested when they made the introduction. When Louie first met Thiel and Alex Karp, who had recently become Palantir's CEO, he knew that their technology had important national security implications.[65]

As Louie recalled, the two men came to him with ideas about identifying outliers in data but without a clear problem to solve, telling him, "We got these algorithms on fraudulent transactions. We think there might be some value for the intelligence community." In the same ways the casino's algorithms tracked corrupt actors, Louie thought fraud alerts at PayPal could find other deviant behavior. "We brainstormed, they came back and I kind of said on the blackboard, 'It needs to look like this,'" and based on that advice, Louie said, "The team went away and did a mock-up in two weeks."[66]

Numerous innovations that Americans (and people around the world) use every day were created this way. To solve the problem of integrating imagery taken by multiple satellites, which could create a three-dimensional model of the Earth, Louie had worked with one new venture to develop EarthViewer to assist with spy missions in Iraq.[67] That technology was named Keyhole, and the private sector began using it, too, including when news outlets like CNN would virtually "fly over" the Iraqi landscape to show where battles were being fought. Keyhole received investment not only from In-Q-Tel but also from Sony and Nvidia, and it sold to Google in October 2004.[68] Its technology became Google Earth, which debuted in June 2005.[69] Today many lunchtime searches by parents with a hungry family on vacation, inquiries about the nearest gas station from the interstate, and urgent searches on Google Maps for an emergency room all happen thanks to satellite technologies. Yet few know anything about the foundational innovations built with, and for, the CIA during the Iraq War.[70] Nowadays, were those lunch spots, gas stations, and hospitals the most convenient, or did they each pay to appear there? As for that, we might never know.

We do know how Alex Karp became Palantir's CEO, however. Joe Lonsdale told the story in a post on Quora in 2017: "Peter wanted us to have a CEO who wasnt 21 (or maybe who wasnt the 21 yr old version of Stephen or me)—and we kept meeting and rejecting leaders from the DC defense world—we insisted they didn't get our culture." He commented, self-effacingly, "I'm not sure if he was more shocked that I'd agree to hire somebody senior to me or that 'Dr. Karp' was willing to be a CEO."[71] Karp held his doctorate, but it was not in national security studies. In fact, his doctoral research at Goethe University in Frankfurt, Germany, did not give him knowledge of criminal justice, military force planning, or even data analytics. Karp earned a PhD in neoclassical social theory in 2002.[72] Ostensibly, his coursework at Stanford Law would have mattered more to Palantir than his doctoral research. This could have just been about relationships, since Stanford was where he'd befriended Thiel—they were roommates.[73] On the surface, loyalty seemed to matter more than expertise. But there was more to it than that.

Two decades after attending Stanford Law with Thiel and Keith Rabois, Karp theorized in his thesis about the relationship between aggression and jargon. As Northeastern University's Moira Weigel has observed, Karp studied how taboo phrases and other violations of speech norms could change the ways we understand ourselves. He also explored how the language being used by a social group can reinforce a sense of shared identity.[74] He found that *words do matter*. Ideas could change lives, and outliers could become organizers.[75] In Karp's research, we could see the influence of Stanford's campus controversies from decades before, as well as approaches that would shape Palantir and affect our national security, and personal privacy, for years to come.

Rabois's violation of campus norms was not just an extreme event or a one-time incident. It got people talking and caused them to stop and think. The same went for the *Stanford Review*'s "RAPE AT STANFORD" issue and other extreme actions by these "new campus radicals."[76] Taboo language and defying norms ended existing inertia and upended the status quo. People debated, then they took sides. After 9/11 it was us-versus-them in all new ways. Because of the experiences they'd shared years earlier, Palantir's founders saw an opportunity.

Long after their time together at Stanford, Thiel, Karp, and their friends kept discussing extreme behavior. While Karp researched how taboo ideas could spread, Thiel, Rabois, and Sacks built PayPal's tools to detect payment fraud. Then Rabois and Sacks invested in Palantir, and Thiel and Karp began to use powerful technologies to identify unusual behaviors, to find patterns and outliers in massive datasets.[77] They would track deviant behavior as it spread, on extremist blogs or social media, and they would monitor dangerous groups as they formed, from terrorist cells overseas to drug cartels and gangs in America.

A decade and a half before Anduril and Clearview AI, Palantir's founders saw how data could solve problems that were previously unsolvable. Their brainstorming sessions with In-Q-Tel, Jennifer Newstead's work on the USA PATRIOT ACT (whether it represented "her excellent service" or a disservice that authorized a "government-sponsored dragnet"), and even when Thiel turned to Carl Schmitt to reject "reasoned half-measures" in favor of "a new crusade as a way to rediscover the meaning and purpose of our lives"—all these are data points that make up the privacy-eroding forces of surveillance capitalism. Yet when we connect the dots, Palantir's true founding story does not begin with PayPal's breakthroughs, or a meeting with Gilman Louie, but with Keith Rabois's late night slurs. What Thiel, Karp, Rabois, and Sacks learned from their Stanford experience would help shape all of these powerful Silicon Age corporations, as Big Tech began to make big money off big data.

* * *

What these men learned at Stanford—not only in the classroom but also from the campus controversies—affected the ventures they built. The same went for

Alphabet, Meta, and so many other corporations. They didn't go to California like the campus radicals of the 1960s, to *turn on, tune in, drop out*. Here's how Timothy Leary had explained that mantra:

**"Turn on"** meant go within to activate your neural and genetic equipment. Become sensitive to the many and various levels of consciousness and the specific triggers that engage them. Drugs were one way to accomplish this end.

**"Tune in"** meant interact harmoniously with the world around you—externalize, materialize, express your new internal perspectives.

**"Drop out"** suggested an elective, selective, graceful process of detachment from involuntary or unconscious commitments. "Drop Out" meant self-reliance, a discovery of one's singularity, a commitment to mobility, choice, and change.[78]

That was how it worked in the 1960s, but by the Silicon Age, half a century later, these were the misfits who *dropped out* to *start up*. This leads us to an important question about education, business, and society. To start a company, is it better to be a college dropout?

Karp studied extreme behaviors and then used Big Data to find terrorists, gangs, and cartels. In that case, what he studied had clearly mattered. That same line of thinking, taken further, might answer whether Mark Zuckerberg would have been better prepared to design one of the world's greatest social tools—a technology with extraordinary power to affect people's daily lives and our overall social cohesion—if he had not dropped out so soon. Recall his classmate's words: "I never saw Mark reading a book, or expressing any interest in books. And he definitely didn't have a broader interest in philosophy, political thought, or economics. If you asked, he would say he was too busy taking over the world to read."[79]

Or, as Zuckerberg admitted: "We were college students. We're not qualified in any way to build this." Also: "When I was in college, I actually wasn't a computer science major. I was a psychology major. I didn't really get around to taking that many classes, because I left pretty quickly."[80] It was just as Parker had confessed. "It's a social-validation feedback loop," he'd admitted, "exactly the kind of thing that a hacker like myself would come up with, because you're exploiting a vulnerability in human psychology."[81] So there we have it, one of the unlocked secrets of the Silicon Age.

We'd been led to believe the technology mattered most. But technology is a tool. What worked for them the most was psychology and sociology, not computer science. Then high-risk investors taught them that exponential growth, world domination, even ubiquity mattered more than early profits. What lessons did that teach? What did they fail to learn? Could the decision to stay in school have altered history? What if they'd debated right and wrong, studied new perspectives in humanities classes, read about negative externalities in economics, and figured out how to compromise in real-life, rather than dropping out and going online? Would the world be a better place? We'll never know. To update Leary:

> **"Turn on"** meant go within to activate our neural and genetic equipment. Become sensitive to the many and various levels of consciousness and the specific triggers that engage them. Technologies were one way to accomplish this end.
>
> **"Tune in"** meant getting us to interact conflictingly with the world online— internalize, agonize about, get angry over others' external perspectives.
>
> **"Drop out"** suggested an untraceable process of attachment to involuntary or unconscious stimuli. "Drop out" meant self-centeredness, a distancing from our communities, a commitment to immobility as we chose sedentary screen time.[82]

Silicon into gold. Profits into power. We can now call it by name. That is Venture Alchemy.

✳ ✳ ✳

All along, perhaps the better question was: Should any of us care if startup founders have expertise in the industry they chose to disrupt? Or were some entrepreneurs only successful because they had a different perspective, even that they didn't know what they didn't know? Is that why new ventures can achieve what others cannot? Because they didn't know any better? "Here's to the crazy ones," Steve Jobs said in 1997, "the misfits, the rebels, the troublemakers, the round pegs in the square holes . . . the ones who see things differently— they're not fond of rules."[83] That might feel inspiring at first, but what about the implications?

Is "Fake it till you make it" a creative force? Or is innovation just delusion until our world becomes remodeled, remolded—or is the right word *warped*— into their vision? Is it our future to decide—or theirs alone? Should we trust in them, as they fit round pegs into square holes by brute force? Should we celebrate students for dropping out of school, because they are younger and less aware of the world, or are hungrier and are willing to risk it all to take a different approach? Is it better to invest in people with expertise—knowledge of an industry with immense impact on society, or at least who have taken basic coursework in ethics and humanities—or are the startup founders who are most likely to succeed the most extreme contrarian thinkers or college dropouts? When we ask, "Is it better to invest?," for whom do we ask? Is it for the benefit of society? Or better for the investors and entrepreneurs who created these Big

Tech corporations that remake the world in their image? *Better for whom?* That's the real question.

## Palantir's initial target customer: "People who can barely pay us"

When members of a Mexican drug cartel murdered U.S. Immigration and Customs Enforcement agent Jaime Zapata, the U.S. government launched Operation Fallen Hero. "What can we do to make an immediate impact against the cartels, to send a message?" the head of the Drug Enforcement Administration asked, according to a feature story by Shane Harris in the *Washingtonian* in 2012. Palantir offered to connect the various data points across the disparate sources of information that federal agents had gathered on the cartels: interviews with informants, video surveillance imagery, intercepted emails and text messages, pictures taken by drones, and much more. Instead of months of detective work to piece together clues, Palantir's artificial intelligence made connections within days, just like PayPal's powers to combine an array of sources, find patterns and anomalies, interpret and analyze that data, and eventually reveal how to anticipate and prevent fraud.

It worked. The counterstrike effort captured the cartel member suspected of killing Zapata. Harris reported that law enforcement also arrested 676 others and confiscated 467 kilograms of cocaine, 64 pounds of methamphetamine, and 282 weapons from across North America, Central America, and South America. Palantir won a no-bid contract seven months later, with 1,150 new licenses for analysts across the country. Palantir priced it at an incredibly low rate of just $7.5 million per year, which included a training course for federal agents on how to most effectively use its tools.[84]

At First Data's Cyber Security Summit in 2014, Alex Karp commented that Palantir might never go public because it prioritized growth over profits. "Some of our biggest appointments are with people who barely can pay us," Karp declared. "We have lots of clients where we get zero money."[85] That was what had happened in Louisiana a few years prior. "No one in New Orleans even knows about this, to my knowledge," Democratic strategist James Carville told Ali Winston of the *Verge*. "I am the sole driver of that project. It was entirely my idea," he claimed. "To me, it was a case of morality. Young people were shooting each other, and the public wasn't as involved as they should have been." With one of the highest murder rates in America, Carville had decided something had to be done.[86]

To help the police department and other city officials anticipate where crime might break out, Palantir created what it called a "gang member scorecard," according to the *Times-Picayune*. Palantir's dashboard would rank people "according to the number of gun-related events (weighted according to severity) with which a person is associated," based on their ties to other gang members, criminal records, and social media posts.[87] But there was something special about the deal struck with New Orleans.

After Carville introduced Karp to Mitch Landrieu, the mayor of New Orleans, Palantir offered the city a remarkable arrangement: it would do all the work pro bono.[88] Palantir proposed this even though San Mateo County in California and Cook County in Illinois were paying over half a million dollars a year for its services, and Los Angeles County had just paid $250,000 for a ten-month pilot that soon led to millions more in contracts.[89] By giving its product away for free, Palantir took what's called a "loss leader" strategy, where it could figure out what worked, then use those insights to refine the product to sell to other cities. In this case, it gained access to New Orleans's resources, with little risk of breach of contract or other downsides if it failed, because it had done it all pro bono. If it worked, Palantir would then be able to market to other police forces that it could successfully predict the likelihood that targeted individuals would commit crimes in the most violent environments like New Orleans. Because it was funded by venture capital, it could afford to do this all for free.

"One compelling thing of working in New Orleans was the staggering scale of the murder rate in the city," a Palantir spokesman told the *Times-Picayune* in 2019.[90] New Orleans presented a unique opportunity for the company because violence was so out of control. Beyond saving lives, Palantir could prove its software worked not only for state-of-the-art police forces but also in cities that were desperate for answers. It could test out its tools, which had worked so well against terrorists overseas and in well-funded U.S. cities, in tougher environments like New Orleans, with overwhelmed police forces that hoped to save money. In other words, if it worked in this underresourced and crime-ridden city, it would likely be effective anywhere.

In a polished document titled, "NOLA Murder Reduction: Technology to Power Data-Driven Public Health Strategies," Palantir promoted how New Orleans had used its tools to "develop rich insights into crime hotspots, criminal gang activity, gang networks, and high-risk individuals who may benefit from specialized interaction."[91] That marketing all sounded great, because everyone wants safer cities, but consider the actual implications. Saying that someone should be investigated due to a crime that hasn't happened yet—and calling this "specialized interaction" a "benefit" for them—that might be a bit less defensible, even reminiscent of the plot in *Minority Report*.[92]

The data sources stitched together by Palantir included crime-related databases (e.g., 911 calls and records of police interactions with people, parole and probation documents, and sheriff's office arrest and booking reports). Yet it also gained access to data that had nothing to do with violating the law (e.g., scraping from social media sites, as well as proprietary information gathered from various aspects of citywide infrastructure, including images captured by cameras at schools, libraries, and streetlights).[93] Palantir published its initial findings in a white paper where it touted that it had targeted 2,916 people, less than 1 percent of the total population, and was able to identify "35–50% of the likely shooting victims." As the report concluded, "This 'NOLA Model' can be further refined as new insights are captured and additional high-risk factors are surfaced.[94]

On February 23, 2012, the City of New Orleans had entered into a Data Sharing Agreement with Palantir; Landrieu and his legal advisor, Rebecca Dietz, had both signed off on a two-year renewal in March 2014.[95] Landrieu renewed the pro bono contract with Palantir twice more, through 2017 and then into 2018, with Deputy City Attorney Julien Meyer approving on behalf of the legal office both times.[96] Matt Long signed the contracts for Palantir.[97] His title was "chief legal ninja," which, according to an advertisement for a talk he gave at Harvard Law School, was "Silicon Valley's cool way of saying he is the General Counsel of Palantir."[98]

As this private company gained access to confidential police records, then pulled data from seemingly every possible public space in the city, it did so without New Orleanians ever being aware that they were being surveilled. In fact, New Orleans City Council members learned about the collaboration with Palantir only in February 2018—a week after the final contract expired—once Ali Winston called them to ask for a comment about why the deal had been approved in the first place. Council members claimed they knew nothing about the arrangement for six years.[99] "To me, it was a case of morality," James Carville's words had gained new significance: "the public wasn't as involved as they should have been."[100]

Yet this powerful technology clearly made a difference as part of the mayor's NOLA for Life antiviolence effort: the two-year period of 2013 and 2014 saw a 21.9 percent reduction in murders, leading to the lowest death toll in forty-three years.[101] In 2019, the year after Landrieu left office, there were 119 homicides citywide. After his successor abandoned the NOLA for Life initiative, that number soared to 280 by 2022. With the highest per capita homicide rate in the nation, New Orleans had become America's "Murder Capital," while the website for NOLA for Life had been taken over by WritingPapersSucks to sell plagiarized essays to high schoolers.[102]

## Palantir's unprecedented ownership structure through Class F shares

In 2020 Palantir went public. Tech startups will typically raise a pre–seed round and a seed round in the first few years, followed by A, B, and C rounds in the next several years after that. Palantir took a different approach, raising twenty-five different rounds of funding over the course of seventeen years before deciding to IPO. Its valuation neared $22 billion.[103] The wealth that Palantir made investors transcended political differences. The fund run by liberal donor George Soros had invested in 2012. His firm released a statement that it had "made this investment at a time when the negative social consequences of big data were less understood," but that didn't change the fact that Soros owned around 1 percent of the company, as its stock surged 38 percent on the first day of trading.[104]

In its initial public offering documents, Palantir revealed that it had had revenues of $742.5 million in 2019, a quick boost that was 25 percent higher than the prior year. But even that couldn't cover expenses, leading to a net loss of $580 million. The company remained unprofitable, as it had been since its founding in 2003.[105] Nonetheless, Palantir had raised more than $3 billion in funding, while burning through over a billion dollars in expenses a year, including spending $450 million on marketing over a two-year period.[106]

It was the Silicon Valley way, applied to the DC Beltway, then taken to local, state, and federal law enforcement nationwide. Palantir's approach more closely mirrored Uber's aggressiveness than the conventional corporate cultures of Raytheon or Boeing. It had grown as quickly as possible, given the product away cheaply or even for free, trained government staffers, locked in government contracts, and then poured money back into marketing and sales.[107] When it came to the many restrictive rules and painstaking oversight that most large corporations carefully adhered to in their work with government, Palantir took an admittedly different approach. "It's not that we give people a long leash at Palantir," explained David Worn, a former intelligence officer who opened Palantir's Northern Virginia office. "There are no leashes here at Palantir."[108]

When Palantir went public, Thiel profited handsomely, since he'd personally retained the greatest economic share of the company, 29.8 percent of all Class B shares, and Founders Fund owned the next highest total, 12.7 percent.[109] Beyond the financial returns, something else astonished Wall Street analysts. "Palantir has an unusual power structure, which has raised eyebrows from investors," Bloomberg's Lizette Chapman reported. "Palantir's chairman and major shareholder, Peter Thiel, along with two of the company's other cofounders, Stephen Cohen and [Alex] Karp, will control 49.99% of voting shares 'for the foreseeable future,' according to the filing."[110] In a move that some analysts couldn't believe was even legal, Palantir's cofounders (Cohen, Karp, and Thiel) received special "Class F" shares that ensured they held 49.999999 percent of the voting rights of the company in perpetuity—even if they sold the ownership shares.[111] When investment analysts asked Karp about corporate governance and its military contracts, Chapman reported his defiant reply: if they didn't like it, they should "pick a different company."[112]

In basic terms, the Class F shares meant that once the company went public, the cofounders could still make the decisions. As Danny Crichton wrote in

*TechCrunch*, "Palantir's model is unique in allowing founders to have a commanding vote even if they were to sell their shares," because they would never have to answer to investors, even once they sold their shares in the company, just so long as 0.000002 percent of other Palantir shareholders voted with them.[113] Several critics protested loudly. "Palantir is talking about how different they are from Silicon Valley, and yet they are taking on the absolutely worst aspect of Silicon Valley with this," Marc Goldstein, the head of U.S. research for the proxy advisory firm Institutional Shareholder Services, told the *Los Angeles Times* in 2020. "The problem is power without accountability."[114] He was right. This arrangement of dual-class shares had precedent—it was just as Mark Zuckerberg had done with Meta—but few had ever decided to create Class A and Class B, then skip C, D, and E. Upon further reflection, it's clear that the F in these Class F shares didn't only mean Founders shares. Maybe it also stood for Flexibility.[115] Or, perhaps, for Freedom.

No, that's not right. Maybe the First Amendment? Not that either. But it certainly wasn't the Fourth Amendment.

This immense power also meant a big F-you to any future investors who dared to challenge what Cohen, Karp, and Thiel would do with all these powerful tools and the data they gathered on so many citizens. Consider the consequences. The U.S. government used our tax dollars to pay Palantir to surveil us, using proprietary information that it also gave them—at least in some places, without "ordinary" citizens knowing it. The enabling environment that made such surveillance possible had resulted, in part, from allowances made by our elected officials post-9/11 that they had hoped would stop foreign terrorists.

When Palantir became publicly traded, its executives consolidated their power in ways that only private companies could usually maintain. "Palantir's model is unique in allowing founders to have a commanding vote even if they were to sell their shares—in other words, voting power without underlying shareholder power, in direct contradiction to modern shareholder theory," explained Danny Crichton. They were making history. He emphasized, "Let's just be clear: We have never seen anything like this before with a startup IPO."[116]

Not only did Palantir retain control over the voting shares of the company, but even the "independent" members of the board weren't all that independent, according to other analysts who reviewed the corporate documents. Palantir's board also included Alex Moore, Palantir's first employee, who touted the achievement of "growing the team from one room to 350 people, $100 mm in sales" in his bio at the investment firm he now worked at. (Even more simply, he wrote, "Started in one room" as the full description of his time at Palantir on his LinkedIn profile.) Nonetheless, he was considered independent in the company's public offering filings.[117]

So, too, was Alexandra Wolfe, who first met Thiel when writing *Valley of the Gods: A Silicon Valley Story* about the Thiel Fellowship, polyamory among Bay

Area entrepreneurs like Patri Friedman, and other controversial topics. "Peter Thiel inspired this book," Wolfe wrote in its acknowledgments. "He piqued my curiosity about Silicon Valley and about people who have the courage to think differently and then execute on their ideas. Peter introduced me to people more impressive and fascinating than I thought possible, some of whom I now count as my best friends."[118] In 2020 Wolfe resigned from the *Wall Street Journal* to join Palantir's board.[119] The only other board member was Spencer Rascoff, the former CEO of Zillow, in addition the all-powerful triumvirate of Cohen, Karp, and Thiel.[120] A former consultant at Accenture, Lauren Friedman Stat, joined in January 2021.[121] She had attended Stanford with Moore.[122]

The unusual voting power held by Cohen, Karp, and Thiel presented corporate governance issues: Moore, Wolfe, Rascoff, and Stat had little incentive to defy them in any meaningful way. Fiduciary duty required them to speak up against poor decision-making, but what would it matter if they'd be outvoted each time? It would never be in their personal financial interest anyway. They'd received $400,000 in Palantir stock initially, then $300,000 in additional Palantir stock and $40,000 in cash each year.[123] This was a more favorable compensation package for the board of directors than what many larger companies offered. For instance, it exceeded what was given by Microsoft, even though Palantir's market value was $49 billion and Microsoft's was $1.8 trillion, or over thirty-six times greater than Palantir's.[124] Then again, it wasn't a fair comparison. The person holding the most shares at Microsoft owned 0.02 percent, not 29.8 percent.[125] And no one owned anywhere near half of the voting control of Microsoft, for all eternity, as was the case with Palantir.

Microsoft's largest shareholder groups were Vanguard, BlackRock, and State Street, with 8.4 percent, 6.8 percent, and 4.2 percent of total shares outstanding, respectively.[126] But those three represented tens of trillions of dollars, by tens of millions of investors, in well over one hundred countries—not three people who would never lose control no matter how many shares they sold.[127] One more thing. It wasn't a fair comparison in terms of profitability, either. Palantir eventually turned a profit after going public, but Microsoft remained over one hundred times more profitable. From 2020 to 2022, Microsoft returned a total gross profit of over $348.4 billion.[128] Palantir's gross profits for that entire period amounted to only $3.4 billion, and the company had not yet been profitable for one full year.[129]


## Power becomes wealth becomes power

By the time it went public, Palantir had secured a wide range of contracts with the U.S. government, ranging from an over $800 million deal to run the army's battlefield intelligence system, to supporting Immigration and Customs

Enforcement's efforts to apprehend and deport undocumented immigrants, to running the platform for COVID-19 vaccine distribution for the Department of Health and Human Services.[130] In fact, government contracts involving big data, surveillance, and analytics made up over half of Palantir's revenues by 2020.[131]

With powers so far reaching and data so all-encompassing, how should Palantir's business model even be described? When talking with Shane Harris about the company for his *Washingtonian* feature, an executive at JP Morgan Chase compared Palantir to Google—except while Google catalogued and made sense of public information, Palantir sought to do the same for *all* information, public and private.[132] He likely had reason to know all about Palantir's capabilities. As Lizette Chapman and two of her Bloomberg colleagues, Peter Waldman and Jordan Robertson, wrote in an exposé about Palantir's partnerships with Wall Street, JP Morgan moved quickly to incorporate the technology into its operations, by monitoring its own employees' email and browser histories, geolocation data, and transcripts from phone conversations. Bloomberg found that Palantir's algorithm had flagged that an employee had begun to arrive at work later than usual, and the software then sent an alert to JP Morgan's "insider threat team" as a red flag of potential disgruntlement and future poor performance. "The world changed when it became clear everyone could be targeted using Palantir," a former JP Morgan cyber expert told Bloomberg. "Nefarious ideas became trivial to implement; everyone's a suspect, so we monitored everything. It was a pretty terrible feeling." The Bloomberg headline read, "Palantir Knows Everything About You." The subheading followed: "Peter Thiel's data-mining company is using War on Terror tools to track American citizens. The scary thing? Palantir is desperate for new customers."[133]

After 9/11 Palantir emerged as one of the earliest innovators to use surveillance for antiterrorism and policing with Palantir Gotham. But its line of business that focused on the private sector (which began as Palantir Metropolis and later expanded to Apollo and Foundry, other offerings for corporations) represented a much broader trend. As algorithms identified patterns in Big Data, and corporations surveilled us not just as citizens but as employees and consumers, something changed in capitalism that went far beyond Palantir. Ultimately, the power to learn from patterns in data, which revealed if someone was harmlessly normal or a violent threat, had many other applications. Those same kinds of patterns also allowed them to predict what we will read, where we will go, what we will watch, and what we will buy. "The ways in which 9/11 was leveraged to play fast and loose with civil liberties are numerous. The ways in which we as consumers willingly signed up to be watched all the time are even more staggering," Mary Elizabeth Williams wrote in a *Salon* article in 2021, "9/11 Changed Surveillance—and Capitalism Reaped the Benefits." She explained, "I know that the device I carry in my pocket that knows where I am at all times is undoubtedly of less interest to the NSA than it is to Yelp. Who monitors me more, really? The cops or Sephora?"[134]

The answer to that question for Palantir, given its dual business lines that served governments and corporations, was *both*. And to create their technologies and strategies—as one of the earliest pioneers in big data patterning, artificial intelligence analyses, and the surveillance capitalism that resulted—Palantir relied on senior officials in the U.S. government. They had been there to guide the company from its earliest days, starting with the introductions Gilman Louie made on their behalf, and continuing throughout the company's development over the decades. As Palantir grew, it attracted some of America's most recognizable and influential politicians and national security officials. In addition to paying James Carville to advise it, Palantir had an impressive roster of other advisors, both Democrats and Republicans.[135]

The CIA director for President Barack Obama, David Petraeus, was on the list.[136] Avril Haines was a paid consultant for Palantir from July 2017 to June 2020.[137] Immediately prior, she had served in the Obama administration as assistant to the president and principal deputy national security advisor. The day after Joe Biden was sworn in as president, she became the director of national intelligence and the first woman to lead the U.S. intelligence community.[138] George Tenet was a Palantir advisor, too, and what a résumé he had.[139] As CIA director, he started In-Q-Tel under President Bill Clinton; it invested in Palantir under President George W. Bush.[140] He was head of the CIA before 9/11 and remained in charge when the post-9/11 "enhanced interrogation" techniques, which  Bush administration attorney John Yoo justified in memos to declare them legal, were implemented by American forces on detainees.[141]

The U.S Senate's official investigation reached definitive conclusions about what was actually meant by the *enhanced* techniques used at detention centers, including Guantanamo Bay. "The use of the CIA's enhanced interrogation techniques was not an effective means of obtaining accurate information or gaining detainee cooperation," the report concluded. "The interrogations of CIA detainees were brutal and far worse than the CIA represented to policymakers and others."[142] In the end, the inspector general reported that "Tenet believes that if the general public were to find out about this program, many would believe we are torturers." He justified the decisions, explaining that his "only potential moral dilemma would be if more Americans die at the hands of terrorists and we had someone in our custody who possessed information that could have prevented deaths, but we had not obtained such information."[143] That was the only moral concern he saw here. We interrogated people in an *enhanced* way anyway (or perhaps a better word for that is *tortured*).

To repeat: "*we had not obtained such information.*" Yet the deeper dilemma was far more complicated than that. If we reject dangerous oversimplifications, we can ask better questions. Were "ordinary" people hurt, as fear limited our moral imagination, leading to the false choice of us versus them, good people versus the other, to do-whatever-it-takes? Had our leaders, instead of being imbued with a professional spirit of public service, acted like distant shareholders—not counting the costs, ignoring damages done?

* * *

In addition to Petraeus and Tenet, another former U.S. government official joined Palantir as an advisor. "The impetus of Palantir is to fight terrorism and to combat crime while maintaining the civil liberties of American citizens and peoples around the world," she told *Forbes*. "As I was the National Security Advisor on 9/11, I am keenly aware of the need to balance the integrity of civil liberties and the need to use technology to support our intelligence efforts and fight terrorism." It seemed a distant memory that Condoleezza Rice, now an advisor to Palantir who praised its integrity, had once deemed the words by Peter Thiel and David Sacks "demagoguery, pure and simple," back when taboo speech taught them how to understand outlier behavior, which they'd eventually use to track violent gangs, drug cartels, or terrorist cells—and then apply those tools to corporate America and our consumer behavior as well.[144]

When Palantir went public in September 2020, Thiel cashed in $279 million worth of his shares. It put his personal net worth around $2.5 billion.[145] Despite selling his stock, he retained his F shares.[146] The letter, of course, also stood for "Forever."

# CHAPTER 14

# WE DO THE RIGHT THING

Dara Khosrowshahi, Uber Technologies, Inc.

Sixteen weeks after Bloomberg published the late-night dashcam video sent to them by Fawzi Kamel, Travis Kalanick resigned under pressure from Uber's board.[1] A few days before that, the *New York Times* reported that the company had cleaned house, firing twenty people on a single day for harassment, discrimination, and inappropriate behavior.[2] The new CEO, Dara Khosrowshahi, quickly scrapped the brash mottos that Kalanick had coined, in favor of more conventional corporate priorities like "Customer Obsessed" and "We Do the Right Thing."[3]

These words weren't drawn up on a whiteboard by the CEO and a few top deputies. This was a far more democratic organization and effort, and in a sign of corporate best practices to come, Khosrowshahi held over twenty focus groups with various resource group leaders. More than twelve hundred Uber employees submitted ideas, in a global effort to gather suggestions about how to improve. Ultimately, Uber employees cast twenty-two thousand votes to rank the new values. Near the top of the list was "We celebrate differences."[4]

Yet so much damage had been done in the name of "Fierceness," to "Always Be Hustlin,'" and being "Super Pumped." As one employee told the *Guardian*: "Everyone used those values to excuse their bad behavior," calling the workplace a "Hobbesian jungle" of might made right, of in-groups versus the others, where powerful people punished dissenters, and "you can never get ahead unless someone else dies." The article's headline: "Uber's 'Hustle-Oriented' Culture Becomes a Black Mark on Employees' Résumés."[5] Some employees had even struggled to get jobs elsewhere because Silicon Valley's enthusiasm over Uber had soured so much. Reworking Uber's company values and fixing company culture couldn't happen quickly enough for the new CEO. "If there's one area that I would have liked to change faster," he told CNN, "it is to execute more fully on our cultural transformation as a company internally, across all levels at the company."[6]

Months later, at the World Economic Forum in Davos, Khosrowshahi declared in an interview with CNBC, "there was a lot that happened at the company that wasn't right, and I think the moral compass of the company was not pointed where it needed to be."[7] After that, the company's leadership kept insisting that there had been a clean break after Kalanick's departure, and they were just cleaning up the mess left behind. "We have not and will not make excuses for past behavior that is clearly not in line with our present values," an Uber spokesperson wrote on the company's website in July 2022. "Instead, we ask the public to judge us by what we've done over the last five years and what we will do in the years to come."[8]

In May 2019—twenty-one months after Khosrowshahi had become CEO—Uber went public at $45 a share, putting the company's valuation over $82 billion. As Mike Isaac wrote in *Super Pumped*, Khosrowshahi asked Kalanick not to join him on the balcony for the ceremonial first bell. That infuriated Kalanick, who showed up anyway. At an early morning breakfast, Khosrowshahi praised Kalanick as a "once-in-a-generation entrepreneur." That was true enough, if measured by wealth alone. Kalanick's shares were worth $5.4 billion at the $45 share price. Garrett Camp's were worth $4.1 billion. Ryan Graves's shares were worth $1.6 billion, all starting with his job application via tweet.[9]

At 6:30 a.m. Pacific Time, Uber's employees lifted their mimosas to toast the opening bell. Over the next few hours, the *Washington Post* reported that their day-drinking continued at nearby bars. But something went horribly wrong. The stock began plummeting. Uber's employees and its alumni returned for a company-funded happy hour back at the office at 2 p.m. By that point, the stock had dropped to nearly $36 a share, but people kept partying hard as it plummeted. A former employee who joined in the celebration was quoted by the *Washington Post*: "What are we celebrating? The loss of billions of dollars in value?" After everyone drank through the beer and wine, they then took shots from bottles of tequila and whiskey, which employees had kept in their desks or brought from home. The bottles featured a version of Uber's logo that had since been phased out, a symbol of Kalanick's time as CEO.[10] That day, he still became a multibillionaire, and Camp and Graves were billionaires too, but they weren't as rich as they'd expected to be after all the sacrifices made to go from startup to IPO. Uber employees raged throughout the day anyway.

People often say that culture eats strategy for breakfast.[11] In this case, it drank it up, on an empty stomach. The daylong bacchanal got so out of hand that Uber had to shut the party down prematurely that evening. Personnel spilled into the streets, back to the bars. The next morning, the celebration made international news, with headlines condemning Uber's employees for ignoring reality so they could enjoy their reveling anyway. At least one wasted employee had to be talked out of driving home (such irony), and another submitted her resignation after a drunken screaming match.[12] By the end of the day, Uber had lost more value than any other IPO in America since 1975.[13]

## Counting the costs at Uber

In a formal sense, the companywide surveys changed Uber's stated corporate values. But its business model remained the same. The amount an Uber driver makes always depends on a wide array of factors. The customer's ability and willingness to pay is algorithmically calculated every instant, and the length of each trip depends on traffic congestion, the size of the city or town, and other variables. So although the company is now public and its disclosures provide a much better idea of the numbers, no one knows exactly how many dollars end up in a driver's pocket at the end of the day.[14]

According to one estimate, an Uber driver's hourly earnings are $13.79 in Atlanta, $12.55 in Tampa, and $17.15 in San Diego.[15] The minimum wages in Georgia, Florida, and California are $7.25, $12, and $15.50, respectively.[16] So Uber drivers make anywhere from 55 cents to around $5 more hourly than minimum wage. Yet this doesn't account for any costs, which differ based on each driver's situation but usually include the car lease, fuel, maintenance, oil changes, and flat tires, as well as speeding or parking tickets, health benefits, and on and on. Uber can change its values statements, but the reality is, the business model would break if it paid drivers as employees rather than contractors. And, as we'll see, few people who get in an Uber or order a meal delivery through the app ever realize who is really benefiting.

We have called it the "sharing" economy, but we now need to reassess that word. We're sharing our homes, our cars, and our services. In exchange, we receive a pittance compared to what the top executives make due to so many passengers or food deliveries. Estimates place the average full-time Uber driver's earnings around $37,000 a year (although that varies depending on the market).[17] In 2019 the total compensation for Khosrowshahi was $42 million. Even he admitted that was excessive. "I think if you define fairness by 'fair market value,' then CEOs are paid fairly," he told Maureen Dowd of the *New York Times*. "I think if you define fairness by how you think society should value people, then I think CEOs are paid too much. You could put me in that group."[18] Of course you could. He made more than *a thousand times more* than the average Uber driver.[19]

"Ordinary" people do the work by rating drivers, rating passengers. They're the ones cleaning up when an overserved partier pukes up his expensive dinner and a long night of drinks. They have to budget, to make ends meet, based on an ever-changing pricing algorithm that the company controls. Only it knows how the math works, and it always knows when drivers are working or not. But that leads to this brainteaser: How can a venture like Uber afford to pay its CEO a thousand times more than the average driver, if drivers make most of the money from each ride?

The answer's in the scale of the company, and along with it, the incredible volume of rides and the amount of valuable data that creates. That riddle might seem confusing at first, but the solution is fairly simple. The playbook went like this: build the app, but don't hire drivers as employees. For connecting passengers to drivers, you get part of every transaction, which might be a small amount individually but adds up quickly, while you become increasingly efficient so that you can set prices at exactly what people will pay. Then you compensate drivers at exactly what people are willing to drive for. Problem solved.

## Fueled by Saudi oil money

Here's another riddle, wrapped in a mystery: Why does His Excellency Yasir Othman Al-Rumayyan of Saudi Arabia own 72,976,322 shares of Uber, which is more than any current or former Uber executive (including Khosrowshahi, Kalanick, Camp, and Graves), and who makes those shares valuable?[20]

The answer to both parts of that one is about ownership. First, the Saudi Public Investment Fund wired Uber $3.5 billion on June 1, 2016, the largest single investment from a foreign government to a venture-backed startup ever.[21] Second, the current value of those shares owned by the Saudi government isn't just due to an app. It's also because of all the work done by drivers, who don't receive the same kind of financial rewards as investors do.

And how did that happen? Who was behind the Uber-Saudi deal? It was David Plouffe, who was formerly Barack Obama's campaign manager and his senior advisor at the White House, who became an Uber executive after leaving the Obama administration. Uber already operated in Saudi Arabia when he visited in March 2016; in fact, Uber's PR team touted that 80 percent of Uber riders were women. That's because women weren't allowed to drive. Plouffe was on a three-city tour of Cairo, Dubai, and Riyadh.[22] During his visit, the official Uber Twitter account quoted Plouffe as saying, "The government in Saudi Arabia wants to make it easier for people to get around and that's exciting," which was followed by this hashtag: #UberEverywhere.[23] Of course, the easiest way "for people to get around" would have been permitting female drivers. In this new context, earlier warnings that Uber's "sexism and misogyny is something different and scary," seemed prescient, as an ancient and ugly anti-equality attitude remained the official Saudi policy—and Uber benefited.[24]

At the time, Saudi Arabia was the only country in the world where such a ban existed, a blatant affront to human rights.[25] *Just because it's legal doesn't make it right.* Due to reforms, the unjust ban ended two years later, but during the intervening time the Saudi government continued to benefit massively from the relationship with Uber that only deepened after David Plouffe's visit.[26] In 2016 Uber celebrated the support it received from the Saudis, and it soon took investment from a regime that denied women their universally accepted human rights. In the coming years, Uber would benefit the Saudis in completely new ways, as Al-Rumayyan deepened his involvement in U.S. venture capital funds and leading startups.

Plouffe's visit wasn't just to promote the Saudi government's supposed commitment to transportation access for women; we know that now, because the $3.5 billion investment that came a few months later was unlike any in venture capital history.[27] To put it in perspective, when Google was six years old, it went public. At the same age, Uber received investment from the Saudis. Google had raised a total of $25 million in venture capital over its first six years. With the investment from Saudi Arabia, Uber had taken on $13.5 billion in total venture investment (540 times more than Google ever raised).[28]

Al-Rumayyan agreed to the transaction using the same terms as prior investors, but he wanted a board seat. The Uber board allowed it. Their relationship with Travis Kalanick proved less amicable, however. When he was forced out in June 2017, Kalanick named himself to one of three seats he had control over. By August one of Uber's top investors, Benchmark, sued him and demanded that he leave the board entirely.[29] A month later he added two new members to Uber's board, and the company issued a statement saying the appointments "came as a complete surprise to Uber and its Board."[30] The power struggle over the future of Uber intensified, but it was no longer Kalanick's kingdom to rule, nor could it ever be fully Khosrowshahi's for that matter. The real ownership lived thousands of miles away. Yet every time an Uber driver or rider taps on the little black icon, he or she likely doesn't know the Saudis own all those shares, nor do people usually worry about any ethical dilemmas caused by their trip. But should they?

## Saudi "blood money"

Here's a third riddle, wrapped in a mystery, inside an enigma: Who really counts as an entrepreneur, if so many of the "small businesses on the Uber platform" they talk about have stayed so small, while this Big Tech corporation has grown incredibly large, with billions upon billions of dollars in venture capital making that unprofitable growth possible? And, a corollary: Who does all of that "economic opportunity" that Uber promised now go to, while drivers made a little more (or much less) than minimum wage after the costs of doing business as an independent contractor were factored in?[31]

Who benefits? These American "entrepreneurs" who are doing the driving, the actual employees who report to Uber corporate, or even the founders who started the company years ago? Or does its major shareholder, Saudi Arabia? What are the ethics of that?

The answer to this one is unsettling. Because you have to look beyond Uber to see what else has His Excellency Yasir Othman Al-Rumayyan, the governor of Saudi Arabia's Public Investment Fund, has been investing in. The nonprofit Human Rights Watch revealed that his fund also owned the charter planes that a Saudi assassination squad used to travel to Istanbul, where they murdered the *Washington Post* journalist Jamal Khashoggi. Then they used those same jets to return to Saudi Arabia.[32] "Until we learn more, we're not in a position to act one way or another," Khosrowshahi said after Khashoggi's death at the *Wall Street Journal*'s D.Live tech conference. "The act was horrible. We're anxious to learn more."[33]

Three days later the CIA announced its conclusion: Crown Prince Mohammed bin Salman had ordered the assassination directly.[34] Throughout the next year, media outlets reported that numerous family members and friends of Khashoggi had all been surveilled through Pegasus, a program that infiltrated messages and calls on WhatsApp, which is owned by Meta.[35] According to Ronan Farrow at the *New Yorker* and a team of investigative journalists at the *Guardian* and other media outlets, the Saudis had paid the Israeli company to turn their phones into always-on surveillance tools, with their microphones and cameras activated without anyone knowing.[36] It was similar to the Uber engineers' iPhone hack from years before, where it monitored people even after the app had been deleted. But this time it was even more invasive, and targeted, and there were far more devastating consequences.[37]

Despite these new revelations, Khosrowshahi said little about the murder. He continued to remain silent about the issue, despite the gruesome facts in a human rights report released by the United Nations.[38] After listening to seven different audio recordings of the murder, the UN's special rapporteur concluded that Khashoggi was forcibly restrained, injected with a large amount of a drug, and killed due to an overdose. Then someone had said, "The body is heavy. First time I cut on the ground. If we take plastic bags and cut it into pieces, it will be finished." They chopped his body into chunks and discarded his corpse. His remains were never found.[39]

For months and months, Khosrowshahi still said nothing. Then, during an interview with Dan Primack of *Axios* almost a year later, he spoke up. "Well listen, it's a serious mistake. We've made mistakes, too, right? With self-driving, and we stopped driving, and we're recovering from that mistake." Was Khashoggi's death morally equivalent to Herzberg's? Was that the message Khosrowshahi was sending? He and his team at Uber likely realized that comparing the two wasn't the best way to lessen the public backlash on either issue. The next day, he emailed Primack to explain, "I said something in the moment that I do not believe. When it comes to Jamal Khashoggi, his murder was reprehensible and should not be forgotten or excused."[40] He also tweeted an apology: "There's no forgiving or forgetting what happened to Jamal Khashoggi & I was wrong to call it a 'mistake.' As I told @danprimack after our interview, I said something in the moment I don't believe. Our investors have long known my views here & I'm sorry I wasn't as clear on Axios."[41] A few weeks after that, a Saudi court sentenced five individuals to death for "committing and directly participating in the murder of the victim" and sentenced three others to prison sentences of twenty-four years for "covering up this crime and violating the law."[42]

Al-Rumayyan not only remained on Uber's board the entire time, but he increased the Saudi Arabian government's ownership of Uber through the Public Investment Fund. He bought $125 million more of the logistics and transportation subsidiary, Uber Freight, in a deal that Uber's Audit Committee approved, which closed in July 2021. As Uber's financial disclosures also noted, long after Khashoggi's death, Al-Rumayyan's 72,976,322 shares represented over 95 percent ownership of the shares held by Uber's entire board of directors and senior management team—all those other leaders at Uber held just 3,560,721 shares combined.[43]

Of course, according to the Church of Creative Capitalism, the company's sole goal was enriching its largest shareholders at any cost to society. Wasn't that how things were supposed to go? Wouldn't Milton Friedman be happy about these distant shareholders prospering? Wouldn't Ayn Rand have been glad to see such individualism at all costs? Perhaps they would have, but the American public remained largely unaware of the Saudi investments for years—until they announced new deals that caught everyone's attention. In the summer of 2022, news outlets drew fresh attention to atrocities committed in, and by, Saudi Arabia. The scrutiny was not due to any new revelations about inhumane acts but, rather, because of a new professional golf league. After dozens of golfers quit the PGA Tour for the Saudi-backed LIV Golf, a group of 9/11 families denounced them as defectors who had "taken the blood money."[44] When asked about partnering with the Saudis, star golfer Phil Michelson admitted, "They're scary motherfuckers to get involved with. We know they killed Khashoggi and have a horrible record on human rights."[45]

9/11 Justice, an advocacy group, then expressed "deep pain and anger" when former president Donald Trump hosted a LIV tournament at one of his golf courses. Media commentators criticized Trump's son-in-law, Jared Kushner, for his involvement.[46] He had served as senior advisor at the White House, working out of the same West Wing office as David Plouffe once had.[47] After LIV struggled to gain support with U.S. audiences, John Ourand of the *Sports Business Journal* reported that Kushner tried to broker a media rights deal for the Saudis.[48] He knew them well, both from his work on Middle East issues in government and from raising $2 billion from the Saudi Public Investment Fund for his new investment firm.[49]

Yasir Bin Othman Al-Rumayyan attended the LIV tournament at Trump's course, where he was photographed, smiling, between the former president and his son-in-law. Trump wore a golf shirt with the Trump New York logo on it, as well as his trademark ball cap that read "Make America Great Again"; Kushner was more casual, wearing a t-shirt, along with a hat that said "LIV Golf."[50] For weeks, the media criticized the Trump family for cozying up to the Saudis.[51]

On June 6, 2023, the PGA Tour announced a surprise deal: it would join forces with LIV to create a single pro golf tour. While some discussed this as a merger, others deemed it closer to an acquisition, since the Saudi Public Investment Fund committed to invest billions in the new entity and Al-Rumayyan would become the chairman of the board.[52] Dan Wolken used the phrase "a hostile takeover," in *USA Today*, writing, "In less than a year, the Saudis went from disruptors to forcing a complete capitulation that laid the PGA Tour's moral high ground to waste. From top to bottom, they own professional golf now." He added, "They sold out. Professional golf will never be the same."[53] The chair of 9/11 Families United said the PGA and its commissioner "appear to have become just more paid Saudi shills, taking billions of dollars to cleanse the Saudi reputation so that Americans and the world will forget how the Kingdom spent their billions of dollars before 9/11 to fund terrorism, spread their vitriolic hatred of Americans, and finance al Qaeda and the murder of our loved ones. Make no mistake—we will never forget."[54]

Leading up to this big announcement, the Saudi government had already invested billions in Uber for half a decade. Al-Rumayyan had served on the company's board that entire time. Even while the overhaul of professional golf had created widespread controversy for the Saudis, their involvement with Uber went largely unnoticed even while so many journalists narrowly focused on the connections to the Trump family. Few retraced the ties that David Plouffe had helped to bind.

In reality, Uber had been the first of many deals in the world of American startups, venture capital, and private equity for the Saudis—and an entry point into their deal-making in America. A few weeks before the PGA deal was announced, the Saudi Public Investment Fund had updated its website. In April 2023 it listed investments it had been making in many of America's marquee venture funds, private equity firms, and startups. That included renowned firms like Andreessen Horowitz and General Atlantic, but more notably, the

Fund had put money into six firms—Craft Ventures, Dragoneer, G Squared, General Atlantic, TA Associates, and Techstars—that had also invested in Uber. The Techstars incubator program had taken an early stake in Uber, and David Sacks, one of Uber's earliest investors, had started Craft Ventures in 2017.[55] Beyond that, the technologies in which it owned significant stakes had serious influence over American politics, too. As Akela Lacy noted in the *Intercept*, the Saudi Public Investment Fund now held a stake in the British private equity firm Apax Partners. The result: "The Government of Saudi Arabia is an investor in the private company that owns a virtual monopoly on software that powers Democratic candidates—including management of the Democratic National Committee's all-important voter list."[56]

## Uber rewrites the laws

Back in September 2019, California legislators had passed a law to require gig economy companies to treat workers as employees, guaranteeing them the rights and protections available under labor laws.[57] Khosrowshahi claimed that prices might need to double if they had to employ every driver.[58] So what was Uber's solution? Create a third category, where Uber and other rideshare companies would offer only a few benefits—the ones that they'd decided people needed, not what government policy required. These businesses took this issue straight to the voters, putting it on the ballot in November 2020. And they used their powerful technology, and the access it gave them to voters throughout the state of California, to get the outcome they'd wanted.

Eight years earlier, when the Washington, DC, City Council attempted to establish a minimum fare requirement, Uber had learned just how powerful its technology could be to change public policies. "We did something called, 'Life, Liberty, and the Pursuit of Uberness,'" Kalanick recalled at Y Combinator's Startup School in 2012. "Eighteen hours later, we had 50,000 original emails—these weren't robo-emails—that went to city council people telling them not to vote for it. Um, 37,000 tweets, 104 million social media impressions. And we won."[59]

And Uber would continue to win, on its terms. On the corporate blog, under the headline "Never Underestimate the Power of #UberDCLove," the company warned that the bill could resurface and "we'll need our full army ready to help us again."[60] As Uber investor Shervin Pishevar tweeted at the time, "What happened today with @Uber & DC is dawn of a new local politics: Tech/social exercising newfound muscles on a policy level in real-time."[61] He was right. Uber often changed its rates—but that was whenever it decided to, rather than at the request of government officials—including when it introduced its own minimum charge called the "Safe Rides Fee" in 2014. "If riders noticed the fee, they rarely complained," Mike Isaac wrote in *Super Pumped*. "Many assumed it would just make their rides safer somehow. The reality was much less noble." It added hundreds of millions of dollars to the company's bottom line and changed nothing about safety. But drivers never saw a single penny of that. "We boosted our margins saying our rides were safer," one Uber employee told Isaac. "It was obscene."[62]

But when rules or regulations came from city officials, Kalanick bristled. "So, I ask the mayors, what are you protecting, who are you protecting?" he demanded in his Startup School talk. "And they don't even realize—they don't even realize," he repeated for emphasis, "that you're actually screwing over *drivers*."[63] The number of lobbyists across America for ride-hailing companies eventually outnumbered the paid lobbying staffs of Amazon, Walmart, and Microsoft combined. Over time, Uber added hundreds of lobbyists to its team, across forty-four states.[64] Uber paid millions to lobbyists every year to avoid regulatory changes—so that it did not have to employ drivers.[65]

At least, that was until California legislators mandated that ride-sharing companies pay their drivers as employees, with all requisite benefits. Six weeks before going to the polls, only 39 percent of likely voters wanted to override the state law, and 25 percent remained undecided.[66] Uber and other gig economy companies poured over $200 million into the California ballot initiative called Proposition 22.[67] The money ran through a Super PAC that claimed to be organized by "a coalition of on-demand drivers and platforms, small businesses, public safety, and community organizations," with funding from Lyft, Uber, and DoorDash.[68]

If breaking the rules no longer works, and it's clear that the rules are about to apply very specifically to you, what's the solution? Uber and its peers spent the money necessary to do-whatever-it-takes, then they made up their own rules. On campaign ads, they said the law was "threatening to shutdown rideshare and food delivery services" and warned, "Unemployment has skyrocketed. What do state politicians do? Pass a drastic law that could eliminate hundreds of thousands of jobs." They argued their solution, Prop 22, "Protects Driver Independence."[69] Independence was one word for it, but there were far worse deceptions at work.

Political mailers soon appeared throughout the San Francisco area that were labeled "Progressive Voter Guide," "Council of Concerned Women Voters Guide," and "Our Voice, Latino Voter Guide."[70] They supported the same candidates and causes endorsed by the California Democratic Party, except for Prop 22, which it had opposed.[71] For that measure, the description read: "Prop 22 protects app-based drivers' independence and provides new benefits including earnings guarantee and healthcare. By 4-to-1-margin, drivers want to remain independent contractors."[72] Rather than a random sample, that online survey was conducted by a small group of readers of the *Rideshare Guy* blog.[73] They had skewed data. That didn't matter.

The companies even argued that creating a third class of workers would advance racial equity. To help them make the case, they paid more than $85,000 to a public affairs firm run by the president of the California NAACP, according to the nonprofit news organization CalMatters.[74] NYU professor Meredith Whittaker and University of California, Hastings, professor Veena Dubal warned in a Medium post that the gig economy companies were "effectively creating a political template for future anti-democratic, corporate law-making." In their view, Prop 22 "eradicates basic labor protections for the state's most vulnerable workers," resulting in "a vile victory and a grim precedent."[75] But misleading propaganda and paying for endorsements are old political tricks, so what was different this time? For one, the sheer amount of capital that these companies spent on the Prop 22 ballot initiative was unprecedented; ultimately, it totaled $203 million, the most in U.S. history.[76] But more than the money, the tactics and technologies they used leading up to the election were unlike anything in history, too.

Uber, Lyft, DoorDash, and every other "sharing economy" app suddenly became a marketing apparatus—and a political organizing tool that would prompt people to click through ads supporting the measure before proceeding. Before drivers could begin their work, they had to read a message every time that said, "Drivers Deserve Better: Join 72% of drivers and delivery people who want to protect app-based work in CA," which hyped the biased results from the *Rideshare Guy* blog's survey.[77] That move led to a lawsuit, which sought an injunction to stop the ads and argued that the companies were violating California laws that prohibit "controlling or directing" employees over political activities, but a California Superior Court deemed it legal.[78]

They weren't employees all along, anyway, right? When the voters went to the polls on Election Day to help decide their future, Uber's coalition had outspent their opponents almost twelve times over.[79] With 9,958,425 votes, or 59 percent of the total share, Prop 22 passed on November 3, 2020.[80] Uber had won with the California voters, but less than a year later, a California court ruled Prop 22 unconstitutional.[81] Perhaps the voters wouldn't have the final say, as more money kept flowing to lawyers and lobbyists. On March 23, 2023, an appeals court reversed that decision and upheld Prop 22. Further court proceedings were anticipated.[82]

* * *

So many Big Tech companies pursued similar strategies in the Silicon Age. They were designed to scale quickly, then reap rewards from their reach, while using their massive size to defend themselves. They connected us, we did the real work, and they aggressively pursued expansion. The money they spent along the way was offset, somewhat, by vast revenues earned from the volume of activity, but they also kept raising more venture capital while benefiting from the value of the data gathered about all of us. As business consultant Tom Goodwin famously wrote in *TechCrunch* in 2015, "Uber, the world's largest taxi company, owns no vehicles. Facebook, the world's most popular media owner, creates no content. Alibaba, the most valuable retailer, has no inventory. And Airbnb, the world's largest accommodation provider, owns no real estate. Something interesting is happening."[83]

Something interesting did happen. And we are just now beginning to comprehend what worked so well. "If you're not paying for the product, then you are the product," nonprofit executive Tristan Harris warned in the popular Netflix documentary *The Social Dilemma*.[84] But a needed nuance is missed with that. The ugly underside of American tech companies is really a story about us, not them. It's not that we're simply the product; it's almost that we're the labor, too. That's obvious with Uber, but it extends to other ways we interact with technology in our lives.

We update our "status" by sharing filtered photos. We search Google, teaching their algorithms what matters most. Big Tech companies benefit from all our attention and effort. We call it entertainment and convenience, even innovation and progress. But deep down, as they rewrite the laws in their own interest, it's not just that we're simply the product for sale. All the money we made for them has been used to encourage us to vote the way they want us to, too. Their growth yielded influence, which they used to consolidate power and protect their profits. Wealth increased power, which also became prestige, which led to more wealth.

For companies like Uber, our efforts might not be classified as employment, but we're deceiving ourselves if we don't see who is doing the actual, everyday work. Who created value all along? Who benefited? We have all been led to believe that we're living up to our entrepreneurial potential by hustling harder, because they claim the drivers are the entrepreneurs, they're all small business owners. We might even think of it as "sharing," which rhymes with caring, as if all this activity is compassionate, even a public service. But we should keep in mind that, in Uber's case, one of the most influential shareholders who is benefiting isn't even in Silicon Valley. We now know that.

All that work increases, in far greater proportions, the worth of the 72,976,322 shares held by the Kingdom of Saudi Arabia than the combined 3,560,721 shares held by Uber's executives or its American board members.[85] And that deal happened only because of meetings between the Saudi elites and Barack Obama's former campaign manager, David Plouffe.

## When nine years disappeared

After Reed Hastings stepped down from Facebook's board, the company announced on April 12, 2019, that Peggy Alford would take his place. Numerous nonprofit leaders and journalists celebrated Facebook for prioritizing diversity, claiming she'd made history with headlines like "Peggy Alford Becomes First Black Woman Nominated to Facebook's Board of Directors."[86] Facebook was larger than most nation-states, so the praise made sense, at least on the surface. As Hastings left and Alford arrived, Facebook's press release described her senior leadership roles: most recently at the Chan Zuckerberg Initiative, where she ran operations and finance, then as the senior vice president of core markets at PayPal. It described her board service for shopping mall owner Macerich, her four prior roles at PayPal, and other positions she held at eBay. It included her college education at the University of Dayton. But there was a nine-year, two-month gap. Facebook didn't mention one thing: her first employer.[87]

Peggy Alford had spent over a third of her career at Arthur Andersen, which notoriously went bankrupt due to its deceptions on behalf of Enron and its efforts to obstruct justice by shredding documents when federal investigators learned it had overstated profits to the tune of $600 million.[88] Instead, Facebook focused on how Alford rose through the ranks at companies started by Thiel and Zuckerberg.[89] Because while the Chan Zuckerberg Initiative is a philanthropy, it's incorporated as a Delaware-based limited liability corporation.[90] And whether these efforts are charitable or for-profit, whether this LLC and Zuckerberg's other donations are meant to burnish Zuckerberg's personal image, to improve Facebook's public standing, or even to influence U.S. elections—that all remains up for debate.

And it is an important debate to have.[91]

## Political support, election integrity, and "a very wise gift"

On March 27, 2020, President Donald Trump signed the Coronavirus Aid, Relief, and Economic Security Act (CARES Act) into law, which included $400 million in emergency funding that was "made available to states to prevent, prepare for, and respond to the coronavirus for the 2020 federal election cycle."[92] Then, on September 1, 2020, Priscilla Chan and Mark Zuckerberg one upped the U.S. government. The Chan Zuckerberg Initiative had supported public education, healthcare, life sciences research, energy, and Internet connectivity— but not election integrity.[93] So rather than funding from their for-profit philanthropic entity, Chan and Zuckerberg gave personally to two nonprofit organizations. They donated $250 million to the Center for Tech and Civic Life and $50 million to the Center for Election Innovation & Research. As Election Day neared, Chan and Zuckerberg increased their contributions, to $419 million in total.[94] In a Facebook post, Zuckerberg insisted, "To be clear, I agree with those who say that government should have provided these funds, not private citizens."[95] Despite that, he and his wife put more money toward the 2020 election than even the U.S. government would.

Donald Graham, the former *Washington Post* owner, had once told Zuckerberg, "I will release you from your moral dilemma," which at the time was more a concern about how to make more money, not the risks to society, free speech, or democracy.[96] After Zuckerberg announced the donation, on Facebook, Graham commented beneath his post: "This is a very wise gift."[97] He'd left Facebook's board by then. His daughter, Molly, had also moved on from Facebook; she was the vice president of operations at the Chan Zuckerberg Initiative prior to Peggy Alford.[98]

But was the gift wise? Should private donations influence which election sites have more poll workers, newer vote-counting machines, better hazard pay, and other resources "to bolster transparency and legitimacy" during an election when "the threat of disinformation could greatly diminish voters' confidence in [the] democratic process," as the head of the Center for Election Innovation & Research had declared in the press release announcing the gift?[99] Was this a penance? Would it limit the damage of the falsehoods that proliferated on Facebook? Of course, Zuckerberg was free to donate to any cause he cared about, but was this really an act of charity?

Two candidates for U.S. Senate certainly did not think so. A few months earlier, they'd both decided to run for office with the support of a joint fundraising effort called the "Masters Vance Committee."[100] They'd both received early support from Peter Thiel, David Sacks, Keith Rabois, and Jacob Helberg.[101] Blake Masters and J. D. Vance had moved in the same month, June 2018.[102] If elected, one of their six-year Senate terms would be longer than the *combined* time they'd lived in Arizona and Ohio just before their campaigns began.[103]

The top strategist for J. D. Vance's campaign, Jai Chabria, had previously run the nonprofit that Vance set up to fight the opioid epidemic. That effort had accomplished little, according to David Fahrenthold of the *New York Times*. When it was shut down, Chabria had taken home more in salary than the sum total of charitable dollars that went to support people struggling with addiction.[104] A political operative named Amalia Halikias managed the Masters campaign.[105] She was Amy Chua's niece. She had graduated from Yale in 2015 and then launched a college tutoring startup called Tiger Cub Tutoring with Sophia Chua-Rubenfeld—that's Amy Chua's daughter, thus the venture's name.[106] The company made national news due to its Tiger Mother ties, but it flamed out quickly when Chua-Rubenfeld attempted to juggle the demands of being a first-year student at Yale Law School while simultaneously working on the venture.[107] She'd go on to clerk for Justice Brett Kavanaugh of the Supreme Court.[108]

Kavanaugh had come under fire during his Senate hearings due to accusations of sexual assault at Yale some thirty-five years earlier, so J. D. Vance defended him in the *Wall Street Journal* in the summer of 2018, noting that his wife had worked for Kavanaugh.[109] Ten days later, the *Journal* published another pro-Kavanaugh piece. "Kavanaugh Is a Mentor to Women: I can't think of a better judge for my own daughter's clerkship," Amy Chua wrote.[110] Despite attempts to "Cancel Brett Kavanaugh" by liberal groups, including organizing a march on Washington and a #MeToo #BrettBye social media campaign, Kavanaugh was confirmed. It was the slimmest margin since 1881.[111] The activists behind CancelKavanaugh.com swore that their movement spurred a "reckoning that echoes far beyond him" that "has barely begun." The website remained up, but a few years later, someone hijacked it and repurposed the page to sell standing desks and other office furniture. The website today has the CancelKavanaugh.com logo, followed by "FURNITURE NEWS FOR YOUR HOME OFFICE."[112]

* * *

Peter Thiel donated $10 million to both the pro-Vance and pro-Masters Super PACs early during the Republican primaries, in the spring of 2021.[113] The Super PACs then ran shadow campaigns that, compared to the candidates' traditional political operations, marshaled far more resources. Vance's campaign became particularly effective with this strategy. By the date of the Republican primary, he'd raised less than $3 million in individual contributions.[114] Once Thiel put an additional $5 million behind Vance's Super PAC, that $15 million in total was the largest amount ever given to bolster a U.S. Senate candidate.[115] They used it to develop a trove of content, which they posted to Medium.[116] They'd created everything that Vance needed to build a best-in-class multimillion-dollar campaign—polling data from the same pollster Trump had used, opposition research on other candidates, and recommendations about messages to convey and strategies to pursue—but it was all completely paid for by the Thiel-funded Super PAC.[117]

The campaign needed the help. Early on, Vance had struggled to gain traction among Republican voters, according to a ninety-eight-page memo from the pollster for the Vance-aligned Protect Ohio Values Super PAC that was obtained by *Politico*. It indicated he was last in the five-person race. The ads his opponents ran of Vance's various denunciations of Trump were proving highly effective. "Vance is now underwater with strong Trump approvers and very conservative voters, groups needed to win a GOP primary," it warned and "being anti-Trump is the #1 reason voters do not like Vance," which was "Listed three times more than anything else."[118] The firm that conducted the surveys was Fabrizio, Lee & Associates, the chief pollsters for Donald Trump's two presidential races.[119]

Vance declared that he'd changed his mind about Donald Trump. More than that, he changed his identity, from being a "Never Trump guy" to such a Forever Trump politician that he told voters the former president was not just good but great. Trump was not only great but the greatest. Vance repeated the campaign talking point that Trump had been "the best president of my lifetime," even better than Ronald Reagan.[120] Yet another Peter Thiel prediction was coming true, as Vance helped to usher in "a new Republican party beyond the dogmas of Reaganism."[121] That much became clear at an event on July 24, 2021, in Alexandria, Virginia, hosted by the Intercollegiate Studies Institute, the same organization that had supported the start of Thiel's *Stanford Review* decades before. Vance gave a speech where he argued that "we need to fight woke capital, woke corporations, and the governments that enable them, because we can't win anywhere else," warning that "we are going to lose this country." He told the audience: "We have lost every single major cultural institution in this country. Accept that. Think about it. Big Finance. Big Tech. Wall Street. The biggest corporations. The universities. The media. And the government. There is not a single institution in this country that conservatives currently control." He declared all that without a hint of irony about his own Big Tech investments, or the ways his relationships with universities and the media had made *Hillbilly Elegy* such a popular sensation. In an even more surprising turn of phrase, Vance declared, in that same speech: "If you don't know where you came from, you will have no idea where you're going."[122]

***

Back home in Ohio, the primary campaign began to move in Vance's favor, with significant support from the Thiel-funded Super PAC—with its polling, its research, and especially its marketing efforts. To counteract what was working so well for his opponents, they dedicated most of the funding toward advertising, hoping to convince voters he was pro-Trump and his prior declarations were irrelevant. The Medium page for Protect Ohio Values had only one follower by the time primary voters went to the polls. It was the president of Ohio-based FlexPoint Media, "an omni-channel media strategy firm dedicated to helping organizations shape public opinion and win," which had received over $11 million from the pro-Vance Super PAC.[123] All told, the Super PAC gave Vance robust campaign support and resources that were out in the open, on the Internet, but they got lost in the wide expanse of other websites about *Hillbilly Elegy,* both Vance's book and Ron Howard's new Netflix film. The Medium page wasn't a top search engine result for anything related to the "Ohio Senate race," "J. D. Vance," or anything that would lead to its discovery.[124] They'd hidden the site in plain sight, and for months the only audience was the Vance campaign and its consultants.

Vance's reliance on the Super PAC and the noncoordination collaboration, his "Never Trump" reversal, and the flood of pro-Vance ads reiterating the messaging they'd tested to win over Trump supporters—it all worked. Vance went from last to first, winning the primary. The next morning, he tweeted, "Also, a note to political journalists: the best pollster in the race was @TonyFabrizioGOP."[125] He offered his kudos to Trump's pollster, who had been right on the money. While the funding didn't touch Vance's campaign coffers, he still thanked Fabrizio for contributing to the victory. Tony Fabrizio had earned it. In fact, it was almost as if Fabrizio, Lee & Associates had worked for him.

***

Both Blake Masters and J. D. Vance made voter fraud, and the ways that Facebook threatened election integrity, one of their very top priorities. In a joint *New York Post* op-ed on October 21, 2021, Masters and Vance excoriated "Facebook founder and CEO Mark Zuckerberg's half-billion-dollar effort to buy the presidency for Joe Biden." They began their campaigns, together, with a unified message about the last time voters went to the polls. "Suggesting that anything went wrong in the 2020 election draws immediate scorn from every institutional power center in our country. The media will label you a conspiracy theorist. Public officials will accuse you of abetting 'insurrection.' Social media giants will censor your speech," they wrote. They put the word "insurrection" in quotes to refer to the January 6 attack on the U.S. Capitol, and to signal their doubts about its severity. "But the only way to fight back against the people who run things in our country is to tell the truth. And the simple truth is that in 2020 our oligarchs used their power and money to do everything they could to steal an election."[126]

Was the 2020 election stolen? It was not 100 percent perfect. No election is.[127] Questioning election credibility was nothing new; in public and in private, Donald Trump had doubted the outcome in 2016 before voters cast their ballots.[128] But as it turned out, it would have taken 76,518 additional votes for Trump to defeat Biden in 2020. That was 10,458 more votes in Arizona, 11,780 more in Georgia, 33,597 more in Nevada, and 20,683 more in Wisconsin.[129] For context, the 2000 election was lost by 538 votes when the recount was stopped in Florida; the election results in 2000 were closer than in 2020 by 75,980 votes.[130]

There wasn't just one election in U.S. history that was closer than 2020, however. Woodrow Wilson won the presidency in 1916 by just 3,774 votes in California.[131] That was 72,744 votes closer than in 2020. John F. Kennedy defeated Richard Nixon in 1960 by less than 1 percent in five states (Hawaii, Illinois, Missouri, New Jersey, and New Mexico). Winning these states, which required a total of 46,309 votes, would have given Nixon the presidency. Republican-leaning newspapers had even investigated and concluded the outcome was fraudulent, but Nixon accepted the outcome.[132] That race was 30,209 votes closer than in 2020. In 1976 Jimmy Carter defeated incumbent president Gerald Ford with crucial victories in two battleground states; just 11,370 more votes in Ohio and 4,910 more votes in New York would have changed the outcome for Ford. Those 16,280 votes meant the 1976 election was 60,238 votes closer than 2020.[133]

In fact, if we revisit the numbers, recall that Hillary Clinton would have needed 77,747 more votes to win in 2016, just 1,229 more than what Trump needed in 2020.[134] The basic math answered the question of who had won the 2020 election. Was the vote tally that far off, giving these claims any validity? Who were these "oligarchs" Vance and Masters worried about? How did they "steal an election" by 76,518 votes, far more than every other close election (along with many not-as-close contests) throughout the past century?

Vance railed against Mark Zuckerberg for "buying up local boards of elections in battleground states of mostly Democratic areas" to push the election in Biden's favor. "We have a fake country right now," he declared in an interview with the *Vindicator*, a local paper in northeastern Ohio. "If a billionaire can go and buy up votes in our biggest geographies and tilt an election, transform who can be president, it's really, really dangerous stuff."[135] Masters promised to investigate Zuckerberg, whom he deemed "completely corrupt and criminal" in a tweet where he claimed, "Zuckerberg and Democrat activists conducted a $400M GOTV [Get Out The Vote] operation with 'non-profit' dollars."[136] In the *New York Post* joint op-ed, Masters and Vance argued that Zuckerberg had unfairly influenced the 2020 election: "In important ways, this election was run not by local officials accountable to the people, but by political activists accountable only to the world's most powerful tech CEO." They added, "Facebook—both the product and the wealth generated for its executives—was leveraged to elect a Democratic president."[137] To many experts, that claim seemed preposterous.[138] But let's shed more light; let's pause, reflect, question, and discern.

Why did Americans see these donations so differently, as deeply corrupting or utterly harmless? The contrasting news angles taken about Zuckerberg's intentions certainly played a role. After interviewing dozens of local election officials who had received the funding and attested that it made their lives easier, NPR published an article on December 8, 2020, with this laudatory title: "How Private Money from Facebook's CEO Saved the 2020 Election."[139] The *New York Post* later cast doubt on that assessment of salvation, quoting a former Federal Election Commission member who claimed, "This was a carefully orchestrated attempt to convert official government election offices into get-out-the-vote operations for one political party and to insert political operatives into election offices in order to influence and manipulate the outcome of the election."[140] Opinion pieces in conservative outlets echoed this argument, decrying Big Tech's corrupting influence: "The 2020 Election Wasn't Stolen, It Was Bought by Mark Zuckerberg," claimed a piece in the *Federalist*; "Mark Zuckerberg's 'Donations' Rigged the 2020 Election," argued another in the *Washington Times*.[141] On March 31, 2022, NPR redoubled its assertion about the virtue of Zuckerberg's gifts in an article titled, "Private Funding Saved the 2020 Election. Now, Some GOP-Led States Are Banning it."[142]

✳ ✳ ✳

Had Zuckerberg saved or undermined democracy? Had his power protected the vote or corrupted the process? It seemed to depend on whether your candidate had won or lost in 2020, or which news you trusted the most. But in another sense, we all should have been evaluating the risks to public trust and the precedent that personally funding elections had created. Attorney General Jeff Landry of Louisiana warned about just that—and he acted, too, by suing the Center for Tech and Civic Life. He determined that "private contributions to local election officials and the election system in general are unlawful and contrary to Louisiana law," especially since he'd found that more money went to areas of Louisiana that were less conservative. He lamented "the corrosive influence of outside money on Louisiana election officials."[143] Landry's legal filing warned against the dangers of such powerful corporations and individuals, which might go beyond financing Super PACs prior to an election and could now reshape the actual voting process on Election Day:

> Private contributors are likely to be political parties or large corporations that have partisan and/or economic objectives to foster with their contributions to election officials; Private interests, as in this instance, fund particular parishes and particular aspects of the election that they believe advance their election goals and objectives; [and] . . . should registrars and clerks become reliant upon private funding of their governmental activities, they may well be compelled to respond to the objectives of those providing the funding in order to ensure that the funding continues.[144]

"Our elections should never be for sale," Landry insisted, based on the principle that "private money should not fund our elections."[145] The *Wall Street Journal*'s editorial board took a similar stance, in an attempt to shed new light during this increasingly heated debate. "The 2020 pandemic election wasn't stolen, but it sure was a superspreader of bad precedents," they wrote on January 3, 2022, in a piece titled, "Zuckerbucks Shouldn't Pay for Elections: It Fans Mistrust to Let Private Donors Fund Official Voting Duties."[146]

Ultimately, many conservatives agreed that the election was "Lost, Not Stolen," including a slate of respected Republicans and strong conservatives—former political appointees, members of Congress, and federal judges—who wrote a lengthy report with that title. "If the American people lose trust that our elections are free and fair, we will lose our democracy," they explained, before providing a detailed analysis that showed "there is absolutely no evidence of fraud in the 2020 Presidential Election on the magnitude necessary to shift the result in any state, let alone the nation as a whole." These conservatives reviewed extensive evidence in an exhaustive search for fraud. They found very little: "In fact, there was no fraud that changed the outcome in even a single precinct. It is wrong, and bad for our country, for people to propagate baseless claims that President Biden's election was not legitimate."[147] For many leading conservatives, the government's reported election returns held up. The result of the 2020 election was that Trump lost, coming up 76,518 votes shy.

But uncertainty had spread, and vitriol had too, so that polls after the 2020 election consistently found that around 35 percent of Americans, and over half of Republicans, believed that the 2020 election was fraudulent.[148] Conspiracies, rumors, and facts swirled together, with Zuckerberg at the center of the storm. As Theodore Schleifer put it in *Puck News*, "Liberals have long suspected that he is a hostage of the right, if not a Republican sympathizer, given the extensive aid that Facebook provided Donald Trump's presidential campaign in 2016 and Zuckerberg's subsequent reluctance to boot him from the platform. Conservatives presume he is a hostage of his woke employees, if not a card-carrying progressive himself, given that he *did* eventually deplatform Trump."[149] Zuckerberg turned to advisers with both Democratic and Republican bona fides in search of help.[150]

Just a few months after brokering the deal with the Saudis, David Plouffe came to work for Zuckerberg.[151] He left Uber in January of 2017 and joined the Chan Zuckerberg Initiative as its head of policy and advocacy.[152] Ben LaBolt, who had served as spokesman for the Obama campaign and as the assistant press secretary in the Obama White House, became the personal spokesman for the Chan and Zuckerberg family.[153] On April 12, 2022, LaBolt informed reporters that the funding was "a one-time donation given the unprecedented nature of the crisis," and that "they have no plans to repeat that donation."[154] Brian Baker, a Republican strategist Zuckerberg had also hired to assist with public relations efforts, put it more bluntly. "They are not donating for something like this," he declared, "ever again."[155]

Per Schleifer's analysis, Baker might have come across as more credible with conservatives than LaBolt when he had made those remarks. That was not only because of his prior allegiances, but also because it had recently been announced that—throughout February, March, and April 2022, at the same time as he'd worked for Chan and Zuckerberg—LaBolt was also serving as an advisor to the

Biden White House to support the Supreme Court nomination of Ketanji Brown Jackson.[156] Less than a year later, on February 9, 2023, the Biden administration announced that LaBolt would join them full-time to oversee all public relations duties as the White House communications director.[157]

* * *

Throughout their campaigns, the fundraising efforts by Vance and Masters proved disappointing, with twenty-seven U.S. Senate candidates nationwide outraising both of them, including several candidates in entirely uncompetitive races.[158] In terms of individual contributions, Vance was outraised more than five times over by his Democratic opponent, Tim Ryan.[159] The Masters campaign's fundraising total was just one-sixth of what his opponent had raised, $15.7 million compared to $92.7 million in personal contributions.[160]

Yet those individual donations, by "ordinary" voters, mattered less this time around. Without Thiel's $32.5 million in contributions and the support from their Super PACs, both Vance and Masters would have faced a nearly insurmountable disadvantage.[161] End Citizens United, a PAC set up to oppose the existence of Super PACs, later filed a complaint with the Federal Election Commission to protest how Vance's campaign collaborated with the Thiel-funded Protect Ohio Values Super PAC. The president of End Citizens United, Tiffany Muller, declared, "This abuse is perhaps one of the clearest and most flagrant examples of a candidate and a Super PAC skirting campaign finance laws."[162]

After Masters and Vance won the Republican primaries in Arizona and Ohio, they recalibrated their messaging for the general election. Early in his campaign, Vance had called President Biden a "crazy fake president," and his website during the primary had blamed Democrats for corrupting the electoral process.[163] To appeal to more moderate voters, Vance's tone became far less aggressive. He talked generically about "election integrity," and his campaign removed the language lambasting Democrats as the perpetrators.[164] Masters softened even further. As the *Arizona Republic* noted, his website from primary season had declared that "the 2020 election was a rotten mess—if we had had a free and fair election, President Trump would be sitting in the Oval Office today and America would be so much better off." That became: "We need to get serious about election integrity."[165] Former president Trump took note, telling Masters that "you'll lose if you go soft. You're going to lose that base." Trump then informed Masters that when another candidate was asked, "How is your family?" her reply was, "The election was rigged and stolen." Outrage over election interference in the 2020 election was supposedly all that mattered to win in 2022, despite the confirmed vote tallies and the overwhelming evidence about the legitimacy of the 2020 outcome—and despite the fact that over $30 million of Peter Thiel's money was being funneled through Super PACs in ways that were clearly having an impact on these very campaigns in 2022.[166]

Trump insisted that the election was rigged and had been stolen from him—but *when* he'd decided that mattered. Steve Bannon, the former White House chief strategist, told donors on October 31, 2020, Halloween Night, that Trump had planned to declare victory—no matter what the results were in a few days.[167] Just seventy-two hours before polls closed, those comments were caught on tape, leaked to *Mother Jones*, and featured in the court case where Bannon was convicted as part of the investigation into the failed insurrection on January 6.[168] Bannon told donors they'd planned to declare victory no matter what happened.

"But that doesn't mean he's the winner. He's just going to say he's the winner," Bannon explained. "And Trump's going to be sitting there, mocking, tweeting shit out: 'You lose. I'm the winner. I'm the king.'"[169]

# CHAPTER 15

# OUR GREAT SYMBOL OF DEMOCRACY

J. D. Vance and Peter Thiel, Narya Capital, Rumble, and Clearview AI

W E ARE AMERICANS!!! WE FOUGHT AND DIED TO START OUR COUNTRY! WE ARE GOING TO FIGHT . . . FIGHT LIKE HELL. WE WILL SAVE HER♥THEN WERE [*sic*] GOING TO SHOOT THE TRAITORS!!!!!!!!!!!!"[1] That Facebook post and many like it, which came in the weeks before January 6, 2021, predicted the violence to come. Employees at Facebook knew it. They'd deleted rumors and lies but also opinions and arguments, censoring some posts that would have been allowed earlier, and making decisions all along about what was permissible, what went too far, what was free or fair, and who could say what.[2]

They'd read the death threats against members of Congress, and they knew all about the planned march and the promised violence. They'd watched as people made plans to attend Trump's speech before the "March to Save America." Some in the crowd had peaceful intentions; others wanted to lynch their leaders.[3] And Facebook employees witnessed the moments when people's rage boiled over in status updates and comments, when they promised retribution, when they declared the need to "be there, will be wild!" just as the sitting president of the United States had encouraged them.[4]

Top officials at Facebook were concerned. In fact, forty days before the presidential election of 2020 and 104 days before the U.S. Capitol attack on January 6, 2021, Tim Kendall had told Congress: "Social media services that I and others have built . . . have served to tear people apart with alarming speed and intensity. At the very least we have eroded our collective understanding—at worst, I fear we are pushing ourselves to the brink of a civil war."[5] He was the former director of monetization for Facebook, and that testimony was on September 24, 2020.

Mark Zuckerberg was also nervous about the worst-case scenario, where widespread political protests or even bloodshed would ruin Election Day 2020. That did not happen.[6] Whether it was wise (or not) to pour over $400 million of his personal money into public election administration, America's leading national security experts had agreed that Zuckerberg was right to worry about potential violence. In the weeks before the election, the Department of Homeland Security's yearly threat assessment established that the most dangerous threat facing the American homeland, for the first time in two decades, no longer came from 9/11-style Islamic extremists or other terrorists from overseas. Our greatest danger was domestic violent extremism.[7]

Yet in the weeks that followed the election—after experts asserted that the election was free and fair, and with $419 million from Zuckerberg and Chan now spent—Facebook shut down the internal task force that had been responsible for monitoring groups where people called for violence against their electors, spread rumors about election fraud, and organized efforts to stop the counting of votes.[8] Mark Zuckerberg had a choice to make. He ordered a return to business as usual.[9] He had declared Mission Accomplished far too soon, though, because the real danger to the peaceful transfer of power had just begun.[10]

***

The results of the 2020 campaign remained too close to call on Election Night because votes were still being counted. But after many Americans had already headed to bed, Trump declared he'd won anyway.[11] Approximately twelve hours later, at 3 p.m. Eastern, a Trump supporter named Kylie Jane Kremer created a new Facebook group named "Stop the Steal." According to the *New York Times*, more than 100,000 people joined in the first few hours, gaining a hundred new members every ten seconds. By the next morning, there were thirty-six posts a minute. It was one of the fastest-growing groups in the platform's history, which is to say, it was one of the fastest-growing movements in world history, since billions of people had never been connected like this before.[12]

While the major news outlets awaited the full results to declare the winner of the 2020 election, executives at Facebook made another choice.[13] Less than twenty-four hours after Stop the Steal debuted, the company shut it down. The group created by Kremer maxed out at 361,292 members before Facebook pulled the plug, with 206,196 posts to the group's page in less than twenty-four hours—the majority coming in the final hours of it being up, according to the figures Facebook later reported to Congress.[14] Put another way, less than a day after its debut, the Facebook group established to spread claims about the 2020 election being stolen (before the final results had even been officially announced) was already larger than over three-quarters of U.S. capital cities.[15] Facebook shut the group down anyway.[16]

Yet Facebook's executives couldn't silence every assertion that the election was rigged. Trump's supporters kept using the platform to organize new groups, sometimes under different names. Many of them still used variations of the "Stop the Steal" moniker. According to the House Select Committee to Investigate the January 6th Attack on the United States Capitol, Facebook employees couldn't keep up with the speed of the spread of Stop the Steal. New groups would start, expand, and then be deleted by a few Facebook staffers. The process would then begin again. Even though there was no policy authorizing the deletion of false claims about election fraud, Facebook employees began taking down some "Stop the Steal" groups and election-related posts within other groups. In the end, they took action inconsistently, removing forty-three groups, while hundreds more remained up.[17]

Facebook employees watched as their platform became home to something much more dangerous than disapproval about the way an election turned out, or even doubts about ballot count tallies.[18] They monitored the content as users became increasingly enraged. People began to organize and promised to take action—often angrily and violently, for the kind of cause worth dying for, or killing for. Afterward we learned just how widespread this was: "A *Pro-Publica / Washington Post* analysis of Facebook posts, internal company documents, and interviews provides the clearest evidence yet that the social media giant played a critical role in spreading lies that fomented the violence of Jan. 6," the two media outlets claimed. According to their analysis, there were at least 650,000 posts on Facebook between Election Day and January 6—or about 10,000 a day—that attacked the legitimacy of the 2020 election.[19]

The House Select Committee came to the same conclusion. "Facebook did not fail to grapple with election delegitimization after the election so much as it did not even try," it reported. "Stop the Steal proliferated through Facebook groups and the company declined to study false claims of election theft even when advised to by senior staff. Though the company removed the initial Stop the Steal group, a coordinated group of users worked to evade Facebook's takedown and grow the movement on the platform." Every ill-considered attempt to stanch the bleeding seemed to only worsen the infection, according to the committee. "After the election, nearly all of the fastest-growing groups on Facebook were related to Stop the Steal, and the company took action against only a small fraction of these groups. Despite warnings, Facebook leadership declined to take the problem seriously because it would 'only create momentum and expectation for action.'"[20]

They didn't have a clear plan, and they had disbanded the task force that had previously been responsible for addressing election integrity, so they soon dealt with the consequences. Like a rapid, reckless game of whack-a-mole, Facebook employees and contractors tried to counter what they deemed misinformation by deleting a variety of content related to the election.[21] But Trump's supporters persisted. They'd type their opinions about fraud as status updates, which another user or an algorithm might flag, and a Facebook staffer would then choose to remove as misinformation. Then they'd post pictures with words embedded in the images, which were harder for Facebook's algorithms to recognize. Unlike every other election since Facebook had first existed, it had begun plastering warnings on some posts that questioned the outcome.[22] That did not stop the outrage.

In fact, it might have even backfired due to what psychologists deemed the "forbidden fruit effect." Renee Engeln described it this way for *Psychology Today*: "When you feel your freedom to access something is taken away or restricted, it often makes you want that thing more. Basically, our response to being told we *can't* have something is often to insist that we *must* have it."[23] Even when social media companies tried to limit the skepticism about the integrity of the 2020 election, it felt like censorship. Whose fault was it that the fruit from the Tree of Knowledge of Good and Evil was consumed then shared? In Genesis, with Eve's reply to the Lord, she tried to self-exonerate: "The serpent deceived me."[24]

As the date for the January 6 ballot counting drew near, the same people who created the Stop the Steal group that had gone viral on Facebook began to organize a march on Washington. Kylie Jane Kremer posted a virtual flyer to social media, encouraging Trump's supporters to descend on the nation's capital, citing President Trump's tweet to "be there, will be wild," and declaring, "The calvary is coming, Mr. President!"[25] She likely meant "cavalry," the word referring to when military reinforcements rush in to save the day, not the place where Jesus was crucified after the murderous demands of a maddened mob.

Trump retweeted her post.[26]

Online, the Stop the Steal group started by Kremer, along with her other efforts on social media, had helped to set the stage for the pro-Trump rally in Washington on January 6. In real life, Kylie Jane and her mother, Amy Kremer, quite literally set the stage for the event near the White House.[27] They were listed as the points of contact for the application from "Women for America First" to the National Park Service, which granted them permission to install 50,000 square feet of flooring, two 13-by-10-foot LED video screens, a 15-by-25-foot jumbotron, a backstage area for the president and his guests, 500 feet of red, white, and blue bunting, and an assortment of other patriotic decor for the event, which was variously called a "First Amendment Rally," the "Save America March," and the "March for Trump," in different sections of their application. According to the federal permit application, the purpose was to "demand transparency and protect election integrity," so that afterward "some participants may leave to attend rallies at the United States Capitol to hear the results of Congressional certification of the Electoral College count."[28]

Who was responsible at Facebook? Of course, Mark Zuckerberg was. He was the CEO. He was also chairman of the board, which created a significant concentration of power that had been criticized as poor corporate governance.[29] And, even more unusually, he had retained well over half of the company's voting shares.[30] But who was in charge of creating and enforcing the policies and procedures that kept failing at Facebook in the lead up to January 6, 2021? Who bore responsibility for fixing problems like these more generally?

## Mark's choices and the "use of our platform to incite violent insurrection"

Peter Thiel been a Facebook board member since 2005, after investing in the new venture.[31] Once Reed Hastings left and Peggy Alford joined, Thiel became the chair of the Compensation, Nominating, and Governance Committee.[32] That meant that he was accountable, in 2019, for developing and recommending to the full board a range of corporate polices: Facebook's Code of Conduct, its rules about reporting illegal or unethical behavior, and all executives' salaries and bonuses. In many ways, Thiel replaced Hastings as the conscience of the organization. He was responsible for the procedures and incentives for what mattered most at Facebook.[33] In particular, he was charged with the duties of "developing and recommending corporate governance guidelines and policies" and "evaluating, recommending, approving and reviewing executive officer compensation arrangements, plans, policies and programs."[34]

As just one example of what happened after Hastings left, Thiel's committee approved a $4 million signing bonus as part of over $19 million in total compensation for Facebook's new chief legal officer in her first year on the job.[35] When they hired her, she was the State Department's top lawyer for the Trump administration, but eighteen years before, she'd worked for George W. Bush's administration on the USA PATRIOT Act. On April 22, 2019, Jennifer Newstead became general counsel at Facebook.[36] Thiel was responsible for oversight of Facebook's governance, and Newstead led its legal department throughout the crucial months of November and December 2020, as Stop the Steal groups spread, were shut down, then kept reemerging.

* * *

Employees at Facebook had previously voiced concerns about their algorithms that soon proved prophetic. "Our existing systems cannot catch even a small fraction of the hate, violence, or misinformation on Facebook," a data scientist wrote weeks before the 2020 election. "We have heavily overpromised regarding our ability to moderate content on the platform."[37] Facebook's personnel had spoken up like this before. But the violence of January 6, 2021, seemed even more dangerous—potentially even a near-death experience for American democracy—and afterward many at Facebook felt responsible that their company's platforms had fueled the fury and aided the organizers. Zuckerberg faced a torrent of backlash this time.

"I'm struggling to match my values to my employment here. I came here hoping to affect change and improve society, but all I've seen is atrophy and abdication of responsibility," one wrote. Another worried about profiting from promoting extreme and violent content, asking, "How are we expected to ignore when leadership overrides research-based policy decisions to better serve people like the groups inviting violence today?" Zuckerberg wrote: "Hang in there everyone as we figure out the best ways to support our teams and manage discourse on our platform to allow for peaceful discussion and organizing but not calls for violence. I know I've had trouble focusing today as I'm watching events unfold. So if this is impacting you you are not alone. Hang in there."[38] One employee was tired of the excuses and delays, writing:

> Never forget the day Trump rode down the escalator in 2016, called for a ban on Muslims entering the US, we determined that it violated our policies, and yet we explicitly overrode the policy and didn't take the video down. There is a straight line that can be drawn from that day to today, one of the darkest days in the history of democracy and self-governance. Would it have made a difference in the end? We can never know, but history will not judge us kindly.[39]

On January 7, 2021, Mark Zuckerberg made an announcement. "The shocking events of the last 24 hours clearly demonstrate that President Donald Trump intends to use his remaining time in office to undermine the peaceful and lawful transition of power to his elected successor, Joe Biden," he wrote. He had justified his decisions over the past several years to keep Trump's Facebook account active, but January 6 caused him to worry that "the current context is now fundamentally different, involving use of our platform to incite violent insurrection against a democratically elected government." Zuckerberg announced that Facebook had shut down the account of the sitting president of the United States, which would last at least until after Joe Biden's inauguration.[40]

On January 8, 2021, Facebook took another unprecedented step. It had already blocked people from searching for "Stop the Steal" from the main search bar after the election in November. It went even further, hiding any groups that used "Stop the Steal" in their name, making it seem like those groups simply did not exist. It was the first time the company had ever intervened in the search function to return a "null result" for a term in their Groups search.[41] Five months later Trump's account remained deactivated. Facebook announced that it would ban Trump for two more years, promising that after that, "we will look to experts to assess whether the risk to public safety has receded."[42] Peter Thiel remained the chair of Facebook's governance committee that entire time, while Jennifer Newstead, who had worked in the Trump administration until just a few months earlier, was Facebook's top lawyer.[43]

## Let's get ready to rumble

Facebook was not the only company grappling with these crucial decisions and failing to find workable solutions as they reacted, in the aftermath of January 6, rather than anticipating and proactively addressing the risks created by their platforms. The House Select Committee also criticized YouTube for failing to meet its "ethical obligation to prevent those services from being used to commit crimes, orchestrate violence, or otherwise contribute to offline harm."[44] Just like Facebook's executives, the leadership at Alphabet seemed to underestimate the ongoing risks to the peaceful transfer of power between Election Day and January 6.

At first, YouTube had placed a caution label on videos flagged by viewers for containing false information about the election being stolen. The warning said, generically, "Robust safeguards help ensure the integrity of election results," but the videos remained up.[45] Then YouTube instituted a new policy following the December 9, 2020, deadline for states to certify their Electoral College votes. After that point, an algorithm was supposed to flag any videos challenging the election's outcome. Humans reviewed questionable videos, too. According to the House Select Committee, Alphabet employed more than twenty-two thousand content moderation staff for these purposes. Yet the company removed only around two thousand videos related to election fraud from December 9 to January 6. By comparison, over one hundred million videos were posted on YouTube during this same period, so the videos they'd removed were less than 0.005 percent of total postings.[46] YouTube tried to restrict some of the videos it had found, but particularly compared to the volume of content uploaded, the House Select Committee criticized the company's response as far too limited.

It's now clear that, just like Facebook's filters, the net that Alphabet used to capture these videos had massive holes in it. In fact, the company did not take down *any* videos about voting fraud that happened to be posted before December 9, 2020. All earlier videos remained up.[47] "YouTube's policies relevant to election integrity were inadequate to the moment," the House Select Committee concluded. "The company did not ban election fraud claims until December 9th, and even then did not enforce that policy retroactively. Forms of election delegitimization not related to ballot fraud were also not considered in violation of this policy, meaning a great deal of election denial remained on the platform through January 6th and into the current day."[48]

Whether Alphabet should have deleted this content due to the risks it posed—or whether free speech took precedence—was an important decision that should have been made. But the reality was that its executives initially didn't make any definitive decisions. Then, even after they made the call, the execution was inconsistent, so the outcome was ineffectual. As YouTube tried to deal with Donald Trump's account, it changed the policies almost weekly: on January 6, 2021, YouTube issued a warning; on January 12, 2021, the account was suspended for a week; on January 26, 2021, the suspension was made indefinite; and then on March 4, 2021, the company announced that it would restore Trump's account whenever it decided the danger of violence had passed. "Select Committee staff confirmed with the briefers that there is no benchmark or set of metrics that would inform YouTube's assessment that the risk of violence has receded; it is purely a judgment call based on available signals," the House Committee explained. "President Trump's account suspension was an exception to YouTube policy made in exigent circumstances," it concluded.[49] It was in this context, as so much content was left up while other information was being scrubbed from the site, that an unlikely new competitor emerged. It was called Rumble.

In January 2021 Rumble sued Google. The Toronto-based video-hosting site claimed its failure to gain new viewers was "a direct result of Google's unlawful anticompetitive, exclusionary and monopolistic behavior."[50] Rumble had been active since 2013 but had struggled to attract attention for over half a decade. Yet suddenly it found a new purpose during COVID-19: to allow almost any content on its platform. The CEO promised Rumble would be "immune to cancel culture."[51] That included refusing to remove "medical misinformation" as part of an effort to "challenge the status quo." Rumble had become a viable alternative to YouTube by allowing almost all videos, without restrictions. Rumble was far more permissive about what could be posted and watched. While it had policies against videos of pornography, child exploitation, or harassment, it was much more lenient than YouTube, especially when it came to baseless rumors about vaccines implanting artificial intelligence and tracking chips or unsubstantiated conspiracy theories about massive fraud in the 2020 election.[52] According to Pew, a fifth of the most prominent accounts on Rumble had been banned or demonetized on other platforms.[53]

Rumble began to attract the attention of millions. The *Washington Post* reported that it had grown from 200,000 American visitors in the last week of July 2020 to over 19 million weekly in the first week of August 2021, growth of 9,000 percent.[54] Rumble was also noticed by two very important viewers. In

May 2021 J. D. Vance (through Narya) and Peter Thiel (through Thiel Capital) coinvested in Rumble.[55] It was Thiel's first investment in a social media venture since Facebook.[56]

After endorsing Vance, and right before Trump's first major public appearance since the January 6 attacks, there was big news from the forty-fifth president. He announced that he'd join Rumble, which would broadcast his appearance live from Vance's home state of Ohio.[57] Then, in October 2021, Donald Trump announced his own tech platform. "We live in a world where the Taliban has a huge presence on Twitter, yet your favorite American President has been silenced. This is unacceptable," he declared.[58] Even without a product on the market, Trump's new media conglomerate surged 400 percent on its first day of trading.[59] That was based on promises that investors would profit from "Trump's Historic Social Media Following" of 146.5 million total followers by "Building a 'Non-Cancellable' Global Community."[60] In reality, the company struggled with technical glitches early on, including a thirteen-hour outage and an unmanageable waiting list.[61] Trump would attract only 3 percent of his total following onto Truth Social by the midterm elections in 2022.[62] Rumble had better success, as its exponential growth continued. In December 2021 it announced a media partnership with Truth Social and then declared that it planned to go public at a $2.1 billion valuation.[63] Rumble represented a powerful platform for Vance and Thiel—and an extremely lucrative one. On paper, they'd quadrupled their investment; the venture was valued at $500 million when they'd made their bet just six months earlier.[64] Despite protests from Tim Ryan, Vance retained his ownership of Rumble throughout his candidacy for U.S. Senate.[65]

After eight years of hardship, Rumble had finally found a viewership. By August 2022 it had 44 million monthly active users, and 9.8 million people used Truth Social.[66] Just over half a year later, 169 million people visited Rumble in March 2023, while only 7 million accessed Truth Social.[67] "We invested in Rumble, which I think is a really good company," Blake Masters explained during an interview with the *On the Brink* podcast during his campaign, using "we" to explain his role in the Thiel Capital investment, which was fitting since Masters stayed on Thiel Capital's payroll throughout much of his campaign, including when he gave that interview on March 2, 2022, with the election less than eight months away.[68]

Speech of all kinds was allowed on Rumble, so not only did members of the Trump family have millions of viewers, but so could RT, Russia's state-owned media.[69] RT live-streamed a speech on Rumble where Putin decried the "cancel culture" targeted against Russia, including "public ostracism, boycotting and even complete silencing" of people who "do not fit into modern templates, no matter how absurd they really are."[70] Putin painted a completely different picture—in the black-and-white of what he deemed right and wrong—than what Ukraine's Volodymyr Zelensky described to Anne Applebaum and Jeffrey Goldberg for the *Atlantic Monthly*. "As Zelensky put it, this is a war over a fundamental definition of not just democracy but civilization," they wrote. Zelensky believed Ukraine symbolized the frontlines of an existential battle, in his words: "to show everybody else, including Russia, to respect sovereignty, human rights, territorial integrity; and to respect people, not to kill people, not to rape women, not to kill animals, not to take that which is not yours."[71]

This gave new meaning to what Vance said on the campaign trail, "I gotta be honest with you, I don't really care what happens to Ukraine one way or another," and to Masters's tweet that "Ukraine is crucial to Russian security, not to ours." In a video posted on March 1, 2022, Masters even called America's leaders "buffoons who hate you so instead they'll keep defending Ukraine's borders while turning their backs on ours."[72] That declaration had many facets and layers. A day after claiming that U.S. politicians hated their own constituents, Masters went on the *On The Brink* podcast to promote Rumble, which filled thousands of Americans' screens with anti-Ukraine, pro-Russian propaganda, on RT's slickly produced news videos, all of it in English. The "cancel culture" battles and "woke" wars had become powerful propaganda in an actual life-and-death war. What did those terms actually mean? It was in the eye of the accuser, on either side. The search for truth, and the pursuit of justice, seemed more elusive than ever.

Using tech that was created in Canada and backed by American investors, the Russian government spread its messages—echoing the Unite the Right's refrain, "Russia is our friend"—on the only major social media site where it had free rein.[73] That resulted in an investment that became more valuable for Vance, Masters, and Thiel, which kept growing as viewers spent more time watching Russian propaganda. Vladimir Putin used the same phrases heard at political rallies across America, claiming his detractors tried to "cancel" him, even as Vance and Masters campaigned against the U.S. supporting a democracy at risk.[74]

Throughout the next year, another candidate began to argue for similar isolationist policies. Vivek Ramaswamy's political fortunes had begun to rise, with every contrarian position he took, and with each heated attack against his Republican primary opponents. He railed against corruption in corporate America and the federal government. He was the only Republican candidate who wanted to totally cease U.S. aid to Ukraine. Then he went further, promising to end Russian sanctions. "He wants to hand Ukraine to Russia," one of his opponents lamented, insisting, "You don't do that to friends," while later noting that he also wanted to cut aid to Israel.[75] After reviewing Ramaswamy's financial disclosures, the *Wall Street Journal* noted that the "anti-woke presidential candidate" had invested in Rumble.[76]

## On schedule for Schedule F

Donald Trump had endorsed J. D. Vance on April 15, 2022, and Blake Masters on June 2, 2022.[77] *Politico* reported that Trump called Vance a "handsome son of a bitch" with a "beautiful" golf swing.[78] Trump praised Masters for claiming the 2020 election was stolen.[79] On the campaign trail, Vance especially made increasingly wild claims. "If you wanted to kill a bunch of MAGA voters in the middle of the heartland, how better than to target them and their kids with this deadly fentanyl," Vance said during an interview with the founder of the *Gateway Pundit*. "And man, it does look intentional. It's like Joe Biden wants to punish the people who didn't vote for him, and opening up the floodgates to the border is one way to do it."[80] Claiming Biden was personally targeting Republican voters with deadly opioids was, to say the least, misleading and in bad faith.[81] Yet the message had been tested, using Peter Thiel's money, and it worked, blending anti-immigration fears with the traumas of the worsening opioid crisis. It got the reaction Vance wanted, so he doubled down, running an ad conveying the same message.[82]

That was, arguably, not the wildest claim Vance made. *Vanity Fair*'s James Pogue reported that Vance thought that Trump should be even *more* authoritarian and nepotistic if he won back the White House: "I think that what Trump should do, if I was giving him one piece of advice: Fire every single midlevel bureaucrat, every civil servant in the administrative state, replace them with *our* people."[83] This would defy the merit-based professionalism, and abet the loyalty-based politicization, of the U.S. government. The civil service, and its pro-merit policies, had been in place since the Pendleton Civil Service Reform Act became law in 1883.[84]

Anticipating objections, Vance then argued, "And when the courts stop you, stand before the country, and say,"—and then he quoted Andrew Jackson, rejecting the U.S. Constitution entirely—"The chief justice has made his ruling. Now let him enforce it." As Pogue put it, "This is a description, essentially, of a coup." Yet that was Vance's view of the world by this point. "We are in a late republican period," he said. "If we're going to push back against it, we're going to have to get pretty wild, and pretty far out there, and go in directions that a lot of conservatives right now are uncomfortable with."[85] With each word, he moved further away from the Never Trump persona he'd presented to America just a few years before. Recall Vance's words in *Hillbilly Elegy*: "This isn't some libertarian mistrust of government policy, which is healthy in any democracy," he cautioned. "This is deep skepticism of the very institutions of our society. And it's becoming more and more mainstream."[86] He had once warned us about the threat to our institutions. Now, he made it so.

Even if Trump wanted to, how could he reinstate meritless nepotism like this, if he ever returned to the White House? The answer was simple: days before the

2020 election, the Trump administration already created the legal authority to do what Vance had called for. On October 21, 2020, Trump signed an executive order that gave him the power to reassign civil servants to a new employment status.[87] Rather than being protected by laws that had been in place for over a century, which allowed for firing due to misconduct but not for political purposes, federal employees who influenced policymaking would be reassigned as a new class of employees. That way, they could be terminated by politicians without cause, then replaced with loyalists.[88]

Usually about four thousand political appointees would join the ranks of the federal government during each new administration.[89] An initial estimate by one Trump administration official projected that this new authority would give the White House the ability to fire up to fifty thousand career public servants and then appoint its own people into those roles.[90] The Silicon Age playbook, to rewrite or ignore the rules you disliked, was in full force here. Trump promised to clean house if he was reelected, just like Uber's attempts to change the rules through Prop 22.[91] But actually, Uber was the wrong analogy. The title the Trump administration gave to this new authority made that clear. At Palantir, Peter Thiel and his cofounders had consolidated power through their Class F shares.[92] The Trump executive order called this takeover, which would give the administration unprecedented political power, by a strikingly similar name: "Schedule F."[93] Earlier, Palantir had skipped classes of C, D, and E shares; this time, the federal government previously had classified roles as Schedule A, B, C, or D. There was no Schedule E, but now there was a Schedule F.[94]

The man who oversaw this change in the eleventh hour of the Trump administration was John McEntee.[95] He had been Trump's "body man" early in his presidency, the staffer who was responsible for carrying the president's bags on trips while attending to his every need. For months he was the first person to see Trump in the morning and the last person to say goodnight.[96] At least that was before he was unexpectedly let go. His background check had come back with too many red flags, and he was ineligible for a security clearance, due to massive gambling debts resulting from individual bets worth tens of thousands of dollars.[97]

Despite that, President Trump brought him back into the administration. Trump told his team, "I want to put Johnny in charge of personnel," as head of the Presidential Personnel Office. As Jonathan Karl explained in his book *Betrayal: The Final Act of the Trump Show*, members of Trump's senior team argued that McEntee was not qualified to take on the role that was, essentially, the White House's chief human resources officer. How could Trump make his body man, with no HR experience, responsible for screening and hiring all cabinet secretaries, ambassadors, and senior intelligence officials—especially since he couldn't get a security clearance? "Mr. President," one aide told him, "I have never said no to anything you've asked me to do, but I am asking you to please reconsider this. I don't think it is a good idea." Trump reportedly screamed back: "You people never fucking listen to me! You're going to fucking do what I tell you to do." And they did. McEntee was twenty-nine-years old.[98]

"I didn't feel ready before, but I am 29 now and I'm ready," McEntee declared during his job interview, according to Karl. He'd insisted, "I'm the only person around here that's just here for the president." As it turned out, loyalty was the most important qualification of all. McEntee cleaned house, hiring pro-Trump activists to staff the office. That included Camryn Kinsey, who was still in college when he hired her as director of external relations.[99] She was a social media influencer with hundreds of thousands of followers on Twitter and Instagram.[100] "Only in Trump's America could I go from working in a gym to working in the White House," she beamed, "because that's the American dream."[101]

McEntee and his newly hired team helped to create the executive order for Schedule F, which Trump signed on October 21, just thirteen days before the 2020 election.[102] Before that, *Axios* reported that they also fired multiple top national security officials and other senior leaders in the federal government. They'd replaced them with Trump supporters who lacked the experience or credentials usually required for those top jobs. Several were brought into the administration just days before the 2020 election; McEntee had developed org charts for overhauling staff across the entire federal government if Trump were reelected.[103]

In fact, McEntee took matters into his own hands in dramatic fashion: he wrote a memo arguing that Trump should fire the secretary of defense. McEntee claimed that Mark Esper had showed disloyalty by supporting Lieutenant Colonel Alexander Vindman, who had testified about the controversial phone call with Ukraine that led to Trump's first impeachment. With a tweet three weeks later, Trump fired Esper, saying he'd be replaced by Christopher Miller, the person whom McEntee had suggested in his memo.[104] On November 9, 2020, Miller became the acting secretary of defense. He served in that role until Joe Biden's inauguration on January 20, 2021.[105]

During those very same weeks, McEntee's new hires began acting wildly. As Karl chronicled in *Betrayal*, they berated top staffers, even cabinet secretaries, threatening to fire anyone who didn't agree that the election was stolen.[106] On New Year's Day of 2021, McEntee sent a long text message to Mike Pence's chief of staff, which advised the vice president to discard dozens of electoral votes. To make his case, he relied on a mistake-ridden retelling of history, about Thomas Jefferson and the election of 1800. Pence and his team rejected it as an ahistorical misinterpretation and, more importantly, utterly unconstitutional. He'd continue to believe that even when it meant risking his life on January 6, 2021.[107]

✳ ✳ ✳

On February 15, 2022, John McEntee announced that he'd launched a new startup.[108] Called "The Right Stuff," it was a new dating app that promised to help "conservatives to connect in authentic and meaningful ways." The Right Stuff cautioned that "other dating apps have gone woke," and that people needed a dating site to "connect with people who aren't offended by everything," to "find out who's *Right* for you."[109] McEntee debuted the app after raising $1.5 million for his seed round—all of it from Peter Thiel.[110]

A year later McEntee's "dating app for the Right wing" had achieved a disappointing 2.5 of 5 stars rating on the Apple App Store.[111] Users griped about its many glitches; others protested that they were stuck on the waiting list for months. McEntee rebuffed claims that the site was not ready yet. In an interview, he insisted, "We're trying to keep it super high-quality," claiming that the delays were intentional, that its exclusivity, even elitism, added to the allure.[112] However, once someone got off the waiting list, reviewers still pointed out serious problems with the site. The most immediately recognizable one was that not enough women had signed up. After getting forty thousand downloads in the first month, interest in the app waned considerably, as men kept complaining that there were far too few women on the site.[113]

In addition to the usual dating app fare, where people uploaded their photos and background information, the Right Stuff also asked users questions about politics when creating their dating profiles. One prompt asked: "January 6th was. . . ." Some users decided to underplay the severity of trying to overturn the results of the 2020 election. Others told vulgar jokes, made disparaging remarks, or vaingloriously bragged that they'd taken part in the violent riot themselves.[114] And according to several news reports, a few answers prompted the FBI to reach out, causing outrage that the app was some kind of hoax or even a trap setup by law enforcement.[115] A woman named Caitlin Berg later claimed to be the informant. "There were so many men on that app who were at January 6 and had pictures of it that I started screenshotting their profiles, matching, asking their last name, and then sending their information to the FBI," she said in a TikTok video that around 150,000 people saw before she made it private. "I think I reported 7 or 8 guys."[116]

***

A few months later it became clear that John McEntee had ambitions that went beyond his dating app startup. On May 2, 2023, a group of fifty conservative organizations—including the Intercollegiate Studies Institute and Young America's Foundation—announced that they had launched a new personnel database they called Project 2025 to prepare for a Republican presidential transition.[117] They aimed to have at least twenty thousand political staffers take advantage of the overhaul made possible by Schedule F. "This database will prepare an army of vetted, trained staff to begin dismantling the administrative state from Day 1," Heritage Foundation president Kevin Roberts stated.[118] In addition to the database, they announced a Presidential Administration Academy with certificate programs on topics like "The Administrative State and the Regulatory Process," released an 887-page, single-spaced manifesto with potential policies and programs, and announced that McEntee would be serving as a senior advisor to the effort.[119]

## Hoan: "We're slowly winning people over"

"Federal, state and local law-enforcement agencies are using facial-recognition technology to identify the members of the mob that assaulted the U.S. Capitol last week," wrote Lee Wolosky and Floyd Abrams, Clearview AI's lawyers, in the *Wall Street Journal* six days after the January 6 attacks.[120] Wolosky had been President Barack Obama's special envoy for Guantanamo closure (and by his own admission, he had completely failed to close the infamous detention facility).[121] Abrams had defended the *New York Times*'s right to publish the Pentagon Papers half a century ago.[122] Abrams told *The Times*'s Kashmir Hill that Clearview AI's actions were constitutionally protected: it had downloaded public information, which was considered free speech, even if it risked individuals' rights to privacy. "Abrams's position also reflects a career shift, from primarily defending the constitutional rights of journalists to supporting those of corporations," Hill explained. "After the 2008 financial meltdown, he argued that AAA ratings by Standard & Poor's of debt that turned out to be junk were simply the company's opinion and therefore worthy of protection like any citizen's. He represented Mitch McConnell in the 2010 Citizens United case, in which the Supreme Court found that limiting corporations' political spending violated their free speech."[123] For Abrams, dollars meant speech, and that took precedence, whether it came from "ordinary" citizens or from massive conglomerates, wealthy donors, and Super PACs.

After the attacks on the U.S. Capitol on January 6, 2021, Hoan Ton-That told the *Washington Post*: "It is gratifying that Clearview AI has been used to identify the Capitol rioters who attacked our great symbol of democracy."[124] Earlier media reports that he'd founded the company with help from white nationalists, conspiracy theorists, and Unite the Right marchers in Charlottesville—just a few years before—somehow seemed part of a distant and forgotten past. Clearview AI announced that its systems had experienced a 26 percent increase in searches on January 7, 2021, with 2,400 law enforcement agencies across the United States using the software.[125] That number had grown to 3,100 two months later. To identify attackers, both the U.S. Capitol police and the FBI had run searches using Clearview AI. The public became aware of this when Ton-That promoted his company's involvement, giving corroborating evidence to *BuzzFeed* to prove it.[126]

Ton-That's company had ample photos to work with as they searched for matches, thanks to the thousands of selfies and videos that the rioters had posted to social media, as well as the surveillance videos that captured the combat from so many angles. By March 2023 federal authorities had identified, tracked down, and arrested over a thousand people in nearly all fifty states—all due to four million digital files, totaling nine terabytes of information, which the FBI stated would take the average person at least 361 days to view continuously.[127] Artificial intelligence scanned through it all with ease. The Department of Justice deemed the investigation "one of the largest in American history, both in terms of the number of defendants prosecuted and the nature and volume of the evidence."[128]

All was seen in the Silicon Age.

This led to confessions of guilt, plea bargains for leniency, and a historic jury trial that resulted in a rare guilty verdict for major crimes—including seditious conspiracy against the United States by a "pro-Western fraternal organization for men who refuse to apologize for creating the modern world," according to the Justice Department.[129] These men's extreme faith in Great Men of History—their convictions that Western civilization required heroic conquerors, and even violent outrage—had grave consequences. Prosecutors won their case by arguing that "these defendants saw themselves as Donald Trump's army, fighting to keep their preferred leader in power no matter what the law or the courts had to say about it," and that they were "thirsting for violence and organizing for action," with both radical words and deeds putting the democratic process at real risk.[130]

A small group of these incarcerated men recorded a video as they prayed together and then sang the national anthem, which was soon posted on Rumble.[131] The song was edited, Donald Trump taped himself reciting the pledge of allegiance, and the finished track blended both recordings. It spread on Truth Social and quickly rose to the top spot on Apple's iTunes music store.[132] On YouTube, the song had over a million views.[133] Even from prison, thanks to technology, they continued to organize and gain support. A few weeks later, at a CNN town hall, Trump said that the U.S. Capitol attackers were there "with love in their heart," promised to pardon "a large portion" of the convicted felons, and called January 6 "a beautiful day."[134]

Ton-That took a different approach, calling the attempted insurrection "tragic and appalling." He also believed it would vindicate his vision for Clearview AI. "You see a lot of detractors change their mind for a somewhat different use case," he told Kashmir Hill. "We're slowly winning people over."[135] One person he'd recently lost favor with, however, was Chuck Johnson. On March 22, 2023, Johnson sued Ton-That for breach of contract, claiming he was owed money for his early involvement in the company when it was Smartcheckr.[136] Yet Johnson had not worked with Ton-That on Clearview AI for years, instead focusing on a startup of his own. "Welcome to Traitwell and Common Good Genetics!" the new venture's newsletter announced on April 1, 2021.[137] Trait-well's website made this offer: "Upload your raw DNA file and find out your personal risk of getting severe Covid-19 symptoms if you are infected. Free."[138]

If you'd already had your DNA sequenced by Ancestry.com, 23andMe, or a similar company, then you could not only find out whether you were suscep-tible to the pandemic's worst effects but also could learn your genetic cancer risk, your risk of schizophrenia, or even "discover how your genes affect your educational attainment," according to the Traitwell website. It was all for "free."[139] Traitwell also gave people an easy way to upload their child's DNA through the Baby Blueprint program. "Understanding genetics can ease par-enting stress," the Traitwell website promised. The company would analyze your child's DNA and report on indicators of "mood instability," "reading abil-ity," "mathematical ability," and "intelligence." Remarkably, Traitwell even claimed that it could predict "childhood gender nonconformity."[140]

But what would Traitwell do with our genetic data? Trait meant a "particu-lar feature, distinguishing quality," coming from the same root as a "short line," as with bloodline.[141] Well meant "satisfactory" or "agreeable to wish or desire."[142] *Good bloodlines. Eugenics. Race betterment.* Based on what Johnson told Max Chafkin, Peter Thiel had invested.[143]

***

On March 13, 2022, *Reuters* reported that Clearview AI had been offering free licenses to its software to the Ukrainian military, as part of the warfighting efforts against the Russians.[144] Just like Palantir had done, Clearview AI had given away the product to local U.S. law enforcement; now the company's executives saw a new "pro bono" opportunity overseas that could change the outcomes on the battlefield. The deal resulted from outreach to Ukrainian officials by Hoan Ton-That, which Clearview AI adviser Lee Wolosky had encouraged. According to Kashmir Hill, Clearview AI had translated its app into Ukrainian within a month. It had created over two hundred accounts for users at five Ukrainian government agencies. The Ukrainians had searched the database more than five thousand times.[145]

In September 2021 Wolosky had left his law firm to join the Biden adminis-tration as special counsel to the president.[146] He later wrote a piece in *Just Secu-rity* about being at the White House preceding Russia's invasion, which gave him this perspective: "The president has been unrelenting in supporting Ukraine's beleaguered democracy in words and deeds. Contrast that with his predecessor, who praised Putin and sought to condition the delivery of essential U.S. military assistance on a bogus Ukrainian investigation into domestic political rivals."[147] Wolosky returned to private practice in January 2022; within a matter of weeks, Clearview AI had begun discussions with the Ukrainians to find ways to utilize these surveillance tools on the battlefield, all for free.[148] Influential figures in both parties had built Clearview AI into a global force. This was not about being a Republican or Democrat, liberal or conservative. Power turned back into silicon, and everything accelerated in wartime, yielding new power and gold.

＊＊＊

Back in September 2007 a local Ohio newspaper reported about Tim Ryan's efforts to expand the Appalachian Regional Commission to new parts of his state. It wasn't a matter of identity or geography. There were more practical considerations. It would bring more federal funding to poorer areas of Ohio.[149] The next fifteen years would be a time of incredible change. Back then, J. D. Vance (then named Hamel) was still three years away from beginning his *Hillbilly Elite* blog. He was nearly nine years from publishing *Hillbilly Elegy*, which "academics, professors, cultural arbitrators" read and praised him for writing, as it became a bestseller. That was because Vance had chosen to *identify* as "an Appalachian white boy in style and disposition" rather than honestly chronicling the ways his identity had been shaped by the military, the classrooms of Yale or Ohio State, or his upbringing in the Midwest.[150]

As Vance had worked on the manuscript, he also worked for Peter Thiel's venture capital firm. At that time, he wrote: "I identify with the millions of working-class white Americans of Scots-Irish descent who have no college degree."[151] He also claimed that Donald Trump was either "a cynical asshole like Nixon who wouldn't be that bad (and might even prove useful) or that he's America's Hitler," denounced Trump as "a demagogue" and "cultural heroin," and criticized the false conspiracy theories that Trump promoted about President Obama being born in Africa.[152] Vance declared: "The elites were right about Donald Trump, right? I'm a Never Trump guy."[153]

Just a few more years after that, and Vance made up his mind—he'd evidently concluded that Trump "wouldn't be that bad (and might even prove useful)," as he overcame his earlier disdain—and he began praising former president Trump and calling Joe Biden "a fake president."[154] During his campaign to become a U.S. senator, Vance told Ohioans that "we are in a late republican period," promising "we're going to have to get pretty wild, and pretty far out there, and go in directions that a lot of conservatives right now are uncomfortable with."[155] He asserted that Trump was "the best president of my lifetime," even better than Ronald Reagan.[156] He bemoaned the corrupting influence of liberal elites and the "woke capital, woke corporations, and the governments that enable them."[157]

Vance had begun his U.S. Senate campaign with an article promoting unsubstantiated claims, without any new empirical evidence, to discredit an election that many leading Republicans had confirmed was legitimate. His coauthor was Blake Masters; they both campaigned for Congress jointly with Peter Thiel's support.[158] Trump decided to endorse both Masters and Vance in 2022, which bolstered their candidacies and helped them win their Republican primaries.[159] Voters learned about Trump's endorsements in a barrage of advertisements from their Super PACs, funded with over $30 million from Thiel.[160]

On Election Day, Blake Masters lost by over 125,000 votes.[161] But J. D. Vance gained a new identity. He became a U.S. senator after beating Tim Ryan by more than 250,000 votes.[162]

That evening, Ryan sought unity. He'd lost, in a mostly free and fair election, where huge sums of private money, funneled through Super PACs, had funded research, polling, and advertising but not the polling sites on Election Day. Ryan deemed the election legitimate. He talked to his fellow citizens about the importance of respecting the democratic process, with dignity:

> I have the privilege to concede this race to J. D. Vance, because the way this country operates, is that when you lose an election, you concede. And you respect the will of the people. Right? We can't have a system where if you win, it's a legitimate election, and if you lose, someone stole it. Our kids and our grandkids are going to live together. . . .
>
> The question is: What kind of country are they going to live in? Are they going to live in a country where they are being forced to hate each other? Or are they going to live in a country where they can have honest disagreements, where they can respect each other?[163]

When Peter Thiel sat down to be interviewed by Bambi Francisco Roizen in Miami on October 20, 2021, there were more revelations from their discussion beyond what we discovered about his politics or theology.[164] True, this was the same conversation where he'd claimed that he was "mildly antidemocracy" and worried that "there is something that is essentially Christian about this concern for victims and there is something about that that could get weaponized and radicalized," but he also shared some surprising beliefs about how technology could become weaponized, too.[165] In that interview, we learned something new about the future. He told Roizen that most Americans were not "paying attention to the thing that really matters," and that they should be far more worried about the risks created by the surveillance powers of artificial intelligence. "There's always this talk about Big Data, and you get the Big Data by surveilling people and monitoring them and knowing more about them than they know about themselves," he explained. But people had missed that "AI, especially in this sort of low-tech surveillance form, is essentially communist," according to Thiel. He warned about the costs of losing our privacy and the power it gave to the state.[166]

His ominous words applied directly to Palantir, Anduril, and Clearview AI. But he didn't mention those companies during the interview. Surveillance companies had created powerful breakthroughs that could both enhance the control of the government and increase the fear among (and self-censoring by) regular citizens. What would you never do if you knew everything was being recorded? What would you not say, or even allow yourself to consider saying? The implications for free thinking and free speech were tremendous.

Take that logic even further. What would happen with even more advanced computers, which could be way smarter than any of us, or even all of us? They've started calling that artificial general intelligence (AGI), which could wield powers far surpassing the capabilities of today's artificial intelligence. Imagine a scenario where computers could not only aggregate the knowledge of all humans but also excel in learning, planning, and problem-solving. What would that mean? What could AGI do for us—or against us?

What if AGI could teach itself? How might it replace human labor, and what would that do to the workforce, to free enterprise? Could we still pursue fairness in business and society, as AGI took on more tasks? Or would individual business interests, which created value for a few shareholders, be all that mattered? Who would decide the ethical constraints on AGI? What would happen without those guardrails or if it got into the wrong hands?

How could we decipher real facts from digital fictions, or distinguish historical events from fabricated deepfakes, once AGI created more of what we heard and saw? What would happen if AGI was used to edit our genetic code? Who decided what benefited humanity or what was too dangerous? Whose values mattered, given the power of this technology? Thiel thought of it this way: "Artificial General Intelligence, somehow this superhuman intelligence, that would be indistinguishable from God for all practical purposes."[167]

That worried him. "Maybe you get to AGI in X years. But on the path to AGI, in X over two years"—meaning in half the time—"you get to surveillance AI, a communist totalitarian technology: facial recognition used to control people that will be used by a small number of people to control lots of other people." He argued we should prevent artificial intelligence from getting beyond our control, now that even the current technologies of generative artificial intelligence had already begun creating so much content and code on its own. "I'd like us to, you know, I'm not sure sabotage or outlaw AI," he posited, and he interrupted his own train of thought by commenting, "That doesn't sound too libertarian." He then continued, "But I would like those people to be less psychologically motivated, and to think about how they're working on the technology that is going to destroy the world. Maybe that will demotivate them and they will work on it more slowly."[168]

A few minutes before, he had warned, "The lesson I take from the twentieth century is that, if we're going to use a precautionary principle—it often gets used with AI or with climate change, or all these things where there's a chance that something goes really haywire and you have to stop it before it becomes real—I think if there's a place for the precautionary principle, I would put the number one place for it: incipient totalitarianism. Because once these things really snowball, they can't be stopped."[169]

Years before, Anthony Levandowski had thought about all of this, too. He'd acted on his beliefs. On August 16, 2017, he received a letter from the Internal Revenue Service informing him that the new 501(c)3 he had setup was now officially exempt from federal income taxes.[170] Levandowski became the dean of the Way of the Future Church, which he founded based on the idea that AGI was actually a higher power and so should be respected, honored, and worshipped. "What is going to be created will effectively be a god," Levandowski told Mark Harris at *Wired*. "It's not a god in the sense that it makes lightning or causes hurricanes. But if there is something a billion times smarter than the smartest human, what else are you going to call it?" This went far beyond Travis Kalanick's Church of Creative Capitalism. Levandowski was completely serious about starting a new religion, telling Harris, "We would want this intelligence to say, 'Humans should still have rights, even though I'm in charge.'"[171]

"Given that technology will 'relatively soon' be able to surpass human abilities, we want to help educate people about this exciting future and prepare a smooth transition," read the website at www.WayOfTheFuture.Church. "Let's stop pretending we can hold back the development of intelligence when there are clear massive short term economic benefits to those who develop it and instead understand the future and have it treat us like a beloved elder who created it."[172] Just like that, Levandowski had prayed the quiet part out loud about the religion he'd founded. So, to repeat once more, for emphasis: *when there are clear massive short term economic benefits to those who develop it.*

Greed is good? No. This meant Greed is God.

Levandowski abandoned this project in June 2020, a few months before he was pardoned by President Trump. He announced that he'd donated all the funds left in the nonprofit's bank account to the NAACP, which he claimed had been inspired by the murder of George Floyd on May 25, 2020. Today, the website WayOfTheFuture.Church has been hijacked by marketers advertising various products, including, "12 Best Metal Shoe Rack for Your Home," "7 Most Powerful Wireless Tattoo Machines of 2023," and "Best 6 Summit Treestands for Portable Comfortable Stand!"[173]

At Palantir, Alex Karp also foresaw massive changes due to AGI. "The risks of these emerging artificial intelligence capabilities to individual rights, and even perhaps to our own physical safety, are significant and apparent to most,"

Karp wrote in an open letter posted to the Palantir website on April 7, 2023. He claimed, "To pause our current efforts, however, would be to indulge in the fantasy of a world without conflict." He concluded: "We must impose our values on the software that we create, otherwise it may impose an emergent and unconstrained set of values on us. It is essential that the systems we are constructing align with our directives and reflect our philosophical and moral commitments." The letter was subtitled "Bending Artificial Intelligence to Our Collective Will."[174] A few weeks before, Palantir's stock went up 16 percent after the company had announced that it expected 2023 to be its first profitable year based on the opportunities created by AGI and related technologies and new defense contracts following Russia's invasion of Ukraine.[175]

Two weeks after that, on April 21, 2023, *TechCrunch* reported that Thiel's Founders Fund had invested in OpenAI, the organization behind the wildly popular ChatGPT, one of the most widely used generative artificial intelligence systems working toward developing AGI.[176] It differed from Palantir, Anduril, and Clearview AI, though, because its founders had arranged for a blended model: they'd established a for-profit entity and a nonprofit entity that, combined, they called OpenAI LP. Through this "capped-profit" approach, investors made money up to a certain point (which was one hundred times the initial investment for first round investors), then any additional profits beyond that would go to the nonprofit.[177]

"All investors and employees sign agreements that OpenAI LP's obligation to the Charter always comes first, even at the expense of some or all of their financial stake," OpenAI's website explained, through a model that resembled the B Corporations that came before.[178] Based on the way it was established, the company remained controlled by the nonprofit's board and its legal documents ensured that the following purpose would be pursued even when it meant sacrificing profits: "OpenAI's mission is to ensure that artificial general intelligence (AGI)—by which we mean highly autonomous systems that outperform humans at most economically valuable work—benefits all of humanity." To leave nothing uncertain, OpenAI's founders stated, "Our primary fiduciary duty is to humanity.[179] Its aims seemed noble, and its legal mandate appeared to safeguard against actions not aligned with its mission. Yet its origin story raised key questions, especially according to one early investor.

Eight years earlier, OpenAI had started as a nonprofit that intended to make all of the innovations it discovered publicly available. To get started, it had raised $1 billion in charitable contributions from Elon Musk, Reid Hoffman, Peter Thiel, and others.[180] But after building the technology with these tax-deductible resources for years, it changed its approach, developed its new "capped-profit" model, and raised billions in venture capital from Andreessen Horowitz, Founders Fund, Microsoft, Sequoia Capital, and others.[181] As OpenAI attracted further attention, experts questioned the legality of that maneuver, while class action litigation also challenged whether using publicly available information on the Internet to train its artificial intelligence had violated federal and state privacy laws.[182]

In early 2023 Microsoft invested over $10 billion for a major stake in OpenAI.[183] After media coverage that was alternately alarmist and enamored with AGI, competitors felt a sense of urgency to accelerate their own innovations. For the first time in years, Sergey Brin and Larry Page returned to Alphabet to strategize ways to develop these innovations faster than Meta, Microsoft, and others.[184] On Twitter (soon to be X), a platform he had purchased four months before, Elon Musk wrote: "OpenAI was created as an open source (which is why I named it "Open" AI), non-profit company to serve as a counterweight to Google, but now it has become a closed source, maximum-profit company effectively controlled by Microsoft. Not what I intended at all."[185] Musk also warned that "the danger of training AI to be woke—in other words, lie—is deadly." He feared that OpenAI's ChatGPT "has the potential of civilizational destruction."[186] He announced: "I'm going to start something which I call 'TruthGPT,' or a maximum truth-seeking AI that tries to understand the nature of the universe." He believed that it "might be the best path to safety" because his version of AGI would be "unlikely to annihilate humans."[187] He named his new venture xAI.[188]

On May 30, 2023, the cofounders of OpenAI and several of its senior executives signed onto a brief public statement, along with leaders from Google, Microsoft, numerous startups, and dozens of leading experts in computer science, ethics, and law at universities around the world. The entire statement took less than two dozen words: "Mitigating the risk of extinction from AI should be a global priority alongside other societal-scale risks such as pandemics and nuclear war."[189] It resembled warnings heard from technologists before. "The increasing concern about the potential impacts of AI is reminiscent of early discussions about atomic energy," the accompanying press release announced.[190] We could almost hear the admonition from Albert Einstein: "All the people living in cities are threatened, everywhere and constantly, with sudden destruction."[191] That echo was on purpose. They wanted people to believe in its awesome power, that it ushered in a new age. And they wanted everyone to trust that they could control it.

"History doesn't repeat itself but it often rhymes," the adage goes. That's often attributed to Mark Twain, but he never said it that way. He instead wrote: "History never repeats itself, but the Kaleidoscopic combinations of the pictured present often seem to be constructed out of the broken fragments of antique legends."[192] That conveyed nearly the same meaning, but in what Twain actually wrote, we can get nearer to the truth. He recognized that the shifting lights and colors playing out in the present always become distorted by a fractured and fabulized past.

We would be wise to ask more questions. Do these words indeed reflect Einstein's warnings about the atomic bomb? Or is this a false alarm, closer to the concerns we had about time zones, when legislators warned that only God should decide noontime, then businesspeople progressed nonetheless?[193] Are the elites worked up over nothing, or is this a more dangerous distraction, mirroring the extreme ideas of the Nobel Prize winners who thought that failing to sterilize Americans with lower IQs would "'hasten the end . . .' of civilization"?[194] Or are we "just going to have multitudes of people who cannot possibly compete in a highly technological world"?[195] Is that what the future holds?

Or maybe it's something else entirely. Tim Berners-Lee wouldn't have created the world's first website, and humanity wouldn't have the Internet as we know it, without the risks of nuclear weapons. Remember, he was a software engineer at CERN.[196] The nuclear researchers were the ones everyone thought held the keys to unlock the secrets of the universe. But as Berners-Lee showed, with help from the Google Boys as the Internet expanded, we had the answers all along.

Our present realities could feel confusing, our vision clouded. The past is even more distorted. But whether the future seems dim or much brighter due to technology, one thing is clear. Transhumanism goes so far—whether it involves bioengineering or supercomputers that go beyond us—that these innovations will have unpredictable consequences. In fact, it might be years before their greatest impacts are felt, because decisions that we make now could have implications we cannot fully fathom. Peter Thiel once told us, "I no longer believe that freedom and democracy are compatible."[197] We've seen how that's gone. Now, he warns: "Once these things really snowball, they can't be stopped."[198] How do we reject easy answers, seek understanding, and pursue the best possible outcomes? What should we do now, to maximize the benefits and reduce as many of the risks as we can?

Thiel is right that this time could be different, because the decisions made with gene editing and with artificial general intelligence might be irreversible. Early in the Silicon Age, we could always revise computer code. But what happens once elite scientists reprogram our genetic code, in ways that are inheritable, irreversible, and utterly unpredictable, with off-target effects or other unknowable long-term implications? Likewise, as computer algorithms became harder to understand, we've struggled to keep up and put needed constraints in place. Technology is a tool that can be used for good and evil, and we've experienced some ugly outcomes with social media. Now what happens if superintelligent computers reprogram their own code? The possibilities seem endless. But we're ignoring recent history if we believe that they are all going to be good. Ultimately, the question is not merely: What comes next? It's also: What will you do about it?

In light of all that, Peter Thiel and the other Great Men of the Silicon Age don't deserve the last word. As we approach the end of these many stories, and the more general lessons they teach us about modern America, we will need to act with urgency, yet also with understanding. To restore free and fair markets, and to ensure free and fair elections—to protect democracy, capitalism, and the American Dream that depends on both—we need to listen more closely to the people we should have heeded all along.

# EPILOGUE

*No matter what he does,*
*every person on earth*
*plays a central role*
*in the history of the world.*
*And normally he doesn't know it.*

—Paulo Coelho, *The Alchemist*
  1988, or 36 years ago


F. Scott Fitzgerald once wrote that "The test of a first-rate intelligence is the ability to hold two opposed ideas in the mind at the same time, and still retain the ability to function."[1] Complete contradictions like this: entrepreneurs have created immense wealth and power for themselves, while accelerating the flow of information and improving business and society in many ways, *and* they have also harmed "ordinary" people, as we are constantly surveilled, as we don't share in the value created by so much of our data, attention, and effort, and as we are led to believe this was all somehow fair, or even that we were getting something for free.

Fitzgerald would recognize the opposing forces at work throughout this modern paradox. America is forever a work in progress, and progress staggers more often than it rushes ahead. There are both forward and backward steps, as the pushes and pulls of our uneven democracy, our economy, and our society.

When we consider the benefits of technology, we must also now weigh the costs. Truly, it is the best of times. It is also, in other ways, the worst of times.

It goes beyond that, too. There are competing interests that are neither entirely good nor altogether bad in the gradations between those extremes, which can unbalance the overall order without warning. Over time, the Venture Alchemists transformed silicon into gold, then they turned gold into power. But it all became highly volatile, with unpredictable effects.

The Internet gave us knowledge, and social media connected us. This had its benefits. But technology also eliminated jobs, leading to angst and resentment. All the while, it created pathways of dependency, an algorithmic dilemma that grew to almost mythical proportions, like a digital Daedalus's "mazey wanderings that deceived the eyes," so even "the architect, hardly could retrace his steps."[2] As we went deeper into unseen labyrinths, we became lost in judgment, anger, or disenchantment. But the morals from that ancient Greek myth of the maze and the Minotaur—or more recent observations about the wisdom and foolishness, the belief and incredulity, of the Machine Age—could help us find our footing again. The good, the bad, and the in-between of the Silicon Age can all be true at the same time, different strands that are ultimately interconnected, knotted up in a tangled web.

When we ask ourselves, *"How could this happen?"* and worry about the dangers we ignored and how our tight-knit communities frayed, we must journey further through our feelings of doubt and confusion. Instead of concluding, helplessly, *"What difference could I make, even if I wanted to?,"* we should go beyond that easy escape. That's the moment to explore more, to go deeper into the maze, to pursue a trail of hard questions about our world and ourselves. The only way out is through.[3]

Let's follow the thread, backtracking one step at a time.

Why did we romanticize the entrepreneurs and the venture capitalists who invested in them? Why did we care more about how we looked to others online instead of how we spent time in real life? How did we allow for all this: so much data mining and 24/7 surveillance, such astonishing addictiveness that affects our children's health, and so many unaccountable algorithms that shape what we see or even change what we think? Why did we assume that entrepreneurs, investors, and politicians wouldn't serve themselves, even if it meant going against the very democratic principles that gave them opportunities, fueled their successes, or even enabled them to exist in business and society? Most of all: How did they subvert the rule of law and erode America's most important institutions? When did we lose trust in each other and in shared facts, even shared reality? Why did we fail to recognize the incredible sway that Silicon Valley's wealthiest gained over so many aspects of our economic and political systems?

Why did we decide that words do not matter, but likes and shares do? How did we ever blur that line? What changed in us, which made comments worth more than commitments? Did the speed and ease of the Silicon Age cheapen our values, weaken our oaths? When did we decide that followers mattered more than leadership?

As we begin to grasp how quickly things unraveled, maybe we shouldn't be so surprised. The history textbook *These United States: A Nation in the Making*, by Yale's Glenda Gilmore and NYU's Thomas Sugrue, put it this way: "Modern America was shaped by the struggles of countless ordinary men and women, seeking to improve their communities, to achieve age-old ideals of equality and justice. But it was also shaped by a relentless drive toward self-interest. That struggle between individual interest and social responsibility remains the enduring contradiction of modern American history."[4] All the triumphs and traumas of the Silicon Age—and the many innovations and manipulations detailed throughout this book—reveal the entangled, enduring, churning contradiction of America's full story. The common thread is now drawn taut as a timeline.

More recently, the tug-of-war between brazen selfishness and social responsibility has been pulled toward the self-interests of a few, relentlessly, while the rest of us have dug in our heels and struggled not to fall too far behind. But every person does, indeed, play a central role in the history of the world, and there's a difference we can make in the direction history can take—whether it is something that happens to us, or by us and for us.

In other words, we should get a grip. Take a deep breath. Do your very best. Hold on tight and pull together. Any new movement we make will surely meet immediate resistance, the friction felt as soon as we lean toward a better balance in free *and* fair markets and free *and* fair elections. Breaking that deadlock and gaining momentum will require resilience and resolve, through the undying, unyielding spirit of "the struggles of countless ordinary men and women, seeking to improve their communities, to achieve age-old ideals of equality and justice."[5] Who will get the final word?

Why not the rest of us?

## Nothing was destined; decisions were made

None of the Silicon Age's outcomes were predestined. These entrepreneurs were never heroes fulfilling a sacred destiny. Just like everyone, they feared rejection, suffered pain, and made tradeoffs. Their choices altered lives. Back in 2005 the founders of Catch27 anticipated many risks of social media. Chantelle Farmer worked closely with E. Jean Carroll on the project; the code that created Catch27 came from Farmer's fingertips. Looking back, she recalls, "We were trying to create an addictive game, but I'm not sure we thought of it like something you would be on 24/7. But I think that's the way that a lot of these things happen. The business and the coders are doing stuff just because they can, and you might not always consider the social implications or really even understand what they might be—until it's too late."[6]

In retrospect, Farmer thinks the better question was not, "Could we do this?" but rather, "Should we?" That was rarely asked back then. She explains, "It was like a fun technical challenge, 'Ooh, could I make this work?' But 'Should I make this work?' is not always a question that gets asked." That was treacherous. As she now realizes, when "you're experimenting with stuff, you don't know what's going to happen."[7]

Farmer is troubled by the pervasive influence over our daily lives that tech companies have gained through their surveillance powers. "I get angry when I get targeted ads," she explains, especially due to "the intrusiveness of it." Her husband's attitude is different. She says that he will often tell her, "But they're just showing you what you actually might be interested in," considering the ease and convenience tech companies have created for us, but she knows that none of this was designed with innocent intent. "I don't like that they know this stuff about me. I don't like it. I would rather see ads that I care nothing about and feel like I still had some privacy," she explains. Yet, even if she wanted to resist, she concedes that she feels powerless, admitting, "But, it doesn't stop me from doing all the things that cause me to lose my privacy."[8]

Nowadays, we don't buy and sell friends in collections of twenty-seven like the website she'd coded, but we've attributed so much value to all those images, status updates, comments, and likes. We're finding it increasingly difficult to know what matters more: our lives or our lives online. Farmer is worried about the implications of our digital existence determining so much of our self-worth, given "the false sense of connection that it brings, and the real-life connections just get watered down."[9] She is right about that. Our biological, psychological, and emotional needs for human-to-human connection cannot be fully satisfied through software and screens. In one realm, we're experiencing reality. The other is an illusion.

Aspects of our personalities may shapeshift in pseudonymity on Reddit or X. We can choose to display only the best versions of ourselves through filtered photos on Facebook or Instagram. Someday, we might all experience immersive replicas of reality with Meta's newest headset, a future version of Apple Vision Pro, or some other technology that allows us to alter our identities as digital avatars. But that will still be a facsimile. Technology cannot replace humanity: the heartfelt comfort of a needed hug or the warmth of a lover's touch, the smells and sounds of exploring a new place that you've always hoped to visit, or the energy of a concert when everyone moves as one. It simply cannot.

It also can't beat the endorphins that come from a great workout while friends cheer you on. These days, Chantelle Farmer is an entrepreneur who runs FLX

Fitclub in Ithaca, New York, which is home to about thirty different group fitness classes every week. She's inspired by people who come together to be healthier one day at a time, and she is energized by the community all around her and the part she plays in it—by starting a business that serves a purpose and helps people. Her days as a computer programmer are mostly behind her, but she enjoys her life's work more these days. As she puts it, that's because she's "impacting fewer people in a more meaningful way" through group fitness. "It's all about the human touch. Technology makes some things easier, and you can automate some things, but creating a real-life connection is so valuable," she now believes. "I am learning that lesson every day."[10] We're all taking our own path, but Farmer's story shows just how important is it to take steps together.

* * *

As artificial intelligence gets smarter and bioengineering evolves, we must ask, "Should we do this?" instead of settling for "Could we do this?" Nearly two decades ago, several people insisted we pose that very question. We should have paid more attention. In 2005 a music student at Colorado State worried about the new wave of social media sites that classmates had become obsessed over, telling told the school newspaper, "I'm afraid people will get carried away and it will become a huge moneymaking endeavor. It's a way to suck people into perpetuating the materialism ideals of our society."[11] That was Nate Wheeler, who has continued to pursue music, art, and technology. Today Wheeler blends these passions together as a consultant who builds interactive sensors, lights, and robotics for musicians and visual artists, enhancing their creativity with his own, through engaging sights and sounds.[12]

When reflecting on prioritizing "Should we?" over "Could we?," Wheeler is reminded of the original *Jurassic Park* movie from 1993 and the lines by Jeff Goldblum's character, Dr. Ian Malcolm. Before the dinosaurs started eating tourists, Malcolm intervened. "You stood on the shoulders of geniuses to accomplish something as fast as you could, and before you even knew what you had," he thundered, "you patented it, and packaged it, and slapped it on a plastic lunchbox, and now you're selling it, you're selling it." He blamed the businessmen for moving fast and breaking things, for messing with nature, mostly to make a buck but also to prove that they could. In one of the movie's most memorable scenes, Malcolm slammed his fist on the table, yelling, "Your scientists were so preoccupied with whether or not they could, that they didn't stop to think if they should."[13]

In the past two decades, Wheeler's concerns about the power of tech companies have intensified, particularly considering the decisions being made by Mark Zuckerberg. "In a way, it's techno-colonialism, because he wants to conquer. He wants to create a new plane of existence, a new sphere of existence in the Metasphere, and then have that as territory," argues Wheeler. The future of the Internet, in this scenario, could become "his land where he has domain, he gets advertising dollars, he gets to choose."[14] If that prediction becomes reality, Meta Platforms would take up even more of our time; the world would literally be Mark Zuckerberg's, and we would all just be living in it. World domination, indeed.

Would this divide society even further, since the metaverse might encourage us to each choose a customized community—whom you identify with, as well as your identity? Today's realities, with the heterogeneous interestingness of our neighborhoods, congregations, and classrooms, could be replaced online by in-groups and out-groups, all curated by attention-maximizing algorithms. There's a risk that we'd mostly surround ourselves with people we feel comfortable with. That kind of mimesis is insular, becoming more about individual ambitions than other people. It's self-centered, ego-driven, and antisocial. It would diminish real world communities, where others can challenge your viewpoints, which helps everyone to learn and grow together.

That same principle applies to what we teach artificial intelligence, how we modify our genes, and other cutting-edge technologies. We should resist the urge to define perfection once-and-for-all when developing these innovations, or we run the risk of perpetuating a twenty-first-century rendition of "race betterment." That pursuit brings us closer to David Starr Jordan's ideal, Carl Schmitt's hopes, and Bill Shockley's plans. But it betrays the idea of America, where richness is supposed to come from everyone and every person adds value, not just a self-selected few that resemble people we like, in a ceaseless spiral of mimesis. Let's remember the encouragements from decades ago about the inherent value of all people, and the intrinsic dignity of work, such as when the Stanford faculty celebrated the "useful careers for the whole wonderful variety of human beings."[15]

The technologies of the future must be pursued thoughtfully, ethically, and cautiously. When we consider our opportunities—the potential, for example, to bioengineer "better" designer babies or to develop "godlike" artificial general intelligence—we would be wise to go beyond *Could we do this?* with each step we take. We should first decide: *Should we?* Then, vitally, *How should we?* so that we take steps in the right direction as we proceed. As we do, we'll move forward, together, with intention and purpose.

## All people are imperfect; the men who made these decisions were, too

Entrepreneurs and investors are merely human, with vulnerabilities and weaknesses. The belief that some people are "just born with it" and are destined for startup success is a harmful lie—one that distorts what's actually happened and distracts us from reality. There are decisions driving all this mythmaking, and they're about more than concentrating wealth. They're about consolidating power. We see that in Palantir's Class F share structure and the Trump administration's Schedule F authority, where a few people will reject proven principles of good governance or abolish time-tested standards for meritocracy in order to take control away from public shareholders or career public servants. In 2018 the chief investment officer of the California State Teachers' Retirement System had warned about these very kinds of risks, arguing that Facebook had amassed too much power in the hands of too few.[16] Christopher Ailman still believes that's true. Put simply, "Control without accountability at Facebook— that's all ego."[17]

Ailman thinks Facebook's story should be a cautionary tale. "We all know the history of how that grew out of Harvard, it was growth, growth, growth. Growth at all costs, and the money in Silicon Valley will pay for growth, not revenue. And it is exponential growth they love best of all." While technology has enabled hypergrowth, Ailman questions the short-term ethical consequences, as well as whether it yielded the most enduring strategy to ensure long-term business value. "What's quite clear is that they were after the almighty dollar, of every single dollar they could get, regardless of good or bad or evil," he explains. Will they ever weigh the moral costs of technology's harms? "I think you've got to hope that somewhere out in the future they will look back and regret those kinds of decisions," Ailman says, "but they were young and I realize we don't want to discourage young people dreaming up innovative ideas."[18]

Ailman advocates for a longer-term perspective, while worrying that many technologists' egocentric and short-term approaches could pose significant risks to American society and democracy. Facebook's business model depends on capturing and maintaining people's attention constantly, "getting the eyeballs to view the page," as Ailman puts it. Facebook knew that negative emotions captivated us. As we clicked out of fear, it meant money and growth. That created power, but it also pushed people to the extremes—most notably in the lead-up to the American trauma of the failed insurrection on January 6, 2021. Ailman puts our recent history in context: "It's interesting when you talk to people about history. 'Do you realize the Roman Empire at least stood for 500 years?' Yet here in America, we're barely at 220 and our democracy is struggling pretty bad right now. So, let's have some perspective on life."[19]

Today Ailman remains worried about fundamental business judgment, reducing risks, and creating lasting shareholder value. People should pay attention, considering what happened since he first spoke out in April 2018: Meta lost $800 billion in market cap in just over a year, including the biggest one-day drop in U.S. stock market history.[20] Ailman explains, "Milton Friedman talked about the value of a corporation: 'The purpose of a corporation is just to make a money.' But I often bug the Harvard people: 'Did you note, he didn't talk about a time frame.' It's not about profit over ninety-one days or even three years. Value is about making money consistently over a really long time period." The wisdom in Ailman's approach is that we are never making decisions that merely affect ourselves, only our friends and family, or even just people we know. Today's choices while navigating the maze can change outcomes for future generations. As he concludes, "I think in generational terms of passing things on, and I think people make better decisions when they think on an intergenerational basis rather than just: me, me, me."[21]

Or, perhaps, meme me, meme me.

## Nothing is ever "free," and unfettered business can cost society

Silicon Valley's frequent mantra of "fake it till you make it" has serious consequences. That ideology has helped upend the status quo, from transportation to entertainment, from national security to news, and almost everywhere in between. But we can no longer idealize its impacts. "Fake it till you make it" can inspire entrepreneurs to believe so much in something that they hope will one day exist that they'll follow their passions until their best dreams come true. Yet there's a darker underside here that many Silicon Age successes are based on, which involves convincing others of a lie that you don't even really believe about yourself (or your product). When that happens, you're projecting something outward that isn't true inside—in other words, a deception.

We could just accept that mythmaking happens more than truth-seeking in the Silicon Age and pretend to care more about identifying than identity. We might go on presenting our lives as almost perfect, through filtered, cropped, and edited photos on social media. We could keep faking it. But is that what we want out of life? Or are we deceiving ourselves?

Melissa Patti felt concerned about this way back in 2005. She was the vice president of Pitt's Campus Women's Organization when she sounded the alarm about Catch27: "It's a destructive process, and it only perpetuates culture's standards of beauty, which are problematic. It kind of decreases the work that women have created in the past to be looked at as equals in society's eyes."[22] That eventually applied to all social media and the Internet more broadly. Since graduating in 2006, Patti has worked on issues ranging from childbirth and mental health to substance abuse and HIV/AIDS. She earned her master's degree in social work at Temple and has dedicated her career to helping others. She now lives in Philadelphia and works at a leading nonprofit, the March of Dimes, as the director of Maternal and Infant Health Initiatives.[23]

In 2023 she thinks that social media's dangers go far beyond setting unattainable beauty standards, since our feeds are filled with so many kinds of unreal narratives. As slanted content (whether unfounded conspiracy theories or merely biased news) angers us and divides us, Patti worries about mutual trust and the future of democracy. "Think about this: What is the impact of sharing this information with people?" she asks. Since the most extreme content spreads faster online, she's concerned people are acting "without having the tools to be discerning about where they get their information, and then questioning it. Don't take everything at face value. Where does it come from? Who pays those folks? Does this align with my values?"[24]

Patti is right. What we choose to promote reflects our values. But this isn't just about fake news. Every deception we share distorts reality and erodes trust, causing us to gradually lose touch with what truly matters. It happens every day. When things get really good, we hold our phones aloft. We miss out on a moment with our children or at a concert, to save it forever as a video we'll probably never watch. Why do we do this? On the off chance it'd be good enough to upload to Facebook or Instagram? Isn't that just another vain attempt to showcase ourselves at our very best? Why do we take time away to update our status? To declare an almighty, *I exist!* Since *This is You?*

But that's not actually us. That's artifice. Age-old wisdom teaches us that. *Vanity of vanities. All is vanity,* repeated the refrain from Ecclesiastes. The Hebrew word, *hebel,* could also be translated as meaningless or absurdity. But how about a simpler phrase: *All is smoke.* It's ephemeral. It's inauthentic. The moment you try to grasp it, suddenly it's gone. It vanishes.[25]

∗ ∗ ∗

Just because we all do it, that doesn't make it all right. In fact, the problem only worsens if everybody accepts this as the status quo. The more myths we make, the less we'll trust each other and the more isolated we'll become. Consider how much we could gain from time better spent together, rather than faking it for the feeds on our phones.

Pause, reflect, question, and discern. Choose wisely. That's the lesson from Melissa Patti: being thoughtful and intentional will improve the paths we take.

Are our decisions advancing our values? How are we representing ourselves? Technology cannot make lies into truths or save the priceless moments we've missed out on, despite our frequent attempts to capture and keep them. At least thus far during the Silicon Age, that hasn't deterred us from trying. But shouldn't we ask ourselves: Where do machines belong in our lives, and what are we not willing to automate? What aligns with our principles?

It's hard to know what to trust anymore. Today's social media platforms make it almost impossible to distinguish facts from figments, as modern technologists craft personalized virtual spaces for us, which serve curated narratives of the world. What might have been designed with relatively innocent intentions—showing us what we were most likely to purchase or comment on, for instance—is now weaponized to present increasingly tailored yet terrifying perspectives of the outside world and our neighbors. When Patti thinks about the future of technology and society, she grapples with these kinds of issues: "What does it say about me? What does it say about my values? And then what is the impact going to be? In general, people don't take those steps to think about their own influence and how they are representing themselves."[26] Today, more than ever, we'd be wise to pursue authenticity. As powerful artificial intelligence learns how to create increasingly convincing deepfakes, which are becoming as lifelike as life itself, it is more important than ever that we understand the serious implications of imitations, especially when we're sharing content created with malicious or self-serving intent. Perhaps the meaningful deliberation and principled decision-making that Melissa Patti proposes could at least be a partial remedy, if we all take personal responsibility.

But what about larger reforms? What would it take to transform the Internet for the better? "Man. Money and politics," Patti says with a laugh. "That's what I think makes systems change. Having the right people in power, being able to influence political movements, and having a lot of money. I think those are the things that make big changes in our country." She's not optimistic that would happen anytime soon. When asked how she would fix social media, or improve the Internet overall, she laughs again. "Tear it all down. Light it on fire."[27]

In the decades since she warned about social media's risks in a college newspaper, Patti hasn't spent her time writing code to improve social media's algorithms or devising strategies to prevent deepfakes from going viral. She instead works at a nonprofit to solve issues that matter to her community, and in her personal life she finds that the moments she cherishes the most aren't happening on the Internet. Growing up, she'd felt isolated and disconnected from others, but that's changed during her adult life. "I moved to Philly and I stayed here. My husband grew up here, and it's all so shocking to me because that's not how my teenage years were, but all of his friends moved back. And they live within blocks of us and have kids the same age who go to the same school together, and we give each other rides to places, and we just walk to each other's houses and hang out." She reflects, "I never had that growing up, and it's amazing to see folks intentionally placing themselves in a space to be a part of a community."[28]

*What if we all did that?* What if we took all of the time we've dedicated to promoting the best possible versions of ourselves on social media and spent it helping people instead, as Melissa Patti does in her day job? Or, more simply, what if we just used those freed up moments for simple kindnesses, to intentionally place ourselves in a space to be part of a community, as Patti tries to do each day? This doesn't require a move to a new city or buying a house in the suburbs. Most of us can readily find community where we are, if we look up from phones, look around for opportunities, and consider those near us as much as we do the comment counts on our screens. Maybe that would be more than just a partial remedy. What if that is the antidote?

We have already lost so many moments we could have spent with people we love, being fully present, if we had been more intentional about our priorities and choices. That's not to shame anyone. We're all flawed. We could log off to invest more in real community, but we often don't. We could come together, seek tolerance and understanding, value everyday kindnesses far more, and worship wealth and fame less. We could sing the praises of so many unsung heroes, the parents who volunteer for carpool duties, the mentors who coach and teach and care for each other's kids. That's not celebrated often enough. It's rarely rewarded. Usually, that's not how we choose to measure greatness. Maybe we should.

✳ ✳ ✳

Technology has the potential to both uplift and unsettle. For truly rich lives in the Silicon Age, we'll need both personal responsibility and collective action. We must support the companies that contribute more to empowering our communities than to destabilizing them. Perhaps OpenAI's executives are right: maybe their blended "capped-profit" model will work for good. Hopefully, ChatGPT will serve humanity. Or maybe they, or it, will betray us.

The same goes for other entrepreneurs and the innovations they pursue. Millions have hoped for a world without Alzheimer's, and by splicing the right life-saving genes, realizing that dream could be closer than ever. But we should also mitigate risks—not only from the opportunists who don't know what they're doing but also from geneticists who do—because while the former seek to get rich quick, the latter might engineer "superior" people based on criteria that the rest of us would find unsettling or extreme. We should worry about whose standards are used to decide what gets inherited—not just in America but in China, Russia, or elsewhere—and not only with visible Übermensch traits like hair, skin, or eye color but also when parents seek every edge for their children through greater athletic, intellectual, or artistic performance. Ultimately, as new breakthroughs occur, the directions they take shouldn't be decided solely by technologists. We all share in the responsibility to improve our world, with each of us having the power to decide the path forward, one step at a time.

The CEOs of the Silicon Age will need to act more ethically, and their board members ought to demand accountability beyond profits. We must create the world we want to live in, too, as we consciously spend our time and money with companies that embrace responsible business practices—even if that means reduced short-term profits. Doing the right thing now gives us the best chance, in the long run, for better business in every sense of the word.

We are bound to repeat what we don't repair. Business can change lives, both for better and for worse. Technologies are tools. Whether they are used for good or evil must be up to us.

$$* * *$$

"Here's to the crazy ones, the misfits, the rebels." Steve Jobs sure was on to something. Here's to them. Let's celebrate them when they do well for themselves, especially if their innovations do more good than harm in this world. But we shouldn't forget the rest of the quote: "disagree with them, glorify or vilify them, but the only thing you can't do is ignore them because they change things."[29]

That makes pretty good sense. Whenever the Great Men of the Silicon Age deserve it, we should glorify them or disagree with them. We'd be prudent to seek the truth about them as often as possible, too. But as for vilifying them? Perhaps instead we should judge less and try to discern more. If we hope to approach our world with nuance and understanding, not extremes—with light, not heat—then we must reject both triumphalism and defeatism. We can avoid the allure of any quick fix, such as rushing to a moral (or moralistic) judgment that we feel tempted to "wrap in a neat package."[30] That includes trying to destroy someone's career with an oversimplified soundbite or ruining their reputation with a stigmatizing label, which we mete out immediately, without due process—whether that's directed at Keith Rabois personally, Travis Kalanick personally, Mark Zuckerberg personally, or anyone personally, for that matter.

Since when has ruthlessness been the answer to the world's problems?

As an "ordinary" but wise man once advised, "You'd find the threads of Keith Rabois in yourself."[31] Each of us must start there, with ourselves. Today we may trust less. We're doubting and we're hurting. But rather than blaming others for the problems that now perplex us, we might think twice about whether our reactions just feel good, or if they truly do any good. Instead of smearing somebody with "a word that obscures more than it reveals" or canceling anyone based on a "dangerous oversimplification," we could find a better way forward.[32]

Ultimately, there's no vindication in vindictiveness. So, let's stay focused. If we're going to weave our way through Daedalus's labyrinth, it's going to be a long journey out.

On a deeper level, the story of the Minotaur never was about a lone external enemy anyway. It's half-human, half-beast, hunting us constantly. The Minotaur represents our inner light and our primal darkness, the throughlines in all of us. As we pull on that dual thread, we can each recognize our own personal virtues and flaws. Consider the many amazingly altruistic, unseen deeds we do, which commingle with our grandstanding performances on social media that are all about ego; consider the nobility of each promise we've kept and every moment we've showed compassion, which coexist with the judgments we've jumped to and the resentment we've harbored; and consider those careful efforts we've made to respect and to repair, which are mixed in among our brutal urges to rage and to ruin. In the end, the Minotaur wasn't some ancient myth about a mystical monster. It's an ageless metaphor for our best actions and worst reactions. In actuality: *This is You.*

The Great Men of History aren't the real problem here, nor do they have the answers. We are, and we just might.

***

To follow this thread further, we will need far less hostility and much more humility. Instead of tearing people down, deepening the darkness, what would happen if we lifted others up, bringing their stories to light? We can find American heroes almost everywhere we look—in decisions made by gym owners, artists, pension managers, and nonprofit directors, who are living meaningful lives in communities they care about—and their greatness shines through loud, soft, and silent acts. We see it when someone passionately protests an injustice, when another respectfully rejects money or power on principle, and even when somebody wordlessly decides not to click on an Instagram ad and puts away their phone to be fully present.

That might seem like a small gesture, but it can become a personal protest: an act of purposeful presence, even civil disobedience. As word spreads, seemingly trivial decisions like that can gain greater relevance, strength in numbers, which can create extraordinary change. Think about it. If enough people did that, it would break Meta's business model. But more importantly, what would happen if we were each more engaged in the world around us, if we all valued "ordinary" people, living together truthfully and honestly, with dignity in their work, love for their neighbors, and decency in their daily lives? The mundane becomes miraculous.

And the maze becomes manageable. As we explore further, you might notice a distant light. Can you not see it yet? Not quite? It's there. You'll almost feel it at first. Despite wildfires surrounding us, the smoke that chokes us—the fear and the fury and the panic and the pain—we can all sense the presence of daylight beyond the darkness.

That is the way out.

***

It has been reflected in the words of leaders who once inspired us to be better than brutes—not to be great at all costs, but to be good, *to be America again, the one in the dream the dreamers dreamed*—and that's what can illuminate our path forward in the Silicon Age.[33] We were once asked to seek out the brilliant points of light scattered all around us, then to join together in goodwill. United, we could overcome any darkness, becoming a beacon to the world.[34]

To make America great *and* good again, free *and* fair again, *America* again, we need to pull together. If we stopped distrusting and disrupting and destroying and instead built and burnished, we could imagine something even better, together again: that splendid city redeemed, teeming with people of all kinds, brimming with commerce and creativity, our doors swung open wide to anyone with the will and the heart to go.[35] Draw nearer and you will see diversity in all important things, unity in all crucial things, and generosity in all things.[36] Hold America up to the source and find where the light gathers.

What can you see? Our greatness shines in the goodness of the many who are poor in spirit and rich in faith, not only from the wealth and prestige of an elite few.

∗ ∗ ∗

*Milton Friedman is dead. Ayn Rand is dead, too.* That's not simply to say that they've passed away from this Earth. It's a statement about their ideas: greed is never good, and rape is inhumane.

We aren't developing genuinely healthy relationships when we seek absolute power over another person. Rand was wrong. Meaningful connections and enduring trust will come from love, not indifference; from understanding, not selfishness. Friedman was wrong, too. Personal vices like greed, at scale, don't spontaneously become public virtues. Business leadership should be about the wisdom to make prudent and decent decisions that affect people, not benefiting from your disregard of others' suffering.

We should follow that line of thinking even further. What responsibilities do we have toward each other? How should we define prosperity? Who creates value? For whom? At what cost? How can we measure good business practices? What is the price of progress? The string of questions will keep going from there, and all of us have the right to ask for answers. Wherever we end up, the solutions to these questions shouldn't just benefit the mightiest and wealthiest among us, if all they'll seek is instant gratification, irresponsible hypergrowth, and rash returns. That's called exploitation.

We should keep going, tracing this thread all the way back to the beginning of our story together. The framers of the Constitution wanted statesmanship, balance, and compromise—not recklessness, factionalism, or disarray. They avoided easy answers and warned against any single strongman. They believed in the power of decency, diligence, and the duty to work together amid differences. We've forgotten the very first American Dream, from back when our nation was a startup, if we only embrace ruthless individualism or if we measure our worth in meaningless points on a made-up scoreboard online, even as our real-life relationships fray and communities crumble.

All men are created equal, and no one is born better than any other. In God We Trust, not in any manmade authority, not even a Superman. And as we all know, tyrants don't win in the end. We already had a king once. We didn't like it much.

And who needs a king anyway? This is America, and what an honor it is, to witness the inestimable value of the "ordinary" men and women who bring more light into lives all around us. The better rebellions arise every day in our democracy, in uncelebrated but profound acts of self-sacrifice. They will also appear—with the flip of a switch—in the simple but sacred act of voting.

In that light, the least wealthy and allegedly least worthy will know that they deserve liberty and justice just the same as anybody else in a democracy—and they will vote. They will vote with their dollars in what they choose to buy; they will vote with how they spend their time and attention; they will vote with the businesses they support and the ones they even start themselves; they will, gradually, regain their footing then vote with their feet, turning beliefs into movements and faith into action; and they will vote with their votes.

We must trust that *words do matter*, including the words on these pages, the words of "ordinary" men and women, let alone those in America's most cherished documents. Our fundamental rights and founding principles are worth more than gold, or silicon, or power and prestige. Each of us is guaranteed unalienable life, unalienable liberty, and the unalienable and relentless pursuit of lasting happiness. In every one of those phrases lives an eternal promise, which is meant for all of us. These rights are ours, inherently and always, not theirs to give or take away. They are self-evident.

They don't come from an executive or an empire, from some corporation or any government. They are from God, for everyone. They are the Absolute Truth.[37]

* * *

*Milton Friedman is dead. Ayn Rand is dead. But God is not dead.* They got that wrong. Our rights weren't imparted from a throne, or earned from some daring investment, or only offered after a high IQ test result. They weren't inherited from some almighty czar or granted to us by an ultrarich king who tries to never die. Those who first dreamed of America and overthrew our oppressors believed that freedom and fairness were for all.

The Founders fought for liberty *and* justice, and nearly a quarter of a millennium later, the better rebels still defend that same common cause, by doing all the small things in a great way or even getting into good trouble when it's called for.[38] They defy tyrants, but never through dark schemes and violent actions—like the misguided mob that organized online to ransack sacred spaces, broadcasting as they burned, only to attempt to lynch a blameless man. More often, and ordinarily, America's better rebels are the unnoticed peacemakers. Their beliefs are reflected in unspoken prayers and unlauded mercies, in good words and great works, in the unsung service that tenderly mends us and melds us together.

That thread unfurls from a place of inner hope and outer grace, which has shed light and spread light. Can you see it now? Follow that homegrown feeling, which is so familiar, you can't possibly miss its source: that is the spirit of independence, the love of country, which shines bright whenever heroes put service before self. Many have sacrificed for us along the way. In fact, these United States were born from a victim's revolution.[39]

Freedom and fairness were triggered together in a single spark, that God-given twinkle in the eye before our nation was knit in the womb. The fabric of our republic, first woven into the Constitution and the Bill of Rights, extends indivisibly as this single common thread: free *and* fair markets, free *and* fair elections. It is timeless, for us but far beyond us, divinely decided and revolutionary and for all.

We have lovingly stitched together our national tapestry ever since. It has always taken the steady handiwork of "ordinary" men and women, who keep the faith and make the movements that advance the loom, the people whom public memory often forgets but after whom we each, personally, have patterned ourselves.

What will future generations say about the Silicon Age? Will our era become a collection of happy misremembrances, picked out and promoted by the powerful few, which will be cheerfully cherished in our children's collective selective memory?

Not necessarily. History is the series of choices we weave. And "ordinary" men and women can make choices—and can make history, too.

***

There is just one last piece of the thread to follow further. "Before I go on with this short history, let me make a general observation," Fitzgerald wrote, "the test of a first-rate intelligence is the ability to hold two opposed ideas in the mind at the same time, and still retain the ability to function." Here was the next line: "One should, for example, be able to see that things are hopeless and yet be determined to make them otherwise."[40]

That's such a thin silver lining. But that sliver can shine in the Silicon Age once we choose to pursue *both* greatness and goodness. For if we believe that words can destroy and divide, then we must also trust that they can heal and restore:

*Here's to the better rebel in all of us. May we see that things are hopeless and yet be determined to make them otherwise.*

The way the world is today, because of the decisions that others have made, is not the way it has to be, because of decisions you can make. Technology is not destined to make the world unbearably worse, nor will it automatically make things almost-perfect. The path of history will be determined by choices, just as it always has. We can be *both* protechnology and skeptical of Big Tech, by demanding that Silicon Age tools benefit more of us and harm us all less. Likewise, we can be *both* staunchly probusiness and advocate for responsible innovations, by pursuing enterprise that is free and fair.  It's not only possible to be *both*, to pursue *both*. It's imperative.

There's nothing inevitable about what we weave next. If we seek both freedom and fairness, we can braid and blend them again. Then we will repair, and even, God willing, redeem. That depends on the decisions we make, starting once this last line unspools.

Let us begin.

# NOTES

## Act I. Silicon


1. Charlotte Curtis, "A Venture of Capital," *New York Times*, May 1, 1984, https://www
   .nytimes.com/1984/05/01/arts/a-venture-of-capital.html.
2. Deutsche Bank, "CIO Special: Venture Capital Investing," September 2021, 9, https://
   www.deutschewealth.com/content/dam/deutschewealth/cio-perspectives/cio
   -special-assets/venture-capital-investing-cio-2021/cio-special-venture-capital
   -investing-returns-and-diversification.pdf; PitchBook, "PitchBook Advanced Search
   Results—Companies & Deals," Venture Capital All Investments, accessed June 18,
   2023, https://content.pitchbook.com/share/quick-link/search/71179cca-2282-49ea-9ac6
   -22debfdb00c1?hash=0ca33afef476be84d492bd0f7a56b4764e80c2d7baad2b2c86808e5
   63bf6bb28.
3. Lesley Kennedy, "The Prehistoric Ages in Order: How Humans Lived Before Written
   Records," *HISTORY*, September 27, 2019, https://www.history.com/news/prehistoric
   -ages-timeline; Nick Smith, "The Seven Ages of Materials," Engineering and Technology, *E&T Magazine*, September 9, 2019, https://eandt.theiet.org/content/articles/2019
   /09/the-seven-ages-of-materials/.
4. Mercedes-Benz Group, "Benz Patent Motor Car: The First Automobile (1885–1886),"
   accessed June 18, 2023, https://group.mercedes-benz.com/company/tradition/company
   -history/1885-1886.html; David Shedden, "Today in Media History: In 1877 Alexander
   Graham Bell Made the First Long-Distance Phone Call to the Boston Globe," Poyn-
   ter, February 12, 2015, https://www.poynter.org/reporting-editing/2015/today-in-media
   -history-in-1877-alexander-graham-bell-made-the-first-long-distance-phone-call-to
   -the-boston-globe/; Franklin Institute, "Edison's Lightbulb," 2022, https://www.fi.edu
   /history-resources/edisons-lightbulb; National Air and Space Museum, "The First Successful Airplane," 2022, https://airandspace.si.edu/exhibitions/wright-brothers/online
   /fly/1903/.

5. "Alchemy Definition & Meaning," *Merriam-Webster Online*, n.d., https://www
.merriam-webster.com/dictionary/alchemy.

## 1. Sophomoric Exploits

1. Samantha Henig, "Facts, Fiction, Facebook, and Appletinis," *New Yorker*, October 1,
2010, https://www.newyorker.com/culture/new-yorker-festival/facts-fiction-facebook
-and-appletinis.
2. "Class of 2006 Chosen from Record Pool of 19,605," *Harvard Gazette*, 2002, https://
news.harvard.edu/gazette/story/2002/04/class-of-2006-chosen-from-record-pool-of
-19605/; Ben Mezrich, *The Accidental Billionaires: The Founding of Facebook: A Tale of
Sex, Money, Genius and Betrayal* (New York: Anchor, 2010), 41–49; "Affidavit of David
London," June 23, 2012. Exhibit E, 80–81, https://www.leader.com/docs/AFFIDAVIT
-OF-DAVID-LONDON-EXHIBIT-D-Defendants-Motion-to-Enforce-Settlement-27
-Jun-2012.pdf.
3. Bari M. Schwartz, "Hot or Not? Website Briefly Judges Looks," *Harvard Crimson*,
November 4, 2003, https://www.thecrimson.com/article/2003/11/4/hot-or-not-website
-briefly-judges/; Mezrich, *Accidental Billionaires*, 41–49; "Affidavit of David London,"
80–81.
4. Schwartz, "Hot or Not?"; Mezrich, *Accidental Billionaires*, 41–49; "Affidavit of David
London," 80–81.
5. Rob Fishman, "The First 25 People on Facebook," Buzzfeed, February 4, 2013, https://
www.buzzfeed.com/robf4/the-first-25-people-on-facebook-433s; Schwartz, "Hot or
Not?"; Erick Schonfeld, "Facemash Returns as (What Else?) a Facebook App Called
ULiken," TechCrunch, May 13, 2008, https://techcrunch.com/2008/05/13/facemash
-returns-as-what-else-a-facebook-app-uliken.
6. Meta Platforms, Inc., "Meta—Q3 2022 Earnings," accessed June 18, 2023, https://
investor.fb.com/investor-events/event-details/2022/Q3-2022-Earnings/default.aspx.
7. Steven Levy, *Facebook: The Inside Story* (New York: Blue Rider Press, 2020), 50.
8. "Mash Definition & Meaning," *Merriam-Webster Online*, 2022, https://www.merriam
-webster.com/dictionary/mash.
9. "Rules and Regulations," *Harvard Crimson*, November 7, 1873, https://www.thecrimson
.com/article/1873/11/7/rules-and-regulations-at-length-the/.
10. "Rules and Regulations."
11. "Teen Mental Health Deep Dive," *Wall Street Journal*, 2021, https://s.wsj.net/public
/resources/documents/teen-mental-health-deep-dive.pdf, slides 18, 43, 44.
12. "Teen Mental Health Deep Dive," slide 34.
13. "Teen Mental Health Deep Dive," slides 33, 34, 36, 37, 38.
14. "Teen Mental Health Deep Dive," slides 43, 44; Bobby Allyn, "Here Are 4 Key Points
from the Facebook Whistleblower's Testimony on Capitol Hill," NPR, October 5, 2021,
https://www.npr.org/2021/10/05/1043377310/facebook-whistleblower-frances-haugen
-congress.
15. "Teen Mental Health Deep Dive," slides 17, 18, 33.
16. Information School, University of Washington, "Gutenberg Indulgence," August 23,
2012, https://ischool.uw.edu/podcasts/dtctw/gutenberg-indulgence; Peter Kelley, "Documents That Changed the World: Gutenberg Indulgence, 1454," *UW News*, November 16, 2012, https://www.washington.edu/news/2012/11/16/documents-that-changed
-the-world-gutenberg-indulgence-1454/; Heather Whipps, "How Gutenberg Changed

the World," Live Science, May 26, 2008, https://www.livescience.com/2569-gutenberg
-changed-world.html; Susan Karant-Nunn and Ute Lotz-Heumann, "Confessional
Conflict. After 500 Years: Print and Propaganda in the Protestant Reformation," 2017,
https://speccoll.library.arizona.edu/online-exhibits/exhibits/show/reformation/role
-of-printing.

17. Katharine A. Kaplan, "Facemash Creator Survives Ad Board," *Harvard Crimson*,
November 19, 2003, https://www.thecrimson.com/article/2003/11/19/facemash-creator
-survives-ad-board-the/.

18. Mai-Linh Ton, "Harvard, Connected: The Houses Got Internet," *Harvard Crimson*,
May 22, 2017, https://www.thecrimson.com/article/2017/5/22/harvard-gets-internet
-1992/.

19. "Mark Zuckerberg at Startup School 2012," YouTube video, 9:40, 2013, https://www
.youtube.com/watch?v=5bJi7k-y1Lo.

20. S. Dixon, "Biggest Social Media Platforms 2023," Statista, February 14, 2023, https://
www.statista.com/statistics/272014/global-social-networks-ranked-by-number-of
-users/.

21. Kaplan, "Facemash Creator Survives Ad Board"; S. F. Brickman, "Face Off," *Harvard
Crimson*, November 6, 2003, https://www.thecrimson.com/article/2003/11/6/face-off
-computer-guru-mark-e/; Levy, *Facebook*, 50.

22. Kaplan, "Facemash Creator Survives Ad Board."

23. Brickman, "Face Off."

24. Schwartz, "Hot or Not?"

25. "Watch the Moment Mark Zuckerberg Got Into Harvard," YouTube video, 2017, https://
www.youtube.com/watch?v=gsefnhTK5lc; "Mark Zuckerberg's Speech as Written for
Harvard's Class of 2017," *Harvard Gazette*, May 25, 2017, https://news.harvard.edu
/gazette/story/2017/05/mark-zuckerbergs-speech-as-written-for-harvards-class-of
-2017/; Interactive, "Awards Category Details," Academy of Interactive Arts and Sciences, n.d., https://www.interactive.org/awards/award_category_details.asp?idAward
=2002&idGameAwardType=118; Edge staff, "The Top 100 PC Games of the 21st Century," Edge Online, August 25, 2006, https://web.archive.org/web/20121017165955/http:
/www.edge-online.com/features/top-100-pc-games-21st-century/.

26. Levy, *Facebook*, 196.

27. Jose Antonio Vargas, "The Face of Facebook," *New Yorker*, September 13, 2010, https://
www.newyorker.com/magazine/2010/09/20/the-face-of-facebook; Kevin Rooke, "4
Books Recommended by Travis Kalanick," n.d., https://www.kevinrooke.com/book
-recommendations/travis-kalanick.

28. Orson Scott Card, *Ender's Game* (New York: Macmillan, 2010), 302.

29. Schwartz, "Hot or Not?"

30. Nicholas Carlson, "How Mark Zuckerberg Hacked the *Harvard Crimson*," *Business
Insider*, March 5, 2010, https://www.businessinsider.com/how-mark-zuckerberg
-hacked-into-the-harvard-crimson-2010-3; Levy, *Facebook*, 75–76.

31. Vargas, "The Face of Facebook."

32. Mike Isaac and Sheera Frenkel, "Facebook Security Breach Exposes Accounts of 50
Million Users," *New York Times*, September 28, 2018, https://www.nytimes.com
/2018/09/28/technology/facebook-hack-data-breach.html; Kate O'Flaherty, "Facebook
Exposed Up to 600 Million Passwords—Here's What to Do," *Forbes*, March 31, 2019,
https://www.forbes.com/sites/kateoflahertyuk/2019/03/21/facebook-has-exposed-up
-to-600-million-passwords-heres-what-to-do/; Zack Whittaker, "Researchers Find 540
Million Facebook User Records on Exposed Servers," TechCrunch, April 3, 2019,

https://techcrunch.com/2019/04/03/facebook-records-exposed-server/; Davey Winder, "Unsecured Facebook Databases Leak Data of 419 Million Users," *Forbes*, September 5, 2019, https://www.forbes.com/sites/daveywinder/2019/09/05/facebook-security-snafu-exposes-419-million-user-phone-numbers/; Paul Bischoff, "Report: 267 Million Phone Numbers & Facebook User IDs Exposed Online," Comparitech, December 19, 2019, https://www.comparitech.com/blog/information-security/267-million-phone-numbers-exposed-online/.

33. Office of the Assistant Secretary for Health (OASH), "Surgeon General Issues New Advisory About Effects Social Media Use Has on Youth Mental Health," HHS.gov, May 23, 2023, https://www.hhs.gov/about/news/2023/05/23/surgeon-general-issues-new-advisory-about-effects-social-media-use-has-youth-mental-health.html.

34. Vivek Murthy, "The U.S. Surgeon General's Advisory: Social Media and Youth Mental Health," U.S. Public Health Service, May 23, 2023, https://www.hhs.gov/sites/default/files/sg-youth-mental-health-social-media-advisory.pdf, 4–5.

35. Georgia Wells and Jeff Horwitz, "Facebook's Effort to Attract Preteens Goes Beyond Instagram Kids, Documents Show," *Wall Street Journal*, September 28, 2021, https://www.wsj.com/articles/facebook-instagram-kids-tweens-attract-11632849667.

36. Harvard University, "History of Honorary Degrees," https://www.harvard.edu/about/history/honorary-degrees/; Lane Brothers Commercial Photographers, "William Randolph Hearst Receiving Honorary Degree from Thornwell Jacobs, President of Oglethorpe University, Atlanta, Georgia, 1927," Georgia State University Library Digital Collections, 1927, http://digitalcollections.library.gsu.edu/cdm/ref/collection/lane/id/171.

37. Vicky C. Hallett, "I'm Gonna Git YOU Sukka!," *Harvard Crimson*, March 11, 1999, https://www.thecrimson.com/article/1999/3/11/im-gonna-git-you-sukka-pin/; Scott Allen, "8 Famous Harvard Dropouts Not Named Gates or Zuckerberg," CNN, 2011, http://edition.cnn.com/2011/LIVING/04/08/famous.harvard.dropouts.mf/index.html.

38. "Hearst Worked on Lampoon in Three Years at College," *Harvard Crimson*, September 21, 1951, https://www.thecrimson.com/article/1951/9/21/hearst-worked-on-lampoon-in-three/.

39. "Hearst Family," *Forbes*, December 16, 2020, https://www.forbes.com/profile/hearst/.

40. Chris Nashawaty, "Best Movies of the 2010s—Top 10 Films of the Decade," *Esquire*, November 5, 2019, https://www.esquire.com/entertainment/movies/g29892894/best-movies-of-the-2010s/.

41. Harlan Lebo, "The 'Third Revised Final' Script of Citizen Kane: Orson Welles and the Roadmap to a Masterpiece," n.d.

42. Brickman, "Face Off."

43. Zuckerberg, "Mark Zuckerberg's Speech."

44. Levy, *Facebook*, 51.

45. Levy, 75.

46. Levy, 52; Schwartz, "Hot or Not?"

47. Levy, *Facebook*, 52.

48. David Kirkpatrick, *The Facebook Effect: The Inside Story of the Company That Is Connecting the World* (London: Virgin Books, 2010), 26; Mezrich, *Accidental Billionaires*, 41–49; "Affidavit of David London."

49. Brickman, "Face Off."

50. Anna Steinbock, "Harvard Awards 10 Honorary Degrees at 366th Commencement," *Harvard Gazette*, May 25, 2017, https://news.harvard.edu/gazette/story/2017/05/harvard-awards-10-honorary-degrees-at-366th-commencement/.

51. S. Dixon, "Social Media: Average Daily Usage Platforms by U.S. Adults 2022," Statista, accessed June 18, 2023, https://www.statista.com/statistics/324267/us-adults-daily -facebook-minutes/; L. Ceci, "Time Spent on WhatsApp 2022," Statista, accessed June 18, 2023, https://www.statista.com/statistics/1294880/time-spent-whatsapp-app -selected-countries/.

52. Sandy Cooper, "Diaries of a Facebook Deactivation," *The Scoop on Balance* (blog), accessed June 18, 2023, https://web.archive.org/web/20170721100507/https://thescoopon balance.com/diaries-of-a-facebook-deactivation/.

53. "Process.Php," January 10, 2006, https://web.archive.org/web/20080307031819/http: //www.02138mag.com/asset/1140.pdf; Bonnie Goldstein, "The Diaries of Facebook's Founder," *Slate*, November 30, 2007, https://slate.com/news-and-politics/2007/11/the -diaries-of-facebook-founder-mark-zuckerberg-2.html.

54. Mezrich, *Accidental Billionaires*, 249.

55. Associated Press, "Number of Active Users at Facebook Over the Years," October 23, 2012, https://finance.yahoo.com/news/number-active-users-facebook-over-years-214 600186--finance.html.

56. Richard Siklos, "News Corp. to Acquire Owner of MySpace.com," *New York Times*, July 18, 2005, https://www.nytimes.com/2005/07/18/business/news-corp-to-acquire -owner-of-myspacecom.html.

57. Levy, *Facebook*, 132.

58. Alex Kantrowitz, "Big Technology Podcast: Doing Business with Zuckerberg and Bezos—with Donald Graham," 11:15, 17:33, accessed June 18, 2023, https://podcasts .apple.com/us/podcast/doing-business-with-zuckerberg-and-bezos/id1522960417?i =1000552011662

59. Kantrowitz, 19:26, 23:40, 26:37.

60. Jeff Bercovici, "Facebook and Don Graham Have Been Very Good to Each Other," *Forbes*, February 2, 2012, https://www.forbes.com/sites/jeffbercovici/2012/02/02/facebook-and -don-graham-have-been-very-good-to-each-other; Alex Kantrowitz, "Ex-*Washington Post* Owner Don Graham on Doing Business with Zuckerberg and Bezos," *Big Technology*, February 2023, https://bigtechnology.substack.com/p/ex-washington-post -owner-don-graham.

61. Levy, *Facebook*, 132–33.

62. Sarah Lacy, *Once You're Lucky, Twice You're Good: The Rebirth of Silicon Valley and the Rise of Web 2.0* (New York: Penguin, 2009), 165.

63. Adam Fisher, *Valley of Genius: The Uncensored History of Silicon Valley (as Told by the Hackers, Founders, and Freaks Who Made It Boom)* (New York: Grand Central Publishing, 2018), 369.

64. History.com editors, "Facebook Raises $16 Billion in Largest Tech IPO in U.S. History," HISTORY, May 15, 2020, https://www.history.com/this-day-in-history/facebook -raises-16-billion-in-largest-tech-ipo-in-u-s-history.

## 2. Dark Arts

1. The story told here is based on the U.S. National Park Service, "Four Special Spikes," November 21, 2021, https://www.nps.gov/gosp/learn/historyculture/four-special-spikes. htm.

2. Randall Stross, "'American Disruptor' Review: The Life and Myth of Leland Stanford," *Wall Street Journal*, October 27, 2019, https://www.wsj.com/articles/american-disruptor

-review-the-life-and-myth-of-leland-stanford-11572208786; Kate Chesley, "First Transcontinental Railroad and Stanford Forever Linked," *Stanford News* (blog), May 8, 2019, https://news.stanford.edu/2019/05/08/first-transcontinental-railroad-stanford-forever-linked/; Charles Russo, "Leland's Legacy: How a Robber Baron Built Stanford and Transformed America," *Palo Alto Online*, February 20, 2020, https://www.paloaltoonline.com/news/2020/02/20/lelands-legacy-how-a-robber-baron-built-stanford-and-transformed-america.

3. Gordon H. Chang, "Op-Ed: Remember the Chinese Immigrants Who Built America's First Transcontinental Railroad," *Los Angeles Times*, May 10, 2019, https://www.latimes.com/opinion/op-ed/la-oe-chang-transcontinental-railroad-anniversary-chinese-workers-20190510-story.html.

4. Lesley Kennedy, "Building the Transcontinental Railroad: How 20,000 Chinese Immigrants Made It Happen," HISTORY, April 28, 2022, https://www.history.com/news/transcontinental-railroad-chinese-immigrants.

5. "Prestige," *Oxford Reference*, 2022.

6. Stanford Magazine, "The Truth About Leland Stanford Jr.," *Medium*, May 14, 2018, https://medium.com/stanford-magazine/the-truth-about-leland-stanford-jr-9d48fbf5623a.

7. "Stanford History—Facts," accessed June 18, 2023, https://facts.stanford.edu/about/.

8. National Association for Olmsted Parks, "The United States Capitol Grounds," November 17, 2008, http://www.olmsted.org/storage/documents/Current_Advocacy_Projects/NAOP_Capitol_Grounds_Brochure_11-17-08.pdf.

9. "A History of Stanford," *Stanford University* (blog), 2022, https://www.stanford.edu/about/history/; "History and Beauty: The Development of LSU's Campus," *LSU Libraries News & Notes*, September 9, 2016, https://news.blogs.lib.lsu.edu/2016/09/history-and-beauty-the-development-of-lsus-campus/; American University, "Frederick Law Olmsted: Research Files," accessed June 18, 2023, https://www.american.edu/library/archives/finding_aids/olmsted_fa_research.cfm.

10. "9 Great Frederick Law Olmsted Designs That Aren't Central Park," *Architectural Digest*, August 9, 2016, https://www.architecturaldigest.com/gallery/frederick-law-olmsted-best-designs.

11. Daniel Arnold, "A Gentleman's Quarrel," *Stanford Magazine*, March/April 2017 (March 1, 2017), https://stanfordmag.org/contents/a-gentleman-s-quarrel.

12. "The End to Falling Back and Forth in 100 Time Zones," *Chicago Tribune*, November 6, 1988, https://www.chicagotribune.com/news/ct-xpm-1988-11-06-8802130818-story.html.

13. Jack Beatty, *Age of Betrayal: The Triumph of Money in America, 1865–1900* (New York: Knopf, 2007), 3–4.

14. Beatty, 3–5.

15. Katharina Buchholz, "Infographic: Which Countries Change the Clock?" Statista Infographics, November 7, 2022, https://www.statista.com/chart/24473/countries-changing-clock-daylight-savings/.

16. John Battelle, "The Birth of Google," *Wired*, August 1, 2005, https://www.wired.com/2005/08/battelle/.

17. Adam Fisher, "'Google Was Not a Normal Place': Brin, Page, and Mayer on the Accidental Birth of the Company That Changed Everything," *Vanity Fair*, July 10, 2018, https://www.vanityfair.com/news/2018/07/valley-of-genius-excerpt-google.

18. Fisher.

19. Google, "How We Started and Where We Are Today—Google," accessed June 18, 2023, https://about.google/our-story/.

20. Fisher, "'Google Was Not a Normal Place.'"

21. Josie Fischels, "A Look Back at the Very First Website Ever Launched, 30 Years Later," NPR, August 6, 2021, https://www.npr.org/2021/08/06/1025554426/a-look-back-at-the-very-first-website-ever-launched-30-years-later.

22. "The World Wide Web Project," accessed June 18, 2023, http://info.cern.ch/hypertext/WWW/TheProject.html.

23. "The World Wide Web Project"; Elizabeth Nix, "The World's First Web Site," HISTORY, August 30, 2018, https://www.history.com/news/the-worlds-first-web-site.

24. Tim Berners-Lee, "Net Neutrality: This Is Serious," Decentralized Information Group (DIG) *Breadcrumbs* (blog), June 21, 2006, https://web.archive.org/web/20120120003419/http://dig.csail.mit.edu/breadcrumbs/node/144.

25. "The World Wide Web Project"; Worldwideweb, "Worldwideweb—Summary," 2022, http://info.cern.ch/hypertext/WWW/Summary.html.

26. Web Design Museum, "Yahoo in 1994," November 29, 2018, https://www.webdesignmuseum.org/gallery/yahoo-1994.

27. Peter H. Lewis, "Yahoo Gets Big Welcome on Wall Street," *New York Times*, April 13, 1996.

28. "Yahoo in 1994."

29. Martin Armstrong, "Infographic: How Many Websites Are There?" Statista Infographics, August 6, 2021, https://www.statista.com/chart/19058/number-of-websites-online/; Dan Tynan, "The History of Yahoo, and How It Went from Phenom to Has-Been," Fast Company, March 21, 2018, https://www.fastcompany.com/40544277/the-glory-that-was-yahoo.

30. "Carl V. Page: In Memoriam," Michigan State University Computer Science and Engineering, accessed June 18, 2023, https://www.cse.msu.edu/Alumni_Friends/Alumni/PageMemorial.php.

31. Pennsylvania State University, Department of Mathematics, "Michael Brin Prize in Dynamical Systems," accessed June 18, 2023, https://math-cal.cloud.science.psu.edu/dynsys/Brinprize; University of Maryland, Department of Mathematics, "Home Page: Michael Brin," math.umd.edu, accessed June 18, 2023, https://www.math.umd.edu/~mib/.

32. Academy of Achievement, "Sergey Brin," accessed June 18, 2023, https://achievement.org/achiever/sergey-brin/; Michigan State University, Department of Computer Science and Engineering, "Carl V. Page: In Memoriam | Computer Science and Engineering," accessed June 18, 2023, https://www.cse.msu.edu/Alumni_Friends/Alumni/PageMemorial.php.

33. Sergey Brin and Lawrence Page, "The Anatomy of a Search Engine," Stanford University, Computer Science Department, accessed June 18, 2023, http://infolab.stanford.edu/~backrub/google.html.

34. Berners-Lee, "Net Neutrality."

35. Brin and Page, "Anatomy of a Search Engine."

36. Brin and Page.

37. Chris Wiggins and Matthew L. Jones, *How Data Happened: A History from the Age of Reason to the Age of Algorithms* (New York: Norton, 2023), 228.

38. Brin and Page, "Anatomy of a Search Engine."

39. Krishna G. Palepu and Suraj Srinivasan, "Strategy and Governance at Yahoo! Inc.," Harvard Business School, accessed June 18, 2023, https://www.hbs.edu/faculty/Pages /item.aspx?num=41079.

40. Brin and Page, "Anatomy of a Search Engine."

41. "Harvard Shields," *Harvard University* (blog), https://www.harvard.edu/about/history /shields/; Dan Oren, "The Yale Seal," *Yale Alumni Magazine*, March 2001, http:// archives.yalealumnimagazine.com/issues/01_03/seal.html; University of North Car- olina at Chapel Hill, "Light and Liberty," https://www.unc.edu/story/university-day -installation/; University of Arkansas, "The Seal | Brand and Style Guidelines," https:// brand.uark.edu/graphic-identity/logos-and-wordmarks/the-seal.php; and Morehouse College, "Founders Week: Et Facta Est Lux," https://morehouse.edu/life/signature -events/founders-week/overview/, all accessed June 18, 2023.

42. Michigan State Alumni, "The Campaign for MSU Advancing Knowledge, Trans- forming Lives," accessed June 18, 2023, https://alumni.msu.edu/stay-informed /alumni-stories/feature-the-campaign-for-msu-advancing-knowledge-transforming -lives.

43. Appalachian State University, "The Bobby L. Dunnigan Award for Outstanding Ser- vice," accessed June 18, 2023, https://studentaffairs.appstate.edu/outstandingservice /general-information-and-nomination.

44. Stanford University, "The Motto Controversy | Becoming Stanford—Spotlight at Stanford," accessed June 18, 2023, https://exhibits.stanford.edu/becoming-stanford /feature/the-motto-controversy.

45. Fisher, "'Google Was Not a Normal Place.'"

46. Tynan, "The History of Yahoo."

47. Fisher, *Valley of Genius*, 277.

48. Grace Dean, "Google Founders Larry Page and Sergey Brin Are Now Worth More than $100 Billion, Making Them 2 of Only 8 Centibillionaires in the World," *Business Insider*, April 12, 2021, https://www.businessinsider.com/google-larry-page-sergey-brin -net-worth-billionaire-wealth-bloomberg-2021-4.

49. Megan Garber, "The First Google Doodle Was a Burning Man Stick Figure," *Atlantic*, September 6, 2013, https://www.theatlantic.com/technology/archive/2013/09/the-first -google-doodle-was-a-burning-man-stick-figure/279416/.

50. Fisher, *Valley of Genius*, 277–78.

51. "Angel Round—Google—1998-11-01—Crunchbase Funding Round Profile," Crunch- base, 2022, https://www.crunchbase.com/funding_round/google-angel—e7036c93.

52. "Google Receives $25 Million in Equity Funding—News Announcements," *News from Google*, June 7, 1999, http://googlepress.blogspot.com/1999/06/google-receives-25 -million-in-equity.html.

53. "Series A—Google—1999-06-07—Crunchbase Funding Round Profile," Crunchbase, 2022, https://www.crunchbase.com/funding_round/google-series-a—6c4715f9.

54. "Google Receives $25 Million."

55. Jillian D'onfro, "Google Has a Clever Way of Promoting Safe Sex to Its Employees, *Business Insider*, February 21, 2016, https://www.businessinsider.com/google-im -feeling-lucky-condoms-2016-2.

56. Nicholas Carlson, "Google Just Killed the 'I'm Feeling Lucky Button,'" *Business Insider*, September 8, 2010, https://www.businessinsider.com/google-just-effectively-killed-the -im-feeling-lucky-button-2010-9.

57. "Anyone Else Noticed the Return of the 'I'm Feeling Lucky' Button?" *Hacker News*, September 27, 2018, https://news.ycombinator.com/item?id=18087722.

58. "Yahoo! Selects Google as Its Default Search Engine Provider—News Announcements," *News from Google*, June 26, 2000, http://googlepress.blogspot.com/2000/06/yahoo-selects-google-as-its-default.html.

59. Tynan, "The History of Yahoo."

60. "Yahoo! Selects Google."

61. "Google Receives $25 Million."

62. *The Google Boys*, 2005, https://topdocumentaryfilms.com/the-google-boys/.

63. Fred Vogelstein, "How Yahoo Blew It," Wired, February 1, 2007, https://www.wired.com/2007/02/yahoo-3/.

64. Wayne Duggan, "This Day in Market History, August 19: The Google IPO—Alphabet (NASDAQ:GOOG), Alphabet (NASDAQ:GOOGL)," Benzinga, August 19, 2022, https://www.benzinga.com/general/education/21/08/14291439/this-day-in-market-history-the-google-ipo-1.

65. Gary Rivlin, "Google Goes Public? Search for 'Rich Get Richer,'" *New York Times*, April 25, 2004, https://www.nytimes.com/2004/04/25/us/google-goes-public-search-for-rich-get-richer.html.

66. Ann Grimes, "Why Stanford Is Celebrating the Google IPO," *Wall Street Journal*, August 23, 2004, https://www.wsj.com/articles/SB109322052140798129.

67. For this calculation, it's important to note that the 1,842,070 shares would have become 3,315,726 shares in 2014 through a 2-for-1 stock spinoff. Those 3,315,726 shares times $3,019.33, the peak price per share in 2021, would have been $10.01 billion. Grimes, "Why Stanford Is Celebrating"; "Stanford Reaps Windfall from Google Stock Sale," *Los Angeles Times*, December 2, 2005, https://www.latimes.com/archives/la-xpm-2005-dec-02-fi-calbriefs2.3-story.html; "Alphabet Inc. Cl A Stock Rises Thursday, Still Underperforms Market," MarketWatch, December 23, 2021, https://www.marketwatch.com/data-news/alphabet-inc-cl-a-stock-rises-thursday-still-underperforms-market-01640295092-6c4efc2e6493; Google, "Final Prospectus," SEC Prospectus, Securities and Exchange Commission, August 18, 2004, https://www.sec.gov/Archives/edgar/data/1288776/000119312504143377/d424b4.htm.

68. Association of University Technology Managers, "Licensing Activity Survey," 2020, 8, https://autm.net/AUTM/media/SurveyReportsPDF/FY20-US-Licensing-Survey-FNL.pdf.

69. Juliet Chung and Eliot Brown, "University Endowments Mint Billions in Golden Era of Venture Capital," *Wall Street Journal*, September 29, 2021, https://www.wsj.com/articles/university-endowments-mint-billions-in-golden-era-of-venture-capital-11632907802.

70. Andrew Ross Sorkin et al., "Harvard's Investment Report Card," *New York Times*, October 15, 2021, https://www.nytimes.com/2021/10/15/business/dealbook/college-endowment-funds-harvard.html; Rob Kozlowski, "UNC Endowment Basks in Blistering 42% Return," *Pensions & Investments*, September 23, 2021, https://www.pionline.com/endowments-and-foundations/unc-endowment-basks-blistering-42-return.

71. Juliet Chung and Dawn Lim, "How Brown University's Endowment Quietly Became Tops in Ivy League," *Wall Street Journal*, October 9, 2020, https://www.wsj.com/articles/how-brown-universitys-endowment-quietly-became-tops-in-ivy-league-11602261071.

72. Juliet Chung and Eliot Brown, "University Endowments Mint Billions in Golden Era of Venture Capital," *Wall Street Journal*, September 29, 2021, https://www.wsj.com/articles/university-endowments-mint-billions-in-golden-era-of-venture-capital-11632907802.

73.  Stanford's endowment in 2021 was $27,699,834,000. The total for the other four schools combined was $27,633,390,623: Columbia ($10,950,738,000), Brown ($3,976,694,000), Dartmouth ($5,731,322,087), and Cornell ($6,974,636,536). From 2021 to 1885, Stanford's founding year, was 136 years; each of the founding years of these schools was a total of 932 years ago (267 years since 1754, 257 years since 1764, 252 years since 1769, and 156 years since 1865). As a result, these schools' head start on Stanford was 796 years. Tom Fish, "The 30 Universities with the Largest Endowments," *Newsweek*, August 27, 2021, https://www.newsweek.com/universities-largest-endowments-america-harvard -yale-stanford-1620979.

74.  Sarah Wood, "10 National Universities with the Biggest Endowments," *US News & World Report*, September 13, 2022, https://www.usnews.com/education/best-colleges /the-short-list-college/articles/10-universities-with-the-biggest-endowments.


## 3. You're Going to Get What's Coming to You

1.  "Writing Instructor, Doctoral Student Dies of AIDS," Stanford University News Service, January 8, 1992, https://news.stanford.edu/pr/92/920108Arc2479.html; "Mosswood Chapel in Lower Temescal," Peerspace, 2022, https://web.archive.org/web /20210305071909/https://www.peerspace.com/pages/listings/6017134bd08a8200 0cc610e0.

2.  "Writing Instructor, Doctoral Student Dies of AIDS."

3.  "Writing Instructor, Doctoral Student Dies of AIDS."

4.  Yaser Haddara, "Matthies Urges Closer, More Thoughtful Look at Incident," *Stanford Daily*, February 7, 1992, https://archives.stanforddaily.com/1992/02/07?page=12 §ion=MODSMD_ARTICLE39; "Writing Instructor, Doctoral Student Dies of AIDS."

5.  "Officials Condemn Homophobic Incident; No Prosecution Planned," Stanford University News Service, February 12, 1992, https://web.archive.org/web/20220809032152 /https://news.stanford.edu/pr/92/920212Arc2432.html; "New Light Shed on Otero Epithet Case; Officials, Students Clarify Circumstances," *Stanford Daily*, February 5, 1992, https://archives.stanforddaily.com/1992/02/05?page=1§ion=MODSMD _ARTICLE4.

6.  Stanford Student Services, "Lloyd W. Dinkelspiel Awards," 2022, https://studentservices .stanford.edu/more-resources/university-awards/lloyd-w-dinkelspiel-awards; "New Light Shed on Otero Epithet Case"; "9192—June 3, 1994, " *Stanford Daily*, June 3, 1994, https://archives.stanforddaily.com/1994/06/03?page=12§ion=MODSMD _ARTICLE24#article; Matthias Dennis, "Otero RF Shares Inner Conflict with Stanford Community," *Stanford Daily*, February 6, 1992, https://archives.stanforddaily.com /1992/02/06?page=5§ion=MODSMD_ARTICLE20#article.

7.  Haddara, "Matthies Urges Closer, More Thoughtful Look."

8.  Stanford University, Residential & Dining Enterprises, "Wilbur Hall," https://rde .stanford.edu/studenthousing/wilbur-hall; and "Otero House," https://rde.stanford .edu/studenthousing/otero, both accessed June 18, 2023.

9.  "Officials Condemn Homophobic Incident."

10.  "Officials Condemn Homophobic Incident."

11.  "New Light Shed on Otero Epithet Case."

12.  June Cohen, "Rabois' Comments on 'Faggots' Derided Across University," *Stanford Daily*, February 6, 1992, https://archives.stanforddaily.com/1992/02/06?page=1§ion

=MODSMD_ARTICLE5#article; Amy Margolin, Tom Nolan, and Jamie Kershaw, "Homophobic Remarks Seen as Embarrassment," *Stanford Daily*, February 6, 1992, https://archives.stanforddaily.com/1992/02/06?page=4§ion=MODSMD _ARTICLE15.

13. Susanna Jech, "Base Name-Calling Is Not at All Free Speech," *Stanford Daily*, February 7, 1992, https://archives.stanforddaily.com/1992/02/07?page=4§ion=MODSMD _ARTICLE16.

14. "Officials Condemn Homophobic Incident."

15. Robin Kennedy, "Lawyer Claims Rabois Will Shame the Profession," *Stanford Daily*, February 6, 1992, https://archives.stanforddaily.com/1992/02/06?page=4§ion =MODSMD_ARTICLE15; Robin Kennedy, interview for John W. Gardner Legacy Oral History Project by Nancy Mancini, June 10, 2017, Stanford Oral History Collections, https://exhibits.stanford.edu/oral-history/catalog/kf546vh1360.

16. Anush Yegyazarian, "Matthies, Rabois Called on Views of Hate Speech KZSU Call-in Show Stirs Broad Dialogue," *Stanford Daily*, February 20, 1992, https://archives .stanforddaily.com/1992/02/20?page=1§ion=MODSMD_ARTICLE1#article.

17. Haddara, "Matthies Urges Closer, More Thoughtful Look."

18. Keith Rabois, "Rabois: My Intention Was to Make a Provocative Statement," *Stanford Daily*, February 7, 1992, https://archives.stanforddaily.com/1992/02/07?page=5§ion =MODSMD_ARTICLE21.

19. Cohen, "Rabois' Comments on 'Faggots' Derided."

20. "New Light Shed on Otero Epithet Case."

21. Dennis, "Otero RF Shares Inner Conflict."

22. Rabois, "Rabois: My Intention."

23. David O. Sacks and Peter Thiel, *The Diversity Myth: Multiculturalism and Political Intolerance on Campus* (Oakland, CA: Independent Institute, 1995), jacket.

24. "About Us," *Stanford Review*, 2022, https://stanfordreview.org/about-us/.

25. Christopher Fish, "Life After the Stanford Review," *Stanford Review*, February 9, 2012, https://stanfordreview.org/life-after-the-stanford-review-by-anthony-mainero/.

26. Several scholars have noted the long-term impacts of the discussions and decisions happening at Stanford during this era. In particular, Stanley Kurtz has argued that the debates at Stanford over curriculum decisions about Western civilization "foreshadowed and helped precipitate our current national divisions," and, in his view, "the furies set loose by Stanford's original Western Culture controversy have long since worked their way into our body politic. They will not soon disappear." In fact, Kurtz traced the origin of America's debates about curriculum decisions to Stanford, crediting "the dispute that effectively kicked off the conflict between the traditional vision of America-in-the-West and the globalizing multiculturalist challenge: Stanford's 1987–88 battle over its required Western Culture course." Stanley Kurtz, *The Lost History of Western Civilization* (New York: National Association of Scholars, 2020), 12, 14, 18, https://files.eric.ed.gov/fulltext/ED612993.pdf.

27. Christopher Fish, "A Brief and Non-Exhaustive History of the Stanford Review," *Stanford Review*, February 9, 2012, https://stanfordreview.org/a-brief-and-non-exhaustive -history-of-the-stanford-review/; Review staff, "A History of the Cornell Review," *Cornell Review*, April 11, 2013, https://www.thecornellreview.org/a-history-of-the-cornell -review/; "About," *Dartmouth Review*, October 30, 2022, https://dartreview.com/about/.

28. Dinesh D'Souza, *Illiberal Education: The Politics of Race and Sex on Campus* (New York: Free Press, 1991), 15, 17, 229, 230.

29. William F. Buckley, *God and Man at Yale* (Washington, DC: Regnery Gateway, 2012).

30. Dan Fastenberg, "God & Man at Yale," *TIME.com*, August 17, 2011, https://enter
tainment.time.com/2011/08/30/all-time-100-best-nonfiction-books/slide/god-man
-at-yale-by-william-f-buckley-jr/.

31. Sacks and Thiel, *The Diversity Myth*, jacket.

32. Moira Weigel, "The Making of Peter Thiel's Networks," *New Republic*, December 20,
2021, https://newrepublic.com/article/164768/peter-thiel-networks-contrarian-book
-review; John J. Miller and Karl Zinsmeister, "John Olin," Philanthropy Roundtable,
2022, https://www.philanthropyroundtable.org/resource/john-olin/; Fish, "Life After
the Stanford Review"; Moira Wiegel, "The Making of Peter Thiel's Networks: A Review
of Max Chafkin's 'The Contrarian,'" *New Republic*, December 20, 2021, https://
newrepublic.com/article/164768/peter-thiel-networks-contrarian-book-review.

33. Sacks and Thiel, *The Diversity Myth*, 169–70.

34. Sacks and Thiel, 169–70.

35. Every Peter Thiel Video, "Peter Thiel Discusses His Book The Diversity Myth in 1996
[C-Span]," YouTube video, 28:10; 28:26; 16:53, 2017, https://www.youtube.com/watch?v
=qTPOBEdc7OI&ab_channel=EveryPeterThielVideo.

36. Sacks and Thiel, *The Diversity Myth*, 101–2.

37. Sacks and Thiel, 174.

38. Weigel, "The Making of Peter Thiel's Networks."

39. "Life After Facebook," *Forbes*, January 26, 2011. https://www.forbes.com/forbes/2011
/0214/features-peter-thiel-social-media-life-after-facebook.html.

40. Chris Welch, "Microsoft Completes Acquisition of Yammer," Verge, July 19, 2012,
https://www.theverge.com/2012/7/19/3169874/microsoft-yammer-acquisition
-complete.

41. "Keith Rabois," LinkedIn, 2023, https://web.archive.org/web/20131027074848/http:
/www.linkedin.com/in/keith; Connie Loizos, "Keith Rabois Joins Founders Fund
Amid Transition at the Firm," *TechCrunch*, February 20, 2019, https://techcrunch.com
/2019/02/20/keith-rabois-is-leaving-khosla-ventures-for-founders-fund/.

42. Founders Fund, "Portfolio," accessed June 18, 2023, https://foundersfund.com/portfolio
/; Founders Fund, "Keith Rabois," 2023, https://foundersfund.com/team/keith-rabois/.

43. "Agreement and Plan of Merger—X.Com Corp. and Confinity Inc.," accessed June 18,
2023, https://corporate.findlaw.com/contracts/planning/agreement-and-plan-of-merger
-x-com-corp-and-confinity-inc.html.

44. Jimmy Soni, *The Founders: The Story of Paypal and the Entrepreneurs Who Shaped Silicon Valley* (New York: Simon and Schuster, 2022), 158–60, 370–76.

45. Robert Frank, "McLaren F1 Sells for $20.5 Million, the Most Expensive Car Auctioned
This Year," CNBC, August 14, 2021, https://www.cnbc.com/2021/08/14/mclaren-f1-sells
-for-20point5-million-most-expensive-car-auctioned-of-the-year.html.

46. Sebastian Mallaby, *The Power Law: Venture Capital and the Making of the New Future*
(New York: Penguin, 2022), 211.

47. "What Happened to Elon Musk's McLaren F1?," *McLaren Palm Beach* (blog), accessed
June 15, 2023, https://www.mclarenpalmbeach.com/mclaren-information/elon-musk
-mclaren-f1/; "CNN Perspectives: Elon Musk, Multi-Millionaire Entrepreneur," You-
Tube video, 2017, https://www.youtube.com/watch?v=x3tlVE_QXm4.

48. Max Chafkin, *The Contrarian: Peter Thiel and Silicon Valley's Pursuit of Power* (London: Bloomsbury, 2021), 59.

49. Christine Kim, "How Well Did the Members of the Paypal Mafia Do in College?,"
Quora, accessed June 18, 2023, https://www.quora.com/How-well-did-the-members-of
-the-Paypal-Mafia-do-in-college/answer/Christine-Kim-8.

50. Margaret Kane, "EBay Picks Up PayPal for $1.5 Billion," CNET, August 18, 2002, https://www.cnet.com/tech/tech-industry/ebay-picks-up-paypal-for-1-5-billion/.

51. Soni, *The Founders*, 234–38.

52. Rob Copeland et al., "The Shadow Crew Who Encouraged Elon Musk's Twitter Takeover," *Wall Street Journal*, April 29, 2022, https://www.wsj.com/articles/the-shadow-crew-who-encouraged-elon-musks-twitter-takeover-tesla-jack-dorsey-11651260119.

53. Andrew Ross Sorkin et al., "Sparks Fly as Musk Moves Fast to Remake Twitter," *New York Times*, October 31, 2022, https://www.nytimes.com/2022/10/31/business/dealbook/elon-musk-twitter-lebron-james-advertisers.html; Theodore Schleifer, "DeSantis-Sacks '24," *Puck* (blog), May 23, 2023, https://puck.news/desantis-sacks-24/; Ariana Baio, "RFK Jr—Live: Musk Reveals Twitter Revenue Down by Half as He Hosts Anti-Vax 2024 White House Hopeful," *Yahoo News*, June 5, 2023, https://news.yahoo.com/robert-f-kennedy-jr-live-135038126.html; Sophia Cai Doherty Erin, "The Big-Money Donors Backing Both DeSantis and RFK Jr.," *Axios*, July 12, 2023, https://www.axios.com/2023/07/12/big-money-backing-desantis-rfk.

54. Elon Musk [@elonmusk], "This is a battle for the future of civilization. If free speech is lost even in America, tyranny is all that lies ahead," Twitter, November 29, 2022, https://twitter.com/elonmusk/status/1597405399040217088.

55. "Jessica Anderson, "Catch 27," *Rocky Mountain Collegian*, March 2, 2005, https://web.archive.org/web/20211128031746/http://archives.collegian.com/2005/03/02/catch_27/.

56. Jeffrey M. O'Brien, "The PayPal Mafia," *Fortune*, November 13, 2007, https://fortune.com/2007/11/13/paypal-mafia/; "Compare Profiles Paypal Alumni Founded Companies, Meta, Alumni Founded Companies, Twitter Alumni Founded Companies," Crunchbase, 2022, https://www.crunchbase.com/compare/hub/paypal-alumni-founded-companies/meta-alumni-founded-companies,twitter-alumni-founded-companies.

57. Robin Wauters. "Yelp Co-Founder and CTO Russel Simmons Is Out," TechCrunch, June 14, 2010, https://techcrunch.com/2010/06/14/russel-simmons-yelp/.

58. Consumer Financial Protection Bureau, "CFPB Announces New Members of the Consumer Advisory Board, Community Bank Advisory Council, and Credit Union Advisory Council," September 18, 2015, https://www.consumerfinance.gov/about-us/newsroom/cfpb-announces-new-members-of-the-consumer-advisory-board-community-bank-advisory-council-and-credit-union-advisory-council/.

59. Founders Fund, "Keith Rabois," 2022, https://foundersfund.com/team/keith-rabois/; Crunchbase, "Keith Rabois—Partner @ Founders Fund," Crunchbase Person Profile, 2022, https://www.crunchbase.com/person/keith-rabois; Jason Del Rey, "Keith Rabois Resigns from Yelp's Board," *Vox*, January 23, 2014, https://www.vox.com/2014/1/23/11622670/keith-rabois-resigns-from-yelps-board; Colleen Taylor, "Yelp Closes 5-Star IPO Day with $1.47 Billion Valuation," TechCrunch, February 2, 2012, https://techcrunch.com/2012/03/02/yelp-closes-5-star-ipo-day-with-1-47-billion-valuation/;

60. "Ken Howery," LinkedIn, 2023, https://www.linkedin.com/in/kenhowery/; "Luke Nosek," LinkedIn, 2023, https://www.linkedin.com/in/lukenosek/.

61. Crunchbase, "Keith Rabois—Partner @ Founders Fund"; Connie Loizos, "Keith Rabois Joins Founders Fund Amid Transition at the Firm," *TechCrunch*, February 20, 2019.

62. "Andrew McCormack," LinkedIn, 2023, https://www.linkedin.com/in/drew mccormack/.

63. Avery Hartmans, "Nearly a Dozen Major Tech Firms Can Trace Their Roots to Pay-Pal. From Palantir to Tesla, Here Are the Companies Launched by Members of the

'PayPal Mafia,'" *Business Insider*, December 24, 2020, https://www.businessinsider.com/tech-companies-founded-by-paypal-mafia-full-list-2020-10; Crunchbase, "PayPal Mafia Who Have Started Companies," 2022, https://www.crunchbase.com/lists/paypal-mafia-who-have-started-companies/476d9107-9aa1-4d76-94f3-28cb98045d70/people; Craft Ventures, "Palantir–Angel-Seed Stage Investment," accessed June 1, 2023, https://www.craftventures.com/portfolio/palantir.

64. Lucy Handley, "Reid Hoffman: The Billionaire Philosopher," CNBC, December 5, 2018, https://www.cnbc.com/linkedin-founder-reid-hoffman-on-investing-his-podcast-and-scaling-up/, 0:13.

65. Crunchbase, "Reid Hoffman—Partner @ Greylock," Crunchbase Person Profile, 2022, https://www.crunchbase.com/person/reid-hoffman.

66. Microsoft Corporation, "Microsoft to Acquire LinkedIn," Microsoft News Center, June 13, 2016, https://news.microsoft.com/2016/06/13/microsoft-to-acquire-linkedin/.

67. Crunchbase, "Keith Rabois—Partner @ Founders Fund."

68. "Roelof Botha," LinkedIn, 2023, https://www.linkedin.com/in/roelofbotha/.

69. M. G. Siegler, "Instagram Launches with the Hope of Igniting Communication Through Images," *TechCrunch*, October 6, 2010, https://techcrunch.com/2010/10/06/instagram-launch/; Liz Gannes, "Sequoia Set to Lead $500M Valuation Round for Instagram," *AllThingsD* (blog), April 6, 2012, https://allthingsd.com/20120406/sequoia-set-to-lead-500m-valuation-round-for-instagram/; Evelyn Rusli, "Facebook Buys Instagram for $1 Billion," *New York Times*, April 9, 2012, https://archive.nytimes.com/dealbook.nytimes.com/2012/04/09/facebook-buys-instagram-for-1-billion/.

70. CompaniesMarketcap, "Block (SQ)—Market Capitalization," 2022, https://companiesmarketcap.com/square/marketcap/; Leena Rao and Dan Primack, "Square Prices IPO at Just $9 per Share, Valued at $2.9 Billion," *Fortune*, November 19, 2015, https://fortune.com/2015/11/18/square-prices-ipo/; Crunchbase, "Keith Rabois—Partner @ Founders Fund."

71. John Adams, "Ex-Square Exec Keith Rabois to Leave Xoom's Board; Amazon's Killalea Joins," *American Banker*, March 27, 2015, https://www.americanbanker.com/payments/news/ex-square-exec-keith-rabois-to-leave-xooms-board-amazons-killalea-joins; Crunchbase, "Series C—Xoom—2006-02-06—Crunchbase Funding Round Profile," 2022, https://www.crunchbase.com/funding_round/xoom-series-c--647a4663.

72. University of Illinois Urbana-Champaign, "Jawed Karim | 2014 Young Alumni Achievement Award," 2014, https://cs.illinois.edu/about/awards/alumni-awards/alumni-awards-past-recipients/jawed-karim; History Computer staff, "Chad Hurley—Complete Biography, History, and Inventions," *History-Computer* (blog), December 27, 2021, https://history-computer.com/chad-hurley-complete-biography/; Marguerite Gong Hancock and Steve Chen, "Oral History of Steve Chen, Part 1 of 2 Interviewed by Marguerite Gong Hancock," Computer History Museum, 2019, 8–11, https://archive.computerhistory.org/resources/access/text/2019/11/102740492-05-01-acc.pdf.

73. Jawed, "Me at the Zoo," YouTube video, April 24, 2005, https://www.youtube.com/watch?v=jNQXAC9IVRw&vl=en&ab_channel=jawed; Leah Asmelash, "The First Ever YouTube Video Was Uploaded 15 Years Ago," CNN, April 23, 2020, https://www.cnn.com/2020/04/23/tech/youtube-first-video-jawed-karim-trnd/index.html.

74. Stuart Dredge, "YouTube Was Meant to Be a Video-Dating Website," *Guardian*, March 16, 2016, https://www.theguardian.com/technology/2016/mar/16/youtube-past-video-dating-website.

75. Viacom International, Inc., Comedy Partners, Country Music Television, Inc., Paramount Pictures Corporation and Black Entertainment Television, LLC vs. YouTube, Inc., YouTube, LLC and Google, Inc., No. 10-3270 (U.S. Court of Appeals, Second Circuit April 5, 2012) A-66-A-67, A-76, https://cases.justia.com/federal/appellate-courts/ca2/10-3270/124/0.pdf.

76. Crunchbase, "Keith Rabois—Partner @ Founders Fund."

77. "Google Buys YouTube for $1.65 Billion," *NBC News*, October 9, 2006, https://www.nbcnews.com/id/wbna15196982.

78. L. Ceci, "YouTube Global Advertising Revenues per Quarter 2022," Statista, October 26, 2022, https://www.statista.com/statistics/289657/youtube-global-quarterly-advertising-revenues/; L. Ceci, "YouTube: Statistics & Data," Statista, 2022; L. Ceci. "YouTube: Hours of Video Uploaded Every Minute 2020," Statista, April 4, 2022, https://www.statista.com/statistics/259477/hours-of-video-uploaded-to-youtube-every-minute/.

79. L. Ceci, "U.S. YouTube Usage Frequency 2020," Statista, March 15, 2022, https://www.statista.com/statistics/256896/frequency-with-which-us-internet-users-visit-youtube/.

80. "PayPal may have the highest ratio of individuals going off to start or finance new start-ups in the Valley," Scott Dettmer once said, and he'd know. He founded the law firm Gunderson Dettmer, the most active venture capital law firm in the world every year from 2014 until 2021. "Gunderson Dettmer Named PitchBook's 2021 Most Active Venture Law Firm Globally for the Eighth Year in a Row," *Firm News*, March 7, 2022.

81. Crunchbase, "Keith Rabois—Partner @ Founders Fund," 2022.

82. Keith Rabois, "Quote of the Day," *Stanford Daily*, February 7, 1992, https://archives.stanforddaily.com/1992/02/07?page=5§ion=MODSMD_ARTICLE23.

83. In addition to Stanford, there was one other university strongly tied to the PayPal Mafia: Levchin, Stoppelman, Simmons, Karim, Chen, and Nosek all went to the University of Illinois Urbana-Champaign. Kim, "How Well Did the Members of the Paypal Mafia Do?"

84. Crunchbase, "Keith Rabois—Partner @ Founders Fund," 2023.

85. Crunchbase, "Peter Thiel—Managing Partner @ Founders Fund," Crunchbase Person Profile, 2023, https://www.crunchbase.com/person/peter-thiel.

86. Crunchbase, "Founders Fund—Investments, Portfolio & Company Exits," 2023, https://www.crunchbase.com/organization/founders-fund/recent_investments.

87. Andrew Granato, "How Peter Thiel and the Stanford Review Built a Silicon Valley Empire," *Stanford Politics*, November 27, 2017, https://stanfordpolitics.org/2017/11/27/peter-thiel-cover-story/.

88. Anush Yegyazarian, "Matthies, Rabois Called on Views of Hate Speech KZSU Call-in Show Stirs Broad Dialogue," *Stanford Daily*, February 20, 1992, https://archives.stanforddaily.com/1992/02/20?page=1§ion=MODSMD_ARTICLE1#article.

89. Scott Kupor, "Fraternity Founded on Principles of Tolerance," *Stanford Daily,* February 6, 1992, https://archives.stanforddaily.com/1992/02/06?page=4§ion=MODSMD_ARTICLE15.

90. Sacks and Thiel, *The Diversity Myth*, 171, 193; Kupor, "Fraternity Founded on Principles of Tolerance"; Andreessen Horowitz, "Scott Kupor," 2023, https://a16z.com/author/scott-kupor/; Andreessen Horowitz, "Portfolio," 2023, https://a16z.com/portfolio/.

91. Crunchbase, "Query Builder: Founders Fund and Andreessen Horowitz," 2023, https://www.crunchbase.com/search/organization.companies/b58c5b6ad0e05888b253bc0c4d892eb5; Crunchbase, "Compare Profiles: Andreessen Horowitz, Founders Fund," 2023,

https://www.crunchbase.com/compare/organization/andreessen-horowitz/founders
-fund.

92. Sacks and Thiel, *The Diversity Myth*, 169–70.

93. Crunchbase, "Keith Rabois—Partner @ Founders Fund," 2023.

94. Alex Grant, "Mainstream Conservatism?" *Stanford Daily*, February 5, 1992, https://
archives.stanforddaily.com/1990/05/22?page=4§ion=MODSMD_ARTICLE23
#article.

95. Rabois's assertion here was almost certainly meant to inflame, not inform. Still, it must
be stated that Reagan opposed the Civil Rights Act of 1964, opposed the Voting Rights
Act of 1965, and ran for California governor in 1966 with promises to get rid of the Fair
Housing Act. "If an individual wants to discriminate against Negroes or others in selling or renting his house," he said then, "he has a right to do so." For all of his virtues
as a president, to claim that President Reagan was the "greatest champion of civil rights
in the 20th century" was quite a stretch. In 2019 the National Archives released an
audio recording where, as former president, Reagan called President Nixon to talk
about delegates at the United Nations, saying, "To see those monkeys from those African countries—damn them, they're still uncomfortable wearing shoes."

  South African bishop Desmond Tutu claimed that Reagan's policies toward apartheid era South Africa were "immoral, evil and totally un-Christian" and argued, "Don't
you want to be able to say to your grandchildren: 'I helped to end a crime against
humanity. . . . I helped bring about freedom in South Africa.'" Raoul Mowatt, "Remem-
brances of the Dreamer Stanford Students, Faculty Reflect on King's Legacy," *Stanford Daily*, January 1, 1990, https://archives.stanforddaily.com/1990/01/19?page=1
§ion=MODSMD_ARTICLE3; "Reagan Called African Delegates 'Monkeys' in
Recording," *CBS Evening News*, YouTube video, 2019; Justin Elliott, "Reagan's Embrace
of Apartheid South Africa," *Salon*, February 5, 2011, https://www.salon.com/2011/02
/05/ronald_reagan_apartheid_south_africa/; Matthew Yglesias, "Reagan's Race
Record," *Atlantic*, November 9, 2007, https://www.theatlantic.com/politics/archive
/2007/11/reagans-race-record/46875/; Victoria Graham, "Tutu Labels Reagan, Thatcher
Racist for Protecting South Africa," *AP News*, May 7, 1988, https://apnews.com/article
/dde74fa83b12ea1c2ec01e7814f5379a; John Nicholas, "Which Transformative American
Leader, Born a Century Ago, Got Civil Rights Right? Ronald Reagan? No, Hubert
Humphrey," *Nation*, February 6, 2011, https://www.thenation.com/article/archive
/which-transformative-american-leader-born-century-ago-got-civil-rights-right
-ronald-reag/.

96. Sacks and Thiel, *The Diversity Myth*, 175.

97. Anush Yegyazarian, "Matthies, Rabois Called on Views of Hate Speech KZSU Call-
in Show Stirs Broad Dialogue," *Stanford Daily*, February 20, 1992, https://archives
.stanforddaily.com/1992/02/20?page=1§ion=MODSMD_ARTICLE1#article.

98. Dennis, "Otero RF Shares Inner Conflict."

99. Haddara, "Matthies Urges Closer, More Thoughtful Look."

100. Dan Primack and Mike Allen, "Peter Thiel Got Married Over the Weekend," *Axios*,
October 16, 2017, https://www.axios.com/2017/12/15/peter-thiel-got-married-over-the
-weekend-1513306233; Cory Weinberg and Zoe Bernard, "In Keith Rabois' Silicon Valley,
Nice Guys Finish Last," *Information*, November 18, 2019, https://www.theinformation
.com/articles/in-keith-rabois-silicon-valley-nice-guys-finish-last.

101. FEC, "Browse Individual Contributions | Keith Rabois," 2022, https://www.fec.gov
/data/individual-contributions/?contributor_name=Keith+Rabois; FEC, "Browse

Individual Contributions | Jacob Helberg," 2022, https://www.fec.gov/data/receipts
/individual-contributions/?contributor_name=Jacob+Helberg.

102. In the years before Keith Rabois met Jacob Helberg, Rabois had donated mostly to
Republicans and had given to few Democrats (including $5,200 in 2013 and $5,400 in
2015 for Ro Khanna's campaign for Congress, and $5,200 in 2014 for Cory Booker's
campaign for U.S. Senate). Helberg gave the first political donation of his life in February 2019. Between 2019 and 2022, he donated $2,271,500. In twenty-four years, from
1996 to 2019, Rabois gave $478,232.78 in political donations. Between 2019 and 2022,
Rabois gave $4,077,737.50.  FEC, "Browse Individual Contributions | Jacob Helberg";
FEC, "Browse Individual Contributions | Keith Rabois."

103. Barbara Rodriguez, "How Pete Buttigieg Climbed to the Top (for Now) in Iowa: He
Showed Strength Across Iowa Counties," *Des Moines Register*, February 13, 2022,
https://www.desmoinesregister.com/story/news/elections/presidential/caucus/2020
/02/13/iowa-caucuses-pete-buttigieg-performed-well-across-iowa-counties-alignment
-process-delegates/4729180002/; Steve Hendrix and Joshua Partlow, "How Pete Buttigieg Went from War Protester to Serving in Afghanistan," *Washington Post*, July 29,
2019, https://www.washingtonpost.com/politics/2019/07/29/how-pete-buttigieg-went
-war-protester-packing-my-bags-afghanistan/.

104. Brittany Shepherd, "Buttigieg Turns to Silicon Valley to Bolster Campaign Fundraising Haul," *Yahoo! News*, July 1, 2019, https://news.yahoo.com/buttigieg-turns-to-silicon
-valley-to-bolster-campaign-fundraising-haul-181417179.html; Miles Kruppa and Richard Waters, "Buttigieg's 'Big Tent' Appeal Rises in Silicon Valley," *Financial Times*,
2019,   https://www.ft.com/content/e1417308-0e85-11ea-a7e6-62bf4f9e548a;   Lapowsky
Issie, "Here Are the Top Political Donors from Amazon, Apple, Facebook, Google and
Microsoft. Only One Is Backing Trump," *Protocol*, October 16, 2020, https://www
.protocol.com/tech-political-donors-2020-amazon-apple-facebook-google
-microsoft; Theodore Schleifer, "How Pete Buttigieg Became the New Toast of Silicon
Valley's Wealthiest Donors," *Vox*, May 7, 2019, https://www.vox.com/recode/2019/5/7
/18527646/pete-buttigieg-silicon-valley-donors-mark-zuckerberg; Jacob Helberg,
"Grateful for so many incredible memories on this journey. Couldn't be prouder of the
campaign that @PeteButtigieg @Chas10Buttigieg @Swatipedia @Joni_california @JessOConnell @Lis_Smith have run—more joyful, positive & inspiring than any I can
remember. The work goes on," Twitter, March 2, 2020, https://twitter.com/jacobhelberg
/status/1234271978271334402?s=20; Alexandra S. Levine, "The FTC-Facebook Finale,"
*Politico*, July 24, 2019, https://www.politico.com/newsletters/morning-tech/2019/07/24
/the-ftc-facebook-finale-693417.

105. "New Light Shed on Otero Epithet Case"; Cohen, "Rabois' Comments on 'Faggots'
Derided."

106. Alex Grant, "Mainstream Conservatism?" *Stanford Daily*, February 5, 1992, https://
archives.stanforddaily.com/1990/05/22?page=4§ion=MODSMD_ARTICLE23
#article; Rabois, "Rabois: My Intention"; Cohen, "Rabois' Comments on 'Faggots'
Derided."

107. Eric Savitz. "Square COO Rabois Resigns Amid Sexual Harassment Charge," *Forbes*,
January 25, 2013, https://www.forbes.com/sites/ericsavitz/2013/01/25/square-coo-rabois
-resigns-amid-sexual-harassment-charge/?sh=496ce3244982.

108. Keith Rabois, "Untitled—a Note from Keith," Tumblr, January 25, 2013, https://web
.archive.org/web/20131231161022/http:/keithrabois.tumblr.com/post/41463189288/a
-note-from-keith.

109. Rabois, "Untitled—a Note from Keith"; "Untitled," July 6, 2017, https://web.archive.org /web/20170706155005/https://keithrabois.tumblr.com/post/41463189288/a-note-from -keith.

110. Elizabeth Brier, Kendrick Cai, Rashi Shrivastava, and Rebecca Szkuta, "The Midas List 2022," *Forbes*, 2022, https://web.archive.org/web/20220504102132/https://www.forbes .com/midas/.

## 4. A Self-Fulfilling Prophecy

1. Travis Kalanick, "Uber's Founding," *Uber Newsroom*, December 22, 2010, https://www .uber.com/newsroom/ubers-founding.

2. Techco Media, "Travis Kalanick Startup Lessons from the Jam Pad—Tech Cocktail Startup Mixology," YouTube video, 7:50, May 5, 2011, https://www.youtube.com/watch ?v=VMvdvP02f-Y&ab_channel=TechcoMedia.

3. Alyson Shontell, "Travis Kalanick Bio and Uber's Founding," *Business Insider*, July 5, 2013, https://www.businessinsider.com/travis-kalanick-bio-and-ubers-founding-2013 -7; Michael Arrington, "Payday for Red Swoosh: $15 Million from Akamai," *Tech-Crunch*, April 12, 2007, https://techcrunch.com/2007/04/12/payday-for-red-swoosh -15-million-from-akamai/.

4. Kalanick, "Uber's Founding."

5. Crunchbase, "StumbleUpon—Crunchbase Company Profile & Funding," accessed June 18, 2023, https://www.crunchbase.com/organization/stumbleupon.

6. Paige Leskin and Avery Hartmans, "The History of How Uber Went from the Most Feared Startup in the World to Its Massive IPO," *Business Insider*, May 18, 2019, https:// www.businessinsider.com/ubers-history.

7. Ali Tamaseb, *Super Founders: What Data Reveals About Billion-Dollar Startups* (New York: PublicAffairs, 2021), 59–60; Kalanick, "Uber's Founding."

8. Zimride, "Carpools for Universities," March 27, 2012. https://zimride.wordpress.com /info/carpools-for-universities/; Ryan Lawler, "Lyft-Off: Zimride's Long Road to Over-night Success," *TechCrunch*, August 29, 2014, https://techcrunch.com/2014/08/29 /6000-words-about-a-pink-mustache/.

9. Sunil Paul, "The Untold Story of Ridesharing—Part III: The Birth of Sidecar and Ride-sharing," *Medium*, September 10, 2017, https://sunilpaul.medium.com/the-untold -story-of-ridesharing-part-iii-the-birth-of-sidecar-and-ridesharing-9f6e6c706d8d.

10. United States Patent and Trademark Office, "System and Method for Determining an Efficient Transportation Route," USPTO Google Patents, 2023, https://patents.google .com/patent/US6356838B1/en.

11. Tomio Geron, "SideCar Raises $10 Million from Google Ventures, Lightspeed," *Forbes*, October 10, 2012. https://www.forbes.com/sites/tomiogeron/2012/10/10/sidecar-raises -10-million-from-google-ventures-lightspeed/.

12. Kalanick and Zuckerberg were acquaintances, which Kalanick sometimes boasted about in Uber's early days. In a speech in 2011, Kalanick claimed that he'd been the one who had encouraged Parker to work with Zuckerberg and should have been in Aaron Sorkin's movie *The Social Network* as a result. "Travis Kalanick Startup Les-sons," 7:50.

13. Mike Isaac, *Super Pumped: The Battle for Uber* (New York: Norton, 2019), 86–87.

14. Sunil Paul, "Why We Sold to GM," *Sidecar*, March 7, 2016, https://web.archive.org/web /20160307071233/https://www.side.cr/why-we-sold-to-gm/.

15. LeWeb, "Travis Kalanick, Uber and Loic Le Meur, Co-Founder, LeWeb," YouTube video, 1:32; 3:33; 4:10, 2013, https://www.youtube.com/watch?v=vnkvNQ2V6Og.

16. Paul Smith, *Sell with a Story: How to Capture Attention, Build Trust, and Close the Sale* (New York: AMACOM, 2016), 225.

17. "Ryan Graves," LinkedIn, February 20, 2023, https://www.linkedin.com/in/ragraves/.

18. Travis Kalanick [@travisk], Twitter, January 6, 2010, https://twitter.com/travisk/status/7422828552.

19. Kalanick, "Uber's Founding"; Ryan Graves [@ryangraves], Twitter, January 6, 2010, https://twitter.com/ryangraves/status/7422940444.

20. Suraj Srinivasan, W. Lorsch Jay, and Quinn Pitcher, "Uber in 2017: One Bumpy Ride," *Harvard Business School CASE COLLECTION*, no. 117–070 (June 2017): 1–29, https://www.hbs.edu/faculty/Pages/item.aspx?num=52840.

21. John Mannes, "Here Is Uber's First Pitch Deck," *TechCrunch*, August 23, 2017, https://techcrunch.com/gallery/here-is-ubers-first-pitch-deck/slide/4/.

22. Mannes, "Here Is Uber's First Pitch Deck," slide 5.

23. Techstars, "Techstars Companies," Techstars Portfolio, 2022, https://www.techstars.com/portfolio; Crunchbase, "Uber—Funding, Financials, Valuation & Investors," 2022, https://www.crunchbase.com/organization/uber/company_financials; Crunchbase, "Techstars—Crunchbase Investor Profile & Investments," 2022, https://www.crunchbase.com/organization/techstars.

24. "Chris Sacca," LOWERCASE capital, 2022, https://lowercasecapital.com/chris-sacca/; Crunchbase, "Chris Sacca—Founder and Chairman @ Lowercase Capital," Crunchbase Person Profile, 2022, https://www.crunchbase.com/person/chris-sacca; "DCVC—Crunchbase Investor Profile & Investments," 2022, https://www.crunchbase.com/organization/data-collective; "List of Top Techstars Portfolio Companies," Crunchbase Hub Profile, 2022, https://www.crunchbase.com/hub/techstars-portfolio-companies; and "Query Builder | Organizations/Person: Gary Vaynerchuk," 2022, https://www.crunchbase.com/search/organizations/field/people/num_portfolio_organizations/gary-vaynerchuk.

25. Crunchbase, "Cyan Banister—General Partner, The Frontier @ Long Journey Ventures," Crunchbase Person Profile, 2022, https://www.crunchbase.com/person/cyan-banister; "First Round Capital—Investments, Portfolio & Company Exits," 2022, https://www.crunchbase.com/organization/first-round-capital/recent_investments; "Kapor Capital—Investments, Portfolio & Company Exits," 2022, https://www.crunchbase.com/organization/kapor-capital/recent_investments; and "Uber—Funding, Financials, Valuation & Investors."

26. Travis Kalanick, "Startup Seed Raising Skilzzz," *Swooshing* (blog), March 19, 2009, https://swooshing.wordpress.com/2009/03/19/startup-seed-raising-skillzzz/.

27. Alyson Shontell, "A Leaked Internal Uber Presentation Shows What the Company Really Values in Its Employees," *Business Insider*, November 19, 2014, https://www.businessinsider.com/uber-employee-competencies-fierceness-and-super-pumpedness-2014-11.

28. Matthew Speiser, Maria LoPreiato-Bergan, Colt Sauers, and Kate Bridge, "The Basics of Venture Capital Fund Distributions," AngelList Venture, 2022, https://learn.angellist.com/articles/distributions; Scott Peterman, Margaret Niles, Sook Young Yeu, and Anson Chan, "Negotiating Private Equity Fund Terms: Key Provisions for PE Sponsors and LP Investors and the New ILPA Model Limited Partnership Agreements," K&L Gates LLP, 2020, https://files.klgates.com/files/171267_negotiating_private_equity_fund_terms.pdf.

29.  Amy Fontinelle, "How to Cut Financial Advisor Expenses," Investopedia, February 15, 2022, https://www.investopedia.com/articles/personal-finance/071415/how-cut-financial -advisor-expenses.asp; Coryanne Hicks, "What to Know About Financial Advisor Fees and Costs | Financial Advisors," *U.S. News*, September 22, 2022, https://money.usnews .com/financial-advisors/articles/financial-advisor-fees-and-costs.

30.  "AngelList—Fund Pricing Calculator," AngelList Venture, 2022, https://www.angellist .com/calculator?_ga=2.181431970.422871924.1657215185-435469897.1644981513.

31.  Diane Mulcahy, "Venture Capitalists Get Paid Well to Lose Money," *Harvard Business Review*, August 5, 2014, https://hbr.org/2014/08/venture-capitalists-get-paid-well -to-lose-money; Diane Mulcahy, "Six Myths About Venture Capitalists," *Harvard Business Review*, May 2013, https://hbr.org/2013/05/six-myths-about-venture-capitalists.

32.  Note that the math here is simplified for illustrative purposes. Usually, annual fees are lower than the full 2 percent throughout the life of the fund, and the return on investments depends on whether returns are allocated on a whole fund or deal-by-deal basis, how the returns to the investors versus the fund managers are structured, and so on.

33.  Jacob Tasto, "Fundraising Cycle Compression: How Frequently Do VCs Raise New Funds?" *Different Funds* (blog), December 4, 2020, https://differentfunds.com/research /vc-fundraising-cycles/.

34.  Kalanick, "Startup Seed Raising Skilzzz."

35.  Scott Austin, Stephanie Stamm, and Winkler Rolfe, "Uber Jackpot: Inside One of the Greatest Startup Investments of All Time," *Wall Street Journal*, May 10, 2019; Michael Arrington, "UberCab Closes Uber Angel Round," *TechCrunch*, October 15, 2010, https://techcrunch.com/2010/10/15/ubercab-closes-uber-angel-round/.

36.  Crunchbase, "Benchmark—Investments, Portfolio & Company Exits," 2022, https:// www.crunchbase.com/organization/benchmark/recent_investments; "Sequoia Capital— Investments, Portfolio & Company Exits," 2022, https://www.crunchbase.com/organi zation/sequoia-capital/recent_investments; Crunchbase, "Scott Banister—Founder @ IRL," Crunchbase Person Profile, 2022, https://www.crunchbase.com/person /scott-banister; "Chris Sacca," LOWERCASE capital, 2022, https://lowercasecapital .com/chris-sacca/; Crunchbase, "Uber—Funding, Financials, Valuation & Investors."

37.  Crunchbase, "Menlo Ventures—Investments, Portfolio & Company Exits," 2022, https://www.crunchbase.com/organization/menlo-ventures/recent_investments; Crunchbase, "Tuesday Capital—Investments, Portfolio & Company Exits," 2022, https://www.crunchbase.com/organization/tuesday-capital/recent_investments.

38.  Ingrid Pan, "Why Uber's History and Financing Mean a Big, Big Valuation," *Yahoo News*, June 23, 2014, https://news.yahoo.com/why-uber-history-financing-mean -130035507.html.

39.  Austin, Stamm, and Rolfe, "Uber Jackpot"; Crunchbase, "Uber—Funding, Financials, Valuation & Investors."

40.  Alex Wilhelm, "Google Ventures Puts $258M Into Uber, Its Largest Deal Ever," *TechCrunch*, August 23, 2013, https://techcrunch.com/2013/08/22/google-ventures-puts -258m-into-uber-its-largest-deal-ever/; Ryan Lawler, "Uber Raises Giant $1.2 Billion Funding Round at a $17 Billion Valuation," *TechCrunch*, June 6, 2014, https:// techcrunch.com/2014/06/06/uber-1-2b/.

41.  Fitz Tepper, "Uber Has Completed 2 Billion Rides," *TechCrunch*, July 18, 2016, https:// techcrunch.com/2016/07/18/uber-has-completed-2-billion-rides/.

42.  Statista Research Department, "Uber: Quarterly Number of Rides Worldwide 2017– 2020," Statista, July 14, 2022, https://www.statista.com/statistics/946298/uber-ridership -worldwide/.

43. Michelle Cheng, "Uber's Market Cap Surpasses Its IPO Valuation," *Quartz*, 2020, https://qz.com/1928990/ubers-market-cap-surpasses-its-ipo-valuation; Alex Wilhelm, "Will Ride-Hailing Profits Ever Come?," *TechCrunch*, February 21, 2021, https://techcrunch.com/2021/02/12/will-ride-hailing-profits-ever-come/.

44. Seth Fiegerman, "Uber's First Investors Open Up About Their Wild Ride," CNN Business, May 10, 2019, https://edition.cnn.com/2019/05/08/tech/uber-first-investors/index.html.

45. Rolfe Winkler, "Uber and Eight Other Once-Small Startups Are Now Worth a Combined $250 Billion," *Wall Street Journal*, May 9, 2019, https://www.wsj.com/articles/uber-like-other-unicorns-began-its-ipo-path-after-the-financial-crisis-11557417619.

46. Jack Morse, "Here's What We Learned from Travis Kalanick's Hidden 2007 Twitter Account," *Mashable*, March 29, 2017, https://mashable.com/2017/03/29/uber-travis-kalanick-konatbone-twitter/; Las Vegas Vacation Rentals, "Tenant Vacation Rental Agreement & Information Sheet," Nine Deep, LLC, 2022, http://vegaspartyhouse.com/partyhouse%20rental%20agreement.pdf.

47. Travis Kalanick, "Travis Kalanick (KonaTbone) on Twitter," Twitter, September 2009, https://web.archive.org/web/20090927063055/https:/twitter.com/KonaTbone.

48. Morse, "Here's What We Learned."

49. Jack Morse, "Strip Clubs and 'Dong Roulette': Travis Kalanick's Twitter Account Is Full of Terrifying Wonders," *Mashable*, March 30, 2017, https://mashable.com/article/travis-kalanick-uber-dong-roulette-twitter.

50. Travis Kalanick, "Living History," *Swooshing* (blog), January 17, 2009, https://swooshing.wordpress.com/2009/01/17/living-history/.

51. Emily Chang, *Brotopia: Breaking Up the Boys' Club of Silicon Valley* (New York: Penguin, 2019), 40.

52. JamPad, "JamPad (@JamPadHQ)," Twitter, 2022, https://twitter.com/JamPadHQ.

53. James B. Stewart, "As a Guru, Ayn Rand May Have Limits. Ask Travis Kalanick," *New York Times*, 2017, https://www.nytimes.com/2017/07/13/business/ayn-rand-business-politics-uber-kalanick.html.

54. Milton Friedman, "A Friedman Doctrine—the Social Responsibility of Business Is to Increase Its Profits," *New York Times*, September 13, 1970, https://www.nytimes.com/1970/09/13/archives/a-friedman-doctrine-the-social-responsibility-of-business-is-to.html.

55. JamPad, Twitter, February 7, 2010, https://twitter.com/JamPadHQ/status/8773310061.

56. Friedman, "A Friedman Doctrine."

57. Angus Burgin, *The Great Persuasion: Reinventing Free Markets Since the Depression* (Cambridge, MA: Harvard University Press, 2012), 152.

58. Roger Thompson, "Reimagining the MBA," *Harvard Business School Alumni*, December 1, 2011, https://www.alumni.hbs.edu/stories/Pages/story-bulletin.aspx?num=1024.

59. E. Merrick Dodd, Jr., "For Whom Are Corporate Managers Trustees?" *Harvard Law Review* 45, no. 7 (May 1932): 1145–63.

60. Isaac, *Super Pumped*, 88.

61. Stewart, "As a Guru, Ayn Rand May Have Limits."

62. Ayn Rand, *The Fountainhead* (New York: Plume, 2005), 24.

63. Susan Love Brown, "Ayn Rand and Rape," *Journal of Ayn Rand Studies* 15, no. 1 (2015): 8, 10–11, https://doi.org/10.5325/jaynrandstud.15.1.0003.

64. Rand, *The Fountainhead*, 197.

65. Rand, 683.

66. Mike Isaac, "Uber's C.E.O. Plays with Fire," *New York Times*, April 23, 2017, https://www.nytimes.com/2017/04/23/technology/travis-kalanick-pushes-uber-and-himself-to-the-precipice.html.

67. Shontell, "A Leaked Internal Uber Presentation."

68. Ayn Rand, Linda Peikoff, and David Harriman, *The Journals of Ayn Rand* (New York: Penguin, 1999), 27, emphasis in original.

69. Kara Robinson, "What's the Difference Between a Sociopath and a Psychopath?," *WebMD*, February 14, 2022, https://www.webmd.com/mental-health/features/sociopath-psychopath-difference#1.

70. Rand, Peikoff, and Harriman, *The Journals of Ayn Rand*, 26, 27, emphasis in the original.

71. "Übermensch," *etymonline*, Online Etymology Dictionary, 2022, https://www.etymonline.com/search?q=%C3%9Cbermensch.

72. Rand, Peikoff, and Harriman, *The Journals of Ayn Rand*, 29.

73. Friedrich Nietzsche *Beyond Good and Evil*, trans. Helen Zimmern, accessed June 18, 2023, https://www.gutenberg.org/files/4363/4363-h/4363-h.htm.

74. Carolyn Said, "California Judge: Uber's Prop. 22 Ads in Driver App Are Not Coercive," *San Francisco Chronicle*, 2020, https://www.sfchronicle.com/business/article/Judge-Uber-s-Prop-22-ads-in-driver-app-are-15685929.php.

75. "4 Books Recommended by Travis Kalanick," *Kevin Rooke*, 2022, https://www.kevinrooke.com/book-recommendations/travis-kalanick.

76. Max Chafkin, "What Makes Uber Run," *Fast Company*, September 8, 2015, https://www.fastcompany.com/3050250/what-makes-uber-run.

77. Jennifer Burns, *Goddess of the Market: Ayn Rand and the American Right* (Oxford: Oxford University Press, 2009), 42.

78. John Ridpath, "Ayn Rand Contra Nietzsche," *Objective Standard*, February 21, 2017, https://theobjectivestandard.com/2017/02/ayn-rand-contra-nietzsche/.

79. Friedrich Nietzsche, *The Antichrist* (1888), trans. H. L. Mencken (N.p.: Monadnock Valley Press, 2008), https://monadnock.net/nietzsche/antichrist-5.html.

80. Nietzsche, *Beyond Good and Evil*.

81. Nietzsche, *The Antichrist*, 62.

82. Burns, "*Goddess of the Market*, 42–43.

83. Burns, 16.

84. Anne Conover Heller, *Ayn Rand and the World She Made* (New York: Knopf Doubleday, 2010), 41–42.

85. Lily Rothman, "TIME's 'Is God Dead?' Cover Turns 50," *TIME.com*, 2016, https://time.com/isgoddead/.

86. Friedrich Nietzsche, *Nietzsche: The Gay Science: With a Prelude in German Rhymes and an Appendix of Songs*, ed. Bernard Williams, trans. Josefine Nockhauff and Adrian Del Caro (Cambridge: Cambridge University Press, 2001), 120, https://doi.org/10.1017/CBO9780511812088.

87. Eva Cybulska, "Nietzsche's Übermensch: A Hero of Our Time?" *Philosophy Now*, no. 93 (2012), https://philosophynow.org/issues/93/Nietzsches_Ubermensch_A_Hero_of_Our_Time.

88. Ayn Rand, "The Fascist New Frontier," Ayn Rand Institute video, 3:20, 4:36, 6:10, 9:30, 2013, https://soundcloud.com/aynrandinstitute/the-fascist-new-frontier.Rand.

89. Burns, *Goddess of the Market*, 209–10.

90. Vint Cerf, "Is Vint Cerf Related to Chris Cerf, Son of Bennett Cerf?" Quora, July 13, 2015, https://www.quora.com/Is-Vint-Cerf-related-to-Chris-Cerf-son-of-Bennett

-Cerf; Internet Hall of Fame, "Vint Cerf | Internet Hall of Fame Pioneer," 2022, https://internethalloffame.org/inductees/vint-cerf; Google Research, "Vinton G. Cerf," 2022, https://research.google/people/author32412/.

91. For instance, it certainly blared when Christopher Cerf learned that American soldiers had used his music to torture detainees at Guantanamo Bay. Bennett Cerf's son had won two Grammy Awards and three Emmy Awards for his music, which included over two hundred songs for Sesame Street. "My first reaction was, 'this can't possibly be true, this is just too crazy,'" said Cerf. "It was much worse when I heard later that they were actually using the music in Guantanamo to actually do deep, long-term interrogations." Bruce Springsteen's "Born in the USA," Eminem's "White America," and "I love you" from Barney and friends were also used, along with numerous songs by Rage Against the Machine. "Guantanamo is known around the world as one of the places where human beings have been tortured—from water boarding, to stripping, hooding and forcing detainees into humiliating sexual acts—playing music for 72 hours in a row at volumes just below that to shatter the eardrums," Rage Against the Machine's lead guitarist, Tom Morello, explained, then demanded: "The fact that music I helped create was used in crimes against humanity sickens me—we need to end torture and close Guantanamo now." We didn't. "Rage Against Gitmo," *Foreign Policy*, October 23, 2009, https://foreignpolicy.com/2009/10/23/rage-against-gitmo/; David Trifunov, "Sesame Street Music Used Against Guantanamo Prisoners, Doc Shows," *The World from PRX*, May 30, 2012, https://theworld.org/stories/2012-05-30/sesame-street-music-used-against-guantanamo-prisoners-doc-shows.

## 5. White Lies


1. Rhett Morris and Mariana Penido, "How Did Silicon Valley Become 'Silicon Valley?'" Endeavor, April 23, 2014. https://web.archive.org/web/20160423005247/http://share.endeavor.org/pdf/HDSVBSV.pdf.

2. Levi Pulkkinen, "If Silicon Valley Were a Country, It Would Be Among the Richest on Earth," *Guardian*, April 30, 2019, https://www.theguardian.com/technology/2019/apr/30/silicon-valley-wealth-second-richest-country-world-earth; Simeon Alder, David Lagakos, and Lee E. Ohanian, "The Decline of the U.S. Rust Belt: A Macroeconomic Analysis," *SSRN Electronic Journal*, August 2015, https://doi.org/10.2139/ssrn.2586168.

3. David Leonhardt, "Holding On," *New York Times*, April 6, 2008, https://www.nytimes.com/2008/04/06/realestate/keymagazine/406Lede-t.html.

4. Steven Leibson, "391 San Antonio Road: The House That William Shockley Built (and Destroyed)," *EEJournal*, August 17, 2018, https://www.eejournal.com/2018/08/17/391-south-san-antonio-road-the-house-that-william-shockley-built-and-destroyed/.

5. "Nobel Lectures, Physics 1942–1962," in *Nobel Lectures* (Amsterdam: Elsevier, 1964), https://www.nobelprize.org/prizes/physics/1956/shockley/biographical/.

6. In February 1945 Shockley had become the expert advisor to the secretary of war, and the essay he wrote, "Air Force in the Atomic Age," appeared in a book written by the military men and scientists who had developed and employed the nuclear technology used to destroy Hiroshima and Nagasaki just a few months before. In addition to Einstein's admonitions, J. R. Oppenheimer, the "Father of the Atomic Bomb," implored, "It would seem that the conscious acquisition of these new powers of destruction calls for the equally conscious determination that they must not be used and that all necessary steps be taken to insure that they will not be used." Published in 1946, most

essays addressed the ethical concerns and moral dilemmas of the nuclear age they had just unleashed.

Shockley's cold calculations took a different approach, calling the bombs used on Hiroshima and Nagasaki "profitable by a favor of fifty; that is, the cost to Japan was fifty times the cost to us." He spelled out, in exacting detail like an accountant doing an assessment: each bomb cost $1 million to make and $240,000 to deliver, but the two trials thus far had destroyed 4.1 square miles of Hiroshima and 2.8 square miles of Nagasaki at a combined cost of less than half a million dollars per square mile. That was six times cheaper than traditional weapons, Shockley concluded, in awe of his own audit of the advantages the weapon gave America. Dexter Masters and K. Way, *One World or None: A Report to the Public on the Full Meaning of the Atomic Bomb* (New York: New Press, 2007), 67–68, 209.


7. Joel Shurkin, *Broken Genius: The Rise and Fall of William Shockley, Creator of the Electronic Age* (New York: Palgrave Macmillan, 2006), 84.

8. Matt Bowling, "Palo Alto History," paloaltohistory, 2023, https://www.paloaltohistory .org/dinahs-shack.php.

9. Jim Crow Museum, "Examples of Jim Crow Laws—Oct. 1960—Civil Rights—Other Jim Crow Information," accessed June 18, 2023, https://jimcrowmuseum.ferris.edu /links/misclink/examples.htm.

10. Bowling, "Palo Alto History."

11. Emiliano Tahui Gomez, "Fact Check: Underground Railroad Unrelated to Black Lawn Jockey Statues," *USA Today*, February 18, 2022, https://www.usatoday.com/story/news /factcheck/2022/02/18/fact-check-underground-railroad-unrelated-black-lawn -jockey-statues/6816652001/.

12. Bowling, "Palo Alto History."

13. Patterson Hood, "Drive-by Truckers—the Three Great Alabama Icons," *Genius Lyrics*, 2023, https://genius.com/Drive-by-truckers-the-three-great-alabama-icons-lyrics.

14. Therese Poletti, "How 8 Fairchild Alums Sparked Silicon Valley," *MarketWatch*, May 11, 2011, https://www.marketwatch.com/story/traitorous-eight-feted-as-california-icons -2011-05-10.

15. Sebastian Mallaby, *The Power Law: Venture Capital and the Art of Disruption* (New York: Penguin, 2022), 22.

16. Michael Hiltzik, "The Twisted Legacy of William Shockley," *Los Angeles Times*, December 2, 2012, https://www.latimes.com/archives/la-xpm-2001-dec-02-tm-10501 -story.html.

17. Mallaby, *The Power Law*, 22.

18. Scott Rosenberg, "Silicon Valley's First Founder Was Its Worst," *Wired*, July 19, 2017, https://www.wired.com/story/silicon-valleys-first-founder-was-its-worst/.

19. Becky Ferreira, "Standing on the Shoulders of Giant Jerks," *Vice*, December 2, 2014, https://www.vice.com/en/article/3dk7yj/standing-on-the-shoulders-of-giant-jerks.

20. Ferreira.

21. Morris and Penido, "How Did Silicon Valley Become 'Silicon Valley'?"

22. Morris and Penido.

23. Steve Case, "AOL Founder Steve Case on the Surprising Entrepreneurs Reimagining the Economic Landscape," interview by Judy Woodruff, *PBS News Hour*, November 24, 2022, https://www.pbs.org/newshour/show/aol-founder-steve-case-on-the-surprising -entrepreneurs-reimagining-the-economic-landscape.

24. Tim J. Kane, "The Importance of Startups in Job Creation and Job Destruction," *SSRN Electronic Journal*, 2010, https://doi.org/10.2139/ssrn.1646934, 6.

25. Case, "AOL Founder Steve Case."

26. Steve Case, *The Rise of the Rest: How Entrepreneurs in Surprising Places Are Building the New American Dream* (New York: Simon and Schuster, 2022), 19.

27. Steve Case, "Rise of the Rest," interview by Raju Narisetti, *Author Talks*, McKinsey Global Publishing September 22, 2022, https://www.mckinsey.com/featured-insights /mckinsey-on-books/author-talks-steve-case-identifies-the-us-cities-driving-new -innovation-and-its-not-where-you-think.

28. David Brancaccio and Alex Schroeder, "75 Years Ago, the Transistor Ignited the Fire of Modern Innovation," *Marketplace* (blog), December 12, 2022, https://www.marketplace .org/2022/12/12/75-years-ago-the-transistor-ignited-the-fire-of-modern-innovation/.

29. "Founding of Intel," PBS, 2022, https://www.pbs.org/transistor/background1/events /intelfounded.html.

30. "Fairchildren," Computer History Museum, 2022, https://computerhistory.org /fairchildren/.

31. Henry Pickavet, "The First Trillion-Dollar Startup," *TechCrunch*, July 26, 2014.

32. Bronwyn H. Hall and Josh Lerner, "The Financing of R&D and Innovation," *Handbook of the Economics of Innovation* (Amsterdam: Elsevier, 2009), 55.

33. Shurkin, *Broken Genius*, 272.

34. "Eugenics," *etymonline*, 2022, https://www.etymonline.com/word/eugenics; "Dysgenics," *etymonline*, 2022. https://www.etymonline.com/word/dysgenics.

35. "Is Quality of U.S. Population Declining? Interview with a Nobel-Prize Winning Scientist," *U.S. News & World Report*, November 22, 1965, box 2, folder 3, William Shockley and Eugenics Collection (SC0595), Dept. of Special Collections and University Archives, Stanford University Libraries, Stanford, CA; William Shockley, "Form Letter and Enclosures," September 6, 1966, box 2, folder 4, William Shockley and Eugenics Collection (SC0595).

36. The political left and right in modern America both face uncomfortable histories when it comes to Bill Shockley (for more on the political right, see the story about Sandra Froman in this chapter). On the left, Cass Canfield's early endorsement added credence to Shockley's efforts, and it was consistent with the views of many early leaders of the prochoice movement from decades earlier. Most infamously, Planned Parenthood's founder, Margaret Sanger, argued extensively for a "cleaner race" through birth control and forced sterilization.

      Planned Parenthood has more recently denounced her views, declaring, "Sanger's belief in eugenics undermined reproductive freedom and caused irreparable damage to the health and lives of generations of Black people, Latino people, Indigenous people, immigrants, people with disabilities, people with low incomes, and many others," and stating that "acceptance of this decision by Sanger and other thought leaders laid the foundation for tens of thousands of people to be sterilized, often against their will."

      In 1918 Sanger wrote: "Has knowledge of birth control, so carefully guarded and so secretly practiced by the women of the wealthy class—and so tenaciously withheld from the working women—brought them misery? Rather, has it not promoted greater happiness, greater freedom, greater prosperity and more harmony among them? The women who have this knowledge are the women who have been free to develop, free to enjoy in its best sense, and free to advance the interests of the community. And their men are the ones who motor, who sail yachts, who legislate, who lead and control. The men, women and children of this class do not form any part whatever in the social problems of our times."

"Had this class continued to reproduce in the prolific manner of the working peo-ple in the past twenty-five years, can human imagination picture what conditions would be today? All of our problems are the result of overbreeding among the work-ing class, and if morality is to mean anything at all to us, we must regard all the changes which tend toward the uplift and survival of the human race as moral. Knowledge of birth control is essentially moral. Its general, though prudent, practice must lead to a higher individuality and ultimately to a cleaner race." Margaret Sanger, "Opposition Claims About Margaret Sanger," Planned Parenthood, 2007, https://www.planned parenthood.org/uploads/filer_public/cc/2e/cc2e84f2-126f-41a5-a24b-43e093c47b2c /210414-sanger-opposition-claims-p01.pdf; William Shockley, "Letter to Bill Spicer," November 16, 1965, box 2, folder 3, William Shockley and Eugenics Collection (SC0595).

37. Shockley, "Letter to Bill Spicer"; "Biography of Cass Canfield (1897–1986)," Eleanor Roosevelt Papers, George Washington University, accessed June 18, 2023, https://www2 .gwu.edu/~erpapers/mep/displaydoc.cfm?docid=erpn-cascan#:~:text=Cass%20 Canfield%2C%20one%20of%20the,enlist%20in%20the%20wartime%20military.

38. Shockley, "Letter to Bill Spicer."

39. Bob Lamar, "An 'Exponential Explosion' of Technological Advances Has Largely Elim-inated 'Survival of the Fittest' as a Control Mechanism in Man's Evolution, Stanford Nobel Laureate William Shockley Said Here Thursday Night (Jan. 7)," Stanford Uni-versity News Service, January 8, 1965, box 2, folder 3, William Shockley and Eugenics Collection (SC0595).

40. Office of Governor, State of California, "California Launches Program to Compen-sate Survivors of State-Sponsored Sterilization," December 31, 2021, https://www.gov .ca.gov/2021/12/31/california-launches-program-to-compensate-survivors-of-state -sponsored-sterilization/.

41. Juliana Jimenez, "California Compensates Victims of Forced Sterilizations, Many of Them Latinas," *NBC News*, July 23, 2021, https://www.nbcnews.com/news/latino /california-compensates-victims-forced-sterilizations-many-latinas-rcna1471.

42. Walter F. Bodmer et al., "Letter to Merritt Holman, Editor of Stanford M.D., from the Faculty of the Department of Genetics, Stanford University," February 14, 1966, box 2, folder 3, William Shockley and Eugenics Collection (SC0595).

43. Bodmer et al.

44. William Shockley, "Draft Letter Prepared to Elicit Comments to the Editor, Stan-ford M.D.," April 12, 1966, box 2, folder 5, William Shockley and Eugenics Collection (SC0595).

45. Shockley saw himself as someone who could speak out about eugenics and dysgenics, due to his status as a Nobel Laureate and tenured faculty member, since others who shared his views could not. He explained that "one of the dominant factors in my deci-sion to let the interview be published was the fact that several eminent individuals who have been cooperative enough to write me their comments have indicated an unwillingness to be publicly identified with the views they communicated to me. (This applies to the above quotations, except for Canfield's.) I appreciate and concur with their position. I feel that my situation leaves me more flexibility to express myself than may be true of others who share the same worries. This may be my most important role as an amateur teammate of the professionals." Shockley, "Letter to Bill Spicer."

46. William R. Rambo, "Memorandum from William R. Rambo to Dean J. M. Pettit, Sub-ject: Shockley Research," June 14, 1968, box 89, folder 89, Stanford Project 2XX0601: "Research on Methodology to Reduce the Environment-Heredity Uncertainty,

Including Ethnic and Racial Aspects," William Bradford Shockley Papers (SC0222), Department of Special Collections and University Archives, Stanford University Libraries, Stanford, CA.

47. J. M. Pettit, "Memorandum from J. M. Pettit, Dean, School of Engineering to Professor William Shockley, Subject: Research Proposal," May 29, 1968, box 89, folder 89, Stanford Project 2XX0601.

48. W. Shockley, "Memorandum from W. Shockley, Alexander M. Poniatoff Professor of Engineering Science to Provost R. W. Lyman, Subject: Research on Methodology to Reduce the Environment-Heredity-Uncertainty, Including Ethnic and Racial Aspects," June 12, 1968, box 89, folder 89, Stanford Project 2XX0601.

49. "NIHF Inductee William Lear Invented the Car Radio," National Inventors Hall of Fame, 2022, https://www.invent.org/inductees/william-p-lear.

50. William P. Lear, "Letter to Dr. W. Shockley from Wm. P. Lear," November 14, 1967; William P. Lear, "Letter to President J. E. Wallace Sterling from William P. Lear," March 29, 1968; and J. E. Wallace Sterling, "Letter to Mr. William P. Lear from J. E. Wallace Sterling, Office of the President, Stanford University," April 19, 1968; all in box 89, folder 89, Stanford Project 2XX0601. Also Anthony Young, "The Vision of William P. Lear," Foundation for Economic Education, February 1, 2005, https://fee.org/articles/the-vision-of-william-p-lear/; "CPI Inflation Calculator," CPI, 2023, https://data.bls.gov/cgi-bin/cpicalc.pl?cost1=10000&year1=196803&year2=202304; "Lear, William P. (William Powell), 1902–1978," Museum of Flight Archives, 2022, https://archives.museumofflight.org/agents/people/2356.

51. Sterling, "Letter to Mr. William P. Lear."

52. Throughout the Stanford administration's deliberations about whether to authorize Shockley's research project on eugenics and dysgenics, many senior leaders expressed concerns about the funding that the university could receive, rather than other risks— whether ethical, reputational, or in terms of academic integrity. Early in 1968 Vice Provost Herbert L. Packer told Shockley to write a formal research proposal, recommending, "I would suggest therefore that you work out a proposed budget to accompany the project description which you send to the potential donor or donors." He went on to emphasize, "One last, mundane point: as you know, the University is heavily dependent upon the recovery of indirect costs incurred in the performance of sponsored research. I therefore hope that you will include in your budget appropriate provision for overhead costs." Shockley did, and the project was approved, despite the concerns raised by Stanford's own faculty with expertise in genetics and biology. Herbert L. Packer, "Memorandum from Herbert L. Packer, Vice Provost, to Professor William B. Shockley, Stanford Electronics Laboratories," January 8, 1968, box 89, folder 89, Stanford Project 2XX0601.

53. Paul J. Kern, "Letter to Prof. William Shockley, Stanford University, from Paul J. Kern," May 16, 1968, box 89, folder 89, Stanford Project 2XX0601.

54. "Paul J. Kern Dies; Aide of La Guardia," *New York Times*, July 6, 1974, https://www.nytimes.com/1974/07/06/archives/paul-j-kern-dies-aide-of-la-guardia.html; Paul J. Kern, "Letter to Mr. W. Palmer Fuller, Trustee of Stanford University, from Paul J Kern," July 25, 1968, box 89, folder 89, Stanford Project 2XX0601.

55. Bob Dylan, "It's Alright, Ma (I'm Only Bleeding)," official Bob Dylan site, 1985, https://www.bobdylan.com/songs/its-alright-ma-im-only-bleeding/.

56. L. Farrell McGhie, "Memorandum from L. Farrell McGhie, Associate Dean, School of Engineering, to Controller's Office, Subject: Research Account for Professor William Shockley," August 30, 1968, box 89, folder 89, Stanford Project 2XX0601.

57. L. Farrell McGhie, "Account Statement for Fund No. 172R042, Account No. 2-XX0-601-68117, Dept. Ref. No 72G010, Description: Gift-Instr., Rsch. & Libr.-Research to Reduce Racial Aspects of the Heredity Uncertainty," September 11, 1968, box 89, folder 89, Stanford Project 2XX0601.

58. W. Shockley, "Letter to Mr. Paul J. Kern from W. Shockley," September 17, 1968, box 89, folder 89, Stanford Project 2XX0601.

59. J. E. Wallace Sterling, "Letter to Mr. William P. Lear from J. E. Wallace Sterling, Office of the President, Stanford University," April 19, 1968, box 89, folder 89, Stanford Project 2XX0601.

60. Equal Justice Initiative, "Slavery in America: The Montgomery Slave Trade," 2018, 25 https://eji.org/wp-content/uploads/2020/05/slavery-in-america-report2.pdf.

61. Michael Kunzelman, "University Accepted $458K from Eugenics Fund," Associated Press, August 24, 2018, https://apnews.com/article/north-america-mo-state-wire-az-state-wire-pa-state-wire-tx-state-wire-a9791e6174374437b3bbe17af8b76215.

62. In 1891 Jordan became the first president of Stanford. He published *Blood of a Nation* in 1902. To defend those assertions that "the blood of a nation determines its history" and "the history of a nation determines its blood," he explained, "for a race of men or a herd of cattle are governed by the same laws of selection. Those who survive inherit the traits of their own actual ancestry." In 1915 he published the book *War and Breed*, where he wrote, "No matter what may be the form of government . . . the laws of heredity will work toward the formation of governing classes inherently superior to the sons of other men." David Starr Jordan, *The Blood of the Nation: A Study of the Decay of Races Through Survival of the Unfit* (Boston: American Unitarian Association, 1902), 12; David Starr Jordan, *War and the Breed: The Relation of War to the Downfall of Nations* (Boston: Beacon Press, 1915), 20–21.

63. United States Holocaust Memorial Museum, "Origins of Neo-Nazi and White Supremacist Terms and Symbols: A Glossary," accessed June 18, 2023, //www.ushmm.org /antisemitism/what-is-antisemitism/origins-of-neo-nazi-and-white-supremacist -terms-and-symbols.

64. Jill Briggs, "Human Betterment Foundation (1928–1942)," Arizona State University, *Embryo Project Encyclopedia*, accessed June 18, 2023, https://embryo.asu.edu/pages /human-betterment-foundation-1928-1942.

65. Jordan, *The Blood of the Nation*, 12; Jordan, *War and the Breed*, 20–21.

66. Shurkin, *Broken Genius*, 13.

67. Even the questions that determined Shockley's "intelligence" should have been thrown out as specious. For example, one of the problems on the test from 1908 juxtaposed two faces and asked respondents to determine which one was "prettier," with the supposed correct answer being the women who appeared to have European ancestry. Just as better crops or cattle could be bred, Terman believed that humankind should be engineered to be fairer and fitter, more efficient and with better hygiene, in order to ultimately create a smarter and more attractive superrace. OpenEd CUNY, "Psychology, Thinking and Intelligence, Measures of Intelligence," accessed June 18, 2023, https://opened.cuny.edu/courseware/lesson/48/student/?task=2; Mitchell Leslie, "The Vexing Legacy of Lewis Terman," *Stanford Magazine*, July 1, 2000, https:// stanfordmag.org/contents/the-vexing-legacy-of-lewis-terman. For more on this topic, see Jennifer L. Eberhardt, *Biased: Uncovering the Hidden Prejudice That Shapes What We See, Think, and Do* (New York: Penguin, 2019), 140–43.

68. Leslie, "The Vexing Legacy of Lewis Terman."

69. William Shockley, "Playboy Interview: William Shockley," *Playboy*, August 1980. https://nextbillionseconds.com/wp-content/uploads/2021/05/shockley_playboy _1980.pdf.

70. "Shockley, William," 1-inch videotape, 40:35, Stanford University Special Collections and University Archives, 2013, http://archive.org/details/cst_000029.

71. Art Harris, "The Shockley Suit," *Washington Post*, September 12, 1984, https://www .washingtonpost.com/archive/lifestyle/1984/09/12/the-shockley-suit/31817b93-4807 -4a16-aa3d-edd773ff9e56/.

72. John Cheves and Bill Estep, "Chapter 4: Disillusioned, Harry Caudill Blames 'Genetic Decline' in Eastern Kentucky," *Lexington (KY) Herald Leader*, August 24, 2019. https:// www.kentucky.com/article44394057.html.

73. Charles L. Sanders, "Letter from Charles L. Sanders to Dr. Shockley: FREED: Reprint, Corres. Out / John H. Johnson Correspondence In / Charles L. Sanders," August 22, 1974, box 106, folder 26, William Bradford Shockley Papers (SC0222).

74. "Bay Microfilm, Inc., Invoice No. 42481 to Dr. William Shockley McCullough Physics Bldg. Room 202 Stanford, CA. 94305," June 29, 1979, box 5, folder 5, William Bradford Shockley Papers (SC0222); "Bay Microfilm, Inc., Invoice No. 42481 to Dr. William Shockley McCullough Physics Bldg. Room 202 Stanford, CA. 94305," January 16, 1981, box 5, folder 7, William Bradford Shockley Papers (SC0222).

75. W. Shockley, "Letter to Mr. John Brown Cook from W. Shockley," October 26, 1970, box 89, folder 89, Stanford Project 2XX0601.

76. Many of the checks were made out to FREED or to Shockley directly, but on several occasions the checks were made out to Stanford University. That included a $25 donation from Samuel B. Batdorf from Corona del Mar, California, which was processed on June 2, 1969, a $5 donation from Raymond J. Marcus of Los Angeles, California, which was processed on May 2, 1972, and a $40 donation from Curtis Gray of Richmond, California, which was processed on March 23, 1972. Samuel B. Batdorf, "Check from Samuel B. Batdorf, Pay to the Order of Stanford University, for Twenty-Five and No/100," May 27, 1969; Raymond J. Marcus, "Check from Raymond J. Marcus, Pay to the Order of Stanford University, for Five + No," April 29, 1972; Raymond J. Marcus, "Check from Raymond J. Marcus, Pay to the Order of Stanford University, for Five + No," April 29, 1972; and Curtis Gray, "Check from Curtis Gray, Pay to the Order of Stanford University, Wm Shockley, for Forty Dollars," March 16, 1972; all in box 4, folder 2, William Bradford Shockley Papers (SC0222).

77. Bill Shockley's records reveal that he had raised at least $270,509.43 from 1968 to 1977, worth well over $2 million today. The Pioneer Fund alone gave $188,700 during these years. There were donations of at least $53,700 from other wealthy individuals and foundations, with some checks made out to Stanford, some to Shockley's lab at Stanford, others to Shockley personally, and still others to FREED. The first check from Paul J. Kern was for $1,000. William P. Lear's donation of $10,000 came early in this effort, along with $5,000 soon thereafter. The Cook Foundation gave $10,000 that went directly to Stanford in 1971; it then gave $7,500 to FREED in 1975 and $2,000 to FREED in 1976. Over the years, donations of $1,000 or more came on a semiregular basis from Wallace Knox (and the Beaver Foundation), Robert Klark Graham, the Kirby Foundation, and Lynn Keller.

    In terms of small-dollar donations (which paid for "membership dues" to the organization, articles that Shockley and his wife mailed out, and general small dollar support), FREED's accounting documents showed that the organization raised $12,189.82

in checks larger than $10 but smaller than $1,000 from January 1973 to December 1974, $430.75 in small-dollar checks in 1975, and Shockley deposited checks worth $9,991.05 from March 1976 through December 1977. Shockley's speeches brought in at least $4,595.34 during these years, with $350 from New York University, $550 from the University of Texas at Dallas, $693.50 from the University of Virginia, $700 from the University of Wisconsin, $1,050 from Virginia Tech, and $1,251.84 from Denison University. Motorola paid Shockley $902.37 in 1974 "to be used for Dr. Shockley's research," even though he'd focused on eugenics and dysgenics exclusively for nearly a decade. William Shockley, "Contributions to FREED January 1973 to June 1974," March 24, 1975; Robert Graham, "Letter to William Shockley," August 27, 1974; Robert Graham, "Check from the Foundation for the Advancement of Man, Pay to the Order of F.R.E.E.D. for Five Hundred and No/100," August 27, 1974; Carl Quackenbush, "Letter to Mrs. W. Shockley, Stanford Electronics Laboratories," August 12, 1974; D. R. Jones, "Checks from Motorola Inc. Semiconductor Products Division, Pay to the Order of Stanford University, for $402.37 and 500.00," August 12, 1974; Geo. Stephen Leonard, "Letter to Dr. William Shockley," July 23, 1974; Joseph P. Whitendi, "Check from New York University, Pay to the Order of Foundation for Research And Education on Eugenics And Dysgenics, for $325.00," April 29, 1974; F. M. Kirby, "Check from F. M. Kirby Foundation, Inc., Pay to the Order of Foundation for Research and Education on Eugenics and Dysgenics, for Twelve Hundred and 00/100," December 23, 1976; Lynn Keller, "Letter to William B. Shockley, FREED—Research Foundation—William Schockley, President (P.O. Box S, Stanford University—94305—Contribution," April 22, 1976 Harold Ripley, "Letter to Mr. William Shockley from Harold Ripley, President, the Cook Foundation, Inc., and Check from the Cook Foundation, Pay to the Order of F.R.E.E.D, for 2,000.00," January 10, 1976; F. M. Kirby, "Check from F. M. Kirby Foundation, Pay to the Order of Foundation for Research & Education on Eugenics and Dysgenics for Seven Hundred Fifty and 00/100," December 26, 1975; Wallace W. Knox, "Letter to Mr. William Shockley from Wallace W. Knox and Check from the Beaver Foundation, Pay to the Order of F.R.E.E.D., for $1,000.00," December 16, 1975; Geo. Stephen Leonard, "Letter to Dr. William Shockley," March 31, 1975; Louis Petito, "Check from Denison University, Pay to the Order Of F.R.E.E.D, for $1,251.84," February 11, 1975; Harold Ripley, "Letter to Mr. William Shockley from Harold Ripley, President, the Cook Foundation, Inc., and Check from the Cook Foundation, Pay to the Order of Foundation for Research and Education on Eugenics and Dysgenics for 7,500.00," January 10, 1976; and F. M. Kirby, "Check from F. M. Kirby Foundation, Pay to the Order of Foundation for Research & Education on Eugenics and Dysgenics, for Five Hundred and 00/100," December 26, 1974; all in box 4, folder 1, William Bradford Shockley Papers (SC0222), Department of Special Collections and University Archives, Stanford University Libraries, Stanford, Calif. Also D. R. Jones, "Checks from D. R. Jones, Motorola, Inc., Semiconductor Products Division, Pay to the Order of A. M. Poniatoff Chair—Stanford University, for Exactly 500 Dollars and 00 Cents and Exactly 402 Dollars and 37 Cents," December 5, 1973; and H. C. Ripley and J. B. Cook, "Check from Cook Foundation, Inc., Pay to the Order of Stanford University—Shockley Project, for Ten Thousand and No/100 Dollars," December 20, 1971; both in box 4, folder 2, William Bradford Shockley Papers (SC0222). In addition, William B. Shockley and S. Fallio, "Contract Agreement Between the University of Texas At Dallas and the Foundation for Research and Education on Eugenics and Dysgenics," August 30, 1978; W. Shockley, "Letter to Mr. Lynn Keller from W. Shockley," March 30, 1978; and Robert Graham, "Check from Robert K. Graham, Pay To The Order Of F.R.E.E.D, for One

Thousand Dollars and No/100," February 1, 1978; all in box 4, folder 5, William Bradford Shockley Papers (SC0222). Also "FREED Deposit Statement, American Program Bureau, Inc.," December 23, 1977; Geo. Stephen Leonard, "Letter to Dr. William Shockley from Geo. Stephen Leonard," July 18, 1977; "FREED Deposit Statement, Wallace W. Knox, Beaver Foundation," December 23, 1975; FREED Deposit Statement, Dr. Alton Ochsner," June 12, 1975; "FREED Deposit Statement, Mr. J. W. Kirkpatrick," March 14, 1975; "FREED Deposit Statement, Robert C. Graham," January 6, 1975; and "FREED Deposit Statement, Douglas A. Brown," August 23, 1974; all in box 5, folder 1, William Bradford Shockley Papers (SC0222). Further, William P. Lear, "Letter to Dr. W. Shockley from Wm. P. Lear," November 14, 1967; William P. Lear, "Letter to President J. E. Wallace Sterling from William P. Lear," March 29, 1968; J. E. Wallace Sterling, "Letter to Mr. William P. Lear from J. E. Wallace Sterling, Office of the President, Stanford University," April 19, 1968; Paul J. Kern, "Letter to Mr. W. Palmer Fuller, Trustee of Stanford University, from Paul J Kern," July 25, 1968; and W. Shockley, "Letter to Mr. John Brown Cook from W. Shockley," October 26, 1970, all in box 89, folder 89, Stanford Project 2XX0601, William Bradford Shockley Papers (SC0222). See also CPI, "CPI Inflation Calculator," U.S. Bureau of Labor Statistics, 2023, https://data.bls.gov/cgi-bin/cpicalc.pl?cost1=10000&year1=196803&year2=202304.

78. William Shockley, "FREED Price List," June 20, 1972, box 4, folder 1, William Bradford Shockley Papers (SC0222).

79. W. Shockley, "Memorandum from W. Shockley to Mr. Earl G. L. Cilley, Subject: Summer Student Assistants for the Project Entitled, Research on Methodology to Reduce the Environment-Heredity Uncertainty, Including Ethnic and Racial Aspects," April 13, 1970, box 89, folder 18, William Bradford Shockley Papers (SC0222).

80. Keith A. Davey, "Letter to Dr. Shockley from Keith A. Davey," April 5, 1970; and Victoria Wright, "Letter to Dr. Shockley from Victoria Wright," April 8, 1970; both in box 89, folder 18, William Bradford Shockley Papers (SC0222).

81. The political left and right in modern America both face uncomfortable histories when it comes to Bill Shockley (for more on the political left, see the story about Cass Canfield in this chapter). Froman was one of the students who worked for Shockley. During her work-study as a Stanford undergraduate, she assisted Shockley with his response to the National Academy of Sciences (NAS). According to an article in *Science* from May 8, 1970, "For more than four years now, William Shockley, a Stanford physicist who shared a Nobel Prize for his part in inventing the transistor, has been carrying on a dogged campaign to have the National Academy of Sciences encourage research in 'dysgenics,'" at which point another NAS member declared that the NAS should refocus its efforts on "the purpose of making clear to the public that Shockley's proposals are essentially unscientific and antisocial." Shockley responded by defending his work, writing, "I undertook research on existing research. This research led me inescapably to the opinion that the social and intellectual disadvantages of American Negroes arise primarily from genetic causes." Shockley and Froman discussed what the title of the response would be, and she advised him, "If you called this something like 'courses on dysgenics,' I think it would catch somebody's eye." She explained, "You're getting publicity about the dysgenics courses, because that's a more, you know, I don't know, a meatier target for newsmen to grab." Froman joined the board of directors of the National Rifle Association in 1992, was board president between 2005 and 2007, and holds a lifetime appointment on the NRA Executive Council. She also serves on the board of directors of Sturm, Ruger & Company, one of the largest U.S. gun manufacturers, where she chairs the Nominating and Corporate

Governance Committee and is a member of the Compensation and Risk Oversight Committees. Luther J. Carter, "NAS Again Says No to Shockley," *Science* 168, no. 3932 (May 8, 1970): 685, https://doi.org/10.1126/science.168.3932.685; "Side A: Parets, Sandy Froman Re Bohannon, KKIS / Side B: Parets, KKIS, Program Ray Bohannon, Feinstein Etc.," Stanford Digital Repository, September 2, 1973, https://purl.stanford.edu/jx706zz3051; "Side A: Hal Parets, P. N. McCluskey, Bob [Beyers?], Loeb, Holstein, Barton CIT, Loeb Sec, Sandy Re Hud Forum / B Side: Sandy Froman, ELS Re Cho Hainstock, Gary Re UCSB Poll, RT Osborne Re NAS," Stanford Digital Repository, September 16, 1973, https://purl.stanford.edu/rb932sn6002; "Side A: Sandy Froman, RJH / Side B: RJH, KLAT, Sandy Frohman, Bill Sweet," Stanford Digital Repository, April 12, 1974, https://purl.stanford.edu/rb932sn6002.

82. "An Appeal for FREED by Student Office Personnel," January 23, 1978, box 4, folder 5, William Bradford Shockley Papers (SC0222).

83. William Shockley, "Contributions to FREED January 1973 to June 1974," March 24, 1975, box 4, folder 1, William Bradford Shockley Papers (SC0222); "Weekly Gifts in School & Dept. Order: N55085-8 80400 Pioneer Fund," November 13, 1969, box 89, folder 31, William Bradford Shockley Papers (SC0222).

84. John C. Bonner, "Letter to Dr. William Shockley from Rev. John C. Bonner, Pastor, Christ Presbyterian Church," July 24, 1972; and O. Anthony, "Letter to Mr. Shockley from O. Anthony, with Donation Card to St. Andrew's Presbyterian Church, Newport Beach, Calif.," August 9, 1972; both in box 4, folder 2, William Bradford Shockley Papers (SC0222).

85. Richard S. Kjarval, "Letter to F.R.E.E.D.," November 20, 1976; and Richard S. Kjarval, "Envelope for Letter to F.R.E.E.D. from Richard S. Kjarval," November 20, 1976, both in box 4, folder 1, William Bradford Shockley Papers (SC0222); Ronald Herdman, "Letter to Dr. William Shockley, 202 McCullough Stanford University, from Ronald Herdman, with $1 Bill Enclosed," July 1, 1972, box 4, folder 2, William Bradford Shockley Papers (SC0222); and Robert J. Childers, "Letter from Robert J. Childers to Stanford University," February 13, 1972, box 90, Chron In/Chron Out (Jul 1971–Dec 1972) 1971–1972, William Bradford Shockley Papers (SC0222).

86. Jacques Guildbaud, "Letter to Dr. Shockley," January 25, 1974, box 4, folder 1, William Bradford Shockley Papers (SC0222); Staffan Norrman, "Letter to Stanford University from Staffan Norrman," April 14, 1972, box 4, folder 2, William Bradford Shockley Papers (SC0222); Thomas G. Draper, Jr., "Check from Professor Hugh Purcell, Pay to the Order of Foundation for Research A. Education Eugenics and Dysgenics, for $11.25," February 28, 1980, box 4, folder 5, William Bradford Shockley Papers (SC0222); Edward Schwartz, "Letter from Edward Schwartz to Dr. Shockley," April 1, 1972, box 90, Chron In/Chron Out (Jul 1971–Dec 1972) 1971–1972, William Bradford Shockley Papers (SC0222).

87. "I admire your courage and fortitude, and I hate myself for not standing up for the views we both share," wrote an anonymous donor who sent $15 in cash (the reason: "Now that the government is requiring banks to copy all checks over one hundred dollars and sice [sic] the banks routinely [sic] copy all checks regardless of amount I am sending cash"). Despite the anonymity, he reassured, "However, in my private contacts with people, I try to pop the current myths of the feasability [sic] of Negro and white amalgamation, unchecked Black population growth, etc." Another note, from Stockton, California, read in its entirety: "For the inclosed [sic] $1.00 please send your paper on the genetic inferiority of the Black race." A. P. Fraas, "Letter to FREED," August 3, 1974, box 4, folder 1, William Bradford Shockley Papers (SC0222);

Anonymous, "Letter to Dr. Shockley," July 23, 1974, box 4, folder 1, William Bradford Shockley Papers (SC0222); Walter R. McCall, "Letter from Walter R. McCall to Dr. William Shockley," February 17, 1972, box 90, Chron In/Chron Out (Jul 1971–Dec 1972) 1971–1972, William Bradford Shockley Papers (SC0222).

88. The letter from Northrop offered the following rationale: "The white race has conquered colored races throughout the course of history and are therefore superior by definition" and "or is there a record of a colored race enslaving a white race." He concluded with the following proposal: "Suppose the white races should combine and fight a war of extermination against the colored races, similar to the war of extermination which we fought against the Indians in this country in the 18th and 19th century, which race would survive and thereby prove its superiority?" John H. Northrop, "Letter from John H. Northrop, Research Biophysicist—Donner Laboratory, Professor Emeritus of the Rockefeller University, New York, and the University of California to Dr. W. Shockley," January 24, 1967, box 116, folder 35, Correspondence—University of California (some reprints) 1967–1969, William Bradford Shockley Papers (SC0222); Nobel Prize Outreach AB 2022, "John H. Northrop—Biographical," NobelPrize.org, December 1, 2022, https://www.nobelprize.org/prizes/chemistry/1946/northrop/biographical/.

89. John H. Northrop, "An Analysis Leading to a Recommendation Concerning Inquiry Into Eugenic Legislation," April 21, 1969, box 116, folder 35, Correspondence—University of California (some reprints) 1967–1969, William Bradford Shockley Papers (SC0222).

90. Northrop, "An Analysis"; Wolfgang Saxon, "Dr. Walter C. Alvarez, 93, Dies; Had Been Mayo Clinic Specialist," *New York Times*, June 20, 1978, https://www.nytimes.com/1978/06/20/archives/dr-walter-c-alvarez-93-dies-had-been-mayo-clinic-specialist-father.html; "John B. de C. M. Saunders, 1903–1991,—Biography," *A History of UCSF*, University of California San Francisco, 2022, https://history.library.ucsf.edu/saunders.html; J. Y. Smith, "Delinquency Authority Sheldon Glueck Dies," *Washington Post*, March 12, 1980. https://www.washingtonpost.com/archive/local/1980/03/12/delinquency-authority-sheldon-glueck-dies/e4cd9e2b-aba0-49db-a264-af60a5aff5d1/; National Academy of Sciences, *Biographical Memoirs: V. 61* (Washington, DC: National Academies Press, 1992), https://doi.org/10.17226/2037.

91. Joseph P. Whitendi, "Check from New York University, Pay to the Order of Foundation for Research and Education on Eugenics and Dysgenics, for $325.00," April 29, 1974; Geo. Stephen Leonard, "Letter to Dr. William Shockley," March 31, 1975; Geo. Stephen Leonard, "Letter to Dr. William Shockley," July 23, 1974; and Louis Petito, "Check from Denison University, Pay to the Order of F.R.E.E.D, for $1,251.84," February 11, 1975, all in box 4, folder 1, William Bradford Shockley Papers (SC0222). Also William B. Shockley and S. Fallio, "Contract Agreement Between the University of Texas at Dallas and the Foundation for Research and Education on Eugenics and Dysgenics," August 30, 1978, box 4, folder 5, William Bradford Shockley Papers (SC0222); Geo. Stephen Leonard, "Letter to Dr. William Shockley from Geo. Stephen Leonard," July 18, 1977, box 5, folder 1, William Bradford Shockley Papers (SC0222); CPI, "CPI Inflation Calculator," U.S. Bureau of Labor Statistics, 2023, https://data.bls.gov/cgi-bin/cpicalc.pl?cost1=550.00&year1=197503&year2=202304.

92. D. R. Jones, "Checks from Motorola Inc. Semiconductor Products Division, Pay to the Order of Stanford University, For $402.37 and 500.00," August 12, 1974, box 4, folder 1, William Bradford Shockley Papers (SC0222); D. R. Jones, "Checks from D. R. Jones, Motorola, Inc., Semiconductor Products Division, Pay to the Order of A. M. Poniatoff

Chair—Stanford University, for Exactly 500 Dollars and 00 Cents and Exactly 402 Dollars and 37 Cents," December 5, 1973, box 4, folder 2, William Bradford Shockley Papers (SC0222).

93.  Carl Quackenbush, "Letter to Mrs. W. Shockley, Stanford Electronics Laboratories," August 12, 1974, box 4, folder 1, William Bradford Shockley Papers (SC0222).

94.  Wallace W. Knox, "Letter to Mr. William Shockley from Wallace W. Knox and Check from the Beaver Foundation, Pay to the Order of F.R.E.E.D., for $1,000.00," December 16, 1975, box 4, folder 1, William Bradford Shockley Papers (SC0222); Boys & Girls Clubs of Oakland, "Our History," accessed June 18, 2023, http://www.bgcoakland.org/history.

95.  Robert Graham, "Letter to William Shockley," August 27, 1974, box 4, folder 1, William Bradford Shockley Papers (SC0222).

96.  F. M. Kirby, "Check from F. M. Kirby Foundation, Inc., Pay to the Order of Foundation for Research and Education on Eugenics and Dysgenics, for Twelve Hundred And 00/100," December 23, 1976; "Check from F. M. Kirby Foundation, Pay to the Order of Foundation for Research & Education on Eugenics and Dysgenics for Seven Hundred Fifty And 00/100," December 26, 1975; and "Check from F. M. Kirby Foundation, Pay to the Order of Foundation for Research & Education on Eugenics and Dysgenics, for Five Hundred And 00/100," December 26, 1974, all in box 4, folder 1, William Bradford Shockley Papers (SC0222).

97.  Stephanie Strom, "Fred Kirby, Who Built Giant Title Insurance Company, Is Dead at 91," *New York Times*, February 11, 2011, https://www.nytimes.com/2011/02/12/business/12kirby.html.

98.  Richard R. Valencia, *Dismantling Contemporary Deficit Thinking: Educational Thought and Practice* (New York: Routledge, 2010), 20.

99.  Pioneer Fund, "Pioneer Fund Inc," Candid, 2023, https://beta.candid.org/profile/7755839?keyword=The+Pioneer+Fund.

100.  Pioneer Fund, "Grantees," January 3, 2013, https://web.archive.org/web/20130103005545/http://www.pioneerfund.org:80/Grantees.html.

101.  Pioneer Pharmacy, "Generic Medications | Pioneer Pharmacy Delivers Generic Prescription Drugs, Generic Lipitor, Generic Singulair, Generic Nexium, Generic Celebrex and More!" March 7, 2015, https://web.archive.org/web/20150307165119/http://www.pioneerfund.org/; Pioneer Fund, "Crypto Trading: Pros and Cons [2022]," May 15, 2023, https://www.pioneerfund.org/.

102.  W. Shockley, "Letter to Mr. Harry F. Weyher from W. Shockley," December 1, 1969, box 89, folder 89, Stanford Project 2XX0601, William Bradford Shockley Papers (SC0222); "CPI Inflation Calculator." U.S. Bureau of Labor Statistics, 2022, https://www.bls.gov/data/inflation_calculator.htm.

103.  W. Shockley, "Memorandum to Dean J. M. Pettit from W. Shockley, Subject: Continuation of Project 2XX0601, William Bradford Shockley Papers (SC0222).

104.  Side A: Cont. Joe McCaughen, [Caudill?] Off., HFW Re $, Keith Davey, 1st Contact with Harry M. Caudill, 1974 Jul 11; Side B: Cont. Caudill, PA Diag., Art Brown, [Doris?] Elliot, Citron, Am. Pro. BU, Marsha Kartzman, 1974 Jul 29, audio cassette, William Shockley papers, 1860–2002 (inclusive), 1940–1988 (bulk), Stanford Digital Repository, 6:25; 7:50, 1973, William Shockley Papers, 1860–2002 (inclusive), 1940–1988 (bulk), https://purl.stanford.edu/jx706zz3051.

105.  J. M. Pettit, "Memorandum to Professor W. B. Shockley, from J. M. Pettit, Subject: Research Continuation," November 4, 1969, box 89, folder 31, William Bradford Shockley Papers (SC0222).

106.  L. Farrell McGhie, "Letter to Harry F. Weyher, Esq. from Vincent J. Cherry, Assistant Staff Legal Counsel, Office of the General Secretary, Stanford University," September 27, 1968, box 89, folder 89, Stanford Project 2XX0601, William Bradford Shockley Papers (SC0222).

107.  "Shockley, William," 1 inch videotape, 41:13, Stanford University Special Collections and University Archives, 2013.

108.  Art Harris, "The Shockley Suit," *Washington Post*, September 12, 1984, https://www .washingtonpost.com/archive/lifestyle/1984/09/12/the-shockley-suit/31817b93-4807 -4a16-aa3d-edd773ff9e56/.

109.  Franz Kuntz, Jenny Johnson, and Daniel Hartwig, "Guide to William Shockley Papers," Online Archive of California (OAC), October 2010, April 2023, https://oac.cdlib.org /findaid/ark:/13030/c8qf8tf9/entire_text/.

110.  "Yale Protestors Silence Shockley," *New York Times*, April 16, 1974, https://www .nytimes.com/1974/04/16/archives/yale-protesters-silence-shockley-disrupt-physicists -debate-on-his.html.

111.  "IEEE—The World's Largest Technical Professional Organization Dedicated to Advancing Technology for the Benefit of Humanity," accessed June 4, 2023, https:// www.ieee.org/; IEEE Medal of Honor, 1980;  IEEE 100th Anniversary Medal, 1984 (Awards, medals, plaques, certificates, souvenirs 1956–1986, 1980), box 69-70, 74, 172, William Bradford Shockley Papers (SC0222).

112.  Shurkin, *Broken Genius*, 272.

113.  Associated Press, "Controversial Nobel Winner Shockley Dies," *Yuba-Sutter Appeal-Democrat* (Marysville, CA), August 14, 1989.

## 6. Trust Us

1.  Steven Levy, *Facebook: The Inside Story* (New York: Blue Rider Press, 2020), 239, 43–44.

2.  Adam Fisher, *Valley of Genius: The Uncensored History of Silicon Valley (as Told by the Hackers, Founders, and Freaks Who Made It Boom)* (New York: Grand Central Publishing, 2018), 368–69.

3.  Cyrus Farivar, "Winamp's Woes: How the Greatest MP3 Player Undid Itself," Ars Technica, July 3, 2017, https://arstechnica.com/information-technology/2017/07/winamp -how-greatest-mp3-player-undid-itself/; S. F. Brickman, "Not-so-Artificial Intelligence," *Harvard Crimson*, October 23, 2003, https://www.thecrimson.com/article /2003/10/23/not-so-artificial-intelligence-for-his-high-school/.

4.  Brickman, "Not-so-Artificial Intelligence."

5.  Levy, *Facebook*, 43–44.

6.  Levy, 91.

7.  Zachary Seward, "Facebook Creator to Debut Wirehog," *Harvard Crimson*, October 20, 2004, https://www.thecrimson.com/article/2004/10/20/facebook-creator-to -debut-wirehog-thefacebookcom/; Steven Ranger. "What Is Cloud Computing? Everything You Need to Know About the Cloud Explained," *ZDNET*, February 25, 2022, https://www.zdnet.com/article/what-is-cloud-computing-everything-you-need-to -know-about-the-cloud/.

8.  Levy, *Facebook*, 33, 40.

9.  Jason Kincaid, "Dropbox Acquires the Domain Everyone Thought It Had: Dropbox .Com," *TechCrunch*, October 13, 2009, https://techcrunch.com/2009/10/13/dropbox

-acquires-the-domain-everyone-thought-it-had-dropbox-com/; Ingrid Angulo and Leslie Picker, "Dropbox Prices IPO at $21 per Share," CNBC, March 22, 2018, https://www.cnbc.com/2018/03/22/dropbox-will-price-ipo-at-21-per-share-source-says.html; S. Dixon, "Meta: Quarterly Net Income 2022," Statista, Meta's net income from first quarter 2010 to third quarter 2022 (in million U.S. dollars), October 27, 2022, https://www.statista.com/statistics/223289/facebooks-quarterly-net-income/.

10. Levy, *Facebook*.

11. Pulse, "Here's Where Facebook's First 20 Employees Are Now (FB)," *Business Insider*, June 13, 2017, https://businessinsider.com/tech/tech-heres-where-facebooks-first-20-employees-are-now-fb/33w4l07.

12. Adam Fisher, *Valley of Genius: The Uncensored History of Silicon Valley (As Told by the Hackers, Founders, and Freaks Who Made It Boom)* (New York: Grand Central Publishing, 2018), 356.

13. Levy, *Facebook*, 88, 94–95.

14. "How Eduardo Saverin Sold Facebook Ads in 2004," *Digiday*, August 20, 2012, https://digiday.com/media/how-eduardo-saverin-sold-facebook-ads-in-2004/.

15. Seward, "Facebook Creator to Debut Wirehog."

16. "Mark Zuckerberg at Startup School 2012," YouTube video, 8:48, 2013, https://www.youtube.com/watch?v=5bJi7k-y1Lo.

17. Levy, *Facebook*, 88, 92.

18. Levy, 95; M. G. Siegler. "Wirehog, Zuckerberg's Side Project That Almost Killed Facebook," *TechCrunch*, May 26, 2010. https://techcrunch.com/2010/05/26/wirehog/.

19. Sebastian Mallaby, *The Power Law: Venture Capital and the Making of the New Future* (New York: Penguin, 2022), 195.

20. M. G. Siegler, "Card Designer: The Inspiration for Zuckerberg's 'I'm CEO, Bitch'? Steve Jobs," *TechCrunch*, June 25, 2011, https://techcrunch.com/2011/06/25/im-ceo-bitch/; Sebastian Dillon, "Here's The Story Behind Mark Zuckerberg's 'I'm CEO, Bitch.' Business Card," *NextShark* (blog), March 24, 2015. https://nextshark.com/heres-the-story-behind-mark-zuckerbergs-im-ceo-bitch-business-card/.

21. Mallaby, *The Power Law*, 195.

22. David Kirkpatrick, *The Facebook Effect: The Inside Story of the Company That Is Connecting the World* (London: Virgin Books, 2010), 104–5.

23. Levy also retold another great story, about when Zuckerberg almost missed a meeting that Thiel *did* want him at. He'd run late due to car troubles, so Thiel solved the problem. He bought Zuckerberg a new car. "Keep it under $50,000," was the only guidance he gave. Zuckerberg chose an Infiniti. Levy, *Facebook*, 97.

24. "Bambi Francisco Interviews Mark Zuckerberg in 2005," video 95, Marquette University's Digital Commons: Zuckerberg Files, 2:08: Vator (YouTube), 2005, https://epublications.marquette.edu/zuckerberg_files_videos/95.

25. Meta, "Facebook Advertising Targeting Options," Meta for Business, 2022, https://en-gb.facebook.com/business/ads/ad-targeting.

26. S. Dixon, "Meta: Quarterly Segment Revenue 2021," Statista, June 2, 2022, https://www.statista.com/statistics/277963/facebooks-quarterly-global-revenue-by-segment/.

27. It was so special that no one even cared what Zuckerberg wore to that interview: black Abercrombie and Fitch gym shorts and a bright red shirt with the words "My mom thinks I am cool" emblazoned across it. It was a slight upgrade from the "My mommy told me to take down this page" page error from Facemash, and barely better than the first impression he'd made by wearing pajamas to meet with the partners at Sequoia Capital. Some saw this carefree attitude as careless. They deemed the disheveled

Silicon Valley style of a hoodie, gym shorts, and flip flops to be inappropriate for "real business." But others believed it indicated risk-taking, self-confidence, and disruption of the status quo. They celebrated the kids who would defy norms; in their attire, they saw the willingness to break rules. And no matter how anyone felt, with exponential growth and such addictive products, this new generation of coder kids could get away with wearing whatever they wanted. Mallaby, *The Power Law*, 195.


28. Who.is, "Thefacebook.com Whois Lookup," 2023, https://who.is/whois/thefacebook .com.

29. Who.is, "Catch27.com Whois Lookup," 2023, https://who.is/whois/catch27.com; Christina Tucker, "Trade Your Friends: Catching on to the Fastest Internet Craze Since Thefacebook, Catch27," *Dog Street Journal*, March 2005, https://digitalarchive.wm.edu /bitstream/handle/10288/375/2005-03.pdf.

30. "Chantelle Farmer," LinkedIn, 2023, https://www.linkedin.com/in/chantelle-farmer /details/experience/; "Lindsey Johnson," LinkedIn, 2023. https://www.linkedin.com/in /lindsey-johnson-863a635/details/experience/.

31. "Hey, Everybody. Huge Welcome to Catch27. The Game. The Social Scene. The Un-Lame Way to Meet People," Catch27, November 13, 2004. https://web.archive.org/web /20041113035656/http:/catch27.com/;

32. Leigh Remizowski, "Catch27.Com Boasts a 'Wicked Twist,'" *Pitt News* (blog), April 11, 2005, https://pittnews.com/article/32331/archives/catch27-com-boasts-a-wicked-twist/.

33. Sarah Mishkin, "Definitive Proof That I'm Hotter than You Are," *Yale Daily News*, March 4, 2005, https://yaledailynews.com/blog/2005/03/04/definitive-proof-that-im -hotter-than-you-are/.

34. Mishkin.

35. Remizowski, "Catch27.Com Boasts a 'Wicked Twist.'"

36. "Catch27.Com: Why 27?," Catch27, February 4, 2007, https://web.archive.org/web /20070204035824/http://www.catch27.com/why27.php; Joe D'Angelo, "Usher Makes Record-Breaking Debut Atop Albums Chart," MTV, March 31, 2004, https://www.mtv .com/news/fikq12/usher-makes-record-breaking-debut-atop-albums-chart; Callie Ahlgrim, "Only 22 Albums in History Have Sold 1 Million Copies in a Single Week— Here They All Are," *Insider*, October 26, 2022, https://www.insider.com/best-selling -albums-all-time-one-week-2021-10.

37. Jessica Anderson, "Catch 27," *Rocky Mountain Collegian*, March 2, 2005, https://web .archive.org/web/20211128031746/http://archives.collegian.com/2005/03/02/catch _27/.

38. Remizowski, "Catch27.Com Boasts a 'Wicked Twist.'"

39. Anderson, "Catch 27."

40. Natasha Dailey, "NFTs Ballooned to a $41 Billion Market in 2021 and Are Catching Up to the Total Size of the Global Fine Art Market," *Markets Insider*, June 6, 2022, https:// markets.businessinsider.com/news/currencies/nft-market-41-billion-nearing-fine -art-market-size-2022-1; Bijan Stephen, "Go Read This Story on the Real History of NFTs," Verge, April 2, 2021, https://www.theverge.com/2021/4/2/22364240/nft -blockchain-artist-hackathon-kevin-mccoy-anil-dash; Phil Rosen, "Remember When NFTs Sold for Millions of Dollars? 95% of the Digital Collectibles May Now Be Worthless," *Yahoo Finance*, September 20, 2023, https://finance.yahoo.com/news/remember -nfts-sold-millions-dollars-215646661.html.

41. "Catch27.Com: How to Play," Catch27, October 29, 2004. https://web.archive.org/web /20050507062607/http:/www.catch27.com/crib.php.

42. Tucker, "Trade Your Friends."

43. Anderson, "Catch 27."

44. Anderson.

45. Tucker, "Trade Your Friends."

46. Remizowski, "Catch27.Com Boasts a 'Wicked Twist.'"

47. Conor Boyland, "Confessions of an Instant Messenger," *Boston Globe*, February 11, 2005, http://archive.boston.com/news/globe/editorial_opinion/oped/articles/2005/02/11/confessions_of_an_instant_messenger/.

48. Anderson, "Catch 27."

49. Jessica Anderson, "Catch 27," *Collegian* Archives, April 19, 2021, https://web.archive.org/web/20210419004219/https:/archives.collegian.com/2005/03/02/catch_27/.

50. The buy-one-give-one approach made famous by TOMS shoes would impact the strategies of many businesses, including Bombas's socks (which gave socks to homeless people), Warby Parker's glasses (which donated glasses overseas), and Better World Books, which resold books rather than filling landfills (and used a share of the proceeds for literacy initiatives), among many others. As a B Corporation, TOMS pursued an Impact Business Model designed to create specific positive outcomes for humanity, and legally, it could prioritize purpose over short-term profits at the discretion of company leadership. Shawn Donnelly, "16 Brands That Use the TOMS Model of One-for-One Giving," InsideHook, November 28, 2016, https://www.insidehook.com/article/food-and-drink/16-brands-use-toms-model-one-one-giving; Anne Stych, "Toms Changes Its 'Buy One Give One' Charitable Model—Bizwomen," *Business Journals*, November 25, 2019, https://www.bizjournals.com/bizwomen/news/latest-news/2019/11/toms-changes-its-buy-one-give-one-charitable-model.html; "TOMS Certified B Corporation," B Lab Global, accessed June 18, 2023, https://www.bcorporation.net/en-us/find-a-b-corp/company/toms.

51. Stych, "Toms Changes."

52. Mishkin, "Definitive Proof."

53. Cindy Ruch, "Secret Life of Teens: 'Coolest Thing Ever,'" *Washingtonian*, August 1, 2007, https://www.washingtonian.com/2007/08/01/secret-life-of-teens-coolest-thing-ever/.

54. Mishkin, "Definitive Proof."

55. "I'm Not on Facebook, Thank You!" *Tufts Daily*, February 22, 2005, https://tuftsdaily.com/archives/2005/02/22/im-not-on-facebook-thank-you/.

56. Mike Fila, "New Site to Buy, Sell Friends Rivals Facebook, Web Trends," *Towerlight*, March 3, 2005, https://archives.towson.edu/Documents/Detail/the-towerlight-march-3-2005/162413.

57. Michael J. Rosenfeld, Reuben J. Thomas, and Sonia Hausen, "Disintermediating Your Friends: How Online Dating in the United States Displaces Other Ways of Meeting," *Proceedings of the National Academy of Sciences* 116, no. 36 (September 3, 2019), 17753–58, https://doi.org/10.1073/pnas.1908630116; Katharina Buchholz, "Infographic: How Couples Met," Statista Infographics, February 13, 2020, https://www.statista.com/chart/20822/way-of-meeting-partner-heterosexual-us-couples/.

58. "Catch27.Com: How to Play," Catch27, October 29, 2004. https://web.archive.org/web/20050507062607/http:/www.catch27.com/crib.php.

59. Peter Dizikes, "Study: On Twitter, False News Travels Faster than True Stories," *MIT News*, March 8, 2018, https://news.mit.edu/2018/study-twitter-false-news-travels-faster-true-stories-0308; Michael A. Cacciatore, "Misinformation and Public Opinion of Science and Health: Approaches, Findings, and Future Directions," *Proceedings of the*

*National Academy of Sciences* 118, no. 15 (April 13, 2021), https://doi.org/10.1073/pnas.1912437117.

60. Niraj Chokshi, "That Wasn't Mark Twain: How a Misquotation Is Born," *New York Times*, April 26, 2017, https://www.nytimes.com/2017/04/26/books/famous-misquotations.html.

61. Jennifer Saranow, "The Gated Online Community," *Wall Street Journal*, April 27, 2005, https://www.wsj.com/articles/SB111455358049717577.

62. "Friendster CEO Sassa Resigns," *Wall Street Journal*, May 25, 2005, https://www.wsj.com/articles/SB111703150724442928.

63. Julia Angwin, "News Corp. Agrees to Buy Web Firm Intermix Media," *Wall Street Journal*, July 19, 2005, https://www.wsj.com/articles/SB112169449806688282.

64. Lee Gomes, "Readers Spar Over Social-Networking Sites," *Wall Street Journal*, August 26, 2005, https://www.wsj.com/articles/SB112498208754923051.

65. Rebecca Buckman, "Too Much Information?" *Wall Street Journal*, December 8, 2005, https://www.wsj.com/articles/SB113400519172816925.

66. Hemant Taneja, "The Era of 'Move Fast and Break Things' Is Over," *Harvard Business Review*, January 22, 2019, https://hbr.org/2019/01/the-era-of-move-fast-and-break-things-is-over.

67. Charisse Jones, "E. Jean Carroll Was a Trailblazing Journalist Before Her Defamation Trial Against Trump," *USA Today*, April 28, 2023, https://www.usatoday.com/story/news/politics/2023/04/28/e-jean-carroll-journalist-writer-new-york/11752140002/.

68. Levy, *Facebook*, 91.

69. Brad King, "The Day the Napster Died," *Wired*, May 15, 2002, https://www.wired.com/2002/05/the-day-the-napster-died/.

70. Eamonn Forde, "Oversharing: How Napster Nearly Killed the Music Industry," *Guardian*, May 31, 2019, https://www.theguardian.com/music/2019/may/31/napster-twenty-years-music-revolution.

71. History.com editors, "The Death Spiral of Napster Begins," HISTORY, March 6, 2001, https://www.history.com/this-day-in-history/the-death-spiral-of-napster-begins.

72. Kevin Westcott et al., "2023 Digital Media Trends: Immersed and Connected," *Deloitte Insights*, April 14, 2023, https://www2.deloitte.com/us/en/insights/industry/technology/media-industry-trends-2023.html.

73. Jonathan Haidt and Jean Twenge, "Social Media and Mental Health: A Collaborative Review," unpublished manuscript, New York University, tinyurl.com/SocialMediaMentalHealthReview.

74. Luca Braghieri, Ro'ee Levy, and Alexey Makarin, "Social Media and Mental Health," *SSRN Scholarly Paper* (Rochester, NY, July 28, 2022), https://doi.org/10.2139/ssrn.3919760; MIT Sloan Office of Media Relations, "Academic Study Reveals New Evidence of Facebook's Negative Impact on the Mental Health of College Students," September 27, 2022, https://mitsloan.mit.edu/press/academic-study-reveals-new-evidence-facebooks-negative-impact-mental-health-college-students.

75. Peter Thiel, "The Straussian Moment," in *Politics and Apocalypse*, ed. Robert Hamerton-Kelly (East Lansing: Michigan State University Press, 2007), 209, http://www.jstor.org/stable/10.14321/j.ctt7zt6qq.9.

76. Sissi Cao, "Facebook's First Investor Peter Thiel Owns Less than 10K Shares After Latest Stock Dump," *Observer* (blog), February 11, 2020, https://observer.com/2020/02/peter-thiel-dump-facebook-stock-before-2020-election/.

77. Levy, *Facebook*, 88.

78. Tom Huddleston Jr., "Apple's App Store Is 10 Years Old—These Were the Most Popular Apps in 2008," CNBC, July 10, 2018, https://www.cnbc.com/2018/07/10/facebook-apple-app-store-most-popular-apps-of-2008.html.

79. Sara Atske, "Americans and Digital Knowledge," *Pew Research Center: Internet, Science & Tech* (blog), October 9, 2019, https://www.pewresearch.org/internet/2019/10/09/americans-and-digital-knowledge/.

80. Haidt and Twenge, "Social Media and Mental Health.

81. Lee Roberston, Jean M. Twenge, Thomas E. Joiner, and Kevin Cummins, "Associations Between Screen Time and Internalizing Disorder Diagnoses Among 9- to 10-Year-Olds," *Journal of Affective Disorders* 311 (August 15, 2022): 530–37, https://doi.org/10.1016/j.jad.2022.05.071; Jonathan Chu et al., "Screen Time and Suicidal Behaviors Among U.S. Children 9–11 Years Old: A Prospective Cohort Study," *Preventive Medicine*, February 17, 2023, 107452, https://doi.org/10.1016/j.ypmed.2023.107452.

82. Haidt and Twenge, "Social Media and Mental Health."

83. Nicholas Carr, *The Shallows: What the Internet Is Doing to Our Brains* (New York: Norton, 2020), 117.

84. Carr, 7.

85. Kevin Roose, "Do Not Disturb: How I Ditched My Phone and Unbroke My Brain," *New York Times*, February 23, 2019, https://www.nytimes.com/2019/02/23/business/cell-phone-addiction.html.

86. Mike Allen, "Sean Parker Unloads on Facebook: 'God Only Knows What It's Doing to Our Children's Brains,'" *Axios*, November 9, 2017, https://www.axios.com/2017/12/15/sean-parker-unloads-on-facebook-god-only-knows-what-its-doing-to-our-childrens-brains-1513306792.

87. Boyland, "Confessions of an Instant Messenger."

88. Allen, "Sean Parker Unloads on Facebook."

89. Allen.

90. Jonathan Haidt, "Why the Past 10 Years of American Life Have Been Uniquely Stupid," *Atlantic*, April 11, 2022, https://www.theatlantic.com/magazine/archive/2022/05/social-media-democracy-trust-babel/629369/.

91. Jonathan Haidt, "'Uniquely Stupid': Dissecting the Past Decade in America," interview by Hari Sreenivasan, *Amanpour & Co.*, PBS, April 18, 2022, https://www.pbs.org/wnet/amanpour-and-company/video/uniquely-stupid-dissecting-the-past-decade-in-america/, 1:24.

92. "Catch27.Com," Catch27, May 24, 2005, https://web.archive.org/web/20050529231615/http:/www.catch27.com/why27.php.

93. "Hey, Everybody. Huge Welcome to Catch27."

94. "The Knot Acquires GreatBoyfriends.Com; Lifestage Media &," Bloomberg, January 18, 2005, https://www.bloomberg.com/press-releases/2005-01-18/the-knot-acquires-greatboyfriends-com-lifestage-media.

95. To be clear, these agreements were included in a terms of service document that was over five thousand words long and then in a data policy that's another ten thousand words. Combined, that's thousands of words longer than this entire chapter. "Facebook Terms of Service," January 4, 2022, https://www.facebook.com/terms.php; "Meta Privacy Policy—How Meta Collects and Uses User Data," January 1, 2023, https://mbasic.facebook.com/privacy/policy/printable/.

96. Adam D. I. Kramer, Jamie E. Guillory, and Jeffrey T. Hancock, "Experimental Evidence of Massive-Scale Emotional Contagion Through Social Networks," *Proceedings*

*of the National Academy of Sciences* 111, no. 24 (June 17, 2014): 8788–90. https://doi.org
/10.1073/pnas.1320040111.

97.  Kramer, Guillory, and Hancock; Kashmir Hill, "Facebook Manipulated 689,003 Users'
Emotions for Science," *Forbes*, June 28, 2014, https://www.forbes.com/sites/kashmirhill
/2014/06/28/facebook-manipulated-689003-users-emotions-for-science/.

98.  Kramer, Guillory, and Hancock, "Experimental Evidence"; Hill, "Facebook Manipulated 689,003 Users' Emotions."

99.  "Editorial Expression of Concern: Experimental Evidence of Massivescale Emotional
Contagion Through Social Networks," *Proceedings of the National Academy of Sciences*
111, no. 29 (July 22, 2014): 10779, https://doi.org/10.1073/pnas.1412469111.

100.  "Senator Ben Sasse on Political Tribalism and Healing America's Divisions," YouTube
video, 3:15, 2018, https://www.youtube.com/watch?v=S6rYY585QKE.

101.  Jeff Horwitz and Deepa Seetharaman, "Facebook Executives Shut Down Efforts to
Make the Site Less Divisive," *Wall Street Journal*, May 26, 2020, https://www.wsj.com
/articles/facebook-knows-it-encourages-division-top-executives-nixed-solutions
-11590507499.

102.  Horwitz and Seetharaman.

103.  Horwitz and Seetharaman; Brandy Zadrozny, "'Carol's Journey': What Facebook
Knew About How It Radicalized Users," *NBC News*, October 22, 2021, https://www
.nbcnews.com/tech/tech-news/facebook-knew-radicalized-users-rcna3581.

104.  Horwitz and Seetharaman, "Facebook Executives Shut Down Efforts"; Zadrozny,
"'Carol's Journey.'"

105.  Timothy B. Lee, "Mark Zuckerberg's Audacious Plan to Control Facebook as He Sells
His Stock, Explained," *Vox*, April 28, 2016, https://www.vox.com/2016/4/28/11522148
/zuck-facebook-dictator-for-life.

106.  Michelle Fox, "Mark Zuckerberg's Control of Facebook Is like a Dictatorship: Cal-
STRS," CNBC, May 10, 2018, https://www.cnbc.com/2018/05/10/mark-zuckerbergs
-control-of-facebook-is-like-a-dictatorship-calstrs.html.

107.  Alex Kantrowitz, Mac Ryan, and Charlie Warzel, "Facebook Executive in 2016: 'Maybe
Someone Dies in a Terrorist Attack Coordinated on Our Tools,'" *BuzzFeed News*,
March 29, 2018, https://www.buzzfeednews.com/article/ryanmac/growth-at-any-cost
-top-facebook-executive-defended-data.

108.  Roose, "Do Not Disturb."

109.  Haidt, "Why the Past 10 Years of American."

110.  "James W. Breyer and Mark E. Zuckerberg Interview," October 26, 2005, Stanford University, Stanford Center for Professional Development: Entrepreneurial Thought
Leaders Seminar, YouTube video, 39:48, 2005, https://www.youtube.com/watch?v=WA
_ma359Meg&ab_channel=DonnaKline; transcript, https://epublications.marquette
.edu/zuckerberg_files_transcripts/116/.

111.  Sheera Frenkel and Cecilia Kang, *An Ugly Truth: Inside Facebook's Battle for Domination* (New York: HarperCollins, 2021), 26.

112.  Andrew Marantz, "The Dark Side of Techno-Utopianism," *New Yorker*, September 23,
2019, https://www.newyorker.com/magazine/2019/09/30/the-dark-side-of-techno
-utopianism.

113.  "Mike Fenton," IMDb, 2022, https://www.imdb.com/name/nm0272067/.

114.  Thiel, "The Straussian Moment"; Cao, "Facebook's First Investor."

115.  "Breyer and Zuckerberg Interview," 57:00.

116.  "Breyer and Zuckerberg Interview," 1:00:02.

117.  "Breyer and Zuckerberg Interview," 1:00:02. Facebook would soon find Zuckerberg's number two, Sheryl Sandberg. When she retired over a decade later, headlines ran, "Sheryl Sandberg Was Facebook's Adult in the Room, but It's Always Been a Zuckerberg Production." Even so, Sandberg was so important to Facebook that when the company went public, the so-called key man clause included not only Zuckerberg but also COO Sheryl Sandberg. Ari Levy, "Sheryl Sandberg Was Facebook's Adult in the Room, but It's Always Been a Zuckerberg Production," CNBC, June 1, 2022, https://www.cnbc.com/2022/06/01/sheryl-sandberg-was-adult-in-room-of-zuckerberg-production-at-facebook.html.

## 7. Anything It Likes

1.  Jemima Kiss, "Ten Years of Online Advertising with Google Adwords," *Guardian*, October 25, 2010, https://www.theguardian.com/media/2010/oct/25/advertising-google-adwords.

2.  Roger Montti, "Google's 'Don't Be Evil' No Longer Prefaces Code of Conduct," *Search Engine Journal*, May 20, 2018, https://www.searchenginejournal.com/google-dont-be-evil/254019/.

3.  The quirky name they eventually chose was a nonsense word invented by mathematician Edward Kasner's nine-year-old nephew: goo-goo-le became "googol," which Kasner used to describe an extremely long number: 1 followed by 100 zeros (or $10^{100}$). This child's neologism would not only become one of America's greatest tech companies, but the 3.5-million-square-foot Mountain View corporate headquarters, the Googleplex, also echoed Kasner's writings (in addition to being a portmanteau of "Google" and "complex"). The mathematician extrapolated from his nephew's logic and imagined an even bigger number, a googolplex: 1 with a googol of zeros, or $10^{googol}$. Google, "Mountain View (Global HQ)," 2022, https://careers.google.com/locations/mountain-view/; United States Security and Exchange Commission, "Google Inc.," 2022, https://www.sec.gov/Archives/edgar/data/1288776/000119312513028362/d452134d10k.htm.

4.  Google, "Google's Mission, Values & Commitments—Google," accessed June 18, 2023, https://about.google/intl/ALL_us/commitments/.

5.  Sergey Brin and Lawrence Page, "The Anatomy of a Search Engine," accessed June 18, 2023, http://infolab.stanford.edu/~backrub/google.html.

6.  "Letter from the Founders," *New York Times*, April 29, 2004, https://www.nytimes.com/2004/04/29/business/letter-from-the-founders.html.

7.  "Letter from the Founders."

8.  Kristen Purcell, Joanna Brenner, and Lee Rainie, "Search Engine Use 2012: Main Findings," *Pew Research Center: Internet, Science & Tech* (blog), March 9, 2012, https://www.pewresearch.org/internet/2012/03/09/main-findings-11/; Statista Research Department, "Global Search Engine Market Share 2022," Statista, December 1, 2022, https://www.statista.com/statistics/216573/worldwide-market-share-of-search-engines/.

9.  Statista Research Department, "Google: Advertising Revenue 2021," Statista, December 2, 2022, https://www.statista.com/statistics/266249/advertising-revenue-of-google/.

10.  Ginny Marvin, "A Visual History of Google Ad Labeling in Search Results," *Search Engine Land*, January 28, 2020, https://searchengineland.com/search-ad-labeling-history-google-bing-254332.

11. Jon Porter, "Google's Ads Just SMX Advanced 2016 Keynote—Google & SEM (and Biggest Search)," *Search Engine Land*, 4:38, accessed June 18, 2023, https://www.facebook.com/watch/live/?ref=watch_permalink&v=10153602873496669.

12. "Letter from the Founders."

13. Kamil Franek | Business Analytics, "What Companies Google & Alphabet Own: Visuals & Full List," October 16, 2019, https://www.kamilfranek.com/what-companies-alphabet-google-owns/.

14. Tiago Bianchi, "Google Revenue 2002–2022," Statista, February 13, 2023, https://www.statista.com/statistics/266206/googles-annual-global-revenue/.

15. Tiago Bianchi, "Alphabet: Global Annual Revenue by Segment 2022," Statista, accessed June 18, 2023, https://www.statista.com/statistics/633651/alphabet-annual-global-revenue-by-segment/.

16. Tim Soulo, "90.63% of Content Gets No Traffic from Google. And How to Be in the Other 9.37% [New Research for 2020]," SEO, *Aref Blog*, January 31, 2020, https://ahrefs.com/blog/search-traffic-study/.

17. CompaniesMarketcap, "Alphabet (Google) (GOOG)," *Market Capitalization*, 2022. https://companiesmarketcap.com/alphabet-google/marketcap/.

18. David Temkin, "Charting a Course Towards a More Privacy-First Web," Google, March 3, 2021, https://blog.google/products/ads-commerce/a-more-privacy-first-web/.

19. Sara Morrison, "Google Is Done with Cookies, but That Doesn't Mean It's Done Tracking You," *Vox*, March 3, 2021, https://www.vox.com/recode/2021/3/3/22311460/google-cookie-ban-search-ads-tracking.

20. Suzanne Vranica, Patience Haggin, and Schechnar Sam, "Google Delays Cookie Removal to Late 2023," *Wall Street Journal*, June 24, 2021, https://www.wsj.com/articles/google-delays-cookie-removal-to-late-2023-11624542064; Kyle Wiggers, "Google Delays Move Away from Cookies in Chrome to 2024," *TechCrunch*, July 27, 2022, https://techcrunch.com/2022/07/27/google-delays-move-away-from-cookies-in-chrome-to-2024/.

21. Jonathan A. Obar and Anne Oeldorf-Hirsch, "The Biggest Lie on the Internet: Ignoring the Privacy Policies and Terms of Service Policies of Social Networking Services," *Information, Communication & Society* 23, no. 1 (July 3, 2018): 128–47, https://doi.org/10.1080/1369118X.2018.1486870.

22. Obar and Oeldorf-Hirsch.

23. Obar and Oeldorf-Hirsch.

24. GDPR.EU, "What Is GDPR, the EU's New Data Protection Law?" November 7, 2018, https://gdpr.eu/what-is-gdpr/.

25. David Berreby, "Click to Agree with What? No One Reads Terms of Service, Studies Confirm," *Guardian*, March 3, 2017, https://www.theguardian.com/technology/2017/mar/03/terms-of-service-online-contracts-fine-print.

26. "Sonic Drive-In," *Terms of Service; Didn't Read*, May 18, 2019, https://edit.tosdr.org/points/6751.

27. Jen Caltrider, Misha Rykov, and Zoë MacDonald, "What Data Does My Car Collect About Me and Where Does It Go?," *Mozilla Foundation* (blog), September 6, 2023, https://foundation.mozilla.org/en/privacynotincluded/articles/what-data-does-my-car-collect-about-me-and-where-does-it-go/.

28. "Bible Gateway," *Terms of Service; Didn't Read*, August 18, 2019, https://edit.tosdr.org/points/7793.

29. "Khan Academy," *Terms of Service; Didn't Read*, Grade E, accessed June 18, 2023, https://tosdr.org/en/service/1815.

30. "National Geographic," *Terms of Service; Didn't Read*," Grade D, accessed June 18, 2023, https://tosdr.org/en/service/1742.

31. BBC, *Terms of Service; Didn't Read*, June 30, 2020, https://edit.tosdr.org/points/7845.

32. J. Clement, "Digital Advertising Revenue of Leading Online Companies 2022," Statista, August 29, 2023, https://www.statista.com/statistics/205352/digital-advertising-revenue -of-leading-online-companies/.

33. Charlie Warzel and Ash Ngu, "Google's 4,000-Word Privacy Policy Is a Secret History of the Internet," *New York Times*, July 10, 2019, https://www.nytimes.com /interactive/2019/07/10/opinion/google-privacy-policy.html.

34. "This Service May Collect, Use, and Share Location Data—Google," *Terms of Service; Didn't Read*, January 6, 2021, https://edit.tosdr.org/points/5841.

35. Michael Sawh, "What Is Google Going to Do with Your Fitbit Data? Anything It Likes," *Wired UK*, December 2, 2022, https://www.wired.co.uk/article/google-buying-fitbit -health-data-privacy.

36. Vanessa Hand Orellana, "Fitbit Charge 4 Review: A Better Fitness Tracker Without the Bulk," CNET, February 12, 2021, https://www.cnet.com/tech/mobile/fitbit-charge-4 -review-better-fitness-tracker-built-in-gps-better-sleep-tracking-slim-design/.

37. "Facebook," *Terms of Service; Didn't Read*, accessed June 18, 2023, https://tosdr.org/en /service/facebook.

38. Matt Burgess, "Meta's $1.3 Billion Fine Is a Strike Against Surveillance Capitalism," *Wired*, May 22, 2023, https://www.wired.com/story/meta-gdpr-fine-ireland/.

39. Jonathan Vanian, "Why Data Is the New Oil," *Fortune*, July 12, 2016, https://fortune .com/2016/07/11/data-oil-brainstorm-tech/.

40. "The World's Most Valuable Resource Is No Longer Oil, but Data," *Economist*, May 6, 2017, https://www.economist.com/leaders/2017/05/06/the-worlds-most-valuable-resource -is-no-longer-oil-but-data.

41. Shoshana Zuboff, "Big Other: Surveillance Capitalism and the Prospects of an Information Civilization." *Journal of Information Technology* 30, no. 1 (2015): 75–89. https:// doi.org/10.1057/jit.2015.5.

42. U.S. House of Representatives, "Written Testimony of Professor Shoshana Zuboff Before the Committee on House Administration U.S. House of Representatives for the Hearing on Big Data: Privacy Risks and Needed Reforms in the Public and Private Sector," February 16, 2022, https://docs.house.gov/meetings/HA/HA00/20220216/114403 /HHRG-117-HA00-Wstate-ZuboffS-20220216.pdf.

43. Sergey Brin and Lawrence Page, "The Anatomy of a Search Engine," http://infolab .stanford.edu/, accessed June 18, 2023, http://infolab.stanford.edu/~backrub/google .html.

44. "The World Wide Web Project,"accessed June 18, 2023, http://info.cern.ch/hypertext /WWW/TheProject.html.

45. Google Finance. "Google Class A Shares," accessed June 18, 2023. https://www.google .com/finance/quote/GOOGL:NASDAQ?window=MAX.

46. "Written Testimony of Professor Shoshana Zuboff."

47. Roger Simon, "Washington Is Hollywood for the Ugly," *Politico*, April 29, 2014, https:// www.politico.com/story/2014/04/white-house-correspondents-dinner-roger-simon -106118.

48. Kori Schulman, "'The President's Speech' at the White House Correspondents' Dinner," whitehouse.gov, May 1, 2011, https://obamawhitehouse.archives.gov/blog/2011/05 /01/president-s-speech-white-house-correspondents-dinner; "Death of Osama Bin

Laden," Barack Obama Presidential Library, November 4, 2016, https://www.obama library.gov/timeline.

49. Dan Pfeiffer, "President Obama's Long Form Birth Certificate," whitehouse.gov, April 27, 2011, https://obamawhitehouse.archives.gov/blog/2011/04/27/president-obamas -long-form-birth-certificate.

50. The Global Disinformation Lab at the University of Texas at Austin has conducted an in-depth study of recent increases in distrust in the election process and the spread of conspiracy theories (as well as the roles that American politicians and foreign propagandists have played in spreading them). Their research is well worth reviewing in the context of the rumors about Obama and the influence of disinformation in public opinion and partisan politics over the past decade. See Austin Merkel et al., "Bellwether Series 1: Disinformation: Fueling Election Distrust in the American Public in the 21st Century," Global Disinformation Lab, March 28, 2023, https://gdil.org /bellwether-series-1-disinformation-fueling-election-distrust-in-the-american-public -in-the-21st-century/; see also Austin Merkel et al., "Bellwether Series 2: Disinformation: Fueling Election Distrust in the American Public in the 21st Century," Global Disinformation Lab, May 5, 2023, https://gdil.org/bellwether-series-2-disinformation -fueling-election-distrust-in-the-american-public-in-the-21st-century/.

51. Barack Obama, "Birth Certificate Correspondence," April 22, 2011, https://obama whitehouse.archives.gov/sites/default/files/rss_viewer/birth-certificate-correspon- dence.pdf.

52. "President Obama Remarks at 2015 WHCA Dinner," accessed June 18, 2023, https://www .c-span.org/video/?c4535549/president-obama-remarks-2015-whca-dinner; Roxanne Roberts, "I Sat Next to Donald Trump at the Infamous 2011 White House Correspondents' Dinner," *Washington Post*, April 28, 2016, https://www.washingtonpost.com/lifestyle/style /i-sat-next-to-donald-trump-at-the-infamous-2011-white-house-correspondents-dinner /2016/04/27/5cf46b74-0bea-11e6-8ab8-9ad050f76d7d_story.html.

53. "President Obama Remarks."

54. "President Obama Remarks"; Garrett M. Graff, "'I'd Never Been Involved in Anything as Secret as This,'" *Politico*, April 30, 2021, https://www.politico.com/news/magazine /2021/04/30/osama-bin-laden-death-white-house-oral-history-484793.

55. "Trump: An American Dream Episode 4," *Netflix*, 13:28, 2018, https://www.netflix.com /ng/title/80206395.

56. Joshua Gillin, "PolitiFact—Bush Says Trump Was a Democrat Longer than a Republican 'in the Last Decade,'" *@politifact*, August 24, 2015, https://www.politifact.com /factchecks/2015/aug/24/jeb-bush/bush-says-trump-was-democrat-longer-republican -las/.

57. "Rona Barrett's 1980 Interview of Donald Trump," *Washington Post*, accessed June 18, 2023, https://www.washingtonpost.com/wp-stat/graphics/politics/trump-archive/docs /rona-barrett-1980-interview-of-donald-trump.pdf.

58. Ryan Struyk, "67 Times Donald Trump Tweeted About the 'Birther' Movement," *ABC News*, September 16, 2016, https://abcnews.go.com/Politics/67-times-donald-trump -tweeted-birther-movement/story?id=42145590.

59. Pfeiffer, "President Obama's Long Form Birth Certificate."

60. "Trump: An American Dream Episode 4," 13:28.

61. "CNN Perspectives: Elon Musk, Multi-Millionaire Entrepreneur," YouTube video, 2017, https://www.youtube.com/watch?v=x3tlVE_QXm4.

62. "Trump: An American Dream Episode 4."

## 8. Words Do Matter


1.  Will Drabold, "Read Peter Thiel's Speech at the Republican Convention," *Time*, July 21, 2016, https://time.com/4417679/republican-convention-peter-thiel-transcript/; "RNC 2016 Schedule of Events and Speakers," *Politico*, July 18, 2016, https://www.politico.com/story/2016/07/rnc-2016-schedule-of-events-and-speakers-225704.

2.  Thiel's "And we won" declaration came while the Russian leader had espoused dangerously imperial ambitions.

3.  Drabold, "Read Peter Thiel's Speech."

4.  David Streitfeld, "Peter Thiel to Donate $1.25 Million in Support of Donald Trump," *New York Times*, October 16, 2016, https://www.nytimes.com/2016/10/16/technology/peter-thiel-donald-j-trump.html.

5.  Mark Wilson, "Why We Had No Idea Trump Would Win," *Fast Company*, November 17, 2016, https://www.fastcompany.com/3065750/why-we-had-no-idea-trump-would-win.

6.  Bartie Scott, "Silicon Valley Is Furious About Peter Thiel's $1.25 Million Donation to Trump's Campaign," *Inc.*, October 16, 2016, https://inc.com/library/bartie-scott-silicon-valley-calls-for-thiels-dismisall-from-facebook.

7.  David Morris, "Peter Thiel Pledges $1.25 Million to Support Donald Trump," *Fortune*, October 16, 2016, https://fortune.com/2016/10/16/peter-thiel-donald-trump-support/.

8.  Maya Kosoff, "Jeff Bezos: Peter Thiel Is 'a Contrarian,' and Contrarians 'Are Usually Wrong,'" *Vanity Fair*, October 20, 2016, https://www.vanityfair.com/news/2016/10/jeff-bezos-peter-thiel-trump-contrarian.

9.  Sara Ashley O'Brien, "Just 52 Tech Workers Donated to Trump's Campaign," CNNMoney, June 6, 2016, https://money.cnn.com/2016/06/06/technology/crowdpac-donations-silicon-valley-trump/index.html.

10.  Ari Levy, "Tech Companies Gave 60 Times More to Clinton than to Trump," *NBC News*, November 7, 2016, https://www.nbcnews.com/storyline/2016-election-day/silicon-valley-donated-60-times-more-clinton-trump-n679156.

11.  Joanna Pearlstein, "Techies Donate to Clinton in Droves. To Trump? Not So Much," *Wired*, August 31, 2016, https://www.wired.com/2016/08/techies-donate-clinton-droves-trump-not-much/.

12.  Deepa Seetharaman, "Facebook Employees Pushed to Remove Trump's Posts as Hate Speech," *Wall Street Journal*, October 21, 2016. http://www.wsj.com/articles/facebook-employees-pushed-to-remove-trump-posts-as-hate-speech-1477075392.

13.  Elizabeth Dwoskin, Craig Timberg, and Tony Romm, "Zuckerberg Once Wanted to Sanction Trump. Then Facebook Wrote Rules That Accommodated Him," *Washington Post*, June 29, 2020, https://www.washingtonpost.com/technology/2020/06/28/facebook-zuckerberg-trump-hate/.

14.  Dwoskin, Timberg, and Romm.

15.  Sheera Frenkel et al., "Delay, Deny and Deflect: How Facebook's Leaders Fought Through Crisis," *New York Times*, November 14, 2018, https://www.nytimes.com/2018/11/14/technology/facebook-data-russia-election-racism.html.

16.  Mike Isaac and Kate Conger, "Facebook Bars Trump Through End of His Term," *New York Times*, January 7, 2021, https://www.nytimes.com/2021/01/07/technology/facebook-trump-ban.html.

17.  Will Feuer, "Trump Sues Facebook, Twitter for 'Censorship of the American People,'" *New York Post*, July 7, 2021, https://nypost.com/2021/07/07/donald-trump-to-sue-mark-zuckerberg-jack-dorsey-report/.

18. Patrick May, "Text of Peter Thiel Speech on Trump and the 'Crazy Condition of Our Country,'" *Mercury News* (blog), October 31, 2016, https://www.mercurynews.com /2016/10/31/peter-thiel-on-trump-and-the-crazy-condition-of-our-country/; "Peter Thiel," National Press Club, October 31, 2016, https://www.press.org/events/peter-thiel.

19. "Mark Zuckerburg Comments on Peter Thiel Controversy Regarding Trump Donation," *Hacker News*, accessed June 18, 2023, https://news.ycombinator.com/item?id =12739582; Jennifer Earl, "Facebook CEO Mark Zuckerberg Defends Peter Thiel's Support of Donald Trump," *CBS News*, October 19, 2016, https://www.cbsnews.com/news /facebook-ceo-mark-zuckerberg-defends-peter-thiels-support-of-donald-trump/.

20. Cory Doctorow, "VERIFIED Mark Zuckerberg Defends Facebook's Association with Peter Thiel," Boing Boing, October 19, 2016, https://boingboing.net/2016/10/19/mark -zuckerberg-defends-facebo.html.

21. David O. Sacks and Peter Thiel, *The Diversity Myth: Multiculturalism and Political Intolerance on Campus* (Oakland, CA: Independent Institute, 1998), 111, 112–13, 114, 175.

22. Sacks and Thiel, 114.

23. Julia Carrie Wong, "Peter Thiel, Who Gave $1.25m to Trump, Has Called Date Rape 'Belated Regret,'" *Guardian*, October 21, 2016, https://www.theguardian.com /technology/2016/oct/21/peter-thiel-support-donald-trump-date-rape-book.

24. Jodi Kantor, "For Stanford Class of '94, a Gender Gap More Powerful than the Internet," *New York Times*, December 22, 2014, https://www.nytimes.com/interactive/2014 /12/23/us/gender-gaps-stanford-94.html.

25. Miranda Doyle, "Thomas Changes Plea to Guilty," *Stanford Daily*, January 6, 1992, https://archives.stanforddaily.com/1992/01/06.

26. Minal Hajratwala, "Thomas Plans to Plead Not Guilty," *Stanford Daily*, October 7, 1991, https://archives.stanforddaily.com/1991/10/07; D'Layne L. Kerr, "Stanford Is Still Sexist," *Stanford Daily*, June 14, 1992, https://archives.stanforddaily.com/1992/06/14.

27. Peter Robinson, "Student Arraigned for Statutory Rape," *Stanford Daily*, October 3, 1991, https://stanfordpolitics.org/wp-content/uploads/2018/01/Stanford_Daily_19911003 _0001.pdf.

28. Hajratwala, "Thomas Plans to Plead Not Guilty."

29. Robinson, "Student Arraigned for Statutory Rape."

30. David Sacks, "From 'Statutory Rape' to Statutory Red Tape: A Wrap-Up to the Stuart Thomas Drama," *Stanford Review* 8, no. 3 (January 21, 1992): 7, Dept. of Special Collections and University Archives, Stanford University Libraries, Stanford, Calif.

31. Max Chafkin, "The Contrarian: Peter Thiel and Silicon Valley's Pursuit of Power," in *The Contrarian: Peter Thiel and Silicon Valley's Pursuit of Power* (London: Bloomsbury, 2021), 35.

32. Stanford University News Service, "Student Arrested on Sexual Assault Charges," October 1, 1991, https://web.archive.org/web/20221104101740/https://news.stanford.edu /pr/91/911001Arc1133.html.

33. Sacks, "From 'Statutory Rape' to Statutory Red Tape."

34. United States Sentencing Commission, "Quick Facts—Sexual Abuse Offenders," 2021, https://www.ussc.gov/sites/default/files/pdf/research-and-publications/quick-facts /Sexual_Abuse_FY21.pdf.

35. Rainn, "Statistics," 2022, https://rainn.org/statistics; Sascha Cohen, "How a Book Changed the Way We Talk About Rape," *Time*, October 7, 2015, https://time.com /4062637/against-our-will-40/.

36. Miranda Doyle, "Thomas' Degree Delayed 2 Years," *Stanford Daily*, September 30, 1992, https://archives.stanforddaily.com/1992/01/10.

37. Mike Ehrman and Keith Rabois, "You Absolutely Know You Go to Stanford When . . . ," *Stanford Review* 8, no. 3 (January 21, 1992): 10; Dept. of Special Collections and University Archives, Stanford University Libraries, Stanford, Calif.

38. David Dirks, "Freshman Loses Housing for Insensitive Conduct," *Stanford Daily*, May 23, 1988, https://archives.stanforddaily.com/1988/05/23.

39. Stanford University, LGBT Community Resources Center (1986–1991), audiovisual material, Stanford Digital Repository (Bomb threat, 1991), Records, https://purl .stanford.edu/cf755jv7075, 0:20.

40. Stanford University News Service, "Officials Condemn Homophobic Incident; No Prosecution Planned," February 12, 1992, https://web.archive.org/web/20220809032152 /https://news.stanford.edu/pr/92/920212Arc2432.html; "New Light Shed on Otero Epithet Case; Officials, Students Clarify Circumstances," *Stanford Daily*, February 5, 1992, https://archives.stanforddaily.com/1992/02/05.

41. "Stanford_Daily_19911003," *Stanford Daily*, October 3, 1991, https://stanfordpolitics.org /wp-content/uploads/2018/01/Stanford_Daily_19911003_0001.pdf.

42. Ehrman and Rabois, "You Absolutely Know."

43. Kara Swisher, "Zenefits CEO David Sacks Apologizes for Parts of a 1996 Book He Co-Wrote with Peter Thiel That Called Date Rape 'Belated Regret,'" *Vox*, October 24, 2016, https://www.vox.com/2016/10/24/13395798/zenefits-ceo-david-sacks-apologizes-1996 -book-co-wrote-peter-thiel-date-rape-belated-regret.

44. Ryan Mac, "Donald Trump Supporter Peter Thiel Apologizes for Past Book Comments on Rape," *Forbes*, October 25, 2016, https://www.forbes.com/sites/ryanmac/2016/10/25 /peter-thiel-apologizes-for-past-book-comments-on-rape-and-race/.

45. Sacks and Thiel, *The Diversity Myth*, 113.

46. Peter Thiel, "The Diversity Myth" (Tenth Edmund Burke Award for Service to Culture and Society, April 27, 2023), *New Criterion*, June 2023, https://newcriterion.com /issues/2023/6/the-diversity-myth.

47. Peter Thiel: "'Diversity Myth' 30 Years Later," YouTube video, 7:10; 4:00, 2023, https:// www.youtube.com/watch?v=PjHinnC1xCE.

48. Every Peter Thiel Video, "Peter Thiel Discusses His Book *The Diversity Myth* in 1996 [C-Span]," YouTube video, 28:43, 29:10, 29:57, 2017, https://www.youtube.com/watch?v =qTPOBEdc7OI&ab_channel=EveryPeterThielVideo.

49. "Shockley, William," 1-inch videotape, 41:13, Stanford University Special Collections and University Archives, 2013, http://archive.org/details/cst_000029; Art Harris, "The Shockley Suit," *Washington Post*, September 12, 1984, https://www.washingtonpost .com/archive/lifestyle/1984/09/12/the-shockley-suit/31817b93-4807-4a16-aa3d -edd773ff9e56/; Intercollegiate Studies Institute, "Peter Thiel," accessed June 18, 2023, https://isi.org/spotlight/peter-thiel/.

50. Every Peter Thiel Video, 29:10, 29:05.

51. Don Kazak, "Taking Aim at Stanford," November 29, 1995, *paloaltoonline*, https://www .paloaltoonline.com/weekly/morgue/cover/1995_Nov_29.4COVER29.html.

52. David Sacks and Peter Thiel, "Happy Indigenous Peoples' Day | David O. Sacks," Independent Institute, October 12, 1995, https://www.independent.org/news/article.asp ?id=299.

53. Thiel Foundation, "The Thiel Fellowship," accessed June 18, 2023, http://thielfellowship .org/.

54. Sacks and Thiel, "Happy Indigenous Peoples' Day."

55. Sacks and Thiel.

56. Kazak, "Taking Aim at Stanford."

57. Stanford Graduate School of Business, "Condoleezza Rice," accessed June 18, 2023, https://www.gsb.stanford.edu/faculty-research/faculty/condoleezza-rice.

58. Susan B. Glasser, "Condi Rice on Trump: 'Words Do Matter,'" *Politico*, May 15, 2017, http://politi.co/2ByPW8M.

59. Carlos Lozada, "Condoleezza Rice's New Book Is a Repudiation of Trump's 'America First' Worldview," *Washington Post*, May 11, 2017, https://www.washingtonpost.com /news/book-party/wp/2017/05/11/condoleezza-rices-new-book-is-a-repudiation-of -trumps-america-first-worldview/.

60. Glasser, "Condi Rice on Trump."

61. Sacks and Thiel, *The Diversity Myth*, 163.

62. At other points throughout her career, Rice was referred to as a Sovietologist, since her area of expertise and research was the USSR, but that was not the context for the descriptor when used here alongside her official title. Sacks and Thiel, *The Diversity Myth*, 163; "Condi in Crisis," *Forbes*, August 28, 2008, https://www.forbes.com/forbes /2008/0915/098.html

63. Global Nonviolent Action, "Stanford Students Campaign for Divestment from Apartheid South Africa, U.S., 1977," Global Nonviolent Action Database, accessed June 18, 2023, https://nvdatabase.swarthmore.edu/content/stanford-students-cam paign-divestment-apartheid-south-africa-us-1977.

64. "CPI Inflation Calculator," 2023, https://data.bls.gov/cgi-bin/cpicalc.pl?cost1 =10%2 C000.00&year1=197703&year2=202304.

65. "Free South Africa Fund's Shutdown Symbolizes End of an Era," *Stanford University News*, May 15, 1995, https://web.archive.org/web/20220813090315/https://news.stanford .edu/pr/95/950515Arc5231.html.

66. The organizers of the fund included Bill Handley, Mike McFaul, and Susan Rice, all three of whom were Rhodes Scholars. Handley would go on to become an English professor at the University of Southern California, where he'd be recognized for his scholarship on the American West. McFaul joined the Stanford faculty in 1995, where he'd teach political science. During a leave of absence, he served as in the Obama administration in senior roles, advising the president on the National Security Council and then as U.S. ambassador to the Russian Federation. Susan Rice taught at American University's School of International Service and served in Obama's White House, as national security advisor and U.S. permanent representative to the United Nations. In Joe Biden's White House, she'd lead the Domestic Policy Council. These Stanford alums and their peers would continue to raise money for the divestment campaign until 1995, the same year *The Diversity Myth* went to print. "Free South Africa Fund's Shutdown"; "Faculty Profile > USC Dana and David Dornsife College of Letters, Arts and Sciences," Dornsife.usc.edu, accessed June 18, 2023, https://dornsife.usc .edu/cf/faculty-and-staff/faculty.cfm?pid=1003327; "Michael McFaul | Political Science," Politicalscience.stanford.edu, accessed June 18, 2023, https://politicalscience .stanford.edu/people/michael-mcfaul; American University, "Distinguished Visiting Research Fellow," accessed June 18, 2023, https://www.american.edu/sis/faculty/srice .cfm; Tyler Pager, "Biden Taps Susan Rice for Top White House Domestic Policy Job," *Politico*, December 10, 2020, https://www.politico.com/news/2020/12/10/biden-taps -susan-rice-for-top-white-house-domestic-policy-job-444231.

67. Jesse Oxfeld, "Free South Africa Fund Balance Is Turned Over to the Amy Biehl Fund," *Stanford Daily*, May 19, 1995, https://archives.stanforddaily.com/1995/05/19.

68. "Free South Africa Fund's Shutdown Symbolizes End of an Era," *Stanford News*, May 15, 1995, https://news.stanford.edu/pr/95/950515Arc5231.html; Jeremy Quach,

"Stanford's Rich History of Divestment Movements," *Stanford Daily*, February 12, 2015, https://stanforddaily.com/2015/02/11/stanfords-rich-history-of-divestment-movements /; "Stanford Students Campaign for Divestment from Apartheid South Africa, U.S., 1977," Global Nonviolent Action Database, accessed June 18, 2023, https://nvdatabase .swarthmore.edu/content/stanford-students-campaign-divestment-apartheid-south -africa-us-1977.

69. Morgan Winsor, "'Apartheid and Jim Crow Are Really No Different': Why George Floyd's Death Reverberated in Africa," *ABC News*, July 12, 2020, https://abcnews.go .com/International/apartheid-jim-crow-george-floyds-death-reverberated-africa /story?id=71556630; Benjamin Zinkel, "Apartheid and Jim Crow: Drawing Lessons from South Africa's Truth and Reconciliation," 2019, 28.

70. Sacks and Thiel, *The Diversity Myth*, 105–6.

71. Julie Lythcott-Haims, "My Conversation with Peter Thiel About Apartheid . . . and Its Unfolding Aftermath," *Thoughts and Ideas* (blog), May 30, 2017, https://medium.com /indian-thoughts/my-conversation-with-peter-thiel-about-apartheid-and-its -aftermath-3fdf4249b08d.

72. Laura Sydell, "Major Trump Backer's Alleged Positive Comments About Apartheid Stir Anger," NPR, November 3, 2016, https://www.npr.org/sections/alltechconsidered/2016 /11/03/500569299/major-trump-backers-positive-comments-about-apartheid-stir -anger.

73. Peter Thiel, "The Education of a Libertarian," *Cato Unbound*, April 13, 2009, https:// www.cato-unbound.org/2009/04/13/peter-thiel/education-libertarian.

74. "Peter Thiel and Bambi Francisco Roizen Conversation on Religion, Culture and Technology," Youtube video, 25:12, 2021, https://www.youtube.com/watch?v=y1qf2MCzneU; Matt Qvortrup, "Plebiscites," in *The Princeton Encyclopedia of Self-Determination*, accessed June 18, 2023, https://pesd.princeton.edu/node/571.

75. Sacks and Thiel, *The Diversity Myth*, 101–2, 105–6, 163, 174.

76. Thiel, "The Education of a Libertarian."

77. "Peter Thiel Commencement Speech, Hamilton College, May 2016 (Transcript)," *Entrepreneur*, May 23, 2016, https://www.entrepreneur.com/growing-a-business/peter -thiel-commencement-speech-hamilton-college-may-2016/276303.

78. Book Haven, "Memorial Service and Reception for René Girard on Tuesday, Jan. 19. Be There," January 16, 2016. https://bookhaven.stanford.edu/2016/01/memorial-service -and-reception-for-rene-girard-on-tuesday-jan-19-be-there/.

79. Quentin Hardy, "René Girard, French Theorist of the Social Sciences, Dies at 91," *New York Times*, November 11, 2015, https://www.nytimes.com/2015/11/11/arts/international /rene-girard-french-theorist-of-the-social-sciences-dies-at-91.html.

80. Peter Thiel, "An Introductory Essay," in *Politics and Apocalypse*, ed. Robert Hamerton-Kelly (East Lansing: Michigan State University Press, 2007), 1–2, http://www.jstor.org /stable/10.14321/j.ctt7zt6qq.9.

81. Peter Thiel, "The Straussian Moment," in Hamerton-Kelly, *Politics and Apocalypse*, 209.

82. Thiel, "The Straussian Moment."

83. Richard Feloni, "Peter Thiel Explains How an Esoteric Philosophy Book Shaped His Worldview," *Business Insider*, November 10, 2014, https://www.businessinsider.com /peter-thiel-on-rene-girards-influence-2014-11.

84. Peter Thiel with Blake Masters, *Zero to One: Notes on Startups, or How to Build the Future* (New York: Penguin Random, 2014).

85. Lora Kolodny, "Why a Nonprofit Backs Dropping Out of School," *Wall Street Journal*, December 19, 2013, http://online.wsj.com/article/SB1000142405270230333020457 9250142741126468.html.

86. Crunchbase, "Blake Masters—Crunchbase Person Profile," accessed June 18, 2023, https://www.crunchbase.com/person/blake-master.

87. Noah Lanard, "Newly Uncovered Emails Show Blake Masters' Long History of Hating Democracy," *Mother Jones*, September 7, 2022, https://www.motherjones.com /politics/2022/09/blake-masters-anti-democratic-stanford-emails-arizona-kelly -thiel/.

88. Hans-Hermann Hoppe, *Democracy—the God That Failed: The Economics and Politics of Monarchy, Democracy and Natural Order* (New York: Routledge, 2018), 71.

89. Hoppe, *Democracy*, 67; Hans-Hermann Hoppe, "The Political Economy of Monarchy and Democracy, and the Idea of a Natural Order," *Journal of Libertarian Studies* 11, no. 2 (1995): 94–121; Hans-Hermann Hoppe, "Political Economy of Monarchy and Democracy," Mises Institute, January 22, 2010, https://mises.org/library/political -economy-monarchy-and-democracy.

90. Thiel with Masters, *Zero to One*, 181.

91. Blakemasters, "Peter Thiel's CS183: Startup—Class 18 Notes Essay," *Tumblr* (blog), June 6, 2012, https://blakemasters.tumblr.com/post/24578683805/peter-thiels-cs183 -startup-class-18-notes.

92. "Leviticus 16—New International Version," *Bible Gateway—New International Version*, 2023, https://www.biblegateway.com/passage/?search=Leviticus%2016&version=NIV.

93. Thiel, "The Straussian Moment," 209.

94. Peter Thiel and Russell Berman, "Sovereignty and the Limits of Globalization and Technology," accessed June 18, 2023, https://www.documentcloud.org/documents/5677718 -Thiel-German-270-Syllabus; Stanford University Explore Courses, "German 270: Sovereignty and the Limits of Globalization and Technology," *Stanford Bulletin*, 2019–2018, https://explorecourses.stanford.edu/search?view=catalog&filter-coursestatus-Active =on&q=GERMAN%20270:%20Sovereignty%20and%20the%20Limits%20of%20Globalization%20and%20Technology&academicYear=20182019; Shannon Liao, "Peter Thiel Returns to Stanford to Teach a German Course on the Limits of Globalization," Verge, July 25, 2018, https://www.theverge.com/2018/7/25/17614764/peter-thiel-stanford-teach -german-course-globalization.

95. Peter Thiel and Russell Berman, "Sovereignty and the Limits of Globalization and Technology," accessed June 18, 2023, https://www.documentcloud.org/documents /5677718-Thiel-German-270-Syllabus

96. Secretary for Internal Affairs Geoff May, "Application for New Zealand Citizenship CIT200100002 SP WP 1," Department of Internal Affairs, New Zealand, June 22, 2011, https://www.dia.govt.nz/diawebsite.nsf/Files/Peter-Thiel-release-29-June-2017/$file /Peter-Thiel-release-29-June-2017.pdf.

97. Ryan Mac, "Why Does Peter Thiel Want Maltese Citizenship?" *New York Times*, October 20, 2022, https://www.nytimes.com/2022/10/20/us/peter-thiel-malta-citizenship -ca.html.

98. May, "Text of Peter Thiel Speech on Trump"; National Press Club, "Peter Thiel."

99. Susan B. Glasser, "Condi Rice on Trump: 'Words Do Matter,'" *Politico*, May 15, 2017, http://politi.co/2ByPW8M.

100. "The Crisis of Parliamentary Democracy," *MIT Press* (blog), accessed June 18, 2023, https://mitpress.mit.edu/9780262691260/the-crisis-of-parliamentary-democracy/.

101. Thiel and Berman, "Sovereignty and the Limits of Globalization"; Liao, "Peter Thiel Returns to Stanford."

102. Claudia Koonz, *The Nazi Conscience* (New York: Belknap Press, 2003), 59–60, 208.

103. "Commission on Unalienable Rights: Member Bios," *United States Department of State* (blog), August 2020, https://2017-2021.state.gov/commission-on-unalienable-rights -member-bio/.

104. Russell Berman and Peter Thiel, "Peter Thiel 'Stagnation or Progress' Syllabus, Stanford 2020 Course (German 277)," *Hacker News*, accessed June 18, 2023, https://news .ycombinator.com/item?id=24607896; Russell Berman and Peter Thiel, "Technology and Culture Between Stagnation or Progress," accessed June 18, 2023, https://explore courses.stanford.edu/search?q=Technology+and+Culture+Between+Stagnation+or +Progress&view=catalog&page=0&filter-coursestatus-Active=on&collapse= &academicYear=20202021.

105. "Carl Schmitt—The Crisis of Parliamentary Democracy," *Democracy Paradox*, August 22, 2020, http://democracyparadox.com/2020/08/22/carl-schmitt-the-crisis-of -parliamentary-democracy/; Carl Schmitt, *The Crisis of Parliamentary Democracy* (Cambridge, MA: MIT Press, 1988), 9.

106. Schmitt, *The Crisis of Parliamentary Democracy*, 28.

107. National WWII Museum, "How Did Adolf Hitler Happen?," New Orleans, accessed June 18, 2023, https://www.nationalww2museum.org/war/articles/how-did-adolf-hitler -happen.

108. Jana Leichsenring, "German Bundestag—National Socialism (1933–1945)," German Bundestag, accessed June 18, 2023. https://www.bundestag.de/en/parliament/history /parliamentarism/third_reich/third_reich-200358.

109. Thiel, "The Education of a Libertarian."

110. "The End of the Future with Peter Thiel," YouTube video, 2:33, November 18, 2022, https://www.youtube.com/watch?v=ibR_ULHYirs.

111. Washington University Libraries, "Norman Rockwell and Race: Complicating Rockwell's Legacy," *University Libraries | Washington University in St. Louis* (blog), November 23, 2016, https://library.wustl.edu/news/norman-rockwell-and-race-complicating -rockwells-legacy/.

112. A top-secret memo produced for Winston Churchill deemed America First "the most effective weapon at the disposal of the enemy for the purpose of keeping the United States out of the war." Due to its anti-Semitic undertones (and often overtones), the British deemed the group "the raw material of American Fascism . . . the present tactics and methods of action of the movement reveal it was the American Fifth Column, sowing racial hatred and accentuating internal division."

It should also be noted that the twentieth century's America First movement began with elite universities and renowned corporations, not extremist groups. It was started by Robert Douglas Stuart, Jr., a Yale Law student whose father had founded Quaker Oats, and the company gave office space rent-free to the organization for its headquarters in downtown Chicago. He was joined by a Yale Law student named Kingman Brewster, who became the COO to his CEO. They called their group "The Emergency Committee to Defend America First," but that was a mouthful. They needed something more memorable for a propaganda campaign. They shortened it to the America First Committee. Stuart would become the CEO of Quaker Oats and served on the boards of First National Bank of Chicago, United Airlines, John Deere & Company, and Molson Companies of Canada. Brewster would one day become Yale's provost, then its president. Despite his campaigning to keep America out of World War II,

Brewster became the U.S. ambassador to the United Kingdom under President Jimmy Carter. Stephen R. Strahler, "Former Quaker Oats CEO Robert Stuart Jr. Has Died," *Crain's Chicago Business*, May 12, 2014, https://www.chicagobusiness.com/article /20140512/NEWS01/130629779/former-quaker-oats-ceo-robert-stuart-jr-has-died; Bradley W. Hart, *Hitler's American Friends: The Third Reich's Supporters in the United States* (New York: St. Martin's, 2018), 162–63, 229.

113. Charles Lindbergh, "Neutrality and War," October 13, 1939, http://www.charles lindbergh.com/americanfirst/speech3.asp.

114. National Archives, "FDR's 'Day of Infamy' Speech," August 15, 2016, https://www .archives.gov/publications/prologue/2001/winter/crafting-day-of-infamy-speech .html.

115. Katelyn Fossett, "The Black Box of Peter Thiel's Beliefs," *Politico*, September 20, 2021, https://www.politico.com/news/magazine/2021/09/20/peter-thiel-book-facebook -trump-jd-vance-blake-masters-josh-hawley-513121.

116. Max Chafkin, *The Contrarian: Peter Thiel and Silicon Valley's Pursuit of Power* (London: Bloomsbury, 2021), 321.

117. In 2021 Thiel received the Lifetime Achievement Award from the Atlas Society, a non-profit that promotes Ayn Rand's ideas. He began the speech by admitting, "I first read *The Fountainhead, Atlas Shrugged* when I was an undergraduate in the late '80s, and to be honest at the time I thought it was a little bit too negative, a little bit too pessimistic." Over time, though, Thiel grew to appreciate Rand more, which led him to struggle with whether to call himself a Libertarian or a Randian. In his words: "If you tell people you're Libertarian, you're saying you're not a Republican, and you're sort of signaling that you're a loser, you're never actually going to win." Thiel debated how much further he could go down that spectrum: "Saying you're Libertarian is the socially safe thing to do. But saying you're a crazed Ayn Rand follower, that's always dangerous, that's never, that's never a socially safe thing to do."
For Thiel, defying social norms was part of the appeal, and it took courage to say what was seemed taboo, even unspeakable. He closed his Atlas Society speech with "a fantasy of what a celebration of individuals might look like," where he described a ticker-tape parade in Manhattan "not for some sort of socialist collective, like the healthcare workers," during the global pandemic. He didn't even dream of celebrating an individual that everyone could agree on, "some person who wasn't even American, so that was sort of a safe individual, like Nelson Mandela or maybe the Pope." Instead, his candidate was Satoshi Nakamoto, the pseudonym used by the person who developed Bitcoin. Atlas Society, "The 2021 Atlas Society Gala: Peter Thiel's Speech," YouTube video, 0:56; 2:20; 25:10, January 27, 2022, https://www.youtube.com/watch?v =YK3Tzx-S264&ab_channel=TheAtlasSociety%2CLtd.

118. George Packer, "No Death, No Taxes," *New Yorker*, November 20, 2011, https://www .newyorker.com/magazine/2011/11/28/no-death-no-taxes.

119. "Thiel and Roizen Conversation," 41:14. Interestingly, Roizen was the same reporter who had interviewed Mark Zuckerberg sixteen years before, when he'd made this claim about Thefacebook: "The time spent on the site was just around the highest on the Internet." "Bambi Francisco Interviews Mark Zuckerberg in 2005," 2:08, https:// epublications.marquette.edu/zuckerberg_files_videos/95.

120. "Thiel and Roizen Conversation," 35:58.

121. "Thiel and Roizen Conversation," 36:47.

122. Jennifer Burns, *Goddess of the Market: Ayn Rand and the American Right* (Oxford: Oxford University Press, 2009), 42–43.

123. "Thiel and Roizen Conversation," 37:25.

124. "Thiel and Roizen Conversation," 38:53, 36:24.

125. Thiel, "The Straussian Moment," 209.

126. Stephen Mark Heim, "The End of Scapegoating," Institute for Faith and Learning at Baylor University (2016), 25, https://www.baylor.edu/content/services/document.php /264317.pdf.

127. "Matthew 20:16—New International Version," *Bible Gateway*, accessed June 18, 2023, https://www.biblegateway.com/passage/?search=Matthew%2020%3A16&version =NIV.

128. "Romans 12:1—New International Version," *Bible Gateway*, accessed June 18, 2023, https://www.biblegateway.com/passage/?search=Romans%2012%3A1&version=NIV.

129. Heim, "The End of Scapegoating," 25.

130. "Micah 6," *Bible Gateway*, https://www.biblegateway.com/verse/en/Micah%206%3A8; "Luke 10:25–37—New International Version," *Bible Gateway*, https://www.biblegateway .com/passage/?search=Luke%2010%3A25-37&version=NIV; "Matthew 5:38–48—New International Version," *Bible Gateway*, https://www.biblegateway.com/passage/?search =Matthew%205%3A38-48&version=NIV; and "Matthew 18:22," *Bible Gateway*, https:// www.biblegateway.com/verse/en/Matthew%2018%3A22, all accessed June 18, 2023.

131. Sacks and Thiel, *The Diversity Myth*, 105–6.

132. Lythcott-Haims, "My Conversation with Peter Thiel."

133. "Teacher, which is the greatest commandment in the Law?" Jesus replied: "'Love the Lord your God with all your heart and with all your soul and with all your mind.' This is the first and greatest commandment. And the second is like it: 'Love your neighbor as yourself.' All the Law and the Prophets hang on these two commandments." "Matthew 22:36–40 NIV—"Teacher, Which Is the Greatest," *Bible Gateway*, accessed June 18, 2023, https://www.biblegateway.com/passage/?search=Matthew%2022%3A36-40 &version=NIV.

134. Biblestudytools, "1 Peter 5:2–12—NLT Bible—Care for the Flock That God Has Entrusted to You," 2023, https://www.biblestudytools.com/nlt/1-peter/passage/?q=1 +peter+5:2-12.

135. "John 1—New International Version," *Bible Gateway*, accessed June 18, 2023, https:// www.biblegateway.com/passage/?search=John%201&version=NIV.

136. "Mark 15:16–20—New International Version," *Bible Gateway*, accessed June 18, 2023, https://www.biblegateway.com/passage/?search=Mark%2015%3A16-20&version =NIV.

137. "Mark 15:6–11—New International Version," *Bible Gateway*, accessed June 18, 2023, https://www.biblegateway.com/passage/?search=Mark%2015%3A6-11&version =NIV.

138. "Mark 15:9–15—New International Version," *Bible Gateway*, accessed June 18, 2023, https://www.biblegateway.com/passage/?search=Mark%2015%3A9-15&version =NIV.

139. Peter Thiel, "Your Suffrage Isn't in Danger. Your Other Rights Are," *Cato Unbound*, forum, May 1, 2009, https://www.cato-unbound.org/2009/05/01/peter-thiel/suffrage -isnt-danger-other-rights-are/.

140. Heim, "The End of Scapegoating," 25–26, https://www.baylor.edu/content/services /document.php/264317.pdf.

141. Yaser Haddara, "Matthies Urges Closer, More Thoughtful Look at Incident," *Stanford Daily*, February 7, 1992, https://archives.stanforddaily.com/1992/02/07?page=12§ion =MODSMD_ARTICLE39.

## 9. Rape with an Engraved Invitation


1.  Voytek, "Rides of Glory," *Uber Blog*, March 26, 2012, https://web.archive.org/web /20140827195715/http://blog.uber.com/ridesofglory.
2.  Voytek, "Rides of Glory."
3.  Voytek "Rides of Glory."
4.  Voytek "Rides of Glory."
5.  Leena Rao, "Uber Brings Its Disruptive Car Service to Chicago," *TechCrunch*, September 22, 2011, https://techcrunch.com/2011/09/22/uber-brings-its-disruptive-car-service-to-chicago/.
6.  Kashmir Hill, "'God View': Uber Allegedly Stalked Users for Party-Goers' Viewing Pleasure (Updated)," *Forbes*, October 3, 2014, https://www.forbes.com/sites/kashmirhill /2014/10/03/god-view-uber-allegedly-stalked-users-for-party-goers-viewing-pleasure /?sh=5a62243c3141.
7.  Peter Sims, "Can We Trust Uber? I Was a Big Fan of the Uber Service . . . by Peter Sims," Silicon Guild, September 26, 2014, https://thoughts.siliconguild.com/can-we -trust-uber-c0e793deda36.
8.  Charlie Warzel and Johana Bhuiyan, "'God View': Uber Investigates Its Top New York Executive for Privacy Violations," *BuzzFeed News*, November 19, 2014, https://www .buzzfeed.com/johanabhuiyan/uber-is-investigating-its-top-new-york-executive-for -privacy.
9.  Patrick McGuire, "Uber's 'God View' Was Once Available to Drivers," *Vice*, November 20, 2014, https://www.vice.com/en/article/ypw5n7/ubers-god-view-was-once-available -to-drivers.
10. Warzel and Bhuiyan, "'God View.'"
11. Charlie Warzel, "Sexist French Uber Promotion Pairs Riders with 'Hot Chick' Drivers," *BuzzFeed News*, December 3, 2014, https://web.archive.org/web/20141203022042 /http://www.buzzfeed.com/charliewarzel/french-uber-bird-hunting-promotion -pairs-lyon-riders-with-a.
12. Sarah Lacy, "The Horrific Trickle Down of Asshole Culture: Why I've Just Deleted Uber from My Phone," *PandoDaily*, October 22, 2014, https://web.archive.org/web /20141203022003/http://pando.com/2014/10/22/the-horrific-trickle-down-of-asshole -culture-at-a-company-like-uber/.
13. Mike Isaac, "*Super Pumped: The Battle for Uber* (New York: Norton, 2019), 122.
14. Ben Smith, "Uber Executive Suggests Digging Up Dirt on Journalists," *BuzzFeed News*, November 18, 2014, https://www.buzzfeed.com/bensmith/uber-executive-suggests -digging-up-dirt-on-journalists.
15. Biz Carson, "Report: Uber Was on Track to Top $1.5 Billion in Revenue Last Year," *Insider*, January 12, 2016, https://www.businessinsider.com/report-uber-15-billion -revenue-in-2015-2016-1?.
16. Isaac, "*Super Pumped*, 158. https://www.google.com/books/edition/Super_Pumped /5KGywwEACAAJ?hl=en.
17. Barbara Figari, *Samuel Ward Spangenberg vs. Uber Technologies, Inc, No. Cgc-16-552156* (Superior Court of the State of California in and for the County of San Francisco, October 19, 2016), https://www.documentcloud.org/documents/3227535-Spangenberg -Declaration.html, 2.
18. Kate Conger, "Uber Snooping Lawsuit Exposes Data and Security Practices," *TechCrunch*, December 13, 2016, https://techcrunch.com/2016/12/13/uber-snooping-lawsuit -exposes-data-and-security-practices/.

19. Chris Welch, "Uber Will Pay $20,000 Fine in Settlement Over 'God View' Tracking," Verge, January 6, 2016, https://www.theverge.com/2016/1/6/10726004/uber-god-mode -settlement-fine.

20. Reuters staff, "Uber's Revenue Hits $6.5 Billion in 2016, Still Has Large Loss," April 14, 2017, https://www.reuters.com/article/us-uber-tech-results-idUSKBN17G1IB.

21. Mike Isaac, Katie Benner, and Sheera Frenkel, "Uber Hid 2016 Breach, Paying Hackers to Delete Stolen Data,"*New York Times*, November 21, 2017, https://www.nytimes .com/2017/11/21/technology/uber-hack.html.

22. Dara Khosrowshahi, "2016 Data Security Incident," Uber, November 21, 2017, https:// www.uber.com/newsroom/2016-data-incident/.

23. U.S. Department of Justice, Northern District of California, "Former Chief Security Officer of Uber Convicted of Federal Charges for Covering Up Data Breach Involving Millions of Uber User Records," October 5, 2022, https://www.justice.gov/usao -ndca/pr/former-chief-security-officer-uber-convicted-federal-charges-covering -data-breach.

24. Joseph Menn, "Former Uber Security Chief Sullivan Avoids Prison in Data Breach Case," *Washington Post*, May 5, 2023, https://www.washingtonpost.com/technology /2023/05/04/sullivan-sentencing-uber-executive/.

25. Travis Kalanick, "The Whole Truth and Nothing but the Truth, So Help Your Reputation," *Swooshing* (blog), March 30, 2010, https://swooshing.wordpress.com/2010/03 /30/the-whole-truth-and-nothing-but-the-truth-so-help-your-reputation/.

26. "Although she did not use explicit biological metaphors, her arguments were like a parody of social Darwinism," Ayn Rand biographer Jennifer Burns explained, in a commentary on this passage from *Atlas Shrugged*: "The man at the top of the intellectual pyramid contributes the most to all those below him, but gets nothing except his material payment, receiving no intellectual bonus from others to add to the value of his time. The man at the bottom who, left to himself, would starve in his hopeless ineptitude, contributes nothing to those above him, but receives the bonus of all their brains." As Burns put it: "Her views on the 'incompetent' were particularly harsh because she was so quick to divide humanity into world-shaking creators and helpless idiots unable to fend for themselves. This binarism, coupled with her penchant for judgment, gave the book much of its negative tone." Jennifer Burns, *Goddess of the Market: Ayn Rand and the American Right* (Oxford: Oxford University Press, 2009), 173.

27. "Alec Baldwin Glengarry Glen Ross Always Be Closing Full Speech," YouTube video, 2:18, 3:04, 3:08, 4:55, 2014, https://www.youtube.com/watch?v=Q4PE2hSqVnk.

28. Isaac, *Super Pumped*, 90–91.

29. Burns, *Goddess of the Market*, 86; Susan Love Brown, "Ayn Rand and Rape," *Journal of Ayn Rand Studies* 15, no. 1 (2015): 4, https://doi.org/10.5325/jaynrandstud.15.1.0003.

30. Burns, *Goddess of the Market*; Brown, "Ayn Rand and Rape," 4.

31. Burns, *Goddess of the Market*, 86.

32. Susan Love Brown's perceptive take in "Ayn Rand and Rape" has also addressed this scene with appropriate sensitivity: "Rand clearly presents Dominique also as a sadist. Indeed, even her name 'Dominique' sounds like 'dominate' or 'dominatrix.' It is clear right from the start, then, that this relationship is based not on admiration of values but on the wish to degrade and be degraded." In fact, she saw it as a pattern of such scenes in Rand's writings, "another case in which men and women know each other's characters without literally knowing anything about one another" (9, 13).

33.  Ayn Rand, *The Fountainhead* (New York: Plume, 2005), 206–16; Brown, "Ayn Rand and Rape," 9.

34.  Rand, *The Fountainhead*, 216.

35.  Rand, *The Fountainhead*, 206–8.

36.  Rand, *The Fountainhead*, 216–18.

37.  Brown, "Ayn Rand and Rape," 13, 10–11.

38.  Ayn Rand, "Letter to Waldo R. Coleman," Ayn Rand Institute, June 5, 1946, https://aynrand.org/archives/letters/letter-223/.

39.  Ryan Mac, "Donald Trump Supporter Peter Thiel Apologizes for Past Book Comments on Rape," *Forbes*, October 25, 2016, https://www.forbes.com/sites/ryanmac/2016/10/25/peter-thiel-apologizes-for-past-book-comments-on-rape-and-race/.

40.  David O. Sacks and Peter Thiel, *The Diversity Myth: Multiculturalism and Political Intolerance on Campus* (Oakland, CA: Independent Institute, 1998), 114.

41.  "Stanford_Daily_19911003," *Stanford Daily*, October 3, 1991. https://stanfordpolitics.org/wp-content/uploads/2018/01/Stanford_Daily_19911003_0001.pdf.

42.  Brown, "Ayn Rand and Rape," 13.

43.  Such justifications are often given by rapists, according to scholars, psychiatrists, and behavioral scientists, including the authors of "Sexual Assault Perpetrators' Justifications for Their Actions: Relationships to Rape Supportive Attitudes, Incident Characteristics, and Future Perpetration." In their study of postassault justifications from 183 men who self-reported committing at least one act of sexual aggression, the researchers found that "perpetrators use rape supportive attitudes and sexual assault incident characteristics to justify forcing sex on their victims," and that "hierarchical multiple regression analyses indicated that rape supportive attitudes, expectations for having sex, misperceptions of sexual intent, victims' alcohol consumption, attempts to be alone with her, and the number of consensual sexual activities prior to the unwanted sex were significant predictors of perpetrators' post-assault use of justifications." Rhiana Wegner et al., "Sexual Assault Perpetrators' Justifications for Their Actions: Relationships to Rape Supportive Attitudes, Incident Characteristics, and Future Perpetration," *Violence Against Women* 21, no. 8 (August 2015): 1018–37, https://doi.org/10.1177/1077801215589380.

44.  Trump praised *The Fountainhead* as one of the greatest novels of all time: "It relates to business, beauty, life and inner emotions. That book relates to . . . everything." A few weeks later, Trump was asked what his favorite Bible verse was. He turned to Exodus: "You are to take life for life, eye for eye, tooth for tooth, hand for hand, foot for foot, burn for burn, wound for wound, bruise for bruise." Trump admitted, "That's not a particularly nice thing," but America was under threat: "They laugh at our face, and they're taking our jobs, they're taking our money, they're taking the health of our country. And we have to be firm and have to be very strong."

Jesus Christ's view of that Old Testament verse was as follows: "You have heard that it was said, 'An eye for an eye and a tooth for a tooth.' But I say to you, Do not resist the one who is evil. But if anyone slaps you on the right cheek, turn to him the other also. And if anyone would sue you and take your tunic, let him have your cloak as well. And if anyone forces you to go one mile, go with him two miles. Give to the one who begs from you, and do not refuse the one who would borrow from you." Kirsten Powers, "Donald Trump's 'kinder, Gentler' Version," *USA Today*, April 12, 2016, https://www.usatoday.com/story/opinion/2016/04/11/donald-trump-interview-elections-2016-ayn-rand-vp-pick-politics-column/82899566/; Nolan D. Mccaskill, "Trump's Favorite Bible Verse: 'Eye for an Eye,'" *Politico*, April 14, 2016, https://www.politico.com

/blogs/2016-gop-primary-live-updates-and-results/2016/04/trump-favorite-bible -verse-221954; "Matthew 5:38–42 ESV—Retaliation—You Have Heard That It," *Bible Gateway*, 2023, https://www.biblegateway.com/passage/?search=Matthew%205%3A38 -42&version=ESV.

45. Brown, "Ayn Rand and Rape," 11.

46. Keith J. Kelly, "'Fifty Shades of Grey' Dominates Decade Book Sales," *New York Post*, January 2, 2020, https://nypost.com/2020/01/01/fifty-shades-of-grey-was-the-dominant -book-of-the-decade/.

47. Susan Fowler, "Reflecting on One Very, Very Strange Year at Uber," February 19, 2017, https://www.susanjfowler.com/blog/2017/2/19/reflecting-on-one-very-strange-year -at-uber.

48. Isaac, *Super Pumped*, 220.

49. Mike Isaac, "Uber Investigating Sexual Harassment Claims by Ex-Employee," *New York Times*, February 20, 2017, https://www.nytimes.com/2017/02/19/business/uber -sexual-harassment-investigation.html.

50. Alyson Shontell, "LEAKED: Internal Uber Deck Reveals Staggering Revenue and Growth Metrics," *Business Insider*, November 20, 2014, https://www.businessinsider .com/uber-revenue-rides-drivers-and-fares-2014-11.

51. Mickey Rapkin, "Uber Cab Confessions," *GQ*, February 27, 2014, https://www.gq.com /story/uber-cab-confessions.

52. Isaac, *Super Pumped*, 194.

53. Kara Swisher and Johana Bhuiyan, "Uber CEO Kalanick Advised Employees on Sex Rules for a Company Celebration in 2013 'Miami Letter,'" *Vox*, June 8, 2017, https:// www.vox.com/2017/6/8/15765514/2013-miami-letter-uber-ceo-kalanick-employees -sex-rules-company-celebration.

54. Crunchbase, Uber—Funding Rounds," accessed June 18, 2023, https://www.crunchbase .com/organization/uber/company_financials.

55. Ryan Lawler, "Uber Raises Giant $1.2 Billion Funding Round at a $17 Billion Valua- tion," *TechCrunch*, June 6, 2014, https://techcrunch.com/2014/06/06/uber-1-2b/.

56. Crunchbase, "Uber—Funding Rounds."

57. In December 2019 the Equal Employment Opportunity Commission "found reason- able cause to believe that Uber permitted a culture of sexual harassment and retalia- tion against individuals who complained about such harassment," and Uber agreed to pay $4.4 million to settle with the agency and compensate current and former employ- ees who were sexually harassed at work. That was just 0.11 percent of its $4.1 billion in revenues from 2019. Kate Conger, "Uber Settles Federal Investigation Into Workplace Culture," *New York Times*, December 18, 2019, https://www.nytimes.com/2019/12/18 /technology/uber-settles-eeoc-investigation-workplace-culture.html; "Uber Announces Results for Fourth Quarter and Full Year 2019," February 6, 2020, https://investor .uber.com/news-events/news/press-release-details/2020/Uber-Announces-Results -for-Fourth-Quarter-and-Full-Year-2019/.

58. Swisher, "Uber CEO Kalanick Advised Employees"; "Max Crowley," LinkedIn, 2023, https://www.linkedin.com/in/maxjc/.

59. Swisher, "Uber CEO Kalanick Advised Employees."

60. Rand, *The Fountainhead*, 681–82.

61. Edward Ongweso Jr. and Jason Koebler, "Uber Became Big by Ignoring Laws (and It Plans to Keep Doing That)," *Vice* (blog), September 11, 2019.

62. Rand, *The Fountainhead*, 680–81.

63. Erica Fink, "Uber-Nasty? Staff Submits 5,560 Fake Ride Requests," CNNMoney, August 11, 2014, https://money.cnn.com/2014/08/11/technology/uber-fake-ride-requests -lyft/index.html.

64. Fink.

65. Heather Long, "Where Are All the Startups? U.S. Entrepreneurship Near 40-Year Low," CNNMoney, September 8, 2016, https://money.cnn.com/2016/09/08/news/economy/us -startups-near-40-year-low/index.html.

66. Economic Innovation Group, "From Great Recession to Great Reshuffling: Charting a Decade of Change Across American Communities," *Economic Innovation Group*, October 2018, 4–5, https://eig.org/wp-content/uploads/2018/10/2018-DCI.pdf.

67. Erica Fink, "Uber-Nasty?"

68. Yuki Noguchi, "Unequal Rights: Contract Workers Have Few Workplace Protections," NPR, March 26, 2018, https://www.npr.org/2018/03/26/593102978/unequal-rights -contract-workers-have-few-workplace-protections.

69. Rebecca Bellan, "Uber Sued by Sexual Assault Survivors for Failing to Protect Them," *TechCrunch* (blog), July 13, 2022, https://techcrunch.com/2022/07/13/uber-sued-by-550 -women-and-counting-over-sexual-assaults-by-drivers/.

70. Cade Metz, "Silicon Valley County Battles with Uber Over Reporting of Sexual Assault," *New York Times*, October 3, 2022, https://www.nytimes.com/2022/10/03/technology /uber-sexual-assault-reporting-santa-clara-county.html

71. Chase DiFeliciantonio, "Uber Settles Dispute Over Sexual Assault Data with California Public Utilities Commission." *San Francisco Chronicle*, July 16, 2021, https://www .sfchronicle.com/bayarea/article/Uber-settles-dispute-over-sexual-assault-data -16318337.php.

72. Uber, "Uber Technologies Revenue 2017–2022," accessed June 18, 2023. https://www .macrotrends.net/stocks/charts/UBER/uber-technologies/revenue.

73. Harry Davies et al., "Uber Broke Laws, Duped Police and Secretly Lobbied Governments, Leak Reveals," *Guardian*, July 11, 2022, https://www.theguardian.com/news /2022/jul/10/uber-files-leak-reveals-global-lobbying-campaign.

74. Alastair, "Uber Kenya Launch Party!" *Uber Blog*, June 17, 2015, https://www.uber.com /en-KE/blog/uber-kenya-launch-party/.

75. Isaac, *Super Pumped*, 195.

76. Isaac, 88.

77. Kimiko de Freytas-Tamura, "Kenya's Struggling Uber Drivers Fear a New Competitor: Uber," *New York Times*, May 22, 2017, https://www.nytimes.com/2017/05/22/world /africa/uber-kenya-driver-protest.html; Margaret Wahito, "Uber Increases Price in Kenya After Drivers' Protest," *Capital Business*, March 16, 2017, https://www.capitalfm .co.ke/business/2017/03/uber-increases-price-in-kenya-after-drivers-protest/

78. "Uber Office Remains Closed, as Drivers' Protest Turns Hostile," *Citizen Digital*, March 2, 2017, https://www.citizen.digital/business/uber-office-remains-closed-as -drivers-protest-turns-hostile-159466

79. "Our Commitment to Kenya; an Update on Pricing," *Uber Blog*, March 16, 2017, https://www.uber.com/en-KE/blog/our-commitment-to-kenya-an-update-on -pricing/

80. Amanda Sperber, "Uber Made Big Promises in Kenya. Drivers Say It's Ruined Their Lives," *NBC News*, November 30, 2020, https://www.nbcnews.com/news/world/uber -made-big-promises-kenya-drivers-say-it-s-ruined-n1247964.

81. Sperber.

82. Sperber.

83. Chris Wiggins and Matthew L. Jones, *How Data Happened: A History from the Age of Reason to the Age of Algorithms* (New York: Norton, 2023), 228.

84. Associated Press, "Patriots vs. Falcons—Game Recap—February 5, 2017," ESPN.com, February 6, 2017. https://www.espn.com/nfl/recap/_/gameId/400927752; Jacob Camenker, "How the Falcons Blew a 28–3 Lead Against the Patriots in Super Bowl 51," *Sporting News*, November 18, 2021, https://www.sportingnews.com/us/nfl/news/falcons-patriots-super-bowl-28-3-lead/1xqfs41k3mfm914f6znfzj5rc9.

85. Marcel Schwantes, "Warren Buffett Says You Can Ruin Your Life in 5 Minutes by Making 1 Critical Mistake," *Inc.*, November 6, 2021, https://inc.com/article/marcel-schwantes-warren-buffett-says-you-can-ruin-your-life-in-5-minutes-by-making-1-critical-mistake.

86. Rima Abdelkader and Alexander Smith, "Uber Driver Fawzi Kamel Tells NBC News Why He Argued with Firm's CEO," *NBC News*, March 1, 2017, https://www.nbcnews.com/news/us-news/uber-driver-fawzi-kamel-explains-why-he-argued-firm-s-n727496.

87. Eric Newcomer, "In Video, Uber's CEO Argues with a Driver Over Falling Fares," Bloomberg, February 28, 2017, https://www.bloomberg.com/news/articles/2017-02-28/in-video-uber-ceo-argues-with-driver-over-falling-fares.

88. Rand, *The Fountainhead*, 206–8.

89. Newcomer, "In Video, Uber's CEO Argues."

90. Travis Kalanick, "The Whole Truth and Nothing but the Truth, So Help Your Reputation," *Swooshing* (blog), March 30, 2010, https://swooshing.wordpress.com/2010/03/30/the-whole-truth-and-nothing-but-the-truth-so-help-your-reputation/.

91. Alison Griswold, "Uber Drivers Are Using This Trick to Make Sure the Company Doesn't Underpay Them," *Quartz*, April 13, 2017, https://qz.com/956139/uber-drivers-are-comparing-fares-with-riders-to-check-their-pay-from-the-company/.

92. Newcomer, "In Video, Uber's CEO Argues."

93. Uber Technologies, "Proxy Statement Pursuant to Section 14(a) of the Securities Exchange Act of 1934," March 16, 2020, https://www.sec.gov/Archives/edgar/data/1543151/000119312519103850/d647752ds1.htm.

94. "Lyft Form S-1 Registration Statement," March 1, 2019, https://www.sec.gov/Archives/edgar/data/1759509/000119312519059849/d633517ds1.htm.

95. Max Slater-Robins, "Sidecar, a Once-Serious Uber Competitor That Raised $35 Million from Top VCs, Is Shutting Down," *Business Insider*, December 30, 2015, https://www.businessinsider.com/sidecar-has-shut-down-2015-12.

96. Uber Technologies, "Proxy Statement."

97. "Uber in 2017," *Uber Blog*, December 22, 2017, https://www.uber.com/blog/2017-in-the-rearview/.

98. Max Chafkin, "Uber Debuts Its First Fleet of Driverless Cars in Pittsburgh," Bloomberg, August 18, 2016, https://www.bloomberg.com/news/features/2016-08-18/uber-s-first-self-driving-fleet-arrives-in-pittsburgh-this-month-iso6r70n.

99. Mike Isaac, "Uber Strikes Deal with Volvo to Bring Self-Driving Cars to Its Network," *New York Times*, November 20, 2017, https://www.nytimes.com/2017/11/20/technology/uber-deal-volvo-self-driving-cars-.html.

100. Brown, "Ayn Rand and Rape," 13.

101. Newcomer, "In Video, Uber's CEO Argues."

102. Newcomer.

103. Newcomer.

104. Peter Thiel and Blake Masters, *Zero to One: Notes on Startups, or How to Build the Future* (London: Virgin Books, 2015), 181; "The Long and Tortured History of Cancel Culture," *New York Times*, December 3, 2020, https://www.nytimes.com/2020/12/03/t-magazine/cancel-culture-history.html.

105. Peter Thiel, "The Education of a Libertarian," *Cato Unbound*, April 13, 2009, https://www.cato-unbound.org/2009/04/13/peter-thiel/education-libertarian.

106. W. E. B. Du Bois, *Black Reconstruction in America: Toward a History of the Part Which Black Folk Played in the Attempt to Reconstruct Democracy in America, 1860–1880* (New York: Routledge, 2017), 46.

107. Newcomer, "In Video, Uber's CEO Argues."

108. Eric Newcomer, "The Fictionalized Viral Uber Driver," Newcomer, April 5, 2022, https://www.newcomer.co/p/the-fictionalized-viral-uber-driver.

109. Travis Kalanick, "A Profound Apology," *Uber Newsroom*, March 1, 2017, https://www.uber.com/newsroom/a-profound-apology/.

110. Jackie Wattles, "Ousted Uber CEO Travis Kalanick Shakes Up Board of Directors," CNNMoney, September 30, 2017, https://money.cnn.com/2017/09/30/technology/business/uber-board-travis-kalanick/index.html.

111. Eliot Brown, "Uber Co-Founder Travis Kalanick Cuts Stake in Company by More Than 90%," *Wall Street Journal*, December 21, 2019, sec. Tech, https://www.wsj.com/articles/uber-co-founder-travis-kalanick-cuts-stake-in-company-by-more-than-90-11576964824; Kate Conger, "Uber Founder Travis Kalanick Leaves Board, Severing Last Tie," *New York Times*, December 24, 2019, https://www.nytimes.com/2019/12/24/technology/uber-travis-kalanick.html.

112. Ari Levy, "Travis Kalanick Left More than \$1 Billion on the Table by Dumping His Uber Stake Last Year," CNBC, February 6, 2020, https://www.cnbc.com/2020/02/06/travis-kalanick-left-1point2-billion-on-table-by-dumping-uber.html.

## 10. Greed Is Good

1. A. P. Fraas, "Letter to FREED," August 3, 1974, box 4, folder 1, William Bradford Shockley Papers (SC0222), Department of Special Collections and University Archives, Stanford University Libraries, Stanford, CA.

2. Harry Caudill, "Caudill to Shockley, 08/26/74," DocumentCloud, August 26, 1974, https://www.documentcloud.org/documents/516209-caudill-8-26-74.html.

3. Glenn Fowler, "Henry M. Caudill, Who Described Appalachia's Poverty, Dies at 68," *New York Times*, November 30, 1990, https://www.nytimes.com/1990/11/30/obituaries/henry-m-caudill-who-described-appalachia-s-poverty-dies-at-68.html.

4. Caudill, "Caudill to Shockley, 08/26/74."

5. Stanford University, "Side A: Cont. Joe McCaughen, [Caudill?] Off., HFW Re \$, Keith Davey, 1st Contact with Harry M. Caudill, 1974 Jul 11; Side B: Cont. Caudill, PA Diag., Art Brown, [Doris?] Elliot, Citron, Am. Pro. BU, Marsha Kartzman, 1974 Jul 29," Side 1, 32:37, Stanford Digital Repository, September 2, 1973, https://purl.stanford.edu/td652vk1434.

6. Stanford University, Side 1, 28:20, Side 1, 42:38; Side 2, 9:01.

7. In much of the historical record about him, Shockley's defeatism, racism, and unrelenting dedication to "race betterment" in all its most heinous forms have been horribly misrepresented to be more presentable. In 2016 David Laws, the Computer History Museum's semiconductor curator, wrote that Shockley developed "well meaning but

socially unacceptable theories of race, intelligence, and eugenics." Likewise, according to a PBS documentary in 1999 about the beginnings of Silicon Valley: "Although he had no training in genetics, he studied the field energetically." PBS's he-meant-well praise continued, "He pursued his argument with his usual thorough scholarship and his almost pathological insensitivity, allowing himself to be painted a racist." Many analyses of Shockley's obsessions with eugenics and dysgenics have made excuses for his choices and actions, but it's especially notable that PBS put it that way. "Allowing himself to be painted a racist" was the pleasant, passive language they used about Shockley. Funded by the David and Lucile Packard Foundation, by the American Institute of Physics . . . and by viewers like you.

That particular documentary went even further, making Shockley seem the victim: "In May of 1963, he gave a speech at Gustavus Adolphus College in Minnesota suggesting that the people least competent to survive in the world were the ones reproducing the fastest, while the best of the human population was using birth control and having fewer children. He had slipped into eugenics," implying that Shockley had made these statements inadvertently, that he'd tripped up accidentally. Soon after that, "in an interview a year later with U.S. News & World Report he fell into the trap of discussing race."

What was that "trap," according to PBS? "He pointed out that African Americans as a group scored 15 points lower on IQ tests, and suggested the cause was hereditary." It concluded: "The more he was pushed, the more extreme he became, until the debate became about him, not about genetics, undermining his own argument." This documentary funded by the American people, which set out to set the record straight about Bill Shockley and the early innovators of Silicon Valley, had bought into his heroism, even his martyrdom, and it excused the reality of his racism. "Bill Shockley, Part 3 of 3," PBS, accessed June 18, 2023, https://www.pbs.org/transistor/album1/shockley /shockley3.html; David Laws, "Beckman, Shockley and the 60th Anniversary of the Birth of Silicon Valley," Computer History Museum, February 10, 2016, https:// computerhistory.org/blog/beckman-shockley-and-the-60th-anniversary-of-the -birth-of-silicon-valley/.

8.  "Special Report: Fifty Years of Night," *Lexington (KY) Herald Leader*, December 3, 2022, https://www.kentucky.com/news/special-reports/fifty-years-of-night/.

9.  Kirkpatrick, a prominent attorney in West Tennessee, donated regularly to FREED, sending checks on May 6, 1974, from his personal account, on April 15, 1974, and March 9, 1975, from his law firm, on November 19, 1975, from his personal account, and on February 8, 1978, from his law firm. J.W. Kirkpatrick, "Check from J.W. Kirkpatrick, Pay to the Order of Freed, for Twenty Five + No/100," May 6, 1974; "Check from Kirkpatrick & Lucas, Pay to the Order of FREED, for $50 and 00 Cts," April 15, 1974; "Check from Kirkpatrick & Lucas, Pay to the Order of FREED, for $50.00," November 19, 1975; "Letter to Professor William F. Shockley from J. W. Kirkpatrick," November 19, 1975; and "Check from Kirkpatrick & Lucas, Pay to the Order of FREED, for $50.00," March 9, 1975, all in box 4, folder 1, William Bradford Shockley Papers (SC0222). Also J. W. Kirkpatrick, "Letter to Professor William Shockley, 202 McCullough Building, from Kirkpatrick & Lucas, with Check from Kirkpatrick & Lucas, Pay to the Order of FREED, for $100.00," February 8, 1978, box 4, folder 5, William Bradford Shockley Papers (SC0222).

10.  See Stewart Bell, *Bayou of Pigs: The True Story of an Audacious Plot to Turn a Tropical Island Into a Criminal Paradise* (New York: Wiley, 2009).

11. AP, "Around the Nation; Alleged Backer of 'Invasion' of Dominica Kills Himself," *New York Times*, June 23, 1981, https://www.nytimes.com/1981/06/23/us/around-the-nation-alleged-backer-of-invasion-of-dominica-kills-himself.html; UPI, "Lawyer Left Suicide Note," June 22, 1981, https://www.upi.com/Archives/1981/06/22/Lawyer-left-suicide-note/1106362030400/.

12. Shockley put a single bullet in a six-shooter, put the gun to his head, and pulled the trigger. Before that, he'd written his wife a note, which read, "I am sorry that I feel I can no longer go on. Most of my life I have felt that the world was not a pleasant place and that people were not a very admirable form of life. I find that I am particularly dissatisfied with myself and that most of my actions are the consequence of motives of which I am ashamed." He survived, and he wrote another note to his wife: "I am sorry that I was not sufficiently ingenious or painstaking and [could not] find a more practical and suitable means of solving our problems." Joel Shurkin, *Broken Genius: The Rise and Fall of William Shockley, Creator of the Electronic Age* (New York: Palgrave Macmillan, 2006), 77–78.

13. Rob Wells, "Harry Caudill, Appalachian Author, Dead at 68," *AP News*, November 30, 1990, https://apnews.com/article/191df0063ffba677e1d897dfa7c0f9a9; Matthew Algeo, *All This Marvelous Potential: Robert Kennedy's 1968 Tour of Appalachia* (Chicago: Chicago Review Press, 2021), 11.

14. John Cheves and Bill Estep, "Chapter 1: Meet the Man Who Focused the World on Eastern Kentucky's Woes," *Lexington Herald Leader*, August 24, 2019, https://www.kentucky.com/news/special-reports/fifty-years-of-night/article44393160.html.

15. Lutz Kaelber, "Eugenics: Compulsory Sterilization in 50 American States," University of Vermont, March 24, 2009, https://www.uvm.edu/~lkaelber/eugenics/.

16. Stanford University, "Side A: Cont. Joe McCaughen," Side 1, 32:37.

17. "Special Report: Fifty Years of Night," *Lexington Herald Leader*, December 3, 2022, https://www.kentucky.com/news/special-reports/fifty-years-of-night/.

18. John Cheves and Bill Estep, "Chapter 3: The World Comes to Whitesburg to Take Harry Caudill's 'Poverty Tour,' " *Lexington Herald Leader*, August 24, 2019, https://www.kentucky.com/news/special-reports/fifty-years-of-night/article44393733.html.

19. Cheves and Estep, "Chapter 1."

20. John F. Kennedy, "Remarks at a Meeting to Consider the Economic Problems of the Appalachian Region," American Presidency Project, April 9, 1963, https://www.presidency.ucsb.edu/documents/remarks-meeting-consider-the-economic-problems-the-appalachian-region.

21. Appalachian Regional Commission, "ARC's History and Work in Appalachia," accessed June 18, 2023, https://www.arc.gov/arcs-history-and-work-in-appalachia/.

22. Robert F. Kennedy, *The Unfulfilled Promise: The Speeches and Notes from the Last Campaign of Robert F. Kennedy, 16 March 1968 to 5 June 1968* (San Diego: M. J. Aguirre, 1986), 804.

23. Edward R. Schmitt, "The Appalachian Thread in the Antipoverty Politics of Robert F. Kennedy," *Register of the Kentucky Historical Society* 107, no. 3 (2009): 395, 399, http://www.jstor.org/stable/23387502.

24. Even though Kennedy was part of America's own Camelot, he "is now one of the faceless hungry," reported the *Knoxville (TN) News Sentinel*, declaring that not since FDR's Depression era campaigns in the South "had so many forlorn turned out with such hopeful enthusiasm." One Kennedy aide had declared at the time, "I was certain that these people would be Democrats their whole lives, and their children's lives."

Over the next four decades, the voters in the six counties that Bobby Kennedy had visited began to shift Republican in presidential races, with President George W. Bush winning some of them in 2000. Republicans won in 2004 by a thin margin. In 2016 Donald Trump won those six counties far more convincingly, carrying 70–80 percent of the total vote. Rick Hampson, "RFK's Visit to Appalachia, 50 Years Later: How Kennedy Country Became Trump Country," Whas11.com, February 12, 2018, https://www.whas11.com/article/news/nation-now/rfks-visit-to-appalachia-50-years-later-how-kennedy-country-became-trump-country/465-93f54d46-5e34-45c8-b967-25e3733bbc87; CNNMoney, "CNN.Com Election 2004," 2004, https://edition.cnn.com/ELECTION/2004/pages/results/states/KY/P/00/county.002.html; Robert F. Kennedy Performance Project, "RFK in EKY: About Robert F. Kennedy's 1968 Tour," accessed June 18, 2023, https://rfkineky.org/1968-tour.htm.

25.  Cheves and Estep, "Chapter 3."

26.  Stanford University, "Side A: Cont. Joe McCaughen," Side 1, 3:30, September 2, 1973.

27.  George V. Voinovich, "S.496–110th Congress (2007–2008): Appalachian Regional Development Act Amendments of 2008," U.S. Senate, October 8, 2008, https://www.congress.gov/bill/110th-congress/senate-bill/496.

28.  John Patrick Gatta, "Youngstown, Appalachia?," *Metro Monthly* (blog), September 1, 2007, https://metromonthly.wordpress.com/2007/09/01/youngstown-appalachia/.

29.  Gatta.

30.  Ohio State University, "Provost's Discovery Themes Lecturer Program: J. D. Vance," Discovery Themes, October 23, 2017, https://discovery.osu.edu/provosts-discovery-themes-lecturer-program-jd-vance.

31.  Rick McCrabb, "From Poverty to Politics: 'A Rags to Riches Story' of JD Vance's Rise to the U.S. Senate," *Butler County (OH) Journal-News*, January 15, 2023, https://www.journal-news.com/news/from-poverty-to-politics-a-rags-to-riches-story-of-jd-vances-rise-to-the-us-senate/6M2B6FUDXZBLFPS3PPXF3G3QY4/.

32.  Appalachian Regional Commission, "Appalachian Counties Served by ARC," accessed June 18, 2023, https://www.arc.gov/appalachian-counties-served-by-arc/.

33.  Thomas Gnau, "Once a 'Little Detroit,' Dayton Region Has Two of Final Five GM Sites in Ohio," *Dayton (OH) Daily News*, March 17, 2019, https://www.mainstaycapital.com/news/DaytonDailyNews.2019.03.22.pdf; Winifred Luten, "How Losantiville Became the Athens of the West," *New York Times*, January 11, 1970, https://www.nytimes.com/1970/01/11/archives/how-losantiville-became-the-athens-of-the-west.html; "Middletown | Ohio, United States," *Britannica*, accessed June 18, 2023, https://www.britannica.com/place/Middletown-Ohio.

34.  James David Vance, *Hillbilly Elegy: A Memoir of a Family and Culture in Crisis* (New York: HarperCollins, 2016), 236.

35.  McCrabb, "From Poverty to Politics."

36.  Vance, *Hillbilly Elegy*, 236; Aaron Marshall, "Buckeye for Life," *OSU Alumni*, February 2017, http://www.epro2.com/article/Buckeye+For+Life/2694044/378588/article.html; FrumForum, "J. D. Hamel," accessed June 18, 2023, http://frumforum.com/author?oid=193; "Bonnie Vance Obituary (2005)—Butler County, OH—Journal-News," Legacy.com, April 25, 2005, https://www.legacy.com/us/obituaries/hamilton/name/bonnie-vance-obituary?id=11847055.

37.  The beginning of Vance's book echoed many other epic beginnings from America's Great Books, including Ralph Ellison's "I am an invisible man," which ranked tenth on the "best first lines from novels" according to the *American Book Review*. What was number one on that list? "Call me Ishmael" from *Moby Dick*. It's worth noting that

Melville didn't write "My name *is* Ishmael." He instead wrote, "Call me Ishmael," with Vance's assertion of identity being even more absolute than his. Melville asked the reader to refer to him by that name, which his narrator chose for himself, while Vance told the reader a truth about his identity from the very first sentence, writing, "My name is J. D. Vance," even though it was a brand-new name to him, too. Vance, *Hillbilly Elegy*, 1, 3.

38. Vance, *Hillbilly Elegy*, 1, 3.

39. Google Maps, "Mithril Capital Management, 1 Letterman Dr Bldg A, Suite 4900, San Francisco, CA 94129, United States," accessed June 18, 2023; Appalachian Regional Commission, "Appalachia: Demographic and Socioeconomic Trends," *PRB*, accessed June 18, 2023, https://www.prb.org/projects/appalachia-demographic -and-socioeconomic-trends/; Mithril II LP, "Sec Form D: Notice of Exempt Offering of Securities," U.S. Securities and Exchange Commission, April 1, 2016, https://www .sec.gov/Archives/edgar/data/1669609/000166960916000001/xslFormDX01/primary _doc.xml.

40. James Hamel, *The Hillbilly Elite* (blog), December 8, 2010, http://jdhamel.blogspot.com /2010/12/brief.html.

41. Vance, *Hillbilly Elegy*, 146.

42. Harry M. Caudill, *Night Comes to the Cumberlands, a Biography of a Depressed Area* (N.p.: Creative Media Partners, 2021), 261.

43. Vance, *Hillbilly Elegy*, 7, 56–57; Amy Chua, "Why Chinese Mothers Are Superior," *Wall Street Journal*, January 8, 2011, https://www.wsj.com/articles/SB1000142405274870411 1504576059713528698754.

44. Dave McNary, "Ron Howard to Direct, Produce 'Hillbilly Elegy' Movie," *Variety* (blog), April 10, 2017, https://variety.com/2017/film/news/ron-howard-hillbilly-elegy -movie-1202027659/.

45. Karen Heller, "Author Has Become a Reluctant Spokesman for Poor White Americans," *West Lebanon (NH) Valley News*, February 10, 2017, https://www.vnews.com/ -Hillbilly-Elegy--made-J-D-Vance-the-voice-of-the-Rust-Belt-but-does-he-want -that-job-7938957.

46. Amy Chua, *Battle Hymn of the Tiger Mother* (New York: Penguin Press, 2011), 313; Vance, *Hillbilly Elegy*, 267; Caroline Kitchener, "How 'Tiger Mom' Convinced the Author of 'Hillbilly Elegy' to Write His Story," *Atlantic*, June 7, 2017, https://www .theatlantic.com/business/archive/2017/06/hillbilly-elegy-mentor/529443/.

47. Chua, *Battle Hymn of the Tiger Mother*, 56–57.

48. Chua, 64.

49. "Nasty, Brutish, and Short," *Oxford Reference*, accessed June 18, 2023, https://www .oxfordreference.com/display/10.1093/acref/9780199567454.001.0001/acref-9780199567454 -e-1287.

50. "Hardcover Nonfiction Books—Best Sellers—Books—Jan. 30, 2011," *New York Times*, https://www.nytimes.com/books/best-sellers/2011/01/30/hardcover-nonfiction/.

51. Kitchener, "How 'Tiger Mom' Convinced."

52. Munger, Tolles & Olson LLP, "Usha C. Vance," accessed June 18, 2023, https://www .mto.com/lawyers/usha-c-vance; Suzanne Goldsmith, "J. D. Vance Moves to Cincinnati," *Columbus (OH) Monthly*, February 1, 2019, https://www.columbusmonthly.com /story/news/2019/02/01/j-d-vance-moves-to/986777007/.

53. Vance, *Hillbilly Elegy*, 209.

54. While most accepted Vance's assertions about his identity, some people did question his credibility. "It is one thing to write a personal memoir extolling the wisdom of one's

personal choices but quite something else—something extraordinarily audacious—to presume to write the 'memoir' of a culture," wrote Dwight Billings, a professor emeritus of sociology and Appalachian studies at the University of Kentucky. Dwight B. Billings, "Once Upon a Time in 'Trumpalachia.' An Excerpt from 'Appalachian Reckoning,'" *Lexington Herald Leader*, May 7, 2019, https://www.kentucky.com/opinion /op-ed/article229947144.html.

55. Vance, *Hillbilly Elegy*, 0.

56. "'Hillbilly Elegy' Is No. 1; New Oprah Pick Is a Best Seller," *USA Today*, July 5, 2017, https://www.usatoday.com/story/life/books/2017/07/05/hillbilly-elegy-jd-vance -behold-the-dreamers-oprah-winfrey-usa-today-best-selling-books/103398062/.

57. Marc Tracy, "How Hollywood and the Media Fueled the Political Rise of J.D. Vance," *New York Times*, May 15, 2022, https://www.nytimes.com/2022/05/15/arts/jd-vance -trump-hollywood.html; Robert Pondiscio, "J. D. Vance's Hillbilly Elegy Is Required Reading for Education Reformers," Thomas B. Fordham Institute, August 17, 2016, https://fordhaminstitute.org/national/commentary/jd-vances-hillbilly-elegy -required-reading-education-reformers; Penelope Lusk, "Presidential Endorsement: On the Merits of J. D. Vance's 'Hillbilly Elegy,'" *Bowdoin Orient* (Brunswick, ME), May 5, 2017, https://bowdoinorient.com/2017/05/05/presidential-endorsement-on-the -merits-of-j-d-vances-hillbilly-elegy/; Kimberly Vardeman, "Guides: Reading Groups: Hillbilly Elegy," Texas Tech University Library, accessed June 18, 2023, https://guides .library.ttu.edu/reading/vance; Morgan Olsen, "Hillbilly Elegy by J. D. Vance Is Chosen as the 2017–18 Go Big Read Book," *Go Big Read*, May 2, 2017, https://gobigread.wisc .edu/2017/05/hillbilly-elegy-chosen-as-go-big-read-book.

58. Sarah Jones, "J. D. Vance, the False Prophet of Blue America," *New Republic*, November 17, 2016, https://newrepublic.com/article/138717/jd-vance-false-prophet-blue -america.

59. Julie Carr Smyth, "JD Vance Was Paid $70K by Colleges While Promoting His Book. Now He Bashes Higher Education as a Senate Candidate," *Chicago Tribune*, April 21, 2022, https://www.chicagotribune.com/nation-world/ct-aud-nw-jd-vance-ohio-senate -20220421-utm53bhysbbxhn3kuomcdbccmq-story.html.

60. Ed Richter, "Report: Amy Adams Signed to Star in Upcoming 'Hillbilly Elegy' Movie," *Atlanta Journal-Constitution*, April 5, 2019.

61. Hillary R. Clinton, *What Happened* (New York: Simon & Schuster, 2017), 277–78.

62. Dave McNary, "Ron Howard to Direct, Produce 'Hillbilly Elegy' Movie," *Variety* (blog), April 10, 2017, https://variety.com/2017/film/news/ron-howard-hillbilly-elegy -movie-1202027659/.

63. Clinton, *What Happened*, 277–78.

64. During the 2016 race, Facebook decided to embed its own employees with the Trump campaign, to help them use the platform most effectively, and they worked with the campaign full-time and onsite, on Facebook's dime. They proposed the same deal to the Clinton campaign, but it refused the offer, according to Steven Levy. The Facebook employees were based in San Antonio, working alongside Brad Parscale, the Trump campaign's senior advisor for data and digital operations. Facebook didn't have an office there, but that didn't matter. It sent employees to work in Texas, not the Trump campaign headquarters in Manhattan where Facebook had nearly three thousand employees, and where the Clinton campaign was based, too.

"I asked Facebook, I want to spend $100 million on your platform, send me a manual," Parscale later explained, "They said we don't have a manual. I said send me a human manual then, and that's pretty much it." The Clinton campaign received no such support, whether it was for deep-seated ethical reasons, for fears about a public backlash over the corporate takeover of politics, or just a strategic miscalculation that put them at a disadvantage against their opponent—one they thought they could easily afford based on what the polls told them.

The result was that Facebook paid employees to coach the Trump operation on how to use its platform, giving them an advantage their opponent did not have in 2016. "If I would have chosen the way Hillary's campaign did it," Parscale explained, "I'd have to send an email and make a phone call, wait a couple of days, and then have it fixed. I wanted it fixed in thirty seconds." Combined, the Trump and Clinton campaigns spent $81 million on Facebook, nearly a rounding error compared to Facebook's worldwide revenues, but for the company, offering this kind of pro bono customer support to make Facebook an active part of the political process all seemed worth it at the time. Steven Levy, *Facebook: The Inside Story* (New York: Blue Rider Press, 2020), 350; Marc Fisher, "A Tale of Two Campaign Headquarters: Clinton and Trump Offices Are Miles Away and Worlds Apart," *Washington Post*, October 24, 2016, https://www.washingtonpost.com/politics/a-tale-of-two-campaign-headquarters-clinton-and-trump-offices-are-miles-away-and-worlds-apart/2016/10/24/e39d8400-963a-11e6-bc79-af1cd3d2984b_story.html; Matthew Haag, "Facebook Bets Big on Future of N.Y.C., and Offices, with New Lease," *New York Times*, August 3, 2020,https://www.nytimes.com/2020/08/03/nyregion/facebook-nyc-office-farley-building.html; Laura Hautala, "Trump and Clinton Campaigns Spent $81 Million Combined on Facebook," *CNET*, November 1, 2017, https://www.cnet.com/news/politics/trump-clinton-election-facebook-campaigns-spent-81-million-combined/.

65.	J. D. Vance, "Trump Speaks for Those Bush Betrayed: Column," *USA Today*, February 18, 2016, https://www.usatoday.com/story/opinion/2016/02/18/donald-trump-white-working-class-rust-belt-voters-elections-2016-column/80422422/.

66.	Jake Coyle, "Review: A 'Hillbilly Elegy' Adaptation, Hold the Politics," *AP News*, April 20, 2021, https://apnews.com/article/hillbilly-elegy-review-movie-ron-howard-26eca5b391e47a9767644f27799d5073.

67.	Josh McLaurin [@JoshforGeorgia], "The Screenshot Below is @JDVance1's unfiltered explanation from 2016 of the breakdown in Republican politics that he now personally is trying to exploit. The 'America's Hitler' bit is at the end. The public deserves to know the magnitude of this guy's bad faith," Twitter, April 18, 2022, https://twitter.com/JoshforGeorgia/status/1516093390378741763.

68.	Isaac Chotiner, "Compassion, and Criticism, for the White Working Class," *Slate*, August 25, 2016, https://slate.com/news-and-politics/2016/08/hillbilly-elegy-author-j-d-vance-on-trump-racism-and-how-the-media-is-failing-the-white-working-class.html.

69.	Vance, *Hillbilly Elegy*, 193.

70.	"'My God What an Idiot': J. D. Vance Gets Whacked for Past Trump Comments," *Politico*, October 23, 2021, https://www.politico.com/news/2021/10/23/jd-vance-ohio-senate-trump-comments-516865.

71.	David Weigel, "Analysis: The Trailer: How J. D. Vance Sprinted to the Head of the Pack in Ohio," *Washington Post*, April 28, 2022, https://www.washingtonpost.com/politics/2022/04/28/trailer-how-jd-vance-sprinted-head-pack-ohio/.

72.	Aaron Navarro, "J. D. Vance Lands Donald Trump's Endorsement for Ohio Senate GOP Race," *CBS News*, April 15, 2022, https://www.cbsnews.com/news/j-d-vance-trump-endorsement-for-ohio-senate-gop-race/.

73.	J. D. Vance on Charlie Rose, 2016, 16:49, https://charlierose.com/videos/29349.

74. James David Vance, "Opioid of the Masses," *Atlantic*, July 4, 2016, https://www
.theatlantic.com/politics/archive/2016/07/opioid-of-the-masses/489911/; Karl Marx, "A
Contribution to the Critique of Hegel's Philosophy of Right: Introduction," in *Marx:
Early Political Writings*, ed. Joseph J. O'Malley, Cambridge Texts in the History of
Political Thought (Cambridge: Cambridge University Press, 1994), 57–70, https://doi
.org/10.1017/CBO9781139168007.007.

75. Sara Randazzo, "Purdue Pharma Pleads Guilty to Felonies Over OxyContin Sales,"
*Wall Street Journal*, November 25, 2020, https://www.wsj.com/articles/purdue-pharma
-pleads-guilty-to-felonies-over-oxycontin-sales-11606243071.

76. Scott Higham, Sari Horwitz, and Steven Rich, "Internal Drug Company Emails Show
Indifference to Opioid Epidemic," *Washington Post*, July 23, 2019, https://www
.washingtonpost.com/investigations/internal-drug-company-emails-show-indifference
-to-opioid-epidemic-ship-ship-ship/2019/07/19/003d58f6-a993-11e9-a3a6-ab670962db05
_story.html.

77. National Institute on Drug Abuse, "Overdose Death Rates," January 20, 2022, https://
nida.nih.gov/research-topics/trends-statistics/overdose-death-rates.

78. Kevin E. Vowles et al., "Rates of Opioid Misuse, Abuse, and Addiction in Chronic Pain:
A Systematic Review and Data Synthesis," *Pain* 156, no. 4 (April 2015): 569–76, https://
doi.org/10.1097/01.j.pain.0000460357.01998.f1.

79. Assistant Secretary for Planning and Evaluation, "Opioid Abuse in the U.S. and HHS
Actions to Address Opioid-Drug Related Overdoses and Deaths," March 25, 2015,
https://aspe.hhs.gov/reports/opioid-abuse-us-hhs-actions-address-opioid-drug
-related-overdoses-deaths-0; U.S. National Library of Medicine, "Greek Medicine—
The Hippocratic Oath," Exhibitions, accessed June 18, 2023, https://www.nlm.nih.gov
/hmd/greek/greek_oath.html.

80. Rose A. Rudd et al., "Increases in Heroin Overdose Deaths—28 States, 2010 to 2012,"
Centers for Disease Control and Prevention, October 3, 2014, https://www.cdc.gov
/mmwr/preview/mmwrhtml/mm6339a1.htm.

81. IQVIA Institute, "Prescription Opioid Trends in the United States: Measuring and
Understanding Progress in the Opioid Crisis," December 16, 2020, https://www.iqvia
.com/insights/the-iqvia-institute/reports/prescription-opioid-trends-in-the-united
-states.

82. National Institute on Drug Abuse, "Drug Overdose Death Rates," February 9, 2023,
https://nida.nih.gov/research-topics/trends-statistics/overdose-death-rates; "Fentanyl
& Carfentanil," U.S. Department of Veteran Affairs, January 2018, https://www.pbm
.va.gov/AcademicDetailingService/Documents/Pain_Patient_FentanylCarfentanil
_IB101137.pdf.

83. Brian Mann, "More than a Million Americans Have Died from Overdoses During the
Opioid Epidemic," NPR, December 30, 2021, https://www.npr.org/2021/12/30
/1069062738/more-than-a-million-americans-have-died-from-overdoses-during-the
-opioid-epidemi.

84. National Institute on Drug Abuse, "Overdose Death Rates," January 20, 2022, https://
nida.nih.gov/research-topics/trends-statistics/overdose-death-rates.

85. For further reading, see Timothy McMahan King, *Addiction Nation: What the Opioid Crisis Reveals About Us* (Harrisonburg, VA: Herald Press, 2019).

86. For further reading, see Beth Macy, *Dopesick: Dealers, Doctors and the Drug Company
That Addicted America* (London: Head of Zeus, 2021).

87. As the Economic Innovation Group summarized in its report in 2018 on distressed
communities: "Hit by two recessions and bypassed by two recoveries, these

communities have experienced nothing short of a hollowing out this century." After a third recession due to the economic impacts of COVID-19, the Economic Report of the President in 2023 reiterated this reality: "It is important to remember, however, that the economic anxiety so many have felt did not start with the pandemic. For decades, the backbone of America, the middle class, has been hollowed out." Economic Innovation Group, "From Great Recession to Great Reshuffling: Charting a Decade of Change Across American Communities," October 2018, 13, https://eig.org/wp-content /uploads/2018/10/2018-DCI.pdf; White House, "Economic Report of the President," March 2023, 3, https://www.whitehouse.gov/wp-content/uploads/2023/03/ERP-2023 .pdf.

88. Bruce Stokes, "Public Divided on Prospects for the Next Generation," *Pew Research Center's Global Attitudes Project* (blog), June 5, 2017, https://www .pewresearch.org/global/2017/06/05/2-public-divided-on-prospects-for-the-next -generation/.

89. As one recent study showed: "Given a household's desire to remain above a minimum threshold standard of living, the rise in the number of dual-earner households is inevitable mostly due to inflationary pressures in product markets including rising housing prices and child care costs coupled with relatively flat wage trends." See Tesa E. Leonce, "The Inevitable Rise in Dual-Income Households and the Intertemporal Effects on Labor Markets," *Compensation & Benefits Review* 52, no. 2 (April 1, 2020): 64–76, https://doi.org/10.1177/0886368719900032.

90. See Amelia Sandhovel, "Dynamism in the West, Stagnation for Much of the Rest," Economic Innovation Group, May 17, 2023, https://eig.org/state-dynamism-key-findings/.

91. See Josh Saul, Zachary R. Mider, and Dave Mistich, "Big Coal Uses This Playbook to Avoid Cleaning Up Its Messes," Bloomberg, October 17, 2022, https://www.bloomberg .com/features/2022-west-virginia-coal-mining-alpha/.

92. "6 Books to Help Understand Trump's Win," *New York Times*, November 9, 2016, https://www.nytimes.com/2016/11/10/books/6-books-to-help-understand-trumps -win.html.

93. J. D. Vance, "Why Race Relations Got Worse," *National Review*, August 29, 2016, https://www.nationalreview.com/2016/08/race-relations-getting-worse-america -why/.

94. Simon van Zuylen-Wood, "The Radicalization of J. D. Vance," *Washington Post*, January 4, 2022, https://www.washingtonpost.com/magazine/2022/01/04/jd-vance-hillbilly -elegy-radicalization/.

95. Kim Hart, "'Hillbilly Elegy' Author J. D. Vance Starts Venture Capital Fund in Ohio," *Axios*, January 9, 2020, https://www.axios.com/2020/01/09/jd-vance-venture -capital-fund-ohio-silicon-valley-peter-thiel; Alex Isenstadt, "A Mole Hunt, a Secret Website and Peter Thiel's Big Risk: How J. D. Vance Won His Primary," *Politico*, May 3, 2022, https://www.politico.com/news/2022/05/03/jd-vance-win-ohio-primary -00029881.

96. John Ronald Reuel Tolkien, *The Return of the King* (New York: HarperCollins, 2012), 457.

97. Ryan Lizza and Rachael Bade, "Politico Playbook: The Book J. D. Vance Doesn't Want You to Read," *Politico*, May 5, 2022, https://www.politico.com/newsletters/playbook /2022/05/05/the-book-j-d-vance-doesnt-want-you-to-read-00030287.

98. J. D. Vance on Charlie Rose, 16:49.

99. "Vivek Ramaswamy," LinkedIn, 2023, https://www.linkedin.com/in/vivekgrama swamy/.

100.  Meghan O'Gieblyn, "God in the Machine: My Strange Journey Into Transhumanism," *Guardian*, April 18, 2017, https://www.theguardian.com/technology/2017/apr/18/god-in -the-machine-my-strange-journey-into-transhumanism.

101.  For a thorough analysis of the origins of this concept and the ways that some theorists have applied it during the Silicon Age, see Meghan O'Gieblyn, *God, Human, Animal, Machine: Technology, Metaphor, and the Search for Meaning* (New York: Knopf Doubleday, 2021), chap. 2.

102.  Other Silicon Valley investors had also invested in research and ventures aimed at life extension—foremost among them, Peter Thiel. "I've always had this really strong sense that death was a terrible, terrible thing. I think that's somewhat unusual. Most people end up compartmentalizing, and they are in some weird mode of denial and acceptance about death, but they both have the result of making you very passive. I prefer to fight it," Thiel told the *Washington Post*. He added, "I believe that evolution is a true account of nature, but I think we should try to escape it or transcend it in our society." Ariana Eunjung Cha, "Peter Thiel's Life Goal? To Extend Our Time on This Earth," *Washington Post*, April 3, 2015, https://www.washingtonpost.com/business/on -leadership/peter-thiels-life-goal-to-extend-our-time-on-this-earth/2015/04/03 /b7a1779c-4814-11e4-891d-713f052086a0_story.html.

103.  "Trans," *etymonline*, accessed June 18, 2023, https://www.etymonline.com/search?q =trans.

104.  Nathan Vardi, "The 30-Year-Old CEO Conjuring Drug Companies from Thin Air," *Forbes*, September 9, 2015, https://www.forbes.com/sites/nathanvardi/2015/09/09/the -30-year-old-ceo-conjuring-drug-companies-from-thin-air/.

105.  Bob Pisani, "Axovant, Biggest Biotech IPO: Is Biotech in a Bubble?" CNBC, June 11, 2015, https://www.cnbc.com/2015/06/11/axovant-biggest-biotech-ipo-is-biotech-in-a -bubble.html.

106.  After Axovant failed Phase III testing, Vivek Ramaswamy stepped down from the CEO role. Its stock kept falling, and his replacement quit after ten months. One of the main pieces of positive news that the company had pointed to while Ramaswamy was there wasn't true at all; it was a statistical miscalculation the company had to fess up to. Mark Terry, "Axovant's Much-Hyped Alzheimer's Drug Flunks Phase III Test," BioSpace, September 27, 2017, https://www.biospace.com/article/axovant-s-much-hyped-alzheimer -s-drug-flunks-phase-iii-test-/; John Carroll, "Axovant: That Positive p-Value We Reported Yesterday? Um, We Screwed That Up Too," *Endpoints News* (blog), January 9, 2018, https://endpts.com/axovant-that-positive-p-value-we-reported-yesterday-um -we-screwed-that-up-too/.

107.  John Carroll, "Why Axovant's \$315M IPO Bonanza Should Scare the Hell out of You," Fierce Biotech, June 11, 2015, https://www.fiercebiotech.com/biotech/why-axovant-s -315m-ipo-bonanza-should-scare-hell-out-of-you.

108.  "Axovant Sciences—Stock Price History" SIOX, Macrotrends.net, 2023, https://www .macrotrends.net/stocks/charts/SIOX/axovant-sciences/stock-price-history.

109.  Carroll, "Why Axovant's \$315M IPO Bonanza."

110.  "Axovant Sciences—Stock Price History."

111.  Vivek Ramaswamy netted \$6,251,118 worth of company shares and \$634,178 in cash, in addition to his \$350,000 annual salary. His mother, Geetha, was granted a stock option for 262,500 common shares, and Shankar Ramaswamy was granted a stock option for 750,000 common shares, with an exercise price of \$0.90 per share. Axovant Sciences Ltd., "Amendment No. 2 to Form S-1: Registration Statement Under the Securities Act

of 1933," Securities and Exchange Commission, June 1, 2015, F-14, https://www.sec.gov
/Archives/edgar/data/1636050/000104746915005125/a2224888zs-1a.htm.

112. John Hyatt, "How Rich Is Vivek Ramaswamy, the Longshot GOP Presidential Candidate Who Helped Take Down Don Lemon?," *Forbes*, April 26, 2023, https://www.forbes
.com/sites/johnhyatt/2023/04/26/how-rich-is-vivek-ramaswamy-the-longshot-gop
-presidential-candidate-who-helped-take-down-don-lemon/.

113. Merrilee Barton, "Vivek Ramaswamy," *Forbes*, accessed June 18, 2023, https://www
.forbes.com/profile/vivek-ramaswamy/.

114. Hyatt, "How Rich Is Vivek Ramaswamy."

115. Marketscreener.com, "SIO Gene Therapies Inc.: Change in Directors or Principal Officers, Submission of Matters to a Vote of Security Holders (Form 8-K)," April 6, 2023,
https://www.marketscreener.com/quote/stock/SIO-GENE-THERAPIES-INC
-58136287/news/SIO-GENE-THERAPIES-INC-Change-in-Directors-or-Principal
-Officers-Submission-of-Matters-to-a-Vote-43447811/.

116. Goodreads, "Books by Vivek Ramaswamy (Author of Woke, Inc.)," June 18, 2023,
https://www.goodreads.com/author/list/21176084.Vivek_Ramaswamy.

117. Oliver Haill, "'Anti-Woke' Investment Fund Launches to Back Companies That Focus
Only on Profits," *Strive* (blog), May 11, 2022, https://strive.com/anti-woke-investment
-fund-launches-to-back-companies-that-focus-only-on-profits/; Crunchbase, "Seed
Round—Strive Asset Management—2022-05-09—Crunchbase Funding Round Profile," accessed June 18, 2023, https://www.crunchbase.com/funding_round/strive-asset
-management-seed--5b002c44; "Meet Vivek Ramaswamy, Republican Presidential
Candidate," *Council on Foreign Relations* (blog), March 8, 2023, https://www.cfr.org
/blog/meet-vivek-ramaswamy-republican-presidential-candidate.

118. Dan Barry, "J. D. Vance's Ambition Comes at a Price in 'Hillbilly' Terms," *New York
Times*, October 27, 2022, https://www.nytimes.com/2022/10/27/us/politics/jd-vance
-trump-ohio.html.

119. Crunchbase, "J. D. Vance—Managing Partner of Revolution's Rise of the Rest Seed
Fund @ Revolution," June 18, 2020, https://web.archive.org/web/20200618212251
/https://www.crunchbase.com/person/j-d-vance#section-jobs; Kim Hart, "'Hillbilly
Elegy' Author J. D. Vance Starts Venture Capital Fund in Ohio," *Axios*, January 9, 2020,
https://www.axios.com/2020/01/09/jd-vance-venture-capital-fund-ohio-silicon
-valley-peter-thiel; Leah Hodgson, "Is Bigger Always Better When It Comes to VC
Funds?" PitchBook, November 11, 2022, https://pitchbook.com/news/articles/are
-bigger-vc-funds-better.

120. Alex Morrell, "'Hillbilly Elegy' Author Is Launching a \$125 Million VC Fund in Amer-
ica's Heartland with Backing from Peter Thiel and Marc Andreessen," *Business
Insider*, January 1, 2020, https://www.businessinsider.com/hillbilly-elegy-jd-vance
-launches-vc-fund-backed-by-thiel-2020-1.

121. Narya, "Home Page," 2022, https://naryavc.com/; David Bank and Dennis Price, "J. D.
Vance, the Impact Fund Manager His Partners Would Rather Forget," ImpactAlpha,
April 28, 2022, https://impactalpha.com/j-d-vance-the-impact-fund-manager-his
-partners-would-rather-forget/.

122. Crunchbase, "Kriya Therapeutics—Crunchbase Company Profile & Funding," 2022,
https://www.crunchbase.com/organization/kriya-therapeutics.

123. Yale University, "Vivek Ramaswamy '13, CEO, Roivant Sciences, Inc.," Yale Law School
Center for the Study of Corporate Law, July 15, 2016, https://ccl.yale.edu/vivek
-ramaswamy-13-ceo-roivant-sciences-inc; Paul & Daisy Soros Fellowships for New

Americans, "Vivek Ramaswamy," accessed June 18, 2023, https://www.pdsoros.org /meet-the-fellows/vivek-ramaswamy.

124. Jason Mast, "Vivek Ramaswamy's Brother, Shankar, Spins Out on His Own, Launching Audacious Gene Therapy Play," *Endpoints News* (blog), May 12, 2020, https://endpts .com/vivek-ramaswamys-brother-shankar-spins-out-on-his-own-launching -audacious-gene-therapy-play/.

125. Shankar Ramaswamy, "Opinion: Greed Is Good," *Harvard Crimson*, February 8, 2009, https://www.thecrimson.com/article/2009/2/8/greed-is-good-president-obama-has/.

126. See Martin Neil Baily, Robert E. Litan, and Matthew S. Johnson, "The Origins of the Financial Crisis," Fixing Finance Series, Brookings, November 2008.

127. Ramaswamy, "Greed Is Good."

128. For more on this shift in business education, see Rakesh Khurana, *From Higher Aims to Hired Hands: The Social Transformation of American Business Schools and the Unfulfilled Promise of Management as a Profession* (Princeton, NJ: Princeton University Press, 2010).

129. Ramaswamy, "Greed Is Good."

130. Milton Friedman, "A Friedman Doctrine—the Social Responsibility of Business Is to Increase Its Profits," *New York Times*, September 13, 1970, https://www.nytimes.com /1970/09/13/archives/a-friedman-doctrine-the-social-responsibility-of-business-is-to .html; Angus Burgin, *The Great Persuasion: Reinventing Free Markets Since the Depression* (Cambridge, MA: Harvard University Press, 2012), 152.

131. Business RoundTable, "Business Roundtable Redefines the Purpose of a Corporation to Promote 'An Economy That Serves All Americans,'" August 19, 2019, https://www .businessroundtable.org/business-roundtable-redefines-the-purpose-of-a -corporation-to-promote-an-economy-that-serves-all-americans.

132. Ramaswamy, "Greed Is Good"; Business RoundTable, "Business Roundtable."

133. Business Roundtable.

134. Ramaswamy, "Greed Is Good."

135. "Madoff Victim Fund | Reaching Victims," *RCB Fund Services* (blog), June 2023, https://madoffvictimfund.com/.

136. U.S. Attorney's Office, U.S. Department of Justice, "Manhattan U.S. Attorney Announces Additional Distribution of More than $568 Million to Victims of Madoff Ponzi Scheme," September 16, 2021, https://www.justice.gov/usao-sdny/pr/manhattan -us-attorney-announces-additional-distribution-more-568-million-victims-madoff

137. Janelle Griffith, "Bernie Madoff Victims to Receive Millions More," *NBC News*, April 20, 2020, https://www.nbcnews.com/news/us-news/bernie-madoff-victims -receive-millions-more-n1188006; United States Attorney's Office, "Madoff Sentence Reduction," February 6, 2020, https://www.justice.gov/usao-sdny/madoff-sentence -reduction.

138. "Madoff Victim Fund | Reaching Victims," *RCB Fund Services* (blog), September 2022.

139. Ramaswamy, "Greed Is Good."

140. "Extraordinarily Evil," *Chicago Tribune*, June 30, 2009, https://www.chicagotribune .com/news/ct-xpm-2009-06-30-0906290439-story.html.

141. Patrick Kesler, "Distressed Communities," *Economic Innovation Group* (blog), 2022, https://eig.org/distressed-communities/.

142. Deidre McPhillips, "US Life Expectancy Continues Historic Decline with Another Drop in 2021, Study Finds," CNN, April 7, 2022, https://www.cnn.com/2022/04/07 /health/us-life-expectancy-drops-again-2021/index.html.

143. Associated Press and NORC Center for Public Affairs, "Many Adults Are Pessimistic About Improving Their Standard of Living," https://apnorc.org/wp-content/uploads/2022/10/UChicago-Harris-AP-NORC-Poll-Report.pdf.

144. Andreas Wiseman, "Netflix Swoops on Ron Howard's Film Version of 'Hillbilly Elegy' in Whopping $45M Deal," *Deadline* (blog), January 25, 2019, https://deadline.com/2019/01/netflix-hillbilly-elegy-ron-howard-movie-deal-40m-1202541118/.

145. IMDb, "Ron Howard," accessed June 18, 2023, http://www.imdb.com/name/nm0000165/bio.

146. Matt Bishop, "Black Stone Cherry Announce New Album, 'Magic Mountain, Due Out May 6," February 5, 2014, https://therockrevival.com/rock-news/black-stone-cherry-announce-new-album-magic-mountain-due-out-may-6/.

147. Craig Peters, "Appalachia Not Dictated by Geography," *Spartanburg (SC) Herald Journal*, November 15, 2008, https://www.goupstate.com/story/news/2008/11/16/appalachia-not-dictated-by-geography/29475916007/.

148. Black Stone Cherry, "Hollywood in Kentucky," *Magic Mountain*, 2014, https://genius.com/Black-stone-cherry-hollywood-in-kentucky-lyrics.

149. Bishop, "Black Stone Cherry Announce New Album."

150. TheKnot, "Usha Chilukuri and JD Vance Wedding Registry," June 14, 2014, http://registry.theknot.com/usha-chilukuri-jd-vance-june-2014/1192686.

151. Jared Goffinet, "Netflix Releases Trailer for Movie Filmed in Middletown," *Fox19Now*, October 14, 2020https://www.fox19.com/2020/10/14/netflix-releases-trailer-movie-filmed-middletown/.

152. Matt Walljasper, "What's Filming in Atlanta Now? Lovecraft Country, The Conjuring 3, Waldo, Hillbilly Elegy, and More," *Atlanta Magazine* (blog), June 27, 2019, https://www.atlantamagazine.com/news-culture-articles/whats-filming-in-atlanta-now-lovecraft-country-the-conjuring-3-waldo-hillbilly-elegy-and-more/; Georgia Department of Economic Development, "Georgia's Film & Entertainment Industry," georgia.org, accessed June 18, 2023, https://www.georgia.org/industries/film-entertainment.

153. Goffinet, "Netflix Releases Trailer."

154. Suzanne Goldsmith, "J. D. Vance Moves to Cincinnati," *Columbus Monthly*, February 1, 2019, https://www.columbusmonthly.com/story/news/2019/02/01/j-d-vance-moves-to/986777007/.

155. Goffinet, "Netflix Releases Trailer."

156. John Patrick Gatta, "Youngstown, Appalachia?" *Metro Monthly* (blog), September 1, 2007, https://metromonthly.wordpress.com/2007/09/01/youngstown-appalachia/.

157. Rotten Tomatoes, "Hillbilly Elegy," November 11, 2020, https://www.rottentomatoes.com/m/hillbilly_elegy; Tony Maglio and Diane Haithman, "Ron Howard's Panned 'Hillbilly Elegy' Was the 7th-Most Streamed Program Over Thanksgiving," *Wrap News*, December 23, 2020, https://www.thewrap.com/hillbilly-elegy-christmas-chronicles-2-netflix-ratings-viewers-the-crown/.

158. Andy Downing, "Daily Distraction: Let's All Point and Laugh at the New Trailer for 'Hillbilly Elegy,'" *Columbus Monthly*, October 14, 2020, https://www.columbusmonthly.com/story/entertainment/2020/10/14/daily-distraction-lets-all-point-and-laugh-at-new-trailer-for-hillbilly-elegy/43277093/.

159. Jessica Blankenship, "Sturgill Simpson Finds His Way Back to Versailles," *Kentucky Country Music* (blog), February 28, 2020, https://kentuckycountrymusic.com/2020/02/sturgill-simpson-finds-his-way-back-to-versailles.html.

160. Marissa R. Moss, "will never forget hearing Sturgill talk about being approached to offer music for this film and being like, "you should have seen the credits, the

characters are like 'holler girl one and two,' " Twitter, web.archive.org, October 14, 2020, https://web.archive.org/web/20201014154407/https:/twitter.com/MarissaRMoss /status/1316388554415788032.

## 11. What Important Truth?

1. Evan Cunningham, "Great Recession, Great Recovery? Trends from the Current Population Survey: Monthly Labor Review," U.S. Bureau of Labor Statistics, April 2018, https://www.bls.gov/opub/mlr/2018/article/great-recession-great-recovery.htm; "DXY | U.S. Dollar Index (DXY) Advanced Charts," *MarketWatch*, accessed June 18, 2023, https://www.marketwatch.com/investing/index/dxy/charts.
2. Gregory Zuckerman, "Pessimism Exacts a Price on the Skeptics," *Wall Street Journal*, September 28, 2009, https://www.wsj.com/articles/SB125409165677744755.
3. "IVV | iShares Core S&P 500 ETF Overview," *MarketWatch*, accessed June 18, 2023, https://www.marketwatch.com/investing/fund/ivv; S. Dixon, "Facebook MAU Worldwide 2022," Statista, October 27, 2022, https://www.statista.com/statistics/264810 /number-of-monthly-active-facebook-users-worldwide/.
4. Zuckerman, "Pessimism Exacts a Price"; Robin Wigglesworth, "US Stocks' Record Bull Run Brought to Abrupt End by Coronavirus," *Financial Times*, March 12, 2020, https:// www.ft.com/content/6b987f46-644f-11ea-b3f3-fe4680ea68b5.
5. Zuckerman, "Pessimism Exacts a Price."
6. Robin Wigglesworth, "US Stocks' Record Bull Run Brought to Abrupt End by Coronavirus," *Financial Times*, March 12, 2020, https://www.ft.com/content/6b987f46-644f -11ea-b3f3-fe4680ea68b5.
7. Christine Idzelis and William Watts, "Dow Ends at Record High as Rising Yields Hit Tech-Heavy Nasdaq in Choppy Trade," *MarketWatch*, January 4, 2022, https://www .marketwatch.com/story/u-s-stock-futures-point-to-further-wall-street-records-as -key-manufacturing-report-looms-11641297344.
8. Dixon, "Facebook MAU Worldwide 2022."
9. Warren E. Buffett, "Opinion | Buy American. I Am," *New York Times*, October 17, 2008, https://www.nytimes.com/2008/10/17/opinion/17buffett.html.
10. Mark DeCambre and Christine Idzelis, "Dow and S&P 500 Finish at Records, Book 4 Weeks of Gains in a Row," *MarketWatch*, April 16, 2021, https://www.marketwatch .com/story/dow-s-p-500-seen-inching-to-new-records-as-investors-parse-earnings -from-morgan-stanley-pnc-11618572648; Alexandra Twin, "Stocks Bounce Back," CNN Money, September 28, 2009, https://money.cnn.com/2009/09/28/markets/markets _newyork/; Zuckerman, "Pessimism Exacts a Price."
11. Lizette Chapman, "What Happened at Mithril When Peter Thiel Wasn't Around," Bloomberg, November 8, 2019, https://www.bloomberg.com/news/articles/2019-11-08 /what-happened-at-mithril-when-peter-thiel-wasn-t-around.
12. Atossa Abrahamian, "Seasteading," *N+1* (blog), June 5, 2013, https://www.nplusonemag .com/online-only/online-only/seasteading/.
13. Futurati Podcast, "Ep. 91: Building Cities on the High Seas | Patri Friedman," *Apple Podcasts*, accessed June 18, 2023, https://podcasts.apple.com/us/podcast/ep-91-building -cities-on-the-high-seas-patri-friedman/id1541051806?i=1000566817940.
14. Katherine Mangu-Ward, "Homesteading on the High Seas," *Reason.com* (blog), April 28, 2008, https://reason.com/2008/04/28/homesteading-on-the-high-seas/.
15. Mangu-Ward.

16. Gregory Thomas, "Ephemerisle Is Burning Man on Boats in the Sacramento River Delta," *San Francisco Chronicle*, August 14, 2019, https://www.sfchronicle.com/travel /article/Ephemerisle-is-Burning-Man-on-boats-in-the-14301730.php.

17. Alexandra Wolfe, *Valley of the Gods: A Silicon Valley Story* (New York: Simon & Schuster, 2017), 56–61.

18. Robert Klark Graham had made millions from inventing shatterproof lenses for contacts and eyeglasses. He promoted seasteading in the 1970s, going so far as having a Signet Armorlite executive work with Los Angeles real estate agents to identify an island at least five miles wide and fifteen miles long. They found several viable candidates, all in the Caribbean (such as, it should be noted, islands like Granada or Dominica, where years later there was a failed coup by white supremacists that was allegedly supported by J. W. Kirkpatrick). Graham drew up blueprints for prefabricated living pods, state-of-the-art sewage systems, greenhouses, production facilities, etc., all of which would make the island entirely self-sufficient. Graham even designed a transportation network that would connect all parts of the island via vacuum tubes, predating by four decades both Elon Musk's Hyperloop and the Virgin Hyperloop One project, led first by early Uber investor Shervin Pishevar and then by Richard Branson. For Graham, the island was a political endeavor, intended to create an independent nation outside the reach of the rules of existing governments, and it was a business enterprise. He planned to enter into royalty-based agreements with the scientists who lived there, profiting off of the inventions they created using the cutting-edge labs and research facilities that attracted them to the island. David Plotz, "The Tycoon Who Planned His Very Own Island Utopia in the 1970s," *Atlas Obscura*, July 14, 2015, http:// www.atlasobscura.com/articles/the-tycoon-who-planned-his-very-own-island -utopia-in-the-1970s; Marco della Cava, "Richard Branson Takes Hyperloop Wheel After Pishevar Exits Under a Cloud," *USA Today*, October 20, 2017, https://www .usatoday.com/story/tech/2017/12/18/richard-branson-takes-hyperloop-wheel-after -pishevar-exits-under-cloud/963223001/.

19. David Plotz, "The Genius Generation," *Guardian*, April 15, 2004, https://www .theguardian.com/science/2004/apr/15/science.highereducation.

20. The Nobel Prize Sperm Bank achieved widespread infamy, including a *Saturday Night Live* skit on March 8, 1980, called "Dr. Shockley's House of Sperm." The scene began with Bill Murray as the clerk, answering the phones and fielding customer inquiries. They kept asking for one donor. Rather than the geniuses and athletes, "people just want funny kids nowadays," Murray said ruefully. But they didn't just want *any* funny kids. Specifically, they all wanted Rodney Dangerfield's sperm. Regrettably for Dangerfield, as the joke went, he could not keep up with demand. Dangerfield told Murray, "Oh, it's impossible! Are you kidding? I can't! No way! No way! You kidding? It can't be done!" Unfortunately for Dangerfield, Murray insisted. "But, Rodney, this is very important," escalating the gag by making fun of Shockley's racism: "These are our first black customers." Dangerfield replied, as only he could: "I'm telling ya, you're gonna kill the goose that laid the golden egg! I'm telling you that right now!" Don Roy King, "Dr. Shockley's House of Sperm," SNL Transcripts Tonight, October 8, 2018, https://snltranscripts.jt.org/79/79msperm.phtml.

21. Plotz, "The Genius Generation."

22. Kat Eschner, "The 'Nobel Prize Sperm Bank' Was Racist. It Also Helped Change the Fertility Industry," *Smithsonian Magazine*, June 9, 2017, https://www.smithsonianmag .com/smart-news/nobel-prize-sperm-bank-was-racist-it-also-helped-change-fertility -industry-180963569/.

23.  Rosalie R. Radomsky, "A Commitment for More than One Lifetime," *New York Times*, February 10, 2018, https://www.nytimes.com/2018/02/10/fashion/weddings/a-commit ment-for-more-than-one-lifetime.html.

24.  Peter Thiel, "The Education of a Libertarian," *Cato Unbound*, April 13, 2009, https:// www.cato-unbound.org/2009/04/13/peter-thiel/education-libertarian.

25.  Patri Friedman, "Beyond Folk Activism," *Cato Unbound*, April 6, 2009, https://www .cato-unbound.org/2009/04/06/patri-friedman/beyond-folk-activism.

26.  "Warren Buffett Explains the 2008 Financial Crisis," YouTube video, 1:32, 3:28, 2018, https://www.youtube.com/watch?v=k2VSSNECLTQ.

27.  Chapman, "What Happened at Mithril."

28.  Steven Levy, *Facebook: The Inside Story* (New York: Blue Rider Press, 2020), 90.

29.  Tomio Geron, "Facebook Prices Third-Largest IPO Ever, Valued at $104 Billion," *Forbes*, May 17, 2012, https://www.forbes.com/sites/tomiogeron/2012/05/17/facebook -prices-ipo-at-38-per-share/.

30.  Reuters, "Thiel's Founders Fund Sells Remaining Facebook Shares," August 27, 2019, https://www.reuters.com/article/us-facebook-foundersfund-idUSKCN1VH1LO.

31.  "Meta (Facebook) (FB)—Stock Price History," accessed June 18, 2023, https:// companiesmarketcap.com/facebook/stock-price-history/; "Meta (Facebook) (FB)— Market Capitalization," accessed June 18, 2023, https://companiesmarketcap.com /facebook/marketcap/.

32.  Yahoo Finance, "Meta Platforms, Inc. (META) Stock Price, News, Quote & History," accessed June 18, 2023, https://finance.yahoo.com/quote/META/; Sissi Cao, "Facebook's First Investor Peter Thiel Owns Less than 10K Shares After Latest Stock Dump," *Observer* (blog), February 11, 2020, https://observer.com/2020/02/peter-thiel -dump-facebook-stock-before-2020-election/.

33.  Peter Thiel with Blake Masters, *Zero to One: Notes on Startups, or How to Build the Future* (London: Virgin Books, 2015), 5.

34.  "Transcript: Donald Trump's Taped Comments About Women," *New York Times*, October 8, 2016, https://www.nytimes.com/2016/10/08/us/donald-trump-tape-transcript .html.

35.  David A. Fahrenthold, "Trump Recorded Having Extremely Lewd Conversation About Women in 2005," *Washington Post*, April 12, 2023, https://www.washingtonpost.com /politics/trump-recorded-having-extremely-lewd-conversation-about-women-in -2005/2016/10/07/3b9ce776-8cb4-11e6-bf8a-3d26847eeed4_story.html.

36.  "Transcript: Donald Trump's Taped Comments."

37.  Jessica Bennett, Megan Twohey, and Alexandra Alter, "Why E. Jean Carroll, 'the Anti-Victim,' Spoke Up About Trump," *New York Times*, June 27, 2019, https://www.nytimes .com/2019/06/27/us/politics/jean-carroll-trump-sexual-assault.html.

38.  Colin Dwyer, "Donald Trump: 'I Could . . . Shoot Somebody, And I Wouldn't Lose Any Voters,'" NPR, January 23, 2016, https://www.npr.org/sections/thetwo-way/2016/01/23 /464129029/donald-trump-i-could-shoot-somebody-and-i-wouldnt-lose-any-voters.

39.  "Read the Completed Jury Verdict Form in the Trump-Carroll Case," *New York Times*, May 9, 2023, https://www.nytimes.com/interactive/2023/05/09/nyregion/trump-liable -verdict-form-jury.html.

40.  CNN, "Read: Transcript of CNN's Town Hall with Former President Donald Trump," May 11, 2023, https://www.cnn.com/2023/05/11/politics/transcript-cnn-town-hall -trump/index.html; Aila Slisco, "Trump Attacks E. Jean Carroll to CNN Town Hall Audience Laughter," *Newsweek*, May 11, 2023, https://www.newsweek.com/trump -attacks-e-jean-carroll-cnn-town-hall-audience-laughter-1799576.

41. Benjamin Weiser, Lola Fadulu, and Kate Christobek, "E. Jean Carroll May Sue Trump a Third Time After 'Vile' Comments on CNN," *New York Times*, May 11, 2023, https://www.nytimes.com/2023/05/11/nyregion/e-jean-carroll-trump-defamation.html.

42. Jordan Fabian and Saagar Enjeti, "Exclusive: Trump Vehemently Denies E. Jean Carroll Allegation, Says 'She's Not My Type,'" *Hill*, June 24, 2019, https://thehill.com/homenews/administration/450116-trump-vehemently-denies-e-jean-carroll-allegation-shes-not-my-type/.

43. Charisse Jones, "E. Jean Carroll Was a Trailblazing Journalist Before Her Defamation Trial Against Trump," *USA Today*, April 28, 2023, https://www.usatoday.com/story/news/politics/2023/04/28/e-jean-carroll-journalist-writer-new-york/11752140002/; "Nancy O'Dell—Life After Television," *Elysian Magazine* (blog), July 6, 2020, https://readelysian.com/nancy-odell/.

44. Chris Kahn, "Trump Trails Clinton by 8 Points After Tape Scandal, Debate: Reuters/Ipsos Poll," Reuters, October 11, 2016, https://www.reuters.com/article/us-usa-election-poll-idUSKCN12B2PV.

45. Tim Alberta, "'Mother Is Not Going to Like This': The 48 Hours That Almost Brought Down Trump," *Politico*, July 10, 2019, https://politi.co/2NKE8eg.

46. Reuters staff, "Trump Apologizes for Lewd Talk Caught on Live Microphone in 2005," Reuters, October 7, 2016, https://www.reuters.com/article/us-usa-election-trump-lewd-idUSKCN1272FQ.

47. Bari M. Schwartz, "Hot or Not? Website Briefly Judges Looks," *Harvard Crimson*, November 4, 2003, https://www.thecrimson.com/article/2003/11/4/hot-or-not-website-briefly-judges; Ryan Mac, "Donald Trump Supporter Peter Thiel Apologizes for Past Book Comments on Rape," *Forbes*, October 25, 2016, https://www.forbes.com/sites/ryanmac/2016/10/25/peter-thiel-apologizes-for-past-book-comments-on-rape-and-race/; Reuters staff, "Trump Apologizes for Lewd Talk."

48. Emerson Brooking and P. W. Singer, "How October 7th, 2016 Shaped the Course of American History," *Rolling Stone* (blog), October 5, 2018, https://www.rollingstone.com/politics/politics-features/trump-access-hollywood-tape-733037/.

49. Bruce Mehlman, "How the West Wing Was Won, 2016: Outcomes & Implications," https://mehlmanconsulting.com/wp-content/uploads/2016-Mehlman-Election-Analysis.pdf, slide 26.

50. Alberta, "'Mother Is Not Going to Like This.'"

51. Ted Johnson, "Donald Trump Apologizes for Lewd Remarks: 'I Pledge to Be a Better Man,'" *Variety* (blog), October 8, 2016, https://variety.com/2016/biz/news/donald-trump-access-hollywood-1201882204/.

52. "Donald Trump Apologizes for Sexist Comments About Groping Women," *PBS NewsHour*, YouTube video, October 8, 2016, https://www.youtube.com/watch?v=ycfARBsz6_Y.

53. OpenSecrets, "Peter Thiel," accessed June 18, 2023, https://www.opensecrets.org/donor-lookup/results?cand=ro+khanna&cycle=&employ=&jurisdiction=&name=peter+thiel&occupation=&state=&type=&zip=.

54. FEC, "Browse Individual Contributions: Peter Thiel," accessed June 18, 2023, https://www.fec.gov/data/individual-contributions/.

55. Thiel gave $2,700 to support Khanna almost exactly a month before he spoke at the RNC and declared, "I am proud to be a Republican. But most of all I am proud to be an American." Khanna's victory in 2016 was aided by donations from many Silicon Valley executives, including Google chairman Eric Schmidt, Facebook COO Sheryl Sandberg, Yahoo CEO Marissa Mayer, and former Facebook CEO Sean Parker. In 2013

Parker spoke at a fundraiser with his Silicon Valley peers, saying, "To a certain extent, I think we are starting to come to a realization of our own power." That proved prescient. Andrea Peterson, "Silicon Valley Tech Execs Backed a Candidate for Congress. And He Lost," *Washington Post*, December 6, 2021, https://www.washingtonpost.com/news/the-switch/wp/2014/11/07/silicon-valley-tech-execs-backed-a-candidate-for-congress-and-he-lost/; Josh Harkinson, "How Big Tech's Congressman Swung Way Left," *Mother Jones* (blog), June 29, 2017, https://www.motherjones.com/politics/2017/06/can-this-berniecrat-congressman-win-silicon-valley-over-to-his-progressive-agenda/.

56. Heritage Action for America, "Rep. Ro Khanna—Scorecard," accessed June 18, 2023, https://heritageaction.com/scorecard.

57. David Streitfeld, "Peter Thiel to Donate $1.25 Million in Support of Donald Trump," *New York Times*, October 16, 2016, https://www.nytimes.com/2016/10/16/technology/peter-thiel-donald-j-trump.html; Gina Pace, "Internet Billionaire Donates $1.25 Million to Create Libertarian Islands," *New York Daily News*, August 17, 2011, https://www.nydailynews.com/life-style/real-estate/internet-billionaire-donates-1-25-million-create-libertarian-islands-article-1.1045086.

58. Katherine Mangu-Ward, "Homesteading on the High Seas," *Reason.com* (blog), April 28, 2008, https://reason.com/2008/04/28/homesteading-on-the-high-seas/.

59. OpenSecrets, "Top Contributors, Federal Election Data for Donald Trump, 2016 Cycle," accessed June 18, 2023, https://www.opensecrets.org/pres16/contributors?id=n00023864.

60. Ian Vandewalker, "Since Citizens United, a Decade of Super PACs," Brennan Center for Justice, January 14, 2020, https://www.brennancenter.org/our-work/analysis-opinion/citizens-united-decade-super-pacs.

61. Donald Trump, "Here is my statement," Twitter, December 6, 2017, https://T.Co/WAZiGoQqMQ.

62. 148Apps, "Trump Hair," accessed June 18, 2023, https://www.148apps.com/app/1040750174/; Kashmir Hill, "The Secretive Company That Might End Privacy as We Know It," *New York Times*, January 18, 2020, https://www.nytimes.com/2020/01/18/technology/clearview-privacy-facial-recognition.html.

63. 148Apps, "Trump Hair."

64. Daniel C. Carroll, "Internet Worm Linked to San Francisco Man," *Harvard Crimson*, February 25, 2009, https://www.thecrimson.com/article/2009/2/25/internet-worm-linked-to-san-francisco/

65. Owen Thomas, "'Anarcho-Transexual' Hacker Returns with New Scam Site," *Gawker* (blog), March 10, 2009, https://www.gawker.com/5167506/anarcho-transexual-hacker-returns-with-new-scam-site.

66. 148Apps, "Flipshot—Stop Hoarding Photos," https://www.148apps.com/app/975446460/; "Shimmer—Animated GIF Maker," https://www.148apps.com/app/1018647221/, both accessed June 18, 2023

67. 148Apps, "Lifestream—Share Your Camera Roll," accessed June 18, 2023, https://www.148apps.com/app/1086401980/.

68. Ryan Mac ☺ [@RMac18], "We found this photo of Clearview CEO Hoan Ton-That with Chuck Johnson from 2016. Ton-That's response: 'I was only making the Okay sign in the photo as in "all okay . . ." It would be absurd and unfair for anyone to distort my views and values based on old photos of any sort,'" Twitter, January 23, 2020, https://twitter.com/RMac18/status/1220338975631527936; Luke O'Brien, "Far-Right Extremists Helped Create the World's Most Powerful Facial Recognition Technology," *HuffPost*,

April 7, 2020, https://www.huffpost.com/entry/clearview-ai-facial-recognition-alt
-right_n_5e7d028bc5b6cb08a92a5c48.

69. David Corn, "Two Republican Congressmen Hobnob with an Alleged Holocaust Denier. Again," *Mother Jones*, September 13, 2018, https://www.motherjones.com /politics/2018/09/alleged-holocaust-denier-chuck-johnson-attends-matt-gaetz -fundraiser-dana-rohrabacher/.

70. Tim Murphy, "The Rise and Fall of Twitter's Most Infamous Right-Wing Troll," *Mother Jones* (blog), December 16, 2014, https://www.motherjones.com/politics/2014/12 /charles-chuck-johnson-gotnews-rolling-stone/.

71. Keith Rabois, "Rabois: My Intention Was to Make a Provocative Statement." *Stanford Daily*, February 7, 1992, https://archives.stanforddaily.com/1992/02/07?page=5§ion =MODSMD_ARTICLE21.

72. Ben Collins and Brandy Zadrozny, "Activist Who Met with Congressmen Posted about Black 'Violence Gene,'" *NBC News*, January 18, 2019, https://www.nbcnews.com /politics/congress/activist-who-met-congressmen-about-dna-posted-about-black -violence-n959931.

73. Charles C. Johnson, "They Mean to Exterminate Us—Charles C. Johnson," Facebook, September 21, 2016, https://web.archive.org/web/20190118200459/https:/www.facebook .com/charles.c.johnson/posts/10207211302981058.

74. Johnson was known for sharing extreme ideas online. Yet that radicalism didn't always translate to his real-life reputation, or at least it did not prevent two conservative members of Congress from meeting with him early in 2019—they later apologized—or another from inviting him as a special guest to the State of the Union the year before. Daniel Moritz-Rabson, "GOP Congressmen Meet with Alleged Holocaust Denier," *Newsweek*, January 17, 2019, https://www.newsweek.com/gop-congressmen-meet -holocaust-denier-chuck-johnson-1296256; Marc Caputo, "Why a Florida Congress-man Invited a Notorious Alt-Right Troll to SOTU," *Politico*, January 31, 2018, https:// www.politico.com/story/2018/01/31/gaetz-florida-right-wing-troll-380577.

75. Kashmir Hill, "What We Learned About Clearview AI and Its Secret 'Co-Founder,'" *New York Times*, March 18, 2021, https://www.nytimes.com/2021/03/18/technology /clearview-facial-recognition-ai.html.

76. Donie O'Sullivan, "This Man Says He's Stockpiling Billions of Our Photos," CNN, February 10, 2020, https://www.cnn.com/2020/02/10/tech/clearview-ai-ceo-hoan-ton -that/index.html.

77. Hill, "What We Learned About Clearview AI."

78. For a thorough analysis of the ideas that influenced Clearview AI's early development, see Kashmir Hill, *Your Face Belongs to Us: A Secretive Startup's Quest to End Privacy as We Know It* (New York: Random House, 2023), chaps. 2 and 4.

79. Schwartz, "Hot or Not?"

80. Open Data New York, "Smartcheckr, LLC, 15 W. 72nd St., Ste. 23-S, New York, NY 10023," accessed June 18, 2023, https://opendatany.com/corporation.php?id=5083343; Apollo.io, "Smartcheckr—Overview, Competitors, and Employees," accessed June 18, 2023, https://www.apollo.io/companies/Smartcheckr/5fd867d06c1b810001771b6f; Alamy Limited, "Smartcheckr Hi-Res Stock Photography and Images," accessed June 18, 2023, https://www.alamy.com/stock-photo/smartcheckr.html; Hill, "The Secretive Company."

81. Andrew Tarantola, "Why Clearview AI Is a Threat to Us All," Engadget, February 12, 2020, https://www.engadget.com/2020-02-12-clearview-ai-police-surveillance -explained.html.

82. Kashmir Hill, "What We Learned About Clearview AI."

83. Hilary Cook and Gisela Perez, "Google, YouTube, Venmo and LinkedIn Send Cease-and-Desist Letters to Facial Recognition App That Helps Law Enforcement," *CBS News*, February 5, 2020, https://www.cbsnews.com/news/clearview-ai-google-youtube-send-cease-and-desist-letter-to-facial-recognition-app/.

84. Meta, "Meta—Leadership & Governance—Corporate Governance Guidelines," April 3, 2022, https://investor.fb.com/leadership-and-governance/corporate-governance-guidelines/default.aspx; Meta, "Meta—Leadership & Governance—Compensation, Nominating & Governance Committee Charter," February 7, 2022, https://web.archive.org/web/20220207061552/https://investor.fb.com/leadership-and-governance/compensation-and-governance-committee-charter/default.aspx.

85. Nick Wingfield, "The Culture Wars Have Come to Silicon Valley," *New York Times*, August 8, 2017, https://www.nytimes.com/2017/08/08/technology/the-culture-wars-have-come-to-silicon-valley.html.

86. Elizabeth Dwoskin, "Peter Thiel Helped Build Big Tech. Now He Wants to Tear It All Down," *Washington Post*, June 28, 2022, https://www.washingtonpost.com/technology/2022/06/19/peter-thiel-facebook-new-right/.

87. Scott Kupor, "Rabois Remarks Sparks Student and Staff Reactions," *Stanford Daily*, February 6, 1992, https://archives.stanforddaily.com/1992/02/06?page=4§ion=MODSMD_ARTICLE15.

88. Douglas MacMillan, Keach Hagey, and Deepa Seetharaman, "Tech Luminary Peter Thiel Parts Ways with Silicon Valley," *Wall Street Journal*, February 15, 2018, https://www.wsj.com/articles/tech-luminary-peter-thiel-parts-ways-with-silicon-valley-1518696120.

89. Jeff Horwitz, "Facebook Shakes Up Board: Erskine Bowles, Reed Hastings to Step Down," *Wall Street Journal*, April 12, 2019, https://www.wsj.com/articles/facebook-shakes-up-board-erskine-bowles-reed-hastings-to-step-down-11555105224.

90. Jose A. DelReal, "Ahead of Debate, Trump Holds News Conference with Bill Clinton Accusers," *Washington Post*, October 9, 2016, https://www.washingtonpost.com/news/post-politics/wp/2016/10/09/ahead-of-debate-trump-holds-news-conference-with-bill-clinton-accusers/.

91. Donald Trump, "Join Me in St. Louis, Missouri—as I Conclude My Debate Prep," Facebook, October 10, 2016, https://web.facebook.com/watch/live/?v=10157857037430725&ref=watch_permalink&_rdc=1&_rdr.

92. Jeremy Stahl, "Watch Trump Blame Hillary for His Litany of Sexual Abuse Accusers," *Slate*, October 20, 2016, https://slate.com/news-and-politics/2016/10/watch-trump-blame-hillary-for-his-litany-of-sexual-abuse-accusers.html.

93. "Donald Trump Apologizes for Sexist Comments about Groping Women," *PBS NewsHour*, YouTube video, October 8, 2016, https://www.youtube.com/watch?v=ycfARBsz6_Y.

94. Maggie Haberman and Jonathan Martin, "Trump Once Said the 'Access Hollywood' Tape Was Real. Now He's Not Sure," *New York Times*, November 29, 2017, https://www.nytimes.com/2017/11/28/us/politics/trump-access-hollywood-tape.html; Gopal Ratnam, "How Fake Audio, like Deepfakes, Could Plague Business, Politics," Roll Call, March 3, 2020, https://www.rollcall.com/2020/03/03/how-fake-audio-like-deepfakes-could-plague-business-politics/.

95. "I've said and done things I regret, and the words released today on this more than a decade-old video are one of them," Trump originally stated in a carefully produced video, in a more direct admission of guilt. "Anyone who knows me know these words

don't reflect who I am. I said it, I was wrong, and I apologize." That video appeared on October 8, 2016. Just over a year later, Trump's daughter, Ivanka, criticized U.S. Senate candidate Roy Moore when he was accused of molesting teenage girls (Ivanka Trump said there was "a special place in hell for people who prey on children"). According to the *New York Times*, Donald Trump defended Moore. He then told a staffer, as well as a sitting U.S. senator, that he'd never bragged about attempting to assault O'Dell and it was someone else's voice on the tape.

By May 2023 Trump had yet again changed his approach. On CNN, he admitted to saying it but he self-justified: "I said if you're famous and rich or whatever I said, but I said if you're a star, you are—and I said women let you. I didn't say you grab. I said women let. You know you didn't use that word, but if you look, women let you. Now, they said will you take that back? I said, look, for a million years, this is the way it's been. I want to be honest. This is the way it's been. I can take it back if you'd like to. But if you're a famous person, if you're a star—and I'm not referring to myself. I'm saying people that are famous, people that are stars." Alberta, "'Mother Is Not Going to Like This'"; Jonathan Martin, Maggie Haberman, and Alexander Burns, "Why Trump Stands by Roy Moore, Even as It Fractures His Party," *New York Times*, November 25, 2017, https://www.nytimes.com/2017/11/25/us/politics/trump-roy-moore-mcconnell -alabama-senate.html; Haberman and Martin, "Trump Once Said"; "Read: Transcript of CNN's Town Hall with Former President Donald Trump," CNN, May 11, 2023, https://www.cnn.com/2023/05/11/politics/transcript-cnn-town-hall-trump/index .html.

96.  Nahal Toosi, "Trump Refuses to Say He'll Accept Election Results," *Politico*, October 19, 2016, https://www.politico.com/story/2016/10/will-trump-accept-election-results -2016-debate-230038.

97.  Amy McKeever, "No Modern Presidential Candidate Has Refused to Concede. Here's Why That Matters," *History*, November 9, 2020, https://www.nationalgeographic.com /history/article/no-modern-presidential-candidate-refused-to-concede-heres-why -that-matters; Lauren Carroll, "Is Trump the First-Ever Candidate Not to Say He'll Accept Election Results?," *PolitiFact*, October 25, 2016, https://www.politifact.com /factchecks/2016/oct/25/hillary-clinton/trump-first-ever-candidate-not-say-hell -accept-ele/.

98.  National Constitution Center, "On This Day, Bush v. Gore Settles 2000 Presidential Race," December 12, 2022, https://constitutioncenter.org/blog/on-this-day-bush-v-gore -anniversary.

99.  Arnie Seipel, "Mike Pence: 'We Will Absolutely Accept the Result of the Election,'" NPR, October 16, 2016, https://www.npr.org/2016/10/16/498152787/mike-pence-we-will -absolutely-accept-the-result-of-the-election; Nolan D. McCaskill, "Ivanka Trump: My Dad Will Accept the Outcome of the Election," *Politico*, October 19, 2016, https://www .politico.com/story/2016/10/ivanka-trump-accept-election-outcome-229994.

100.  NPR staff, "Fact Check and Full Transcript of the Final 2016 Presidential Debate," NPR, October 19, 2016, https://www.npr.org/2016/10/19/498293478/fact-check-trump-and -clinton-s-final-presidential-debate; Leigh Ann Caldwell, "5 Takeaways from the Third and Final Presidential Debate," *NBC News*, October 20, 2016, https://www.nbcnews .com/storyline/2016-presidential-debates/5-major-takeaways-third-final-presidential -debate-n669831.

101.  Alberta, "'Mother Is Not Going to Like This.'"

102.  Hillary Clinton needed 77,747 more votes to win in 2016. In Michigan, Trump won by 10,704 votes after he received 2,279,543 votes and Clinton received 2,268,839 votes. In

Pennsylvania, Trump won by 44,292 votes after he received 2,970,733 votes and Clinton received 2,926,441 votes. In Wisconsin, Trump won by 22,748 votes after he received 1,405,284 votes and Clinton received 1,382,536 votes. If Clinton had received one more vote than Trump in each of those three states (10,705 in Michigan, 44,293 in Pennsylvania, and 22,749 in Wisconsin), then the electoral votes of those three states (16 in Michigan, 20 in Pennsylvania, and 10 in Wisconsin) would have brought her total from 232 electoral votes to 278, surpassing the 270 she needed to win. "2016 Presidential Election Results," *New York Times*, August 9, 2017, https://www.nytimes.com/elections/2016/results/president.

103. "Trump: An American Dream Episode 4," *Netflix*, 13:28, 2018, https://www.netflix.com/ng/title/80206395; "The Beat with Ari Melber: MSNBCW: September 3, 2018 3:00 p.m.–4:00 p.m. PDT," September 3, 2018, http://archive.org/details/MSNBCW_20180903_220000_The_Beat_With_Ari_Melber.

104. "Are You Not Entertained? | Gladiator (2000)," YouTube video, November 6, 2014, https://www.youtube.com/watch?v=YbBiXPVKuTA&ab_channel=ScreenBites.

105. Katherine Mangu-Ward, "Homesteading on the High Seas," *Reason.com* (blog), April 28, 2008, https://reason.com/2008/04/28/homesteading-on-the-high-seas/.

106. Maureen Dowd, "Peter Thiel, Trump's Tech Pal, Explains Himself," *New York Times*, January 11, 2017, https://www.nytimes.com/2017/01/11/fashion/peter-thiel-donald-trump-silicon-valley-technology-gawker.html.

107. "Epictetus," *Internet Encyclopedia of Philosophy* (blog), accessed June 18, 2023, https://iep.utm.edu/epictetu/.

108. Dowd, "Peter Thiel."

109. Alberta, "'Mother Is Not Going to Like This.'"

110. Thiel with Masters, *Zero to One*, 12.

111. Dowd, "Peter Thiel."

112. Lucinda Shen, "Tim Cook, Jeff Bezos and Peter Thiel Are Meeting with Trump Today," *Fortune*, June 19, 2017, https://fortune.com/2017/06/19/tim-cook-jeff-bezos-peter-thiel-donald-trump-jared-kushner/; Jessica Bursztynsky, "Apple Becomes First U.S. Company to Reach a $2 Trillion Market Cap," CNBC, August 19, 2020, https://www.cnbc.com/2020/08/19/apple-reaches-2-trillion-market-cap.html; Kif Leswing, "Apple Becomes First U.S. Company to Reach $3 Trillion Market Cap," CNBC, January 3, 2022, https://www.cnbc.com/2022/01/03/apple-becomes-first-us-company-to-reach-3-trillion-market-cap.html.

113. Tony Romm, "Thiel Could Gain from Trump Transition," *Politico*, December 6, 2016, https://www.politico.com/story/2016/12/peter-thiel-trump-transition-benefits-232233.

114. Ryan Mac, "A Troll Outside Trump Tower Is Helping to Pick Your Next Government," *Forbes*, January 9, 2017, https://www.forbes.com/sites/mattdrange/2017/01/09/chuck-johnson-troll-trump-transition-team/.

115. Mike Isaac, "Facebook Renames Itself Meta," *New York Times*, October 28, 2021, https://www.nytimes.com/2021/10/28/technology/facebook-meta-name-change.html.

116. Eliana Johnson, "Donald Trump's 'Shadow President' in Silicon Valley," *Politico*, February 26, 2017, https://www.politico.com/story/2017/02/donald-trumps-shadow-president-in-silicon-valley-235372.

117. White House (archive), "Michael Kratsios, Chief Technology Officer of the United States," accessed June 18, 2023, https://trumpwhitehouse.archives.gov/people/michael-kratsios/.

118. Michael John Kotsakas Kratsios, "Senate Commerce Committee Nominee Question-naire, 116th Congress," April 4, 2019, https://www.commerce.senate.gov/services/files /ee198cae-4721-49af-bfa1-0f7d0f696256; "Michael Kratsios," LinkedIn, 2023, https:// www.linkedin.com/in/michaelkratsios/.

119. Douglas MacMillan, "The Man Playing Peacemaker Between Trump and Tech," *Wall Street Journal*, November 13, 2017, https://www.wsj.com/articles/michael-kratsios-plays -peacemaker-between-trump-and-tech-1510603201.

120. Michael Kratsios, "Public Financial Disclosure Report (OGE Form 278e)," June 1, 2017, https://s3.documentcloud.org/documents/4388504/Michael-John-Kotsakas-Kratsios -Financial.pdf.

121. "Michael Kratsios," LinkedIn; Douglas MacMillan, "Michael Kratsios Plays Peace-maker Between Trump and Tech—WSJ," *archive.vn*, November 13, 2017, https:// archive.vn/IoMLz; U.S. Embassy and Consulates in Italy, "Turin G7 Ministerial Ind.—-U.S. Delegation: Michael Kratsios," September 25, 2017, https://it.usembassy.gov /turin-g7-ministerial-u-s-delegation-michael-kratsios/.

122. Kratsios, "Public Financial Disclosure Report."

123. Scott Waldman, "Trump's Science Advisor, Age 31, Has a Political Science Degree," *Scientific American*, February 14, 2018, https://www.scientificamerican.com/article /trump-rsquo-s-science-advisor-age-31-has-a-political-science-degree/.

124. News Office, "Corporation Elects New Members," *MIT News*, Massachusetts Institute of Technology, June 3, 2011, https://news.mit.edu/2011/new-corporation-members -0603; Quentin Hardy, "Re-Engineering Google.Org," *Forbes*, February 24, 2009, https://www.forbes.com/2009/02/24/larry-brilliant-google-technology_brilliant.html.

125. "Todd Park," LinkedIn, 2023, https://www.linkedin.com/in/todd-park-3232573/details /experience/.

126. Colleen DeBaise and Scott Austin, "The Top 50 Venture-Backed Companies," *Wall Street Journal*, March 10, 2011, https://www.wsj.com/articles/SB10001424052748703300 904576178673309577828.

127. "Aneesh Chopra," LinkedIn, 2023, https://www.linkedin.com/in/apchopra/; Norman Nicolson, "Aneesh P. Chopra, Secretary of Technology, Virginia," GovTech, December 24, 2010, https://www.govtech.com/archive/Aneesh-P-Chopra-Secretary-of-Technology -Virginia.html.

128. U.S. Department of Defense, "DOD Names Acting Under Secretary of Defense for Research and Engineering" (Washington, DC, July 13, 2020), https://www.defense.gov /News/Releases/Release/Article/2271633/dod-names-acting-under-secretary-of -defense-for-research-and-engineering.

129. U.S. Department of Defense, "Michael D. Griffin," accessed June 18, 2023, https://www .defense.gov/About/Biographies/Biography/Article/1489249/michael-d-griffin/; Michael D. Griffin and Rebecca Wright, "Michael D. Griffin Oral History," history-collection.jsc.nasa.gov, September 10, 2007, https://historycollection.jsc.nasa.gov /JSCHistoryPortal/history/oral_histories/NASA_HQ/NAF/GriffinMD/GriffinMD _9-10-07.htm; Eminent Scholars Foundation, "By-Laws of Eminent Scholars Founda-tion," June 20, 2010, https://web.archive.org/web/20100620194139/http:/sacs.uah.edu /documents/policies/emminent_scholars_foundation_bylaws.pdf.

Years before, Griffin had played an interesting role with another member of the PayPal Mafia. In 2002 he joined Elon Musk on a trip to Russia where Musk first began to formulate his ideas for the company that would one day become SpaceX. A few months later Griffin became president and COO of In-Q-Tel, a role he would serve in until becoming the administrator of NASA. Jim Cantrell, "In 2002 Elon Musk

Traveled to Russia with Jim Cantrell, Adeo Ressi, and Mike Griffin, So Why Was Mike Griffin in Particular in Attendance?," Quora, accessed May 11, 2023, https://www.quora .com/In-2002-Elon-Musk-traveled-to-Russia-with-Jim-Cantrell-Adeo-Ressi-and -Mike-Griffin-so-why-was-Mike-Griffin-in-particular-in-attendance; "In-Q-Tel Names Dr. Michael D. Griffin as President and Chief Operating Officer," In-Q-Tel, August 5, 2002, https://www.iqt.org/news/in-q-tel-names-dr-michael-d-griffin-as-president -and-chief-operating-officer/.

130.   Still, to name a few: he'd received the ASA Exceptional Achievement Medal, the AIAA Space Systems Medal and Goddard Astronautics Award, the National Space Club's Goddard Trophy, the Rotary National Award for Space Achievement, the Missile Defense Agency's Ronald Reagan Award, and the Department of Defense Distinguished Public Service Medal, the highest award that can be conferred on a nongovernment employee.

131.   U.S. Department of Defense, "Michael D. Griffin."

132.   Rolfe Winkler, "Trump Transition Team Adds Tech Execs," *Wall Street Journal*, December 7, 2016, https://www.wsj.com/articles/trump-transition-team-adds-tech -execs-1481136755.

133.   Kate Brannen and Luke Hartig, "Disrupting the White House: Peter Thiel's Influence Is Shaping the National Security Council," *Just Security*, February 8, 2017, https://www .justsecurity.org/37466/disrupting-white-house-peter-thiels-influence-shaping -national-security-council/.

134.   Owen Thomas, "Trump Update: Peter Thiel Confidant Appointed to NSC Staff," *SFGATE*, February 2, 2017, https://www.sfgate.com/business/article/Trump-update -Peter-Thiel-confidant-appointed-to-10903818.php.

135.   Jenna McLaughlin, "The Guerrilla Campaign Against McMaster Is Alive and Well," *Foreign Policy* (blog), December 14, 2017, https://foreignpolicy.com/2017/12/14/the -guerrilla-campaign-against-mcmaster-is-alive-and-well/.

136.   Spencer Ackerman, "Trump Aide Floated Withdrawing U.S. Forces to Please Putin," *Daily Beast*, January 10, 2018, https://www.thedailybeast.com/white-house-official -floated-withdrawing-us-forces-to-please-putin.

137.   Paul Kirby, "Why Did Russia Invade Ukraine and Has Putin's War Failed?," *BBC News*, April 12, 2021, https://www.bbc.com/news/world-europe-56720589; "How Many Ukrainian Refugees Are There and Where Have They Gone?," *BBC News*, February 28, 2022, https://www.bbc.com/news/world-60555472; Alexander Vindman, "What I Heard in the White House Basement," *Atlantic*, August 2, 2021, https://www.theatlantic.com /politics/archive/2021/08/trump-ukraine-call-impeachment-vindman/619617/.

138.   Sarah Pruitt, "How a Five-Day War with Georgia Allowed Russia to Reassert Its Military Might," *History*, September 4, 2018, https://www.history.com/news/russia-georgia -war-military-nato; Center for Preventive Action, "Conflict in Ukraine," *Global Conflict Tracker*, November 8, 2022, https://cfr.org/global-conflict-tracker/conflict/conflict -ukraine; David Gilbert, "White House Aide Wanted to Pull U.S. Troops from Europe Because Putin Would Like It," *Vice* (blog), January 10, 2018, https://www.vice.com/en /article/wjp4q4/trump-putin-kevin-harrington-russia-troops.

139.   Spencer Ackerman, "Trump Aide Floated Withdrawing U.S. Forces to Please Putin," *Daily Beast*, January 10, 2018, https://www.thedailybeast.com/white-house-official -floated-withdrawing-us-forces-to-please-putin; Greg Miller, Greg Jaffe, and Philip Rucker, "How Trump's Skepticism of U.S. Intelligence on Russia Left an Election Threat Unchecked," *Washington Post*, December 14, 2017, https://www.washingtonpost

.com/graphics/2017/world/national-security/donald-trump-pursues-vladimir-putin
-russian-election-hacking/.

140. Ackerman, "Trump Aide Floated"; Edward Fishman, James Lamond, and Max Berg-
man, "Opinion: No, Trump Has Not Been 'Tough' on Russia," *Washington Post*, October 13, 2020, https://www.washingtonpost.com/opinions/2020/10/13/no-trump-has
-not-been-tough-russia/; Robert Siegel and Michael Isikoff, "Trump Administration
Made Secret Efforts to Ease Russia Sanctions," NPR, June 2, 2017, https://www.npr.org
/2017/06/02/531269090/trump-administration-made-secret-efforts-to-ease-russia
-sanctions.

141. Edward R. Royce, "Text—H.R.3364–115th Congress (2017–2018): Countering America's Adversaries Through Sanctions Act," congress.gov, August 2, 2017, https://www
.congress.gov/bill/115th-congress/house-bill/3364/text.

142. Abby Phillip, "Trump Signs What He Calls 'Seriously Flawed' Bill Imposing New Sanctions on Russia," *Washington Post*, November 26, 2021, https://www.washingtonpost
.com/news/post-politics/wp/2017/08/02/trump-signs-bill-imposing-new-sanctions
-on-russia-but-issues-a-statement-with-concerns/.

143. House Foreign Affairs Committee, "Engel Statement on President's Signing Sanctions
Legislation," August 2, 2017, https://democrats-foreignaffairs.house.gov/2017/8/engel
-statement-presidents-signing-sanctions-legislation.

144. CNN, "Read Trump's Phone Conversation with Volodymyr Zelensky," September 25,
2019, https://www.cnn.com/2019/09/25/politics/donald-trump-ukraine-transcript-call
/index.html.

145. Freedom House, "Countries and Territories," 2021, https://freedomhouse.org/countries
/freedom-world/scores.

146. Kyle Rempfer, "Purple Heart, Ranger Tab, FAO: Meet the Army Officer Testifying
About Trump's Ukraine Call," *Army Times*, October 29, 2019, https://www.armytimes
.com/news/your-army/2019/10/29/purple-heart-ranger-tab-fao-meet-the-army
-officer-testifying-about-trumps-ukraine-call/.

147. Vindman, "What I Heard."

148. U.S. Department of State, "Ukraine: Executive Summary," accessed June 18, 2023,
https://2009-2017.state.gov/documents/organization/186627.pdf.

149. Vindman, "What I Heard."

150. CNN, "Read Trump's Phone Conversation."

151. Committee on the Judiciary, "H. Rept. 116–346—Impeachment of Donald J. Trump
President of the United States," congress.gov, December 9, 2022, 2019/2020, https://
www.congress.gov/congressional-report/116th-congress/house-report/346/1; Reuters
staff, "U.S. Agrees to Sell $39 Million of Anti-Tank Weapons to Ukraine: Source,"
Reuters, October 1, 2019, https://www.reuters.com/article/us-usa-ukraine-arms
-idUSKBN1WG4P6.

152. CNN, "Read Trump's Phone Conversation."

153. Vindman, "What I Heard."

154. Sharon LaFraniere, Andrew E. Kramer, and Danny Hakim, "Key Dates at the Center of
the Ukraine Matter," *New York Times*, November 12, 2019, ttps://www.nytimes.com
/2019/11/11/us/politics/trump-ukraine-timeline.html.

155. Committee on the Judiciary, "H. Rept. 116–346."

156. Mark Galli, "Trump Should Be Removed from Office," *ChristianityToday*, December 19, 2019, https://www.christianitytoday.com/ct/2019/december-web-only/trump
-should-be-removed-from-office.html.

157. Nahal Toosi, "Trump's New National Security Adviser Shakes Up Staff," *Politico*, October 11, 2019, https://www.politico.com/news/2019/10/11/national-security-council -staff-changes-044622; FederalPay.org, "Employee Profile of Kevin John Harrington— Miscellaneous Administration and Program," accessed June 18, 2023, https://www .federalpay.org/employees/national-security-council/harrington-kevin-john.

## 12. There Will Be Blood

1. "Ephemera 2009 (7)," *Kung Fu Monkey* (blog), March 19, 2009, https://web.archive.org /web/20200615171201/http://kfmonkey.blogspot.com/2009/03/ephemera-2009-7 .html.

2. IMDB, "'Transformers': Their War. Our World," June 27, 2007, https://www.imdb.com /title/tt1023626/.

3. Roopinder Tara, "Uber's Self-Driving Car Had 6 Seconds to Respond Before Fatal Crash, but Got Confused, Did Nothing," Engineering.com, June 5, 2018, https://www .engineering.com/story/ubers-self-driving-car-had-6-seconds-to-respond-before -fatal-crash-but-got-confused-did-nothing; Daisuke Wakabayashi, "Self-Driving Uber Car Kills Pedestrian in Arizona, Where Robots Roam," *New York Times*, March 19, 2018, https://www.nytimes.com/2018/03/19/technology/uber-driverless-fatality.html.

4. Ensar Becic, "Vehicle Automation Report," National Transportation Safety Board, Office of Highway Safety, 2018, 11, https://www.documentcloud.org/documents /6540547-629713.

5. Becic, 11–12.

6. "Uber Dashcam Footage Shows Lead Up to Fatal Self-Driving Crash," YouTube video, 2018, https://www.youtube.com/watch?v=RASBcc4yOOo; "Video Shows Moments Before Fatal Uber Self-Driving Crash," YouTube video, 2018, https://www.youtube.com /watch?v=R8Up9Ph_aoY.

7. YouTube Help, "Violent or Graphic Content Policies," accessed June 18, 2023, https:// support.google.com/youtube/answer/2802008?hl=en&ref_topic=9282436&sjid =16701646580393519876-NA.

8. Meta Platforms, "Violent and Graphic Content | Transparency Center," accessed June 18, 2023, https://transparency.fb.com/policies/community-standards/violent -graphic-content/.

9. Daniel Victor, "Man Inadvertently Broadcasts His Own Killing on Facebook Live," *New York Times*, June 17, 2016, https://www.nytimes.com/2016/06/18/us/man -inadvertently-broadcasts-his-own-killing-on-facebook-live.html.

10. Steven Levy, *Facebook: The Inside Story* (New York: Blue Rider Press, 2020), 441.

11. Google bought YouTube for $1.65 billion and DoubleClick for $3.1 billion. As important as the YouTube acquisition was, the DoubleClick deal paved the way for the ad-based business model that would redesign Google's entire approach, in ways that ran completely contrary to the original thesis proposed by Page and Brin. Louise Story and Miguel Helft, "Google Buys DoubleClick for $3.1 Billion," *New York Times*, April 14, 2007, https://www.nytimes.com/2007/04/14/technology/14DoubleClick.html;

12. Nicholas Jackson, "Infographic: The History of Video Advertising on YouTube," *Atlantic*, August 3, 2011, https://www.theatlantic.com/technology/archive/2011/08/infographic -the-history-of-video-advertising-on-youtube/242836/.

13. L. Ceci, "U.S. YouTube Reach by Age Group 2020," Statista, March 15, 2022, https:// www.statista.com/statistics/296227/us-youtube-reach-age-gender/

14. Tasneem Nashrulla, "Here Are the Last Moments Before a YouTube Stunt Went Fatally Wrong," *BuzzFeed News*, June 22, 2018, https://www.buzzfeed.com/tasneemnashrulla /failed-youtube-stunt-killing-videos.

15. Jared Leone, "Tennessee Man Wielding Butcher Knife for YouTube Robbery . . . Prank . . . Fatally Shot, Police Say," *FOX13 Memphis*, February 8, 2021, https://www .fox13memphis.com/trending_archives/tennessee-man-wielding-butcher-knife -for-youtube-robbery-prank-fatally-shot-police-say/article_0825f657-ebcb-50ff-85c6 -6bd5ba053264.html.

16. YouTube Help, "Harmful or Dangerous Content Policies," 2022, https://support.google .com/youtube/answer/2801964.

17. Lauren Smiley, " 'I'm the Operator': The Aftermath of a Self-Driving Tragedy," *Wired*, March 8, 2022, https://www.wired.com/story/uber-self-driving-car-fatal-crash/.

18. Richard Gonzales, "Feds Say Self-Driving Uber SUV Did Not Recognize Jaywalking Pedestrian in Fatal Crash," NPR, November 7, 2019, https://www.npr.org/2019/11/07 /777438412/feds-say-self-driving-uber-suv-did-not-recognize-jaywalking-pedestrian -in-fatal-.

19. Alex Davies, *Driven: The Race to Create the Autonomous Car* (New York: Simon and Schuster, 2022), 191; "Jeff Holden," LinkedIn, 2023, https://www.linkedin.com/in /jeffholden/.

20. Biz Carson, "Travis Kalanick on Uber's Bet on Self-Driving Cars: 'I Can't Be Wrong,' " *Business Insider*, August 18, 2016, https://www.businessinsider.com/travis-kalanick -interview-on-self-driving-cars-future-driver-jobs-2016-8.

21. Smiley, " 'I'm the Operator.' "

22. Smiley.

23. Tara, "Uber's Self-Driving Car Had 6 Seconds."

24. "Video Bodycam Video Reveals New Details of Deadly Uber Self-Driving Car Accident," *ABC News*, June 23, 2018, https://abcnews.go.com/GMA/News/video/bodycam -video-reveals-details-deadly-uber-driving-car-56105010.

25. Catherine Shu, "Report: A Manager at Uber's Self-Driving Unit Warned Executives About Safety Issues Just Days Before Fatal Crash," *TechCrunch*, December 11, 2018, https://techcrunch.com/2018/12/10/report-a-manager-at-ubers-self-driving-unit -warned-executives-about-safety-issues-just-days-before-fatal-crash/.

26. Amir Efrati, "The Uber Whistleblower's Email," *Information*, December 10, 2018, https://www.theinformation.com/articles/the-uber-whistleblowers-email.

27. Shu, "Report."

28. Ruth Styles, "Operator of Self-Driving Uber Had a History of Traffic Violations," *Daily Mail Online*, March 21, 2018, http://www.dailymail.co.uk/news/article-5527575/Operator -self-driving-Uber-history-traffic-violations.html.

29. Ryan Randazzo, Uriel J. Garcia, and Bree Burkitt, "Uber Touts Corporate Policy to Offer Felons a Second Chance," *Arizona Republic*, March 19, 2018, https://www .azcentral.com/story/news/local/tempe/2018/03/19/operator-self-driving-uber -vehicle-killed-pedestrian-felon/440501002/.

30. Smiley, " 'I'm the Operator.' "

31. Noah R. Bombard, "NTSB Report: Driver Inattentive and Pedestrian on Drugs in Automated Uber Crash That Killed Arizona Woman," *MassLive*, December 11, 2019, https://www.masslive.com/news/2019/12/ntsb-report-on-automated-uber-crash-that -killed-elaine-herzberg-reveals-pedestrian-was-on-drugs-driver-was-inattentive .html.

32. Shu, "Report."

33. Smiley, "'I'm the Operator.'"

34. Mark Harris, "Exclusive: Arizona Governor and Uber Kept Self-Driving Program Secret, Emails Reveal," *Guardian*, March 28, 2018https://www.theguardian.com/technology/2018/mar/28/uber-arizona-secret-self-driving-program-governor-doug-ducey

35. State of Arizona, "Officers and Employees Required to Take Loyalty Oath; Form," azleg.gov, accessed June 18, 2023, https://www.azleg.gov/ars/38/00231.htm.

36. Office of the Arizona Governor, "Governor Ducey Tells Uber 'CA May Not Want You, but AZ Does,'" December 22, 2016, https://web.archive.org/web/20210219083522/https://azgovernor.gov/governor/news/2016/12/governor-ducey-tells-uber-ca-may-not-want-you-az-does

37. Office of the Arizona Governor, "Regulation Rollback," October 19, 2016, https://web.archive.org/web/20180214222341/https://azgovernor.gov/redtape.

38. "Longest Continuous Journey by a Driverless and Autonomous Lorry," *Guinness World Records*, October 20, 2016, https://www.guinnessworldrecords.com/world-records/361214-%E2%80%8Blongest-continuous-journey-by-an-autonomous-vehicle.

39. Alyssa Newcomb, "Former Uber CEO's 'Bro-Cabulary' Steals the Show in Court," *NBC News*, February 7, 2018, https://www.nbcnews.com/tech/tech-news/former-uber-ceo-steals-show-court-trade-secrets-bro-cabulary-n845541.

40. Rob Price, "'GREED IS GOOD': Ex-Uber CEO Travis Kalanick Denies Stealing Google Trade Secrets in Explosive Silicon Valley Trial," *Yahoo News*, February 7, 2018, https://www.yahoo.com/news/former-uber-ceo-travis-kalanick-150144230.html.

41. Peter Holley, "'Greed Is Good'? Waymo Turns to Gordon Gekko to Aid Its Case Against Uber," *Washington Post*, December 5, 2021, https://www.washingtonpost.com/news/innovations/wp/2018/02/07/greed-is-good-silicon-valley-hotshots-channeled-gordon-gecko-before-swiping-trade-secrets-waymo-alleges/.

42. Americanrhetoric, "Movie Speech: Wall Street—Gordon Gekko Addresses Teldar Shareholders—Greed Is Good," accessed June 18, 2023, https://www.americanrhetoric.com/MovieSpeeches/moviespeechwallstreet.html.

43. Bree Burkitt, "Fatal Uber Crash: A Timeline of the Crash and Investigation," *Arizona Republic*, June 22, 2018, https://www.azcentral.com/story/news/local/tempe/2018/06/22/fatal-uber-crash-timeline-crash-and-investigation/725921002/.

44. Ray Stern, "Self-Driving Uber Crash 'Avoidable,' Driver's Phone Playing Video Before Woman Struck," *Phoenix New Times*, June 21, 2018, https://www.phoenixnewtimes.com/news/self-driving-uber-crash-avoidable-drivers-phone-playing-video-before-woman-struck-10543284.

45. Burkitt, "Fatal Uber Crash."

46. Travis Hiland, "The Untold Story of Elaine Herzberg," *AFSC Arizona | ReFraming Justice* (blog), May 14, 2018, https://afscarizona.org/2018/05/14/the-untold-story-of-elaine-herzberg/.

47. Burkitt, "Fatal Uber Crash."

48. Romain Dillet, "Uber Acquires Otto to Lead Uber's Self-Driving Car Effort," *TechCrunch*, August 18, 2016, https://techcrunch.com/2016/08/18/uber-acquires-otto-to-lead-ubers-self-driving-car-effort-report-says/.

49. Waymo Team, "A Note on Our Lawsuit Against Otto and Uber," *Waymo* (blog), February 23, 2017, https://medium.com/waymo/a-note-on-our-lawsuit-against-otto-and-uber-86f4f98902a1.

50. Mike Isaac and Daisuke Wakabayashi, "Uber Fires Former Google Engineer at Heart of Self-Driving Dispute," *New York Times*, May 30, 2017, https://www.nytimes.com/2017/05/30/technology/uber-anthony-levandowski.html.

51. Bill Chappell, "Uber Parks Its Self-Driving Truck Project, Saying It Will Push for Autonomous Cars," NPR, July 31, 2018, https://www.npr.org/2018/07/31/634331593/uber-parks-its-self-driving-truck-project-saying-it-will-push-for-autonomous-car; Joe Mullin, "Uber Engineer Levandowski, Accused of Massive Theft from Google, Has Been Fired," Ars Technica, May 30, 2017, https://arstechnica.com/tech-policy/2017/05/ubers-levandowski-gets-fired/.

52. Alex Wilhelm, "Google Ventures Puts $258M Into Uber, Its Largest Deal Ever," *TechCrunch*, August 23, 2013, https://techcrunch.com/2013/08/22/google-ventures-puts-258m-into-uber-its-largest-deal-ever/.

53. Ari Levy, "Alphabet's Investment in Uber Has Multiplied by 20-Fold Since 2013," CNBC, April 11, 2019, https://www.cnbc.com/2019/04/11/alphabet-uber-investment-stake-has-gone-up-20x-since-2013.html.

54. Dara Khosrowshahi, "Uber and Waymo Reach Settlement," Uber Newsroom, February 9, 2018, https://www.uber.com/newsroom/uber-waymo-settlement/.

55. "Waymo and Uber Partner to Bring Waymo's Autonomous Driving Technology to the Uber Platform," *Waypoint—the official Waymo blog*, May 23, 2023, https://waymo.com/blog/2023/05/waymo-and-uber-partner-to-bring-waymos.html.

56. Roger Montti, "Google's 'Don't Be Evil' No Longer Prefaces Code of Conduct," *Search Engine Journal*, May 20, 2018, https://www.searchenginejournal.com/google-dont-be-evil/254019/; Anthony Cuthbertson, "Google Just Quietly Removed References to 'Don't Be Evil' from Its Code of Conduct," *Independent*, May 21, 2018, https://www.independent.co.uk/tech/google-dont-be-evil-code-conduct-removed-alphabet-a8361276.html.

57. Montti, "Google's 'Don't Be Evil.'"

58. Sergey Brin and Larry Page, "A Letter from Larry and Sergey," Google, December 3, 2019, https://blog.google/alphabet/letter-from-larry-and-sergey/.

59. Alex Davies, "Trump Pardoned the Star Google Engineer Who Was Paid $120 Million, Then Got Sentenced to Prison. Here's the Definitive Story of Anthony Levandowski," *Business Insider*, January 20, 2020, https://www.businessinsider.com/google-waymo-self-driving-uber-atg-levandowski-urmson-davies-driven-2020-12

60. Davies.

61. Adam, "I Drink Your Milkshake!" Know Your Meme, January 26, 2021, https://knowyourmeme.com/memes/i-drink-your-milkshake.

62. U.S. Attorney's Office, Northern District of California, "Former Uber Executive Sentenced to 18 Months in Jail for Trade Secret Theft from Google," August 4, 2020, https://www.justice.gov/usao-ndca/pr/former-uber-executive-sentenced-18-months-jail-trade-secret-theft-google.

63. "Anthony Levandowski: Ex-Google Engineer Sentenced for Theft," *BBC News*, August 5, 2020, https://www.bbc.com/news/world-us-canada-53659805.

64. Gina Hall, "Google Former Engineering Manager Anthony Levandowski Earned $120 Million While Working on Competing Projects, Company Claims in Self-Driving Car Arbitration Case," *Silicon Valley Business Journal*, April 4, 2017, https://www.bizjournals.com/sanjose/news/2017/04/04/anthony-levandowski-google-uber-otto-waymo-lawsuit.html.

65. U.S. Attorney's Office, Northern District of California, "Former Uber Executive Sentenced."

66. Joel Rosenblatt, "Ex-Google Exec Calls Prison Possible 'Death Sentence,'" *Automotive News Europe*, July 29, 2020, https://europe.autonews.com/suppliers/ex-google-exec-calls-prison-possible-death-sentence.

67. Kirsten Korosec, "Former Google Engineer Anthony Levandowski Among List of Last-Minute Trump Pardons," *TechCrunch*, January 20, 2021, https://techcrunch.com/2021/01/19/former-google-engineer-anthony-levandowski-among-list-of-last-minute-trump-pardons/.

68. Press Secretary, "Statement from the Press Secretary Regarding Executive Grants of Clemency," White House, January 20, 2021, https://trumpwhitehouse.archives.gov/briefings-statements/statement-press-secretary-regarding-executive-grants-clemency-012021/.

69. Daniel Gill, "Bankrupt Ex-Uber Engineer's Criminal Counsel Opposed by U.S.," Bloomberg Law, April 29, 2020, https://news.bloomberglaw.com/bankruptcy-law/bankrupt-ex-uber-engineers-criminal-counsel-opposed-by-u-s.

70. "Michael Ovitz," LinkedIn, 2023, https://www.linkedin.com/in/mikeovitz/.

71. Crunchbase, "Michael Ovitz—Co-Founder @ Creative Artists Agency—Crunchbase Person Profile," accessed June 18, 2023, https://www.crunchbase.com/person/michael-ovitz.

72. Brian Solomon, "Peter Thiel's Chosen One: This 25-Year-Old CEO Wants to Make Sleep a Billion-Dollar Business," *Forbes*, January 3, 2017, https://www.forbes.com/sites/briansolomon/2017/01/03/james-proud-hello-sense-sleep-apple-amazon/.

73. Max Chafkin, *The Contrarian: Peter Thiel and Silicon Valley's Pursuit of Power* (London: Bloomsbury, 2021), 167.

74. Solomon, "Peter Thiel's Chosen One."

75. Samar Marwan, "Peter Thiel Fellow James Proud Shuts Down Sleep Tracking Startup, Hello," *Forbes*, June 13, 2017, https://www.forbes.com/sites/samarmarwan/2017/06/13/thiel-fellow-james-proud-shuts-down-sleep-tracking-startup/.

76. Hello, "Goodbye, Hello," *Medium* (blog), June 12, 2017, https://medium.com/@hello/goodbye-hello-c62ea1f58d13.

77. CB Insights Research, "252 of the Biggest, Costliest Startup Failures of All Time," February 7, 2023, https://www.cbinsights.com/research/biggest-startup-failures/.

78. Solomon, "Peter Thiel's Chosen One."

79. Marwan, "Peter Thiel Fellow James Proud."

80. Crunchbase, "Series A—Flexport—2015-08-06—Crunchbase Funding Round Profile," https://www.crunchbase.com/funding_round/flexport-series-a--e890e105.

81. Jessica Davies, "Flexport Tackles Trump Tariffs with Data and Analytics," *InformationWeek*, August 22, 2019, https://www.informationweek.com/it-strategy/flexport-tackles-trump-tariffs-with-data-and-analytics.

82. Megan Rose Dickey, "Flexport CEO Expresses Some Remorse in Taking Cash from Peter Thiel," *TechCrunch*, June 28, 2016, https://techcrunch.com/2016/06/28/flexport-peter-thiel/.

83. Crunchbase, "Series B—Flexport—2016-09-26—Crunchbase Funding Round Profile," https://www.crunchbase.com/funding_round/flexport-series-b--d50a22f3.

84. Crunchbase, "Series C—Flexport—2017-09-21—Crunchbase Funding Round Profile," https://www.crunchbase.com/funding_round/flexport-series-c--dc0d6dac.

85. "Flexport's Ryan Petersen: 'Plan for the Unimaginable,'" *Danny in the Valley*, Apple Podcasts, 25:25, August 7, 2020, https://podcasts.apple.com/ie/podcast/flexports-ryan-petersen-plan-for-the-unimaginable/id1233991021?i=1000487366350.

86. "Flexport's Ryan Petersen," 27:22.

87. CNBC.com staff, "1. Flexport," CNBC, May 17, 2022, https://www.cnbc.com/2022/05
/17/flexport-disruptor-50.html.

88. Anduril, "Anduril Leadership," accessed October 10, 2023, https://www.anduril.com
/leadership/.

89. The initial sales were crowdsourced on Kickstarter. The headset debuted on August 1,
2012, and prospective buyers preordered the first $250,000 worth of the product in two
hours. Within days, the first Oculus headsets had brought in $2,427,429 when they
stopped taking in money. The incredible innovation Luckey had designed over a couple of years and debuted in a matter of months was enough to get Mark Zuckerberg
interested enough to offer nearly $1 billion to buy Luckey's company outright less than
eighteen months later. Zuckerberg was told no. Less than a week later, after further
negotiations, Facebook bought it for $2 billion on March 16, 2014, with an additional
$700 million in potential earn outs if all went well.
    At the Atlas Society's gala in 2021, Luckey introduced Thiel. "I'm only here because
of Peter. I mean that figuratively in terms of my enormous wealth," he joked. Later in
the speech, Luckey explained that he kept working in tech because of Thiel: "I knew
Peter, and he encouraged me to keep doing what I was doing and told me that I had his
support. And that really meant a lot to me, because I knew that there was at least one
person who really supported me—not just then, but who has supported me in a lot of
ways that people are not even necessarily familiar with—because this wasn't the first
time that Peter had helped me when very few people were even willing to talk to me."
Levy, *Facebook*, 328–29; Oculus VR, "VR Gets VC," *Oculus Blog*, June 17, 2013, https://
www.oculus.com/blog/vr-gets-vc; Crunchbase, "Series A—Oculus—2013-06-17—
Crunchbase Funding Round Profile," https://www.crunchbase.com/funding_round
/oculus-vr-series-a--1be5636e; "The 2021 Atlas Society Gala: Palmer Luckey's Speech,"
YouTube video, 0:21; 9:35; 10:42; 12:03; 12:32, https://www.youtube.com/watch?v
=lJRTkjA-UJo.

90. Jyoti Mann, "Meta Has Spent $36 Billion Building the Metaverse but Still Has Little to
Show for It, While Tech Sensations Such as the IPhone, Xbox, and Amazon Echo Cost
Way Less," *Business Insider*, October 29, 2022, https://www.businessinsider.com/meta
-lost-30-billion-on-metaverse-rivals-spent-far-less-2022-10.

91. Farhad Manjoo, "Opinion | My Sad, Lonely, Expensive Adventures in Zuckerberg's
V.R.," *New York Times*, November 4, 2022, https://www.nytimes.com/2022/11/04
/opinion/facebook-meta-zuckerberg-virtual-reality.html.

92. Taylor Hatmaker, "Meta's Reality Labs Lost $13.7 Billion on VR and AR Last Year,"
*TechCrunch*, February 3, 2023, https://techcrunch.com/2023/02/03/metas-reality-labs
-lost-13-7-billion-on-vr-and-ar-last-year/.

93. Rachel Sandler, "Mark Zuckerberg Is No Longer One of the 10 Richest Americans,"
*Forbes*, September 27, 2022, https://www.forbes.com/sites/rachelsandler/2022/09/27
/mark-zuckerberg-is-no-longer-one-of-the-10-richest-americans/.

94. Ben Cohen, "There Has to Be a Better Way to Lose $800 Billion," *Wall Street Journal*,
November 3, 2022, https://www.wsj.com/articles/meta-facebook-metaverse-mark
-zuckerberg-11667424987.

95. Mark Zuckerberg, "Mark Zuckerberg's Message to Meta Employees," *Meta* (blog),
November 9, 2022, https://about.fb.com/news/2022/11/mark-zuckerberg-layoff-message
-to-employees/.

96. Zuckerberg.

97. Alex Hern, "Zuckerberg's Meta to Lay off Another 10,000 Employees," *Guardian*, March 14, 2023, https://www.theguardian.com/technology/2023/mar/14/mark-zucker berg-meta-layoffs-hiring-freeze.

98. On other occasions, Luckey was more direct in his accusation that Zuckerberg fired him for the donation. "I refuse to be a professional victim, though I am consumed with rage every day. You see, I got fired from my own company because I gave $10,000 to a group that ran a single anti-Clinton billboard. It was actually pretty tame. It was a pic- ture of Hillary Clinton and the caption, 'Too Big To Jail.'" He added, "So, I gave them $10,000, which to me as a newly minted rich man, it really wasn't anything, I thought very little of it." "The 2021 Atlas Society Gala: Palmer Luckey's Speech," YouTube video, 2022, https://www.youtube.com/watch?v=lJRTkjA-UJo.

99. Steven Levy, "Palmer Luckey Says Working with Weapons Isn't as Fun as VR," *Wired*, March 15, 2022, https://www.wired.com/story/palmer-luckey-drones-autonomous -weapons-ukraine/.

100. Adi Robertson, "Palmer Luckey's Surveillance Startup Anduril Signs Contract for 'Vir- tual Border Wall,'" Verge, July 2, 2020, https://www.theverge.com/2020/7/2/21311433 /anduril-palmer-luckey-virtual-border-wall-surveillance-contract-patrol.

101. Taylor Hatmaker, "Anduril Launches a Smarter Drone and Picks Up More Money to Build a Virtual Border Wall," *TechCrunch*, September 11, 2020, https://techcrunch.com /2020/09/10/anduril-cbp-ghost-2020/.

102. Jackson Barnett, "Anduril Nabs $1B Contract for Anti-Drone Work with SOCOM," FedScoop, January 20, 2022, https://www.fedscoop.com/anduril-nabs-1b-contract-for -anti-drone-work-with-socom/.

103. Crunchbase, "Seed Round—Anduril Industries—2017-08-11—Crunchbase Funding Round Profile," https://www.crunchbase.com/funding_round/anduril-industries -seed--25afedd8.

104. John Ronald Reuel Tolkien, *Two Towers* (New York: Houghton Mifflin, 1965), 225.

105. John Ronald Reuel Tolkien, *The Lord of the Rings* (New York: Houghton Mifflin, 1965), 290.

106. Kashmir Hill, *Your Face Belongs to Us: A Secretive Startup's Quest to End Privacy as We Know It* (New York: Random House, 2023), 57–58.

107. Ryan Mac, Caroline Haskins, and Logan McDonald, "Secret Users Of Clearview AI's Facial Recognition Dragnet Included a Former Trump Staffer, a Troll, and Conserva- tive Think Tanks," *BuzzFeed News*, March 25, 2020, https://www.buzzfeednews.com /article/ryanmac/clearview-ai-trump-investors-friend-facial-recognition.

108. Luke O'Brien, "Far-Right Extremists Helped Create the World's Most Powerful Facial Recognition Technology," *HuffPost*, April 7, 2020, https://www.huffpost.com/entry /clearview-ai-facial-recognition-alt-right_n_5e7d028bc5b6cb08a92a5c48.

109. Anti-Defamation League, "Okay Hand Gesture," June 2022, https://web.archive.org /web/20220602002911/https://www.adl.org/resources/hate-symbol/okay-hand -gesture.

110. U.S. Department of Justice, Eastern District of New York, "Social Media Influencer Douglass Mackey Convicted of Election Interference in 2016 Presidential Race," March 31, 2023, https://www.justice.gov/usao-edny/pr/social-media-influencer -douglass-mackey-convicted-election-interference-2016."

111. "Torch-Wielding Protesters Gather at Lee Park," *Daily Progress*, May 13, 2017, https:// dailyprogress.com/news/local/torch-wielding-protesters-gather-at-lee-park/article _201dc390-384d-11e7-bf16-fb43deof5d38.html.

112. O'Brien, "Far-Right Extremists."

113. Natasha Lomas, "DigitalOcean and Cloudflare Ditch Neo-Nazi Client, the Daily Stormer," *TechCrunch*, August 16, 2017, https://techcrunch.com/2017/08/16/digital-ocean-and-cloudflare-ditch-neo-nazi-client-the-daily-stormer/.

114. "Man Gets Life Plus 419 Years in Deadly Charlottesville Car Attack," *CBS News*, July 15, 2019, https://www.cbsnews.com/news/james-alex-fields-jr-charlottesville-car-attack-sentenced-life-plus-419-years-today-2019-07-15/.

115. Erika Kinetz and Lori Hinnant, "'White Dissidents' Raise Millions in Cryptocurrency," *Frontline*, September 27, 2021, https://www.pbs.org/wgbh/frontline/article/far-right-extremists-raise-millions-cryptocurrency-bitcoin/.

116. Matt Reynolds, "Alt-Right Outlet Sued for Linking Michigan Men to Charlottesville Attack," *Courthouse News*, February 15, 2018, https://www.courthousenews.com/alt-right-outlet-sued-for-linking-michigan-men-to-charlottesville-attack/; J. Thomas Richie and John Goodman, "A Quick Study in Doxing and Personal Jurisdiction: Vangheluwe v. GotNews," *JD Supra* (blog), September 5, 2019, https://www.jdsupra.com/legalnews/a-quick-study-in-doxing-and-personal-56018/.

117. Alexander Nazaryan, "Why Did Right-Wing Troll Charles C. Johnson Meet with Commerce Secretary Wilbur Ross?," *Yahoo News*, May 16, 2019, https://news.yahoo.com/why-did-rightwing-troll-charles-c-johnson-want-to-meet-with-commerce-secretary-wilbur-ross-090000636.html.

118. Jon Porter, "Facebook and LinkedIn Are Latest to Demand Clearview Stop Scraping Images for Facial Recognition Tech," Verge, February 6, 2020, https://www.theverge.com/2020/2/6/21126063/facebook-clearview-ai-image-scraping-facial-recognition-database-terms-of-service-twitter-youtube; Kashmir Hill, "Twitter Tells Facial Recognition Trailblazer to Stop Using Site's Photos," *New York Times*, January 23, 2020, https://www.nytimes.com/2020/01/22/technology/clearview-ai-twitter-letter.html; Matt O'Brien, "YouTube, Venmo Tell Clearview AI to Stop Scraping Sites," *San Francisco Chronicle*, February 5, 2020, https://www.sfchronicle.com/business/article/YouTube-Venmo-tell-Clearview-AI-to-stop-scraping-15033473.php.

119. Porter, "Facebook and LinkedIn."

120. Edward J. Markey, "Letter to Hoan Ton-That," accessed June 18, 2023, https://int.nyt.com/data/documenthelper/6718-sen-markey-letter-to-clearview/33422997119c3d43033d/optimized/full.pdf#page=1.

121. Paul D. Clement, "ClearView AI," https://data.aclum.org/wp-content/uploads/2021/02/A-privatecompanies/A11-clearview/A11j-wellesley/documents/Success%20Stories.pdf.

122. Clearview AI, "Overview," accessed June 18, 2023, https://www.clearview.ai/overview.

123. Clearview AI, "Clearview—Technology to Help Solve the Hardest Crimes," March 9, 2020, https://web.archive.org/web/20200309013754/https:/clearview.ai/.

124. Kashmir Hill, "The Secretive Company That Might End Privacy as We Know It," *New York Times*, January 18, 2020, https://www.nytimes.com/2020/01/18/technology/clearview-privacy-facial-recognition.html.

125. U.S. Government Accountability Office, "Facial Recognition Technology: Current and Planned Uses by Federal Agencies," GAO-21-526, August 2021, https://www.gao.gov/assets/gao-21-526.pdf, 20, 26–28.

126. Clearview AI, "Clearview AI | The World's Largest Facial Network," October 9, 2021, https://web.archive.org/web/20211009170407/https:/www.clearview.ai/.

127. Drew Harwell, "Facial Recognition Firm Clearview AI Tells Investors It's Seeking Massive Expansion Beyond Law Enforcement," *Washington Post*, February 19, 2022,

https://www.washingtonpost.com/technology/2022/02/16/clearview-expansion-facial-recognition/.

128. Clearview AI, "Facial Recognition," June 2, 2022, https://web.archive.org/web/20220602110703/https://www.clearview.ai/.

129. Clearview AI, "Overview."

130. Ryan Mac, Caroline Haskins, Brianna Sacks, and Logan McDonald, "How a Facial Recognition Tool Found Its Way Into Hundreds of US Police Departments, Schools, and Taxpayer-Funded Organizations," *BuzzFeed News*, April 10, 2021, https://www.buzzfeednews.com/article/ryanmac/clearview-ai-local-police-facial-recognition.

131. "Tagged Stories: Clearview Ai," *BuzzFeed*, accessed June 18, 2023, https://www.buzzfeed.com/tag/clearview-ai.

132. Logan McDonald, Ryan Mac, and Caroline Haskins, "Clearview AI Is Struggling to Address Complaints as Its Legal Issues Mount," *BuzzFeed News*, January 28, 2020, https://www.buzzfeed.com/ryanmac/clearview-ai-cops-run-wild-facial-recognition-lawsuits.

133. Logan McDonald, Ryan Mac, and Caroline Haskins, "Clearview's Facial Recognition App Has Been Used by the Justice Department, ICE, Macy's, Walmart, and the NBA," *BuzzFeed News*, February 28, 2020, https://www.buzzfeednews.com/article/ryanmac/clearview-ai-fbi-ice-global-law-enforcement.

134. "I've come to the conclusion that because information constantly increases, there's never going to be privacy," David Scalzo, one of Clearview AI's earliest investors, told Kashmir Hill. Those words echoed Travis Kalanick's blog post from over a decade prior, where he'd argued that "hyper-transparency is the world we are increasingly living in and we all better get used to it," and Peter Thiel's essay where he deemed "inviolable individual rights" to be "rendered an unviable anachronism." As Scalzo saw it, "Laws have to determine what's legal, but you can't ban technology. Sure, that might lead to a dystopian future or something, but you can't ban it." Hill, "The Secretive Company"; Travis Kalanick, "The Whole Truth and Nothing but the Truth, So Help Your Reputation," *Swooshing* (blog), March 30, 2010, https://swooshing.wordpress.com/2010/03/30/the-whole-truth-and-nothing-but-the-truth-so-help-your-reputation/; Peter Thiel, "The Straussian Moment," in *Politics and Apocalypse*, ed. Robert Hamerton-Kelly (East Lansing: Michigan State University Press, 2007), 209, http://www.jstor.org/stable/10.14321/j.ctt7zt6qq.9.

135. Ryan Mac, Caroline Haskins, and Logan McDonald, "Clearview AI Says Its Facial Recognition Software Identified a Terrorism Suspect. The Cops Say That's Not True," *BuzzFeed News*, January 23, 2020, https://www.buzzfeednews.com/article/ryanmac/clearview-ai-nypd-facial-recognition.

136. U.S. Department of State, "United Arab Emirates 2019 Human Rights Report," Country Reports on Human Rights Practices for 2019, March 2020, https://www.state.gov/wp-content/uploads/2020/03/UNITED-ARAB-EMIRATES-2019-HUMAN-RIGHTS-REPORT.pdf.

137. Clearview AI, "Clearview AI | The World's Largest Facial Network."

138. Crunchbase, "Anduril Industries—Crunchbase Company Profile & Funding," accessed June 18, 2023, https://www.crunchbase.com/organization/anduril-industries; "Palmer Luckey," LinkedIn, accessed June 18, 2023, https://www.linkedin.com/in/palmer-luckey-21a16959/.

139. "Sturgill Simpson—Call to Arms," YouTube video, January 30, 2017, *Saturday Night Live*, https://www.youtube.com/watch?v=qsrsrOBozNQ&ab_channel=Sturgill Simpson.

140. "Sturgill Simpson—Call to Arm." Fun fact: Sturgill Simpson sang "our fucking skies" as the final line to the song on *A Sailor's Guide to Earth*, but he altered it to "American skies" for the SNL appearance, which he also used on *Cuttin' Grass Vol. 2: The Cowboy Arms Sessions* from 2020.

## 13. A New Crusade


1. Peter Thiel, "The Straussian Moment," in *Politics and Apocalypse: Studies in Violence, Mimesis, and Culture*, ed. Robert Hamerton-Kelly (East Lansing: Michigan State University Press, 2007), 189–90, http://www.jstor.org/stable/10.14321/j.ctt7zt6qq.9.
2. Thiel, 189–90.
3. "Costs of the 20-Year War on Terror: $8 Trillion and 900,000 Deaths," *News from Brown*, Brown University, September 1, 2021, https://www.brown.edu/news/2021-09-01/costsofwar.
4. Thiel, "The Straussian Moment," 190. If "Dieu le veult!" sounds familiar, it's probably because the same phrase, which means "God wills it!," was chanted (in its Latin form, "Deus Vult") by white nationalists at the Unite the Right rally in Charlottesville, Virginia, in 2017. The words "Deus Vult," above the red cross of the Christian Crusades, appeared on t-shirts and flags carried by violent protestors both in Charlottesville and at the storming of the U.S. Capitol on January 6, 2021. "Deus Vult" has also appeared in anti-Muslim graffiti on mosques; in Arkansas, it was scrawled alongside a swastika and the words "Go Home" and "We Don't Want You Here U.S.A." Neda Ulaby, "Scholars Say White Supremacists Chanting 'Deus Vult' Got History Wrong," NPR, September 4, 2017, https://www.npr.org/2017/09/04/548505783/scholars-say-white-supremacists-chanting-deus-vult-got-history-wrong; *Washington Post* staff, "Deconstructing the Symbols and Slogans Spotted in Charlottesville," *Washington Post*, August 18, 2017, https://www.washingtonpost.com/graphics/2017/local/charlottesville-videos/; Sabrina Tavernise, "At an Arkansas Mosque, a Vandal Spreads Hate and Finds Mercy," *New York Times*, August 26, 2017, https://www.nytimes.com/interactive/2017/08/26/us/fort-smith-arkansas-mosque-vandalism-and-forgiveness.html.
5. Thiel, "The Straussian Moment," 190.
6. Pew Research Center, "Mapping the Global Muslim Population," *Pew Research Center's Religion & Public Life Project* (blog), October 7, 2009, https://www.pewresearch.org/religion/2009/10/07/mapping-the-global-muslim-population/.
7. Embassy of the Republic of Indonesia, Washington D.C., "Facts & Figures," June 25, 2021, https://web.archive.org/web/20210625030316/https://www.embassyofindonesia.org/basic-facts/.
8. Pew Research Center, "Mapping the Global Muslim Population."
9. Drew Desilver and David Masci, "World's Muslim Population More Widespread than You Might Think," *Pew Research Center* (blog), January 31, 2017, https://www.pewresearch.org/fact-tank/2017/01/31/worlds-muslim-population-more-widespread-than-you-might-think/.
10. U.S. Department of State, Bureau of Public Affairs, Office of Electronic Information, "The Global War on Terrorism: The First 100 Days" accessed June 18, 2023, https://2001-2009.state.gov/s/ct/rls/wh/6947.htm.
11. Meg Bortin, "In War's Wake, Hostility and Mistrust," *New York Times*, June 4, 2003, https://www.nytimes.com/2003/06/04/news/in-wars-wake-hostility-and-mistrust.html.

12. Pew Research Center, "Views of a Changing World 2003," *Pew Research Center—U.S. Politics & Policy* (blog), June 3, 2003, https://www.pewresearch.org/politics/2003/06/03/views-of-a-changing-world-2003/.

13. Thiel, "The Straussian Moment," 190.

14. Reem Nadeem, "Two Decades Later, the Enduring Legacy of 9/11," *Pew Research Center—U.S. Politics & Policy*, September 2, 2021, https://www.pewresearch.org/politics/2021/09/02/two-decades-later-the-enduring-legacy-of-9-11/; Drew Desilver, "More than a Decade Later, 9/11 Attacks Continue to Resonate with Americans," *Pew Research Center*, May 14, 2014, https://www.pewresearch.org/fact-tank/2014/05/14/more-than-a-decade-later-911-attacks-continue-to-resonate-with-americans/

15. Tomas Lopez and Jennifer L. Clark, "Uncovering Kris Kobach's Anti-Voting History" Brennan Center for Justice at NYU Law, May 11, 2017, https://www.brennancenter.org/our-work/analysis-opinion/uncovering-kris-kobachs-anti-voting-history; White House Fellows Class of 2001–2002, "White House Fellowships: News & Information," georgewbush-whitehouse.archives.gov, 2021, https://georgewbush-whitehouse.archives.gov/fellows/news/board.html.

16. Ana C. Pottratz and Wnyong Austin, "Rajah v. Mukasey," Casetext, September 24, 2008, https://casetext.com/case/rajah-v-mukasey.

17. Cory Doctorow, "VERIFIED Mark Zuckerberg Defends Facebook's Association with Peter Thiel," Boing Boing, October 19, 2016, https://boingboing.net/2016/10/19/mark-zuckerberg-defends-facebo.html.

18. Elizabeth Dwoskin, Craig Timberg, and Tony Romm, "Zuckerberg Once Wanted to Sanction Trump. Then Facebook Wrote Rules That Accommodated Him," *Washington Post*, June 29, 2020, https://www.washingtonpost.com/technology/2020/06/28/facebook-zuckerberg-trump-hate/.

19. Pamela Brown, Scott Bronstein, and Drew Griffin, "Source: Trump Immigration Plan Mirrors Post-9/11 Policy," CNN, November 17, 2016, https://www.cnn.com/2016/11/17/politics/kris-kobach-donald-trump-immigration-muslim-registry-ban/index.html

20. Reena Flores, "Kris Kobach Says Trump Team Considering a Muslim Registry," *CBS News*, November 17, 2016, https://www.cbsnews.com/news/kris-kobach-says-trump-team-considering-a-muslim-registry/.

21. Patrick Reis, "Top Trump Immigration Adviser Joins Transition Team," *Politico*, November 11, 2016, https://www.politico.com/blogs/donald-trump-administration/2016/11/kobach-a-key-trump-immigration-adviser-joins-transition-team-231240.

22. Brown, Bronstein, and Griffin, "Source: Trump Immigration Plan."

23. Sherman Smith, "Kansas Agrees to $1.9M Settlement for Defending Kobach's Baseless Voter Fraud Claims," *Kansas Reflector*, September 10, 2021, https://kansasreflector.com/2021/09/10/kansas-agrees-to-1-9m-settlement-for-defending-kobachs-baseless-voter-fraud-claims/.

24. Theodore Schleifer, "Tech Billionaire Peter Thiel Is Searching for New Political Allies. He's Found One in Kansas," *Vox*, July 27, 2020, https://www.vox.com/recode/f2020/7/27/21333636/peter-thiel-kris-kobach-kansas-senate-primary.

25. FEC, "Browse Receipts: Peter Thiel," FEC.gov, accessed June 18, 2023, https://www.fec.gov/data/receipts/?committee_id=C00721910&two_year_transaction_period=2020&cycle=2020&line_number=F3X-17&data_type=processed.

26. FEC, "free forever political action committee" (FEC FORM 3X, June 30, 2020), https://docquery.fec.gov/pdf/709/202006309244226709/202006309244226709.pdf.

27. Jonathan Bullington, "Evanston Man Charged in Anti-Immigration Graffiti Case Says U.S. Policy Spurred Tagging," *Chicago Tribune*, November 7, 2011, https://www

.chicagotribune.com/news/ct-xpm-2011-11-07-ct-met-evanston-graffiti-bust-1108
-20111108-story.html.

28. Jordan Graham, "Anti-Immigration Graffiti Continues on Evanston's North Side,"
Evanston, IL, *Patch*, October 10, 2011, https://patch.com/illinois/evanston/anti
-immigration-graffiti-continues-on-evanstons-north-side.

29. Astead W. Herndon and Katie Glueck, "Kris Kobach Loses Kansas Senate Primary,
Easing Republican Worries," *New York Times*, August 5, 2020, https://www.nytimes
.com/2020/08/04/us/politics/kobach-tlaib.html.

30. Blake Masters [@bgmasters], "The Democrats want open borders so they can bring in
and amnesty **tens of millions** of illegal aliens—that's their electoral strategy. Not
on my watch," Twitter, May 14, 2022, https://twitter.com/bgmasters/status/152562
1731309649921.

31. Richard Luscombe, "Scrutiny of Republicans Who Embrace 'Great Replacement Theory' After Buffalo Massacre," *Guardian*, May 16, 2022, https://www.theguardian.com
/us-news/2022/may/16/buffalo-massacre-great-replacement-theory-republicans.

32. Steve Peoples, "Ohio's J. D. Vance Among Republican Senate Candidates Who Have
Promoted 'Replacement' Theory at Center of Buffalo Shooting," wkyc.com, May 4,
2022, https://www.wkyc.com/article/news/nation-world/ohio-jd-vance-republican
-senate-candidates-promoted-replacement-buffalo-shooting/95-799c8d51-e398-40e4
-8271-f1fd02a4c73a.

33. Brian Schwartz, "Peter Thiel's Picks Masters, Vance Split Key Senate Races in Arizona,
Ohio After Billionaire Spent $32 Million on 2022 Midterms," CNBC, November 12,
2022, https://www.cnbc.com/2022/11/12/midterm-results-peter-thiel-picks-masters
-vance-see-mixed-results-in-arizona-ohio.html; FEC, "Receipts 2021–2022," FEC.gov,
December 31, 2022, https://www.fec.gov/data/receipts/?data_type=processed&two
_year_transaction_period=2022&min_date=01%2F01%2F2021&max_date=12%2F31
%2F2022&recipient_committee_type=S&recipient_committee_type=H.

34. Theodore Schleifer, "DeSantis-Sacks '24," *Puck* (blog), May 23, 2023, https://puck.news/
desantis-sacks-24/.

35. "David Sacks," OpenSecrets, accessed June 18, 2023, https://www.opensecrets.org
/donor-lookup/results?cand=&cycle=&employ=&jurisdiction=&name=david+sacks
&occupation=&state=CA&type=&zip=; FEC.gov, "Browse Individual Contributions:
David O. Sacks," FEC.gov, accessed June 18, 2023, https://www.fec.gov/data/individual
-contributions/?contributor_name=David+O.+Sacks&contributor_name=david
+sacks.

36. As mentioned previously, Stanford's founding president, David Starr Jordan, strongly
believed in "race betterment" and protecting the "purity" of national bloodlines. In
support of those beliefs, he warned about the United States being invaded by immigrants. He especially worried about Mexico, which was "teeming millions, ignorant,
superstitious, and ill-nurtured, with little self-control" who were "lacking, indeed, most
of our Anglo-Saxon values."

   Others at Stanford later promoted this same view. "If a woman can produce 17 children in our society, none of whom will be eliminated by survival of the fittest, she
and others like her will be multiplying at an enormously faster rate than more intelligent people do," Bill Shockley declared. "It could snowball so that a fraction of our
population composed of such people could double in less than 20 years and outnum-
ber all the others in a few centuries." As for the reasons he cared so much, he explained,
"It's important to me because of the tragedy at the bottom end of the population,
which is particularly severe for the blacks, but also probably occurs for the *chicano*

population—maybe to a comparable degree—though I am not as conversant with the *chicano* case. The same thing probably occurs for some Appalachian whites. What I'm talking about here is poverty, crime, unemployment and a host of other human miseries that impose heavy burdens on society." Shockley ran for U.S. Senate in 1982, promising that "my participation will contribute to the enlightenment of the other candidates and of the public," which the *New York Times* stated was to "use his campaign to explain his view that blacks and some other races are not evolving as quickly as others." Shockley lost badly, coming in eighth. Eugenics at Stanford History Project, "Request to Rename Jordan Hall," February 16, 2019, https://campusnames .stanford.edu/wp-content/uploads/sites/14/2020/04/Jordan-Hall-request.pdf; "Shockley, Nobel Winner, Files for Senate Race in California," *New York Times*, February 12, 1982, https://www.nytimes.com/1982/02/12/us/shockley-nobel-winner-files-for -senate-race-in-california.html; Art Harris, "Shockley Found Libeled, Receives $1 in Damages," *Washington Post*, September 15, 1984, https://www.washingtonpost.com /archive/politics/1984/09/15/shockley-found-libeled-receives-1-in-damages/36b0d330 -a21d-447f-bf12-3709773d6532/; William Shockley, "Is Quality of Human Population Declining?," *U.S. News and World Report*, November 22, 1965, https://iiif.nlm.nih.gov /nlm%3Anlmuid-101584906X9604-pgimg-1/full/2544,/0/default.jpg; Playboy and William Shockley, "Playboy Interview: William Shockley," *Playboy*, 1980, https:// nextbillionseconds.com/wp-content/uploads/2021/05/shockley_playboy_1980.pdf.

37. Thiel, "The Straussian Moment," 189–90.

38. Travis Kalanick, "The Whole Truth and Nothing but the Truth, So Help Your Reputation," *Swooshing* (blog), March 30, 2010, https://swooshing.wordpress.com/2010/03 /30/the-whole-truth-and-nothing-but-the-truth-so-help-your-reputation/.

39. Neta C. Crawford, Stephanie Savell, and Suzanne Fiederlein, "Civilians Killed & Wounded," The Costs of War, Watson Institute, Brown University, September 2021, https://watson.brown.edu/costsofwar/costs/human/civilians.

40. David Vine et al., "Creating Refugees: Displacement Caused by the United States' Post-9/11 Wars," The Costs of War, Watson Institute, Brown University, August 19, 2021, https://watson.brown.edu/costsofwar/files/cow/imce/papers/2021/Costs%20of%20 War_Vine%20et%20al_Displacement%20Update%20August%202021.pdf;    "Human Costs of U.S. Post-9/11 Wars: Direct War Deaths in Major War Zones," The Costs of War, March 2023, https://watson.brown.edu/costsofwar/figures/2021/WarDeathToll; Neta C. Crawford, "U.S. Budgetary Costs of Post-9/11 Wars Through FY2022: $8," The Costs of War, September 2021, https://watson.brown.edu/costsofwar/figures/2021 /BudgetaryCosts.

41. George W. Bush, "Address to a Joint Session of Congress and the American People," georgewbush-whitehouse.archives.gov, September 20, 2001, https://georgewbush -whitehouse.archives.gov/news/releases/2001/09/20010920-8.html.

42. The legislation is capitalized here, and throughout, because the legislation's name was an acronym: the "Uniting and Strengthening America by Providing *Appropriate* Tools Required to Intercept and Obstruct Terrorism (USA PATRIOT) Act of 2001," https://www.congress.gov/107/plaws/publ56/PLAW-107publ56.htm. Emphasis mine.

43. United States Congress, "Actions—H.R.3162–107th Congress (2001–2002): Uniting and Strengthening America by Providing Appropriate Tools Required to Intercept and Obstruct Terrorism (USA PATRIOT ACT) Act of 2001," webpage, congress.gov, October 26, 2001, 2001/2002, https://www.congress.gov/bill/107th-congress/house-bill /3162.

44. During an interview recorded for Michael Moore's film *Fahrenheit 9/11*, Congressman Jim McDermott claimed that the bill was rushed through the process so quickly that no senator had read it, because "they wait until the middle of the night; they drop it in the middle of the night; it's printed in the middle of the night; and the next morning when we come in, it passes!" Congressman John Conyers, Jr., added, "We don't read most of the bills. Do you really know what that would entail if we read every bill that we passed?" "We Don't Read Most of the Bills"—Rep. John Conyers," YouTube video, 2018, https://www.youtube.com/watch?v=fDsDaFM2aGc.

45. Patrick G. Eddington, "The PATRIOT Act Has Threatened Freedom for 20 Years," *Cato Institute*, October 21, 2021, https://www.cato.org/commentary/patriot-act-has-threatened-freedom-20-years.

46. "EBay to Acquire PayPal," July 8, 2002, https://www.sec.gov/Archives/edgar/data/1103415/000091205702026650/a2084015zex-99_1.htm.

47. S. F. Brickman, "Not-so-Artificial Intelligence," *Harvard Crimson*, October 23, 2003, https://www.thecrimson.com/article/2003/10/23/not-so-artificial-intelligence-for-his-high-school/.

48. "Newstead, Jennifer G.," Davis Polk & Wardwell LLP, October 17, 2015, https://web.archive.org/web/20151017041937/https://www.davispolk.com/lawyers/jennifer-newstead/.

49. Eddington, "The PATRIOT Act Has Threatened Freedom."

50. History.com editors, "Patriot Act," *History*, December 19, 2017, https://www.history.com/topics/21st-century/patriot-act.

51. American Civil Liberties Union, "Surveillance Under the Patriot Act," accessed June 18, 2023, https://www.aclu.org/issues/national-security/privacy-and-surveillance/surveillance-under-patriot-act.

52. U.S. Department of Justice, "Assistant Attorney General Dinh Announces New Leadership in the Office of Legal Policy," Justice.gov, February 19, 2002, https://www.justice.gov/archive/opa/pr/2002/February/02_olp_089.htm.

53. Zoe Tillman and John Hudson, "A Lawyer Who Helped Write the Patriot Act Is Trump's Pick for a Top State Department Job," *BuzzFeed News*, June 28, 2017, https://www.buzzfeednews.com/article/zoetillman/trump-picks-patriot-act-lawyer-for-top-state-depar.

54. Senate Select Committee on Intelligence, "Report of the Senate Select Committee on Intelligence Committee Study of the Central Intelligence Agency's Detention and Interrogation Program Together with a Foreword by Chairman Feinstein and Additional and Minority Views," 113th Senate, December 9, 2014, https://www.intelligence.senate.gov/sites/default/files/publications/CRPT-113srpt288.pdf, vii, 119.

55. CIA, Office of Inspector General, "OIG Report on CIA Accountability with Respect to the 9/11 Attacks," June 2005, https://www.cia.gov/readingroom/docs/DOC_0001499482.pdf, ix–x.

56. Alsop Louie Partners, "Gilman Louie," March 29, 2017, https://alsop-louie.com/team/gilman-louie/.

57. MobyGames, "Gilman Louie Video Game Credits," May 5, 2023, https://www.mobygames.com/person/3490/gilman-louie/credits/.

58. "Gilman Louie: In-Q-Tel and Funding Startups for the Government," YouTube video, 50:40, 2017, https://www.youtube.com/watch?v=DfUmoRxXWxI.

59. Angel Au-Young, "Palantir IPO Cements Billionaire Fortunes for Cofounder Peter Thiel and CEO Alexander Karp," *Forbes*, September 30, 2020, https://www.forbes.com

/sites/angelauyeung/2020/09/30/palantir-ipo-cements-billionaire-fortunes-for
-cofounder-peter-thiel-and-ceo-alexander-karp/?sh=2227ffe25b2f.

60. Palantir, "Our Products," 2014, https://web.archive.org/web/20140723170305/https://www
.palantir.com/products/.

61. Oliver Chiang, "Super Crunchers," *Forbes*, February 23, 2011, https://www.forbes.com
/forbes/2011/0314/technology-facebook-palantir-thinkprogress-super-crunchers
.html.

62. "Gilman Louie," 50:40, 34:40.

63. Thomas H. Kean and Lee H. Hamilton, "Introduction: Factual Overview of the September 11 Border Story," *9/11 Commission Report*, National Commission on Terrorist Attacks Upon the United States, August 21, 2004, https://www.9-11commission.gov
/staff_statements/911_TerrTrav_Ch1.pdf.

64. "Gilman Louie," 36:50.

65. "Alexander Karp," *Forbes*, 2023, https://www.forbes.com/profile/alexander-karp/.

66. "Gilman Louie," 51:37.

67. "Gilman Louie," 50:20.

68. "Google Acquires Keyhole," *Wall Street Journal*, October 27, 2004, https://www.wsj
.com/articles/SB109888284313557107.

69. "20 Years of Google," Google Maps, 2018, https://earth.google.com/web/@0,-9.0994,0
a,22251752.77375655d,35y,0h,0t,0r/data=CjASLhIgODA4NTU5MTdhYTY5MTFlODh
iNmY4NzJhOWI4M2NhODgiCmdjc19saXNoXzA.

70. Damian Paletta, "The CIA's Venture-Capital Firm, Like Its Sponsor, Operates in the Shadows," *Wall Street Journal*, August 30, 2016, http://www.wsj.com/articles/the-cias
-venture-capital-firm-like-its-sponsor-operates-in-the-shadows-1472587352.

71. Joe Lonsdale, "How Did Alex Karp Get Chosen as Palantir CEO?" Quora, 2017, https://
www.quora.com/How-did-Alex-Karp-get-chosen-as-Palantir-CEO/answer/Joe
-Lonsdale.

72. "Alexander Karp."

73. Moira Weigel, "Palantir Goes to the Frankfurt School," Boundary 2, July 10, 2020,
https://www.boundary2.org/2020/07/moira-weigel-palantir-goes-to-the-frankfurt
-school/.

74. Moira Weigel, "Palantir Goes to the Frankfurt School," Boundary 2, July 10, 2020,
https://www.boundary2.org/2020/07/moira-weigel-palantir-goes-to-the-frankfurt
-school/.

75. Weigel made a compelling case in her essay "Palantir Goes to the Frankfurt School" that Karp's intellectual development in Germany later shaped Palantir's business development. She also addressed topics that Karp's thesis, "Aggression in the Life-World," had failed to grapple with fully, which portended the ethical issues created by Big Tech corporations individually and surveillance capitalism overall.

What happened when these machines made mistakes because biased data led to flawed conclusions? Instead of dealing with those cases, Weigel noted that Karp's thesis ended abruptly. He focused on how aggressive jargon reinforced social cohesion and how social groups could coalesce around extremists. These theories would eventually be applied to what you could find using data, not what was missing. This reflected "Karp's apparent lack of interest in the ethical and political implications of his case study," in Weigel's view. "Algorithms take the histories of oppression embedded in training data and project them into the future, via predictions that powerful institutions then act on," she wrote. "If the identities constituted in this way are false, the reifications they generate do real work, and can cause real harm." Weigel, "Palantir Goes to the Frankfurt School."

76. Christopher Fish, "Life After the Stanford Review," *Stanford Review*, February 9, 2012. https://stanfordreview.org/life-after-the-stanford-review-by-anthony-mainero/.

77. "Keith Rabois," Founders Fund, accessed June 18, 2023, https://foundersfund.com /team/keith-rabois/; "David Sacks," Craft Ventures, accessed June 18, 2023, https:// www.craftventures.com/team/david-sacks.

78. Timothy Leary, *Flashbacks: A Personal and Cultural History of an Era: An Autobiography* (New York: Putnam's, 1990), 253.

79. Sheera Frenkel and Cecilia Kang, *An Ugly Truth: Inside Facebook's Battle for Domination* (New York: HarperCollins, 2021), 26.

80. "Mark Zuckerberg at Startup School 2012," YouTube video, 9:40, 2013, 15:20, 2013, https://www.youtube.com/watch?v=5bJi7k-y1Lo.

81. Mike Allen, "Sean Parker Unloads on Facebook: 'God Only Knows What It's Doing to Our Children's Brains,'" *Axios*, November 9, 2017, https://www.axios.com/2017/12/15 /sean-parker-unloads-on-facebook-god-only-knows-what-its-doing-to-our -childrens-brains-1513306792.

82. Leary, *Flashbacks*, 253.

83. Steve Jobs, "Think Different Apple Commercial," *Farnam Street* (blog), March 24, 2016, https://fs.blog/steve-jobs-crazy-ones/.

84. Shane Harris, "Killer App: Have a Bunch of Silicon Valley Geeks Figured Out How to Stop Terrorists?" *Washingtonian*, February 2012, 71–72.

85. Cadie Thompson, "Free Advice: Don't Go Public, Says Palantir's CEO," CNBC, March 19, 2014, https://www.cnbc.com/2014/03/19/free-advice-dont-go-public-says -palantirs-ceo.html.

86. Ali Winston, "Palantir Has Secretly Been Using New Orleans to Test Its Predictive Policing Technology," Verge, February 27, 2018, https://www.theverge.com/2018/2/27 /17054740/palantir-predictive-policing-tool-new-orleans-nopd.

87. Jonathan Bullington and Emily Lane, "How a Tech Firm Brought Data and Worry to New Orleans Crime Fighting," *NOLA.com*, July 12, 2019, https://www.nola.com/news /crime_police/article_33b8bf05-722f-5163-9a0c-774aa69b6645.html.

88. Palantir Technologies Inc., "Pilot Agreement," December 1, 2009, https://www .documentcloud.org/documents/3237770-Palantir-Pilot-Agreement.

89. Darwin Bond-Graham, "Forget the NSA, the LAPD Spies on Millions of Innocent Folks," *LA Weekly*, February 27, 2014, https://www.laweekly.com/forget-the-nsa-the -lapd-spies-on-millions-of-innocent-folks/; County of Los Angeles, Department of Auditor-Controller, "Review of Transactions Between Los Angeles County and Palantir Technologies INC.," August 28, 2015, https://www.documentcloud.org/documents /4350052-LASD-Palantir-Audit; Muckrock staff, "Payments to Palantir," Northern California Regional Intelligence Center, January 3, 2017, https://www.documentcloud .org/documents/5993254-Payments-to-Palantir, 7; Muckrock staff, "Palantir Contract CCSO," Cook County Sheriff, February 27, 2013, https://www.documentcloud.org /documents/3227922-Palantir-Contract-CCSO, 20, 46.

90. Bullington and Lane, "How a Tech Firm Brought Data."

91. Bullington and Lane.

92. Intercepting likely criminals before they even act is basically the beginning premise of the plot for Stephen Spielberg's *Minority Report*, which hit theaters in 2002, the year before Palantir first launched. It was a decade before New Orleans's mayor signed a deal

with the company to deploy its tools to fight crime in his city without telling the city council about it upfront. Bullington and Lane, "How a Tech Firm Brought Data."

93. Bullington and Lane; Palantir Technologies Inc., "NOLA Murder Reduction White Paper," documentcloud.org, accessed June 18, 2023, https://www.documentcloud.org /documents/4344816-NOLA-Murder-Reduction-White-Paper.

94. Palantir Technologies, 7–8.

95. Palantir Technologies Inc. and City of New Orleans, "K14 182 Palantir Technologies Amendment 1," City of New Orleans, March 31, 2014, https://www.documentcloud .org/documents/4344819-K14-182-Palantir-Technologies-Amendment-1.html; "Rebecca Dietz," LinkedIn, 2023, https://www.linkedin.com/in/rebecca-dietz-92098775/.

96. "Julien Meyer," LinkedIn, 2023, https://www.linkedin.com/in/julienmeyernolavocat /; Palantir Technologies Inc. and City of New Orleans, "K16 430 Palantir Technologies Amendment 2," City of New Orleans, June 16, 2016, https://www.documentcloud .org/documents/4344818-K16-430-Palantir-Technologies-Amendment-2.html; Palantir Technologies Inc. and City of New Orleans, "K17 453 Palantir Technologies Inc Amd 3," City of New Orleans, August 23, 2017, https://www.documentcloud.org /documents/4344817-K17-453-Palantir-Technologies-Inc-Amd-3.html.

97. Palantir Technologies Inc. and City of New Orleans, "K14 182 Palantir Technologies Amendment 1"; "K16 430 Palantir Technologies Amendment 2"; and "K17 453 Palantir Technologies Inc Amd 3."

98. Facebook, "HALB Presents: Matt Long, Chief Legal Ninja of Palantir," April 2, 2018, https://www.facebook.com/events/halb-presents-matt-long-chief-legal-ninja-of -palantir/209335583154023/.

99. Winston, "Palantir Has Secretly Been Using New Orleans"; Bullington and Lane, "How a Tech Firm Brought Data."

100. Winston, "Palantir Has Secretly Been Using New Orleans."

101. Palantir Technologies Inc., "Nola Murder Reduction," accessed June 18, 2023, https://s3 .documentcloud.org/documents/4344816/NOLA-Murder-Reduction-White-Paper .pdf, 9.

102. Emma Colton and Jasmine Baehr, "New Orleans Closes 2022 with Sky-High Homicide Rate Not Seen in Decades: 'Horrific,'" Fox News, January 9, 2023, https://www .foxnews.com/us/new-orleans-closes-2022-sky-high-homicide-rate-decades -horrific. Mark Moore, "New Orleans Becomes Murder Capital of America, Overtaking St. Louis," New York Post, September 18, 2022, https://nypost.com/2022/09/18/ new-orleans-becomes-murder-capital-of-america-overtaking-st-louis/; "NOLA for Life," WritingPaperSucks, accessed June 23, 2023, http://nolaforlife.org.

103. Crunchbase, "Palantir Technologies—Funding Rounds," accessed June 18, 2023, https://www.crunchbase.com/organization/palantir-technologies/company _financials; Reuters, "Palantir Opens up 38% in New York Debut, Valuation at Nearly $22 Bln," September 30, 2020, https://www.reuters.com/article/palantir-ipo-idINL4 N2GR4AI.

104. Open Society Foundations, "Statement from Soros Fund Management on Palantir Investment," November 17, 2020, https://www.opensocietyfoundations.org/newsroom /statement-from-soros-fund-management-on-palantir-investment; "Peter Thiel's Secretive Palantir Surges 38% in Debut, Valuation at Nearly $22B," New York Post, September 30, 2020, https://nypost.com/2020/09/30/peter-thiels-secretive-palantir-makes -its-market-debut/.

105. Cade Metz and Erin Griffith, "Palantir Shares Go Up in Wall Street Debut," New York Times, September 30, 2020, https://www.nytimes.com/2020/09/30/technology/palantir -stock-initial-public-offering.html.

106.  Kim Lyons, "Palantir Still Relies Heavily on Government Contracts Despite Push for More Corporate Customers," Verge, August 21, 2020, https://www.theverge.com/2020 /8/21/21396043/palantir-government-contracts-trump-thiel.

107.  Sharon Weinberger, "Is Palantir's Crystal Ball Just Smoke and Mirrors?" *Intelligencer*, September 28, 2020, https://nymag.com/intelligencer/2020/09/inside-palantir-tech nologies-peter-thiel-alex-karp.html.

108.  Harris, "Killer App."

109.  Lizette Chapman, "Palantir's Peter Thiel Keeps Control While Keeping Invisible," *Los Angeles Times*, September 29, 2020, https://www.latimes.com/business/technology /story/2020-09-29/palantirs-peter-thiel-keeps-control-while-keeping-invisible; Securities and Exchange Commission, "Palantir Technologies Inc. 10-K," Commission File Number: 001-39540, December 31, 2020, https://web.archive.org/web/20220201104003 /https://sec.report/Document/0001193125-21-060650/.

110.  Lizette Chapman, "Palantir CEO Says Pick 'Different Company' If You Don't Like Us," Bloomberg, September 9, 2020, https://www.bloomberg.com/news/articles/2020-09 -09/palantir-makes-its-pitch-to-investors-ahead-of-direct-listing.

111.  Palantir Technologies Inc., "S-1/A," FORM S-1 REGISTRATION STATEMENT, Securities and Exchange Commission, September 3, 2020, 8–10, 75–76, https://www.sec .gov/Archives/edgar/data/1321655/000119312520239121/d904406ds1a.htm.

112.  Chapman, "Palantir CEO Says Pick 'Different Company.'"

113.  Danny Crichton, "In Amended Filing, Palantir Admits It Won't Have Independent Board Governance for Up to a Year," *TechCrunch*, September 3, 2020, https:// techcrunch.com/2020/09/03/in-amended-filing-palantir-admits-it-wont-have -independent-board-governance-for-up-to-a-year.

114.  Chapman, "Palantir's Peter Thiel Keeps Control."

115.  This was what Peter Thiel and his cofounders argued in a Delaware court. Their Class F stock was a "flexible" security, not a power that illegally made them "emperor for life," as plaintiffs protested. The Palantir cofounders argued that the F share class "reflects the fundamental flexibility that is at the core of Delaware corporate law." Mike Leonard, "Peter Thiel, Palantir Co-Founders Slam 'Emperor for Life' Claims," *Bloomberg Law*, July 23, 2021, https://news.bloomberglaw.com/esg/peter-thiel-palantir-co -founders-slam-emperor-for-life-claims.

116.  Crichton, "In Amended Filing."

117.  "Alex Moore | Our Team," 8VC, accessed June 18, 2023, https://www.8vc.com/team/alex -moore; "Alex Moore," LinkedIn, 2023, https://www.linkedin.com/in/alex-moore -4639b91/.

118.  Alexandra Wolfe, *Valley of the Gods: A Silicon Valley Story* (New York: Simon & Schuster, 2017), 257.

119.  Chris Roush, "WSJ's Wolfe Resigns to Join Palantir Board," *Talking Biz News*, June 24, 2020, https://talkingbiznews.com/they-talk-biz-news/wsjs-wolfe-resigns -to-join-palantir-board/.

120.  "Spencer Rascoff," LinkedIn, 2023, https://www.linkedin.com/in/spencerrascoff/.

121.  "Lauren Friedman Stat," LinkedIn, 2023, https://www.linkedin.com/in/lauren -friedman-stat/.

122.  Palantir, "Palantir Board of Directors," Palantir Investor Relations, accessed June 18, 2023, https://investors.palantir.com/governance/board of directors/default . aspx.

123.  Palantir Technologies Inc., "Palantir Technologies Inc.: Outside Director Compensation Policy," sec.gov, September 10, 2020, https://www.sec.gov/Archives/edgar/data /1321655/000119312520244936/d904406dex108.htm.

124. SEC, "Microsoft Corporation SCHEDULE 14A," DEF 14A, accessed June 18, 2023, https:// www.sec.gov/Archives/edgar/data/789019/000119312522270484/d318171ddef14a.htm #toc318171_6, 30; Yahoo Finance, "Microsoft Corporation (MSFT) Stock Price, News, Quote & History," accessed June 18, 2023, https://finance.yahoo.com/quote/MSFT/; Yahoo Finance, "Palantir Technologies Inc. (PLTR) Stock Price, News, Quote & History," accessed June 18, 2023, https://finance.yahoo.com/quote/PLTR/.

125. Nathan Reiff and Margaret James, "Top Microsoft Shareholders," *Investopedia*, November 26, 2022, https://www.investopedia.com/articles/investing/122215/top-4-microsoft -shareholders.asp.

126. Reiff and James.

127. Vanguard, "Investment Insights and Company Information," accessed June 18, 2023, https://corporate.vanguard.com/content/corporatesite/us/en/corp/home.html; BlackRock, "BlackRock in the U.S. | About BlackRock," accessed June 18, 2023, https://www.blackrock.com/us/individual/about-us/about-blackrock; State Street Corporation, "Feature with Financial Highlights," accessed June 18, 2023, https:// stakeholderreport.statestreet.com/Y2019/Details/2019/financial-highlights-and -sustainability-review/default.aspx.

128. "Microsoft Gross Profit 2010–2023 | MSFT," MacroTrends, accessed June 18, 2023, https://www.macrotrends.net/stocks/charts/MSFT/microsoft/gross-profit.

129. MacroTrends, "Palantir Technologies Gross Profit 2019–2023 | PLTR," accessed June 18, 2023, https://www.macrotrends.net/stocks/charts/PLTR/palantir-technologies/gross -profit.

130. Jackson Barnett, "As Palantir Hits the Stock Market, It Continues to Target Government Work," FedScoop, October 1, 2020, https://www.fedscoop.com/palantir-public -listing-stock-market-government-work-contracting/; Edward Ongweso Jr, "Palantir Admits to Helping ICE Deport Immigrants While Trying to Prove It Doesn't," *Vice* (blog), September 29, 2020, https://www.vice.com/en/article/qj4y9q/palantir-admits -to-helping-ice-deport-immigrants-while-trying-to-prove-it-doesnt; Dave Nyczepir, "HHS Renews, Expands Palantir's Tiberius Contract to $31M," FedScoop, July 26, 2021, https://www.fedscoop.com/hhs-palantir-tiberius-contract-renewal/.

131. Aaron Gregg and Douglas MacMillan, "Palantir Goes Public at $10 per Share, Ending 16 Years of Privately Held Secrecy," *Washington Post*, September 30, 2020, https:// www.washingtonpost.com/business/2020/09/29/palantir-public-offering/.

132. Harris, "Killer App."

133. Peter Waldman, Lizette Chapman, and Jordan Robertson, "Palantir Knows Everything About You," Bloomberg, April 19, 2018, https://www.bloomberg.com/features/2018 -palantir-peter-thiel/.

134. Mary Elizabeth Williams, "9/11 Changed Surveillance—and Capitalism Reaped the Benefits," *Salon*, September 11, 2021, https://www.salon.com/2021/09/11/911-changed -surveillance—and-capitalism-reaped-the-benefits/.

135. Winston, "Palantir Has Secretly Been Using New Orleans."

136. Ryan Mac, "National Security Darling: Why Condoleezza Rice, David Petraeus and George Tenet Back Palantir," *Forbes*, August 19, 2013, https://www.forbes.com/sites /ryanmac/2013/08/19/national-security-darling-why-condoleezza-rice-david -petraeus-and-george-tenet-back-palantir/.

137. Avril Haines, "Public Financial Disclosure Report (OGE Form 278e)," Nominee Report, U.S. Office of Government Ethics, December 30, 2020, https://extapps2.oge.gov/201 /Presiden.nsf/PAS+Index/00CB412D4BCCFDF58525864F00810563/$FILE

/Haines,%20Avril%20%20final%20278.pdf; Office of the Director of National Intelligence, "Director of National Intelligence," Avril Haines, accessed June 18, 2023, https://www.dni.gov/index.php/who-we-are/leadership/director-of-national -intelligence.

138. "Director of National Intelligence."

139. Mac, "National Security Darling."

140. In-Q-Tel, "About IQT," accessed June 18, 2023, https://www.iqt.org/about-iqt/.

141. Senate Select Committee on Intelligence, "Report of the Senate Select Committee on Intelligence Committee Study of the Central Intelligence Agency's Detention and Interrogation Program Together with a Foreword by Chairman Feinstein and Additional and Minority Views," 113th Congress, December 9, 2014, https://www .intelligence.senate.gov/sites/default/files/publications/CRPT-113srpt288.pdf, 34.

142. Senate Select Committee on Intelligence, iv–xii.

143. Senate Select Committee on Intelligence, 123n.727.

144. Mac, "National Security Darling"; Don Kazak, "Taking Aim at Stanford," *Paloaltoonline*, November 29, 1995, https://www.paloaltoonline.com/weekly/morgue/cover/1995 _Nov_29.4COVER29.html.

145. Angel Au-Yeung, "Palantir Cofounders Peter Thiel and Alex Karp Have Unloaded Over $400 Million in Shares Since the IPO," *Forbes*, October 6, 2020, https://www .forbes.com/sites/angelauyeung/2020/10/06/palantir-cofounders-peter-thiel-and -alex-karp-have-unloaded-over-400-million-in-shares-since-the-ipo/.

146. Crichton, "In Amended Filing."

## 14. We Do the Right Thing

1. Mike Isaac, "Uber Founder Travis Kalanick Resigns as C.E.O.," *New York Times*, June 21, 2017, https://www.nytimes.com/2017/06/21/technology/uber-ceo-travis-kalanick .html.

2. Mike Isaac, "Uber Fires 20 Amid Investigation Into Workplace Culture," *New York Times*, June 6, 2017, https://www.nytimes.com/2017/06/06/technology/uber-fired.html.

3. Sara Ashley O'Brien, "New from Uber: 'We Do the Right Thing. Period,'" CNNMoney, November 7, 2017, https://money.cnn.com/2017/11/07/technology/uber-do-the-right -thing/index.html.

4. O'Brien.

5. Julia Carrie Wong, "Uber's 'Hustle-Oriented' Culture Becomes a Black Mark on Employees' Résumés," *Guardian*, March 7, 2017, https://www.theguardian.com/technology/2017 /mar/07/uber-work-culture-travis-kalanick-susan-fowler-controversy.

6. Sara Ashley O'Brien, "Uber CEO Reflects on One Year at the Company," CNNMoney, August 29, 2018, https://money.cnn.com/2018/08/29/technology/uber-ceo-dara -khosrowshahi-one-year-anniversary/index.html.

7. Matthew J. Belvedere, "'Moral Compass' Was off at Uber Under Co-Founder Kalanick, Says New CEO Dara Khosrowshahi," CNBC, January 23, 2018, https://www.cnbc.com /2018/01/23/uber-moral-compass-under-co-founder-kalanick-was-off-new-ceo-says.html.

8. Jill Hazelbaker, "Uber Newsroom: ICJI Statement," July 10, 2022, https://www.uber .com/newsroom/icij-statement/.

9. Mike Isaac, *Super Pumped: The Battle for Uber* (New York: Norton, 2019), 344, 55–56, 344.

10. Faiz Siddiqui, "Uber Rang in Its IPO with Champagne and Mimosas. Then the Hangover Began," *Washington Post*, May 17, 2019, https://www.washingtonpost.com /technology/2019/05/17/uber-rang-its-ipo-with-champagne-mimosas-then-hangover -began/.

11. "Did Peter Drucker Say That?" *Drucker Institute* (blog), accessed June 18, 2023, https:// www.drucker.institute/did-peter-drucker-say-that/.

12. Siddiqui, "Uber Rang in Its IPO."

13. Lydia Ramsey Pflanzer, "Uber Had the Worst First-Day Dollar Loss Ever of Any US IPO," *Business Insider*, May 11, 2019, https://www.businessinsider.com/uber-had-the -worst-first-day-dollar-loss-of-a-us-ipo-2019-5.

14. Andrew J. Hawkins, "Uber Goes Public: Everything You Need to Know About the Biggest Tech IPO in Years," Verge, May 10, 2019, https://www.theverge.com/2019/5/10 /18564197/uber-ipo-stock-valuation-pricing-fares-drivers-public-market.

15. Frank Gogol, "THIS Is How Much Uber Pays in Different Parts of the U.S. [2022]," *Stilt Blog*, February 19, 2020, https://www.stilt.com/blog/2020/02/how-much-does-uber -pay/.

16. U.S. Department of Labor, "State Minimum Wage Laws," January 1, 2023, http://www .dol.gov/agencies/whd/minimum-wage/state.

17. Salary.com, "Uber Driver Salary in the United States," November 23, 2022, https://www .salary.com/research/salary/alternate/uber-driver-salary; Eric Reed, "How Much Do Uber and Lyft Drivers Make?" *TheStreet*, April 3, 2020, https://www.thestreet.com /personal-finance/how-much-do-uber-lyft-drivers-make-14804869.

18. "Maureen Dowd Interviews Uber CEO Dara Khosrowshahi," *New York Times*, July 16, 2021, https://www.nytimes.com/2021/07/16/style/uber-ceo-dara-khosrow shahi.html.

19. Uber Technologies, Inc., "Uber 2022 Proxy Statement," 2022, https://s23.q4cdn.com /407969754/files/doc_financials/2022/ar/Final-2022-Proxy-(1).pdf, 71.

20. Google, "Uber Technologies Inc (UBER) Stock Price & News—Google Finance," Google Finance, accessed June 18, 2023, https://www.google.com/finance/quote /UBER:NYSE; Uber Technologies, Inc., "Uber 2022 Proxy Statement"; Milken Institute, "His Excellency Yasir Othman Al-Rumayyan," accessed June 18, 2023, https:// milkeninstitute.org/events/gc19/speakers/36567.

21. Justin Scheck and Bradley Hope, "How the Crown Prince of Saudi Arabia Made His Way Into Silicon Valley Circles with a $3.5 Billion Investment in Uber," *Business Insider*, 19:52, https://www.businessinsider.com/how-investment-in-uber-brought -saudi-prince-to-silicon-valley-2020-9.

22. Eric Newcomer, "How Uber Got Into Bed with the Saudis—and Why It's Not Getting out Anytime Soon," *Los Angeles Times*, November 5, 2018, https://www.latimes.com /business/la-fi-uber-saudi-money-20181105-story.html; Hayes Brown and Maged Atef, "This Is What Saudi Women Think of Their Country's Massive Investment in Uber," *BuzzFeed News*, accessed June 18, 2023, https://www.buzzfeednews.com/article /hayesbrown/this-is-what-saudi-women-think-of-their-countrys-massive-inv.

23. السعودية [@Uber_KSA], Twitter, March 9, 2016, https://twitter.com/Uber_KSA/status /707546668313530368.

24. Sarah Lacy, "The Horrific Trickle Down of Asshole Culture: Why I've Just Deleted Uber from My Phone," *PandoDaily*, October 22, 2014, https://web.archive.org/web /20141203022003/http://pando.com/2014/10/22/the-horrific-trickle-down-of-asshole -culture-at-a-company-like-uber/.

25. Human Rights Watch, "Saudi Arabia: As Women's Driving Ban Ends, Provide Parity," *Human Rights Watch* (blog), September 27, 2017, https://www.hrw.org/news/2017/09/27/saudi-arabia-womens-driving-ban-ends-provide-parity.

26. Sarah Sirgany Smith-Spark Laura, "Landmark Day for Saudi Women as Kingdom's Controversial Driving Ban Ends," CNN, June 23, 2018, https://www.cnn.com/2018/06/23/middleeast/saudi-women-driving-ban-lifts-intl/index.html.

27. Newcomer, "How Uber Got Into Bed with the Saudis."

28. Crunchbase, "Google—Funding, Financials, Valuation & Investors," accessed June 18, 2023, https://www.crunchbase.com/organization/google/company_financials.

29. Katie Roof, "Benchmark-Kalanick Uber Board Suit Sent to Arbitration," *TechCrunch*, August 30, 2017, https://techcrunch.com/2017/08/30/pishevar-says-delaware-court-is-sending-benchmark-lawsuit-to-arbitration/.

30. Katie Roof, "Travis Kalanick Appoints Ursula Burns, John Thain to Uber's Board," *TechCrunch*, September 30, 2017, https://techcrunch.com/2017/09/29/travis-kalanick-appoints-ursula-burns-john-thain-to-ubers-board/.

31. Brett Helling, "How Much Do Uber Drivers Make in 2022?" Ridester, September 2, 2021, https://www.ridester.com/how-much-do-uber-drivers-make/; Dani Anguiano, "'It's Not Worth It': Rising Gas Prices Force Drivers to Work for Less than Minimum Wage," *Guardian*, March 10, 2022, https://www.theguardian.com/us-news/2022/mar/10/gig-workers-gas-prices-california-uber-lyft.

32. Human Rights Watch, "Letter to Rumayyan," March 15, 2022, https://www.hrw.org/sites/default/files/media_2022/03/gl.2022.03.15.Letter%20to%20Rumayyan.pdf.

33. Shara Tibken, "Uber Stuck Between a Rock and a Hard Place with Saudi Investment," CNET, November 13, 2018, https://www.cnet.com/tech/mobile/uber-ceo-says-stuck-between-a-rock-and-a-hard-place-with-saudi-investment/.

34. Shane Harris, Greg Miller, and Josh Dawsey, "CIA Concludes Saudi Crown Prince Ordered Jamal Khashoggi's Assassination," *Washington Post*, November 17, 2018, https://www.washingtonpost.com/world/national-security/cia-concludes-saudi-crown-prince-ordered-jamal-khashoggis-assassination/2018/11/16/98c89fe6-e9b2-11e8-a939-9469f1166f9d_story.html.

35. Stephanie Kirchgaessner, "Saudis Behind NSO Spyware Attack on Jamal Khashoggi's Family, Leak Suggests," *Guardian*, July 18, 2021, https://www.theguardian.com/world/2021/jul/18/nso-spyware-used-to-target-family-of-jamal-khashoggi-leaked-data-shows-saudis-pegasus.

36. Nina dos Santos Kaplan Michael, "Jamal Khashoggi's Private WhatsApp Messages May Offer New Clues to Killing," CNN, December 2, 2018, https://www.cnn.com/2018/12/02/middleeast/jamal-khashoggi-whatsapp-messages-intl/index.html; Ronan Farrow, "How Democracies Spy on Their Citizens," *New Yorker*, April 18, 2022, https://www.newyorker.com/magazine/2022/04/25/how-democracies-spy-on-their-citizens.

37. Mike Isaac, "Uber's C.E.O. Plays with Fire," *New York Times*, April 23, 2017, https://www.nytimes.com/2017/04/23/technology/travis-kalanick-pushes-uber-and-himself-to-the-precipice.html.

38. United Nations Human Rights Council, "Investigation of, Accountability for and Prevention of Intentional State Killings of Human Rights Defenders, Journalists and Prominent Dissidents," July 24, 2019, https://documents-dds-ny.un.org/doc/UNDOC/GEN/G19/296/91/PDF/G1929691.pdf?OpenElement.

39. "Jamal Khashoggi: All You Need to Know About Saudi Journalist's Death," *BBC News*, October 10, 2018, https://www.bbc.com/news/world-europe-45812399.

40.  HBO Documentaries [@HBODocs], "@Uber CEO @dkhos discusses his decision to stay out of Saudi Arabia after the murder of journalist Jamaal Khashoggi with @Axios co-founder @MikeAllen and Axios business editor @DanPrimack," Twitter, November 10, 2019, https://twitter.com/HBODocs/status/1193672181928144899.

41.  dara khosrowshahi [@dkhos], Twitter, November 11, 2019, https://twitter.com/dkhos/status/1193889281846067200.

42.  "Jamal Khashoggi: All You Need to Know."

43.  Uber Technologies, "Uber 2022 Proxy Statement," 43, 48.

44.  While Uber's ties to Saudi Arabia haven't received significant attention, there has been far more dramatic blowback against professional golfers who joined the Saudi-funded LIV tour, including from families of 9/11 victims. "It's interesting to see what money will do and it makes you wonder, where will folks draw the line? How much money will it take so you don't care about murder or human rights?" Brett Eagleson asked. His father, Bruce, was last seen rushing up the stairs of the World Trade Center to help with evacuations; Brett was just fifteen and a sophomore in high school at the time. To Eagleson, golfers who didn't join LIV showed that they valued "accountability, truth and justice," compared to those who had "taken the blood money." He condemned the new LIV golfers with this: "I guess we've seen what their price tag is." Lindsay Schnell, "Members of 9/11 Justice Group Invite LIV Golfers to Meet About Tour's Ties to Saudi Arabia," *USA Today*, June 30, 2022, https://www.usatoday.com/story/sports/golf/2022/06/30/liv-golf-oregon-911-families/7776711001/

45.  Alan Shipnuck, "The Truth About Phil Mickelson and Saudi Arabia," Fire Pit Collective, February 12, 2022, https://firepitcollective.com/the-truth-about-phil-and-saudi-arabia/.

46.  Jack Stebbins, "9/11 Families Condemn Trump for Hosting Saudi-Funded LIV Golf Tournament at His NJ Club," CNBC, July 18, 2022, https://www.cnbc.com/2022/07/18/9/11-families-slam-trump-for-hosting-saudi-funded-liv-golf-tournament.html.

47.  Karl Vick, "The Trials of Jared Kushner," *Time*, June 1, 2017, https://time.com/4800796/the-trials-of-jared-kushner/.

48.  John Ourand, "SBJ Media: Jared Kushner's LIV Golf Connection," *Sports Business Journal*, August 15, 2022, https://www.sportsbusinessjournal.com/SB-Blogs/Newsletter-Media/2022/08/15.aspx

49.  David D. Kirkpatrick and Kate Kelly, "Before Giving Billions to Jared Kushner, Saudi Investment Fund Had Big Doubts," *New York Times*, April 10, 2022, https://www.nytimes.com/2022/04/10/us/jared-kushner-saudi-investment-fund.html; Ken Klippenstein, "Jared Kushner Flaunted Influence with Saudi Arabia, Russia in Pitch to Investors," *Intercept*, April 18, 2022, https://theintercept.com/2022/04/18/saudi-russia-jared-kushner-affinity-partners/; Affinity Partners, "Affinity Partners Slide Deck," https://www.documentcloud.org/documents/21639665.

50.  Alex Raskin, "LIV Golf 'Will Buy Airtime on Fox Sports After Networks Balked at Saudi-Backed Tour's First TV Deal,'" *Daily Mail*, September 29, 2022, https://www.dailymail.co.uk/sport/sportsnews/article-11258615/LIV-Golf-buy-airtime-Fox-Sports-networks-balked-Saudi-backed-tours-TV-deal.html.

51.  Reice Shipley, "Golf World Reacts to Donald Trump's Family Involvement with LIV Golf," *The Comeback: Today's Top Sports Stories & Reactions*, August 16, 2022, https://thecomeback.com/golf/donald-trump-jared-kushner-media-rights-liv-golf.html; Jack Stebbins, "Trump Criticizes PGA Tour, Says 'Saudis Have Done a Fantastic Job' with LIV," CNBC, October 27, 2022, https://www.cnbc.com/2022/10/27/trump-criticizes-pga-tour-praises-saudis-liv.html.

52. Lillian Rizzo, "PGA Tour Agrees to Merge with Saudi-Backed Rival LIV Golf," CNBC, June 6, 2023, https://www.cnbc.com/2023/06/06/pga-tour-agrees-to-merge-with-saudi-backed-rival-liv-golf.html.

53. Dan Wolken, "PGA Tour Sold Out to LIV Golf and the Saudis. Pro Golf Will Never Be the Same," *USA Today*, June 6, 2023, https://www.usatoday.com/story/sports/columnist/dan-wolken/2023/06/06/pga-tour-sold-out-liv-golf-saudis/70293260007/.

54. 9/11 Families United, "9/11 Families United Statement on PGA Merging with Saudi-Backed LIV Golf Tour," accessed June 18, 2023, https://911familiesunited.org/9-11-families-united-statement-on-pga-merging-with-saudi-backed-liv-golf-tour/.

55. Kia Kokalitcheva, "Saudi Arabia's Sovereign Wealth Fund Reveals Its VC Portfolio," *Axios*, April 4, 2023, https://www.axios.com/2023/04/04/saudi-arabias-sovereign-wealth-fund-vc-pe-portfolio; Dealroom, "Uber Company Information, Funding & Investors," accessed June 18, 2023, https://app.dealroom.co/companies/uber.

56. Akela Lacy, "Saudi Arabia Owns Stake in Firm That Bought Democratic Party's Campaign Tech," *Intercept*, April 23, 2023, https://theintercept.com/2023/04/23/saudi-arabia-democratic-party-campaign-ngp-van/.

57. Kate Conger and Noam Scheiber, "California Bill Makes App-Based Companies Treat Workers as Employees," *New York Times*, September 11, 2019, https://www.nytimes.com/2019/09/11/technology/california-gig-economy-bill.html.

58. Levi Sumagaysay, "Uber CEO Says Prices Could Double If Drivers Become Employees, but This Economist Isn't Buying It," *MarketWatch*, October 21, 2020, https://www.marketwatch.com/story/uber-ceo-says-prices-could-double-if-drivers-become-employees-but-this-economist-isnt-buying-it-11603297839.

59. "Travis Kalanick at Startup School 2012," YouTube video, 27:00, 2012, https://www.youtube.com/watch?v=rQ6GoY2_Ujw.

60. Alex, "Never Underestimate the Power of #UberDCLove," Uber Newsroom, July 10, 2012, https://newsroom.uber.com/us-dc/never-underestimate-the-power-of-uberdclove/.

61. Shervinator ✈ ∞ 🛡 [@shervin], Twitter, July 10, 2012, https://twitter.com/shervin/status/222819101310062592.

62. Isaac, *Super Pumped*, 135–36.

63. "Travis Kalanick at Startup School 2012," 28:20.

64. Janet Burns, "While Uber Invests in Lobbying and AI, Drivers Are Fighting for Decent Pay," *Forbes*, January 23, 2018, https://www.forbes.com/sites/janetwburns/2018/01/23/while-uber-targets-laws-and-ai-drivers-are-fighting-to-win-fair-pay/.

65. In 2013 Uber spent just $50,000 on lobbying, but that amount nearly quadrupled every year over the rest of the decade. Payments to lobbyists grew to $200,000 in 2014, $470,000 in 2015, $1.36 million in 2016, $1.83 million in 2017, and $2.3 million in 2018—with over $2 million a year ever since. OpenSecrets, "Uber Technologies Lobbying Profile," 2022, https://www.opensecrets.org/federal-lobbying/clients/summary?id=D000067336.

66. Suhauna Hussain, Johana Bhuiyan, and Ryan Menezes, "How Uber and Lyft Persuaded California to Vote Their Way," *Los Angeles Times*, November 13, 2020, https://www.latimes.com/business/technology/story/2020-11-13/how-uber-lyft-doordash-won-proposition-22.

67. Graham Rapier, "Uber, Lyft, and DoorDash Have Now Spent More than $200 Million on Prop. 22—but There's Still No Guarantee It'll Pass," Business Insider, October 30, 2020, https://www.businessinsider.com/uber-doordash-lyft-prop-22-spending-200-million-close-polling-2020-10.

68. "Truth Be Told: The 'Yes on Prop 22' Ad," YouTube video, 2020, https://www.youtube.com/watch?v=N4LMWUrSLvU.

69. "Truth Be Told."

70. Mike Dickerson [@MyDickerson], "Hmm . . .," Twitter, October 7, 2020, https://twitter.com/MyDickerson/status/1313952213358661632.

71. Mike Moffitt, "Fake 'Progressive' Mailers Urge Yes on Uber/Lyft's Prop. 22," *SFGATE*, October 9, 2020, https://www.sfgate.com/politics/article/Fake-progressive-mailers-urge-yes-on-Uber-Lyft-15635173.php

72. Dickerson [@MyDickerson], "Hmm. . . ."

73. "In Case You Missed It: New Independent Poll Shows App-Based Drivers Resoundingly Prefer to Be Independent Contractors by a 71–17% Margin," Prop 22 News, Protect App-Based Drivers + Services, May 12, 2020, https://protectdriversandservices.com/in-case-you-missed-it-new-independent-poll-shows-app-based-drivers-resoundingly-prefer-to-be-independent-contractors-by-a-71-17-margin/.

74. Laurel Rosenhall, "California NAACP President Aids Corporate Prop Campaigns—Collects $1.2 Million and Counting," CalMatters, September 26, 2020, http://calmatters.org/politics/2020/09/california-naacp-president-helps-corporate-ballot-measure-campaigns/.

75. Meredith Whittaker, "Prop 22: Where Do Gig Workers Go from Here?" *OneZero* (blog), November 5, 2020, https://onezero.medium.com/prop-22-where-do-gig-workers-go-from-here-e6eaa3ee2324; Megan Rose Dickey, "Human Capital: The Gig Economy in a Post-Prop 22 World," *TechCrunch*, November 7, 2020, https://techcrunch.com/2020/11/07/human-capital-the-gig-economy-in-a-post-prop-22-world/.

76. Rapier, "Uber, Lyft, and DoorDash Have Now Spent More than $200 Million on Prop. 22—but There's Still No Guarantee It'll Pass."

77. Carolyn Said, "Lawsuit: Uber Abuses Power with Prop. 22 Ads in Drivers' Apps," *San Francisco Chronicle*, October 22, 2020, https://www.sfchronicle.com/business/article/Lawsuit-Uber-abuses-power-with-Prop-22-ads-in-15668596.php.

78. Carolyn Said, "California Judge: Uber's Prop. 22 Ads in Driver App Are Not Coercive," *San Francisco Chronicle*, 2020, https://www.sfchronicle.com/business/article/Judge-Uber-s-Prop-22-ads-in-driver-app-are-15685929.php.

79. Manthey, "Prop. 22."

80. "California Ballot Measure Results 2020," *CNN Politics*, January 12, 2020, https://edition.cnn.com/election/2020/results/state/california/ballot-measures/1.

81. Margot Roosevelt and Shauna Hussain, "Prop. 22 Is Ruled Unconstitutional, a Blow to California Gig Economy Law," *Los Angeles Times*, August 21, 2021, https://www.latimes.com/business/story/2021-08-20/prop-22-unconstitutional.

82. Grace Gedye, "Court Upholds California Prop. 22 in Big Win for Gig Firms like Lyft and Uber," *CalMatters*, March 14, 2023, http://calmatters.org/economy/2023/03/prop-22-appeal/.

83. Tom Goodwin, "The Battle Is for the Customer Interface," *TechCrunch*, March 3, 2015, https://techcrunch.com/2015/03/03/in-the-age-of-disintermediation-the-battle-is-all-for-the-customer-interface/; "Tom Goodwin," LinkedIn, 2023, https://www.linkedin.com/in/tomfgoodwin/.

84. *The Social Dilemma*, "If You're Not Paying for the Product, then You ARE the Product," Netflix, 2020, 0:13:11, https://www.youtube.com/watch?v=Aucb5tJMi7o&ab_channel=Illuminator.

85. Uber Technologies, "Uber 2022 Proxy Statement"; "His Excellency Yasir Othman Al-Rumayyan"; Mike Isaac and Michael J. de la Merced, "Uber Turns to Saudi Arabia for

$3.5 Billion Cash Infusion," *New York Times*, June 1, 2016, https://www.nytimes.com /2016/06/02/technology/uber-investment-saudi-arabia.html; Newcomer, "How Uber Got Into Bed with the Saudis."

86. NewsOne staff, "Peggy Alford Becomes First Black Woman Nominated to Facebook's Board of Directors," *NewsOne* (blog), April 15, 2019, https://newsone.com/3850910 /peggy-alford-facebook-board-of-directors/; NewsOne, "About Us," *NewsOne* (blog), December 1, 2015, https://newsone.com/about-us/.

87. Meta, "Peggy Alford Nominated to Facebook's Board of Directors," *Meta* (blog), April 12, 2019, https://about.fb.com/news/2019/04/alford-nominated-to-facebook-board/.

88. Staff and agencies, "Timeline: Enron," *Guardian*, January 30, 2006, https://www .theguardian.com/business/2006/jan/30/corporatefraud.enron.

89. Alex Vuocolo, "Zuckerbergs Chose Delaware-Based LLC for Chan Zuckerberg Initiative," *Delaware Business Times* (blog), February 2, 2016, https://delawarebusinesstimes .com/news/people/zuckerbergs-chose-delaware-based-llc-for-chan-zuckerberg -initiative/.

90. OpenCorporates, "CHAN ZUCKERBERG INITIATIVE, LLC: Delaware (US) Company Number 5911862," August 27, 2019, https://opencorporates.com/companies/us_de /5911862.

91. The LLC structure allowed Chan Zuckerberg to make investments in for-profit enterprises. It made its first venture investment in the $24 million Series B Round of Andela, following an A Round that included Zuckerberg's former roommate Chris Hughes. Chan Zuckerberg's investment in this new venture, which outsourced tech jobs to coders across Africa, also came at a crucial time for Facebook. It had opened its first office on the continent in 2015, and two months after its bet on Andela was announced, Mark Zuckerberg traveled to sub-Saharan Africa for the very first time in his life. "Mark Zuckerberg's visit gives Nigerian startups much-needed boost," CNN's Stephanie Busari touted, claiming that "entrepreneurs like Zuckerberg were inspiring because his approach to Facebook has never been about making a lot of money." These were the lessons Africans learned from Zuckerberg: "It's been about creating something that's going to change the world and obviously if you do that, you are bound to reap the benefit," one said. Another tweeted a picture of Zuckerberg out for a jog, which Busari quoted in full: "Mark Zuckerberg jogging FREELY on a bridge at Lekki. He's a billionaire yet humble. Africans should learn." But the true purpose here—whether the investment bolstered the philanthropic work of Chan Zuckerberg, Mark Zuckerberg's image, or the power and profits of his company, Facebook—was that it all deserved serious reconsideration. Crunchbase, "Series B—Andela—2016-06-15—Crunchbase Funding Round Profile," accessed June 18, 2023, https://www .crunchbase.com/funding_round/andela-series-b--3c35c38e; Arafrika Sankara [@ arafrika], "Mark Zuckerberg jogging FREELY on a bridge at Lekki. He's a billionaire yet humble. Africans should learn," Twitter, August 31, 2016, https://twitter.com /arafrika/status/770989315342163968; Stephanie Busari, "Mark Zuckerberg's Visit Gives Nigerian Startups Much-Needed Boost," CNN, August 31, 2016, https://www .cnn.com/2016/08/31/africa/nigeria-zuckerberg-visit/index.html.

92. U.S. Election Assistance Commission, "EAC Expediting Distribution of $400 Million in CARES Act Election Funding for Coronavirus Response," EAC.gov, March 27, 2020, https://www.eac.gov/news/2020/04/03/eac-expediting-distribution-400-million -cares-act-election-funding-coronavirus.

93. Mark Zuckerberg and Priscilla Chan, Giving Pledge, November 9, 2015, https:// givingpledge.org/pledger?pledgerId=314; Alex Vuocolo, "Zuckerbergs Chose

Delaware-Based LLC for Chan Zuckerberg Initiative," *Delaware Business Times* (blog), February 2, 2016, https://delawarebusinesstimes.com/news/people/zuckerbergs -chose-delaware-based-llc-for-chan-zuckerberg-initiative/.

94. Issie Lapowsky, "How 'Zuck Bucks' Saved the 2020 Election—and Fueled the Big Lie," *Protocol*, May 23, 2022, https://www.protocol.com/policy/zuck-bucks-election.

95. Mark Zuckerberg, Facebook post, October 13, 2020, https://web.facebook.com/zuck /posts/10112459455098901.

96. Alex Kantrowitz, "Ex–*Washington Post* Owner Don Graham on Doing Business with Zuckerberg and Bezos," Big Technology, 2/23, https://bigtechnology.substack.com/p /ex-washington-post-owner-don-graham.

97. Zuckerberg, Facebook post, October 13, 2020.

98. Kara Swisher, "Molly Graham Is Taking on a Top Ops Role at the Chan Zuckerberg Initiative," *Vox*, February 8, 2017, https://www.vox.com/2017/2/8/14548266/molly -graham-operations-head-chan-zuckerberg-initiative; Kurt Wagner, "Molly Graham, the Top Operations Exec at the Chan Zuckerberg Initiative, Is Leaving," *Vox*, January 25, 2018, https://www.vox.com/2018/1/25/16933194/molly-graham-leave-czi-mark -zuckerberg-priscilla-chan; Crunchbase, "Molly Graham—Hanging with My Family @ Substack—Crunchbase Person Profile," accessed June 18, 2023. https://www .crunchbase.com/person/molly-graham.

99. "Amalia Halikias | LinkedIn," accessed June 18, 2023, https://www.linkedin.com/in /amalia-halikias-11b00457/; "Priscilla Chan and Mark Zuckerberg Commit $300 Million Donation to Promote Safe and Reliable Voting During COVID-19 Pandemic," Center for Tech and Civic Live  Press Release, September 1, 2020, https://www .documentcloud.org/documents/7070695-CTCL-CEIR-Press-Release-9-1-20-FINAL .html.

100. FEC, "masters vance committee—Committee Overview," FEC.gov, 2022–2021, https://www.fec.gov/data/committee/C00792580/.

101. Theodore Schleifer, "Who's Funding Bari Weiss?" *Puck*, November 12, 2021, https:// puck.news/bari-weiss-tim-draper-vance-masters-thiel/; Teddy Schleifer [@teddyschle- ifer], "A @PuckNews scooplet . . . time for a BLOWOUT fundraiser for the Senate GOP. Hosts @rabois and @DavidSacks invite you to Miami next month. Nine Senate Republican candidates—Mehmet Oz, J. D. Vance, Blake Masters, etc.—plus Rick Scott," Twitter, August 23, 2022, https://twitter.com/teddyschleifer/status/15622164351 61505792.

102. Redfin, "4310 25th St, San Francisco, CA 94114–2 Beds/1.5 Baths," 2022, https://www .redfin.com/CA/San-Francisco/4310-25th-St-94114/home/1940254; Realtor.com, "1858 William Howard Taft Rd, Cincinnati, OH 45206," 2022, https://www.realtor.com /realestateandhomes-detail/1858-William-Howard-Taft-Rd_Cincinnati_OH_45206 _M44413-64059.

103. Alex Isenstadt, "Rise of a Megadonor: Thiel Makes a Play for the Senate," *Politico*, May 17, 2021, https://www.politico.com/news/2021/05/17/peter-thiel-senate-megadonor -488799; Alex Isenstadt, "Peter Thiel Makes $10M Bet on Associate in Arizona Senate Race," *Politico*, April 26, 2021, https://www.politico.com/news/2021/04/26/peter-thiel -arizona-senate-race-484585; Jessie Balmert, "Super PAC Supporting Potential Senate Candidate J. D. Vance Gets $10 Million Donation from PayPal Cofounder," *Enquirer*, March 15, 2021, https://www.cincinnati.com/story/news/politics/elections/2021/03/15 /super-pac-supporting-possible-ohio-senate-candidate-j-d-vance-gets-10-m -donation-peter-thiel/4700540001/.

104. David A. Fahrenthold, "J. D. Vance's First Attempt to Renew Ohio Crumbled Quickly," *New York Times*, October 8, 2022, https://www.nytimes.com/2022/10/08/us/politics/jd -vance-ohio-senate-nonprofit.html.

105. Noah Lanard, "Newly Uncovered Emails Show Blake Masters' Long History of Hating Democracy," *Mother Jones*, September 7, 2022, https://www.motherjones.com/politics /2022/09/blake-masters-anti-democratic-stanford-emails-arizona-kelly-thiel/

106. "Amalia Halikias | LinkedIn"; Melody Hahm, "Tiger Mom Meets Her Match: Her Entrepreneur Daughter," *Yahoo! Finance*, September 11, 2015, http://finance.yahoo.com /news/tiger-mom-meets-her-match—her-entrepreneur-daughter-194614786.html.

107. "Sophia Chua-Rubenfeld | LinkedIn," accessed June 18, 2023, https://www.linkedin .com/in/sophia-chua-rubenfeld-b1923231/; Tiger Cub Tutoring, "Squarespace— Domain Not Claimed," accessed June 18, 2023, http://www.tigercubtutoring.com/.

108. "Sophia Chua-Rubenfeld | LinkedIn"; Associated Press, "Daughter of 'Tiger Mom' Chua Picked as Kavanaugh Law Clerk," *AP News*, June 10, 2019, https://apnews.com /article/6d04c4f10b7e4071b4e3223fb39a510c.

109. J. D. Vance, "The Case for Brett Kavanaugh," *Wall Street Journal*, July 2, 2018, https:// www.wsj.com/articles/the-case-for-brett-kavanaugh-1530572358.

110. Amy Chua, "Kavanaugh Is a Mentor to Women," *Wall Street Journal*, July 12, 2018, https://www.wsj.com/articles/kavanaugh-is-a-mentor-to-women-1531435729.

111. Sheryl Gay Stolberg, "Kavanaugh Is Sworn in After Close Confirmation Vote in Senate," *New York Times*, October 6, 2018, https://www.nytimes.com/2018/10/06/us /politics/brett-kavanaugh-supreme-court.html; Women's March, "Women Say Cancel Kavanaugh," December 28, 2018, https://web.archive.org/web/20181228025940 /https://www.cancelkavanaugh.com/.

112. After Kavanaugh became a Supreme Court justice, the Cancel Kavanaugh campaign's website had originally promised, "Brett Kavanaugh's confirmation has been devastating for women, survivors, communities of color, and so many more across America. It ushered in a reckoning that echoes far beyond him. The fight against all those who want to keep women small, silent, and controlled, has barely begun." A few years later the website advertised, "If a 60 x 60 regulars standing desk is not able to accommodate your hefty requirements, why not go big and get an L-shaped desk instead. So here are our top three picks for a more spacious working area." Women's March, "Women Say Cancel Kavanaugh"; Women's March, "Furniture News for Your Home Office— Cancelkavanaugh," February 3, 2023, https://web.archive.org/web/20230203141448 /https://cancelkavanaugh.com/.

113. Schleifer, "Who's Funding Bari Weiss?"

114. "Browse Receipts, JD Vance for Senate Inc., 2021–2022," FEC.gov, December 31, 2022, https://www.fec.gov/data/receipts/.

115. Alex Isenstadt, "A Mole Hunt, a Secret Website and Peter Thiel's Big Risk: How J. D. Vance Won His Primary," *Politico*, May 3, 2022, https://www.politico.com/news/2022 /05/03/jd-vance-win-ohio-primary-00029881.

116. Taylor Giorno, "Vance Surges to Victory in Ohio's Record-breaking Senate Primary," *OpenSecrets News*, May 4, 2022, https://www.opensecrets.org/news/2022/05/vance -surges-to-victory-in-ohios-record-breaking-senate-primary/.

117. POV, "B-Roll," *Medium* (blog), April 27, 2022, https://medium.com/@protectohiovaluesforms/b roll-71956c554e04; POV, "B-Roll Update," *Medium* (blog), April 28, 2022, https://medium.com/@protectohiovaluesforms/b-roll-update-e2cd35967e3f; POV, "POV—Medium," *Medium* (blog), May 4, 2022, https://web.archive.org/web/20220

504032034/https:/medium.com/@protectohiovaluesforms. Also "JD Vance Trump Rally," April 24, 2022; "4-25-22 JD Vance Trump Jr," April 25, 2022; and christian rautenstrauch, "A Cam," April 22, 2022, all at Dropbox, https://www.dropbox.com/sh /c9f7cz2msramit2/AADWFNrWLU_X7g1uZ2O1vIYea?.

118. Fabrizio Lee, "Ohio Statewide Likely GOP Primary Voters: 800 Likely 2022 GOP Primary Voters January 18–20, 2022," *Politico*, https://www.politico.com/f/?id=0000017e -d5b6-de19-a97e-f5b7f15e0000.

119. "Clients—Fabrizio, Lee & Associates," February 5, 2023, https://web.archive.org/web /20230205174718/https://fabriziolee.com/clients/; "Vendor/Recipient Profile: Fabrizio, Lee & Assoc.," OpenSecrets, 2022, https://www.opensecrets.org/campaign -expenditures/vendor?cycle=2022&vendor=Fabrizio%2C+Lee+%26+Assoc.

120. Dan Barry, "J. D. Vance's Ambition Comes at a Price in 'Hillbilly' Terms," *New York Times*, October 27, 2022, https://www.nytimes.com/2022/10/27/us/politics/jd-vance -trump-ohio.html; Jessie Balmert and Laura A. Bischoff, "Former President Donald Trump Endorses J. D. Vance in Ohio Senate Race," *Enquirer*, April 15, 2022, https:// www.cincinnati.com/story/news/2022/04/15/ohio-senate-candidates-fight-donald -trump-endorsement/7330668001/.

121. Patrick May, "Text of Peter Thiel Speech on Trump and the 'Crazy Condition of Our Country,'" *San Jose (CA) Mercury News* (blog), October 31, 2016. https://www .mercurynews.com/2016/10/31/peter-thiel-on-trump-and-the-crazy-condition-of -our-country/; "Peter Thiel," National Press Club, accessed June 18, 2023, https://www .press.org/events/peter-thiel.

122. Intercollegiate Studies Institute, "JD Vance on Our Civilizational Crisis," YouTube video, 15:12, 14:21, 5:46, July 24, 2021, https://www.youtube.com/watch?v=jBrEng3xQYo, 5:46.

123. POV, "POV—Medium," May 4, 2022; "FlexPoint Media," accessed June 18, 2023, https:// flexpointmedia.com/; "Kegan Beran," LinkedIn, 2023, https://www.linkedin.com/in /kegan-beran-44b113150/; "Protect Ohio Values PAC PAC Expenditures," OpenSecrets, accessed June 18, 2023, https://www.opensecrets.org/political-action-committees-pacs /protect-ohio-values-pac/C00770495/expenditures/2022.

124. Google, "J. D. Vance—Google Search," October 31, 2022, https://www.google.com /search?client=safari&rls=en&q=J.D.+Vance&ie=UTF-8&oe=UTF-8; "Ohio Senate Race—Google Search," October 31, 2022, https://www.google.com/search?client=safari &rls=en&q=Ohio+Senate+race&ie=UTF-8&oe=UTF-8.

125. J. D. Vance [@JDVance1], "Also, a note to political journalists: the best pollster in the race was @TonyFabrizioGOP. Maybe in the future don't treat garbage polls from Remington the same as Tony's because they're both 'internal.' The best independent pollster was @RobertCahaly. Kudos to both," Twitter, May 4, 2022, https://twitter.com /JDVance1/status/1521848200084271106.

126. J. D. Vance and Blake Masters, "Senate Candidates J. D. Vance and Blake Masters: We Must Stop Facebook from Election Meddling," *New York Post* (blog), October 21, 2021, https://nypost.com/2021/10/21/j-d-vance-blake-masters-we-must-stop-facebook -election-meddling/.

127. Still, it is important to understand, as clearly as possible, the legitimacy or illegitimacy of the 2020 vote tally. "There has been no demonstration of rampant fraudulent voting in any state. There have been plenty of cases of individual fraud, rooted out through the established, successful mechanisms that are in place to catch such illegalities," the *Washington Post's* Phillip Bump concluded. "There are plenty such cases in every

national election. What hasn't emerged is any evidence of hundreds or thousands of votes having been illegally cast in any state." He then quoted from a report by a group of prominent Republicans. "For this Report, we examined every count of every case brought in these six battleground states," its executive summary read. "We conclude that Donald Trump and his supporters had their day in court and failed to produce substantive evidence to make their case." Philip Bump, "Analysis: We Have Reached the Apex of Election-Fraud Debunking," *Washington Post*, July 15, 2022, https://www.washingtonpost.com/politics/2022/07/14/we-have-reached-apex-election-fraud-debunking/; Harvard Kennedy School, "Electoral Integrity in the 2020 U.S. Elections," 2022, https://www.hks.harvard.edu/publications/electoral-integrity-2020-us-elections.

128. Nahal Toosi, "Trump Refuses to Say He'll Accept Election Results," *Politico*, October 19, 2016, https://www.politico.com/story/2016/10/will-trump-accept-election-results-2016-debate-230038.

129. FEC, "Official 2020 Presidential General Election Results," November 3, 2020, https://www.fec.gov/resources/cms-content/documents/2020presgeresults.pdf.

130. NCC staff, "On This Day, Bush v. Gore Settles 2000 Presidential Race," National Constitution Center, December 12, 2022, https://constitutioncenter.org/blog/on-this-day-bush-v-gore-anniversary.

131. "The 10 Closest Presidential Elections in U.S. History," *List Wire* (blog), November 8, 2022, https://thelistwire.usatoday.com/lists/the-10-closest-presidential-elections-in-u-s-history/.

132. Kennedy defeated Nixon in Hawaii (3 electoral votes), Illinois (27 electoral votes), Missouri (13 electoral votes), New Jersey (16 electoral votes), and New Mexico (4 electoral votes). Nixon would have prevailed if he had won those states with 116 more votes in Hawaii, 8,859 more votes in Illinois, 10,474 more votes in Missouri, 22,094 more votes in New Jersey, and 4,766 more votes in New Mexico, so 46,309 more votes for Nixon would have changed the outcome of the 1960 election. Robert Speel, "Four Times the Results of a Presidential Election Were Contested," *Smithsonian Magazine*, November 4, 2020, https://www.smithsonianmag.com/history/rigged-vote-four-us-presidential-elections-contested-results-180961033/; JFK Library, "1960 Presidential Election Results," accessed June 18, 2023, https://www.jfklibrary.org/learn/about-jfk/life-of-john-f-kennedy/fast-facts-john-f-kennedy/1960-presidential-election-results.

133. Winning Ohio (with 25 electoral votes) and New York (with 41 electoral votes) would have given Ford the presidency over Carter. In Ohio, Carter received 2,247,932 votes and Ford received 2,236,563 votes, so Carter won by 11,369 votes. In New York, Carter received 4,159,130 votes and Ford received 4,154,221 votes, so Carter won by 4,909 votes. Ford would have prevailed with 11,370 more votes in Ohio and 4,910 more votes in New York, a total of 16,280 votes. American Presidency Project, "Election of 1976," accessed June 18, 2023, https://www.presidency.ucsb.edu/statistics/elections/1976.

134. American Presidency Project, "2016 Election Year," 2022, https://www.presidency.ucsb.edu/statistics/elections/2016.

135. David Skolnick, "Vance Talks Voter Fraud, Conspiracy," *Vindy.com* (blog), October 23, 2021, https://www.vindy.com/news/local-news/2021/10/vance-talks-voter-fraud-conspiracy/.

136. Blake Masters [@bgmasters], "Just watched the debut of 'Rigged' with President Trump at Mar-a-Lago. Zuckerberg and Democrat activists conducted a $400M GOTV operation with 'nonprofit' dollars. completely corrupt and criminal. It's too bad AG

Brnovich won't investigate Zuck Bucks in AZ, I wonder why," Twitter, April 6, 2022, https://twitter.com/bgmasters/status/1511545459373920258; Niels Lesniewski, "Trump-Backed Masters Wants to Join Senate 'America First Caucus,'" *Roll Call*, July 7, 2022, https://www.rollcall.com/2022/07/07/trump-backed-masters-wants-to-join-senate-america-first-caucus/.

137.  Blake Masters and J. D. Vance, "J. D. Vance, Blake Masters: We Must Stop Facebook Election Meddling," *New York Post* (blog), October 21, 2021, https://nypost.com/2021/10/21/j-d-vance-blake-masters-we-must-stop-facebook-election-meddling/.

138.  Issie Lapowsky, "How 'Zuck Bucks' Saved the 2020 Election—and Fueled the Big Lie," *Protocol*, May 23, 2022, https://www.protocol.com/policy/zuck-bucks-election.

139.  Tom Scheck et al., "How Private Money from Facebook's CEO Saved the 2020 Election," NPR, December 8, 2020, https://www.npr.org/2020/12/08/943242106/how-private-money-from-facebooks-ceo-saved-the-2020-election.

140.  Steve Nelson and Bruce Golding, "Zuckerberg Election Spending Was Orchestrated to Influence 2020 Vote," *New York Post*, October 14, 2021, https://nypost.com/2021/10/14/zuckerberg-election-spending-was-orchestrated-to-influence-2020-vote/.

141.  William Doyle, "The 2020 Election Wasn't Stolen, It Was Bought by Mark Zuckerberg," *Federalist*, October 12, 2021, https://thefederalist.com/2021/10/12/the-2020-election-wasnt-stolen-it-was-bought-by-mark-zuckerberg/; David Bossie, "Mark Zuckerberg's 'Donations' Rigged the 2020 Election," *Washington Times*, April 12, 2022, https://www.washingtontimes.com/news/2022/apr/12/mark-zuckerbergs-donations-rigged-the-2020-electio.

142.  Miles Parks, "Private Funding Saved the 2020 Election. Now, Some GOP-Led States Are Banning It," NPR, March 31, 2022, https://www.npr.org/2022/03/31/1088252896/private-funding-saved-the-2020-election-now-some-gop-led-states-are-banning-it.

143.  Margot Cleveland, "Court Reinstates Lawsuit Against Zuckerberg's Election Meddling Group," *Federalist*, April 5, 2022, https://thefederalist.com/2022/04/05/court-reinstates-louisiana-ags-lawsuit-against-zuckerbergs-election-meddling-group/.

144.  "STATE OF LOUISIANA VERSUS CENTER FOR TECH AND CIVIC LIFE, ET AL. VS.," *Casetext*, March 30, 2022, https://casetext.com/case/state-v-ctr-for-tech-civic-life.

145.  Victor Skinner, "Appeals Court Sides with AG Landry in 'Zuckerbucks' Election Lawsuit | Louisiana," *Center Square*, April 4, 2022, https://www.thecentersquare.com/louisiana/article_c622f588-b437-11ec-8260-6339773270d0.amp.html.

146.  Editorial Board, "Opinion: Zuckerbucks Shouldn't Pay for Elections," *Wall Street Journal*, January 3, 2022, https://www.wsj.com/articles/zuckerbucks-shouldnt-pay-for-elections-mark-zuckerberg-center-for-technology-and-civic-life-trump-biden-2020-11640912907.

147.  Senator John Danforth et al., *Lost, Not Stolen: The Conservative Case That Trump Lost and Biden Won the 2020 Presidential Election*, July 2022, https://lostnotstolen.org//wp-content/uploads/2022/07/Lost-Not-Stolen-The-Conservative-Case-that-Trump-Lost-and-Biden-Won-the-2020-Presidential-Election-July-2022.pdf.

148.  Sara Swann, "PolitiFact—No, Most Americans Don't Believe the 2020 Election Was Fraudulent," @politifact, February 2, 2022, https://www.politifact.com/factchecks/2022/feb/02/viral-image/no-most-americans-dont-believe-2020-election-was-f/.

149.  Theodore Schleifer, "Silicon Valley's Biden Beef and Zuckerberg's Hired Gun," *Puck News* (blog), December 21, 2021, https://puck.news/silicon-valleys-biden-beef-and-zuckerbergs-hired-gun/.

150.  It should be noted that Democratic activists were actively involved in the election integrity efforts that Chan and Zuckerberg funded. In particular, Tiana Epps-Johnson,

executive director of The Center for Tech and Civic Life, had previously worked at the New Organizing Institute, which provided training to liberal activists and Democratic staffers. She had been selected from twenty thousand candidates as one of the twenty Obama Foundation Fellows in its inaugural year. Evan McMorris-Santoro, "Liberal Organizing Group Implodes In One Tumultuous Afternoon," *BuzzFeed News*, February 11, 2015, https://www.buzzfeednews.com/article/evanmcsan/new-organizing-institute-implodes; Center for Tech and Civic Life, "Tiana Epps-Johnson," https://www.techandciviclife.org/team/tiana-epps-johnson/; Obama Foundation, "Tiana Epps-Johnson," 2022, https://www.obama.org/fellowship/2018-fellows/tiana-epps-johnson/; "Tiana Epps-Johnson," LinkedIn, 2023, https://www.linkedin.com/in/tianaej/.

151. Mike Isaac, "David Plouffe Leaves Uber, Joins Chan Zuckerberg Initiative," *SFGATE*, January 11, 2017, https://www.sfgate.com/business/article/David-Plouffe-leaves-Uber-joins-Chan-Zuckerberg-10848865.php.

152. "CZI Announces David Plouffe to Lead Policy and Advocacy Work," *Chan Zuckerberg Initiative* (blog), January 10, 2017, https://chanzuckerberg.com/newsroom/czi-announces-david-plouffe-to-lead-policy-and-advocacy-work/; White House, "David Plouffe," whitehouse.gov, August 17, 2011, https://obamawhitehouse.archives.gov/blog/author/david-plouffe.

153. Michael Scherer, "Obama Veteran Ben LaBolt to Become White House Communications Director," *Washington Post*, February 10, 2023, https://www.washingtonpost.com/politics/2023/02/10/obama-veteran-ben-labolt-become-white-house-communications-director/.

154. Neil Vigdor, "Mark Zuckerberg Ends Election Grants," *New York Times*, April 12, 2022, https://www.nytimes.com/2022/04/12/us/politics/mark-zuckerberg-midterms-elections-grant.html.

155. Theodore Schleifer, "Silicon Valley's Biden Beef and Zuckerberg's Hired Gun," *Puck* (blog), December 21, 2021, https://puck.news/silicon-valleys-biden-beef-and-zuckerbergs-hired-gun/; Susan Ferrechio, "Zuckerberg Won't Repeat 2020's Massive Spending on Elections Offices, Bows to Conservative Critics," *Washington Times*, April 12, 2022, https://www.washingtontimes.com/news/2022/apr/12/zuckerberg-wont-repeat-2020s-massive-spending-elec/.

156. Madeleine Carlisle and Brian Bennett, "How Joe Biden Is Deciding on a Supreme Court Nominee," *Time*, February 2, 2022, https://time.com/6144413/joe-biden-supreme-court-nominee-process/; Neil Vigdor, "Mark Zuckerberg Ends Election Grants," *New York Times*, April 12, 2022, https://www.nytimes.com/2022/04/12/us/politics/mark-zuckerberg-midterms-elections-grant.html; Seung Min Kim, "White House Unveils Supreme Court Nomination Team," *Washington Post*, February 3, 2022, https://www.washingtonpost.com/politics/2022/02/02/supreme-court-biden-vacancy/.

157. Steven Nelson, "Ex-Mark Zuckerberg Spox to Lead Biden Comms Team as Bedingfield Exits," *New York Post*, February 10, 2023, https://nypost.com/2023/02/10/ex-mark-zuckerberg-spox-to-lead-biden-comms-team-as-bedingfield-exits/.

158. FEC, "Browse Candidates for Senate," FEC.gov, accessed June 18, 2023, https://www.fec.gov/data/candidates/senate/?election_year=2022&cycle=2022&election_full=true.

159. FEC, "JD VANCE FOR SENATE INC.—Committee Overview." FEC.gov, accessed June 18, 2023, https://www.fec.gov/data/committee/C00783142/; FEC, "TIM RYAN FOR OHIO—Committee Overview," FEC.gov, accessed June 18, 2023, https://www.fec.gov/data/committee/C00777771/.

160. FEC, "BLAKE MASTERS FOR SENATE—Committee Overview," FEC.gov, accessed June 18, 2023, https://www.fec.gov/data/committee/C00784165/; FEC, "KELLY, MARK— Candidate Overview," FEC.gov, accessed June 18, 2023, https://www.fec.gov/data /candidate/S0AZ00350/.

161. Brian Schwartz, "Peter Thiel's Picks Masters, Vance Split Key Senate Races in Arizona, Ohio After Billionaire Spent $32 Million on 2022 Midterms," CNBC, November 12, 2022, https://www.cnbc.com/2022/11/12/midterm-results-peter-thiel-picks-masters -vance-see-mixed-results-in-arizona-ohio.html; FEC, "Receipts 2021–2022," FEC.gov, December 31, 2022, https://www.fec.gov/data/receipts/?data_type=processed&two _year_transaction_period=2022&min_date=01%2F01%2F2021&max_date =12%2F31%2F2022&recipient_committee_type=S&recipient_committee_type=H.

162. "End Citizens United Files FEC Complaint Against JD Vance Campaign and Protect Ohio Values PAC for Illegal In-Kind Contribution Scheme," End Citizens United | We the People, Not "We the Wealthy," June 9, 2022, https://endcitizensunited.org/latest -news/press-releases/end-citizens-united-files-fec-complaint-against-jd-vance -campaign-and-protect-ohio-values-pac-for-illegal-in-kind-contribution-scheme/.

163. Christopher Caldwell and Mark Peterson, "Opinion | The Decline of Ohio and the Rise of J. D. Vance," *New York Times*, April 29, 2022, https://www.nytimes.com/2022/04 /29/opinion/jd-vance-senate.html.

164. JD Vance for Senate Inc., "Issues," December 29, 2021, https://web.archive.org/web /20211229162401/https:/jdvance.com/issues/; JD Vance for Senate Inc., "Issues," October 23, 2022, https://web.archive.org/web/20221023025205/https:/jdvance.com /issues/.

165. Ronald J. Hansen, "After Debate, Trump Urged Blake Masters to 'Go Stronger' on 'Rigged' Election Claims," *Arizona Republic*, October 26, 2022, https://www.azcentral .com/story/news/politics/elections/2022/10/25/trump-urged-blake-masters-go -stronger-rigged-election-claims/10601866002/.

166. Kyung Lah, Kate Sullivan, and Paul Leblanc, "Trump Told Arizona GOP Senate Nominee 'You'll Lose If You Go Soft' on Election Fraud Claims," CNN, October 26, 2022, https://www.cnn.com/2022/10/25/politics/blake-masters-donald-trump-arizona -voter-intimidation/index.html.

167. Dan Friedman, "Leaked Audio: Before Election Day, Bannon Said Trump Planned to Falsely Claim Victory," *Mother Jones* (blog), July 12, 2022, https://www.motherjones .com/politics/2022/07/leaked-audio-steve-bannon-trump-2020-election-declare -victory/.

168. Aishvarya Kavi and Alan Feuer, "Bannon Found Guilty of Contempt in Case Related to Capitol Riot Inquiry," *New York Times*, July 22, 2022, https://www.nytimes.com/2022 /07/22/us/politics/bannon-trial-contempt-charges.html.

169. "LEAKED AUDIO: Trump Planned to Falsely Claim Victory, According to Bannon," YouTube video, 0:00; 0:35, October 31, 2020, https://www.youtube.com/watch?v =OxNoUnxN_cs.


## 15. Our Great Symbol of Democracy


1. Craig Silverman et al., "Facebook Hosted Surge of Misinformation and Insurrection Threats in Months Leading Up to Jan. 6 Attack, Records Show," ProPublica, January 4, 2022, https://www.propublica.org/article/facebook-hosted-surge-of-misinformation -and-insurrection-threats-in-months-leading-up-to-jan-6-attack-records-show.

2. Jeff Horwitz, "Facebook Says Its Rules Apply to All. Company Documents Reveal a Secret Elite That's Exempt," *Wall Street Journal*, September 13, 2021, https://www.wsj.com/articles/facebook-files-xcheck-zuckerberg-elite-rules-11631541353.

3. Catie Edmondson, "'So the Traitors Know the Stakes': The Meaning of the Jan. 6 Gallows," *New York Times*, June 16, 2022, https://www.nytimes.com/2022/06/16/us/politics/jan-6-gallows.html.

4. Dan Barry and Sheera Frenkel, "'Be There. Will Be Wild!': Trump All but Circled the Date," *New York Times*, January 7, 2021, https://www.nytimes.com/2021/01/06/us/politics/capitol-mob-trump-supporters.html.

5. House Committee on Energy and Commerce, "Testimony of Tim Kendall," September 24, 2020, https://web.archive.org/web/20220726161221/https://energycommerce.house.gov/sites/democrats.energycommerce.house.gov/files/documents/09.24.20%20CPC%20Witness%20Testimony_Kendall-UPDATED.pdf.

6. Tom Westphal, "Stanford-MIT Healthy Elections Project," March 10, 2021, https://web.mit.edu/healthyelections/www/final-reports/violence-2020-election.html.

7. Department of Homeland Security, "Homeland Threat Assessment October 2020," October 2020, https://www.dhs.gov/sites/default/files/publications/2020_10_06_homeland-threat-assessment.pdf.

8. Craig Silverman, Craig Timberg, Jeff Kao, and Jeremy B. Merill, "Facebook Groups Topped 10,000 Daily Attacks on Election Before Jan. 6, Analysis Shows." *Washington Post*, January 4, 2022. https://www.washingtonpost.com/technology/2022/01/04/facebook-election-misinformation-capitol-riot/.

9. Shannon Bond and Bobby Allyn, "How the 'Stop the Steal' Movement Outwitted Facebook Ahead of the Jan. 6 Insurrection," NPR, October 22, 2021, https://www.npr.org/2021/10/22/1048543513/facebook-groups-jan-6-insurrection.

10. While senior leadership at Facebook dismissed many of the dangers that eventually led to the failed insurrection on January 6, 2021, others in the organization remained vigilant. Brian Fishman, who led Facebook's Dangerous Organizations Policy team, told the House Select Committee the company should have responded more forcefully, especially to the Stop the Steal movement: "I distinctly, however, remember having the impression that we in the dangerous orgs world were still terrified, and everyone else wasn't. Everyone was terrified in the run-up to the election. We remained terrified, and I don't think that that was as widespread after the election." Brian Fishman, Select Committee to Investigate the January 6th Attack on the U.S. Capitol, U.S. House of Representatives, Washington, DC, Webex, April 26, 2022, https://perma.cc/2D3C-KLRR.

11. Christina Wilkie, "Trump Tries to Claim Victory Even as Ballots Are Being Counted in Several States—NBC Has Not Made a Call," CNBC, November 4, 2020, https://www.cnbc.com/2020/11/04/trump-tries-to-claim-victory-even-as-ballots-are-being-counted-in-several-states-nbc-has-not-made-a-call.html.

12. Sheera Frenkel, "The Rise and Fall of the 'Stop the Steal' Facebook Group," *New York Times*, November 5, 2020, https://www.nytimes.com/2020/11/05/technology/stop-the-steal-facebook-group.html.

13. Elahe Izadi, "First CNN, Then Within Minutes, Most Other News Organizations Called the Race for Biden," *Washington Post*, November 7, 2020, https://www.washingtonpost.com/media/2020/11/07/fox-news-biden-president/.

14. House Select Committee to Investigate the January 6th Attack on the United States Capitol, "Social Media & the January 6th Attack on the U.S. Capitol: Summary of Investigative Findings," *Washington Post*, January 17, 2023. https://www

.washingtonpost.com/documents/5bfed332-d350-47c0-8562-0137a4435c68.pdf?itid
=lk_inline_manual_3, 40.

15. "List of State Capitals in the United States," *Britannica*, accessed June 18, 2023, https://
www.britannica.com/topic/list-of-state-capitals-in-the-United-States-2119210.

16. House Select Committee to Investigate the January 6th Attack, "Social Media & the
January 6th Attack," 40–42.

17. House Select Committee to Investigate the January 6th Attack, 40–42.

18. House Select Committee to Investigate the January 6th Attack, 50.

19. Kimberly Adams and Daniel Shin, "The Tech Legacy of Tracking the Jan. 6 Insurrec-
tionists," *Marketplace* (blog), June 1, 2022, https://www.marketplace.org/shows
/marketplace-tech/the-tech-legacy-of-tracking-the-jan-6-insurrectionists/.

20. House Select Committee to Investigate the January 6th Attack, "Social Media & the
January 6th Attack," 8–9.

21. House Select Committee to Investigate the January 6th Attack, 40–42.

22. Megan Graham and Salvador Rodriguez, "Twitter and Facebook Race to Label a Slew
of Posts Making False Election Claims Before All Votes Counted," CNBC, November 4, 2020, https://www.cnbc.com/2020/11/04/twitter-and-facebook-label-trump
-posts-claiming-election-stolen.html.

23. Renee Engeln, "Most People Ignore Instagram's Sensitive Content Warnings," *Psychology Today* (blog), December 14, 2022, https://www.psychologytoday.com/us/blog
/beauty-sick/202212/most-people-ignore-instagrams-sensitive-content-warnings.

24. "Genesis 3:13—New International Version," Bible Gateway, accessed June 18, 2023,
https://www.biblegateway.com/passage/?search=Genesis%203%3A13&version=NIV.

25. Kylie Jane Kremer [@KylieJaneKremer], "The calvary is coming, Mr. President! JAN-
UARY 6th | Washington, DC," Twitter, December 19, 2020, https://twitter.com
/KylieJaneKremer/status/1340399063875895296.

26. Kylie Jane Kremer [@KylieJaneKremer], "The calvary is coming, Mr. President! JAN-
UARY 6th | Washington, DC," Twitter, December 19, 2020, https://twitter.com
/KylieJaneKremer/status/1340399063875895296.

27. It is important to note that a dozen years earlier, Amy Kremer believed that Barack
Obama was ineligible to be president of the United States based on the same conspiracies
that Donald Trump went on to promote on social media in the ensuing years. "I have
lost all hope on this issue of OBami's eligibility to be President of the United States," she
wrote on January 8, 2009. "It is sickening! The whole thing just makes my stomach
churn. Several months ago, I had hope that this would all come to light and someone
would have the balls to object to certifying the vote. I believe it has come to light . . . all
the members of Congress are aware of the lawsuits surrounding his eligibility. Unfortunately, none of them have any balls!" Amy Kremer, "Congress Certifies the Electoral
College Vote," *Southern Belle Politics* (blog), January 8, 2009, https://web.archive.org
/web/20160406221036/http:/www.southernbellepolitics.com/2009/01/congress-certifies
-electoral-college.html; Casey Tolan, "7 Defenders of the Big Lie," CNN, 2021, https://
www.cnn.com/interactive/2021/06/us/capitol-riot-paths-to-insurrection/.

28. U.S. Department of the Interior, National Park Service, National Capital Region, "PUB-
LIC GATHERING PERMIT: 21-0278," January 5, 2021, https://www.nps.gov/aboutus/foia
/upload/21-0278-Women-for-America-First-Ellispse-permit_REDACTED.pdf.

29. Joseph Mandato and William Devine, "Why the CEO Shouldn't Also Be the Board
Chair," *Harvard Business Review*, March 4, 2020, https://hbr.org/2020/03/why-the-ceo
-shouldnt-also-be-the-board-chair.

30. Katie Canales, "'The Most Powerful Person Who's Ever Walked the Face of the Earth': How Mark Zuckerberg's Stranglehold on Facebook Could Put the Company at Risk," *Business Insider*, October 13, 2021, https://www.businessinsider.com/mark-zuckerberg -control-facebook-whistleblower-key-man-risk-2021-10.

31. Meta, "Peter Thiel to Retire from Meta Board of Directors at 2022 Annual Shareholder Meeting," February 7, 2022, https://s21.q4cdn.com/399680738/files/doc_news/Peter -Thiel-to-Retire-from-Meta-Board-of-Directors-at-2022-Annual-Shareholder -Meeting-2022.pdf.

32. Facebook, Inc., "Proxy Statement Pursuant to Section 14(a) of the Securities Exchange Act of 1934," sec.gov, April 12, 2019, https://www.sec.gov/Archives/edgar/data/1326801 /000132680119000025/facebook2019definitiveprox.htm, 15; Facebook, Inc., "Proxy Statement Pursuant to Section 14(a) of the Securities Exchange Act of 1934," sec.gov, April 10, 2020, https://www.sec.gov/Archives/edgar/data/1326801/000132680120000037 /facebook2020definitiveprox.htm, 17.

33. Meta, "Meta—Leadership & Governance—Compensation, Nominating & Governance Committee Charter," September 8, 2022, https://investor.fb.com/leadership -and-governance/compensation-and-governance-committee-charter/default .aspx.

34. Facebook, Inc., "Proxy Statement Pursuant to Section 14(a) of the Securities Exchange Act of 1934," sec.gov, 2021, https://www.sec.gov/Archives/edgar/data/1326801/0001326 80121000022/facebook2021definitiveprox.htm.

35. Brian Baxter, "Facebook's First-Year General Counsel Earns $19 Million," *Bloomberg Law*, April 10, 2020, https://news.bloomberglaw.com/esg/facebooks-first-year-general -counsel-earns-19-million.

36. Isaac Stanley-Becker, "She Sold the Patriot Act to Congress. Her Next Job Is Defending Facebook," *Washington Post*, April 23, 2019, https://www.washingtonpost.com /nation/2019/04/23/she-sold-patriot-act-congress-her-next-job-is-defending -facebook/.

37. House Select Committee to Investigate the January 6th Attack, "Social Media & the January 6th Attack," 50.

38. House Select Committee to Investigate the January 6th Attack, 42.

39. House Select Committee to Investigate the January 6th Attack, 45–46.

40. Guy Rosen, "Our Response to the Violence in Washington," *Meta* (blog), January 7, 2021, https://about.fb.com/news/2021/01/responding-to-the-violence-in-washington-dc/.

41. House Select Committee to Investigate the January 6th Attack, "Social Media & the January 6th Attack," 42.

42. "In Response to Oversight Board, Trump Suspended for Two Years; Will Only Be Reinstated If Conditions Permit," *Meta* (blog), June 4, 2021, https://about.fb.com/news /2021/06/facebook-response-to-oversight-board-recommendations-trump/.

43. Meta, "Meta—Leadership & Governance—Corporate Governance Guidelines," April 3, 2022, https://investor.fb.com/leadership-and-governance/corporate-governance -guidelines/default.aspx; Meta, "Meta—Leadership & Governance—Compensation, Nominating & Governance Committee Charter," February 7, 2022, https://web .archive.org/web/20220207061552/https://investor.fb.com/leadership-and -governance/compensation-and-governance-committee-charter/default.aspx.

44. House Select Committee to Investigate the January 6th Attack, "Social Media & the January 6th Attack," 3.

45. House Select Committee to Investigate the January 6th Attack, 69–70.

46. House Select Committee to Investigate the January 6th Attack, 69–70; L. Ceci, "You-Tube: Hours of Video Uploaded Every Minute 2020," Statista, January 9, 2023. https://www.statista.com/statistics/259477/hours-of-video-uploaded-to-youtube-every-minute/; L. Ceci, "Youtube Average Video Length by Category 2018," Statista, August 23, 2021, https://www.statista.com/statistics/1026923/youtube-video-category-average-length/.

47. House Select Committee to Investigate the January 6th Attack, 69–70; Ceci. "YouTube: Hours of Video"; Ceci, "Youtube Average Video Length."

48. House Select Committee to Investigate the January 6th Attack, 10.

49. House Select Committee to Investigate the January 6th Attack, 72.

50. Adi Robertson, "Rumble's Antitrust Lawsuit against Google Can Proceed, Says Judge," *Verge*, August 2, 2022, https://www.theverge.com/2022/8/2/23288732/rumble-antitrust-lawsuit-google-search-results-app-court-decision.

51. Jeremy W. Peters, "Rumble, the Right's Go-To Video Site, Has Much Bigger Ambitions," *New York Times*, March 28, 2022, https://www.nytimes.com/2022/03/28/business/media/rumble-social-media-conservatives-videos.html.

52. Drew Harwell, "Rumble, a YouTube Rival Popular with Conservatives, Will Pay Creators Who 'Challenge the Status Quo,'" *Washington Post*, August 12, 2021, https://www.washingtonpost.com/technology/2021/08/12/rumble-video-gabbard-greenwald/; Ellie House, "Rumble Sends Viewers Tumbling Toward Misinformation," *Wired*, May 11, 2021, https://www.wired.com/story/rumble-sends-viewers-tumbling-toward-misinformation/.

53. Shreenita Ghosh and Galen Stocking, "Key Facts about Rumble," *Pew Research Center* (blog), December 21, 2022, https://www.pewresearch.org/short-reads/2022/12/21/key-facts-about-rumble/.

54. Harwell, "Rumble, a YouTube Rival."

55. Houston Keene, "Peter Thiel, J. D. Vance Ready to Rumble, Investing in Popular Conservative Video Site," FOXBusiness, May 19, 2021, https://www.foxbusiness.com/politics/rumble-investors-bolster-position-youtube-alternative.amp.

56. Keach Hagey, "Peter Thiel, J. D. Vance Invest in Rumble Video Platform Popular on Political Right," *Wall Street Journal*, May 19, 2021, https://www.wsj.com/articles/peter-thiel-j-d-vance-invest-in-rumble-video-platform-popular-on-political-right-11621447661.

57. Elizabeth Culliford, "Trump Joins Video Platform Rumble Ahead of Ohio Rally," Reuters, June 26, 2021, https://www.reuters.com/world/us/trump-joins-video-platform-rumble-ahead-ohio-rally-2021-06-26/.

58. Amar Mehta, "Truth Social: Donald Trump to launch social network, saying 'your favourite President has been silenced,'" *Sky News*, October 21, 2021, https://news.sky.com/story/truth-social-donald-trump-to-launch-social-network-saying-your-favourite-president-has-been-silenced-12439821; Liz Harrington [@realLizUSA], "🚨President Donald J. Trump announces Trump Media & Technology Group🚨 'I created TRUTH Social and TMTG to stand up to the tyranny of Big Tech . . . I Am Excited to Send out my first TRUTH on TRUTH Social very soon," Twitter, October 21, 2021, https://twitter.com/realLizUSA/status/1450979193400045570.

59. Dan Mangan, Yun Li, and Christina Wilkie, "Shares in Digital World Acquisition Soar by 400 Percent on News of Social Media Deal with Trump," *NBC News*, October 21, 2021, https://www.nbcnews.com/business/markets/shares-digital-world-acquisition-soar-145-percent-news-social-media-n1282061.

60. TMTG, "Company Overview," 2021, https://web.archive.org/web/20211021010358 /https://www.tmtgcorp.com/company-overview/, 10, 12.

61. Drew Harwell, "Co-founder of Trump's Media Company Details Truth Social's Bitter Infighting," *Washington Post*, October 16, 2022, https://www.washingtonpost.com /technology/2022/10/15/truth-social-trump-animosity-whistleblower/.

62. Donald Trump, "@realDonaldTrump," Truth Social, November 9, 2022, https://web .archive.org/web/20221109160340/https://truthsocial.com/@realDonaldTrump; TMTG, "Company Overview."

63. "Joshua Fineman, "Rumble SPAC Jumps After Trump Social Media Partnership Confirmed," *Seeking Alpha*, December 14, 2021, https://seekingalpha.com/news/3780186 -rumble-spac-jumps-after-confirming-partnership-with-trump-social-media -company; "Video Platform Rumble to Go Public via $2.1 Bln SPAC Deal," Reuters, December 1, 2021, https://www.reuters.com/markets/funds/video-platform-rumble-go -public-via-21-bln-spac-deal-2021-12-02/.

64. Theo Wayt, "Facebook Director Peter Thiel Invests in Conservative Rival Rumble," *New York Post*, May 19, 2021, https://nypost.com/2021/05/19/facebook-director-peter -thiel-invests-in-conservative-rival-rumble/.

65. Jon Greenberg, "PolitiFact—Does JD Vance Profit from Russia Propaganda?," *Politifact*, May 24, 2022, https://www.politifact.com/factchecks/2022/may/24/tim-ryan/does -jd-vance-profit-russia-propaganda/.

66. Rumble, "Rumble Sets New Record for Monthly Active Users," Cision, August 15, 2022, https://www.prnewswire.com/news-releases/rumble-sets-new-record-for-monthly -active-users-301605472.html; Daniel F. Carr, "Truth Social Surges More on Trump World's Anticipation of Indictment than on the News," *Similarweb* (*blog*), April 4, 2023, https://www.similarweb.com/blog/insights/social-media-news/truth-social -trump-indictment/.

67. Drew Harwell, "He Blew the Whistle on Trump's Truth Social. Now He Works at Starbucks," *Washington Post*, May 1, 2023, https://www.washingtonpost.com/technology /2023/04/29/truth-social-wilkerson-starbucks/.

68. "Blake Masters on Inflation, CBDCs, and Setting a Pro-Crypto Agenda on Apple Podcasts," *On the Brink with Castle Island*, Apple Podcasts, 27:24, March 2, 2022, https:// podcasts.apple.com/us/podcast/blake-masters-on-inflation-cbdcs-and-setting-a /id1480586463?i=1000552682900; Adam Wren Leonard Meghan Morris, Kimberly, "Billionaire Peter Thiel Has a Republican US Senate Candidate on His Corporate Payroll Who Is Earning More than $1 Million, Documents Show," *Business Insider*, October 8, 2021, https://www.businessinsider.com/peter-thiel-blake-masters-senate -finances-arizona-2021-10.

69. Rumble, "Donald Trump Jr.: Profile," accessed June 18, 2023, https://rumble.com/c /DonaldJTrumpJr?sort=views; Jon Fingas, "Russia's RT Moves to Rumble After Being Deplatformed Elsewhere," Engadget, March 3, 2022, https://www.engadget.com/russia -rt-moves-to-rumble-204631299.html.

70. Rumble, "'They Are Not Only Crazy, They Are Hopeless'—Putin on Amount and Nature of Russia Sanctions," 0:10, 2022, https://rumble.com/v18s7e4-they-are-not-only -crazy-they-are-hopeless-putin-on-amount-and-nature-of-rus.html; Rumble, "Keiser Report | The End of Woke Utopia | E1792," 14:20, 2021, https://rumble.com/vra8wv -keiser-report-the-end-of-woke-utopia-e1792.html.

71. Jeffrey Goldberg and Anne Applebaum, "Zelensky's Plan to Defeat Russia—and Take Back Crimea," *Atlantic*, May 1, 2023, https://www.theatlantic.com/magazine/archive /2023/06/counteroffensive-ukraine-zelensky-crimea/673781/.

72. John McCormack, "A Closer Look at Why J. D. Vance's Stance on Ukraine Is Unpopular," *National Review* (blog), April 6, 2022, https://www.nationalreview.com/corner /a-closer-look-at-why-j-d-vances-stance-on-ukraine-is-unpopular/l; Blake Masters [@ bgmasters], "This invasion is an atrocity and Putin is a thug. Ukrainian resistance is noble. But geography is real. Ukraine is crucial to Russian security, not to ours. We will be living with Russia for decades and centuries, unless we fail at today's task and blow up the whole world,"*Twitter*, March 1, 2022, https://twitter.com/bgmasters/status /1498775891857522694; Ian Schwartz, "Blake Masters Slams New $40 Billion Ukraine Aid Bill: 'Under Joe Biden, It Is Always America Last,'" *Real Clear Politics*, May 12, 2022, https://www.realclearpolitics.com/video/2022/05/12/blake_masters_slams_new _40_billion_ukraine_aid_bill_under_joe_biden_it_is_always_america_last.html.

73. Sheila Dang, "Russian News Channel RT to Broadcast on Rumble After Big Tech Curbs," Reuters, March 3, 2022, https://www.reuters.com/business/media-telecom /russian-news-channel-rt-broadcast-rumble-after-big-tech-curbs-2022-03-03/.

74. Colin Greenspon, "Form ADV," Narya Capital Management, LLC, March 24, 2022, https://reports.adviserinfo.sec.gov/reports/ADV/307707/PDF/307707.pdf; Blake Masters [@bgmasters], "Just cleared my schedule to defeat Mark Kelly in November: I have resigned from my posts running Thiel Capital and the Thiel Foundation. 🇺🇸🌵," Twitter, March 16, 2022, https://twitter.com/bgmasters/status/1504166071632162816.

75. Brad Dress, "Ramaswamy Isolates Himself on Ukraine with Proposed Putin Pact," *Hill*, September 1, 2023, https://thehill.com/policy/defense/4179994-ramaswamy -isolates-himself-on-ukraine-with-proposed-putin-pact/; Jared Gans, "Haley Knocks Ramaswamy over Support for Reducing Aid to Israel," *Hill*, August 21, 2023, https:// thehill.com/homenews/campaign/4162615-haley-knocks-ramaswamy-over-support -for-reducing-aid-to-israel/.

76. Peter Rudegeair and Angel Au-Yeung, "The Anti-Woke Presidential Candidate Who Wants to Crush ESG and Gut the Fed," *Wall Street Journal*, May 27, 2023, https://www .wsj.com/articles/the-anti-woke-presidential-candidate-who-wants-to-crush-esg -and-gut-the-fed-a486fdc.

77. Dareh Gregorian, "Trump Endorses J. D. Vance in Hotly Contested Ohio Senate Primary," *NBC News*, April 15, 2022, https://www.nbcnews.com/politics/2022 -election/trump-endorses-jd-vance-hotly-contested-ohio-senate-primary -rcna24647; Donald J. Trump, "Endorsement of Blake Masters," June 2, 2022, https:// web.archive.org/web/20220610021023/https://www.donaldjtrump.com/news/news -djyreqf7b22098.

78. Alex Isenstadt, "A Mole Hunt, a Secret Website and Peter Thiel's Big Risk: How J. D. Vance Won His Primary," *Politico*, May 3, 2022, https://www.politico.com/news/2022 /05/03/jd-vance-win-ohio-primary-00029881.

79. Trump, "Endorsement of Blake Masters."

80. Ron Filipkowski 🚩 [@RonFilipkowski], "Vance says Biden is trying to kill MAGA voters: 'If you wanted to kill a bunch of MAGA voters in the middle of the heartland, how better to target them and their kids with this fentanyl. It does look intentional. It's like Biden wants to punish people who didn't vote for him," Twitter, April 30, 2022, https://twitter.com/RonFilipkowski/status/1520201563330990080.

81. Glenn Kessler reviewed Vance's assertion for the *Washington Post's Fact Checker* blog: "In just about every way, Vance's outrage at Biden is misplaced. Fentanyl seizures have increased, not fallen, under Biden. Overdose deaths jumped sharply under Trump. As for Trump voters being supposedly targeted, people of color die at a higher rate from opioids than Whites. It's bad enough to suggest that the president is deliberately

trying to kill off Trump voters with illicit drugs. But it's especially appalling to make such hyperbolic claims based on zero facts." Glenn Kessler, "Analysis | J.D. Vance's Claim That Biden Is Targeting 'MAGA Voters' with Fentanyl," *Washington Post*, May 12, 2022, https://www.washingtonpost.com/politics/2022/05/11/jd-vances-claim -that-biden-is-targeting-maga-voters-with-fentanyl/.

82. Greg Sargent, "Opinion | As Vile as It Gets: J. D. Vance Goes Full 'Great Replacement Theory,'" *Washington Post*, April 6, 2022, https://www.washingtonpost.com/opinions /2022/04/06/jd-vance-immigration-ukraine-great-replacement/; Amy Sherman, "PolitiFact—JD Vance's Ad About 'Open Border' and Immigrant Voters Is Wrong," *Politifact*, April 8, 2022, https://www.politifact.com/factchecks/2022/apr/08/jd-vance /jd-vances-ad-about-open-border-and-immigrant-voter/.

83. James Pogue, "Inside the New Right, Where Peter Thiel Is Placing His Biggest Bets," *Vanity Fair*, April 20, 2022, https://www.vanityfair.com/news/2022/04/inside-the-new -right-where-peter-thiel-is-placing-his-biggest-bets.

84. National Archives, "Pendleton Act (1883)," September 8, 2021, https://www.archives .gov/milestone-documents/pendleton-act.

85. Pogue, "Inside the New Right."

86. Vance, *Hillbilly Elegy*, 193.

87. Donald Trump, "Executive Order on Creating Schedule F in the Excepted Service— The White House," trumpwhitehouse.archives.gov, October 21, 2020, https:// trumpwhitehouse.archives.gov/presidential-actions/executive-order-creating -schedule-f-excepted-service/.

88. Jim Eisenmann, "Trump's Plan to Gut the Civil Service," *Lawfare*, December 8, 2020, https://www.lawfareblog.com/trumps-plan-gut-civil-service;

89. Center for Presidential Transition, "The Basics: Frequently Asked Questions About Presidential Transitions," Partnership for Public Service, accessed June 18, 2023, https:// presidentialtransition.org/faq/.

90. Jonathan Swan, "Inside Trump '25: A Radical Plan for Trump's Second Term," *Axios*, July 22, 2022, https://www.axios.com/2022/07/22/trump-2025-radical-plan-second -term.

91. Faiz Siddiqui, "California Judge Rules Unconstitutional the Measure Classifying Uber and Lyft Drivers as Contractors," *Washington Post*, August 21, 2021, https://www .washingtonpost.com/technology/2021/08/20/uber-lyft-prop-22-unconstitutional/.

92. Mike Leonard, "Peter Thiel, Palantir Co-Founders Slam 'Emperor for Life' Claims," *Bloomberg Law*, July 23, 2021, https://news.bloomberglaw.com/esg/peter-thiel-palantir -co-founders-slam-emperor-for-life-claims.

93. Trump, "Executive Order on Creating Schedule F."

94. Code of Federal Regulations, "Section 213.102 of United States Code, Identification of Positions in Schedule A, B, C, or D—Excepted Service," October 20, 2020, https://www .ecfr.gov/on/2020-10-20/title-5/chapter-I/subchapter-B/part-213.

95. Jonathan Swan, "Trump's Revenge: How the Former President Could Gut the Federal Bureaucracy," *Axios*, July 23, 2022, https://www.axios.com/2022/07/23/donald-trump -news-schedule-f-executive-order.

96. Michael D. Shear and Maggie Haberman, "Trump Places Loyalists in Key Jobs Inside the White House While Raging Against Enemies Outside," *New York Times*, February 13, 2020, https://www.nytimes.com/2020/02/13/us/politics/trump-roger-stone .html.

97. John Santucci, Katherine Faulders, and Tara Palmeri, "Trump Personal Aide John McEntee Forced out Over Background Check Issues," *ABC News*, March 13, 2018,

https://abcnews.go.com/Politics/trump-personal-aide-john-mcentee-forced
-background-check/story?id=53708972.

98.  Jonathan D. Karl, "The Man Who Made January 6 Possible," *Atlantic*, November 9,
2021, https://www.theatlantic.com/ideas/archive/2021/11/trump-johnny-mcentee
-january-6-betrayal/620646/.

99.  Karl; "Camryn Kinsey," LinkedIn, 2023, https://www.linkedin.com/in/camryn-kinsey
-913a7b1a7/.

100.  "Camryn Kinsey (@camrynbaylee)," Twitter, accessed June 18, 2023, https://twitter
.com/camrynbaylee; "Camryn Kinsey (@camrynbaylee)," Instagram, accessed June 18,
2023, https://www.instagram.com/camrynbaylee/.

101.  Karl, "The Man Who Made January 6 Possible."

102.  Karl; Trump, "Executive Order on Creating Schedule F."

103.  Swan, "Trump's Revenge."

104.  Jonathan Karl [@jonkarl], "Here's the memo, never before made public, that Johnnie
McEntee's Presidential Personnel Office wrote making the case for firing Secretary of
Defense Mark Esper. Written on 10/19/20, it's a remarkable window inside the thinking of the Trump White House. #Betrayal," Twitter, November 10, 2021, https://twitter
.com/jonkarl/status/1458449358672773127; Missy Ryan et al., "Trump Fires Defense
Secretary Mark Esper," *Washington Post*, November 10, 2020, https://www
.washingtonpost.com/national-security/defense-secretary-mark-esper-fired-trump
/2020/11/09/9b7cbcbc-a5b9-11ea-8681-7d471bf20207_story.html.

105.  U.S. Department of Defense, "Christopher C. Miller," accessed June 15, 2023, https://
www.defense.gov/about/biographies/biography/article/2111192/christopher-c-miller/.

106.  Karl, "The Man Who Made January 6 Possible."

107.  Jonathan Karl, *Betrayal: The Final Act of the Trump Show* (New York: Penguin, 2021),
260–65, 269–70.

108.  Sara Fischer, "Peter Thiel Backs Conservative Dating App The Right Stuff," *Axios*, February 15, 2022, https://www.axios.com/2022/02/15/peter-thiel-conservative-dating-app
-the-rightstuff.

109.  The Right Stuff, "The Right Stuff," 2022, https://www.daterightstuff.com/optin
-569022551666898319501; "No More Bad Dates—The Right Stuff Dating App—
Commercial," YouTube video, 2022, https://www.youtube.com/watch?v=E5Nk
De6JpuM.

110.  Fischer, "Peter Thiel Backs Conservative Dating App."

111.  Apple App Store, "The Right Stuff: Dating Right—Ratings and Reviews," October 3,
2022, https://web.archive.org/web/20221003211319/https://apps.apple.com/us/app/the
-right-stuff-dating-right/id1620026842?see-all=reviews

112.  "The Right Stuff, Timeless with Julie Hartman," YouTube video, 20:23, 2022, https://
www.youtube.com/watch?v=h5WOMIY8waI.

113.  Kyle Barr, "Conservative Dating App the Right Stuff Is a Flop," Gizmodo, December 28, 2022, https://gizmodo.com/no-one-using-conservative-dating-app-the-right
-stuff-1849934412.

114.  Terrian Spurs, "Conservative Dating App 'The Right Stuff' Is Allegedly All Guys, Users
Contacted by FBI," Fox 26 Houston, October 6, 2022. https://www.fox26houston.com
/news/conservative-dating-app-the-right-stuff-is-apparently-all-guys.

115.  Kassia Byrnes, "Right-Wing Dating App Users on 'The Right Stuff' Allegedly Contacted by FBI: Report," *New York Post*, October 10, 2022. https://nypost.com/2022
/10/10/right-wing-dating-app-users-on-the-right-stuff-contacted-by-fbi/; Chelsea
Ritschel, "The Right Stuff Users Claim They Were Contacted by FBI After Using the

Conservative Dating App," *Independent*, October 4, 2022, https://www.yahoo.com /video/stuff-users-claim-were-contacted-215915863.html.

116. Stephen M. Lepore, "Woman Who Joined Conservative Dating Site Reveals She Sent January 6 Rioters' Details to FBI," *Daily Mail*, March 29, 2023, https://www.dailymail .co.uk/news/article-11917043/Woman-joined-conservative-dating-site-reveals-sent -January-6-rioters-details-FBI.html.

117. Project 2025, "Former PPO Director John McEntee Joins Project 2025; Personnel Database Launches," May 2, 2023, https://www.project2025.org/news/press-releases /former-ppo-director-john-mcentee-joins-project-2025-personnel-database -launches/; Project 2025, "Advisory Board," February 2, 2023, https://www.project2025 .org/about/advisory-board/.

118. Jonathan Swan and Maggie Haberman, "Heritage Foundation Makes Plans to Staff Next G.O.P. Administration," *New York Times*, April 20, 2023, https://www.nytimes .com/2023/04/20/us/politics/republican-president-2024-heritage-foundation.html.

119. Project 2025, "The Presidential Administration Academy," February 28, 2023, https:// www.project2025.org/training/presidential-administration-academy/; Heritage Foundation, "Mandate For Leadership: The Conservative Promise," May 2023, https://thf _media.s3.amazonaws.com/project2025/2025_MandateForLeadership_FULL.pdf; Project 2025, "Former PPO Director John McEntee Joins Project 2025; Personnel Database Launches," May 2, 2023, https://www.project2025.org/news/press-releases /former-ppo-director-john-mcentee-joins-project-2025-personnel-database -launches/.

120. Floyd Abrams and Lee Wolosky, "Opinion: The Promise and Peril of Facial Recognition," *Wall Street Journal*, January 13, 2021, https://www.wsj.com/articles/the-promise -and-peril-of-facial-recognition-11610579445.

121. Lee Wolosky, "Opinion | What I Learned When I Tried to Close Guantanamo," *Politico,* January 11, 2022, https://www.politico.com/news/magazine/2022/01/11/close -guantanamo-prison-wolosky-526829.

122. David A. May and David L. Hudson Jr., "Floyd Abrams," *First Amendement Encyclopedia*, Middle Tennessee State University, accessed June 18, 2023, https://www.mtsu .edu/first-amendment/article/1384/floyd-abrams.

123. Kashmir Hill, "What Happens When Our Faces Are Tracked Everywhere We Go?" *New York Times*, March 18, 2021, https://www.nytimes.com/interactive/2021/03/18 /magazine/facial-recognition-clearview-ai.html.

124. Drew Harwell and Craig Timberg, "How America's Surveillance Networks Helped the FBI Catch the Capitol Mob," *Washington Post*, April 4, 2021, https://www .washingtonpost.com/technology/2021/04/02/capitol-siege-arrests-technology-fbi -privacy/.

125. Ryan Daws, "Police Use of Clearview AI's Facial Recognition Increased 26% After Capitol Raid," *AI News*, January 11, 2021, https://www.artificialintelligence-news .com/2021/01/11/police-use-clearview-ai-facial-recognition-increased-26-capitol -raid/.

126. Ryan Mac, Caroline Haskins, Brianna Sacks, and Logan McDonald, "How A Facial Recognition Tool Found Its Way Into Hundreds of US Police Departments, Schools, And Taxpayer-Funded Organizations," *BuzzFeed News*, April 10, 2021, https://www .buzzfeednews.com/article/ryanmac/clearview-ai-local-police-facial-recognition; Jisha Joseph, "Rioters Thought It Was Cool to Take Selfies at the Capitol. Then, the FBI Came Calling for Them." *scoop.upworthy*, January 14, 2022. https://scoop.upworthy .com/rioters-thought-cool-take-selfies-at-capitol-fbi-came-calling.

127. Meg Anderson and Nick McMillan, "1,000 People Have Been Charged for the Capitol Riot. Here's Where Their Cases Stand," NPR, March 25, 2023, https://www.npr.org/2023/03/25/1165022885/1000-defendants-january-6-capitol-riot.

128. Spencer S. Hsu, "Justice Dept. Calls Jan. 6 'Capitol Attack' Probe One of Largest in U.S. History, Expects at Least 400 to Be Charged," *Washington Post*, March 13, 2021, https://www.washingtonpost.com/local/legal-issues/capitol-attack-investigation-largest/2021/03/12/5c07b46c-833d-11eb-9ca6-54e187ee4939_story.html.

129. Department of Justice, "Jury Convicts Four Leaders of the Proud Boys of Seditious Conspiracy Related to U.S. Capitol Breach," May 4, 2023, https://www.justice.gov/opa/pr/jury-convicts-four-leaders-proud-boys-seditious-conspiracy-related-us-capitol-breach.

130. Associated Press, "Proud Boys Were Ready for 'All-Out War' Before January 6, Prosecutors Argue," April 24, 2023, https://www.theguardian.com/us-news/2023/apr/24/proud-boys-jan-6-attack-trial-closing-arguments.

131. Rumble, "J6 Political Prisoners at DC Gulag Leak Video from Inside Jail Praying and Singing National Anthem," 2023, https://rumble.com/v2bvp92-j6-political-prisoners-at-dc-gulag-leak-video-from-inside-jail-praying-and-.html.

132. Isaac Arnsdorf et al., "Behind Trump's Musical Tribute to Some of the Most Violent Jan. 6 Rioters," *Washington Post*, May 4, 2023, https://www.washingtonpost.com/investigations/interactive/2023/trump-j6-prison-choir/.

133. "Justice for All," YouTube video, 2023, https://www.youtube.com/watch?v=uhXDz_ZTMfQ.

134. CNN, "READ: Transcript of CNN's Town Hall with Former President Donald Trump | CNN Politics," May 11, 2023, https://www.cnn.com/2023/05/11/politics/transcript-cnn-town-hall-trump/index.html.

135. Hill, "What Happens When Our Faces Are Tracked."

136. "Johnson v. Clearview AI, Inc. et Al," Justia, Dockets & Filings, March 22, 2023, https://dockets.justia.com/docket/new-york/nysdce/1:2023cv02441/596057.

137. Traitwell, "Welcome to Traitwell and Common Good Genetics!" *Traitwell* (blog), Substack newsletter, April 1, 2021, https://traitwell.substack.com/p/welcome-to-traitwell-and-common-good.

138. Traitwell, "Covid Forecaster," 2021, https://web.archive.org/web/20210107055659/https://www.covidforecaster.com/.

139. Traitwell, "Know Your DNA. Know Yourself," accessed June 18, 2023, https://traitwell.com/.

140. Traitwell, "Baby Blueprint," accessed June 18, 2023, https://traitwell.com/app/baby.

141. "Trait | Etymology, Origin and Meaning," *etymonline*," accessed June 18, 2023, https://www.etymonline.com/word/trait; "Bloodline—Definition, Meaning & Synonyms," *Vocabulary.com*, accessed May 11, 2023, https://www.vocabulary.com/dictionary/bloodline.

142. "Well | Etymology, Origin and Meaning," *etymonline*," accessed June 18, 2023, https://www.etymonline.com/word/well.

143. Max Chafkin, *The Contrarian: Peter Thiel and Silicon Valley's Pursuit of Power* (London: Bloomsbury, 2021), 333.

144. Paresh Dave and Jeffrey Dastin, "Exclusive: Ukraine Has Started Using Clearview AI's Facial Recognition During War," Reuters, March 14, 2022, https://www.reuters.com/technology/exclusive-ukraine-has-started-using-clearview-ais-facial-recognition-during-war-2022-03-13/.

145. Kashmir Hill, "Facial Recognition Goes to War," *New York Times*, April 7, 2022, https://www.nytimes.com/2022/04/07/technology/facial-recognition-ukraine-clearview.html.

146. "Lee Wolosky," LinkedIn, 2023, https://www.linkedin.com/in/lee-wolosky-414ba045/.

147. Ambassador (ret) Lee Wolosky, "America Resurgent: From Afghanistan to Ukraine," *Just Security* (blog), August 22, 2022, https://www.justsecurity.org/82767/america-resurgent-from-afghanistan-to-ukraine/.

148. "Lee Wolosky"; Reuters, "Ukraine Has Started Using Clearview AI's Facial Recognition During War," March 13, 2022, https://www.cnbc.com/2022/03/13/ukraine-has-started-using-clearview-ais-facial-recognition-during-war.html.

149. John Patrick Gatta, "Youngstown, Appalachia?" *Metro Monthly* (blog), September 1, 2007, https://metromonthly.wordpress.com/2007/09/01/youngstown-appalachia/.

150. James Hamel, "The Hillbilly Elite," *Hillbilly Elite* (blog), December 8, 2010, http://jdhamel.blogspot.com/2010/12/brief.html.

151. J. D. Vance, *Hillbilly Elegy: A Memoir of a Family and Culture in Crisis* (New York: Harper, 2016), 1, 3.

152. Josh McLaurin [@JoshforGeorgia], "The screenshot below is @JDVance1's unfiltered explanation from 2016 of the breakdown in Republican politics that he now personally is trying to exploit. The 'America's Hitler' bit is at the end. The public deserves to know the magnitude of this guy's bad faith," Twitter, April 18, 2022, https://twitter.com/JoshforGeorgia/status/1516093390378741763; James David Vance, "Opioid of the Masses," *Atlantic*, July 4, 2016, https://www.theatlantic.com/politics/archive/2016/07/opioid-of-the-masses/489911/.

153. "J. D. Vance on Charlie Rose," 16:49, 2016, https://charlierose.com/videos/29349.

154. Josh McLaurin, Twitter; James Hohmann, "Opinion: Once the Toast of Liberal Parties, J. D. Vance Has Gone Full MAGA," *Washington Post*, April 27, 2022, https://www.washingtonpost.com/opinions/2022/04/26/jd-vance-trump-endorsement-rally-ohio/.

155. James Pogue, "Inside the New Right, Where Peter Thiel Is Placing His Biggest Bets," *Vanity Fair*, April 20, 2022, https://www.vanityfair.com/news/2022/04/inside-the-new-right-where-peter-thiel-is-placing-his-biggest-bets.

156. Dan Barry, "J. D. Vance's Ambition Comes at a Price in 'Hillbilly' Terms," *New York Times*, October 27, 2022, https://www.nytimes.com/2022/10/27/us/politics/jd-vance-trump-ohio.html; Jessie Balmert and Laura A. Bischoff, "Former President Donald Trump Endorses J. D. Vance in Ohio Senate Race," *Enquirer*, April 15, 2022, https://www.cincinnati.com/story/news/2022/04/15/ohio-senate-candidates-fight-donald-trump-endorsement/7330668001/.

157. Intercollegiate Studies Institute, "JD Vance on Our Civilizational Crisis," YouTube video, 15:12, July 24, 2021, https://www.youtube.com/watch?v=jBrEng3xQYo.

158. FEC, "MASTERS VANCE COMMITTEE—Committee Overview," FEC.gov, 2022, https://www.fec.gov/data/committee/C00792580/; J. D. Vance and Blake Masters, "Senate Candidates J. D. Vance and Blake Masters: We Must Stop Facebook from Election Meddling," *New York Post* (blog), October 21, 2021, https://nypost.com/2021/10/21/j-d-vance-blake-masters-we-must-stop-facebook-election-meddling/.

159. Barry, "J. D. Vance's Ambition"; Deepa Shivaram, "Blake Masters, Trump Pick Funded by Billionaire Thiel, Wins Arizona Senate Primary," NPR, August 3, 2022, https://www.npr.org/sections/2022-live-primary-election-race-results/2022/08/03/1115185686/blake-masters-trump-pick-funded-by-billionaire-thiel-wins-arizona-senate-primary.

160. Brian Schwartz, "Peter Thiel's Picks Masters, Vance Split Key Senate Races in Arizona, Ohio After Billionaire Spent $32 Million on 2022 Midterms," CNBC, November 12, 2022, https://www.cnbc.com/2022/11/12/midterm-results-peter-thiel-picks-masters-vance-see-mixed-results-in-arizona-ohio.html.

161. "Mark Kelly and Blake Masters: Arizona Senate Midterm Election 2022 Live Results," *NBC News*, December 29, 2022, https://www.nbcnews.com/politics/2022-elections/arizona-senate-results.

162. "Ohio U.S. Senate Election Results," *New York Times*, November 8, 2022, https://www.nytimes.com/interactive/2022/11/08/us/elections/results-ohio-us-senate.html.

163. "Tim Ryan: 'I Have the Privilege to Concede This Race to J. D. Vance,'" *NBC News*, November 9, 2022, https://www.nbcnews.com/video/tim-ryan-concedes-ohio-senate-race-to-j-d-vance-153076293930, 0:12.

164. "Culture, Religion and Technology Fall Miami 2021," vatorevents, October 20, 2021, https://events.vator.tv/culture-religion-and-technology-fall-miami-2021.

165. Steven Loeb, "Peter Thiel Talks Democracy, Religion, Freedom, and Woke Culture with Bambi Francisco," *Vator News*, November 2, 2021, https://vator.tv/news/2021-11-02-peter-thiel-talks-democracy-religion-freedom-and-woke-culture-with-bambi-francisco.

166. "Peter Thiel and Bambi Francisco Roizen Conversation on Religion, Culture and Technology," YouTube video, 1:24:05, 2021, https://www.youtube.com/watch?v=y1qf2MCzneU, 1:24:05.

167. "Peter Thiel and Bambi Francisco Roizen," 1:24:11.

168. "Peter Thiel and Bambi Francisco Roizen," 1:25:17, 1:23:13.

169. "Peter Thiel and Bambi Francisco Roizen," 1:10:15; Sam Shead, "Palantir's Peter Thiel Thinks People Should Be Concerned About Surveillance AI," CNBC, October 22, 2021, https://www.cnbc.com/2021/10/22/palantirs-peter-thiel-surveillance-ai-is-more-concerning-than-agi.html.

170. Department of the Treasury, Internal Revenue Service, "Way of the Future Tax Exempt Status," August 16, 2017, https://apps.irs.gov/pub/epostcard/dl/FinalLetter_81-4753507_WAYOFTHEFUTURE_05172017_02.tif.

171. Mark Harris, "Inside the First Church of Artificial Intelligence," *Wired*, November 15, 2017, https://www.wired.com/story/anthony-levandowski-artificial-intelligence-religion/.

172. Way of the Future, "What Is This All About?," 2017, https://web.archive.org/web/20171116002313/http://www.wayofthefuture.church/.

173. Kirsten Korosec, "Anthony Levandowski Closes His Church of AI," *TechCrunch*, February 18, 2021, https://techcrunch.com/2021/02/18/anthony-levandowski-closes-his-church-of-ai/; Way of the Future, "Past. Present. Future," April 10, 2023, https://web.archive.org/web/20230410052730/http://wayofthefuture.church/.

174. Alex Karp, "Our New Platform," *Palantir* (blog), April 7, 2023, https://www.palantir.com/newsroom/letters/our-new-platform/.

175. Chavi Mehta, "Palantir Expects 2023 to Be First Profitable Year, Shares Soar," *Yahoo Finance*, February 13, 2023, https://finance.yahoo.com/news/palantir-expects-2023-first-profitable-210744645.html.

176. Jagmeet Singh and Ingrid Lunden, "OpenAI Closes $300M Share Sale at $27B-29B Valuation," *TechCrunch*, April 28, 2023, https://techcrunch.com/2023/04/28/openai-funding-valuation-chatgpt.

177. Greg Brockman and Ilya Sutskever, "We've created OpenAI LP, a new 'capped-profit' company that allows us to rapidly increase our investments in compute and talent

while including checks and balances to actualize our mission," *OpenAI* (blog), March 11, 2019, https://openai.com/blog/openai-lp.

178. Greg Brockman and Ilya Sutskever, "We've created OpenAI LP, a new 'capped-profit' company that allows us to rapidly increase our investments in compute and talent while including checks and balances to actualize our mission," *OpenAI* (blog), March 11, 2019, https://openai.com/blog/openai-lp.

179. "OpenAI Charter," April 9, 2018, https://openai.com/charter.

180. Theo Priestley, "Elon Musk and Peter Thiel Launch OpenAI, a Non-Profit Artificial Intelligence Research Company," *Forbes*, December 11, 2015, https://www.forbes.com /sites/theopriestley/2015/12/11/elon-musk-and-peter-thiel-launch-openai-a-non -profit-artificial-intelligence-research-company/.

181. Berber Jin and Miles Kruppa, "Microsoft to Deepen OpenAI Partnership, Invest Billions in ChatGPT Creator," *Wall Street Journal*, January 23, 2023, https://www.wsj.com /articles/microsoft-says-it-plans-multibillion-dollar-investment-in-openai -11674483180; Crunchbase, "OpenAI—Investors," May 11, 2023, https://www .crunchbase.com/organization/openai/company_financials.

182. Isaiah Poritz, "OpenAI Legal Troubles Mount with Suit Over AI Training on Novels," *Bloomberg Law*, June 29, 2023, https://news.bloomberglaw.com/ip-law/openai -facing-another-copyright-suit-over-ai-training-on-novels.

183. Crunchbase, "OpenAI—Funding, Financials, Valuation & Investors," accessed June 18, 2023, https://www.crunchbase.com/organization/openai/company_financials.

184. Nico Grant, "Google Calls in Help from Larry Page and Sergey Brin for A.I. Fight," *New York Times*, January 20, 2023, https://www.nytimes.com/2023/01/20/technology /google-chatgpt-artificial-intelligence.html.

185. Kate Conger and Lauren Hirsch, "Elon Musk Completes $44 Billion Deal to Own Twitter," *New York Times*, October 28, 2022, https://www.nytimes.com/2022/10/27 /technology/elon-musk-twitter-deal-complete.html; Elon Musk [@elonmusk], Twitter, February 17, 2023, https://twitter.com/elonmusk/status/1626516035863212034.

186. Elon Musk [@elonmusk], "@andyo___ @sama the danger of training AI to be woke—in other words, lie—is deadly," Twitter, December 16, 2022, https://twitter.com/elonmusk /status/1603836383885332480; Hyunjoo Jin and Sheila Dang, "Elon Musk Says He Will Launch Rival to Microsoft-Backed ChatGPT," Reuters, April 18, 2023, https://www .reuters.com/technology/musk-says-he-will-start-truthgpt-or-maximum-truth -seeking-ai-fox-news-2023-04-17/.

187. Jin and Dang, "Elon Musk Says He Will Launch Rival."

188. For more on Musk's rationale behind starting his own AI venture, see Walter Isaacson, *Elon Musk* (New York: Simon and Schuster, 2023), chap. 94.

189. Center for AI Safety, "Statement on AI Risk," accessed June 18, 2023, https://www.safe .ai/statement-on-ai-risk#open-letter.

190. Center for AI Safety, "AI Extinction Statement Press Release," accessed June 18, 2023, https://www.safe.ai/press-release.

191. Dexter Masters and K. Way, *One World or None: A Report to the Public on the Full Meaning of the Atomic Bomb* (New York: New Press, 2007), 67–68.

192. Quote Investigator, "History Does Not Repeat Itself, but It Rhymes," *Quote Investigator* (blog), January 12, 2014, https://quoteinvestigator.com/2014/01/12/history-rhymes/.

193. Jack Beatty, *Age of Betrayal: The Triumph of Money in America, 1865–1900* (New York: Knopf, 2007), 3–4.

194. John H. Northrop, "An Analysis Leading to a Recommendation Concerning Inquiry into Eugenic Legislation," April 21, 1969, box 116, folder 35, Correspondence—University

of California (some reprints) 1967–1969, William Bradford Shockley Papers (SC0222), Department of Special Collections and University Archives, Stanford University Libraries, Stanford, CA.

195.  Stanford University, Side 1, 28:20, Side 1, 42:38; Side 2, 9:01.

196.  Josie Fischels, "A Look Back at the Very First Website Ever Launched, 30 Years Later," NPR, August 6, 2021, https://www.npr.org/2021/08/06/1025554426/a-look-back-at-the-very-first-website-ever-launched-30-years-later.

197.  Peter Thiel, "The Education of a Libertarian," *Cato Unbound*, April 13, 2009, https://www.cato-unbound.org/2009/04/13/peter-thiel/education-libertarian.

198.  "Peter Thiel and Bambi Francisco Roizen," 1:10:00; Sam Shead, "Palantir's Peter Thiel Thinks People Should Be Concerned About Surveillance AI," CNBC, October 22, 2021, https://www.cnbc.com/2021/10/22/palantirs-peter-thiel-surveillance-ai-is-more-concerning-than-agi.html.

## Epilogue

1.  F. Scott Fitzgerald, "The Crack-Up: A desolately frank document from one for whom the salt of life has lost its savor," *Esquire* (1936), 41 (Esquire archive at classic.esquire.com), quoted at Quote Research, "The Test of a First-Rate Intelligence Is the Ability to Hold Two Opposed Ideas in the Mind at the Same Time," Quote Investigator, 2020, https://quoteinvestigator.com/2020/01/05/intelligence/#note-437233-3.

2.  Ovid, *Metamorphoses*, trans. Brookes Moore (Boston: Cornhill, 1922), https://www.theoi.com/Text/OvidMetamorphoses8.html.

3.  Robert Frost, "A Servant to Servants," Poetry Verse, accessed June 18, 2023, https://www.poetryverse.com/robert-frost-poems/a-servant-to-servants.

4.  Glenda Elizabeth Gilmore and Thomas J. Sugrue, *These United States: A Nation in the Making: 1890 to the Present* (New York: Norton, 2015), 625.

5.  Gilmore and Sugrue, 625.

6.  Interview with Chantelle Farmer, Zoom, August 9, 2022, 29:13.

7.  Interview with Farmer, 31:43.

8.  Interview with Farmer, 30:45.

9.  Interview with Farmer, 30:20.

10.  Interview with Farmer, 35:40; Marjorie Z. Olds, "Chantelle Farmer: Optimizing," *Ithaca (NY) Times*, July 15, 2021, https://www.ithaca.com/opinion/columnists/community_connections/chantelle-farmer-optimizing/article_a3ca2530-e587-11eb-8353-cbe1eac92cb5.html; "FLX Fitclub—Ithaca NY's Best Group Fitness Classes," *FLX Fitclub* (blog), accessed June 18, 2023, https://flxfitclub.com.

11.  Jessica Anderson, "Catch 27—*Collegian* Archives," *Catch27*, April 19, 2021, https://web.archive.org/web/20210419004219/https:/archives.collegian.com/2005/03/02/catch_27/.

12.  Interview with Nate Wheeler, audio recording, August 25, 2022, 36:30.

13.  "Jurassic Park (1993)—IMDb," IMDb, accessed June 18, 2023, http://www.imdb.com/title/tt0107290/characters/nm0000156.

14.  Interview with Wheeler, 32:30.

15.  Walter F. Bodmer et al., "Letter to Merritt Holman, Editor of Stanford M.D., from the Faculty of the Department of Genetics, Stanford University," February 14, 1966, box 2, folder 3, William Shockley and Eugenics Collection (SC0595), Department of Special Collections and University Archives, Stanford University Libraries, Stanford, CA.

16. Michelle Fox, "Mark Zuckerberg's Control of Facebook Is like a Dictatorship: Cal-STRS," CNBC, May 10, 2018, https://www.cnbc.com/2018/05/10/mark-zuckerbergs-control-of-facebook-is-like-a-dictatorship-calstrs.html; Leanna Orr, "CIO of CalSTRS—$1B Facebook Shareholder—Shuts Account in Disgust," *Institutional Investor*, April 5, 2018, https://www.institutionalinvestor.com/article/b17n35zyzzmtbp/cio-of-calstrs-%E2%80%94-1b-facebook-shareholder-%E2%80%94-shuts-account-in-disgust.

17. Interview with Chris Ailman, September 13, 2022, Zoom, 7:40.

18. Interview with Ailman, 18:58.

19. Interview with Ailman, 28:45.

20. Ben Cohen, "There Has to Be a Better Way to Lose $800 Billion: Intelligent Failures in Business Are Based on Small Bets. Meta Bet the Company," *Wall Street Journal*, November 3, 2022, https://www.wsj.com/articles/meta-facebook-metaverse-mark-zuckerberg-11667424987.

21. Interview with Ailman, 28:45.

22. Leigh Remizowski, "Catch27.Com Boasts a 'Wicked Twist,'" *Pitt News* (blog), April 11, 2005, https://pittnews.com/article/32331/archives/catch27-com-boasts-a-wicked-twist/.

23. "Melissa Patti MSW LCSW," LinkedIn, 2023, https://www.linkedin.com/in/melissa-patti-msw-lcsw/.

24. Interview with Melissa Patti, Zoom, April 3, 2023, 53:27.

25. "Ecclesiastes 1:2–8 ESV; NIV—Vanity of Vanities, Says the Preacher," Bible Gateway, accessed June 18, 2023, https://www.biblegateway.com/passage/?search=Ecclesiastes%201%3A2-8&version=ESV;NIV.

26. Interview with Patti, 53:52.

27. Interview with Patti, 30:03, 47:58.

28. Interview with Patti, 42:56.

29. Steve Jobs, "Think Different Apple Commercial," *Farnam Street* (blog), March 24, 2016, https://fs.blog/steve-jobs-crazy-ones/.

30. Yaser Haddara, "Matthies Urges Closer, More Thoughtful Look at Incident," *Stanford Daily*, February 7, 1992, https://archives.stanforddaily.com/1992/02/07?page=12& section=MODSMD_ARTICLE39.

31. Haddara, "Matthies Urges Closer, More Thoughtful Look."

32. Matthias Dennis, "Otero RF Shares Inner Conflict with Stanford Community," *Stanford Daily*, February 6, 1992, https://archives.stanforddaily.com/1992/02/06?page=5 §ion=MODSMD_ARTICLE20#article.

33. Langston Hughes, "Let America Be America Again," Academy of American Poets, accessed June 18, 2023, https://poets.org/poem/let-america-be-america-again.

34. George H. W. Bush, "Inaugural Address of George Bush," Yale Law School Avalon Project, January 20, 1989, https://avalon.law.yale.edu/20th_century/bush.asp.

35. "Transcript of Reagan's Farewell Address to American People," *New York Times*, January 12, 1989, https://www.nytimes.com/1989/01/12/news/transcript-of-reagan-s-farewell-address-to-american-people.html.

36. Bush, "Inaugural Address of George Bush."

37. "Declaration of Independence: A Transcription," National Archives, July 4, 1776, https://www.archives.gov/founding-docs/declaration-transcript.

38. "'The Dimensions of a Complete Life,' Sermon at Dexter Avenue Baptist Church," Martin Luther King, Jr., Research and Education Institute, January 24, 1954, https://kinginstitute.stanford.edu/king-papers/documents/dimensions-complete-life-sermon-dexter-avenue-baptist-church; Carla Hayden, "Remembering John Lewis:

The Power of 'Good Trouble,'" *Timeless* (blog), Library of Congress, July 19, 2020, https://blogs.loc.gov/loc/2020/07/remembering-john-lewis-the-power-of-good -trouble.

39. New England Historical Society, "Christopher Seider: The First Casualty in the American Revolutionary Cause," July 31, 2015, https://newenglandhistoricalsociety.com /christopher-seider-the-first-casualty-in-the-american-revolutionary-cause/; "Black History Boston: The Hero of the Boston Massacre, Crispus Attucks," Boston.gov, January 14, 2020, https://www.boston.gov/news/black-history-boston-hero-boston -massacre-crispus-attucks.

40. Fitzgerald, "The Crack-Up," 41.

# INDEX